SIXTH EDITION

BUSINESS AND SOCIETY
A Managerial Approach

Heidi Vernon
Northeastern University

McGraw-Hill
A Division of The McGraw·Hill Companies

BUSINESS AND SOCIETY: A MANAGERIAL APPROACH

Copyright © 1998 by The McGraw-Hill Companies, Inc. All rights reserved. Previous editions © 1980, 1981, 1985, 1990, and 1994, by Richard D. Irwin, a Times Mirror Higher Education Group, Inc. company. Printed in the United States of America. Except as permitted under the United States Copyright Act of 1976, no part of this publication may be reproduced or distributed in any form or by any means, or stored in a data base or retrieval system, without the prior written permission of the publisher.

This book is printed on acid-free paper.

2 3 4 5 6 7 8 9 0 DOC/DOC 9 0 9

ISBN 0-256-21765-3

Senior sponsoring editor: *John E. Biernat*
Marketing manager: *Kenyetta Giles*
Project manager: *Carrie Sestak*
Production supervisor: *Melonie Salvati*
Senior designer: *Crispin Prebys*
Compositor: *Interactive Composition Corporation*
Typeface: *10/12 Times Roman*
Printer: *R. R. Donnelley & Sons Company*

Library of Congress Cataloging-in-Publication Data

Vernon, Heidi (date)
    Business and society : a managerial approach / Heidi Vernon. — 6th ed.
      p.   cm.
    Includes bibliographical references and index.
    ISBN 0-256-21765-3
    1. Industries—Social aspects—United States. 2. Industrial management—United States. 3. Business ethics—United States. 4. United States—Commerce. I. Title.
HD60.5.U5S88   1998
658.4 08—dc21
                                                                                                              97-16986

http://www.mhhe.com

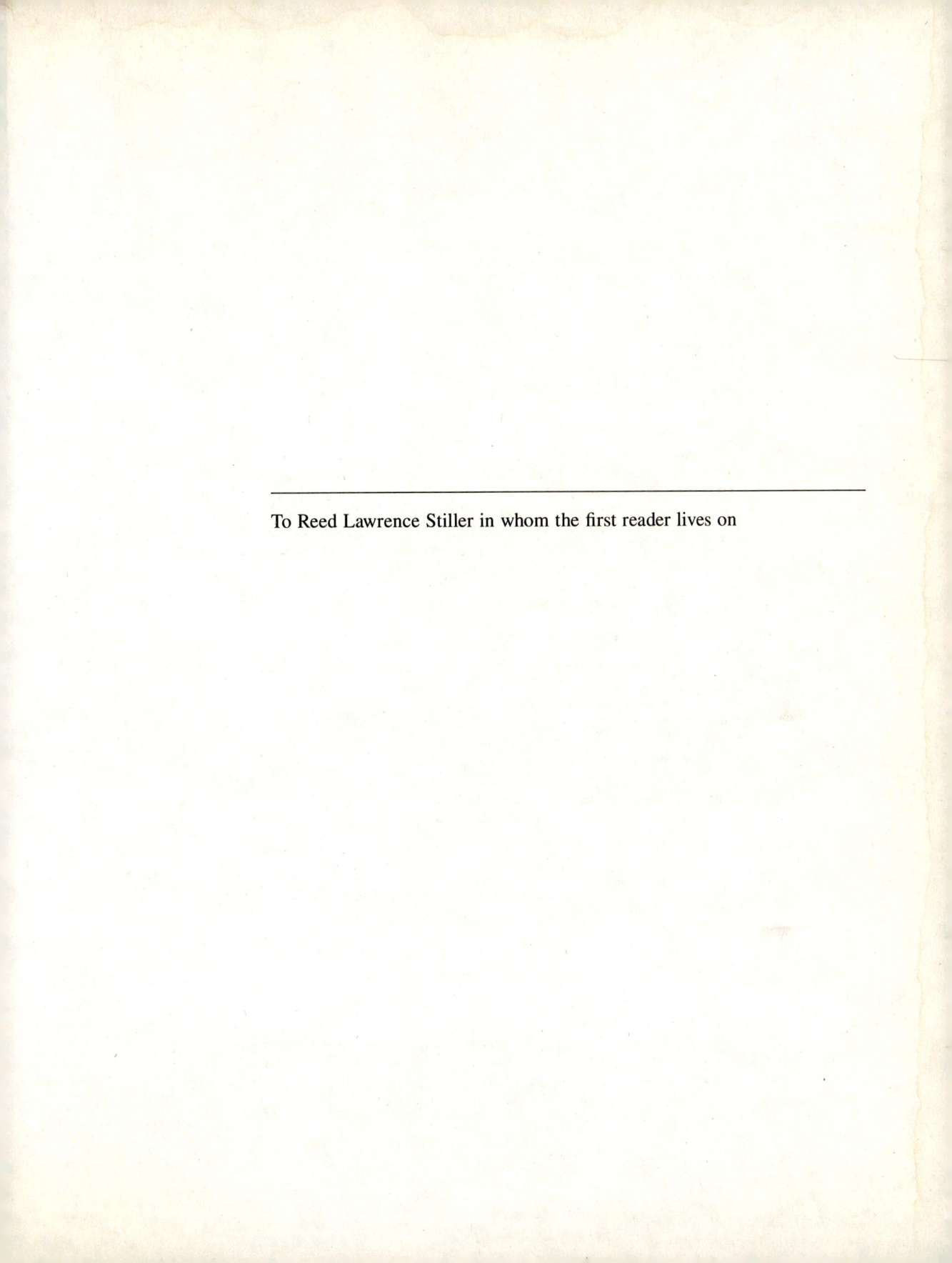

To Reed Lawrence Stiller in whom the first reader lives on

PREFACE

The sixth edition of *Business and Society: A Managerial Approach* is designed to help future managers successfully confront and deal with social issues into the new millennium. This book provides tools and builds skills essential to achieving corporate social goals.

Business and Society: A Managerial Approach is written for upper-level undergraduate and MBA students. Combining academic theory with real hands-on management concerns, it covers a wide range of topics and issues. Each instructor can decide which topics and approaches to emphasize. The book looks at social issues from a business policy/strategy perspective.

New Approaches

The Internet. The sixth edition integrates the use of the Internet in developing and discussing social issues. There are numerous references to web sites where students can find their own information and from which they can begin to surf the Net on their own.

Global Business. The current edition integrates global business issues, cultural issues, and concerns of multinational corporations into each chapter.

Cases. Many more cases appear in this edition than in previous editions. Each chapter begins with a case about a current event or situation that examines real company actions. Minicases are integrated throughout the text to tie together models, theory, and real-life experience. Students can compare their analyses of these cases before and after they have mastered the analytical tools contained in each chapter.

The Beta Pharmaceutical Company, introduced at the end of Chapter 2, continues as the integrative case. In each chapter, Beta's managers face a variety of new problems. Like the cases that introduce the chapters, Beta episodes are based on concerns real companies face daily. All relevant data are documented and taken from real-life situations. Some cases require top managers to take immediate action, while others allow more time for planning and strategy. Each case is followed by questions that help reinforce the case's important points.

This text guides students as they learn to identify social issues and their relevant stakeholders, to avoid crises whenever possible, and to effectively manage those crises that cannot be predicted or avoided. The book also teaches students how to integrate social issues and functional business-area strategies. It combines theory with pragmatic advice and examples of current corporate behavior.

Part I, "Strategic Management of Social Issues," contains six chapters that create the framework within which social issues are discussed throughout the book. It provides models, processes, and tools to help managers handle their social issues.

Chapter 1, "Business and Social Responsiveness," sets the stage by discussing demographic changes and business organization since the last edition was published in 1994. Governmental and political changes are critically important for businesses' decision making. This chapter also discusses the theory of capitalism to establish the ideological context for the book and looks at the historical development of the modern corporation. Chapter 1 stresses the strong linkages between business strategy and the economic, social, and political environments. After making the arguments for and against corporate social responsibility, it concludes—not surprisingly—that social responsibility is a mandatory, not a discretionary, activity. As in later chapters, frequently we address global issues.

Chapter 2, "Strategy Formulation," focuses on decision processes that help managers formulate strategies to achieve social and other business objectives. Macro- and microeconomic, macro- and microsocial, political and legal, and technological environmental forces all affect strategic analysis, the first stage of strategy formulation. The framework for strategy formulation includes the development of a mission statement, defining corporate objectives, making an internal assessment, environmental scanning and analysis, and making strategic choices.

Chapter 3, "Strategy Implementation," introduces the Stakeholder Influence Map (SIM). This matrix model helps identify stakeholders in a systematic way. The chapter analyses stakeholder activities according to their position inside or outside the firm, their interests in particular issues, the depth of their involvement, and their power to affect company strategy. Managing for social responsiveness is a hands-on managerial activity that includes identifying, classifying, and managing issues—and finally, evaluating corporate performance.

Chapter 4, "Crisis Management," discusses managerial strategies for identifying, handling, and resolving crises. The chapter begins with the Dow Corning and breast implants case, offering models for identifying stages in crisis situations. These models are then tied to the Prudential Securities Case and the *Exxon Valdez* disaster. Chapter 4 also makes recommendations for initiating crisis risk analysis and establishing programs to head off potential crises before they arise.

Chapter 5, "Ethics," begins with a discussion of the Barings Bank debacle. The chapter approaches ethics as a major issue to be managed within the company. It suggests ways for managers to make ethics more meaningful than a framed code on the wall. Chapter 5 offers standards and guidelines that increase the likelihood that ethics will be taken seriously by everyone in the firm.

Chapter 6, "The Origins of Big Business," is a topic rarely addressed in business and society books. It is included here because it is invaluable in setting the stage for the topics to come. This chapter discusses U.S. business ideology and links it to present-day management thought.

Part II, "Political and Community Responsiveness," covers the political and legal processes. It looks at ways companies can affect legislation and promote their agendas. Part II deals with the company's ability to conduct its affairs legally, to influence its political and regulatory environment in a positive fashion, and to act as a responsible citizen in the global community.

The discussion of regulation of the Internet is new to this edition. Legislation is just beginning to be written to control access and use of the Internet. Although U.S. courts are reluctant to interfere with the First Amendment, other nations are not so closely bound by a constitution and impartial judiciary. This part also examines the deregulation of the telecommunications industry and the impact of new technologies on social issues.

In recent years philanthropic institutions have been scandal-ridden. United Way and New Era furnish excellent case examples of how good works and reputations can be destroyed by individual unethical behavior. Charity means different things to different cultures. Examples from other countries give a unique perspective to U.S. readers.

Part III, "Managing People and Social Issues," has three chapters that deal with the many issues that directly affect employees. Employees, and society as a whole, expect companies to provide physical, psychological, and economic support. Stakeholders also expect companies to create an environment in which employees perceive they are treated fairly and given opportunities to grow, meet challenges, and find satisfaction.

New concerns about employee privacy are challenging companies. Communication within and outside the company has changed since employees began to use E-mail. There is no doubt that the workplace is more stressful and that employees have less security than before. Many employees are as concerned about access to elder care as to child care.

Ideology about affirmative action has changed dramatically in the past few years. The Clinton administration and the Republican Congress continue to press their opposing views in court battles, the media, and regulatory agency activities. Sexual harassment, which gained visibility as an issue in the Anita Hill–Clarence Thomas case, continues to be a difficult issue to manage.

In 1996 and 1997, unions chose new leadership and begun major organizing campaigns. It is too soon to know what the impact will be in the United States. Union activity in Europe and in other countries takes different forms and relates to management in different ways.

Part IV, "Consumer Welfare," covers consumer information and product safety. The two chapters in this section discuss the evolution of the consumer movement, issues of information dissemination, product promotion, and the duties of the FDA and the FTC. Part IV also explores product safety, total quality management, ISO 9000 and ISO 14000, and the role of the Consumer Product Safety Commission.

Part V, "The Environment," has two chapters on the physical environment and the concluding chapter of the book. Governments, corporations, special interest groups, and individuals are concerned about problems of the shrinking ozone layer, toxic waste disposal, and disappearing rain forests even as they create and perpetuate the problems. Chapter 16 looks at issues of clean air, clean water, and the role of the Environmental Protection Agency in managing the environment. It traces the development of the electric car and the impact of more stringent environmental rules on business. Chapter 17 analyzes the effectiveness of international efforts to clean up the environment. It discusses the tension between policies that promote unfettered economic development and sustainable development.

The final chapter is set in Beta Corporation's boardroom as the company gets ready for its annual meeting. Many of the issues addressed in the preceding 17 chapters are important to Beta's board members.

Heidi Vernon

ACKNOWLEDGMENTS

I would like to thank the following people for their cogent reviews of the sixth edition:

- Anne C. Cowden, *University of California at Sacramento*
- William A. Ward, *Susquehanna University*
- Mary Jane Saxton, *University of Colorado at Denver*
- David Flynn, *Hofstra University*
- George S. Cole, *Shippensburg University*

My deepest thanks go to my aunt, Dr. Corinne Friend. She took on this project at a critical time; her excellent, detailed, and perceptive comments were always on the mark. Her support, advice, love and involvement are appreciated beyond words. My debt to her can never truly be repaid. Dr. F. Gerard Adams broadened my perspective, kept my fingers to the keyboard, and changed my life. My graduate and undergraduate students tested many of these chapters prior to publication. Their comments contributed to the quality of the book.

BRIEF CONTENTS

PART I
STRATEGIC MANAGEMENT OF SOCIAL ISSUES

1 Business and Social Responsiveness   3
2 Strategy Formulation   37
3 Strategy Implementation and Evaluation   83
4 Crisis Management   121
5 Ethics   155
6 The Origins of Big Business   195

PART II
POLITICAL AND COMMUNITY RESPONSIVENESS

7 Managing the Legal and Political Processes   229
8 Regulation   259
9 Regulation and Deregulation from the 1960s to the 1990s   279
10 Philanthropy and Corporate Giving   309

PART III
MANAGING PEOPLE AND SOCIAL ISSUES

11 Workplace Issues for the Late 1990s   351
12 Equal Employment and Affirmative Action   391
13 Unions, Occupational Safety, and Health   429

PART IV
CONSUMER WELFARE

14 Consumers and Information   463
15 Product Use Issues   497

PART V
THE ENVIRONMENT

16 Environmental Issues   531
17 The International Environment   571
18 Beta's Management Challenge   611

Index   619

CONTENTS

PART I

STRATEGIC MANAGEMENT OF SOCIAL ISSUES

1 Business and Social Responsiveness 3

Issues of the Late 1990s 5
   The U.S. Economy 6
   Immigration 7
   Age Segmentation 8
   Gender Issues 10
   Corporate Restructuring 10
   Politics and Change 13
The Nature of Capitalism 15
   Private Property 16
   The Dynamic Nature of Business 18
The Modern Corporation 19
The Linkage between Strategy and the Economic, Social, and Political Environments 21
Social Responsiveness Management 22
   The Firm and Its Larger Environment 23
   Strategy Formulation 24
   Strategy Implementation 24
   Performance Evaluation 24
The Business and Society Responsibility Debate 24
The Scope of Business Responsibility 30
Case: Daiwa Bank 33
Summary 35
Questions 36

2 Strategy Formulation 37

Case: Gillette Company 37
The Environment of Strategy Formulation 39
Elements of the Environment 41
   The Economic Environment 41
   The Social Environment 43
   The Legal and Political Environment 47
   The Technological Environment 47
Strategic Management and Organizational Culture 55
   Values and Leadership 55
   Adaptability to Change 58
A Framework for Strategy Formulation 59
   The Mission Statement 59
   Corporate Objectives 64
   Internal Assessment 65
   Organizational Weaknesses, Social Issues, Visibility, and Vulnerability 67

    Environmental Scanning and
      Analysis 71
    Strategic Choice 73
Summary 76
Project 77
Questions 77
Beta Pharmaceuticals: Introduction 77
Beta Case 2: Strategy Formulation 78

3 Strategy Implementation and Evaluation 83

Case: Stakeholders and Nuclear
  Waste 83
Stakeholder Analysis 86
The Stakeholder Influence Map 87
    Stakeholder Analysis and
      Management 90
    External Direct Forces 92
    Internal Direct Forces 96
    External Indirect Forces 99
    Internal Indirect Forces 101
Stakeholders' Power to Affect Firms'
  Affairs 103
    Stakeholders' Resources 105
    Selection of Alternatives 106
    Managing for Social
      Responsiveness 108
Managing for Social
  Responsiveness 109
    Classification of Major Social
      Issues 109
    Determine Priorities and Collect
      Data 110
    Select a Plan or Policy 110
    Implementation (Action) 112
    Control and Measure
      Performance 112
    The Three-Stage Implementation
      Pattern 114
    The Social Audit 115
Summary 118
Projects 118
Questions 118
Beta Case 3: Strategy Implementation and
  Evaluation 119

4 Crisis Management 121

Case: Dow Corning and Breast
  Implants 122
Crisis Classification 126
    Internally Generated Crisis 126
Environmental Crises: A Special
  Situation 128
A Model for Crisis Management 129
Anatomy of a Major Crisis 132
    The Precrisis or Prodromal Stage 132
    The Crisis Stage 133
    The Postcrisis Stage 133
Prudential Securities, Inc.: An Internally
  Generated Crisis 134
    The Precrisis or Prodromal Stage 134
    The Crisis Stage 138
    The Postcrisis Stage 138
The *Exxon Valdez:* A Major External
  Environmental Accident 140
    The Precrisis or Prodromal
      Stage 142
    The Crisis Stage 142
    The Postcrisis Stage 143
Routine Crises 146
Effective Crisis Management 146
    The Team Approach 146
Crises and the Media 149
Summary 152
Questions 153
Project 153
Beta Case 4: Crisis Management 154

5 Ethics 155

Case: Barings PLC 156
The Background of the Ethics
  Debate 159
    Ideological Arguments 163
    Ethics: Whose Responsibility? 166
    Educating Managers in Business
      Ethics 167
Setting Standards for Ethical Behavior
  in Corporations 170
    Benefits of Guidelines 173
Ethics, Credos, Programs, and
  Codes 173

Ethics Credos 175
Ethics Codes 176
General Code Contents 179
Employee Issues 181
Whistle-Blowing 182
International Ethics 184
Multinational Corporations 188
Summary 189
Projects 192
Questions 193
Beta Case 5: Ethics 194

6 The Origins of Big Business 195

Conditions Supporting Business Development in the United States 196
Plentiful Natural Resources 197
Favorable Social and Political Environments 198
Population Growth and Urbanism 200
The Transportation Revolution 201
Innovations in Communication 202
Technological Developments 203
Stages of Capitalism 205
Prebusiness and Petty Capitalism 205
Mercantile Capitalism 206
Industrial Capitalism 207
Finance Capitalism 210
National Capitalism 216
Summary 223
Questions 224
Beta Case 6: The Origins of Big Business 225

PART II
POLITICAL AND COMMUNITY RESPONSIVENESS

7 Managing the Legal and Political Processes 229

Case: Product Liability Law 230
The Legal Framework 233
The U.S. Constitution 233
Informal Societal Rules 234
Corporations and the Law 235
The Political and Legal Frameworks 237
Corporate Political Stakeholders 237
Major Stakeholders Groups 238
Corporate Political Power 240
The Corporate Political Program 242
Skills of the Political Manager 243
Political and Legal Stakeholder Groups 245
Business Associations 245
Political Action Committees 246
Lobbying and Legislation 247
Passage of Legislation 251
Prelegislative Phase 251
The Legislative Process 252
Administrative Agencies 254
Working with Agencies 255
Summary 256
Projects 256
Questions 257
Beta Case 7: The Legal and Political Arenas 258

8 Regulation 259

Case: Regulation in Our Daily Lives 261
Business Regulation from the 19th Century to World War I 262
Interstate Commerce Act of 1887 262
Sherman Antitrust Act of 1890 265
Federal Trade Commission Act of 1914 267
Consumer Regulation from the 19th Century to World War I 268
Pure Food and Drug Act of 1906 268
Business Regulation Summary 270
World War I to the New Deal 270
Regulation in the New Deal 271

Functional Agencies 271
Economic Agencies 272
Social Agencies 272
Case: The Justice Department and
   Antitrust Legislation 273
Summary 276
Projects 277
Questions 277
Beta Case 8: Regulation 278

9 Regulation and Deregulation from the 1960s to the 1990s 279

Case: Regulation and the Cable
   Industry 279
Regulations in the 1960s 282
From Regulation to Deregulation,
   1960–1978 284
The Carter Administration 285
   The Airline Industry 286
   The Trucking Industry 286
   The Communications Industry 287
The Reagan Administration,
   1980–1988 287
   Airlines 291
   Telephone Industry 291
The Reagan–Bush Transition: The Case
   of the Banking Industry 292
   New Banking Regulation 293
The Clinton Years, 1992–1996 295
   Regulatory Issues in the Clinton
   Administration 297
Summary 305
Questions 306
Beta Case 9: Regulation and
   Deregulation 306
Appendix: U.S. Regulatory
   Agencies 307

10 Philanthropy and Corporate Giving 309

Case: United Way 309
Charitable Organizations 311
   Company Towns 312
Individual Giving 313
   Individual Giving in the 1990s 314
   The Political Controversy 316
   Giving in 1995 318
   New Models for Nonprofit
   Organizations: The Arts as an
   Example 320
Individual Charitable Giving 323
Corporate and Large Foundations 326
How Is Your Money Spent? 329
Case: The Foundation for New Era
   Philanthropy 330
The Strategic Marketing Approach to
   Corporate Giving: Doing Well by
   Doing Good 336
   Cause-Related Marketing 336
An International Perspective on
   Charitable Giving 340
   The British Example 341
   The Japanese Example 343
Summary 345
Questions and Projects 346
Beta Case 10: Community Support and
   Philanthropy 347

PART III

MANAGING PEOPLE AND SOCIAL ISSUES

11 Workplace Issues for the Late 1990s 351

Case: Jennifer Stills' Workday 351
A Changing Labor Force 353
Employee Privacy 354
   The Government and Privacy 356
   Polygraph Testing 357
   Electronic Surveillance in the
   Workplace 359
Stress 362
   Workplace Violence 365
   Guidelines for Preventing Workplace
   Violence 367
Medical Issues in the Workplace 368
   Substance Abuse 369

Disabled Workers 371
   Aids in the Workplace 376
Family and Child Care Benefits 379
   The Family Leave Bill 379
   Child Care 380
   Elder Care 383
Health Care 384
Summary 387
Projects 388
Questions 388
Beta Case 11: Workplace Issues for the 1990s 389

12 Equal Employment and Affirmative Action 391

Case: Diversity Training 391
A Level Playing Field 392
Civil Rights Act of 1964 392
   Background 392
   Employee Qualifications 393
   Title VII of the Civil Rights Act of 1964 394
   Equal Employment Opportunity Commission (EEOC) 395
   Affirmative Action 396
Landmark Supreme Court Decisions 398
   Allan Bakke v *The Regents of the University of California* 399
   United Steelworkers, etc. v *Weber* 400
   Memphis Fire Department v *Shotts* 400
   City of Richmond v *J. A. Croson* 401
Equal Opportunity and Affirmative Action in the 1980s 402
The Civil Rights Act of 1991 403
Changing Views of Affirmative Action, the Mid-1990s and Beyond 405
   The California Plan 406
   Race Discrimination: The Case of Texaco 409

Sexual Harassment 414
   Mitsubishi Motor Manufacturing of America, Inc. (MMMA) 415
   Astra USA, Inc., and Sexual Harassment 418
Age Discrimination 421
   Managing an Aging Workforce 424
   Making the Most of Diversity 425
Summary 426
Questions 427
Projects 427
Beta Case 12: Equal Employment and Affirmative Action 428

13 Unions, Occupational Safety, and Health 429

Case: Jennifer Stills and Workplace Safety 429
The Changing Work Environment 430
Labor Unions 430
   The Development of Nationwide Unions 430
   Union Activity in the 1980s 433
   Labor in the 1990s 435
   European Labor Issues 439
Occupational Safety and Health 444
   Development of Worker Health and Safety Concerns 444
   The Occupational Safety and Health Act 447
   The Reagan and Bush Years 449
   OSHA and the Clinton Administration 451
   Repetitive Stress: A Workplace Safety Issue 453
Management Strategy for Workplace Safety Issues 456
Summary 457
Questions 458
Projects 458
Beta Case 13: Unions and Workplace Safety 459

PART IV

CONSUMER WELFARE

14 Consumers and Information 463

Case: What You Don't Know about
    Drugs . . . 463
Consumerism 464
Regulation and Consumer
    Protection 468
    The Federal Trade Commission 468
The Food and Drug Adminstration 475
Consumers' Sources of
    Information 478
    What is Good Information 482
Advertising 482
    Advertising Goals 482
    Deceptive Advertising 483
Summary 493
Questions 494
Projects 494
Beta Case 14: Consumers and
    Information 495

15 Product Use Issues 497

Case: General Motors and Its Pickup
    Trucks 497
Product Quality 500
    History of Quality Control 500
    Eight Dimensions of Quality 502
Total Quality Management 505
    The Malcolm Baldrige National
      Quality Award 507
    ISO 9000 509
    Sybase, Inc.: A Company That Ate
      the Elephant One Bite at a
      Time 511
    ISO 14000 513
Regulation of Product Safety 515
The Legal Environment 517
Theories of Product Liability 518
    Negligence 518
    Design Defect 520
    Warranty 522
    Strict Liability 523
Case: Cellular Phones and
    Electromagnetic Fields: Are These
    Phones Safe? 524
Summary 525
Questions 526
Projects 526
Beta Case 15: Product Use Issues 527

PART V

THE ENVIRONMENT

16 ENVIRONMENTAL ISSUES 531

Case: Buying and Selling the Right to
    Pollute 531
History of Air and Water Pollution 535
Regulatory Agencies 536
    Council on Environmental Quality
      (CEQ) 536
    Environmental Protection Agency
      (EPA) 536
Clean Air 539
    The Clean Air Act of 1990 541
    The Clean Car 544
Clean Water 548
    Clean Water Act of 1972 548
    Safe Drinking Water Act 551
Hazardous Waste 553
Waste Reduction 555
    Recycling: A Strategy for Reducing
      Waste 555
    Alternative Fuels: Another Strategy
      for Reducing Waste 558
    A Systems Approach to Waste
      Minimization 560
    Waste Management 561
Radioactive Waste in the United
    States 565
Summary 568
Questions 569
Projects 569
Beta Case 16: Environmental
    Issues 570

17 The International Environment 571

Case: The Aral Sea 572
Sustainable Development 573
Trade Policy and the Environment 575
The Environment and the European
    Union 578
  Green Politics 578
  Environmental Policy
    Implementation 580
The Environment and Eastern
    Europe 582
  The Example of Poland 583
  The Example of the Former Soviet
    Union 585
  The Environment and Asia 588
  China: A Nation in Transition 588
  China and the Three Gorges
    Project 590
Development versus the
    Environment 593
  Four Themes 593
International Agreements on the
    Environment: Before Rio and
    Beyond 598
  The Earth Summit, Rio de
    Janeiro 600
Summary 608
Questions 608
Beta Case 17: International
    Environment 609

18 Beta's Management Challenge 611

Index 619

PART I

STRATEGIC MANAGEMENT OF SOCIAL ISSUES

In the last few years of the 20th century, corporations face new economic and social challenges. It is more critical than ever before that managers meet these challenges with organized, comprehensive, and well-developed strategies. Universities and colleges, recognizing their responsibility to train managers of the future, are incorporating strategies for social issues management into their courses.

Part I of this book provides models, processes, and tools to help managers handle the social issues their companies encounter daily. The six chapters in Part I analyze the components of social responsiveness, strategy formulation, strategy implementation, crisis management, and ethics. The chapters provide the historical setting and context for the discussion of social issues and the analytical tools for integrating companies' social issues with their bottom-line business strategies.

CHAPTER 1
BUSINESS AND SOCIAL RESPONSIVENESS

In this chapter we lay a broad groundwork for discussions of social issues in the 1990s. We then go on to discuss how the modern corporation evolved and issues that are central to the debate over the proper roles of business and society.

All corporations have multiple stakeholders. Stakeholders are individuals and groups involved or invested in the company's decisions and its social and economic exchanges. The involvement may be direct or indirect. The example of National Cash Register and the city of Dayton, Ohio, shows how one company's actions in one city can affect many disparate groups of stakeholders.

AT&T acquired National Cash Register Company (NCR) in September 1991. NCR, subsequently renamed AT&T Global Information Solutions, eliminated 20,000 jobs over the next several years. Following NCR's example, companies such as General Motors, Chrysler, Wright-Patterson Air Force Base, and Dayton Press reorganized and downsized, laying off an additional 30,000 workers. As Dayton's locally owned financial institutions were taken over and consolidated, small business owners found it harder to get loans. By 1996, unemployment in inner-city Dayton was 15 percent, compared with 4.8 percent in the surrounding county. Local groups from the Boy Scouts to the United Way lost leadership and financial support in the exodus of workers and diminution of funding. One of the few local bank officers remaining in his downtown job observed, "What is Dayton's identity now? I don't know."[1] Although Dayton has recently attracted high technology firms, it is a very different environment in which to live and work. In the past, most stakeholders judged firms primarily by the quality of their products and services.

---

[1] S. Rimmer, "A Hometown Feels Less Like Home," *New York Times,* March 6, 1966, pp. A1, 16–17.

Companies supplied goods, services, financial opportunities, and security for many millions of people. Stakeholders had an underlying conviction that if firms used their resources to make quality goods and offer quality services at fair prices, the profits they earned would attract investment, provide jobs, and build the economy. In the 1960s, stakeholders began to evaluate firms on how well they managed social issues. Now, as the federal and state governments grow smaller, many of the social functions that used to be performed by government will shift to the private sector. Corporate success will depend on companies' technological progress and their managers' individual growth, development, and creativity.

Globally, corporations will be operating in an increasingly free enterprise environment. Historically, free enterprise has always been a dominant institution in the United States. Since the early 1980s, other countries have turned their large and small government-run corporations back to the private sector. Governments around the world are abandoning central planning in favor of competition. Although some political factions in formerly centrally planned economies are questioning the benefits of selling off state-owned enterprises, the worldwide trend toward privatization is likely to continue almost unabated. Privatization encourages competitiveness which, in turn, helps foster global interactions among firms. Tremendous strides in technology and telecommunications facilitate the development of similar management cultures and styles across national boundaries.

Industrial development has its downside as well as benefits. As manufacturing develops and proliferates, externalities or by-products are not always beneficial. Residue from the production process may harm the environment and society. Along with goods and services, companies create toxic wastes, polluted water, and unhealthy air. In addition, they contribute to unplanned urban sprawl, uneven distribution of wealth, unsafe products, and ethically questionable situations. The corporate propensity to merge, acquire, proliferate, and contract leads to job flight in one area while job opportunities increase elsewhere. Employee uncertainty and insecurity leads to stress, anxiety, and even fear.

Since the 1960s, the debate has sharpened about the elements that constitute a corporation's proper role in society. Diverse groups of stakeholders pressure firms to conform to their own views of proper corporate behavior. Ethnic and racial minorities, environmentalists, consumer advocates, and special-interest lobbyists join regulatory agencies, union leaders, academicians, politicians, and social commentators in demanding that corporations take particular actions. These demands are frequently contradictory and sometimes counterproductive.

The relative power of different groups of stakeholders changes over time. As issues important to one group dissipate or are resolved, new stakeholder groups take up the banner and focus on new local or national concerns. The essential issue for every group is to define the appropriate role of business in an increasingly complex world. Over the past decade, millions of stakeholders in scores of countries have joined the debate. It is incredibly difficult for managers to respond to multiple competing demands on a national basis and even more difficult when stakeholders have global concerns.

Nonetheless, managers must adopt a global view of social issues management. The major challenge for corporations, wherever located, is to develop strategies that help their managers work toward a reasonable definition of their appropriate societal role and do an effective job of implementing and managing social issues.

This chapter begins with a look at the issues of the late 1990s and beyond. It discusses linkages between the social and political environment and corporate strategy. The chapter also explores the nature of capitalism and the meaning of responsibility in business, government, and society.

Issues of the Late 1990s

The economy, social climate, physical environment, and composition of the workforce all help determine the mix and scope of social issues that corporations and their stakeholders face. US and global managers recognize that they need to address a wide spectrum of national and global economic and social con-cerns. They realize there are no easy answers to complex, difficult problems in their own country and even fewer answers to problems in other countries.

Media chronicles of job contraction, underemployment, stagnating incomes, the huge national debt, and ideological malaise may seem dismal. However, companies can formulate and implement strategies to help them survive and thrive into the next century. Opportunities abound for forward-looking individuals and firms that anticipate a future substantially different from the one which they currently operate.

Now and in the beginning of the next century, new technologies will require extensive academic and on-the-job training. Ethical issues will take on a new urgency. United States companies will face uncertainties in the political and legal environments as Congress and the courts change long-standing and hitherto sacrosanct expectations. New laws will be churned out as others are abolished. Outside the United States, the actions of foreign governments will constrain companies in some areas and provide opportunities in others. Every issue will have multiple well-organized stakeholders, both proponents and detractors, who will pursue their own agendas with energy and determination.

To a great extent, managers will be judged by how effectively they identify their stakeholders and then formulate and implement thoughtful, comprehensive corporate strategies at home and abroad. In addition to environmental, legal, and political concerns, strategic planning will have to incorporate crisis management and multiple workplace issues.

The U.S. Economy

In the middle 1990s and later, stakeholders asked many of the same questions as stakeholders earlier in the decade. They wanted to know why business was not delivering on expectations that American society had always taken for granted. People became increasingly discouraged about their opportunity to prosper in an environment they had always taken for granted. Despite a vigorous stock market and low unemployment nationwide, large numbers of citizens seemed to regard job stability, future opportunity, and good pay and benefits as an ideal becoming more and more elusive. In a *Business Week/Harris* poll, 67 percent of Americans said the American dream was getting further out of reach. When asked whether they thought the American dream of equal opportunity, personal freedom, and social mobility had become harder or easier to achieve in the past 10 years, 31 percent said easier, 67 percent said harder, and 2 percent weren't sure.[2]

Traditionally, people believed they should be able to count on business leaders to ensure that American companies were fully competitive with overseas firms. They assumed they and their children would have at least as much financial and job security as had earlier generations. In January 1996, a *Wall Street Journal*/NBC News poll showed that although American baby boomers were reasonably satisfied with their own economic circumstances, they were concerned about their children's future. Fifty-two percent of Americans did not expect their children's generation to achieve a higher standard of living than they enjoyed. Only 41 percent expected their children to be generally better off.[3]

A Time/CNN poll was not quite as pessimistic. Sixty-four percent of the 800 respondents said they believed their children would have better jobs than they did, and 63 percent said their children would have better standards of living.[4] Although this poll was more optimistic, it was clear that large number of people had doubts about their families' future.

There was widespread sentiment that the rich were faring far better than the middle class or the poor. A January 1996 poll conducted by Lake Research and the Terrance Group found that 76 percent of voters believed that the wealthy had gained the most in the past five years. Only 6 percent thought the middle class had gained the most.[5]

Census Bureau data indicate that the share of aggregate household income earned by the middle 60 percent of households (average household income: $31,300) shrank from 52 percent in 1973 to 48 percent in 1993. By

---

[2] *Business Week*/Harris Poll, "America, Land of the Shaken," *Business Week,* March 11, 1996, p. 64.

[3] D. Wessel and G. F. Seib, "Americans, Especially Baby Boomers, Voice Pessimism for Their Kids' Economic Future," *The Wall Street Journal,* January 19, 1996, p. A12.

[4] "Poll: 50% Believe U.S. in Deep Trouble," *Boston Globe,* January 21, 1996, p. 8.

[5] D. L. Boroughs, "Workers Take It on the Chin," *US News & World Report,* January 22, 1996, p. 44.

1995, the total purchasing power of the top 20 percent of U.S. households equaled that of the middle 60 percent.[6] Profound political and social implications exist for policymakers when large segments of the population believe a pervasive financial and social inequality cannot be ameliorated.

The share of total wealth held by the richest 1 percent of families nearly doubled between 1979 and 1989. Between 1989 and 1992, the portion of wealth held by the richest 1 percent declined from 37.1 percent to 30.4 percent. The next richest 9 percent had its share of the nation's wealth grow from 31.2 percent to 36.8 percent.[7] From a middle-class perspective these numbers were almost irrelevant. The gap between the middle class and the holders of the top 10 percent of the nation's wealth was a chasm. The share going to the remaining 90 percent of households rose only 1 percent between 1989 and 1992.[8]

In 1996, 42 percent of all marketable assets belonged to a small group that held a minimum of $2.3 million per family. Middle-income Americans held most of their assets in their home equity and savings. When housing markets leveled off in the mid-1990s, the middle class virtually stopped accumulating savings. The wealthy, however, continued to realize huge gains in the stock market. A 1996 report by the Organization for Economic Co-operation and Development (OECD) determined the United States had the most unequal distribution of wealth among the advanced industrialized nations.[9] Divided by nationality, gender, and age, segments of the population encountered different social and economic environments.

Immigration

Between 1990 and 1994, New York State's population was bolstered by 450,000 immigrants. Demographer William Frey believed that job competition from foreign immigrants pushed residents of some states out of lower-paying, lesser-skilled jobs. He suggested the influx of foreign immigration would keep pressure on less-educated mostly white residents of states like Illinois, Massachusetts, New Jersey, and New York. A possible by-product of immigration could be an exodus of previous residents to states where opportunities were growing. The migration also might create what Frey called balkanization as middle- and lower-middle-class whites leave states with high immigration. In the future, the biggest U.S. cities and some states could become polarized with affluent white professionals at one end and minority immigrants at the other.[10]

---

[6] P. Francese, "America at Mid-Decade," *American Demographics,* February 1995, p. 29.

[7] R. Stevenson, "Rich Are Getting Richer But Not the Very Rich," *New York Times,* March 13, 1996, p. D1.

[8] "Wealth Wars," *Economist,* March 23, 1996, p. 27.

[9] Boroughs, p. 49.

[10] "Where Americans Are Moving," *Fortune,* August 21, 1995, p. 38.

The most recent data suggest that legal immigration has slowed. The March 1996 report of the Immigration and Naturalization Service (INS) showed that for the nation as a whole, legal immigration was 10.4 percent below 1994's total and 20.3 percent below 1993. The INS attributed part of the drop to underutilized employment visas. On the other hand, there has been a 132 percent increase in requests for legal status since the passage of the 1994 law letting immigrants stay in the United States while they apply for visas. At the time the report was issued, 3.5 million people had been approved for admission to the United States and were waiting for family-sponsored preference visas.[11]

In 1996, non-Hispanic whites accounted for three-quarters of the U.S. population. By 2050, non-Hispanic whites will be about one-half of the total population. Already immigration and a relatively high birth rate have led to a surge in the nation's Hispanic population. In 4 of the nation's 10 largest cities Hispanics outnumber blacks.

Asian immigrants were the fastest-growing immigrant group in the United States. Between 1971 and 1990, the number of people from Asia or the Pacific Rim grew 385 percent. By the year 2000, this group is expected to reach 11 million. The number of businesses owned by Asian-Americans grew by 90 percent from 1982 to 1987. A study conducted by Leadership Education for Asian Pacifics reported that Asian immigrants have a substantial role in new company development and have a special ability to attract investment from Asian venture capitalists.[12]

Age Segmentation

Age segmentation also had major social and business implications. The ranks of teenagers, the youngest independent consumers, began to grow in 1992. As baby boomers' babies reached their teen years and immigrant families arrived in the United States, the number of teenagers grew. Demographers predicted the number of teens would rise at twice the rate of the overall population until 2005. In the year 2006, there will be 30.8 million teens, with the bulge peaking in 2010. By then, one in three teens would belong to a minority compared to one in four in the total population.

Teenagers have grown up with different societal expectations and responsibilities than their parents. They also have been exposed to new forms of communication and new levels of technology. Personal computers, worldwide interactive data retrieval, VCRs, CD players, and cellular phones are taken for granted. In 1994, 60 percent of 12 to 17 year olds had their own CD players, and 20 percent belonged to record clubs. About one in nine had a

---

[11] "The Coming-to-America Tide Ebbs," *US News & World Report,* April 8, 1996, p. 6.

[12] C. Goldberg, "Asian Immigrants Help Bolster U.S. Economy, New Report Says," *New York Times,* March 31, 1996, p. 32.

personal credit card. According to a Nickelodeon/Yankelovich Youth Monitor survey, many teens shop for themselves, make their own meals, and do their own laundry.[13] Teens also have experienced their parents' job layoffs and increased family debt. Large numbers have been exposed to violence, AIDS, and adult responsibilities.

In a 1994 survey of 500 teenage students, 73 percent of those aged 12 to 17 declared that violence and crime were major problems in their own lives. One-third of the students said crime was serious in their schools. Many reported they knew people who carried guns and knives to school or knew someone who had been shot.[14] Data bear out these teens' perceptions. The Children's Defense Fund reported in April 1996 that gunfire was the second leading cause of death among children ages 10 to 19 and that firearm deaths were increasing faster among that age group than any other.[15]

In the late 1990s, many teens are growing up in nontraditional one-parent or same-gender-parent families. From the mid-1960s to mid-1990s, the birthrate among unmarried women 15 to 19 years old nearly tripled to 45 births per 1,000. Although it appears that the increase in births among unmarried women may be stabilizing, teenage pregnancy and birth rates continue to grow, albeit at a slower rate.

Older Americans faced different issues and problems. In 1995, about half of all householders were aged 45 and older. The middle-aged segment of householders aged 45 to 54 was growing fastest.[16] Experts predict the 50-60 age group will grow by 50 percent in the decade between 1996 and 2006. By 2030 the group 65 and older will make up 20 percent of the population. A Population Reference Bureau study showed that the elderly over 65 have higher living standards than at any time in U.S. history primarily due to a combination of government programs like Medicare and pension benefits. However, there is considerable poverty among women, the unmarried, and minorities.

A 1995 study by the Rand organization found the top 5 percent of white families with at least one spouse over 70 had wealth of $655,000, seven times the $90,000 held by the median white household. However, white households in the bottom 10 percent had less than $800. Preretirement white households aged 51-61 in the top 5 percent had $300,00 in savings compared to a median of $17,300. The bottom 20 percent had less than $800. Typical black and Hispanic households in these age groups had less than $500 in assets and 4 out of 10 had nothing.[17]

---

[13] L. Zinn, "Teens, Here Comes the Biggest Wave Yet," *Business Week,* April 11, 1994, pp. 76–86.

[14] D. Crispell, "People Patterns," *The Wall Street Journal,* March 10, 1995, p. B1.

[15] "Guns Are No. 2 Cause of Death among the Young, Data Show," *New York Times,* April 9, 1996, p. A16.

[16] Francese, p. 24.

[17] "Gap between Rich, Poor Seen Worse," *Boston Globe,* July 25, 1995, p. 33.

Gender Issues

Working women provided more of the total family income at the end of the 1990s. In 1994, women's labor-force participation rose to 58.8 percent. The increase occurred among all women except those aged 20 to 24. In 1987, women provided 39 percent of the family's income. By 1995, half of working women brought home half the household income. U.S. women formed companies at nearly twice the rate of all businesses between 1987 and 1996. The National Foundation for Women Business Owners said the number of women-owned business increased 78 percent in contrast to the 47 percent increase in the total number of businesses. The report showed that women-owned businesses employed about 26 percent of the American workforce early in 1966.[18]

Education played a major role in women's earning potential. By 1995, among workers under age 35, women accounted for one in three doctors, 4 in 10 mail carriers, and a majority of purchasing agents. In general, however, median salaries of women were lower than their male counterparts. Experts attributed the disparity to several factors; women tended to have shorter tenure in work, did more part-time work, and suffered greater job discrimination than men.[19]

As women gained greater job status and experience in the workplace, men began to change their views of gender roles. Increasingly, men refused to relocate if their companies didn't provide spousal assistance. As Rosalind Barnett, a senior scholar at Radcliffe noted, "Men's and women's work and home lives are like a spider's interconnected web; a tug that occurs at one section of the web sends vibrations all through it."[20]

Corporate Restructuring

The corporate restructuring policies of the early 1990s continued; newspapers and magazines reported daily on mergers and acquisitions. In 1995, domestic mergers totaled more than $450 billion. In just the first week of the second quarter of 1996, merger activity totaled $28.3 billion.[21] News media reported on two huge mergers on April 2, 1996. In one of the largest corporate mergers ever, two regional Bell telephone systems combined. SBC Communication announced it was acquiring Pacific Telesis Group for nearly $17 billion. The deals will create a company providing service to 30 million

---

[18] "Women-Owned Business Boom," *Financial Times,* March 28, 1996, p. 6.

[19] S. Roberts, "Women's Work: What's New, What Isn't," *New York Times,* April 27, 1995, p. B6; T. Lewin, "Women Are Becoming Equal Providers," *New York Times,* May 11, 1995, p. A27.

[20] S. Shellenbarger, "Work & Family," *The Wall Street Journal,* February 14, 1996, p. B1.

[21] S. Lipin, "Megadeals Accelerate Merger Action after a Slowdown in the First Quarter," *The Wall Street Journal,* April 8, 1996, p. A3.

residential and business customers in seven states west of the Mississippi.[22] We discuss the impact of that merger in more detail in Chapter 9.

The same day, Aetna Life and Casualty Company announced it planned to buy U.S. Healthcare, Inc., for $8.8 billion. The combined company—the largest medical benefits company in the nation—will cover 1 in 12 Americans. It will offer health and disability protection, prescriptions, mental health care, vision, and dental care. This deal was the biggest in a wave of consolidation of health care companies.[23] Changes in health care delivery are discussed in Chapter 11.

Mergers, acquisitions, and consolidations are international as well as domestic. As competition for global markets continued to intensify, companies of all nationalities sought cross-border and domestic alliances. Telecommunications companies, entertainment/media, and commercial banking were particularly active industries seeking new partners to meet customer demand and intense global competition. The Bank of Tokyo and Mitsubishi Bank combined to create the world's largest bank. The new bank had assets of $373 billion and was 2.4 percent bigger than Chase Manhattan Bank which had merged with Chemical Bank a few days earlier.[24] Sandoz Ltd. merged with Ciba-Geigy Ltd. in a deal valued at more than $30 billion. British Petroleum and Mobil Corporation merged their European marketing and refining business.[25]

Some companies restructured by splitting into more manageable nimble units. AT&T's 1995 breakup was due, in large part, to global pressures and opportunities. The privatization of telephone companies around the world meant that AT&T and others had to scramble for international alliances. By splitting the company into three parts, AT&T's board could give its attention to the telephone service that accounted for two-thirds of the former company. AT&T's domestic competitors, MCI and Sprint, had already formed tighter European and Asian alliances. The new structure was designed to shed AT&T's image as a slow, hidebound 800-pound gorilla.[26]

Companies and the media seemed to reach a tacit agreement that layoffs and downsizing were simply inevitable. There was no more discussion of whether downsizing was socially responsible behavior. In 1995 and 1996 Wall Street applauded when companies downsized. Investors and analysts seemed to respect the companies that inflicted the deepest cuts and fired the

---

[22] L. Eaton, "Aetna to Buy US Healthcare in Big Move to Managed Care," *New York Times,* April 2, 1996, p. A1.

[23] J. Keller and G. Naik, "SBC-Pac Tel Merger Is Likely to Ring in an Era of Alliances among Baby Bells," *The Wall Street Journal,* April 2, 1996, p. B1.

[24] S. WuDunn, "Opening Day for Biggest Bank in the World," *New York Times,* April 2, 1996, p. D4.

[25] Lipin, p. A8.

[26] T. Jackson, "Giant Bows to Colossal Pressure," *Financial Times,* September 22, 1995, p. 13.

greatest number of workers. Executive pay rose along with corporate profits and productivity.[27]

Ronald Compton, chairman of Aetna Life & Casualty, received a 1996 compensation package of $6.64 million, a 485 percent jump over the previous year. Oracle Corporation Chairman Lawrence J. Ellison's pay went up 387 percent. Delta Airlines, which had announced the elimination of 18,800 jobs since 1991, gave its chief Robert W. Allen a 187 percent increase in 1995. The largest compensation package went to Coca-Cola Chairman Roberto C. Goizueta who received $13.1 million in 1995 and a stock option grant worth more than $25 million.[28]

Unlike CEOs, compensation packages for nonexecutive employees were tied increasingly to performance. In 1995, nearly 50 percent of all companies in a Towers Perrin survey had a variable-pay plan tied to divisions' performance. Base-pay and future merit-pay plans were frozen as companies implemented pay-for-performance programs. The erosion of trust and perception of inequity between top management and workers seemed to be exacerbated by this dual system. One expert noted that "the kind of trust that would be needed to have these [pay plans] function long term probably doesn't exist in a lot of companies."[29]

In March 1996, the *New York Times* published a seven-part series on the downsizing of America. The newspaper's nationwide poll of 1,265 adults conducted December 3 to 6, 1995, found economic insecurity and fear of job loss had eroded the loyalty between employees and their companies. When asked whether companies were more loyal or less loyal to their employees than they were in 1985, 75 percent said they were less loyal. When asked whether workers were more loyal or less loyal in the same time period, 64 percent of respondents said they were less loyal. Seventy percent said they competed with their co-workers more often than in the past; only 20 percent reported they cooperated more.[30]

Between 1979 and the end of 1995, more than 43 million jobs were eliminated nationwide. The U.S. Labor Department's Bureau of Labor Statistics reported 24.8 million blue-collar jobs were lost in occupations like factory work, transportation, mining, and construction. White-collar jobs lost numbered 18.7 million. A University of Michigan study tracking 5,000 families since 1968 found that among the college-educated over 50, the rate of layoffs doubled from the 1980s.

It is true that each year more jobs were created than lost. This factor accounted for the low jobless rate in 1996 even though the rate of layoffs

---

[27] B. D. Butterfield, "Pink Slips *and* Profits," *Boston Globe,* December 31, 1995, p. 56.
[28] J. A. Byrne, "Gross Compensation?" *Business Week,* March 18, 1996, pp. 32–33.
[29] W. Zellner, E. Schine, and G. Smith, "Trickle-Down Is Trickling Down at Work," *Business Week,* March 18, 1996, p. 34.
[30] N. R. Kleinfield, "The Company as a Family, No More," *New York Times,* March 4, 1996, p. A1.

increased. The total number of nonagricultural jobs grew from 90 million in 1979 to 117 million in 1995, even though 43 million jobs were eliminated as just noted. According to the Labor Department, many people who lost full-time jobs were paid less by a new employer or were able to find only part-time work. Among those workers who lost full-time jobs in 1991 or 1992, 35 percent were paid the same or more in 1994. Sixty-five percent were paid less. Twenty-four percent of those who lost their jobs were still unemployed in 1994.[31]

Pollster Daniel Yankelovich warned job insecurity unleashed "a floating anger that [is attaching] itself to all sorts of targets as a form of scapegoating." Polls showed voters were angry at immigrants, blacks, women, government, corporations, welfare recipients, computers, the very rich, and even the concept of capitalism.[32]

Politics and Change

The November 1994 Republican sweep of the House of Representatives drastically changed the political scene. For the first time in 40 years Republicans, led by Speaker Newt Gingrich, controlled the House. The Republican Contract with America set an agenda for social issues.[33]

The Contract included, among other things, a balanced budget amendment, welfare reform, a line-item veto, greater congressional accountability, reform of House rules, term limits, a crime bill, a family reinforcement act, a middle-class tax cut, a constitutional amendment on school prayer, drastic cuts in farm subsidies, and a widespread change in the system of civil litigation. Many of these issues are discussed in greater detail later in the book.

By spring 1996, much of the Republican revolution was stalled. In November and December 1995, federal workers were sent home when President Bill Clinton and the Republican congressional leaders could not agree on routine appropriations bills. Constitutional amendments were defeated and tax cuts vetoed. Some domestic spending cuts were implemented but offset by higher military spending.

Results of Specific Legislative Initiatives

1. *Health care:* Republicans wanted to cut $270 billion from projected spending on Medicare for the elderly and $170 billion from Medicaid for the poor. President Clinton vetoed the bill that also would have encouraged the elderly to enter health maintenance programs and other managed care plans.

---

[31] L. Uchitelle and N. R. Kleinfield, "On the Battlefields of Business, Millions of Casualties," *New York Times,* March 3, 1996, p.1.
[32] Ibid., p. 28.
[33] The complete Contract with America can be accessed through the United We Stand home page. Internet [http://www.telusys.com/newuwsa/html]

2. *Welfare:* The House passed a welfare bill later vetoed by the Clinton administration.

3. *Environment:* The House passed a sweeping environmental reform bill to change the way all environmental laws were enforced; the Senate rejected it. Nevertheless, there were substantial cuts in environmental protection spending. In January 1996, the Republicans, worried about political damage, backed off their tough environmental stand. A Republican pollster reported that only 35 percent of the public would vote to re-elect members of the House who supported the Republican-backed bill for severely cutting financing to the Environmental Protection Agency (EPA).[34]

4. *Agriculture:* Despite promises to radically redesign agricultural subsidies, nothing was done until April 1996. Clinton quietly signed farm legislation that lifted many government controls on farmers although he opposed the key provisions because they "failed to provide an adequate safety net for family farmers." Senator Richard Lugar called the farm bill "the most historic change in American agriculture since the 1930s."[35]

5. *Social issues:* The Contract included a crime bill, middle-class tax cut, dismantling of the federal welfare system, a constitutional amendment on school prayer, and federal money for private and parochial schools. None of these items were passed.

6. *Law enforcement:* President Clinton took the initiative on the law-enforcement issue and vetoed the Republican-passed measures.

7. *Education:* Congress tried to reduce the federal role in education but the unfinished budget left its efforts in doubt.[36]

8. *Line-item veto:* In March 1996, the Senate gave final passage to the line-item veto, a major item in the Contract. The bill, scheduled to become effective in January 1997, prevented President Clinton from exercising the veto in his first term. The Republicans clearly hoped that a Republican would be in the White House when it took effect. The president would be able to cut individual items from the annual spending bills. He also could cancel any tax break that affected 100 or fewer taxpayers and could cancel new entitlement programs or expansion of benefits in existing programs such as Medicare or welfare. Senator Ted Stevens (R-Alaska) said, "It will be the most significant delegation of authority by the Congress to the president since the Constitution was ratified in 1789." Some constitutional scholars asserted that the measure would face a court challenge since the shift in balance of powers required a constitutional amendment.[37]

---

[34] J. H. Cushman, Jr., "GOP Backing Off from Tough Stand over the Environment," *New York Times,* January 26, 1996, p. A1.

[35] "Clinton Signs Law Ending Crop Supports," *Boston Globe,* April 5, 1996, p. 8.

[36] A. Clymer, "GOP Revolution Hits Speed Bumps on Capitol Hill," *New York Times,* January 21, 1996, p. 1.

[37] Internet [http://all-politics.com/news/9603/28/line.item]; C. Georges, "Senate Approves, 69-31, Line-Item Veto," *The Wall Street Journal,* March 29, 1996, p. A3.

As the 1996 presidential campaign heated up, Senate President Robert Dole emerged as the Republican front-runner. By the end of the March Republican primaries, he had more than enough votes to solidify his position going into the summer convention. Political pundits were unwilling to predict what changes would or could be made before the November elections. The only thing that was clear was that American society and enterprise would remain firmly rooted in capitalist ideology. The election of President Clinton to a second term, and the mass return of incumbents to the House and Senate virtually guaranteed that 1997 would bring more of the same legislatively. Although Democrats, Republicans, and Independents often had very different ideas of the meaning of capitalism, there were certain concepts to which all adhered. In the next section, we discuss the ideology of the capitalist system and the evolution of modern U.S. corporations.

The Nature of Capitalism

American ideology is based on capitalism. Essentially a capitalistic system is a system in which the means of production are privately owned and the market operates to guide production and distribute income. Frequently the terms *free enterprise* or *private enterprise* are used interchangeably with capitalism. It is not easy to describe the nature of the system, but some basic features are generally accepted.

The classical theory of capitalism is founded on two fundamental assumptions: (1) human beings are rational creatures capable of understanding the natural order of the universe, and (2) the role of government in the economy can and should be limited. The relationship between these two assumptions led classical economists to believe that if all artificial barriers to economic behavior, such as tariffs, monopolies, and wage controls, were removed, labor, capital, and natural resources would all seek their own economic interests. If government or monopolists who enjoyed unnatural powers in the marketplace did not interfere, the market would benefit everyone in society.

Exhibit 1–1 shows the essential elements of capitalism: (1) private property, (2) economic incentive in the form of the profit motive, (3) a free market system, and (4) political and economic freedom.

Adam Smith first expressed his views on capitalism in *The Wealth of Nations,* published in 1776. Smith argued that every individual continually tries to find the most advantageous way to employ whatever capital he can command. The individual works to enhance his own advantage and not that of society. However, when the individual considers personal advantage, he naturally prefers employment that is most advantageous to the society.[38]

---

[38] A. Smith, *The Wealth of Nations,* vol. 4 (New York: Modern Library, 1937), p. 421.

EXHIBIT 1–1 The Essential Elements of Capitalism

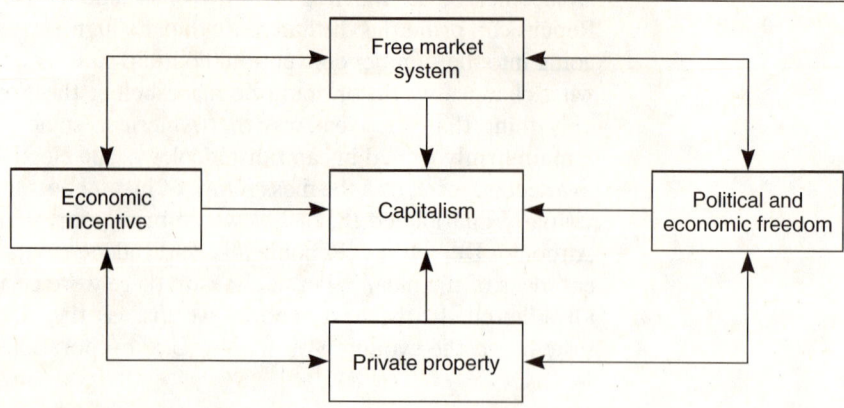

Ralph Waldo Emerson, a 19th-century American writer, also emphasized the importance of individualism. He believed societal structures inhibited individual potential; only in an unfettered social and political system could people develop their potential. In his book *The Conduct of Life and Other Essays,* Emerson wrote that people are inclined by their very nature to be productive and to make money.[39]

In theory, every activity in a free enterprise must return a profit. However, free enterprise or capitalistic systems are never totally pure. Every nation in the world has values and goals that place it on a continuum between free enterprise and a planned economy. Each determines where it lies on the continuum by the priority it gives to specific values and goals.

Private Property

The concept of property as more than land is an essential and significant element of capitalism. John Locke, the 17th-century English economist and philosopher wrote,

> Though the earth and all inferior creatures be common to all men, yet every man has a property in his own person; this nobody has any right to but himself. The labour of his body and the work of his hands, we may say, are properly his. Whatsoever then he removes out of the state that nature hath provided and left in it, he hath mixed his labour with, and joined to it something that is his own, and thereby makes it his property.[40]

In essence, a person who has property or assets also has the right to use them and to enjoy the economic power that ownership conveys. However,

---

[39] R. W. Emerson, *The Conduct of Life and Other Essays* (London: Dent, 1908), pp. 190–213.
[40] T. I. Cook, *Two Treatises of Government by John Locke* (New York: Hafner Publishing, 1947), p. 134.

Locke's notion of property was not universally accepted in 19th-century America. During the late 19th-century, the U.S. courts struggled with the concept. The classic Supreme Court case of *Munn* v. *Illinois* clarified both the meaning of property and epitomized the legal struggle that took place to define the legitimacy of the state to control the use of private property.

In the 1880s, farm organizations put intense political pressure on Illinois state legislators to allow the state to fix rates for grain storage. The law, which favored the farmers, passed the Illinois state legislature in 1883. Grain elevator operators challenged the law, and the case eventually went to the Supreme Court. In 1877, the Court found the state did have the right to regulate private property. Chief Justice Waite, in the majority opinion, reasoned that when "one devotes his property to a use in which the public has an interest, he, in effect, grants to the public an interest in that use, and must submit to be controlled by the public for the common good, to the extent of the interest he has thus created."[41] The Court thereby rejected the argument that the regulation of grain elevator rates was a deprivation of property rights without due process.

Despite *Munn* v. *Illinois* and subsequent cases that expanded the right of the state to regulate private property, it is clear that in most instances the owner of property has right to control it. People may buy, sell, lease, franchise, and engage in a variety of other contractual arrangements regarding their property. Businesspeople who need to control their companies' tangible and intangible resources find this right essential.

Business executives would probably care very little about property and its control if they could not make money managing their resources. The profit motive fuels capitalism. In 1957 Max Lerner argued, "Men's brains and energy work best when they have no hampering restrictions, and when they see an immediacy of relation between effort and reward."[42] More than 40 years later, few would argue with Lerner's view.

Classical theory is not and cannot be fully applied to all political environments. There has never been a time in which every country in the world has operated as a free market based on the profit motive. In trade and business, national interests and pragmatism have always prevailed over theory and ideology.

Milton Friedman wrote about the role of government and business saying "government is necessary to preserve our freedom; yet by concentrating power in political hands, it is also a threat to freedom."[43] Friedman contended that the dilemma could be solved by recognizing two principles.

---

[41] *Munn* v. *Illinois,* 94 U.S. 113 (1877), p. 125.

[42] M. Lerner, *America as a Civilization,* vol. 1 (New York: Simon & Schuster, 1957), p. 268.

[43] M. Friedman, *Capitalism and Freedom* (Chicago: University of Chicago Press, 1961), p. 2.

First, the scope of the government must be strictly limited. According to Friedman, "Its major functions must be to protect our freedom both from the enemies outside our gates and from our fellow citizens: to preserve law and order, to enforce private contracts, to foster competitive markets."[44]

Second, the power exercised by government must be dispersed. In essence, Friedman argued that government should exercise its limited powers at the level closest to the people involved; that is, local communities should resolve issues involving streets, schools, sewers, and the like. The few problems that could not be solved locally would go to the county, the few that were broader yet would go to the state, and only a limited number of issues would find their way to Washington, D.C.

This view of the role of government, especially as it applies to nonintervention in business matters, may be traced directly to Adam Smith. A policy of laissez-faire, under which the government keeps its hands out of economic activities, continues to be central to the debate concerning the roles of business and society.

The Dynamic Nature of Business

Joseph A. Schumpeter, writing in the 1920s, saw economic systems in a process of continuous change. He noted that every process of economic development rested on the preceding development which, in turn, created the prerequisites for what was to follow. He posited that in a competitive environment there was a phenomenon called creative destruction, in which new combinations or firms emerged and old firms were necessarily eliminated. Schumpeter who first wrote *The Theory of Economic Development* as part of the 1934 Harvard Economic Series, characterized the entrepreneur who created these new enterprises as an individual who had the dream and will to create an industrial or commercial success, the will to conquer, "the impulse to fight to prove oneself superior to others, to succeed for the sake, not the fruits of success, but of success itself." Finally, he said, there was "the joy of creating, of getting things done, or simply exercising one's energy and ingenuity." Profit was an additional objective measure of success.[45]

Michael E. Porter writing in *The Competitive Advantage of Nations,* commented that Schumpeter's contribution on competition still holds in the global environment. "Much traditional thinking has embodied an essentially static view focusing on cost efficiency due to factor or scale advantages. Technological change is treated as though it is exogenous, or outside the purview of the theory. As Joseph Schumpeter recognized . . . there is no 'equilibrium' in competition. Competition is a constantly changing the land-

---

[44] Ibid.
[45] J. A. Schumpeter, *The Theory of Economic Development* (New York: Oxford University Press, 1961), pp. 1–94.

scape in which new products, new ways of marketing, new production processes, and whole new market segments emerge."[46]

As new global enterprises emerge and older ones disappear, governments will continue to intervene and participate in free market systems. Theoretically, one key to the existence of a free market system is the absence or paucity of government regulation. Yet in the United States, government regulations dismantle most businesses when they get large enough to constitute a monopoly. In the past two decades, we have seen a great deal of confusion regarding the government's stand on antitrust. Since 1978, the U.S. government has lifted rules that set prices and controlled the entry of new companies.

Government's intervention in business matters changed profoundly in the 1980s and continues to evolve in the 1990s. Throughout the mid-1980s, the Justice Department relaxed merger guidelines. To meet foreign competition and record trade deficits, the Bush and Reagan administrations focused their activities on price fixing and bid rigging rather than on price and territorial arrangements between manufacturers and distributors.[47] We discuss antitrust and what the future may hold for that issue in much greater detail in Chapters 8 and 9.

While the U.S. economy has moved a long way from the vision of Adam Smith, the concepts of a free enterprise economy are deeply rooted in our culture and continue to influence the definition of business as an institution. Since the 19th century, government has played an increasingly active role in economic affairs. Government's intervention in business matters changed profoundly in the 1980s and continues to evolve in the 1990s. As noted earlier, the election of 1994 represented a sweeping change in thinking about government's role. It is highly unlikely that at any time in the foreseeable future the United States will return to the highly regulated environment that existed prior to 1978.

The Modern Corporation

The corporation is another underlying concept central to an understanding of the relationship between business and society in the United States. As a form of business organization, the corporation has played a central role in the evolution of capitalism. While the nation's sole proprietorships and partnerships significantly outnumber corporations, the sales and assets of corporations dwarf other organizational forms. The huge enterprises in the Fortune 500 are almost exclusively corporations.

In the United States, individual states charter corporations to engage in specified types of business activity. Corporations enjoy important legal

---

[46] M. E. Porter, *The Competitive Advantage of Nations* (New York: The Free Press, 1990), p. 20.

[47] "Reagan Turns a Cold Eye on Antitrust," *Fortune,* October 14, 1985, p. 31.

advantages over sole proprietorships and partnerships in that they are characterized by perpetual succession and the personal liability of their owners is limited to the extent of the owners' investment in the corporation. A corporation continues as a legal entity regardless of the physical well-being of its founders and owners. Unlike proprietorships and partnerships, claims against the corporation do not jeopardize the personal property of the owners.

The modern corporation was first defined by the Supreme Court case of *Dartmouth College* v. *Woodward* (1819). In this case, which helped confirm the rights of the corporate form of organization, Chief Justice Marshall described the corporation as "an artificial being, invisible, intangible, and existing only in contemplation of law." In a sense, the corporation is a fictitious person who has the right to sue and can be sued, is protected from claims based on the separate debts of its owners, may own and sell property, and may engage in contracts.

Adolph A. Berle and Gardiner C. Means wrote *The Modern Corporation and Private Property,* an important contribution to our understanding of modern corporations. First published in 1932, this study moved well beyond the debate over the legal form of corporations, focusing instead on their political and social impact. The study's principal concerns were the concentration of economic power among the largest corporations and the separation of corporate ownership and control. The authors noted:

> Corporations have ceased to be merely legal devices through which the private business transactions of individuals may be carried on. Though still much used for this purpose, the corporate form has acquired a larger significance. The corporation has, in fact, become both a method of property tenure and a means of organizing economic life. A corporate system has accrued to it a combination of attributes and powers and has attained a degree of prominence entitling it to be dealt with as a major social institution.[48]

The authors' perception of the corporation as a system of organization is even more relevant in the late 1990s than it was in the beginning of President Franklin D. Roosevelt's New Deal. Today corporations transcend national boundaries and product categories. Their assets, ownership, resources, and power go well beyond the expectations of early scholars and organizational theorists. To a very great degree, corporations touch nearly every part of our daily lives.

The modern corporation has stakeholders or, according to Richard Ells and Clarence Walton, a constellation of interests that exists not only at the core of the organization but at the periphery as well.[49] The direct claimants (stakeholders) of the corporation are owners of stocks and bonds, employees,

---

[48] A. A. Berle and G. C. Means, *The Modern Corporation and Private Property,* rev. ed. (New York: Harcourt Brace Jovanovich, 1967), p. 3.

[49] R. Ells and C. Walton, *Conceptual Foundations of Business* (Burr Ridge, IL: Richard D. Irwin, 1961), pp. 147–63.

customers, and suppliers. The indirect claimants include competitors, local communities, the general public, and governments. A business scholar, Dov Votaw, concluded that the corporation is our way of life because of its economic power and the scope of its influence on almost every facet of the lives of individuals in our society.[50]

In a corporation, ownership interests can be transferred relatively easily. Corporate equity is represented by shares of stock that may be exchanged for cash or other assets. Individuals or groups are able to purchase or sell corporate shares through organized domestic stock markets such as the New York and American stock exchanges. With modern telecommunications individuals can purchase stocks around the world every hour of the day. When the stock markets are closed in New York they are busy in Tokyo, Hong Kong, or Europe. Stock markets selling shares in local and international companies are developing all over the world. Even tiny countries such as Singapore have sophisticated computer systems that allow buyers and sellers to communicate and conduct transactions.

The corporation and its stakeholders play a central role in our study of business and society. We focus on the interaction of large corporations with the business environment along the ideological continuum from planned economy to free enterprise. We also examine systems that are emerging from central planning and are struggling to define their economic, social, and ideological systems. Primarily, we concentrate on companies that are professionally managed, publicly owned, and have multiple profit centers. Generally these companies wield great power and influence and are most often the subject of controversy regarding their role in society.

Managers of large companies must be directly concerned with issues related to the social responsibility of business. While their companies may not necessarily be better or more responsive corporate citizens than smaller concerns, these managers have a greater vested interest in developing methods of improving their strategic management skills in this area of their firms' operations. The process of strategic thinking, planning, and implementation is central to this book's theme. There are explicit links between management strategy and the economic, social, and political environments.

The Linkage between Strategy and the Economic, Social, and Political Environments

Managers in the late 1990s still have much to learn from Peter F. Drucker's 1980 statement that "performance in management . . . means in large measure doing a good job of preparing today's business for the future."[51] Effective managers must deal with daily and future threats and opportunities.

---

[50] D. Votaw, *Modern Corporations* (Englewood Cliffs, NJ: Prentice Hall, 1965), p. 2.
[51] P. F. Drucker, *Managing in Turbulent Times* (New York: Harper & Row, 1980), p. 68.

Businesses must arrange their employees, financial resources, innovativeness, and strategies in ways that will best ensure their success. Two axioms help managers to develop and maintain the perspective or scope of vision necessary to achieve that end.

First, business is not isolated from other institutions nor does it serve a single purpose or a single constituency. Business organizations are linked to a broader social system made up of groups of stakeholders. As we discussed earlier, stakeholders include customers, competitors, suppliers, employees, government, regulatory agencies, legislative bodies, political parties, social activist groups, labor unions, trade associations, educational institutions, shareholders, investors, and the news media. These institutions and components of society each are part of a global network.

American business leaders know well that the geographical boundaries of the United States are easily breached by competitors from Japan, Eastern Europe, the Middle East, the advanced economies of Western Europe, and the burgeoning markets of Asia. Developing countries and emerging economies are important to U.S. interests. Indeed, Commerce Secretary Ron Brown's ill-fated trip to Bosnia in 1996 was designed to promote business which, he hoped, would reduce political instability in the region and favor U.S. business interests.

Second, business faces environmental threats and opportunities. Well-managed companies must deal effectively with the social, political, and legal dynamics of their environment as well as with the more traditional product- and market-focused variables in the economic and technological environments.

Business is a component of broad and constantly changing social systems. It is within these dynamic environments that managers need to initiate change and modify their firms' policies, practices, and strategies. Fundamentally, managers' attention to social responsiveness will, in many cases, enhance their companies' long-run economic performance and profits. The question for managers is how they actually accomplish managing social responsiveness.

Social Responsiveness Management

Igor Ansoff describes management as "the creative and error correcting activity that gives the firm its purpose, its cohesion, and ensures satisfactory return on investment."[52] In Ansoff's view, managers meet the challenge of the environment by using strategy to transform their enterprises. He argues that a firm must have strategies to deal with sociopolitical variables as well as product/market/technology-focused strategies.[53]

---

[52] H. I. Ansoff, "The Changing Shape of the Strategic Problem," in *Strategic Management: A View of Business Policy and Planning,* ed. D. E. Schendel and C. W. Hofer (Boston: Little Brown, 1979), p. 30.

[53] Ibid., p. 43.

Exhibit 1-2 Strategic Components of Social Responsiveness Management

Environment	Strategy Formulation	Strategy Implementation	Performance Evaluation
What problems or strategic issues do we need to deal with in the social/political/legal arenas? Are there related problems in the economic and technological environments?	Who are we, and what are our goals? What are our capabilities and limitations? Which strategic issues are of greatest relevance? What strategy should we pursue?	What operational plans do we need? How should we organize? What information and controls do we need to ensure the strategy is implemented?	What results are we getting? How have organizational units and people performed?

Buchholz and Rosenthal have a broader view of the relationship between business and society. They assert that "no absolute line can be drawn between business and society, for the origin and foundation of business are social in nature. . . . Corporations have to take the perspective of the society as a whole and incorporate the standards of society, even as they remain unique centers of activity that have a creative dimension to add to the total social experience."[54]

These two perspectives point out that managers have challenging strategically focused tasks. Managers must deal with the firm's economic, social, and political tasks while at the same time responding to the demands of a larger societal environment. Corporate social responsiveness, that element of the company's strategy designed to solve the firm's problems or grasp opportunities related to the social, political, and legal environments, should be an integral component of a company's overall strategy. Exhibit 1-2 lists the key elements of social responsiveness management.

The segments of the environment, strategy formulation, strategy implementation, and performance evaluation are covered thoroughly in Chapters 2 and 3. A brief overview of these topics follows.

The Firm and Its Larger Environment

Managers study the environment to identify problems or strategic issues important to the firm. Environmental forces are both internal and external to the company. People, the most basic organizational resource of a company, are largely responsible for the success of the strategy identified by top management. While this book focuses principally on the social, political and legal, and regulatory arenas internal and external to the firm, it also includes related strategic social issues in the economic and technological environments.

---

[54] R. A. Buchholz and S. B. Rosenthal, "Theoretical Foundations of Public Policy: A Pragmatic Perspective," *Business & Society* 34, no. 3 (December 1995), p. 281.

Strategy Formulation

Strategy is the linking mechanism between most organizations and their environments as they seek to achieve their missions, goals, and objectives. Effective strategy and a realistic appraisal of the company's strengths and limitations are management's keys to formulating a clear understanding of those missions, goals, and objectives.

Managers need to assess the environment and determine which issues have the greatest relevance to the company. Once they identify the most important problems or strategic issues, they must determine how best to organize and use the firm's resources to achieve their goals. Strategic choice is the process of deciding which approach is best and selecting among available alternatives.

Strategy Implementation

Merely developing a strategy is not sufficient. To reach a strategic objective, top management must create an implementation plan and assign responsibility for its execution to individuals and units of the organization. Firms also need to create a formal or informal information and control system, if one is not already in place, to monitor the implementation of the strategy. An effective control system keeps track of actual accomplishments and provides an early warning system to detect potential problems.

Performance Evaluation

A strategy has little meaning if no one cares about results. Someone must care whether the company is getting the job done and how well the strategy is being implemented by those responsible for doing so. Managers need to know their performances are being evaluated and how the results they achieve will be reflected in the company's reward system. We discuss this process in greater detail in subsequent chapters.

The Business and Society Responsibility Debate

In recent years, managers have begun to think of corporate social performance as a basic functional area of management. One important reason may be new elements in the business and society responsibility dialog.

The role of business in American society has long been the subject of great debate, analysis, and emotion. The proper role of business was debated both by clergy and politicans. In the colonial period, Puritan ministers exhorted their parishioners to work hard. If a person were poor or failed economically, often it was interpreted that God looked upon this person with disfavor. Wealth and position were seen as signs of God's approval.

The link between God's favor and wealth appears to be re-emerging in the 1990s. The connection between wealth and religion became a hot topic in books, church programs, financial seminars, and spiritual retreats. *The Wall Street Journal* remarked that "God has a new co-pilot: Midas." In Seattle, a lecture by the author of *God Wants You to Be Rich,* drew 500 people, each of whom paid $50 to attend. In the Midwest, community churches developed seminars in personal finance and financial planning.[55] Despite this trend, most discussion of the role of business and society was and continues to be secular.

The framers of the Constitution and other notable thinkers of the time debated the proper roles of business and society. Alexander Hamilton's goal was to foster a strong economy based on commerce, manufacturing, and finance. Hamilton viewed government's role as supporting an environment of order and stability in which business could grow and prosper. Thomas Jefferson, on the other hand, wanted people to remain on the land to produce the basic elements of clothing, shelter, and food. He abhorred the idea of putting people to work in urban factories. Government's proper role, in his view, was to respond to the will of a responsible electorate. Many of Jefferson's contemporaries had grave doubts that an electorate of ordinary people had the capacity or will to be responsible. These skeptical individuals urged the creation of a strong government to limit individual freedom.

As business became an increasingly large and powerful force throughout the 19th century, businesspeople, writers, politicians, and philosophers debated how to define and shape its role. *The Education of Henry Adams* provides a remarkably insightful discussion of the seriousness of the matter.[56] This autobiography of the great-grandson of John Adams and the grandson of John Quincy Adams was published in 1918, the year of Henry Adams's death.

Adams viewed the impact of industrialization on the political process and the values of society with alarm and even horror. "The work of domestic progress is done by masses of mechanical power—steam, electric, furnace, or other—which have to be controlled by a score or two of individuals who have shown the capacity to manage it. The work of internal government has become the task of controlling these men."[57]

Adams, like many patricians of his generation, had little faith that "these men" could or would be controlled. Although they were supposed to be trustees for the public, Adams was convinced they would "control society without appeal" just as they controlled the workers in their factories. He concluded this point by arguing that "modern politics is, at bottom, a struggle

---

[55] A. Sharpe, "More Spiritual Leaders Preach Virtue of Wealth," *The Wall Street Journal,* April 5, 1996, p. B1.

[56] H. Adams, *The Education of Henry Adams* (New York: Modern Library, 1931).

[57] Ibid., p. 421.

not of men but of forces. The men become every year more and more creatures of force, massed about central power-houses."[58]

The debate continued into the 20th century. In *The Limits of Corporate Power,* Ira M. Millstein and Salem M. Katsh observed, "The central issue is corporate control: those forces which operate to constrain the discretionary acts of business corporations—especially, but not exclusively, large corporations. There are those for whom no amount of corporate control is enough; and there are those for whom no amount of corporate control is too much."[59]

David Vogel made some interesting observations about public control over large business corporations in the 1980s.[60] He noted that the public-interest movement of the 1960s dissipated in the 1970s. As deregulatory forces gathered steam during the late 1970s and early 1980s, business interests began to dominate public policy, and corporate forces pressured for economic and tax reform.

Vogel believed business became politically successful because the public deemed the historically liberal tradition of the United States inadequate: "The whole tone of the political agenda has shifted from a focus on corporate abuses to a preoccupation with reforming the regulations enacted to curb these abuses."[61]

Graham K. Wilson made a somewhat related point noting that under the Reagan administration, business became more active and more successful politically than in the previous decade. Wilson asserted that the public shifted its concern from social goals to prices and American competitiveness. This was a change from the 1970s, when public-interest groups seemed likely to alter the very nature of business-government relations.[62]

While some scholars deliberated over the proper balance of business, government, and interest groups, others like Clarence C. Walton, summarized the conservative argument and took a negative view of the broad responsibilities of business. Walton asserted, "the expansion of private power into the public domain will upset the already uneasy balance existing in our society to a point where corporation executives will assume too much power or will be so effectively challenged as to lose their existing freedom of action."[63]

Milton Friedman was the major contemporary proponent of a limited, strictly economic role for business. Friedman argued that business involvement in the social and political arenas was a threat to freedom. He wrote, "If

---

[58] Ibid., p. 423.

[59] I. M. Millstein and S. M. Katsh, *The Limits of Corporate Power: Existing Constraints in the Exercise of Corporate Discretion* (New York: Macmillan, 1981), p. ix.

[60] D. Vogel, "The Inadequacy of Contemporary Opposition to Business," *Daedalus,* Summer 1980, pp. 47–51.

[61] Ibid., p. 49.

[62] G. K. Wilson, *Business and Politics* (Chatham, NJ: Chatham House Publishers, 1985), pp. 42–43.

[63] C. C. Walton, *Corporate Social Responsibilities* (Belmont, CA: Wadsworth, 1967), pp. 57–58.

Exhibit 1–3 Seven Reasons to Abandon the Concept of Corporate Social Responsibility

1. The origins of the concept are suspect, as they derive primarily from the field of economics, and fail to include, among others, history, religion, and culture.
2. The different models of corporate social responsibility all accept the terms of the debate as set forth by Milton Friedman's argument that sees corporations only as profit maximizers.
3. Corporate social responsibility accepts the prevailing business rhetoric of "capitalism: love it or leave it."
4. Corporate social responsibility is inherently conservative—it starts with the standard received wisdom and then attempts to "fix" its unintended consequences.
5. Corporate social responsibility promotes incompetence by leading managers to involve themselves in areas beyond their expertise—that is, repairing society's ills.
6. Corporate social responsibility accepts a view of business and society as separable from each other, each with a distinct ethic, linked by a set of responsibilities.
7. The language of rights and responsibilities is, itself, both limiting and often irrelevant to the world of the practicing manager.

Source: R. E. Freeman and J. Liedka, "Corporate Social Responsibility: A Critical Approach," *Business Horizons,* July–August 1991, p. 93.

economic power is joined to political power, concentration seems almost inevitable. On the other hand, if economic power is kept in separate hands from political power, it can serve as a check and a counter to political power."[64] Friedman and others who saw business as having a central but limited role in society contended that the business of business is business, not social issues or politics.

Those who viewed the role of business more broadly or more positively disagreed with Friedman's position. They concluded that social responsibility is also the business of business. For example, Peter F. Drucker wrote, "Friedman's 'pure' position—to eschew all social responsibility—is not tenable. . . . Business and other institutions of our society . . . cannot be pure, however desirable that may be. Their own self-interest alone forces them to be concerned with society and community and to be predisposed to shoulder responsibility beyond their own main areas of task and responsibility."[65]

R. Edward Freeman and Jeanne Liedka, two leading scholars in the field of business and society, argued that the idea of corporate social responsibility is outmoded.[66] Their rationale, which could not differ more dramatically from Friedman's, is unique and as yet outside the mainstream. Nevertheless, their ideas are creative and thought provoking. They offer seven reasons to abandon the concept of corporate social responsibility, given in Exhibit 1–3.

---

[64] Friedman, p. 16.
[65] P. F. Drucker, *Management: Tasks, Responsibilities, Practices* (New York: Harper & Row, 1974), p. 349.
[66] R. E. Freeman and J. Liedka, "Corporate Social Responsibility: A Critical Approach," *Business Horizons,* July–August 1991, pp. 92–98.

Freeman and Liedka suggested that managers should undertake an "ongoing conversation about corporations and the good life." In their view, corporations should be conceptualized as "a network of relationships [making possible] a social world in which 'caring' has primary significance." In place of social responsibility, they offered Three Propositions for New Conversation:

> **Proposition 1:** Corporations are connected networks of stakeholder interests. This proposition expands the conversation to include suppliers, employees, and customers, among others, making them legitimate partners in the dialogue.
>
> **Proposition 2:** Corporations are places in which both individual human beings and human communities engage in caring activities that are aimed at mutual support and unparalleled human achievement. This proposition pushes us beyond the language of rights and responsibilities to a focus on the ethics of care, which recognizes needs and affirms the self and its linkage with others.
>
> **Proposition 3:** Corporations are mere means through which human beings are able to create and recreate, describe and redescribe, their visions of self and community. This proposition urges us to see the projects of "self creation" and "community creation" as two sides of the same coin, and see in institutions many possibilities for different ways of living together to pursue the joint ends of individual and collective good.[67]

William C. Frederick took a balanced view of corporate social responsibility. He pointed out that disruptions of the ethical, social, and legal fabrics arise within the business system; they are not imposed on business from outside. "The issues and problems that have been at the heart of the social responsibility debate are a natural consequence of the institutionalized quest for profits normally sought through the free market. They represent the raw edge of business values rubbing against the social values of human communities and the ecosystems that sustain those communities."[68]

Conservative commentator Irving Kristol suggested that had business been such a large and powerful institution in the late 18th century, the founders would have provided bounds for it in the Constitution. Instead, they concentrated on government responsibility because they knew about and feared oppressive central states.

The appropriate role of government has been the subject of serious and ongoing debate. There is, however, general agreement about what constitutes individual responsibility or responsiveness. By definition, public servants and the government organizations for which they work are expected to serve the public good and not act selfishly.

Scholarly debate over the connection between business and society heated up in the mid-1990s. The fire was ignited by Edward Freeman's

---

[67] Ibid., p. 96.
[68] W. C. Frederick, "Corporate Social Responsibility in the Reagan Era and Beyond," *California Management Review* 25, Spring 1983, p. 147.

address at the 1993 meeting of the Society for Business Ethics. Freeman asserted that scholars conceptually separate ethics and business. Each realm has its own concepts, language, and logic. Accepting Freeman's dichotomy leads to questions about whether business and society issues can be linked to firms' performance.

Andrew Wicks, analyzed this separation thesis in the broader context of business and society studies. He noted that many scholars think the corporation has separate private and public roles. The private role is to make money for the firm. The public role is to meet the legitimate expectation of stakeholders. Although many authors try to make connections among firms' economic, legal, and ethical activities, in Wicks' view they do not provide the conceptual models for accomplishing this goal. We are left with the notion that economic returns determine how corporations ought to behave. If social responsibility does not preclude economic performance, then corporations should behave in a socially responsible manner. However, if there is a trade-off between financial performance and social responsibility, perhaps corporations should not worry about social responsibility.

Wicks noted that the strategic management literature reinforces the image of stakeholders "outside the walls of the firm as intruders or hostile forces." The literature suggests that the objectives of stakeholder groups became important to managers only to the extent that they had the power to harm or threaten the corporation's goals. The core interest of managers was to focus on the firm's financial well-being, a concept that promoted the separation thesis.

Wicks concluded there was a challenge for business and society scholars in trying to develop concepts that help get around the separation thesis. He urged them to look for new ideas and ways of understanding the firm and capitalism.[69]

Donna Wood, one of the preeminent business and society scholars, answered Wicks by noting that her work did not assert economic objectives were most important and that social objectives were tacked on. She wrote that "the principles of social responsibility . . . explicitly derive from the acceptance of business power by a variety of stakeholders (legitimacy), the rule of relevance determining what responsibilities are held by particular business organizations (public responsibility), and the individual-level *moral values* of managers and other employees (managerial discretion)." Wood, like Wicks, pointed to the importance of intellectual reconciliation in the study of business and society.[70]

The value of this discussion becomes apparent in the rest of this book. The recurring theme is that economic performance and social responsibility

---

[69] A. C. Wicks, "Overcoming the Separation Thesis," *Business & Society* 35, no. 1, (March 1995), pp.89–118.

[70] D. Wood, "Reconciliation Awaits," *Business & Society* 35, no. 1 (March 1995), pp. 119–22.

are intertwined. In some periods, economic issues seem to be preeminent; in others, the focus is on the critical importance of social issues. Most of the time, managers must consider both in determining their corporate strategy. Individual managers' professionalism helps them balance both aspects of corporate performance.

Professionals, whether in government or in private enterprise, are presumed to behave responsibly. "To ensure performance," wrote Wilbert E. Moore, "professionals are obliged to regulate their own conduct by adherence to ethical codes."[71] Writing on the same topic, Everett C. Hughes observed that a "central feature . . . of all professions is the motto . . . *credat emptor* [let the buyer trust]."[72] Alan H. Goldman noted, "The special knowledge of those within each profession relates to a central, even vital, value for their society and the other individuals in it."[73]

One can debate whether managers are, or should be, any more or less professional than lawyers, doctors, architects, or engineers, but nearly everyone agrees that trust in business relationships is important. In fact, a strong case can be made that trust is essential to the long-term survival of any business enterprise.

Therefore, it seems the notion of individual responsibility on the part of managers is fairly clear-cut; individual responsibility is a characteristic of a professional. However, the nature and scope of the responsible behavior are hard to define. Does it mean a business should be run like a social welfare agency? Does it mean corporate managers need merely to obey the law?

The Scope of Business Responsibility

Global Imperatives.   In the 1990s, the business and society debate took on a global perspective. In a 1992 article, Donna J. Wood and Philip L. Cochran discussed business and society in transition. They asserted the global economy requires managers to abandon a narrow domestic perspective. International trade, global stakeholders, and multicultural social and political issues all affect business and necessitate new approaches to balancing stakeholder demands.[74]

In another article, Wood pointed out that multinationals, by their very structure, largely escape national controls.[75] Except for some local operations

---

[71] W. E. Moore, *The Professions: Roles and Rules* (New York: Russell Sage Foundation, 1970), p. 14.

[72] E. C. Hughs, "Professions," in *The Professions in America,* ed. K. S. Lynn (Boston: Houghton Mifflin, 1965), p. 3.

[73] A. H. Goldman, "Professional Values and the Problem of Regulation," *Business and Professional Ethics Journal* 5, Winter 1986, p. 48.

[74] D. J. Wood and P. L. Cochran, "Business and Society in Transition," *Business and Society,* Spring 1992, pp. 1–17.

[75] D. J. Wood, "Toward Improving Corporate Social Performance," *Business Horizons,* July–August 1991, pp. 66–69.

within national boundaries, multinational corporations govern themselves. She had no easy answers as to how multinationals can be held to norms of social responsibility. One partial solution was to develop bilateral and multilateral agreements and regulations among nations to deal with common issues concerning business activities. As Wood noted, negotiation is time-consuming and difficult, and monitoring and enforcing those agreements are even more so.

Wood rejected the notion of world government or comprehensive treaties as solutions to global social responsibility. In her view, the discussion leading to global social responsibility is just beginning. She recommends better training in intercultural management, more research on comparative definitions of corporate social responsibility, greater attention to collaborative social problem solving, less aggressive posturing, and more listening.

These recommendations may seem too general and inadequate to deal with global issues and the problems of controlling corporations that operate outside a framework of law and regulation. But the issue is not whether managers and their firms, wherever they are located, *should* behave responsibly; they must behave responsibly.

Legal and Economic Imperatives. Peter F. Drucker writes that limits to social responsibility are imposed on business by (1) economic realities: "Whenever a business has disregarded the limitation of economic performance and has assumed social responsibilities which it could not support economically it has gotten into trouble," (2) the limits of competence: "To take on tasks for which one lacks competence is irresponsible behavior. It is also cruel. It raises expectations which will then be disappointed," and (3) authority: The most important limitation on social responsibility is the limitation of authority. . . . Where business . . . is asked to assume social responsibility for one of the problems or ills of society and community, management needs to think through whether the authority implied in the responsibility is legitimate. Otherwise it is usurpation and irresponsible."[76]

In their comments on the limits of corporate responsibility, none of these observers suggests that obeying the law is sufficient. All agree it is simplistic to suggest that the law provides answers and guidelines in dealing with every social and political issue. Law often lags behind changing social norms and expectations. For example, long before the federal law was passed barring former executive branch employees from lobbying the government on a particular matter in which they personally and substantially participated while in office, those lobbyists reaped the rewards of decisions they made while working in government.

In some areas, the law is just beginning to be written. For example, biotechnological advances are so new and are proliferating so rapidly that the legal system is lagging behind. Issues include the legal implications for

---

[76] Drucker, *Management*, pp. 345–48.

business and the health care industry of genetic testing. If, for example, a prospective parent chooses to continue a pregnancy knowing the child will have serious, expensive medical problems, should the parent's employer have to bear the financial responsibility through the company medical plan? Can business require prospective parents to have genetic testing to uncover potentially expensive problems?

Business, government, and society all have a major stake in the way legislation is drawn up. If we look at the past as predictive, laws will continue to lag behind issues. Social norms and expectations are changing rapidly, far more rapidly than legislators and lawyers can provide even baseline answers. In short, obeying the law is *necessary* for a socially responsible executive, but probably it is not *sufficient* in the eyes of most observers of corporate policy and practice.

CASE: DAIWA BANK

Prior to September 1995, few Americans outside the banking industry had heard of Daiwa Bank Ltd. The Japanese bank was, in fact, a major player in world banking, particularly in pension trust management and small business loans. It was the 10th largest commercial bank in Japan and the 19th largest in the world. The New York branch, like all other banks that traded in the United States Treasury market, was regulated by the Federal Reserve (the Fed).

On September 26, the Fed charged Daiwa trader Toshida Iguchi with bank fraud. Iguchi was accused of hiding $1.1 billion in losses over the 11 years he worked for Daiwa's New York branch.[77] According to news sources, officials in the Federal Reserve Bank of New York knew there might be problems two years before the scandal broke.

In 1993, Fed president William J. McDonough met with Takeshi Ota, a Daiwa vice president, to discuss Iguchi's trading practices. McDonough told Ota that Iguchi could no longer execute trades and also do the clerical work (called clearing) to record them. Typically, execution and recording are done by different people to prevent cheating or hiding losses. Ota assured McDonough that Daiwa would impose new controls. When told he could not perform both functions, Iguchi chose to take a less prestigious job for lower pay that allowed him to continue the clearing function. This demotion allowed Iguchi to continue to hide the losses.

A little more than a week after the discussion, four senior Daiwa executives from Japan visited the New York Fed to discuss Daiwa's oversight of its trading business. In March 1994, Daiwa's deputy general manager in the international department flew to the United States for meetings with Fed officials in Washington and New York. After these discussions, the Fed apparently took Daiwa's word that procedures were being tightened. Fed officials did not undertake their own investigation. They seemed to be satisfied with Daiwa's assurances that the trading and clearing functions were being separated and this action would prevent problems.[78]

On August 8, 1995, Daiwa officials informally notified Japanese authorities of Iguchi's losses. American authorities were not notified until September 18, ostensibly because Japanese officials wanted to make sure that the losses were real. Initially, the Japanese Ministry of Finance seemed to be relatively unconcerned about Daiwa's losses. A ministry official instructed Daiwa to investigate the losses and report back to him. He did not tell U.S. authorities nor did he check with Daiwa officials for the next six weeks. Daiwa became even more active, raising money it hoped would cut losses once the situation became public.[79]

At an October 1995 hearing in a Manhattan federal court, Iguchi confirmed that senior officials at Daiwa asked him to continue hiding his losses even after he confessed his actions. Iguchi pleaded guilty to six counts of fraud, including money laundering, falsifying bank documents, embezzling $500,000 for his personal use, and misappropriating $1.1 billion in unauthorized trades.[80]

Hiroki Yamaji, a former managing director of Daiwa supported Iguchi's story. He admitted to the Japanese newspaper *Asahi Shimbun* that he and other executives had planned to continue concealing the loss until after the New York branch's half-year closing of books on September 30 and the announcement of the bank's earnings on November 24.[81]

---

[77] Internet [http://pathfinder.com/@@0dccvpPqAAJAQK62/pathfinder/features/daiwa], April 11, 1996.

[78] P. Truell, "Fed Missed Big Opportunity on Daiwa, Ex-Officials Say," *New York Times,* October 19, 1995, p. A1.

[79] G. Baker, "Hidden Behind a Screen of Stability," *Financial Times,* October 24, 1995, p. 17.

[80] N. Shirouzu, "Daiwa Confirms It Told Trader to Hide Losses, *The Wall Street Journal,* October 23, 1995, p. A15.

[81] "Ex-Daiwa Official Cites Cover-Up Plan," *New York Times,* October 23, 1995, p. D3.

In November 1995, the Federal Reserve gave Daiwa 90 days to wrap up its U.S. operations and leave the country. A federal indictment was handed down charging the bank with conspiracy and fraud for hiding the trading losses.

In January 1996, Daiwa agreed to sell its U.S. assets to Sumitomo Bank Ltd. for $3.3 billion. Fifteen U.S. offices and the Daiwa Bank Trust subsidiary were sold for an addition $65 million. Sumitomo was the fourth-largest bank in the world with assets of $556 billion, 30 billion of which were held in the United States.

In February 1996, for technical reasons, U.S. prosecutors agreed to drop some of the charges against Daiwa. Shortly thereafter, the bank pleaded guilty to conspiring to hide $1.1 billion in trading losses from U.S. regulators and agreed to pay a $340 million fine. Daiwa's executives issued a news release saying "We agreed to this settlement as the best business decision for our bank, its customers and its shareholders."[82]

The Daiwa situation had far-reaching consequences. Observers in U.S., Japanese, and European banking circles began to wonder whether the cover-up was isolated or indicative of large-scale problems deliberately kept from public scrutiny. Why, they wondered, did Daiwa's officials and the Ministry of Finance assume such a relaxed attitude?

Japan's banks operate under different rules from U.S., British, and European banks. The Japanese Ministry of Finance, the regulator, enforces the rules in the broader interest of the stability of the entire Japanese financial system, not in the interest of the investor. In fact, the Japanese government seemed to have concluded the scandal was "a family affair." Its major concern was that the nation's banking system's foundation would be shaken. Japanese officials seemed genuinely surprised that U.S. officials would regard their attitude and Daiwa's actions as inappropriate.

Japanese banks are permitted to hide their problems in affiliated companies and do not have to declare results for these affiliates. Prior to 1993, banks did not have to account for their losses in property loans and after 1993, were required to disclose only a small proportion of nonperforming assets.

Japanese accounting rules allowed banks to keep their affiliates' results private. Alicia Ogawa, an analyst for Salomon Brothers in Tokyo, remarked, "You can look at the figures for a bank and they may seem perfectly healthy. But what the investor can't see is that all the problems have been moved to affiliates, and there's no way of knowing."[83]

The Ministry of Finance recommended that banks under their supervision use a practice called carrying a deficit forward. For example, when a transaction produces a loss of $100 billion and a profit of $50 billion, there is a deficit of $50 billion. By carrying the deficit forward the bank can have a deficit of only $20 billion. By entering $30 billion for the current period, financial records are arranged so that another $20 billion deficit is recorded the following year. In five years the $100 billion will be recouped.

Public accountability was further reduced because most Japanese bank shares are owned by companies that have long-term relationships with the bank. Some analysts say that these companies own as much as 80 percent of the bank with which they are related. Unlike individual shareholders in the U.S. system, Japanese corporate owners are more concerned about relationships and stability than disclosure about operating details.[84]

In April 1996, Masahiro Tsuda, the former general manager of Daiwa Bank Ltd.'s New York branch pleaded guilty to one charge of conspiring to defraud the Federal Reserve by failing to disclose $1.1 billion in trading losses. Tsuda said that although he violated American laws, he was told to do so by his superiors at Daiwa and the Japanese Ministry of Finance. He admitted he had taken similar measures in the late 1980s to cover up a $30 million loss. At the hearing he said that Japanese custom was to wait until an internal investigation was completed before reporting an employee's wrongdoing to the authorities. He continued,

---

[82] L. Hays, "Daiwa Bank Pleads Guilty to Conspiring to Hide Loss," *The Wall Street Journal,* February 29, 1996, p. A3.

[83] Ibid.

[84] Internet [http://www.meshnet.or.jp/TAKEMURA/english/vpoint/d-7e.html]

"However, I knew that in the United States such reports should be made more swiftly and that an internal investigation wasn't a justification for not reporting in a timely fashion. I wish to note that I felt I had very little choice but to follow my superiors' instructions and particularly the policy of the Ministry of Finance, which has such great authority over banks such as Daiwa." Sentencing was set for July 1996; Tsuda faced a prison term of up to five years and a fine of $250,000.[85]

---

[85] F. A. McMorris, "Ex-Daiwa Official Pleads Guilty in Failure to Disclose Trade Losses," *The Wall Street Journal,* April 5, 1996, p. B5; K. N. Gilpin, "A Supervisor Pleads Guilty in Daiwa Case," *New York Times,* April 5, 1996, p. D3.

Questions

1. What are the important political issues in the Daiwa Bank Case? Are the issues different in the United States and Japan?
2. In the global arena, what are the implications of conducting business with different standards of corporate, social, and legal responsibility?
3. Both Japan and the United States operate under a capitalist, free market system. What accounts for the two nations' different approaches to managing in social, political, and legal environments?

Summary

This chapter discussed the importance of social issues management to the overall task of managing a modern corporation. It began with a discussion of the economic, political, and social issues that confront today's managers. The chapter also examined capitalism as the fundamental concept underlying the American economic system. The modern corporation emerged from that system and is ideologically molded by the unique political and legal system elaborated by the framers of the Constitution.

Today's managers are central players in the ongoing philosophical debate over the nature of corporate social responsibility. Many economists, historians, organizational behaviorists, and practicing managers have failed to recognize the importance of this debate to corporations globally. In recent years, academics and practitioners have tried to establish a more rigorous and manageable set of criteria for defining the scope of business responsibility.

Social responsiveness management focuses on a company's management as it relates to the social, political, and legal environments. A central objective of this book is to help managers develop an analytical framework and tools that will enable them to manage corporate social responsibility more effectively and systematically. This analytical framework must be based on a solid foundation.

The chapter reviewed some of the issues managers face in the late 1990s. It then looked at the linkage between the environment and company strategy and reviewed the business–government responsibility debate.

The Daiwa Bank case brought out some of the issues global companies face as they deal with ethics, management strategy, and political and legal environments. It emphasized the complexities of doing business in multiple environments. The case also addresses the issue of how companies respond to crises and the demands of stakeholders.

Questions

1. Using the Internet, discuss some of the critical social issues corporations face in the 1990s. The local and national networks are all on the Internet; some of the most useful sites are:
[http://www.321.com/]
[http://www.newslink.org/menu.html]
[http://www.cnn.com]
[http://pathfinder.com]

2. If you were the CEO of a large corporation, how would you resolve the corporate responsibility debate? Be prepared to argue that a company should not get involved in social issues unless it can make a profit on every transaction. Also be prepared to define the social responsibilities every corporation has toward its stakeholders.

3. What are the two fundamental assumptions on which capitalism is based? Which four essential elements derive from those assumptions?

4. What are the major legal characteristics of a corporation? How do they differ from the characteristics of a sole proprietorship or a partnership?

5. If you had been an American manager in the Daiwa Bank in New York, what was your legal responsibility if you discovered the hidden bond sales? What was your moral responsibility, if any? Would you have the same responsibilities if you were working for a U.S. bank in Japan?

CHAPTER 2
STRATEGY FORMULATION

This chapter focuses on decision processes that help managers formulate strategies to achieve social goals and other business objectives. Kenneth R. Andrews's classic definition of corporate strategy is "the pattern of decisions in a company that determines and reveals its objectives, purposes, or goals; produces the principal policies and plans for achieving those goals; and defines the range of business the company is to pursue."[1] A company, like Gillette for instance, may start with a single product and over time develop patterns of strategic decision-making that evolve into strategies for expansion.

---

[1] K. R. Andrews, *The Concept of Corporate Strategy* (Burr Ridge, IL: Richard D. Irwin, 1980), p. 18.

CASE: GILLETTE COMPANY

Early History

King Camp Gillette, the inventor of the Gillette razor, started his career as a salesperson in a hardware store. By the mid-1890s, he had received a number of patents for plumbing products and was hoping to invent an object that "when used once, is thrown away and the customer comes back for more, and with every additional customer you get, you are building a permanent foundation of profit."[2]

Gillette cast about for ideas that would meet these criteria. One morning in 1895, he had an almost mystic experience. As he described it, he was standing in front of a mirror, stropping his straight razor, when "the Gillette razor was born . . . all this [the design] came more in pictures than in thought as though the razor was already a finished thing and held before my eyes. I stood there in a trance of joy at what I saw."

---

[2] H. Vernon-Wortzel, "The Gillette Corporation: The Formative Years," paper delivered at the Academy of Management, August 1983. Research for this paper was based largely on reports in *The Gillette Blade,* the company magazine published between 1917 and 1929.

Gillette worked with several friends and acquaintances to form a company, which they incorporated in 1901 as American Safety Razor Company of Maine. The following year, at Gillette's insistence, the company's name was changed to Gillette Safety Razor Company of Maine. Although Gillette, as president, was the only paid employee, the company quickly fell into debt. "In fact," Gillette later reminisced, "we were busted and apparently done for."

Desperate, the owners turned to a group of New York investors who demanded 51 percent of the stock. Gillette, reluctant to give control of the stock to outsiders, forced the board to reject the New York offer.

After the meeting at which the offer was turned down, Gillette went to his favorite Boston restaurant for lunch. As luck would have it, he met John Joyce, a local financier who had financed some of Gillette's earlier unsuccessful inventions. Gillette had given Joyce a sample razor and 1,000 shares of worthless Gillette company stock. Joyce, hoping to recoup some of his investment, offered the despondent Gillette small but regular infusions of cash in exchange for bonds and a substantial, but not controlling, share in the firm.

Overjoyed, Gillette returned to the office, where he called an impromptu board meeting. The directors quickly approved the Joyce offer. From that moment on, the fledgling company had few major financial problems, although its management had serious managerial disagreements. Gillette and his board frequently quarreled over strategy and control. Gillette became so contentious that top management desperately tried to force him out of the company.

In 1912, the original Maine corporation was reorganized as Gillette Safety Razor Company of Massachusetts. By this time, Gillette had signed over his patents to the company in exchange for a five-year contract and had virtually no part in running the company.

Symbolically as well as managerially, it was the end of an era. The company, which by now was very large and growing, had business worldwide. Professional managers were hired to develop and implement strategy. Despite its early success, it is doubtful that anyone could have predicted Gillette Company's phenomenal growth or conceived of the strategy that would take the company into the 21st century.

Gillette in the Mid-1990s

In the early 1990s, the company began to undertake major global projects. For example, in 1991 it formed a joint venture in St. Petersburg, Russia, to develop a factory with a capacity of 750 million units a year. Between 1991 and 1993, Gillette bought out Turkey's biggest blade maker, Permasharp. It established additional joint ventures and made acquisitions in India, Egypt, Pakistan, and Poland.

The operation with perhaps the greatest potential was begun in 1992. Gillette and Shanghai Razor Blade Factory, China's leading blade maker, agreed to form Gillette Shanghai Ltd., with 70 percent Gillette ownership. With an initial investment of $45 million, the Chinese venture boosted Gillette's market share from 10 to 70 percent of China's rapidly growing billion-blade market.[3]

Gillette's 1994 Annual Report noted that sales totaled $6.07 billion, a 12 percent increase over 1993. It gave the following description of the business: "[Gillette] develops, manufactures, and sells a wide range of products for personal care, such as razor blades, shaving cream, deodorants, skin care products, shampoos, cosmetics, and electric razors; and manufactures and sells writing instruments and household appliances." The company's 32,800 employees work all over the world making and selling these products.[4]

Gillette's global strategy for the next century was well underway. Gillette speeded up its new product development, introducing 20 new products in 1994. Gillette sales in all international markets outside of Western Europe grew by 18 percent in 1994. Units outside the United States generated approximately 70 percent of total sales and operating profits. Long-term growth plans included development of business in "new geographies" such as Eastern Europe, Russia, and China.

Gillette's top management pointed to some major successes in toiletries and cosmetics sales. The com-

---

[3] F. M. Biddle, "The Sun Never Sets," *Boston Globe*, June 27, 1993, p. 51.

[4] KPMG Peat Marwick's Auditors' Report, January 26, 1995.

pany's development of clear gel technology in 1992 substantially aided deodorant product sales. Gillette first introduced gel products into the United States, Canada, and the United Kingdom, markets they considered fairly homogeneous. By 1994, gel products accounted for one-quarter of Gillette's total deodorant sales.

Sales of blades and razors also were considerably higher than in 1993, due to the growth of the Gillette Sensor franchise. The franchise accounted for almost 40 percent of total Gillette and razor sales dollars. By 1994, Sensor razors and cartridges had worldwide distribution.

U.S. and Japanese sales of Braun products also did very well in 1994. Braun electric shavers and oral care products sales increased rapidly. During 1994, the company established a Braun factory in China as part of its new geography strategy. Not all markets prospered however. European sales were down, largely as a result of an unfavorable rate of exchange between the dollar and European currencies and intense competition from European products.

Nevertheless, at the April 1996 annual meeting Gillette announced record first-quarter profits and sales. For the first three months of 1996, sales increased to $1.68 billion, 9 percent over the same period in 1995. Net income went up 17 percent to $230 million. CEO Alfred M. Zein attributed the company's success to the strategy of putting more shavers into the hands of consumers worldwide. Once they used the disposable shavers, the company was successful in getting them to switch to the more profitable premium brands such as Sensor and SensorExcel.[5]

The purchase of Parker Pen in 1994 increased the sale of stationery products. Gillette directors acknowledged that this acquisition boosted domestic and foreign sales of stationery products. In sum, Gillette's board and shareholders seemed well satisfied with the company's performance and its future prospects.

---

[5] A. Pham, "Gillette Sees Growth Spurt Ahead," *Boston Globe,* April 19, 1996, p. 85.

Questions

1. Did the original managers of Gillette Company have a specific strategy? If so, what was it?

2. How important was strategic planning in the early days?

3. How important is strategic planning today?

4. As you read the rest of the chapter, look at what aspects of the economic, social, legal and political, and technological environments have changed since the early 20th century. How have these changes affected the formulation of Gillette's strategy?

The Environment of Strategy Formulation

Managers often find they have more difficulty formulating social issues strategy than they do functional business strategies because bottom-line measures are so fuzzy for social issues. In both cases, managers use many of the same approaches: They study the environment, assess their firms' particular strengths and weaknesses, and analyze the information they have gathered. However, the choices they confront in assessing and measuring social issues programs are often very difficult. In fact, many top managers admit they do not even try to deal with social issues strategically. They simply allocate a budget for social issues and address problems as they arise. Often they do not

EXHIBIT 2–1 Environmental Forces Affecting Social Issues Strategy

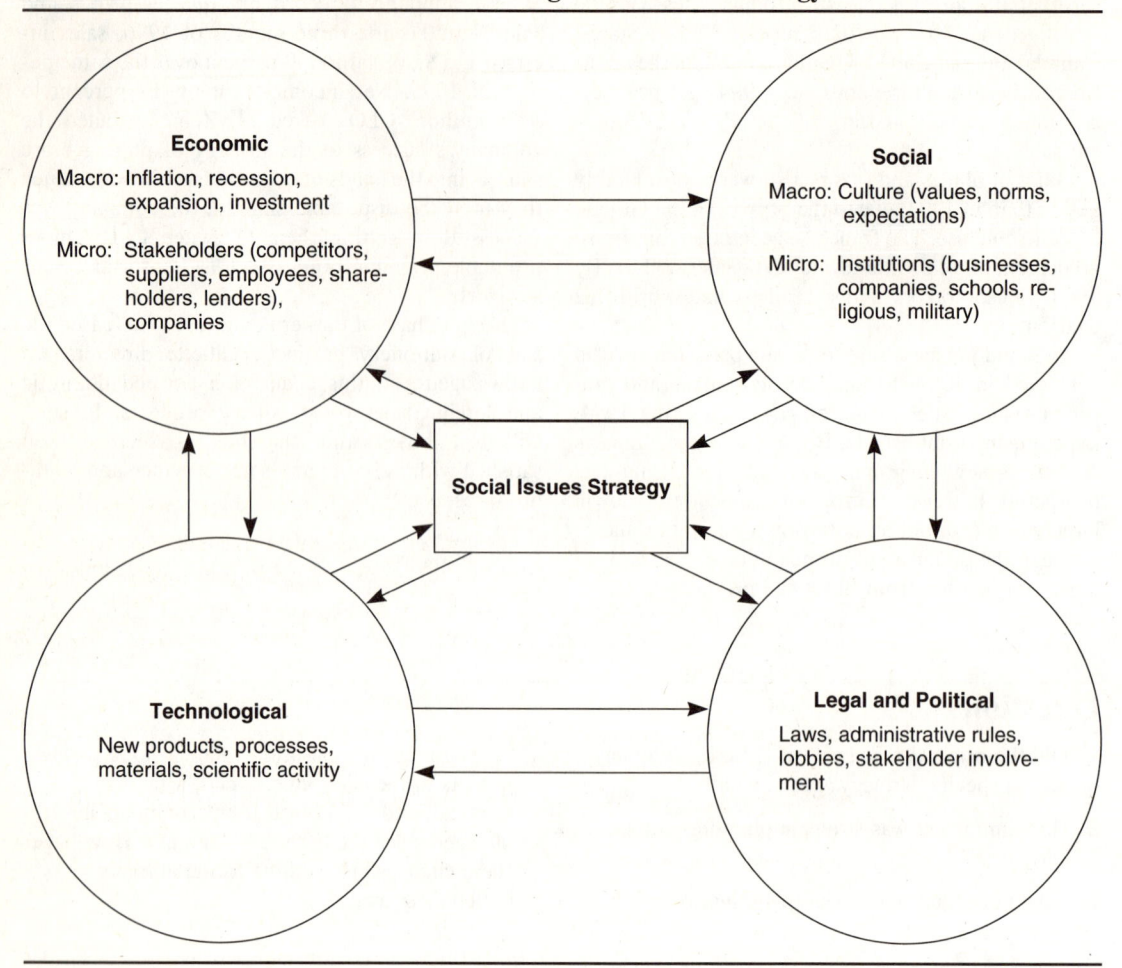

Economic
Macro: Inflation, recession, expansion, investment

Micro: Stakeholders (competitors, suppliers, employees, shareholders, lenders), companies

Social
Macro: Culture (values, norms, expectations)

Micro: Institutions (businesses, companies, schools, religious, military)

Technological
New products, processes, materials, scientific activity

Legal and Political
Laws, administrative rules, lobbies, stakeholder involvement

Social Issues Strategy

Source: Adapted from V. K. Narayanan and L. Fahey, "Environmental Analysis for Strategy Formulation," in *Strategic Planning and Management Handbook,* ed. W. R. King and D. I. Cleland (New York: Van Nostrand Reinhold, 1987), p. 155.

make an organized attempt to set goals and priorities to maximize the use of resources; nor do they follow up to assess results. As we discussed in the previous chapter, this nonstrategic or ad hoc approach to social issues management is becoming increasingly unfeasible in the environment business firms face.

The strategic problem for managers is to choose among social issues. Managers must identify those issues with potentially high impact on their firms and plan how to deal with them in the future. A first step is to understand the multiple environments in which their companies operate.

This chapter begins with a general discussion of environmental analysis and an overview of four basic environmental sectors: (1) economic, (2) social, (3) legal and political, and (4) technological. As we see in Exhibit 2–1, all of these sectors have a potential impact on social as well as business issues.

Elements of the Environment

The Economic Environment

On a macroeconomic level, the economic environment includes broad, sweeping forces such as inflation, recession, and waves of rapid expansion. It also incorporates systemic problems such as uneven income distribution, balance of payments, unemployment, and the rates of saving and capital investment.

These economic forces are highly significant for any business, but they are essentially a given. Any company, regardless of its size and scope, can do little to alter them. The forces affect all industries and all companies within an industry. General economic conditions influence the mood of the public, the nature of the issues likely to receive attention from activist groups, and acts of government.

At a microeconomic level, the company's environment consists of stakeholders such as competitors, suppliers, employees, lenders, and shareholders. (We discuss stakeholders in detail in Chapter 3.) Most managers try to be sensitive to their microeconomic environments. Yet many get caught by surprise in their own markets even when forces for change have been highly visible for some time. When macro- and microeconomic forces combine, the effect on industry can be profound.

American corporations are finally beginning to meet and adjust to changes in both the macro- and microeconomic environments. Increased competition from foreign companies signals a turbulent economic environment for the United States. Since the 1980s, the opponents' jerseys have read The Netherlands, Great Britain, Japan, Canada, and West Germany. Now players also include South Korea, Hong Kong, Singapore, and Taiwan.

The Japanese Example. For years, U.S. industry has looked at the Japanese economic juggernaut with amazement, apprehension, and often not a little envy. In the 1980s, Japanese companies dominated the markets for consumer electronics, semiconductors, and automobiles. Management gurus attributed Japanese success to hard work, thrift, and a superior economic and social system. For the previous 30 years, Japan's economy had grown by 6.5 percent a year.

But Japan's success was compromised by a serious recession beginning in 1991. The value of the yen soared, making Japanese exports less competitive. Economic growth slowed dramatically, and Japanese productivity fell. Between 1992 and 1995, Japan's GDP grew at an average of 0.6 percent a year. From 1990 to 1994, automakers like Nissan closed factories as car production fell by nearly 22 percent.[6] By mid-1993, Japanese productivity ranked in the bottom half of the industrialized nations, well below the rankings of the United States and many European Union countries.[7]

With Japan in a severe economic slump, Japanese companies began to search for ways to minimize the chronic underutilization of their own resources that had reduced corporate earnings. Most companies planned to reduce hiring, offer voluntary retirement, or transfer employees to subsidiaries or suppliers. White-collar employees were particularly vulnerable.

In the boom years of the 1980s, no one really noticed that offices were getting more and more crowded. By 1990, white-collar workers accounted for 56 percent of all manufacturing company employees, up from 47 percent in 1980. In 1994, management consulting firm Proudfoot, Ltd., estimated that Japan's big corporations had 12 percent too many middle managers.

The Japanese Constitution written after World War II stipulated that "all people shall have the right and obligation to work." The notion of lifetime employment had economic and ideological bases going back to Japan's initial industrialization in the mid-19th century. In reality, lifetime employment had always been limited to Japan's large corporations and had only covered between 20 and 30 percent of all workers. However, the concept became part of the mythology of Japan's success. What were the reactions of the Japanese people when faced with the stagnant economy in the 1990s? What strategy would Japanese companies develop to change the new economic and social environment? How would they deal with a discouraged and increasingly angry populace?[8]

In 1996, a poll of 10,000 adult Japanese found that 54 percent of respondents believed that Japan was becoming worse off. Ezra Vogel, author of *Japan as Number One: Lessons for America* (1979) acknowledged there was a "malaise, a deep recognition that they are no longer on the way up. . . . There are no easy answers, and, unlike the past, no unified response."[9]

The 70 to 80 percent of workers not covered by lifetime employment found that management could be just as brutal as in the United States and other countries. Although it was illegal for employers to fire workers without cause and compensation, employers often harassed workers until they quit. A

---

[6] I. Mkunii, S. Oba, and H. Tashiro, "The Failed Miracle," *Time,* April 22, 1996, pp. 60–64.

[7] E. Thompson, "Japan's Struggle to Restructure," *Fortune,* June 28, 1993, p. 84.

[8] B. R. Schlender, "Japan's White Collar Blues," *Fortune,* March 21, 1994, p. 97.

[9] E. W. Desmond, "The Failed Miracle," *Time,* April 22, 1966, pp. 61–64.

Mitsubishi economist believed unemployment could eventually reach 6.5 percent for people aged 16–24. Although this figure is low by U.S. and European standards, it was shocking for a country used to almost full employment.

To add to Japan's woes, the rift between business and government widened. Japan's large industries began to shift production offshore in the early 1990s. This move made it easier to fire Japanese workers and hire replacements in low-wage Asian countries such as Indonesia, Malaysia, and Thailand. Some companies even set up research labs and administrative units in the United States and Europe. The business editor of Japan's leading newspaper *Yomuri Shimbun* wrote, "Japan's remarkable postwar economic development was due largely to a cooperative relationship between government and business." He noted that "conflicts have been emerging in recent years between the Government's 'national interests' and the private-sector's 'corporate interests'."[10]

The Social Environment

As Japan's economic ills frayed the fabric of society, traditional Japanese cultural values seemed to be under attack. Schools and families experienced significant dislocations:

- A 1996 poll showed that 64 percent of parents distrusted teachers and 66 percent were unhappy with their children's education.
- Parents worried about their children's classmates and even teachers who bullied children they thought were too smart or too stupid.
- Competition to enter high status private schools required children to study six and a half days a week and to learn huge amounts of material by rote.

Many Japanese began to worry about crime in the mid-1990s. Unlike the United States and many other countries, violent crime was almost unknown in Japan. Beginning in 1995, murders unrelated to organized crime became more commonplace. An advisory board to the National Police Agency recommended hiring many more police because Japan was "proceeding down the path to becoming a Western-style crime society."[11]

The social environment affects social issues management most directly. As was true in our discussion of the economic environment, it is useful to think of the social environment at both the macro and micro levels. The broad and pervasive influences of culture are most obvious at the macro level. Yet we tend to discount the importance of culture, because it is so deeply

---

[10] A. Pollack, "Shift Offshore Rattles Japan's Economic Bedrock," *New York Times*, January 30, 1996, p. D1.

[11] Desmond, p. 64.

ingrained and subtle that we are unaware of its importance in daily life. Culture has been defined in a number of ways by anthropologists, sociologists, political scientists, and others. The classic historic definition of culture is "that complex whole which includes knowledge, belief, art, morals, law, custom, and any other capabilities and habits acquired by man [or woman] as a member of society."[12]

To understand culture, therefore, it is essential to understand the major attributes of a given society. Culture provides a common framework and acts as a social bond. "Bonds," according to the philosopher Ralph Ross, "may restrain, like chains on a slave, or they may sustain, like the climber's rope."[13] In fact, cultures both restrain and sustain. They do not, however, uniformly respond to environmental forces. Cultural diversity, regardless of similarities or dissimilarities in the physical environment, may be explained by the fact that "culture acts as a set of blinders, or a series of lenses, through which men [and women] view their environments."[14]

We are all aware of the numerous cultures that can exist even within small geographic areas. For example, people on the French side of the Alps have a different language, as well as different political, social, and economic institutions, than their Italian neighbors. Two African tribes within a five-mile radius may have different languages, dress, customs, and hierarchical structures.

Despite its subtle nature, culture may provide a great deal of stability and guidance for a society. While society is often flexible and dynamic in nature, its basic cultural traits endure. A society's body of knowledge, laws, beliefs, and habits result in what sociologist Geert Hofstede calls "a collective programming of the human mind that distinguishes the members of one human group from those of another."[15] Although some writers comment on radical changes, megatrends, and future shock in American society, the social fabric has proven remarkably durable and elastic.

A society's value system is a source of underlying stability. Thomas A. Petit makes the connection between the economic and social environments. He notes that "chief among the determinants of the particular shape which an economic system takes are the dominant social values of the society of which the economy is a part. In every society there is a more or less continuous interaction between social values and . . . institutions."[16]

---

[12] E. B. Tyler, *Primitive Culture,* 3rd Eng. ed. (London: John Murray Publishers, 1891), p. 1.

[13] R. Ross, *Symbols and Civilizations* (New York: Harcourt Brace Jovanovich, 1957), p. 172.

[14] C. Kluckhohn and H. A. Murray, *Personality in Nature, Society, and Culture* (New York: Alfred A. Knopf, 1949), p. 45.

[15] G. Hofstede, "Culture and Organizations," in *International Studies of Man & Organization,* vol. 10, no. 4 (Armon K, NY: M E Sharpe, 1981), p. 24.

[16] T. A. Petit, *Freedom in the American Economy* (Burr Ridge, IL: Richard D. Irwin, 1964), p. 1.

EXHIBIT 2–2 The Relationship among Institutions, Culture, and Individual Values

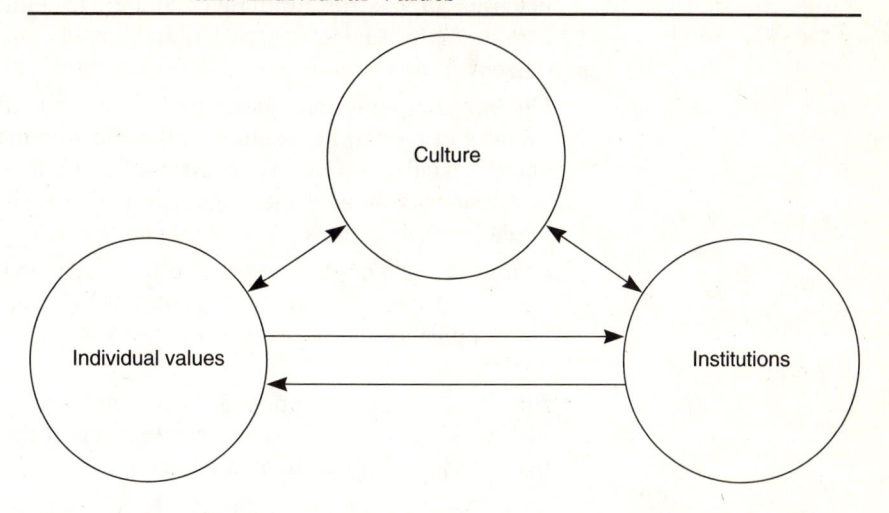

```
                    Culture
                   /      \
                  ↙        ↘
                 ↗          ↖
        Individual values ─→ Institutions
                          ←─
```

Institutions in the Social Environment. Institutional roles are an essential element of culture and value systems. Institutions form microcultures that include religious organizations, social groups, the government, businesses, and schools. People create institutions to gain security, generate a collective sense of purpose and direction, and accomplish certain tasks that are best undertaken as a group. In effect, they bring the individual values they learned early in their lives to the collective values of an institution.

However, as Exhibit 2–2 shows, the transfer of values from individual to institution is not a one-way process.

Richard T. Pascale observes that many corporations develop programs to socialize new members in the values of the company. In this way, the firm perpetuates a distinct microculture of its own by passing its values on to new employees. Pascale notes the value systems of some prospective employees are, and will remain, incompatible with the culture of the firm. He advises companies not to hire these individuals because the desirable reciprocal cultural exchange is unlikely to occur.[17] Pascale does not address issues of diversity in this recommendation but it is clear that he does not suggest establishing a screening device to get around issues such as gender, age, and ethnicity.

The reciprocal transfer of values from individual to institution and from institution to individual carries an expectation that both will realize a return on their investment.

---

[17] R. T. Pascale, "The Paradox of 'Corporate Culture': Reconciling Ourselves to Socialism," *California Management Review* 28, Winter 1985, pp. 26–41.

- Government: most U.S. citizens expect the government to provide schools, hospitals, and a financial safety net as well as national defense and victories in foreign ventures. In return, the government expects tax revenues, civil order, and a modicum of patriotism from citizens.
- Organized religion: provides moral guidance and, to some, the promise of eternal life. Religion also offers community solidarity and the inculcation of a value system for children. In return, parishioners volunteer their time and financial support. Some predicate their actions on their religion's moral guidelines.
- Consumers: expect businesses to offer fair value in products and services, provide employment, contribute to economic growth, and act responsibly. They also expect products to be safe and of good quality.
- Employees: expect compensation commensurate with their services and working conditions that are safe, support their tasks, and respect their rights as human beings.

Most societal institutions are remarkably stable over time. However, if they repeatedly fail to deliver on society's expectations, they can experience the equivalent of a run on the bank. If people withdraw their support and espouse different values, resulting social movements may weaken institutions. Clearly social movements must be compatible with dominant societal values if they are to affect the social order meaningfully. Institutions that do not reflect prevailing values and lose public confidence are particularly vulnerable to attack.

As we mentioned in the previous chapter, now many Americans are highly skeptical of the ability of the political system to deal with social problems. The 1994 congressional elections were dramatic evidence of the public's willingness to withdraw from the bank. The electorate, clearly dissatisfied with the status quo, elected a Republican majority dedicated to nothing less than a societal revolution. Although the subsequent Oklahoma City bombing, militia movements, and Unabomber activities seemed to be isolated examples of societal anomie, polls showed people had a real fear that society was breaking down.

A *US News*/Bozell Worldwide poll conducted in February 1996 found that 9 out of 10 Americans felt incivility was a serious problem. More than 90 percent of respondents believed that incivility contributed to violence; 85 percent agreed it divided the national community and eroded healthy values.[18] There appeared to be a widespread conviction that institutions and movements no longer reflected the American culture's positive social values.

---

[18] J. Marks, "The American Uncivil Wars," *US News & World Report,* April 12, 1996, pp. 66–72.

Social values are not merely free-floating, vague concerns about public confidence in institutions. As they change over time, social values can have an impact on corporate policies and can drastically affect entire industries. For example, the automobile industry had to respond to changing views of pollution control. Access to health care is another social value in a state of flux. Mergers, acquisitions, and consolidations are leading politicians, providers, ethicists, and ordinary citizens to question established convictions about who should be eligible for and pay for a variety of health services.

The Legal and Political Environment

Many cultural conflicts are acted out and sometimes are resolved in the culture's legal and political systems. From culture to culture, these systems vary considerably in the degree and scope of their interaction. Social activists and politicians may use legal and political systems to press for the passage of legislation they believe represents the views of their supporters even more profoundly than those they hold themselves.

For example, Republican Senator Robert Dole severely criticized the Clinton administration's choice of lower court judges. He even vowed to remove the American Bar Association from rating candidates if he were elected president. As the likely Republican candidate, Senator Dole addressed this issue to attract supporters. Candidate Dole's stand on this issue and many others clashed so seriously with his office of Senate Majority Leader, he resigned from the Senate.

Some societies are far more litigious than others. Americans rush into court to resolve problems that are settled by conciliation elsewhere. To maintain an orderly and predictable society, most formal legal systems operate in concert with informal rules of behavior. We discuss the interaction of law and informal societal guidelines throughout the book. Chapters 7, 8, and 9 address the development and passage of laws and legislation.

The Technological Environment

Technological advances in the past decade have been staggering in their number and their societal impact. Technology affects and interacts with every aspect of the cultural, political, and legal environments. Throughout this book, we address societal issues of changing technology and developments in new processes, products, and materials.

Generally, "the technological segment is concerned with the technological progress or advancement taking place in a society. New products, processes, or materials; general scientific activity; and advances in fundamental science . . . are the key concern in this area."[19] Developments such as

---

[19] V. K. Narayanan and L. Fahey, "Environmental analysis for Strategy Formulation," in *Strategic Planning and Management Handbook,* ed. W. R. King and D. I. Cleland. (New York: Van Nostrand Reinhold, 1987), p. 154.

product innovations (videocassette recorders, fax machines, laptop computers) and process innovations (mass merchandising and telemarketing, and the Internet) are examples of events in the technological environment. The technological environment also is linked to the economic, social, and legal and political environments.

When videocassette recorders became household fixtures in the late 1980s, moviemakers and sports promoters began to realize they were not receiving their full potential measure of royalties. Viewers freely copied movies from commercial cassettes or taped restricted sports programs from pay cable stations. Producers and promoters formed lobbying groups to press for laws ensuring they would earn royalties every time the films and sportscasts were shown. The entertainment industry went to court to prevent pirating and to ensure that every rental cassette carried a warning from the FBI forbidding illegal copying.

The proliferation of video rental stores created a new competitive arena that affected the economic environment. Stores in every small town and major city in America rented videocassettes for weekend amusement. People sat at home in front of television sets instead of going to the local movie theater. Television screens got bigger and bigger as multiplex theater screens got smaller and smaller.

For $3 a family could see a movie that would cost $7 per person in a theater. During the 1980s, many local movie theaters closed because they lost customers who had discovered this new form of inexpensive entertainment. Videocassette supermarkets like Blockbuster, used new merchandising techniques that quickly grabbed the rental business from the local drug or convenience store. They sold popcorn, candy, and other snacks so that viewers could have an experience similar to the theater.

Further technological advances, such as high-definition television (HDTV), satellite transmission, and interactive computer programs are profoundly changing the entertainment industry. The rate of change is accelerating as new inventions are ever more quickly developed and adopted. It is difficult to imagine the number and variety of new products that will be available in the next decade.

Mass merchandising is a different kind of technological innovation. In the 1920s, the growth of chain stores began to pose a threat to independent retail businesses. Because chain stores enjoyed relative efficiency by taking advantage of scale economies, they presented tough competition for traditional retailers. In the late 1920s and early 1930s, responding to pressure from local merchants' groups, more than 30 states passed laws imposing discriminatory taxes on chains.[20]

However, legislation could not stop the economic advantages of scale enjoyed by mass merchandisers. Family-owned businesses such as drug-

---

[20] J. C. Palamountain, Jr., *The Politics of Distribution* (Cambridge, MA: Harvard University Press, 1955).

stores, hardware stores, and office suppliers have virtually disappeared over the past 30 years. Large chains such as Walgreen, Osco, and CVS replaced the independent pharmacies. Local hardware chains such as Massachusetts-based Grossman's went out of business because it could not compete with megastores such as Home Depot, Home Quarters, and Wal-Mart.

Between 1986 and 1996, Staples Inc. grew from a single store in Brighton, Massachusetts, to a $3 billion office products superstore chain. The company employs 25,000 people worldwide and, in 1996, was adding 120 stores a year. Competition from Staples, OfficeMax, and Office Depot superstores buried mom-and-pop establishments.[21]

Sophisticated medical and scientific technologies proliferate and create societal controversies. For example, physicians can extract an egg and a sperm from a couple, fertilize the egg in a petri dish, then freeze the embryo for later use. A host mother, who has no genetic link to the child she carries, can be rented to carry the embryo to term. In theory, a woman could give birth to her own great-aunt or uncle, or even a sibling, years after the embryo was frozen.

Medical technology now allows scientists to isolate genetic defects that affect the carrier and generations to come. Should that information be made available to carriers or to their employers? Should the health care industry have the right to refuse to issue insurance to carriers who decide to have children that may inherit the defect? Should the medical community be permitted to do experimental in utero procedures to change the genetic heritage of the fetus? At present, the body of law and regulation covering this new industry is just being developed, and the ethical implications are only beginning to be explored.

What seemed like science fiction 20 years ago is scientifically feasible and even commonplace today. With new technology proliferating, one cannot possibly predict the nature of scientific and business collaborative efforts in the future.

There are numerous examples of industries whose issues touch on all the environments just discussed. The tobacco and cigarette controversy is a useful example.

The Tobacco Industry and the Economic, Social, Legal and Political, and Technological Environments. The debate swirling around smoking and cigarette production involves all the environments discussed earlier. Between World War II and the early 1980s, the issue of whether to smoke changed from a question of health and habit to one of civil rights and social etiquette. Our culture changed from "smoking permitted" to "no smoking allowed." The right to smoke versus the right to live in a smoke-free environment became a burning issue. Exhibit 2–3 highlights the key elements in the tobacco controversy.

---

[21] S. Bailey and S. Syre, "It's His Party," *Boston Globe,* April 26, 1996, p. 89.

EXHIBIT 2–3 Key Events in the Tobacco Controversy

1955	The first Federal Trade Commission (FTC) publishes advertising guidelines.
1964	The surgeon general's report demonstrates a link between cigarette smoking and cancer.
1965	The FTC advertising code passes, requiring a warning label on cigarette packages.
1970	Legislation passes banning cigarette advertising from all broadcast media.
1972	Health warnings made mandatory in all cigarette advertising.
1972	All airlines volunteer to establish no-smoking sections.
1988	The Federal Aviation Administration (FAA) prohibits smoking on all flights of two hours or less.
1990	Complete ban on smoking on all domestic flights.
1995	FDA concludes that nicotine in cigarettes should be regulated as a drug.
1996	Health and Human Services Administration (HHS) issues stricter rules against cigarette sales to minors
1996	Liggett Group offers to settle class-action claims for smoking-related damages.

In the mid-1980s, Philip Morris and R. J. Reynolds Industries, Inc., tried to counter changing attitudes toward smoking. They formulated and implemented strategies to promote prosmoking issues. Reynolds did a direct mailing in a few states to encourage people to oppose possible increases on cigarette taxes. Philip Morris published a magazine to "influence people and make them feel good and warm about Philip Morris."[22]

In 1988, Philip Morris began a national advertising campaign that stressed the economic and political power of smokers. As Guy Smith IV, Philip Morris's vice president for corporate affairs, put it, "Let the politicians take note. You're not just talking special interest group. You're talking swing vote."[23]

But the antismoking trend was clear. By 1988, more than half of American companies had restricted smoking on the job, the Federal Aviation Administration prohibited smoking on domestic air flights of two hours or less, and Northwest Airlines advertised it prohibited smoking on all domestic flights. No-smoking sections in restaurants and no-smoking rooms in hotels became the norm.

Societal sanctions against smoking escalated in 1993, when the Environmental Protection Agency (EPA) reported that secondhand smoke caused about 3,000 nonsmokers to die from lung cancer each year in the United States. The report also asserted that environmental tobacco smoke increased not only the risk of asthma in all children but also the severity of attacks in

---

[22] T. Hall, "Philip Morris Cos. Magazine Promotes Pro-Smoking Issues," *The Wall Street Journal,* July 24, 1985, p. 7.

[23] R. Rothenberg, "New Ads by Philip Morris Stress Power of Smokers," *New York Times,* June 29, 1988, p. 1.

asthma-prone children. Antismoking groups immediately used the EPA report to demand more restrictions on smoking in public places. To avoid liability, shopping malls, restaurants, businesses, and even sports stadiums banned or severely restricted smoking. Philip Morris and RJR Nabisco sued the EPA, claiming the report was unscientific, arbitrary, and capricious. They accused the EPA of manipulating data and failing to follow basic statistical principles.[24]

In 1995, under intense pressure from antismoking groups, the tobacco industry donated $4.1 million to political candidates and parties. The tobacco industry also gave a substantial amount of money to think tanks and other groups that were not legally required to disclose the amount of the gifts. Most of these groups were strongly opposed to the FDA and the policies of its director, David Kessler.

In July 1995, federal proscutors in Washington and New York began probing allegations that tobacco executives perjured themselves before Congress by hiding evidence about the use and addictiveness of nicotine. In April 1994, top executives of the nation's seven largest tobacco companies appeared at congressional hearings. William I. Campbell, then CEO of Philip Morris stated unequivocally that "Philip Morris does not manipulate nor independently control the level of nicotine in our products." All the executives testified under oath they did not think that nicotine was addictive, that cigarettes caused disease, or that their companies manipulated the level of nicotine in tobacco products.[25]

To counter adverse publicity, Philip Morris launched an ad campaign in which it touted the creation of a program to prevent sales of cigarettes to minors. In full-page ads in national newspapers, the company announced it would place a notice on all packs and cartons noting underage sales were prohibited. In addition, Philip Morris vowed it would implement other measures to keep minors from smoking. It would deny merchandising benefits to retailers who were fined or convicted of selling cigarettes to minors and would seek state legislation to prevent minors from buying cigarettes from vending machines.[26]

In August 1995, the Food and Drug Administration (FDA) declared cigarettes a drug. President Clinton instructed the FDA to propose rules that would curtail the sale, distribution, and advertising of cigarettes to minors. Tobacco companies were furious and immediately went to court to try to block the move. Filing a lawsuit in Greensboro, North Carolina, the tobacco industry contended the FDA had no jurisdiction over cigarettes.[27] They

---

[24] N. Tait, "US Tobacco Groups Sue over Report," *Financial Times,* June 23, 1993, p. 6.

[25] V. Novak and A. M. Freedman, "Tobacco Industry Facing 2 Criminal Investigations," *The Wall Street Journal,* July 25, 1995, p. A3; P. J. Hilts, "U.S. Convenes Grand Jury to Look at Tobacco Industry," *New York Times,* July 26, 1995, p. A1.

[26] *The Wall Street Journal,* June 28, 1995, A7.

[27] "Cigarette Regulation Is Formally Proposed; Industry Sues to Halt It," *The Wall Street Journal,* August 11, 1995, p. A1.

accused FDA Commissioner David Kessler of hatching a devious plot to ban cigarettes altogether.

Tobacco companies suffered a second major blow in October. *The Wall Street Journal* uncovered two major confidential internal reports by Brown & Williamson Tobacco Corp (B&W). The first report, drafted in the early 1990s, explained how ammonia scavenged nicotine from tobacco and converted it to a form that had a greater effect on smokers. By using ammonia in the process, manufacturers could actually enhance the nicotine delivery system without actually adding more of the substance. Brown & Williamson's manual said the company added ammonia-releasing chemicals to almost all its menthol brands.

The second document, dated October 1992, was Brown & Williamson's competitive analysis of Philip Morris's Marlboro brand cigarette. The Marlboro analysis traced Philip Morris's use of ammonia technology back to the 1950s, at which time Philip Morris began using tobacco stems, dust, and broken leaves as money-saving fillers. Apparently the ammonia compound acted like a glue to keep the residue together in manufacturing. B&W's report noted that "extractable nicotine contributes to impact in cigarette smoke and this is how ammonia can act as an impact booster."[28]

In December 1995, *The Wall Street Journal* published a confidential Philip Morris draft report dating back several years. The report acknowledged that cigarettes were a "nicotine delivery system" and that nicotine was chemically similar to such drugs as cocaine, morphine, and atropine. A Philip Morris spokesperson responded that "we have acknowledged in public documents that nicotine, like many, many other things, has pharmacological effects, but that doesn't mean that cigarette smoking is addictive."[29]

In January 1996, Jeffrey S. Wigand, a former Brown & Williamson employee, gave a deposition about his career with the tobacco manufacturer. Wigand, who had a PhD in biochemistry and pharmacology, was B&W's research chief until he was fired in 1993. The 137-page deposition covered many subjects but focused on three major points. Wigand charged that his ex-boss, former Chairman Thomas E. Sandefur, lied to Congress in April 1994 about his views on nicotine addiction. He further charged that B&W in-house lawyers repeatedly hid damaging scientific research. Wigand also said that when he told top officials they were using a compound found in rat poison, they insisted the compound remain as an additive in pipe tobacco.

Lawyers for B&W responded that their private detectives had turned up evidence that Wigand had shoplifted, failed to pay child support, and that he

---

[28] A. M. Freedman, "Tobacco Firm Shows How Ammonia Spurs Delivery of Nicotine," *The Wall Street Journal,* October 18, 1995, p. A1.

[29] A. M. Freedman, "Philip Morris Memo Likens Nicotine to Cocaine," *The Wall Street Journal,* December 8, 1995, p. B1.

was fired for being abusive to subordinates. Wigand countercharged, accusing B&W of threatening him and his children.[30]

In February, Mississippi Attorney General Michael Moore filed a $45 billion suit against the tobacco industry. With Jeffrey Wigand as his star witness, Moore's novel suit sought to recover the Medicaid costs of treating tobacco-related diseases. The states of Minnesota, Florida, and Wisconsin brought similar suits.

Mississippi Governor Kirk Fordice filed a suit charging that Attorney General Moore needed to get the governor's permission to sue the tobacco companies. State politics semed to be a major element in the legal actions. Republican Governor Fordice was not eligible for re-election after completing his second term and Democrat Moore was considered a major contender for the position. Fordice rejected Moore's claim that he was pressured by the tobacco industry and its lobbying efforts.[31]

The tobacco industry had to deal with new federal regulations requiring states to discourage teenagers from smoking. The government threatened states with loss of federal grants if they did not block at least 80 percent of the efforts of teenagers to buy cigarettes. State legislatures wrestled with these regulations as well as many additional aspects of tobacco use.

Almost every state legislature found itself embroiled in some aspect of the tobacco controversy. Florida, New York, and New Jersey legislators debated whether their states should be able to sue tobacco companies to get back Medicare expenses on tobacco-related illnesses. Florida, which tried to get back $1.4 billion, had an antismoking law that prevented tobacco companies from defending themselves by arguing that smokers knew the risks. The state, therefore, could rely on broad statistical evidence in its suit, thus greatly improving its chances of winning.

State lawmakers, who found their legislation conflicted with city and town ordinances, began to override local interests. Pennsylvania's lawmakers weighed legislation to stop towns and cities from passing their own tobacco regulations. Michigan wrestled with whether it should restore the rights which it took away in 1993, and New York considered whether to do away with bans on cigarette smoking in restaurants passed by New York City and three counties. By 1996, 27 states had passed laws that pre-empted local legislation.[32] In Exhibit 2–4 we summarize the most recent lawsuits involving the tobacco industry.

---

[30] A. M. Freedman, "Cigarette Defector Says CEO Lied to Congress about His View of Nicotine," *The Wall Street Journal,* January 26, 1996, p. A1.

[31] S. L. Hwang, "State Attorney Has New Hurdle in Tobacco Suit," *The Wall Street Journal,* February 20, 1996, p. B1.

[32] B. J. Feder, "New Federal Rule Helps Intensify Smoking Fight in States," *New York Times,* March 15, 1996, p. A22.

Exhibit 2–4 Key Lawsuits Involving the Tobacco Industry, 1995–1996

Class actions	*Castano* v. *The American Tobacco Co. et al.* is a class action by 60 law firms that sued the major tobacco companies on behalf of every current and past smoker who claimed addiction.
Secondhand smoke	Major tobacco companies sue to challenge the Environmental Protection Agency's (EPA) classification of secondhand smoke as a cause of cancer.
Medicaid payments	Florida, Massachusetts, Minnesota, Mississippi, and West Virginia sue tobacco companies seeking compensation for the expense of treating smoking-related illnesses among Medicaid patients.
Advertising	Major tobacco companies and advertisers sue to block proposed federal regulations restricting advertising and promotion of tobacco products.

Source: B. J. Feder, "A United Front by Tobacco Starts to Crack," *New York Times,* March 14, 1996, p. A1.

On March 13, 1996, lawyers representing millions of class-action claimants in the Castano case (named for Dianne Castano whose husband had died from lung cancer in 1994) agreed to drop the Liggett Group from the suit. Liggett agreed to pay Castano plaintiffs up to 5 percent of its pretax income each year to a maximum of $50 million a year for the next 25 years. Liggett also promised to withdraw from the fight against the FDA's new tobacco regulations discouraging sales to children. The company agreed to contribute to quit-smoking campaigns.[33]

While the Liggett settlement was being negotiated, the Justice Department began anew to look into accusations of fraud and perjury against tobacco executives. Initial investigations had begun in 1993 but not much had happened until Wigand made his disclosures, internal company documents were made public, and Liggett capitulated. By spring 1996, four of the Justice Department's six litigating divisons had taken up tobacco-related issues. The Justice Department's Office of Legal Counsel began to examine First Amendment issues related to tobacco advertising.

In May 1996, the Castano class-action suit suffered a major blow. A three-judge panel in Louisiana ruled unanimously that there were too many differences in plaintiffs' circumstances and too many conflicts among state laws yet to be resolved. As a result of this decision, plaintiffs would be forced to proceed individually or join class-actions suits in state courts. Tobacco companies and Wall Street were euphoric. Major tobacco companies' stock went up immediately. The senior vice president of R. J. Reynolds told the press, "We see this as a clear signal of the beginning of the end of class-action

---

[33] M. Shao, "Tobacco Firm Agrees to Settle Suit," *Boston Globe,* March 14, 1996, p. 1.

litigation involving the tobacco industry." Lawyers for the plaintiffs viewed the ruling as a temporary glitch noting, "It is a procedural setback. But it is not a setback of the theory of the case."[34]

This case raises issues for young and old that transcend economic and social lines. It frames the issue within the U.S. legal and political systems. It points to the balance between the rights of nonsmokers and smokers. It asks who should bear the cost of health care for smokers and how those costs should be allocated. The case also raises questions about the rights of individuals with free will who choose to use a substance even if it harms them and others. It asks what rights local, state, and federal governments have to dictate public and private behavior. The case also explores the technologies available to manufacturers who want to change the natural attributes of raw materials.

Thus far, we have examined the external environment of strategic management. In the next section, we look at strategy formulation within the company.

Strategic Management and Organizational Culture

The business that attempts to plan its functional and social strategies must consider the interactions of the four sectors that make up its total environment. As our cursory overview suggests, the environment is complex and hard to define. Therefore, managers must identify and deal with those particular environmental forces linked most closely to the firm's truly strategic issues.

Managers have a critical responsibility to assess their firms' internal organizational cultures as well as their external environments. People within an organization select among issues they will address and the tools they will use to achieve their objectives. We look next at some of the factors affecting these decisions. Corporate assessment and issue identification go on at all levels of the corporation but top management is responsible for determining the elements and process of strategy formulation.

Values and Leadership

A key issue for general managers (CEO, chairperson of the board, senior vice presidents) is to understand the company's sociocultural environment and determine how and where social issues fit into the firm's overall strategy. The skills that managers must use to deal with the financial, marketing, human resources, and other functional areas of business also apply to social issues.

---

[34] A. Flint, "Court Derails Class-Action Tobacco Suit," *Boston Globe,* May 24, 1996, p. 9.

There is no doubt the personal values and leadership styles of the firm's top managers play a major role in this determination. Chester I. Barnard, the former president of New Jersey Bell Telephone Company, wrote a book in 1938 that anticipated a number of today's business problems.[35]

Barnard observed that the endurance of organizations "depends upon the quality of leadership; and that quality derives from the breadth of the morality upon which it rests." He went on to explain that executive responsibility is "that capacity of leaders by which, reflecting attitudes, ideals, hopes, derived largely from without themselves, they are compelled to bind the wills of men to the accomplishment of purposes beyond their immediate ends, beyond their times."[36] In essence, Barnard was pointing to the importance of scope of vision and the ability to create an organization of people capable of responding thoughtfully and purposefully to the world around them.

Kenneth R. Andrews points out that general managers function as "communicators of purpose and policy."[37] Their values and what they want to do often form the basis for their choice of alternatives. Unless the CEO identifies an issue as critical, institutes mechanisms for dealing with it, and communicates its importance, middle managers are likely to ignore the issue.

Spyros Makridakis, a pioneer in the field of forecasting, notes the difficulties top management faces in planning, formulating, and communicating its purpose and policies. He outlined six elements or steps in successful planning. We discuss the first three in terms of strategy formulation and the remaining three (Implementing the Best Alternative; Monitoring and Controlling Results; and Pursuing versus Abandoning Plans and Planning) in Chapter 3, Strategy Implementation and Evaluation.

1. *Seeing the Need for Planning:* The manager must realize that something needs to be done ahead of time and must understand the consequences if nothing is done. We discuss this process more thoroughly in Chapter 4, Crisis Planning.

2. *Formulating Alternatives*: Once managers have established the need for planning, they must study all the important aspects of the task and, at the same time, determine various alternatives. Managers must have (*a*) knowledge about the planning situation being considered; (*b*) creativity in developing alternatives; and (*c*) realistic, practical alternatives.

3. *Selecting the Best Alternative*: Senior managers must evaluate all alternatives to select the best among them. A personal vision of the future and willingness to take risks is part of each senior manager's decision.[38]

---

[35] C. I. Barnard, *Function of the Executive* (Cambridge, MA: Harvard University Press, 1960).

[36] Ibid., pp. 282–83.

[37] Andrews, p. 7.

[38] S. G. Makridakis, *Forecasting, Planning, and Strategy for the 21st Century* (New York: The Free Press, 1990), pp. 124–25.

Planning for social issues can be more difficult than planning for many functional business situations because issues do not lend themselves to quantitative modeling, results are often difficult to measure, and planners operate in a state of environmental uncertainty. However, there are activist CEOs whose social issues planning lasted well after they retired or moved on.

Edwin Land founded the Polaroid Corporation. Even though it has been many years since he was active in the firm, he still enjoys a semimythical status. His legacy of strong community involvement continues. Polaroid began a minority-training project called Inner City in 1968, well before stakeholder pressure for such a program existed. The project became profitable and trained hundreds of employees for Polaroid and other companies. Polaroid gives financial, administrative, and technical assistance to hundreds of nonprofit institutions in the Greater Boston area and other areas in which Polaroid facilities are located. It offers employees a huge range of courses in career development, information systems, math and science, communication, and management. Land's personal values continue to influence the strategy of the current group of general managers decades after his retirement.

Greg Steltenpohl is still actively involved in Odwalla, Inc., the fresh-fruit beverage company he founded in 1980. It is likely his ideals will persist even after his active participation ceases. From the beginning, Steltenpohl and his colleagues wanted to create a company that "by its nature, didn't wreak havoc on the environment." At the end of 1995, Odwalla's net revenue was $36 million, up from $18.1 million for the prior year. Net income grew by about 200 percent in the same period.

Because Odwalla's juice is neither pasteurized nor contains added preservatives, its shelf life is only two weeks. Odwalla uses its own direct-to-the-store delivery system to serve its 2,000 retail customers. Concerned about emissions from the trucks, Steltenpohl worked with Isuzu to convert its 143 truck delivery fleet from gasoline to natural gas. Odwalla has a comprehensive recycling system that composts all fruit and vegetable waste and converts it into usable products such as livestock feed. Co-CEO Stephen Williamson developed a contract farming system that eliminated the use of herbicides and pesticides. Steltenpohl acknowledges the importance of the founder's vision. "We spent time working on an internal process designed to connect the day-to-day tasks of more than 500 employees with the bigger vision and fundamental values of the company."[39]

From the beginning, George A. Steiner asserts, "the values of top managers are reflected in the network of aims of an enterprise. Whether written or not, these values have the profoundest impact on the direction in which a firm moves and the way it operates."[40] Gerald F. Cavanagh writes that while strategic planning is essential to business success, values are the criteria by

---

[39] M. Scott, "Odwalla, Inc.," *Business Ethics,* November–December 1995, p. 35.
[40] G. A. Steiner, *Top Management Planning* (New York: Macmillan, 1969), p. 144.

which managers make their important decisions.[41] In effect, the personal values of senior managers such as Land, Steltenpohl, Williamson, and others serve as filters through which they view the world and pilot their firms.

Adaptability to Change

Scholars wrestle with the relationship between environmental changes and strategic planning. Strategic planning often is based on a general manager's assessment of how the firm can and should adapt to a changing environment. Her personal values often determine the company's direction in a period of uncertainty. Many scholars agree with H. Igor Ansoff that one of the primary difficulties of strategic issue management is top management's refusal to accept new and unfamiliar issues as relevant.[42]

Perhaps top management's attitude toward change is the key issue; that is the company's willingness to recognize environmental change, adapt to it, or in some instances, even generate change from within. Because managing change is central to an organization's effectiveness in adapting to its turbulent environment, managerial resistance to change limits and inhibits the company's vision.

Resistance to change also helps explain why managers do or do not take action. In recent years, American business leaders have been criticized for their lack of innovativeness and risk taking. William R. Boulton observes organizations that have operated in a stable environment over a long time find it very difficult to change. It is possible that only some sort of crisis can spark a change.[43]

In sum, it is essential that a company's leaders understand and even welcome change rather than perceive it as a threat. They must build an organizational culture in which people are encouraged to try new ideas and approaches to problems. They must view a dynamic environment as a source of challenge and excitement, not something to be ignored in the hope it will go away. If a firm's strategic planning process fails to anticipate change, the firm will likely be unable to set a strategically sound and socially responsive course.

It is worth noting that social change often engenders economic change and vice versa. Consider the potential economic changes resulting from fewer people smoking. Less tobacco is sold, tobacco farmers' incomes fall, farmers sell off their land and enter other occupations. Community solidarity and stability suffer. Farmland is developed to support other industries, and generations of tradition are lost.

---

[41] G. F. Cavanagh, *American Business Values,* 2nd ed. (Englewood Cliffs, NJ: Prentice Hall, 1984), pp. 1, 206.
[42] H. I. Ansoff, "Strategic Issue Management," *Strategic Management Journal* 1, April–June 1980, pp. 131–48.
[43] W. R. Boulton, *Business Policy: The Art of Strategic Management* (New York: Macmillan, 1984), pp. 204–205.

As tobacco manufacturers lose markets in the United States, they begin to acquire new, nontobacco-based companies. They also enter joint ventures with developing-country governments and firms to generate new populations of cigarette smokers abroad. Finally, U.S. consumers who are trying to quit smoking buy nicotine patches, chew nicotine gum, and enter behavior modification programs. All these activities create new economic opportunities, change established markets, and have major societal implications.

A Framework for Strategy Formulation

In *Competitive Strategy,* Michael E. Porter stresses, "The essence of formulating competitive strategy is relating a company to its environment."[44] If a company aligns itself with its environment, it must fit its strategy to the realities of that environment. A company's ability to achieve a strategic fit between itself and its environment depends on management's ability to identify, define, and assess the organization's mission, major objectives, and internal capabilities. Top management must scan and analyze its environment and choose an effective strategy from among a number of options.[45]

In this section we develop more fully those aspects of the strategy formulation process most directly related to the management of corporate social responsiveness. The mission statement is a logical starting point.

The Mission Statement

In spelling out a company's mission or purpose, top management defines its product or market boundaries and provides its people with a sense of direction and purpose. In *A Sense of Mission: Defining Direction for the Large Corporation,* Andrew Campbell and Laura Nash found that in the ideal situation, the sense of mission is established by a company's founders and is revised and extended as the company grows.[46]

In short, the mission statement should answer the following questions:

- Who are we?
- What business are we in?
- What do we stand for?

---

[44] M. E. Porter, *Competitive Strategy: Techniques for Analyzing Industries and Competition* (New York: The Free Press, 1980), p. 3.

[45] See, for example, Boulton, *Business Policy*; L. G. Hrebiniak and W. L. Joyce, *Implementing Strategy* (New York: Macmillan, 1984); P. Lorange and R. F. Vancil, *Strategic Planning Systems* (Englewood Cliffs, NJ: Prentice Hall, 1977); D. E. Schendel and C.W. Hofer, eds., *Strategic Management* (Boston: Little, Brown, 1979); B. Yavitz and W. H. Newman, *Strategy in Action* (New York: The Free Press, 1982); and H. I. Ansoff, *The New Corporate Strategy* (New York: John Wiley & Sons, 1988).

[46] J. A. Kurtzman, "Mission Statements," *Harvard Business Review* (March/April 1993), p. 10.

According to John A. Pearce II, the company mission is "a broadly defined but enduring statement of purpose that distinguishes a business from other firms of its type and identifies the scope of its operations in product and market terms."[47] James C. Collins and Jerry I. Porras define the mission statement as "a clear and compelling goal that serves to unify an organization's efforts. . . . [It] must stretch and challenge the organization, yet be achievable. It translates the abstractness of philosophy into a tangible, energizing, highly focused goal that draws the organization forward."[48]

Some companies restrict their mission statement to a discussion of the economic mission of the enterprise and supplement it with a separate company credo or ethics statement. Others incorporate their basic beliefs or credos into the text of the mission statement. The company generally benefits from defining its commitment to good corporate citizenship whether it uses joint or separate statements.

Johnson & Johnson's (J&J) Credo is a classic example of a mission statement that serves a company well. In September 1982, several Chicago-area residents died of cyanide poisoning after taking Tylenol, a leading over-the-counter pain remedy produced by one of J&J's divisions. Johnson & Johnson immediately announced a recall of more than 90,000 bottles of Extra-Strength Tylenol from the lot that caused the deaths. Even though multiple tests of other bottles in the lot showed no contamination, the company wasted no time in alerting doctors, hospitals, and wholesalers about the possible danger. CEO James E. Burke announced early in the crisis, "It's important that we demonstrate that we've taken every step possible to protect the public, and that there's simply nothing else we can do."[49]

Employees and customers alike understood J&J's public position as the firm struggled with the aftermath of the deaths. As the investigation into the cause of the deaths proceeded, it became clear that J&J was not responsible and that someone had tampered with the packages after distribution. With tremendous fanfare and publicity, J&J introduced a new tamper-resistant package in November 1982. By the end of the year, Tylenol had regained first place among over-the-counter analgesics. J&J's mission statement shows the intertwining of economic and social goals (see Exhibit 2–5). Some mission statements, such as J&J's, broadly define relevant stakeholders.

Nonprofit and state organizations also develop mission statements. Their goal, like that of profit-making corporations, is to unify the organization and define its purpose. The tiny nation of Singapore developed a mission statement for its civil service. The ideals expressed in this statement could just as easily have been written by a corporation (see Exhibit 2–6).

---

[47] J. A. Pearce II, "The Company Mission as a Strategic Tool," *Sloan Management Review* 23, Spring 1982, p. 15.

[48] J. C. Collins and J. I. Porras, "Organizational Vision and Visionary Organizations," *California Management Review* 34 (Fall 1991), p. 42.

[49] *The Wall Street Journal,* October 4, 1982, p. 16.

EXHIBIT 2–5 Johnson & Johnson's Mission Statement

Johnson & Johnson

Our Credo

We believe our first responsibility is to the doctors, nurses and patients, to mothers and all others who use our products and services. In meeting their needs everything we do must be of high quality. We must constantly strive to reduce our costs in order to maintain reasonable prices.
Customers' orders must be serviced promptly and accurately.
Our suppliers and distributors must have an opportunity to make a fair profit.

We are responsible to our employees, the men and women who work with us throughout the world.
Everyone must be considered as an individual.
We must respect their dignity and recognize their merit.
They must have a sense of security in their jobs.
Compensation must be fair and adequate, and working conditions clean, orderly and safe.
Employees must feel free to make suggestions and complaints.
There must be equal opportunity for employment, development and advancement for those qualified.
We must provide competent management, and their actions must be just and ethical.

We are responsible to the communities in which we live and work and to the world community as well.

We must be good citizens—support good works and charities and bear our fair share of taxes.
We must encourage civic improvements and better health and education.
We must maintain in good order the property we are privileged to use, protecting the environment and natural resources.

Our final responsibility is to our stockholders.
Business must make a sound profit.
We must experiment with new ideas.
Research must be carried on, innovative programs developed and mistakes paid for.
New equipment must be purchased, new facilities provided and new products launched.
Reserves must be created to provide for adverse times.
When we operate according to these principles, the stockholders should realize a fair return.

Source: Johnson & Johnson, 1982 *Annual Report.*

EXHIBIT 2–6 Singapore Civil Service

Our Mission
- We work with the elected government to shape Singapore's future, forge a common vision among Singaporeans and transform vision into reality.
- We safeguard the independence, sovereignty, security and prosperity of Singapore.
- We uphold justice and equality, guided by the principles of incorruptibility, meritocracy, and impartiality.

Our Customers
- We provide quality service—responsive, efficient and courteous.
- We treat our customers fairly and honestly, holding to high standards of professionalism, integrity and conduct.
- We do our best to help our customers and meet their needs.

Our Staff
- We value our staff. We maximize their potential through continuing training and development. We encourage them to continuously improve their knowledge, skills, and capabilities.
- We offer our staff challenging and worthwhile responsibilities. We expect them to show commitment, resourcefulness and enterprise. We provide them with the tools, resources and environment to do a good job.
- We require our staff to work well with others. We can develop sound plans and implement them effectively only when people at different levels with diverse abilities work closely together.

Our Beliefs
- *Respect* for individual staff members is the first prerequisite for outstanding service and wholehearted commitment.
- *Change* is essential for continuously maintaining and improving Singapore's international competitiveness in the global economy.
- *Excellence* drives us to be the best that we can be in all that we do.
- *Learning* from others, from feedback and from mistakes is the best way to benefit from experience.
- *Leadership* which is bold, discerning and open to new ideas and insights is crucial for steady progress and superior achievement.

Source: Internet, April 24, 1996 [http://www.gov.sg/rita/intro.html]

In the late 1980s, managers incorporated ethical codes into their companies' mission statements more frequently. Scandals involving insider trading and collusion between the defense industry and government officials over multimillion-dollar contracts rocked the corporate world. Corporations rushed to adopt codes of ethics. The Business Roundtable recommended that top managers implement written codes that explicitly communicate the expectations of top management, develop programs to implement guidelines, and conduct surveys to monitor compliance.[50] We discuss codes of ethics more fully in Chapter 5.

---

[50] J. A. Byrne, "Businesses Are Signing Up for Ethics 101," *Business Week,* February 15, 1988, pp. 56–57.

If the company's mission changes, or if a new mission statement says one thing while employees are experiencing something else, employees and other stakeholders may perceive a gap between the company's stated values and its observable behavior. Then, stakeholders are likely to ignore the social values proclaimed by the mission statement.

AT&T Chairman Robert E. Allen created AT&T's Common Bond statement in 1990. The company conducted focus groups of employees worldwide, challenging them to address three basic questions: What defines AT&T? What's the glue that holds the company together? What do we stand for? After considerable revision, Allen released the statement to senior officers for review and discussion in 1991. More focus groups were held, and in 1992 more changes were made based on the feedback.

Late in 1992 the statement was released to shareholders and employees and was featured in company publications; see Exhibit 2–7. Allen asked his corporate officers to write down what they planned to do to build their behavior and that of their organization around the values. He did his own

---

EXHIBIT 2–7 AT&T's Common Bond Statement

Our Common Bond

Respect for Individuals: We treat each other with respect and dignity, valuing individual and cultural differences. We communicate frequently and with candor, listening to each other regardless of level or position. Recognizing that exceptional quality begins with people, we give individuals the authority to use their capabilities to the fullest to satisfy their customers. Our environment supports personal growth and continuous learning for all AT&T people.

Dedication to Helping Customers: We truly care for each customer. We build enduring relationships by understanding and anticipating our customers' needs and by serving them better each time than the time before. AT&T customers can count on us to consistently deliver superior products and services that help them achieve their personal or business goals.

Highest Standards of Integrity: We are honest and ethical in all our business dealings, starting with how we treat each other. We keep our promises and admit our mistakes. Our personal conduct ensures that AT&T's name is always worthy of trust.

Innovation: We believe innovation is the engine that will keep us vital and growing. Our culture embraces creativity, seeking different perspectives and risks pursuing new opportunities. We create and rapidly convert technology into products and services, constantly searching for new ways to make technology more useful to customers.

Teamwork: We encourage and reward both individual and team achievements. We freely join with colleagues across organization boundaries to advance the interests of customers and shareowners. Our team spirit extends to being responsible and caring partners in the communities where we live and work.

By living these values, AT&T aspires to set a standard of excellence worldwide that will reward our shareowners, our customers, and AT&T people.

Source: Internet April 24, 1996 [http://www.att.com/ar-1994/html3/page14.html]

self-assessment which he reviewed with senior people and came up with an action plan to align his own behavior with espoused values. The entire team of corporate officers engaged in the same exercise. Human resource leaders in the business units used coaches to help them disseminate the process through the entire organization. Employees were urged to see values as part of all their business decisions, not as a separate exercise.

In *AT&T's 1995 Annual Report,* Chairman Allen told the shareholders that September 20, 1995, was the most important day in the reporting year. That was the day he announced plans to separate AT&T into three independent, publicly held corporations. AT&T was to focus on communications services, Lucent Technologies was to offer communications systems and technology, and NCR was to offer computer systems and services. Allen noted that the three companies shared a history of looking to Our Common Bond as a guide to doing business. He noted that "We are making an intense effort to live that value [Respect for Individuals] as we now go through the difficult process of reducing our skilled and capable workforce by about 40,000 jobs, or about 13 percent. . . . Good and talented people will be leaving us because they are not a match for our future needs and size. That can't be helped. . . . The restructuring we're doing now has to be seen in the context of a continuing journey. . . . You don't make a journey of this magnitude without hitting some bumps along the way."[51] It remains to be seen what effect Our Common Bond will have on the cultures of the three new companies and their goals.

Corporate Objectives

Organizations have a hierarchy of objectives. Strategic objectives are those objectives that cover the broadest scope of organizational activities and require the greatest commitment and risk to resources. The companies that seem most successful in achieving their goals are those that have a limited number of crisply defined and well-understood strategic objectives. For example, if diversification is a major objective, the scope of the firm can delineate the diversification effort (compatible with its mission statement) and quantify the objective (e.g., "No more than 20 percent of our revenues is to be derived from any single product line"). Above all, managers should use the process of objective setting to transform broad directions into concrete, measurable action commitments.[52]

According to most scholars of corporate strategy, corporate social responsiveness objectives need to be specific, to avoid apple-pie-and-parenthood statements and, as difficult as it may seem, to be quantifiable whenever

---

[51] *AT&T 1995 Annual Report,* "We're Hatching Three Unusual Start-Ups," pp. 6–7.
[52] A. A. Thompson and A. J. Strickland III, *Strategy Formulation and Implementation* (Dallas: Business Publications, 1980), p. 8.

possible. For example, Polaroid's statement of objectives in environmental affairs notes the company uses state-of-the-art methods to reduce the amount of waste generated per unit of production. The company commits itself to reducing the toxicity volume per unit of production and the level of emissions to all environmental media.[53] These goals are measurable and clearly understandable to both employees and shareholders in the same way as are goals related to financial or market share objectives.

Mintzberg takes a different view of objective setting. In his view "values are the least operational of the elements of the strategic planning model." He says that quantification is possible in principle but "can do terrible injustice in practice to the complex set of values contained in the human system called organization."[54] He is skeptical that objectives provide incentives and are devices of motivation and control.

Many corporate strategists disagree with Mintzberg's analysis. At the hub of Michael Porter's Wheel of Competitive Strategy is a set of goals including "objectives for profitability growth, market share, social responsiveness, etc." The hub contains the company's broad definition of how it wants to compete and its specific and noneconomic objectives.[55] Porter clearly places social responsiveness objectives at the center of the company's activities (see Exhibit 2–8).

Internal Assessment

To a considerable extent, the organization's strengths and weaknesses have a direct impact on the strategic choices the firm makes after assessing its environment. A company's strengths lie in its core competencies or capabilities (what it does especially well).

The Apple Example. In 1984 Apple Computer was, according to *Business Week,* the Magic Kingdom. Two kids in a garage had created a computer. They formed a New Age company in which the only thing that mattered was building computers that could change the world. On January 22, a 60-second commercial shown to 43 million Super Bowl viewers, showed an athlete running into an auditorium filled with corporate types watching a figure on a huge video screen. She broke the screen by hurling a hammer into it. Symbolically, this action destroyed old ways of doing things and introduced the world to the new user-friendly Macintosh.

By 1996 Apple was virtually unrecognizable as an image-making company. Microsoft's Windows' 95 eroded the Mac's market and a decision to license Apple technology to other personal-computer markets didn't work. By 1995, 14 out of 45 vice presidents were fired or had left. Apple's share

---

[53] Polaroid Corporation, 1977 Annual Report, p. 12.
[54] Mintzberg, p. 54.
[55] Porter, *Competitive Strategy,* p. xvii.

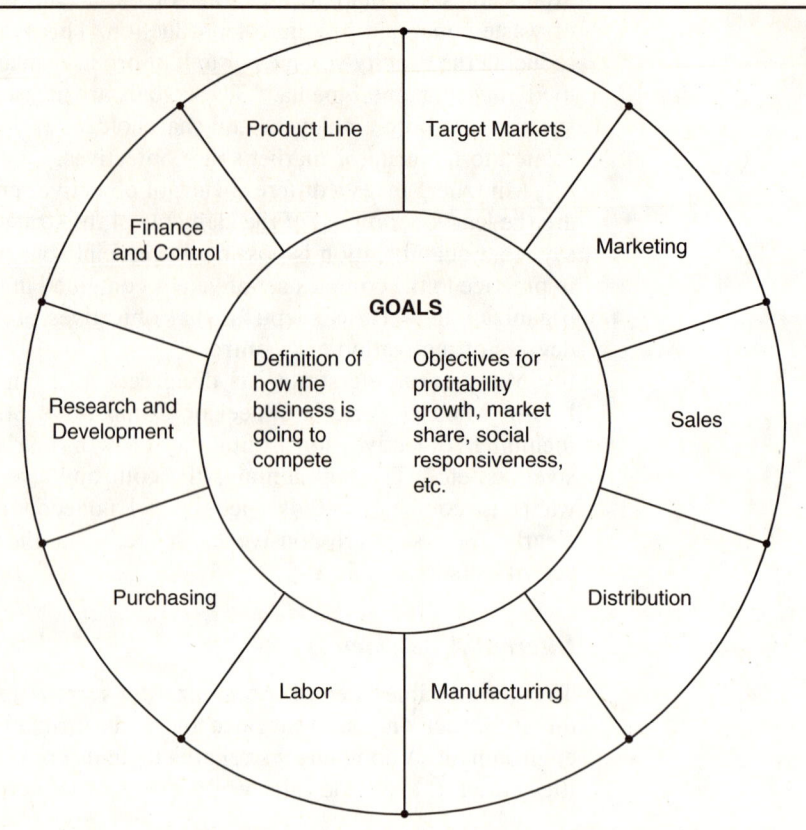

EXHIBIT 2–8 The Wheel of Competitive Strategy

Wheel diagram with center labeled **GOALS**: "Definition of how the business is going to compete" and "Objectives for profitability growth, market share, social responsiveness, etc." Surrounding segments: Product Line, Target Markets, Marketing, Sales, Distribution, Manufacturing, Labor, Purchasing, Research and Development, Finance and Control.

of the world market fell from 8.2 percent in the fourth quarter of 1994 to 7.1 percent in the same quarter of 1995. Apple had lost its technological edge and leadership position. It couldn't get top dollar anymore nor could it stimulate market growth.[56]

Apple's top management, thinking of strategies to rejuvenate the company, began talks with Sun Microsystems Inc. about a Sun buyout. A California job recruiter reported that morale at Apple was very low and that he was getting calls from mid- and upper-management executives looking to leave.[57]

On April 17, 1996, Apple issued a press release in which it reported that net sales were down 18 percent from the second quarter of 1995. The net loss for the quarter was $740 million. Apple's chairman and chief executive

---

[56] K. Rebello, P. Burrows, and I. Sager, "The Fall of an American Icon," *Business Week*, February 5, 1996, pp. 34–42.

[57] J. Carlton, "Uncertainty Over Apple's Future Begins to Hurt Dealers, Spark Employee Jitters," *The Wall Street Journal*, January 31, 1996, p. B3.

officer, Dr. Gilbert F. Amelio said that "with regard to strategic direction the intrinsic multimedia capabilities of Apple's platform place us in a unique position to capitalize on the ongoing convergence of computers and communications." Executive Vice President Fred D. Anderson added, "We've taken decisive action necessary to align the balance sheet with current conditions and to reserve for the necessary restructuring of Apple."[58]

The "Netly News," part of Pathfinder's comprehensive news and entertainment Internet site, was skeptical about Apple's ability to work its way out of its troubles. On April 22, 1996, "Netly News's" Chris Stamper wrote the following about Always Apple, a cheerleading site for Apple customers. "Maybe it's just me. For two months, like someone who's found a dead body decaying in the woods, I've been returning to Always Apple—a site set up by employees to spread good cheer as the company teeters over the brink and into the newspaper headlines."[59]

The critical issue for Apple was whether it had irrevocably lost its vision and its understanding of its core competencies. Did Apple executives understand why Apple was in such trouble and, even more important, could they fix the problems in this fast-changing industry?

Organizational Weaknesses, Social Issues Visibility, and Vulnerability

Organizational weaknesses of companies tend to center around two major areas: (1) resources, both managerial and financial, and (2) negative social issues visibility. Frequently managerial talent is a limited resource. Some companies lack enough talented people to sustain certain types of strategies. A company may have a great idea for a new product line but lack the managerial resources or competencies needed to take advantage of the idea. Inadequate financial resources are another major limitation. Good ideas and good people are essential to success, but the financial strength to carry out a strategy is equally important. When products or top management are highly visible in a negative way, the company becomes more vulnerable to stakeholders' challenges.

Social responsiveness programs create both visibility and vulnerability for a company. Visibility is a double-edged sword. A highly visible company that undertakes a project reflecting cultural values gets rewarded. On the other hand, a company is punished if it acts in a way that is considered wrong or insensitive in terms of those values. Management must consider objectively the firm's vulnerability to stakeholder pressure.

---

[58] To access a vast amount of information about Apple Computer use the Internet address [http://www.apple.com/]. The company has a site called Always Apple set up by employees to boost morale.

[59] Internet [http://pathfinder.com]

Social activists and others seeking change are likely to target highly visible firms that are close to the consumer. Financially weak firms operating in an intensely competitive environment also are vulnerable to challenges focused on social responsibility.

Company visibility depends on several factors: the firm's size, the nature of its products, the services it offers, the customers it serves, and the personalities of key members of its management. As a result of their sheer size and market position, companies in certain industries are more likely than others to be targeted. Oil companies, for example, frequently come under scrutiny for their environmental policies and their pricing strategies by the media, government agencies, and social activist groups.

The Body Shop Example. Anita Roddick, founder of The Body Shop, promoted her company as one that combined good business with socially responsible behavior. In 1976, she opened a small cosmetics shop in Brighton, England. She vowed that all her products were natural and "100 percent pure." In 1984, investment bankers backed her stock and she quickly became a multimillionaire. Touting the purity of her products, she heaped criticism on other cosmetic makers, calling some of them cheats and exploiters of women. Roddick's outspokenness and penchant for publicity turned her into a celebrity. By 1994, she and her husband had an estimated net worth of more than $200 million. Their worldwide empire consisted of 1,050 stores in 45 countries.

Roddick frequently expressed her philosophy. "We see ourselves not just as a creator of profits for our shareholders, but as a force for good, working for the future of the planet. Enlightened capitalism is the best way of changing society for the better. I think you can trade ethically, be committed to social responsibility, global responsibility, empower your employees without being afraid of them. I think you can rewrite the book on business."

Despite a booming market, Roddick and her husband came under intense media scrutiny. Jon Entine, an investigative reporter and TV news reporter, wrote an exposé of The Body Shop, pointing out the gap between the founders' assertions and counterassertions by franchisees, employees, trading partners, and social researchers.[60]

Roddick was frequently interviewed about why she named the company, The Body Shop. Her official story was that she was visiting California in 1971 and got the idea for the name from an auto repair business. Roddick's original partner, Mark Constantine, disputed this story. He said there was an existing cosmetic shop in Berkeley, California, called the Body Shop and she copied the store design, literature, products, and marketing strategies.

From the beginning, The Body Shop asserted that it sold natural products. In 1970, there were no laws governing labeling. Constantine said he and

---

[60] J. Entine, "Shattered Image," *Business Ethics,* September–October 1994, pp. 23–28.

Roddick added synthetic dyes and artificial colors and petrochemical ingredients to the products.

In 1979, the company hired a public-relations expert, Janis Raven, who designed an image of "Anita-the-world-traveler, hobnobbing with bare-breasted native Indians spreading mysterious goop on their faces." Raven later reported they made up "one fable after another."

In 1986, the company faced its first serious challenge from Revlon and the British department store, Marks & Spencer. Roddick hooked up with Greenpeace U.K., promoting the chapter's "Save the Whales" campaign and touting its substitution of vegetable jojoba oil for whale spermaceti. Although it was a very popular campaign in Britain, other chapters pointed to The Body Shop's continued use of petrochemicals. Some Greenpeace chapters refused to promote The Body Shop products, a decision that upset Roddick.

She quickly launched a second promotion that tied her company and other natural cosmetics companies to animal rights groups. As sales soared, Roddick campaigned for environmental causes such as rain forest preservation, recycling, AIDS awareness, and helping Romanian orphans. Roddick's image and fame grew as the company expanded to the United States.

In 1992 and 1993, the Food and Drug Administration (FDA) inspected the company's U.S. manufacturing processes. The reports showed that The Body Shop periodically suspended its standard microbial testing for months, hoping to save time getting the products to the stores. A former quality-control manager declared, "We are under such demand right now that they take the product in right off the truck, fill it up into the bottles, and it goes out the door." The Body Shop was directly violating the Good Manufacturing Practices standards to which it subscribed.

In 1993, the U.S. manufacturer received a shipment of banana shampoo. The manufacturer skipped the required tests on the bulk containers, filled the bottles, and sent one filled bottle to the lab for testing. Before the test results came back, the company shipped the lot of bottled shampoo to regional distribution centers. A week later the test results showed *E. coli* bacteria at levels 1,000 percent above acceptable industry standards. Instead of recalling the shampoo, The Body Shop sent new samples to the lab hoping to get acceptable results. The FDA found that 140 bottles of contaminated shampoo were sold before the batch was recalled. The Body Shop said the incident was a distributor's mistake and that it had instructed distributors to hold the shampoo until lab results came back.

In another example of the gap between rhetoric and fact, The Body Shop apparently did not live up to its corporate philanthropy fact sheet statement. The sheet asserted, "The Body Shop donates an inordinately high percentage of pretax profits to often controversial charitable campaigns." Public record showed that between 1986 and 1993, the company's charitable donations ranged from .36 percent to 1.24 percent of pretax earnings. The average for U.S. companies was 1.9 percent and some companies, like Patagonia, gave as much as 10 percent. After repeated media inquiries, The Body Shop raised its charitable contribution for 1994 to 2.97 percent.

Corporate governance also became an issue for The Body Shop. The company had never had an outside board member. In 1992 the London Stock Exchange established a Code of Best Practices of the Corporate Governance.[61] The Body Shop violated seven provisions of the code. Media criticism and franchisee unhappiness made imperative a move toward more professional management. In 1994, the company vowed to remedy the situation by appointing an outsider who would reorganize the firm and its management systems.

Roddick dismissed Entine's article as "recycled rubbish." Some franchisees rejected Entine's allegations but others agreed that The Body Shop set up their franchises for failure. Stacie and Larry Benes said that The Body Shop chose their location, oversaw the construction of the store, and negotiated the lease with the mall. The costs incurred made it impossible for them to be profitable despite good sales. When they faced personal bankruptcy and losing the many thousands of dollars they had invested, The Body Shop top management would not even discuss their situation.

Other franchisees, suppliers to The Body Shop, cosmetic company executives, customers, and academics commented on Entine's article and the Roddicks' vehement denial of any wrongdoing. Although there were supporters and detractors, Kirk O. Hanson of Stanford University summed it up in his letter to the editor, "I believe the fault lies collectively with the author, The Body Shop itself, and *Business Ethics*. In other words, everyone is to blame for The Body Shop's troubles."[62]

By 1996 the company's share price had dropped 65 percent from its 1992 high. U.S. business was dismal. Competition from the Limited's Bath & Body Works was so successful that The Body Shop actually lost money in its U.S. operations. Only booming sales in Asia propped up the overall earnings picture. The Roddicks' hands-on style and their running battle with the media and critics led former employees to complain that the company lacked a strategic plan. Internal weakness in planning and the absence of solid professional management appeared to overshadow The Body's Shop social and political message.

Currently, it appears the Roddicks are stepping back from day-to-day operations and have hired a managing director to bring in professionals and install tighter processes.[63] Analysts wondered whether The Body Shop and its top management could overcome the combination of internal weaknesses and increasingly fierce competition. It seemed clear that the company's social responsiveness agenda could not overcome organizational weaknesses. There were some who felt that Anita Roddick's strident support of some causes actually hurt the company. The Body Shop's strategy is based

---

[61] Ibid.
[62] "Letters to the Editor," *Business Ethics,* November–December 1994, pp. 4–6.
[63] C. P. Wallace, "Can The Body Shop Shape Up?" *Fortune,* April 15, 1996, pp. 119–20.

on highly visible and sometimes controversial stands. Roddick established herself as an example of high moral character and exemplary values. It was no wonder that her visibility also turned her into a lightening rod for every complaint and contrary perspective.

In April 1966, Kirk O. Hanson issued a social audit commissioned by The Body Shop. Although Hanson gave high marks to the company for its mission statement, corporate philanthropy, and environmental and animal welfare, he was concerned about the company's poor relationship with the media and critics. As he noted, "I believe that until very recently, the company has given more attention to its 'social campaigns' than it has to improving the social impact on its day-to-day business dealings."[64]

Stakeholders hold companies that rely on a high level of consumer trust, such as The Body Shop, to especially rigorous standards. Both the public and the media react particularly strongly when large numbers of lives are at risk or when a company appears to have deliberately betrayed the public trust. Falling short of that standard ensures a great deal of negative publicity and costly litigation. Top managers' visibility or absence of involvement can help either defuse or exacerbate a crisis. In Anita Roddick's case it did both.

Environmental Scanning and Analysis

At some time, all companies face uncertainties in the environment and become vulnerable to stakeholder pressure. Managers can use tools such as scanning to minimize vulnerability to stakeholder pressure and maximize their options. Companies use scanning to alert them to potential changes that might constrain their strategic options.

John E. Fleming describes environmental scanning and analysis as "a process designed to obtain, analyze, and report information relating to issues in the social and political environments."[65] Companies use scanning techniques to try to identify indicators of change in the economic, social, legal and political, and technological environments before they occur. Companies gain time to work out their strategic options before stakeholders apply pressure on them to change. The earlier steps of determining the company's mission, defining its strategic objectives, and assessing its internal strengths and weaknesses are essential prerequisites for an effective scanning and analysis of the firm's environment.

When companies perform these steps properly, they can identify the particular areas of the environment that need to be monitored most closely. The values of senior management and the organization's culture also

---

[64] M. Rose, "Body Shop Draws Some Criticism in 'Social Audit,'" *The Wall Street Journal,* April 19, 1996, p. B7A.

[65] J. E. Fleming, "Public Issues Scanning," in *Corporate Social Performance and Policy,* ed. L. E. Preston (Greenwich, CT: JAI Press, 1981), p. 156.

influence the selection of relevant variables from the environment. Some writers have argued that "systematic and continuous environmental scanning within a comprehensive framework is an essential activity for an ongoing managerial organization . . . comparable to annual budget preparation and review or the preparation of regular operating statements."[66]

The scanning and analysis process consists of four basic elements. Companies must ask:

1. How can we gather the best and most useful information about the environment?
2. What is the competitive environment of the firm?
3. Which participants have the greatest stake in a given issue or management decision?
4. How can we classify the issues into subsets, and how can we manage those issues and evaluate our performance?

Social issues opportunities and threats exist in the environment outside the corporation as well as within the structure of the company itself. The

EXHIBIT 2–9 Home Page of the U.S. Department of Commerce

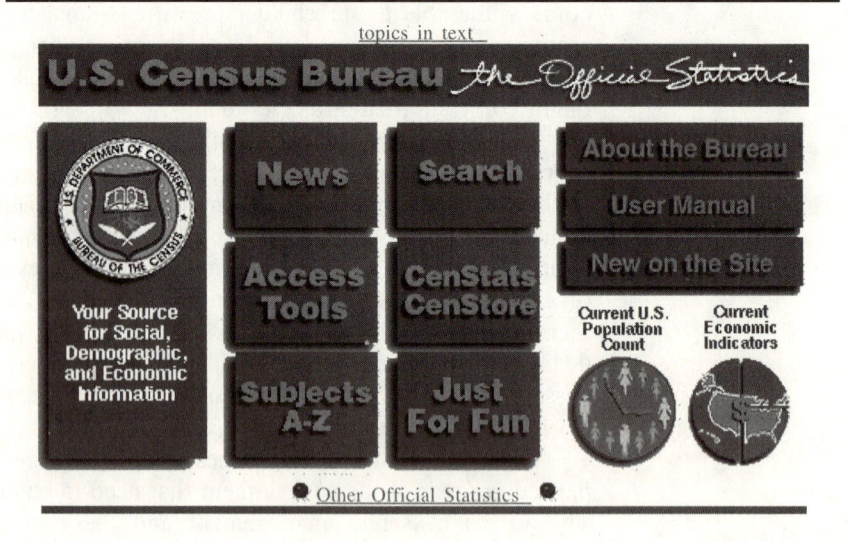

---

[66] L. E. Preston and J. E. Post, *Private Management and Public Policy* (Englewood Cliffs, NJ: Prentice Hall, 1975), p. 107.

company should gather as much data as possible on external issues such as government regulation, consumerism, pollution, energy sources and costs, and taxation. Internally, the company should amass information on compensation and benefit trends, hiring and firing practices, safety, employee stress, and ethics.

A manager can draw on many sources of information. The Internet is the newest and has enormous potential. Let's presume a manager who wants data on economic activity by region throughout the United States accesses the Internet and then types in [http://www.census.gov/]. The home page in Exhibit 2–9 would appear.

By clicking on the box titled Population and Housing, the manager gets Exhibit 2–10. By clicking on Press Releases, the manager can access news releases by subject; note the various options in Exhibit 2–11.

Connecting to the Internet takes only a few minutes and the information is free and readily accessible. Although information on the Internet is likely to be very timely, it may need to be worked into more usable form; in other words, the searcher may get raw data.

The Yankelovich Group, the Opinion Research Corporation, the Roper Organization, the Survey Research Center at the University of Michigan, the Harris Poll, and many other commercial and academic organizations provide potentially helpful environmental studies and trend analyses. Analysts have already taken the data, compiled them into a form, and presented them in terms of other data and trends.

Trade organizations are also good sources of information because they conduct specialized studies for specific companies. In some industries, trade associations undertake ongoing studies of social issues and member activities. For example, the American Council of Life Insurance and the Health Insurance Association of America created the Center for Corporate Public Involvement. Since 1973, the center has published an annual report identifying a number of areas of social concern (e.g., equal employment opportunity, contributions, and environmental issues) and provides a summary of the activities and efforts of 250 member companies. Volunteers scan specific publications for particular kinds of issues and events and each volunteer writes a summary of the relevant item stating what is important. These abstracts go to a committee that looks for emerging trends. As we discuss in the next chapter, the scanning and analysis effort must be systematic and manageable. If the scanning effort is to contribute to improved company performance, it must be an integral part of the firm's overall social responsiveness management process.

Strategic Choice

Having identified and analyzed the issues and parties that have the strongest possible consequences for the firm, management must make strategic decisions about how best to adapt or respond. The process is one of strategic choice. According to Robert H. Miles,

EXHIBIT 2–10   Population and Housing Information

U.S. Census Bureau *the Official Statistics*

New on Our Site

Subscribe to the Census I-Net Bulletin to keep posted about new products and services as well as additions and other changes to our World-Wide Web site. (sample available)

- TechTalk Visit TechTalk, a clearinghouse for product information and related technical assistance. 02/19/97 NEW!!
- Housing Vacancies and Homeownership: Annual Statistics 1996 02/13/97 NEW!!
- Central Cities for Metropolitan Areas of the United States 02/06/97 NEW!!
- Record Linkage Workshop: Agenda The Committee on Applied and Theoretical Statistics of the National Academy of Sciences, the Washington Statistical Society, the Bureau of the Census, the National Agricultural Statistical Service, National Center for Health Statistics, National Science Foundation, the Federal Committee on Statistical Methodology, and The George Washington University are sponsoring or providing support for a two-day workshop on record linkage in Washington, D.C., March 20-21, 1997 02/05/97 NEW!!
- Census Headquarters Employment Opportunities Open Vacancies at the Census Bureau 02/03/97 NEW!!
- The Video Zone Census Bureau video clips--featuring We Measure America, a music video 01/31/97 NEW!!
- Housing Vacancies and Home Ownership, Fourth Quarter 1996 01/29/97 NEW!!
- Survey of Market Absorptions: Third quarter 1996 absorptions (2nd qtr 96 completions) 12/31/96
- 1990-96 Estimates of Population and Components of Change Three tables: ST-96-1 - Annual time series of total populations, 1990-96 ST-96-2 - Demographic Components of Change 1995-96 and Population Change 1990-96 ST-96-e - Annual time series of total populations and components of change, 1990-96 12/30/96
- Property Owners and Managers Survey (POMS) 12/20/96
- Trend Data on Recent Movers and People Living Alone, 1940-1990 12/09/96
- Changing the Way the United States Measures Income and Poverty 12/05/96
- Record Linkage Workshop: Call for Papers 12/05/96
- Historical Tables on Marital Status, Living Arrangements: March 1995 12/04/96
- Historical Tables on Households and Families: March 1995 12/04/96
- 1993 Commmodity Flow Survey U.S. Summmary 10/25/96
- MABLE/GeoCorr Geographic Correspondence Engine Mirror Site 10/23/96
- Housing Vacancies and Home Ownership: Third Quarter 10/22/96
- Population Projections for States by Age, Sex, Race, and Hispanic Origin: 1995 to 2025 10/22/96
- Census Bureau Data on Disability 10/22/96

Exhibit 2–11 News Releases by Subject

U.S. Census Bureau *the Official Statistics*

News Releases By Subject

- Census 2000
- Aging Population
- Agriculture
- Business Ownership Characteristics
- Children
- County Business Patterns
- Disability
- General Economic Census & Survey
- Economic Indicators
- Education
- Fact Sheets
- Families and Households
- Fertility
- Finance, Insurance, and Real Estate
- Governments
- Health Care

- Hispanic Origin Population
- Housing
- Income and Wealth
- International Population
- Manufacturing Industries
- Marital Status
- Mineral Industries
- Mobility
- Population
- Poverty
- Race
- Retail Industries
- Service Industries
- Transportation Industry
- Voting
- Women

To Top of List

This view emphasizes the role of learning and choice in the process of organizational adaptation, and observes not only that complex organizations have the ability to alter themselves to conform to the contingencies—constraints and opportunities—posed by their environment, but that they may exercise considerable influence on the environments in which they operate. Indeed, these choices may range from the manipulation of environmental features to make them more accommodative of organizational goals, strategies, and structures, to the actual choice of the environments in which an organization wishes to operate.[67]

The literature on corporate social responsiveness identifies two strategic approaches to stakeholder pressure: proactive and reactive. A proactive company attempts to anticipate strategic issues and devise approaches to prevent problems from developing. If the anticipatory effort is not successful and a problem develops, the company attempts to respond as quickly and

---

[67] R. H. Miles, *Coffin Nails and Conflict Resolution* (Englewood Cliffs, NJ: Prentice Hall, 1982), p. 11.

effectively as possible. In short, the company strives to be on top of situations and take constructive steps to be a positive force for desirable change. For example, the anticipatory activities of Johnson & Johnson's management allowed the company to handle crises such as the Tylenol scare expertly.

A reactive company deals with problems only after they have developed. Its posture is often defensive. When the firm is required to act, such as following litigation or the passage of new legislation, the initial response is minimal: "We do what the law requires, nothing more, nothing less." These companies act only when forced to; they drag their heels as long as possible and deny responsibility long after it becomes obvious they are responsible for the problems. For the most part, tobacco and asbestos companies have adopted that strategy.

In practice, companies rarely respond in a purely proactive or a purely reactive way. Most companies make reactive responses to some issues and proactive responses to others. For example, a company may institute a training program for minorities that costs a considerable amount of money and managerial time but refuse to address the needs of its workers with disabilities.

Sometimes the response process for a single issue may vary according to its cost to the company. If the cost either in money or adverse publicity is high, the organization may be more inclined to delay action than if the issue is low in cost. Each organization learns how far it has to go to satisfy a particular stakeholder without reorganizing its priorities.

Strategic budgetary and economic considerations appear to weigh extremely heavily in companies' decisions about which social issues to tackle. Gaining public approval, while desirable, does not necessarily guide expenditures.

In Chapter 3, we look in depth at how companies implement social goals based on the formulation of strategies most appropriate for them.

Summary

This chapter concentrated on developing a framework for strategy formulation. It examined the relationship between elements of the corporate environment and a company's social responsiveness. The major sources of change and turbulence flow from a company's economic, social, legal and political, and technological segments of the environment. While formulating strategy, a company interprets environmental forces and issues based on the values of top management. The extent of the firm's response is influenced significantly by the culture of the organization.

In formulating its strategic response, a company must consider its mission and its strategic objectives. It must assess its internal strengths and weaknesses, scan and analyze its objectives, and then make choices among strategic alternatives. Most companies adopt a mixed proactive and reactive response to issues depending on the particular circumstances with which they must deal.

Project

Choose a Fortune 500 firm and ask its public relations department about the company's social issues agenda. Try to assess the environmental forces affecting its social issues strategy. Also, try to identify the major issues in each of the four environments.

Questions

1. What are the major elements of the American macroculture? Is there one identifiable American business culture? If so, what are its elements?

2. Suppose you are the CEO of a large, divisionalized company that makes canned food products. What ideas would you put into the company's mission statement? A consumer complains that a can of your company's string beans was not properly sealed. What guiding concept tells you how to deal with this situation?

3. How would you go about scanning for social issues that your company should address?

4. If you were on the board of Philip Morris, what response would you make to the issue of states seeking to claim Medicare reimbursement? What consequences do you think your action would have?

Beta Pharmaceuticals: Introduction

Beta Pharmaceuticals, Inc., is the integrative case that illustrates some of the issues and problems managers encounter as they formulate and implement social issues strategy. The case can be used segment by segment in conjunction with individual chapters. It can also stand alone as a multipart case that deals with a wide range of social issues affecting stakeholders both within and external to the firm.

BETA CASE 1
STRATEGY FORMULATION

The Economic Environment

Beta Pharmaceuticals, Inc., is a large, global, multidivisional pharmaceutical company headquartered in Detroit. Beta, like other major pharmaceutical companies enjoyed an excellent year in 1995. U.S. sales rose 10 percent to $40.3 billion, the highest level in three years. Beta's total 1995 sales worldwide were $13.6 billion, a jump of more than 12 percent over the previous year. Stock prices for Beta and other major pharmaceutical companies also set record highs. Leading U.S. and European drugmakers were happy with expert predictions that net income was expected to rise by as much as 12 percent in 1996.

Beta and other drug companies were no longer concerned about the Clinton administration's health care reform package that had threatened to have a major impact on the pharmaceutical industry in the early 1990s. For the time being, health care reform was stalled and the Republican Congress was in no mood to rein in drug company profits. The PRIME Institute at the University of Michigan College of Pharmacy noted that the producer list for the 500 most-prescribed drugs, climbed an average of 4.6 percent in 1995, with much of the rise coming in the fourth quarter.

Some drug companies admitted they should have heeded the market forces that drove consolidation of medical supply companies in 1992 as a harbinger of things to come in their industry. Merck and Company, a pharmaceutical industry leader, was the first major company to respond dramatically to the changing economic environment. On July 20, 1993, Merck announced it was setting aside $775 million for restructuring and was paying more than 2,000 employees to take early retirement. Eight days later, Merck announced it would pay $6 billion in stock and cash for Medco Containment Services, Inc., a prescription mail-order seller and discounter.

Restructuring and alliance building continued through the 1990s. Deals between pharmaceutical companies and biotechnology start-ups seemed very attractive. In 1996, the pharmaceutical industry as a whole invested about $3.5 billion in partnering with biotech firms. Switzerland's Ciba paid $2 billion for half of California's Chion in 1994. SmithKline Beecham, one of the most aggressive multinationals, had more than 30 biotech partnerships and over 100 academic alliances by 1996. Pfizer and Bristol-Myers Squibb tied up with U.S.-based biotech firms Immusol and Somatix in the area of gene therapy. Their strategy was pre-emptive. Neither had international gene therapy R&D programs but both wanted to move into the field when it looked more viable. Drug industry experts remained upbeat about pharmabiotech relationships. Their view was that the partnering strategy allowed the biotech industry to avoid consolidation and shrinkage.

Takeover bids and mergers also continued and were designed to boost productivity in manufacturing and marketing. Drug distribution management companies were purchased by Merck, Lilly, and SmithKline Beecham in 1993 and 1994 for more than $12 billion. American Home Products concluded a $10 billion takeover of American Cyanamid in 1995. Hoechst of Germany paid $1.7 billion for Marion Merrill Dow of the United States, and Roche paid $5.3 billion for California's Syntex. Glaxo bid more than $13 billion for Wellcome in the United Kingdom in 1995.

Beta's top management and board of directors concluded that mergers, acquisitions, and consolidation would continue. Some executives speculated that within a few years, only a few large pharmaceutical makers would survive. The rest would fall to declining drug profits, cost containment measures, killing competition, and a trickle of new drugs in the research pipeline. Other top managers disagreed, noting that Glaxo Wellcome, the world's biggest pharmaceutical company had only 5 percent market share, and the top 20 companies controlled less than half of world drug sales. In their view, the industry would remain competitive for the foreseeable future.

Beta's Social Environment

Like other companies in the industry, Beta had to deal with the areas of social concern common to most U.S. businesses. These issues included equal employment opportunity, worker safety and privacy, job creation, and product safety. Environmental issues, such as waste disposal, clean air, and clear-water requirements, had always been a major concern. As a global company, Beta worried about its overseas subsidiaries and their environmental requirements. In the mid-1990s, the pharmaceutical industry in general, and Beta in particular, faced a number of social issues, including AIDS research and drug development, fetal research, biotechnological advances, rampant patent infringements, orphan drugs (drugs used in the treatment of a disease affecting 5,000 or fewer people), and supervision of controlled substances.

Beta's Corporate Organization

Before 1987, Beta had six operating divisions: ethical products, hospital products, consumer products, diagnostics, therapeutics, and pediatrics. See the Beta Pharmaceuticals Organization Chart in Exhibit 2–12.

Late in 1987, Beta concluded negotiations to acquire Intac, Inc., a biotechnology company specializing in gene splicing and genetically engineered drugs. Manufacturing operations for the original divisions and the new biotech division were located in 20 states and eight other countries. In 1996, Beta entered a strategic alliance with Immogetics, a Swiss biotech company specializing in diagnostic testing. Intac's Sam Powell worked directly with Immogetics' corporate officers.

In 1995, Beta began a new generic drug division. The company hired David Shapiro, the vice president of a small, successful generic drug company in New Jersey, to head the division. Like other pharmaceutical companies, Beta had scorned low-priced generic

EXHIBIT 2–12   Beta Pharmaceuticals Organization Chart

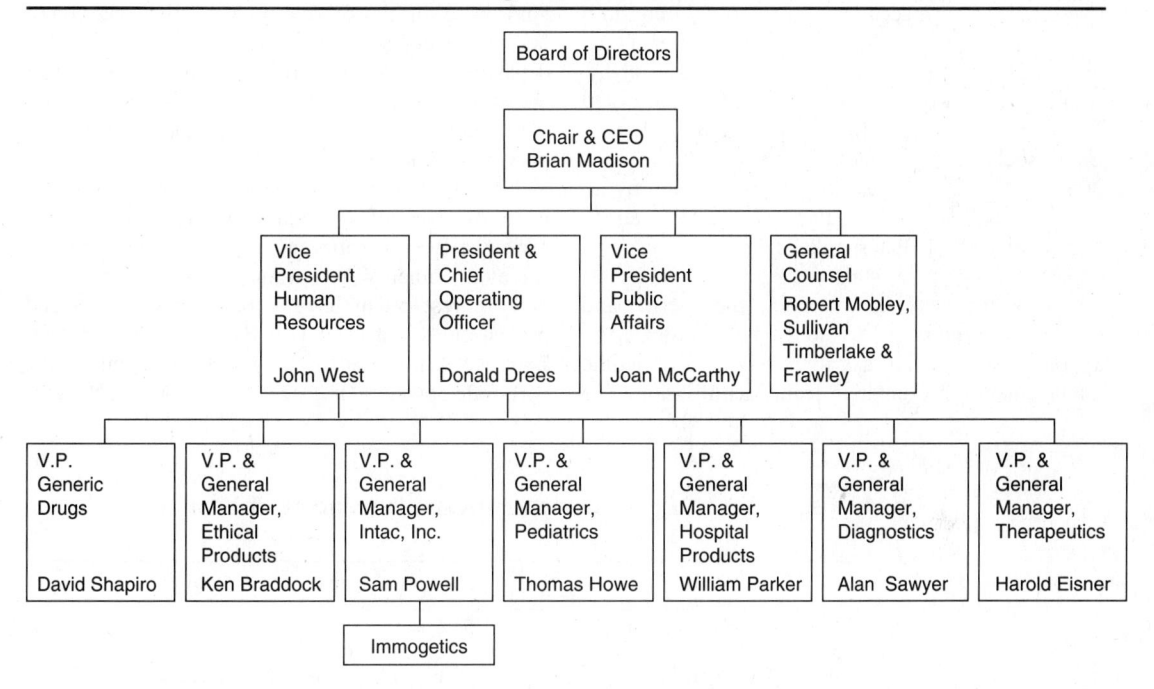

```
                           Board of Directors
                                  |
                            Chair & CEO
                            Brian Madison
                                  |
        ┌─────────────────┬───────┴────────┬─────────────────┐
    Vice              President &        Vice             General
    President         Chief              President         Counsel
    Human             Operating          Public
    Resources         Officer            Affairs           Robert Mobley,
                                                           Sullivan
                                                           Timberlake &
    John West         Donald Drees       Joan McCarthy     Frawley
                                  |
  ┌──────┬──────┬──────┬──────┬──────┬──────┐
 V.P.   V.P. & V.P. & V.P. & V.P. & V.P. & V.P. &
 Generic General General General General General General
 Drugs   Manager,Manager,Manager,Manager,Manager,Manager,
         Ethical Intac,  Pediatrics Hospital Diagnostics Therapeutics
         Products Inc.            Products
 David   Ken     Sam    Thomas   William   Alan     Harold
 Shapiro Braddock Powell Howe    Parker    Sawyer   Eisner
                  |
              Immogetics
```

imitators, holding to the industry line that the copies were not as reliable as the originals. But the opportunities for profit were simply too seductive and the penalty for late entry too great. Beta, like Merck, Marion Merrill Dow, and others, decided to grab a piece of the multibillion-dollar-a-year generic market.

Beta hurried its move into generics because more than 60 important drugs with combined American sales of $8 billion per year had patents that would expire over the next 36 months. A few of Beta's managers suggested that selling a product at a price much lower than that of an identical prototype might kill the market for the more expensive drug. Others argued that doctors often continued to prescribe the brand-name drug. They also noted that although pharmacists could provide a generic unless the doctor specifically forbade it, customers whose drugs were covered by insurance often requested the more expensive version.

Brian Madison, the chairperson and chief executive of Beta Pharmaceuticals, was strongly committed to social responsiveness. Shortly after being named CEO in 1990, Madison hired Joan McCarthy, who had been working for a competitor, and asked her to create a public affairs department to manage Beta's social responsiveness program. McCarthy was one of three executives who reported directly to Madison. She decided her first task was to identify and classify all of Beta's stakeholders.

McCarthy and her staff put together a public affairs department to begin scanning the internal and external environments for social issues. McCarthy appointed an internal task force, taking one middle management representative from each division. The task force's assignment was to generate a list of social issues relevant to the company and identify the specific stakeholder groups concerned with each issue.

After they compiled the list, the task force disbanded and the public affairs department assumed the job of setting priorities to determine the importance of each issue. McCarthy met occasionally with Madison to discuss developing management performance measures. Madison believed it was very important to add the selected issues to the firm's planning and evaluation process. He and McCarthy had a number of inconclusive discussions about how they should undertake this process, and implementation proceeded very slowly.

During the early and mid-1990s, division vice presidents developed yearly and long-range objectives for improving performance in each of the designated areas. Vice presidents told lower-level managers their evaluations would be based in part on their ability to meet those objectives. In practice, financial goals were still the single most important criterion of performance. McCarthy and other members of her department were concerned about the economic pressures on Beta, particularly since the uncertainties of the economic climate were even more acute than in previous years.

The task force identified a number of employee issues that were of particular concern. For example, a review of Beta Pharmaceuticals' employment record revealed women were chronically and substantially underrepresented in the ranks of top management and professionals (category 1 in Exhibit 2–13). In fact, Joan McCarthy was the only vice president on the corporate or general manager level. Women also were

EXHIBIT 2–13 Beta Pharmaceuticals' Percentage of Female Employees

	1979	1981	1983	1995
Category 1 (officials, managers, professionals)	1.64% (n 72)	2.1% (116)	3.66% (177)	4.12% (373)
Category 2 (technicians, sales workers, office and clerical workers)	51.39% (1,886)	51.71% (2,219)	51.22% (2,557)	53.62% (2,833)
Category 3 (craftspeople, operatives, laborers, service workers)	4.83% (1,335)	4.84% (1,424)	7.20% (2,231)	11.65% (3,438)

underrepresented among craftspeople, operatives, laborers, and service workers (category 3). Indeed, the only category in which women were fully represented was category 2, with its tradition of women's jobs such as office and clerical workers. These traditional employment patterns had prevailed during Beta's most successful growth period. McCarthy had been working on this issue for several years and had some success in recruiting women for category 3 jobs. However, she was far from satisfied with the company's progress in bringing women into top management positions.

The Clinton administration had lifted the government directive against the use of fetal tissue in research. Would stakeholders seize this issue and inhibit the company's research opportunities? It seemed that a fierce political battle was brewing between pro-life and pro-choice advocates. Should Beta abandon this area of research?

Beta's management was concerned about potential criticism of the composition of the board of directors. Beta had no women or minorities on its board, and most of the directors were inside managers. The company's law firm had a banker and a senior partner on its board, but there were no executives of other companies, no members of trade organizations, no union representatives, no foreign nationals, and no participants from the Detroit community.

Shareholders were pressuring Beta to change the board's composition to reflect society's diversity and to increase the representation of independent, outside directors on boards. McCarthy and Madison met frequently to discuss the qualifications and numbers of outsiders who should be brought onto the board. While McCarthy and her staff agreed they could set objectives for hiring women and minorities and could develop strategies to achieve this goal, they were less sure about their ability to set objectives for many of the other issues.

They were particularly concerned about developing measures to evaluate middle- and lower-level managers on implementation in nonquantifiable areas. Madison had clearly stated his commitment to social goals when he established McCarthy's public relations department and gave the charge to the task force, but the public affairs department was left with unclear goals and an unknown degree of institutional resistance to change. On the other hand, the company's commitment to social responsiveness generally had met with enthusiasm.

CHAPTER 3
STRATEGY IMPLEMENTATION AND EVALUATION

Strategy formulation and implementation are highly interrelated activities. The concepts and recommendations discussed in Chapter 2 and the issues addressed in this chapter are fundamental to accomplishing corporate goals. This chapter examines the key elements of the process that move the company from analysis toward getting the job done and evaluating the results.

Environmental scanning and analysis, introduced in the previous chapter, link strategy formulation and implementation to evaluation. Once the company has collected the best and most useful information about the economic, social, legal and political, and technological environments, managers must be able to identify the stakeholder issues that directly and indirectly influence the firm.

CASE: STAKEHOLDERS AND NUCLEAR WASTE

In 1994, the United States had 107 nuclear plants. Some had already been shut down because their 40-year life span had expired or safety hazards were too great. Two dozen more plants were scheduled to be closed in the last part of the 1990s. Stakeholder disputes began to reach explosive proportions over what should be done with the plants' spent nuclear fuel and radioactive reactor components.

Nuclear plant managers, a major stakeholder group, tried to deal with ballooning maintenance costs and decreasing safety as plants aged. Managers also had to comply with federal regulations by setting aside funds for the plants' eventual demolition.

Kenneth Harrison, CEO of Oregon's Trojan reactor, faced problems common to the industry. Trojan's chronic maintenance problems forced Harrison to shut the plant down after 17 years, rather than the planned 40 years of operation. Although Trojan's managers had put aside funds for demolition during the plant's lifetime, the utility managed to accrue only $40 million for a task that was projected to cost about $488 million.[1]

---
[1] S. Shulman, "Nuclear Reactors: The High Cost of Early Retirement," *Technology Today,* January 20, 1994, pp. 20–21.

Nuclear plants also were supervised by the Department of Energy (DOE), another major stakeholder. The DOE was charged with providing a permanent repository for high-level radioactive waste. It had proposed boring a tunnel into Nevada's Yucca Mountain and building a vast underground facility. The Yucca Mountain plan would create a labyrinth of bunkers carved beneath the mountain. The bunkers would store thousands of steel cannisters full of radioactive material that would not decay for 10,000 years. The state of Nevada, yet another stakeholder, threatened to fight the implementation of the radioactive dump plan.

Lawmakers in states in which nuclear plants were located encountered complex and often conflicting demands. The Minnesota State Legislature, for example, had a vexing nuclear waste problem. The Red Wing plant owned by the Northern States Power Company ran out of storage space for its nuclear waste although it was only halfway through its projected 40-year life span. The state legislature, anticipating a federal solution, refused to allow the power company to build temporary storage areas.

The Sioux tribe of Native Americans, on whose land the reactor was located, was also very much opposed to Northern States's proposal to build temporary storage facilities since the tribe's Treasure Island casino was located a half-mile from the reactor. The tribe argued that visitors would not come to visit a nuclear dump. Environmentalist groups such as the Prairie Island Coalition Against Nuclear Storage sided with the Sioux although they did not support gambling or the casino.

On the other side of the controversy, the city of Red Wing, in which the plant was located, wanted operations to continue. The city's tax base would be seriously eroded by the plant's closing. The plant's 500 jobs and $22 million in local tax revenues furnished city officials with a persuasive argument to keep it open and to build temporary storage.

Northern States said it would have to buy coal-based replacement power if the plant were forced to shut down. Managers predicted that the 10,000 to 15,000 pounds of sulfur dioxide created each year would greatly exacerbate the problem of acid rain. Acid rain would affect a number of stakeholders: farmers, forestry managers, fishing groups, and ordinary people living in its path. Plant opponents countered the utility's assertion that coal was the only other source of energy with the suggestion that windmills could be used instead.[2] Variations of Minnesota's situation were played out again and again in other states as reactors aged and broke down.

Some Native Americans actively promoted the creation of a national nuclear waste site on their land. A 3,500-member tribe of Mescalero Apaches in New Mexico figured the waste site could bring in $15 to $25 million a year. When combined with the tribe's casino, ski resort, and bingo hall, the Mescaleros believed they would have an integrated and remunerative group of businesses. A spokesperson for the tribe remarked on their entrepreneurial spirit, "We are already a business-minded tribe. We feel this type of venture could be profitable for us."[3]

In 1994, the issue went to a tribal vote. The vote, the largest in recent years, was a surprise to the community which prided itself on following the lead of the tribal president. In this case, the president was unable to convince his people that the dump would earn millions of dollars and not pose a threat to health and safety. The negative vote was based on tribal concerns that the federal government had not given a firm commitment on the final burial spot for spent fuel rods. Descendants of two of the tribe's most honored leaders, Geronimo and Cochise, were on opposite sides of the issue. Silas Cochise managed the waste project; Joseph Geronimo led the opposition.[4]

By the beginning of 1995, more than 70 nuclear generating plants proposed building community repositories for spent nuclear fuel. The United States Court of Appeals for the Sixth Circuit ruled that utilities could build permanent repositories near their plants. Since the Mescalero Apaches had turned down the national center, there was nowhere else to store the 30,000 tons of nuclear waste.

---

[2] M. L. Wald, "Nuclear Waste, with Nowhere to Go," *New York Times,* March 28, 1994, p. A10.

[3] S. Allen, "Tribe Sees Gold in Nuclear Waste," *Boston Globe,* August 9, 1994, p. 1.

[4] G. Johnson, "Apache Tribe Rejects Move to Store Nuclear Waste on Reservation," *New York Times,* February 2, 1996, p. A16.

Stakeholders agreed that the Apache decision, followed by the court decision, made it easier for utilities to build their own storage sites. All agreed it was highly unlikely a national repository would be built before 2010. By then, the DOE estimated there would be 55,000 more tons of spent nuclear fuel.[5]

In February 1995, scientists at the Los Alamos National Laboratory in New Mexico began a public debate over whether the planned underground dump in Yucca Mountain, Nevada, might erupt in a nuclear explosion sending radioactive particles into the ground water or scattering them to the winds. The possibility of an explosion was raised in a private discussion between Dr. Charles D. Bowman and Dr. Francesco Vennari, both physicists at Los Alamos. Lab managers formed three teams with a total of 30 scientists to investigate the idea. The teams rejected the explosion thesis but in March 1995, Bowman and Vennari received support from scientists at the Savannah River nuclear site in South Carolina.

The Savannah River site was a leading center of nuclear waste study. Its scientists focused on the process by which military wastes were melted into glassy logs for underground disposal. Savannah River experts wrote that although they normally dealt with scrapped nuclear arms rather than spent fuel rods, an explosion was certainly a possibility. The danger would come some time far in the future when underground water dissolved the steel cannisters allowing plutonium to seep into the surrounding rock. The report said the physical properties of the rock could help set off a nuclear chain reaction equal to that of a large hydrogen bomb.[6]

In light of this report and continued uncertainty over the efficacy of the Yucca Mountain site, John R. Kasich of the House Budget Committee and Robert S. Walker of the House Science Committee recommended the project be scrapped. In a letter to Representative John R. Ensign, a Nevada Republican who opposed the Yucca Mountain dump, Kasich and Walker pointed to the enormous cost of the project and recommended that the government build an interim storage site instead and undertake a new search for a permanent repository.[7]

Senator Richard Bryan, a Nevada Democrat and Governor Robert Miller raised safety concerns about transporting nuclear waste from sites around the country to Nevada. Bryan called the plan for temporary storage sites "mobile Chernobyl." He noted that "the ecological and economic consequences of Chernobyl were massive, immediate, and will last for tens of thousands of years. If Chernobyl has taught us anything, it is that when dealing with such high-risk matters as nuclear power or nuclear waste, small mistakes can have enormous consequences."[8]

---

[5] K. Schneider, "70 Nuclear Plants on Route to Being Radioactive Dumps," *New York Times,* February 15, 1995, p. A1.

[6] W. J. Broad, "Theory on Threat of Blast at Nuclear Waste Site Gains Support," *New York Times,* March 23, 1995, p. A18.

[7] W. B. Broad, "Two House Leaders Propose Ending Plans for a Permanent Nuclear Waste Site in Nevada," *New York Times,* May 27, 1996, p. 9.

[8] J. Enders, "Atomic Waste Dump Plan Decried as 'Mobile Chernobyl'," *Boston Globe,* June 2, 1996, p. 14.

Questions

1. Who are the stakeholders in this issue? Identify as many stakeholders as possible.
2. Using the Stakeholder Influence Map (Exhibit 3–1), assume that the U.S. government is the corporation. Categorize the stakeholders according to whether they are direct or indirect, internal or external.
3. Can the concerns of all the stakeholders in this issue be resolved?

Stakeholder Analysis

In *Strategy in Action,* Boris Yavitz and William H. Newman note that "success and, indeed, survival of every business depends on either obtaining the support or neutralizing the attacks of key actors in its environment." They go on to explain that "we live in a highly interdependent world. To steer a course through this ever changing structure, we need a keen insight into the behavior of those actors who affect our fate."[9] These key actors are *stakeholders.*

William Safire notes the word *stakeholder* has multiple meanings. In the 19th century, those who worked land in the American West marked off their property with stakes and claimed it as their own. A stake was also a money advance for food, an investment, or a loan. The stakeholder was the person who held the stake of a bet or wager. Safire says H. Igor Ansoff's use of stakeholder in *Corporate Strategy* (1965) established its modern meaning. The *Oxford English Dictionary's* citation says, "The objectives of top management can and frequently do come in conflict with objectives of other *stakeholders* in the firm." A decade later in a *Handbook for British Managers,* Croon and Witlau wrote, "The needs of our 'stakeholders'—i.e., the persons and groups having a direct stake in our organization: the owners, employees . . . customers, suppliers, financiers, managers, the area in which the organization is established, etc."[10]

A stakeholder is any individual or group that believes it has a stake in the consequences of management's decisions and has the power to influence current or future decisions. Stakeholders may be religious groups, employees, unions, environmentalists, or consumerists. They include government agencies (e.g., the Occupational Safety and Health Administration, the Equal Employment Opportunity Commission, the Securities and Exchange Commission), local chambers of commerce, Mothers Against Drunk Driving (MAAD), the National Association for the Advancement of Colored People (NAACP), and the American Association of Retired Persons (AARP). They also may include traditional industry participants such as suppliers, buyers, and competitors. Stakeholders are you, me, our families, and our neighbors. Before embarking on strategy formulation—and certainly before implementing strategy—any manager should ask, "Who are the actors or players who have the greatest stake in a given issue or management decision?"

The stakeholder influence map (SIM) in Exhibit 3–1 provides a conceptual framework for understanding the roles and influence of various stakeholders and issues. This map does not include every player in every circumstance, but it creates a foundation for categorizing people and organizations

---

[9] B. Yavitz and W. H. Newman, *Strategy in Action* (New York: The Free Press, 1982), p. 74.

[10] W. Safire, "Stakeholders Naff? I'm Chuffed," *New York Times Sunday Magazine,* April 28, 1996, p. 26.

involved in implementing and evaluating the firm's social responsiveness strategy.

Stakeholders hold widely varying expectations and opinions about particular issues. Some stakeholders represent the views of large numbers of people; others speak for just a few; still others speak only for themselves. Stakeholders exercise a wide range of power and influence over particular issues and vary greatly in the degree of intensity of their feelings. They may be actively involved in one set of issues and relatively passive in their reactions to another.

Stakeholders play a central role in determining whether or not a company achieves its strategic objectives. All firms face major challenges in balancing the legitimate claims of groups representing a broad range of interests. Suppliers, buyers, employees, consumers, and even environmentalists and clergy all may have vested interests in a particular firm's strategy but have very different claims and expectations. This chapter analyzes stakeholder activities according to their position inside or outside the firm, their interests in a particular issue, the depth of their involvement, and their power to affect company strategy.

The Stakeholder Influence Map

Exhibit 3-1 classifies stakeholders into four groups along two dimensions:

- *Location:* whether stakeholders are internal and work inside the firm's structure or external and work outside the firm.
- *Influence:* whether they influence the firm directly or indirectly.

Although we discuss the stakeholders in each quadrant in detail later in this chapter, a brief identification follows:

- The upper-left quadrant of the SIM includes external stakeholders such as suppliers, customers, and competitors. Although they do not work within the firm, they exert their power directly on managers who formulate and implement strategy. Much of their ability to influence the firm comes from their economic power which affects competition within an industry or industries.
- Employees and the board of directors occupy the lower-left quadrant. They are internal to the company and directly affect its policies.
- A variety of stakeholders external to the firm whose influence varies from issue to issue occupy the upper-right quadrant.
- Unions and shareholders are in the lower-right quadrant. These groups are part of the company family and exert power over the firm intermittently and less directly than do the company's employees.

EXHIBIT 3–1   Stakeholder Influence Map (SIM)

	Direct	Indirect
External	Suppliers Customers Competitors Potential entrants Government	Social activist groups Religious institutions Regulators Local community members Media Trade associations Lobbies and PACs
Internal	Board of directors Employees	Unions Shareholders

Jeffrey S. Harrison and Caron H. St. John present an interesting model for analyzing the interactions between the firm and external stakeholders. They make no distinction between direct and indirect external stakeholders. Instead, they focus closely on today's changing environment in which traditional management hierarchies are weakened, corporations are hollowed out, and management is creating new partnering techniques leading to the achievement of common goals. They ask (1) Can external stakeholders be managed? (2) Which stakeholders deserve high levels of managerial attention? and (3) What are the most recent trends in stakeholder management?[11]

Exhibit 3–2 identifies their seven stakeholder groups. In column 2, the authors list tactics companies employ to manage these stakeholders. They note that organizations adopt two basic postures when managing relationships with stakeholders. The first is to try to protect the organization from environmental uncertainty by using techniques to stabilize and predict environmental influences. The second posture builds on interdependencies created among stakeholders through joint ventures with competitors, cooperative product development, and industry-level lobbying. Column 3 lists the activities based on partnering with external stakeholders.

---

[11] Jeffrey S. Harrison and Caron H. St. John, "Managing and Partnering with External Stakeholders," *Academy of Management Executive* 10, no. 2 (1966), pp. 46–60.

EXHIBIT 3–2 Tactics for Managing and Partnering with External Stakeholders

Stakeholder	Stakeholder Management Tactics	Stakeholder Partnering Tactics
Customer	Customer service departments Marketing research Advertising On-site visits 800 numbers Long-term contracts Product/service development Market development	Customer involvement on design teams Customer involvement in product testing Joint planning sessions Enhanced communication linkages Joint training/service programs Sharing of facilities Financial investments in customer Appointment to board of directors
Suppliers	Purchasing departments Encourage competition among suppliers Sponsor new suppliers Threat of vertical integration Long-term contracts	Supplier involvement on design teams Integration of ordering system with Manufacturing (i.e., Just-in-Time Inventory) Joint information systems Jointly developing new products and applications Coordinated quality control (i.e., T.M.) Simultaneous production
Competitors	Product and service differentiation Technological advances Innovation Speed Price cutting Market segmentation Intelligence systems Corporate espionage*	Kieresu* Joint ventures for research and development Joint ventures for market development Collective lobbying efforts Informal price leadership or collusion* Industry panels to deal with labor and other problems Mergers (horizontal integration)
Government agencies/ Administrators	Legal departments Tax departments Government relations departments Individual firm lobbying efforts Campaign contributions Individual firm political action committees Self-regulation Personal gifts to politicians*	Consortia on international trade and competitiveness Jointly or government-sponsored research Joint ventures to work on social problems such as crime and pollution Joint Foreign development projects Panels on product safety Appointment of retired government officials to the board of directors Participation in government-sponsored initiatives
Local communities/ Governments	Community relations offices Public relations advertising Involvement in community service/politics Local purchases of supplies Employment of local workers Donations to local government organizations Donations to local charities Gifts to local government officials*	Task forces to solve skilled-labor shortages Joint urban renewal programs Cooperative training programs Development committees/boards Employment programs for workers with special needs such as the handicapped Joint education programs
Activist groups	Internal programs to satisfy demands Public/political relations efforts to offset or protect from negative publicity Financial donations	Consultation with members on sensitive issues Joint ventures for research/research consortia Appointment of group representatives to board of directors Jointly sponsored public relations efforts

(continued)

EXHIBIT 3–2 Tactics for Managing and Partnering with External Stakeholders *(continued)*

Stakeholder	Stakeholder Management Tactics	Stakeholder Partnering Tactics
Unions	Avoid unions through high levels of employee satisfaction Avoid unions by thwarting attempts to organize* Hiring of professional negotiators Public relations advertising Chapter XI protection	Mutually satisfactory (win–win) labor contracts Contract clauses that link pay to performance (i.e., profit sharing) Joint committees on safety and other issues of concern to employees Employee development programs Joint industry/labor panels Labor leaders appointed to board of directors included in major decisions

*These tactics are of questionable ethical acceptability to some internal and external stakeholders in the United States and elsewhere.

Harrison and St. John note that effective planning for stakeholder management activities begins with identification of key stakeholders. The organization should establish the strategic importance of stakeholder groups, an activity that helps the organization determine what stakeholder management strategies it should adopt. The authors say there should be a positive relationship between the strength of the alliance and the strategic importance of the stakeholder. The outcome of this analysis should be reduction of litigation, reduced negative publicity, and favorable regulatory policies. The stakeholder influence map (SIM), which continues to be the operating model for this chapter, can be applied to the Harrison and St. John discussion as well as to the Freeman and Porter models that follow.

We now take a closer look at groups of stakeholders using the Freeman and Porter models. The SIM defines the relationship between stakeholders and the firm more closely.

Stakeholder Analysis and Management

In Exhibit 3–3, R. Edward Freeman combines stakeholder analysis with Michael E. Porter's five variables. Freeman refers to the combination as the "six forces that shape strategy."[12] To control the strategy formulation and implementation process, management must build a coalition of diverse stakeholders. The process requires considerable analysis, negotiation, persuasion, and exercise of power. If a company hopes to continue achieving its objectives, its stakeholder management effort must be continuous. As Yavitz and Newman observe, "Shaping external alignments is a never-ending task. Even with the most thorough analysis of each key actor and the wisest choice of relationship, tomorrow will present new problems."[13]

[12] R. E. Freeman, *Strategic Management: A Stakeholder Approach* (Boston: Pitman Publishing, 1984), p. 78.
[13] Yavitz and Newman, p. 85.

EXHIBIT 3–3 Six Forces That Shape Competitive Strategy

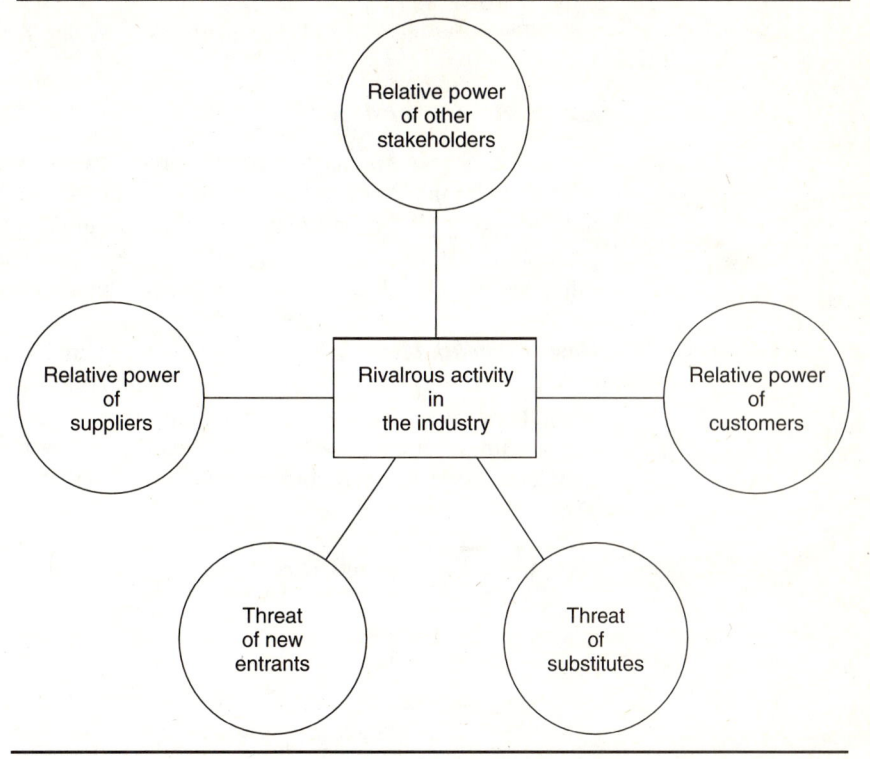

```
                    ┌──────────────┐
                    │Relative power│
                    │   of other   │
                    │ stakeholders │
                    └──────┬───────┘
                           │
  ┌──────────────┐   ┌─────┴────────┐   ┌──────────────┐
  │Relative power│   │  Rivalrous   │   │Relative power│
  │      of      ├───│  activity in ├───│      of      │
  │   suppliers  │   │ the industry │   │   customers  │
  └──────────────┘   └─────┬────┬───┘   └──────────────┘
                           │    │
                    ┌──────┘    └──────┐
             ┌──────┴───────┐   ┌──────┴───────┐
             │    Threat    │   │    Threat    │
             │    of new    │   │      of      │
             │   entrants   │   │  substitutes │
             └──────────────┘   └──────────────┘
```

Source: R. E. Freeman, *Strategic Management: A Stakeholder Approach* (Boston: Pitman Publishing, 1984), p. 78.

Freeman suggests that organizations with high stakeholder-management capability are likely to possess the following attributes:

- They design and implement communication processes with multiple stakeholders.
- They actively negotiate with stakeholders on critical issues and seek voluntary agreements.
- They take a marketing approach to serving multiple stakeholders. They spend heavily on understanding stakeholder needs and use marketing research techniques to segment stakeholders and understand their needs and aspirations.
- In formulating strategy, they draw on members of their management teams who are knowledgeable about stakeholders.
- They take a proactive stance, attempt to anticipate stakeholder concerns, and try to influence their stakeholder environment.

- They allocate resources in a manner consistent with stakeholder analysis.
- Their managers think in stakeholder-serving terms.[14]

External Direct Forces

Michael E. Porter's analytical framework helps managers analyze the impact of these external direct stakeholders. Exhibit 3–4 shows the forces that drive industry competition and play a central role in determining the company's profitability. In the following discussion, we will see how these stakeholders influence the global telecommunications industry.

New or Potential Entrants. New or potential entrants to an industry present current players with all kinds of problems and opportunities. Sometimes new entrants bring substantial resources and have the power to change the rules of the game. For example, those who add capacity may cut prices to utilize their capacity efficiently and increase their market share.

EXHIBIT 3–4   External Direct Forces

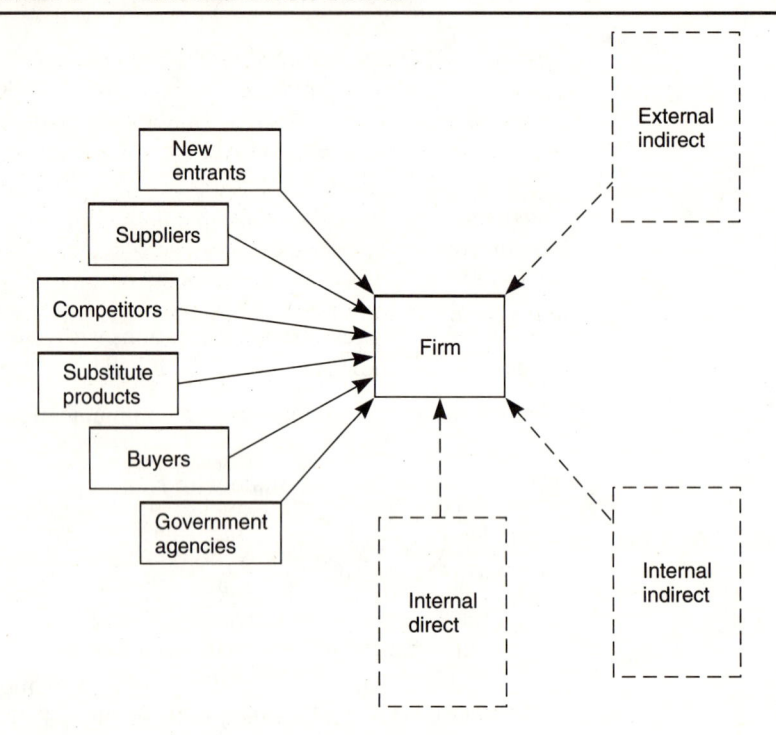

[14] Ibid.

Commercial online services such as CompuServe, Prodigy, and America Online made the Internet accessible to millions of people. Some of these services were extremely expensive because they charged for the time used on each connection. America Online, for example, charged $9.95 for five hours and $216.45 for 75 hours. Small competitors such as Netcom and PsInet sold flat rate access for $20 to $30 a month but often they could not keep up with the demand. Users got angry and frustrated by busy signals instead of connections.

In February 1996, a new entrant announced it would provide Internet access to its regular residential telephone customers. AT&T said its 80 million customers could have Internet service on a plan that gave them five free hours a month for the subscription fee or they could pay a monthly usage fee of $19.95 for unlimited access. Twenty million AT&T phone customers with personal computers and modems could begin the service in March. AT&T provided free software for using the World Wide Web and round-the-clock telephone technical support.

AT&T brought resources that promised to change the entire market. Although rivals MCI and Sprint also offered Internet access, they could not compete with AT&T service. Experts predicted AT&T's entry into the Internet access market would become a central force in industry competition.[15]

Intensity of Rivalry among Existing Competitors. If a number of powerful, aggressive, and well-entrenched competitors exist in an industry, the rivalry is likely to be very intense. On February 8, 1996, President Clinton signed the Telecommunications Act. On April 8, 1996, *Business Week's* Internet service reported that the president had unleashed a "$1 trillion digital free-for-all." The act ended government rules that maintained the barriers among local and long-distance calling, cable TV, broadcasting, and wireless services. According to DRI/McGraw-Hill, the act would "unleash a frenzy of restructuring, mergers, and dealmaking . . . that will account for $1 trillion in annual revenues by the year 2000."[16] Quoting cartoon character Pogo, the subheading of DRI's report observed: "We're surrounded by an insurmountable opportunity."

Substitute Products. Products that may be substituted for the offerings of a given industry place a ceiling on the potential returns of an industry. Perhaps the greatest environmental threat any industry faces is the prospect that someone will develop a product or service that will render the industry's traditional offerings obsolete. This happened to rotary dial phones when their

---

[15] P. H. Lewis, "AT&T's Customers to Get Free Time on the Internet," *New York Times,* February 28, 1996, p. A1; C. Gorman, "AT&T Rewires the Net," *Time,* March 11, 1996, p. 63.

[16] Internet [http://www.businessweek.com/1996/15/b34701.html#table1]

Touch-Tone replacements were integrated into new, worldwide telecommunications systems.

The Internet is beginning to offer services that may make substantial inroads into traditional service provider markets. Now consumers anywhere in the world can bypass travel agents by using the Internet to book their own hotel rooms directly. Travel Web [http://www.travelweb.com] gives immediate access to hotel chains such as Hilton, Marriott, and Hyatt. Holiday Inn Worldwide and IBM collaborated to integrate the hotel chain's reservation and property management system.

Consumers no longer need to be put on hold while airline agents look up the latest airplane fares and connections; they can use Travelocity [http://www.travelocity.com]. Travelocity's slogan is "Maximum power for the do-it-yourself traveler." The service is a collaboration between Worldwide Systems Corp., the leading online destination information provider, and SABRE Interactive, the company that brought travel agents the flight tracking system that allows them to come up with schedules and fares in minutes. Using Travelocity, the traveler has to type in only departure and arrival dates and the options appear on the screen.[17]

Bargaining Power of Buyers. According to Porter, "Buyers compete with the industry by forcing down prices, bargaining for higher quality or more services, and playing competitors against one another—all at the expense of industry profitability."[18] Buyers are in a powerful position if they are large in size, are limited in number, and account for a large percentage of industry participants' total revenues. A buyer's position may be even more powerful if the firm is partially integrated or is capable of integrating backward. Buyers' bargaining power extends to consumers, wholesalers, and retailers. For example, a large retailer of consumer electronics can negotiate better terms with suppliers than can a small, independent retailer. A chain like Toys R Us can pressure suppliers to give it exclusive rights to a specific Barbie® doll or GI Joe.® It also can negotiate a lower price per unit than can a local toy store or even a small chain.

Bargaining Power of Suppliers. Powerful suppliers are in a position to charge higher prices or offer lower levels of service or quality of goods. Weak suppliers, in contrast, must deliver more for less and thus allow industry leaders to enjoy higher profits.

Bell Atlantic, one of the nation's most powerful Baby Bells merged with NYNEX in May 1996. The $23 million merger created an entity that became the second largest telecommunications provider in the United States after

---

[17] "A Traveler's Tour of the Internet," *Boston Globe,* May 19, 1996, p. B7.
[18] M. E. Porter, *Competitive Strategy: Techniques for Analyzing Industries and Competitors* (New York: The Free Press, 1980), p. 24.

AT&T. Why was this merger so important to Bell Atlantic? As discussed earlier, the 1966 Telecommunications Act allowed regional phone companies to enter a number of new businesses and geographical markets. Ray Smith, CEO of Bell Atlantic, and Ivan Seidenberg, NYNEX's CEO, agreed both companies would have to get bigger and more efficient to compete in the new telecom environment. Smith predicted the merger would allow the combined company to grab 30 percent of the regional long-distance market from AT&T and MCI. He vowed the company would grow 10 to 12 percent a year, compared to the 7 percent that was predicted for Bell Atlantic as a separate company.

Smith, who had come up through the Bell System ranks, reached the top spot at Bell Atlantic in 1989. He had substantial opportunity to assess his company's strength and weakness as a supplier, particularly in his pet project of providing video services. In 1993 he tried to merge Bell Atlantic with cable giant TCI in a $30 billion deal. At the time, he likened the deal to the invention of the printing press. The merger was called off, however, in 1994 when TCI stock dropped and Congress passed new cable regulations. Smith's determination to get into the video business as a strong supplier was reflected in his remark about the NYNEX merger: "I don't want to be one of the bit players in a grand play."[19] Perhaps a merged Bell Atlantic would allow Smith to fulfill his dream of delivering phone calls, Internet services, and interactive video to every home from Virginia to Maine.

Government Agencies. Government can directly influence a company's competitive position in many ways. As a large-scale purchaser or supplier, it affects the competitive position of firms from which it buys or to which it sells. Its purchases thus indirectly have an impact on the positions of all other firms in the industry. Governments also can alter the position of a firm or industry by providing subsidies or imposing regulations.

The role of national governments in the telecom industry was brought into sharp focus during the World Trade Organization (WTO) negotiations in April 1996. Under the most-favored nation (MFN) principle, WTO countries must extend the same trading access they give one partner to all their trading partners. Fifty-three nations met in Geneva to discuss ending the monopoly domination of many national phone companies. The effect of state ownership had been to keep prices artificially high. This round of discussions was just the latest in talks that had been underway without resolution for the previous two years.

American negotiators complained that other countries had not offered the United States sufficiently liberal market access in return for opening its own telecommunications sector. Charlene Barshefsky, the U.S. acting trade

---

[19] W. Cohen, K. Hetter, and K. Whitelaw, "A New Telecom Titan," *US News & World Report,* May 6, 1996, pp. 57–58.

representative, said, "Over 40 percent of the world telecom revenues and over 34 percent of global international traffic are not covered by acceptable offers. We will not enter an agreement on these terms."[20]

Rather than risk a showdown, trade negotiators discussed plans to delay the deadline for another year. Renato Ruggiero, the WTO director general proposed keeping existing liberalization offers on the table with hopes of improving them later. Sir Leon Brittan, the European Union's (EU) trade commissioner was particularly critical of the U.S. position. Noting that the EU regretted and deplored the U.S. stance, he said the postponement of the talks was a missed opportunity to help create a global information society.[21] Although industry representatives were vocal stakeholders in this issue, government policies prevailed.

Internal Direct Forces

Employees. As Exhibit 3–5 shows, employees at every level exert internal direct force on corporate decision making. Employee stakeholder force is both economic and noneconomic. Economic issues that overlap with social issues are equal pay for comparable work, equal pay for equal work, and compensation through benefits such as retirement, maternity policies, and medical benefits. Additional issues that directly involve employees include safety and stress in the workplace, privacy, sexual harassment, equal access to training programs, and hiring and firing practices.

The U.S. telecommuncations industry engaged in the same downsizing, reorganization, and layoff activities as other industries in the mid-1990s. In January 1996, AT&T employees came to work to find that 40,000 of them would be terminated. The news was all the more shocking because AT&T had been regarded as a company that offered exceptional security. The typical AT&T manager was 42 years old with 16 years of service and made $55,000 a year, plus $15,000 in miscellaneous benefits. Under the reorganization plan, this manager would receive a package worth more than $30,000. The company offered a lump sum proportion of salary based on the manager's age and years with the company. Each manager would also receive a retraining and relocation stipend, health benefits, and the possibility of being rehired elsewhere in the company. Some employees elected to continue working as long as possible, while others took immediate buyouts.[22] Despite the generosity of the severance package, many workers felt stressed, sad, worried, and

---

[20] P. Lewis, "Telecommunications Talks Postponed as U.S. Balks," *New York Times,* May 1, 1996, p. D1.

[21] F. Williams, "WTO Telecoms Plan under Scrutiny," *Financial Times,* May 1, 1996, p. 7.

[22] R. Hanley, "Today, 2,000 Fewer AT&T Employees," *New York Times,* January 17, 1996, p. B5.

Exhibit 3–5 Internal Direct Forces

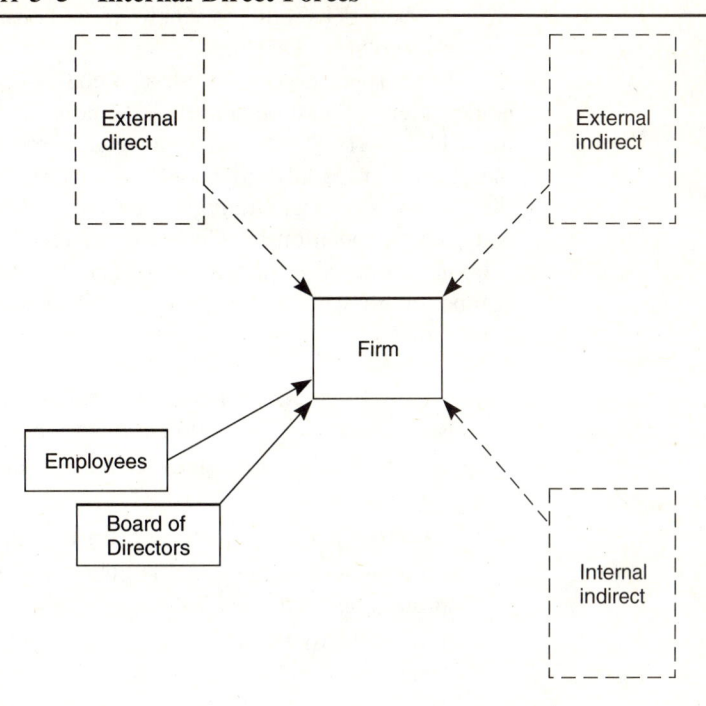

[Diagram: Firm in center receiving solid arrows from Employees and Board of Directors (internal direct), and dashed arrows from External direct, External indirect, and Internal indirect boxes]

even betrayed. As telecommunications companies worldwide reorganized and restructured, former AT&T employees joined thousands of others whose jobs had disappeared.

Boards of Directors. Boards of directors are another group of internal direct stakeholders. Board members set policy for their firms and are responsible for the companies' financial well-being. Often they are involved in the establishment of social issues programs and may even take leadership in this area. In fact, it would be virtually impossible for a company to formulate a social issues agenda without the approval and participation of its board.

Walter J. Salmon wrote in the *Harvard Business Review* that boards have a role in crisis prevention.[23] He noted that board composition and oversight have improved significantly since the 1970s. Salmon pointed to surveys showing the typical board consists of nine outside directors and three inside directors, as opposed to five inside and eight outside directors in the early 1970s. In Salmon's view, the only insiders who belong on boards are the

---

[23] W. J. Salmon, "Crisis Prevention: How to Gear Up Your Board," *Harvard Business Review,* January–February 1993, pp. 68–75.

CEO, the chief operating officer (COO), and the chief financial officer (CFO). The CEO should routinely initiate discussions between board members and senior managers.

Others think corporate board members are better guardians of shareholder interests than outsiders. At some major companies, outside directors make fees of $100,000 a year—as well as extras including a lifelong pension, medical coverage, and contribution of as much as $1 million to a charity of the director's choice. Hoping to develop guidelines for board members, The National Association of Corporate Directors set up a 19-member Blue Ribbon Commission that included senior executives, academics, investors, compensation specialists, and others. The commission urged companies to consider:

- Paying directors primarily in stock, with equity representing a substantial part or total of the compensation.
- Setting a substantial stock-ownership target and deadline for each director.
- Abolishing all benefits programs for board members.
- Banning outside directors or their firms from providing financial or professional services.
- Fully disclosing each director's pay and perquisites in the proxy statement.[24]

The commission stressed that a properly informed board should be able to spot problems early. Although directors should not micromanage (become overly involved with) issues, they have a responsibility to get involved in long-range planning and identify areas of concern. Effective directors speak their minds, engage in constructive discussion, and make tough decisions.

Board composition became an important issue as more women and minorities climbed the corporate ladder. In 1995, women were still very rare on corporate boards, accounting for only 6 percent of directors of Fortune 500 companies. A study published in the *Academy of Management Journal* found even when women were appointed to boards, they were kept off the powerful committees. The investigators concluded that being a man was a significant advantage for appointment to the executive, compensation, and finance committees. Women were more likely to be appointed to the public affairs committee. Although women had a shorter tenure on boards (men had a mean service of 8.8 years compared to women at 5.5 years) "sex bias . . . is the larger explanation."[25]

---

[24] J. S. Lublin, "Give the Board Fewer Perks, A Panel Urges," *The Wall Street Journal,* June 6, 1995, p. B1.

[25] D. Bilimoria and S. K. Piderit, "Sexism on High: Corporate Boards," *New York Times,* February 5, 1995, p. F11.

Catalyst, a women's research group, found that one-third of Fortune 500 companies had at least two female directors. The 1995 Catalyst survey showed that cosmetics, publishing, and apparel companies had the highest number of women while packaging and freight delivery companies had the fewest.[26]

In 1996 a controversy over board composition hit the front page of *The Wall Street Journal.* Sister Doris Gormly of the Sisters of St. Francis of Philadephia wrote a letter to T. J. Rodgers, CEO of Cypress Semiconductor Corporation. Sister Doris was director of corporate social responsibility for her congregation. She looked over the sisters' proxy statements for evidence of women and minorities on the board of directors. When there were no women or minorities, she sent out a three paragraph form letter explaining the order's policy to withhold its votes for boards that didn't include qualified women and minorities.

Rodgers sent off a six-page blistering reply to Sister Doris, saying, "Bluntly stated, a 'woman's view' on how to run our semiconductor company does not help us, unless that woman has an advanced technical degree. . . . You ought to get down from your moral high horse. Your views seem more accurately described as 'politically correct' than Christian."

Rodgers received a great deal of support from corporate leaders. The chairmen of Hewlett-Packard; Advanced Micro Devices, Inc.; and CMP Display Systems Inc. hastened to congratulate him on his stand.

The Wall Street Journal pointed out two conflicting pressures influencing the composition of corporate boards. On one hand, boards are more diversified than before and numerous large corporations such as Wal-Mart and W. R. Grace have adopted policies to support continued diversification. On the other hand, there is a corporate backlash against affirmative action, political correctness, and even the semblance of quotas. There is no doubt that this conflict will continue and activists on both sides will become more strident.[27]

External Indirect Forces

Exhibit 3–6 shows the groups of stakeholders external to the firm in the upper-right quadrant; they wield varying degrees of indirect influence. External indirect stakeholders include social activist groups; some government agencies (especially those not specifically tied to the firm's economic position in the industry); members of the local community; industry trade associations; and religious organizations, lobbies, and political action committees (PACs).

---

[26] J. S. Lublin, "Survey Finds More Fortune 500 Firms Have at Least Two Female Directors," *The Wall Street Journal,* September 28, 1995, p. B16.

[27] E. J. Pollack, "CEO Takes on a Nun in a Crusade against 'Political Correctness'," *The Wall Street Journal,* July 15, 1996, p. A1.

Exhibit 3–6 External Indirect Forces

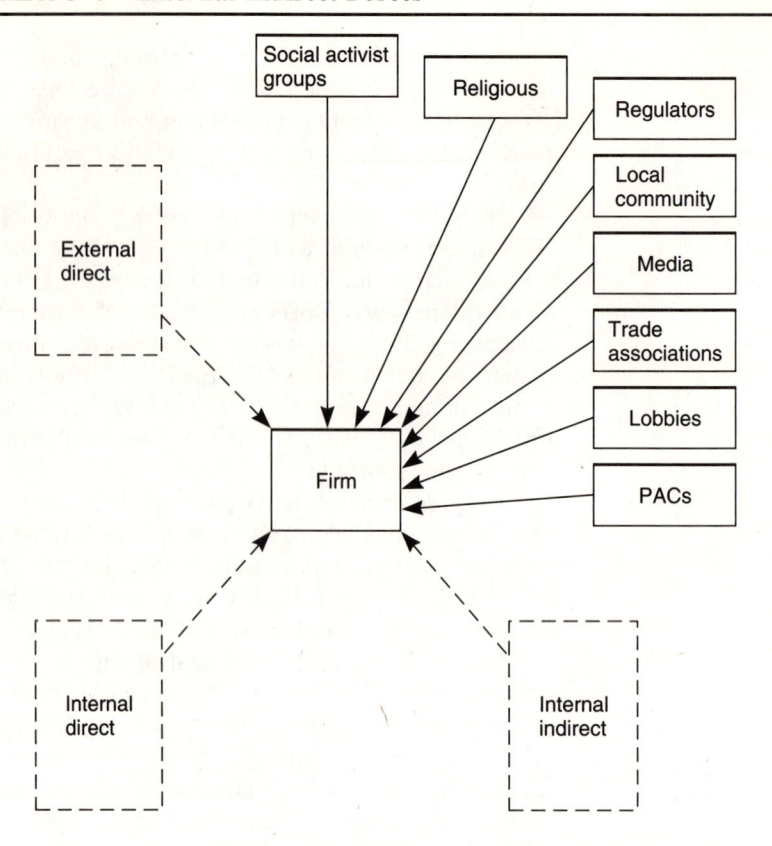

[Diagram: Arrows pointing to "Firm" from Social activist groups, Religious, Regulators, Local community, Media, Trade associations, Lobbies, PACs. Dashed boxes labeled "External direct," "Internal direct," and "Internal indirect" with dashed arrows to the Firm.]

Companies and communities need to coordinate their programs to satisfy all these stakeholders. If, for example, 25 percent of the workforce in a given company needs child care, this need can have profound implications for stakeholders in the local community. If a child care center is located on company property, local providers may lose their livelihood. If it is located in the community, local government agencies may be asked to participate or religious institutions may be chosen as sites. Teachers may need both local and state certification. School-age children may need transportation to the child care center.

Community pressures can interfere with or even stall corporate strategy. Local communities are particularly powerful stakeholders in designing zoning legislation to determine where companies can locate. In Newton, Massachusetts, the controversy over the location of a supermarket dragged on for months. The Stop & Shop chain lobbied the Newton Board of Aldermen for permission to build a megastore on a busy commercial street. Embroiled in the controversy, local business leaders, environmentalists, tax groups, and residents debated the potential consequences. Some nearby merchants were convinced that traffic would turn into gridlock and have deleterious effects on their businesses. Some aldermen predicted an increased tax base that would result in better city services. Others asserted environmental degradation and pollution would occur because the store would draw many more cars into an already crowded area. The issue became so contentious that hitherto friendly neighbors no longer spoke to one another. Stop & Shop continued to spend very substantial amounts of money on legal fees and development plans as it tried to convince these external indirect stakeholders that the business would ultimately benefit the community.

Internal Indirect Forces

As Exhibit 3–7 shows, unions and shareholders are located in the lower-right quadrant of the stakeholder influence map. They are part of the company but do not always influence it directly.

Unions may work with management to develop programs to benefit workers or take an adversarial approach by making demands management is unwilling to consider. Indirectly, union demands affect external competition if workers strike or gain concessions. Unions also can affect the quality of work life within the firm.

EXHIBIT 3–7   Internal Indirect Forces

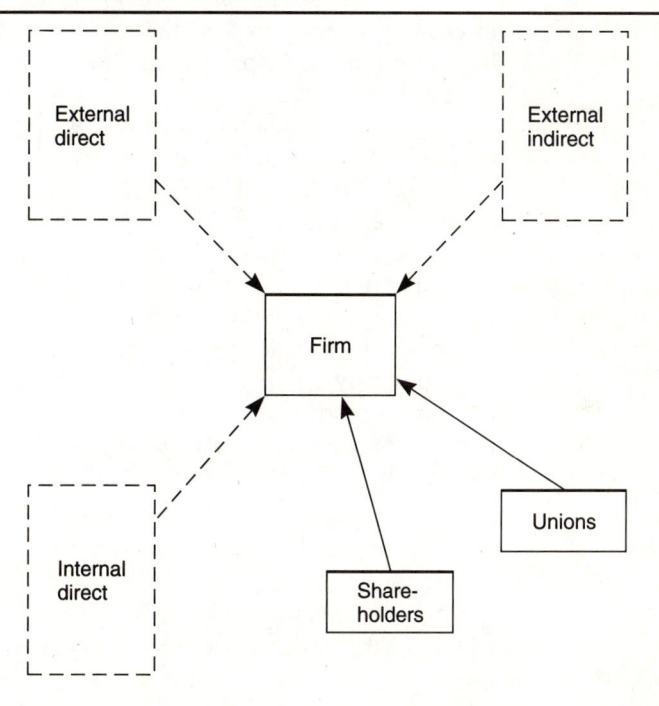

In 1995, John J. Sweeney, the AFL–CIO's new president called for a new social compact between U.S. corporations and workers. In a departure from the usual confrontational stance toward industry, Sweeney urged business to adopt a less greedy, more respectful attitude toward employees. In a major speech to business leaders Sweeney said, "I want to build bridges between labor and management, so that American business can be more successful and American workers can share in the gain." Sweeney exhorted business leaders to help reduce the wage gap between the rich and the rest of the country. He recalled President John F. Kennedy's social compact based on the aphorism, "A rising tide lifts all boats." Nevertheless he noted that large numbers of mergers and acquisitions often were accompanied by layoffs. He asked, "Does a rising tide now sink most ships, except for luxury yachts?"[28] We discuss the role of unions in greater detail in Chapter 13.

Shareholders are another group of internal indirect stakeholders. Traditionally, most were content to sign over their voting proxies to corporate appointees; in recent years, however, a new kind of shareholder has emerged. Large institutional investors, such as pension funds, are taking a real interest in the companies in which they have invested. They are asking tough questions of boards of directors and are not automatically assigning voting proxies for the stock they own. This interaction, called relationship investing, usually concentrates on profits and governance. The U.S. Council on Competitiveness, the congressionally sponsored Competitiveness Policy Council, and the Twentieth Century Fund have all endorsed the idea of relationship investing.

There is no structural reason to exclude social issues from relationship-investing concerns. In fact, the close ties between corporations and these large investors should provide an ideal climate for defining and implementing a social issues strategy.

Supporters of relationship investing point to two major advantages: long-term investing and increased management accountability. Relationship investors provide "patient" capital that focuses on long-term goals. In theory, top managers should be freer to concentrate on productivity and prospects without the pressure of quarterly returns.

Supporters declare that this new breed of large shareholder holds the CEO to account. The board of directors can no longer automatically rubber-stamp decisions made by an imperial leader. In fact, studies show few CEOs are deposed by activist shareholders. A *Wall Street Journal* study determined that large companies are fairly unresponsive to shareholder threats of bad publicity or proxy fights. According to a University of Rochester study, small and midsize companies are much more likely to react to shareholder criti-

---

[28] S. Greenhouse, "Labor Chief Asks Business for a New 'Social Contract'," *New York Times,* December 7, 1995, p. A2.

cism, and their CEOs are slightly more likely to lose their jobs than are those at larger firms.[29] Relationship investing is still a new idea, and its effectiveness and influence have yet to be fully felt and assessed.

Stakeholders' Power to Affect Firms' Affairs

R. Edward Freeman and Daniel R. Gilbert, Jr., point out that "power is an interesting concept . . . because it signifies that those who have it control those who do not."[30] Those who have power have the ability to force things to happen and, in many cases, to override disagreement. Most stakeholders tend to be fairly passive toward a company's affairs unless they see themselves as personally threatened or potentially benefited by the company's actions. If aroused, seemingly powerless stakeholders can exert considerable power.

Drug Companies and the Power of Class Action. In 1996, 40,000 independent mom-and-pop pharmacies settled a class-action suit against 13 big drugmakers. The independents accused the drugmakers of violating the Sherman Antitrust Act by conspiring to overcharge them for drugs while offering big discounts to bulk buyers such as health maintenance organizations (HMOs) and pharmaceutical mail-order firms. HMOs' power to demand discounts came from their control of millions of members who were potential drug company customers.

Retail pharmacists, by comparison, had no power to shift market share from one drug to another. They had to carry all the drugs that physicians might prescribe and could not threaten to exclude any of them. As a result, retail pharmacies and their customers paid more because managed care customers paid less.

At first, individual pharmacies and groups of retailers filed separate lawsuits across the country. Finally in 1994 these suits were brought together in federal court in Chicago. Armies of lawyers on both sides filed hundreds of motions. Court documents revealed that the independents' lawyers hired three top economists to determine if there was evidence of a drug company conspiracy. Robert E. Lucas, Jr., a Nobel Prize winner, wrote, "It is my opinion that the defendant wholesalers in the brand-name prescription

---

[29] "Relationship Investing," *Business Week.* March 15, 1993, pp. 68–75; J. Kim, "Companies to Activists: Let's Make a Deal," *USA Today,* March 23, 1993; S. Mieher, "Shareholder Activism, Despite Hoopla, Leaves Most CEOs Unscathed," *The Wall Street Journal,* May 24, 1993, p. A1.

[30] R. E. Freeman and D. R. Gilbert, Jr., *Corporate Strategy and the Search for Ethics* (Englewood Cliffs, NJ: Prentice Hall, 1988) p. 172.

market have been involved in ongoing price collusion to deny discounts to retail pharmacists at least since the 1980s."[31]

Drug companies were sharply split over whether they could win at the trial scheduled for April 1996. Those that agreed to settle immediately were Abbott Laboratories, American Home Products, American Cyanamid, Bristol-Meyers Squibb, Burroughs Wellcome, Ciba-Geigy, Eli Lilly, Glaxo, Knoll Pharmaceutical, Merck, Pfizer, Schering-Plough, Warner-Lambert, Zeneca, and SmithKline Beecham. Those holding out for trial were Forest Laboratories, Inc.; Johnson & Johnson; Marion Merrill Dow, Inc. (part of Hoechst AG); Rhone-Poulenc Rorer, Inc.; Sandoz Pharmaceuticals; G. D. Searle & Co. (a unit of Monsanto); Hoffman-LaRoche Inc.; and Pharmacia & Upjohn Inc.

On February 10, the 15 drug companies that were willing to settle, formally agreed to pay $408 million, $388 million in cash. Five percent of the total cash payment, $19.2 million, was to go into a nonprofit foundation to promote the interests of independent pharmacies. Under the proposed settlement, the manufacturers would not have to change their practices and individual pharmacies would be free to file new lawsuits against the drug companies in the future. The pharmacies agreed to give up any past claims of conspiring to fix prices against the drug companies under the federal and state antitrust and price discrimination laws.[32]

In April, Judge Charles P. Kocoras of the Federal District Court in Chicago issued a 76-page decision in ordering the trial. The judge said it was "unquestionable" that the companies "had the opportunity to conspire" and noted that internal drug company memos supported the plaintiffs' notion of manufacturer interdependence. He also noted there was a considerable degree of dissension among the companies in terms of their policies.[33] Judge Kocoras then rejected any settlement that failed to require changes in drugmakers' pricing practices.

In May, many of the major drug companies in the original settlement agreed to stop charging pharmacies higher prices than they charged managed care facilities. The agreement was designed to show the judge that they were willing to be cooperative. The judge had found "the record is replete with instances of collusive behavior, parallel conduct, uniformity of responses, mutual awareness of each other's policies and practices, and various incriminating quotes on the part of defendants." It remained unclear whether drug

---

[31] L. P. Cohen and E. Tanouye, "Drug Makers Set to Pay $600 Million to Settle Lawsuit by Pharmacies," *The Wall Street Journal,* January 18, 1996, p. A1.

[32] M. Freudenheim, "Drugmakers Settle Suit on Price Fixing," *New York Times,* February 10, 1996, p. 37.

[33] M. Freudenheim, "Ruling in Price-Fixing Case Provides a Look at Drug Industry," *New York Times,* April 14, 1996, p. 29.

companies would stop discounting altogether or would offer everyone the same discount. Most observers agreed that consumers would reap little or no benefit from either policy. There was nothing in the settlement that required retail pharmacies to pass savings along to customers.[34] The drug companies that were not part of the original settlement continued to wait for the legal process to determine their fate. Whatever the eventual outcome, it was clear that retail pharmacies would never have prevailed if they had not combined their forces and concentrated their power.

The retail pharmacies successfully wielded power through the media and the courts. They took action at the point at which they perceived they could affect company strategy. Unless top managers can anticipate the activity and potential power of stakeholders, they may find themselves simply reacting rather than formulating and implementing a well-thought-out strategy.

Stakeholders' Resources

Porter perceives power differently than Freeman and Gilbert. Porter points out that in economic terms, stakeholders possess power only if their resources influence the elements of return on investment (ROI).[35] When social issues are a concern, stakeholders can affect a firm's financial results through the pressure they apply to its buyers, suppliers, and customers.

After the *Exxon Valdez* disaster, activists tried to organize a boycott of Exxon. The boycott failed for several reasons: The boycotters had few resources compared to the giant oil company. There was no loss of human life, the oil spill was in a remote area, and most observers realized they could not meaningfully affect Exxon's ROI.

In contrast, INFACT's boycott against Nestlé was very successful and sufficiently powerful to interfere with Nestlé's buyer and customer relations. Nestlé had hired women and dressed them like nurses to give samples of infant formula to poor mothers in developing countries. Women who would ordinarily breastfeed their babies were encouraged to use formula. Often the water used to dilute the concentrated formula was contaminated or the price of the formula was too high for mothers to afford. In both cases, mothers who had fed their babies sample formula were no longer physically able to breastfeed. INFACT was a lobbying group organized to attack Nestlé's policy of distributing infant formula. Helpless babies' lives were at stake, the moral outrage was sustainable, and this dedicated group of stakeholder activists pursued the issue over a long period.

---

[34] E. Tanouye, "Drugmakers Alter Antitrust Settlement," *The Wall Street Journal,* May 6, 1996, p. A3.

[35] M. E. Porter, *Competitive Advantage* (New York: The Free Press, 1985), p. 5.

Selection of Alternatives

As noted in Chapter 2, Implementing the Best Alternative is Makridakis's fourth step in the process of planning strategy. Makridakis stresses that planning requires concrete action. Companies must commit resources and overcome organizational resistance to change. There are specific tasks that must be accomplished within a given time. He suggests that companies develop an alternative plan so it can be compared to the best plan. Although Makridakis assumes the company has control over the selection of alternatives, it is not always clear that this is the case.[36]

Managers must determine whether they or stakeholders control the selection of alternative courses of action. The power struggle between stakeholders and managers often revolves around this selection. Active stakeholders try to control management actions and preempt management's choice of alternatives by publicly displaying their particular viewpoints. These stakeholders use common tools such as picket lines, demonstrations, and effective use of the media.

Nuclear Energy and Selection of Alternatives. The debate over whether nuclear energy is a societally acceptable source of energy provides a graphic example of how stakeholders have used their power to dictate management and industry policy. Exhibit 3–8 shows a partial list of nuclear energy stakeholders.

The fiasco at Three Mile Island turned passive stakeholders into active opponents of the development of nuclear energy resources. In 1986, the disaster at the Chernobyl plant in the former Soviet Union further strengthened the position of antinuclear energy forces, particularly those in the United States. Over the next decade, frequent radiation leaks and fires at the site, coupled with reports of genetic damage to people and animals in the area, reinforced antinuclear sentiments in the United States and abroad. The nuclear energy industry was forced to seriously consider the concerns of a variety of stakeholders.

Public-interest groups went to the courts to prevent plants from operating. State politicians refused to file evacuation plans, further stalling the start-up process. Public-interest groups made sure antinuclear energy questions were put on state and local ballots. Stakeholders generated both financial and human resources to constrain the industry's selection of alternative actions. As a result, nuclear power companies gave up on ordering new nuclear facilities.

In addition to the public's concerns about radioactive leaks and potential cancer epidemics, reports of unsafe operations inside a number of nuclear

---

[36] S. G. Makridakis, *Forecasting, Planning and Strategy for the 21st Century* (New York: The Free Press, 1990), p. 126.

EXHIBIT 3–8   Stakeholder Influence Map: Nuclear Energy Issue—Partial List of Stakeholders

	Direct	Indirect
External	Alternative energy suppliers Nuclear Regulatory Commission Banks Creditors Commercial and residential customers	Local governments State governments Media Public interest groups Industry lobbyists Citizens' groups Other environmental groups
Internal	Employees at operating plants Boards of directors of utilities	Unions Construction companies

plants proliferated. Unsafe operating practices continued despite adverse publicity. The Nuclear Regulatory Commission reported the New York Power Authority failed to ensure that certain backup systems were operating properly at its Indian Point 3 plant. Between May 1992 and July 1993, the power authority paid $762,500 in fines for safety violations at Indian Point 3 and an additional $300,000 in fines for problems at the Fitzpatrick nuclear power plant in Scriba, New York.[37]

Industry inertia led to widespread personnel problems and poor managerial practices in other states as well. One stakeholder group, the Institute of Nuclear Power Operations, referred to Philadelphia area's Peach Bottom plant as "an embarrassment to the industry and to the nation. The Nuclear Regulatory Commission eventually closed the Peach Bottom plant because workers were sleeping on the job.[38]

In addition to the stakeholders already mentioned, active players included state and other government officials, local town and city officials, and an assortment of citizens' groups. All had huge stakes in the consequences of managements' decisions about whether to bring new plants online, rehabilitate old ones, or abandon nuclear energy altogether.

---

[37] "Nuclear Regulators Propose $300,000 Fine for New York Plant," *The Wall Street Journal,* July 23, 1993, p. B5.

[38] M. L. Wald, "The Peach Bottom Syndrome," *New York Times,* March 27, 1988, p. F1.

By 1993, the U.S. nuclear industry was on its way to extinction. As noted in the beginning of the chapter, even plants that were still operating were struggling with radioactive waste disposal problems.

Drug Testing and Selection of Alternatives. Company management of substance abuse in the workplace is another issue in which firms can take many alternative actions. This issue involves stakeholders in all quadrants of the stakeholder influence map. Approximately 25 percent of an average workforce abuses either drugs or alcohol.

Companies must address several issues: Should they carry out involuntary testing, voluntary testing, or no testing at all? Should companies develop a drug-free policy as a specific condition of employment? Should they begin a formal program to help alcohol or drug abusers? How should they address employee concerns about confidentiality or job security? Should supervisors be given the responsibility of identifying and reporting abusers? Should managers have to use their operating budgets for rehabilitation programs? Should employers develop their own drug rehabilitation policy or outsource the program? How should managers integrate the firm's activities with the community? Finally, how, if at all, does the firm's strategy affect its competitive position in its industry?

Each of these questions has several answers. But before a company can formulate and implement a strategy to deal with substance abuse, it must correctly assess the power different stakeholders hold and the degree to which each is actively or passively involved in the issue. The company can be sure that as issues continue to evolve, it will receive input from stakeholders who are both external and internal to the firm and are involved both directly and indirectly.

Managing for Social Responsiveness

Makridakis's fifth step in the strategic implementation process is Monitoring and Controlling Results. Managers usually observe that predicted and actual outcomes of plans are seldom the same. There are many reasons why it is so hard to manage plans: forecasts may be inaccurate, competitors may make unexpected moves, resources may be inadequate, the environment may change, and resistance to change may be stronger than predicted. Effective monitoring helps establish why outcomes deviate from the plans and makes it easier for managers to correct their actions.

Even with the most meticulous planning and careful implementation, companies have to abandon some strategic initiatives. Companies may encounter fundamental changes in the environment or marketplace that make implementation unrealistic or simply too expensive in financial or human resources.[39]

---

[39] Makridakis, p. 128.

Managing for Social Responsiveness

Obviously companies cannot attend to all issues, and not all stakeholders care equally about particular issues. To deal systematically and effectively with its complex environment, a firm must answer four questions:

- How can managers identify relevant issues?
- How can they classify issues?
- How can these issues be managed?
- How can managers evaluate performance on the issues?

Peter F. Drucker stresses that "social impacts and social responsibilities are areas in which business—and not only big business—has to think through its role, has to set objectives, has to perform. Social impacts and social responsibilities have to be managed."[40]

Classification of Major Social Issues

After completing its environmental scanning and analysis, the company needs to classify the major social issues it confronts into meaningful subjects. Five major categories cover most of the significant issues even large, diverse enterprises face:

- *Community and political responsiveness:* the effectiveness with which the company manages its affairs in the political and legal environment and responds to the economic and other expectations of the domestic and international communities in which it operates (e.g., job creation, philanthropy).
- *Human investment:* the provision for the physical, psychological, and economic welfare of present, potential, and retired employees. Also includes the creation of an environment in which people are treated fairly and are given an opportunity to grow, meet challenges, and enjoy their jobs.
- *Openness of the system:* the company's willingness to communicate honestly and openly with its employees and external stakeholders. Openness includes relations with the news media, the company's ability to establish an effective governance system and to assure employees of due process and protection of their rights.
- *Consumer welfare:* the provision of quality products and services to prospective buyers in an honest and comprehensive manner to reasonably assure their safety, well-being, and satisfaction.
- *Ecology and energy:* the company's efforts to minimize the negative impact of its operations on the natural environment (water, air, plants, wildlife, microorganisms) and the structural environment (buildings, farms, homes) and to conserve natural resources such as energy.

---

[40] P. F. Drucker, *Management: Tasks, Responsibilities, Practices* (New York: Harper & Row, 1974), p. 325.

Determine Priorities and Collect Data

Exhibit 3–9 combines the preceding five categories, a few selected issues, and several concerned stakeholder groups. Just as a company sets priorities for expenditures in functional areas, it must rank social issues in order of their importance to the firm. Some firms may decide to consider only issues for which reliable data exist or for which they can generate what they consider good data.

However, some social issues are not data-oriented. For example, it is almost impossible to measure the benefit of a contribution to a symphony orchestra or the benefit of hosting a fund-raising gala. Likewise, it is difficult to measure employee satisfaction and greater productivity due to a company-sponsored child care program. Data on such issues are elusive at best.

In reality, most companies do not even care about measuring benefit; key managers are simply committed to a cause. Top management determines the relative urgency of corporate priorities. As is often true in other management decision-making areas, management must make trade-offs in targeting certain social issues. If management decides it is critical to improve the company's record for equal employment opportunity, it may postpone its attention to one or more other issues. Likewise, it may delay introducing a second new product until it is sure its first entrant will succeed. The social assessment system (SAS) we introduce later in this section seems to have its greatest impact on improving a company's social performance when it selects no more than four to six key indicators for attention and corrective action.

Select a Plan or Policy

If possible, companies should measure their current performance before they act. Creativity and cooperation are important to the SAS process in developing sound measures. Three types of measures exist for the quantification of social performance: (1) actual performance, (2) level of effort, and (3) surrogates (substitutes that appear to approximate the underlying phenomenon). Measures of actual performance are possible in certain areas, such as the frequency of disabling injuries, the number of product recalls, or positive media comments.

Managers must be careful when developing measures of actual performance. The data must be consistent in definition and truly represent performance. For example, minority employment is an area for which actual performance measures are available.

Where actual performance may not be readily quantifiable in commonly understood terms, companies may measure the effort expended in dealing with a given problem. For example, annual expenditures for pollution control equipment would be a measure of level of effort.

The third type of measure utilizes surrogates of performance. Employee satisfaction is an example of an important issue that is not readily measurable. Management may use absenteeism, turnover, and measures of worker output as appropriate indicators of employee satisfaction.

EXHIBIT 3-9 Matrix of Issues with Social Consequences and the Affected Stakeholders

	Stakeholders									
Social Issues	Stock-holders	Non-management Employees	Managers	Retired Management and Non-management Employees	Customers	Suppliers	Lenders	Com-petitors	Gov-ernment	Neighbors or Local Com-munities	Activist Groups

Community and political responsiveness
1. Relations with regulatory agencies
2. Corporate giving
3. Support of minority-owned business

Human investment
1. Minority participation
2. Health and safety
3. Treatment of retired workers

Openness of the system
1. Relations with the news media
2. Composition of the board of directors
3. Financial disclosure

Consumer welfare
1. Handling of customer complaints
2. Customer satisfaction
3. Product recalls

Ecology and energy
1. Pollution abatement
2. Energy conservation

Implementation (Action)

Even when managers have satisfactory measures of performance, they may find that achieving the desired result is not easy. Internal company politics can and do distort both the process by which the policy is put into effect and the outcome.[41] However, there are ways to maximize the probability that the organization will actually carry out the plan. The plan should be sold to lower levels of management with enthusiasm, excitement, and goodwill. Lower-level managers should have the opportunity to ask questions and help move the process forward.

As we discussed in Chapter 2, organizations resist change. Managers must think of social change as a problem-solving mechanism. If all levels of the company accept new social goals as a remedy for an existing problem, implementation is likely to be more successful. Top management should closely relate important social goals to the company mission. When managers regard a plan as a fringe activity, the plan encounters organizational resistance.

Money and human resources are critical to social goal implementation. It is not sufficient—and is often counterproductive—to make budgetary increases or assign people to new tasks without ensuring they are used effectively.

Top management support must be ongoing. Top managers must direct resources and legitimize the efforts of those implementing the change. Top managers should not be involved in the day-to-day tasks of implementation. In fact, middle managers in charge of implementation may resent interference from above and may even sabotage top management's efforts.

Bateman and Zeithamel advise top managers to delegate as simply and directly as possible. They urge managers to show how the issue applies to organizational goals, what results are expected, and what problems are likely to occur in implementation. They note that managers must recognize high levels of performance and must stress the positive aspects of the implementation process.[42]

Control and Measure Performance

If management is to incorporate goals into the firm's operations, it must develop and measure success and control for deviations in the plan. These measures can be both objective and subjective. As noted earlier, companies prefer to rely on hard data such as costs, quotas, and industry averages.

---

[41] R. Wernham, "Implementation: The Things That Matter," in *Strategic Planning and Management Handbook,* eds. W. R. King and D. I. Cleland, (New York: Van Nostrand Reinhold, 1987), pp. 439–55.

[42] T. S. Bateman and C. P. Zeithamel, *Management: Function and Strategy* (Burr Ridge, IL: Richard D. Irwin, 1990), p. 379.

Ideally members of an industry should gather as much data as possible to generate a data bank of industry averages. In practice, this sort of participation rarely occurs unless a government agency or a trade association collects statistics. A social assessment system can help greatly in measuring and controlling performance.

The Social Assessment System. Creative management information systems offer the most constructive mechanisms for assessing corporate social performance. These systems are designed to keep management informed about the company's performance in areas of social concern. They are potential control mechanisms, providing management with a basis on which to make decisions about corporate conduct.

Because much of the data a firm gathers are confidential, often the company cannot hire an outside organization to evaluate its social performance. Companies differ in defining the categories of information they gather and analyze. The information may be industry- or company-specific, but the process of generating the needed information involves similar steps.

The social assessment system (SAS) is one form of management information system. It is by no means the only approach and has obvious limitations. However, it is a straightforward system that many large companies use in their efforts to manage social responsiveness.

Unlike financial reporting systems, the SAS disaggregates performance so that no bottom line of "social profit" or "net increase in social assets" is reported to provide an overall grade or score. Instead, the company develops key indicators for those policies and practices that have important social consequences and evaluates them against standards that management or outside agencies consider appropriate. The SAS uses existing data or data generated from corporate records. Therefore, management has discretion regarding whether or not to report social performance externally.

Obviously, certain social issues related to business are beyond management's control. Hence, issues concerning inflation, poverty, or reducing terrorism are not classified as relevant stimuli. The SAS recognizes that while literally hundreds of social issues may be relevant to a given corporation, it is feasible to focus on only a relatively limited number.

A particular company may decide it wants to lead, be equal to, or lag behind industry averages in responding to a given issue. However, with or without industry data, management should assess its own performance over time with regular, periodic analyses. Sometimes external direct or indirect stakeholders impose standards. For example, state or federal agencies, such as the Environmental Protection Agency or the Equal Employment Opportunity Commission, or even community groups, may dictate standards.

In summary, the social assessment system is useful as a confidential management tool. The company identifies the major social issues it considers of greatest relevance. It collects data on present performance and formulates a plan. It sets up objective and subjective performance measures to enable management to periodically measure social performance. Management may then determine whether performance is acceptable and, if not, which corrective steps it should initiate.

The Three-Stage Implementation Pattern

Robert W. Ackerman observed that many corporations move through a remarkably similar three-stage implementation pattern over a period of six to eight years.[43] Although his article first appeared in 1973, the identification and implementation process of social issues remains remarkably constant.

- Stage 1. The chief executive identifies an issue important to him or her and to the company. Usually the CEO considers the choice an issue of corporate responsibility or corporate self-interest.

The CEO begins to talk about the issue to external stakeholders who are either directly or indirectly affected by the issue and may even commit company resources to the issue. Soon the CEO decides the issues should be incorporated into company policy and assigns the responsibility for implementation to the operating units.

Perhaps to the CEO's surprise, little or no action is taken because the company has no established measures of success and no penalties for failure. Also, it is not clear to operating managers that the corporation is seriously committed to the cause. This phase may last for months or even years.

- Stage 2. The president or CEO appoints a staff executive to report on and coordinate the company's efforts. This staff member usually has the title of vice president or director of environmental affairs or consumer affairs. The specialist might even be a lawyer or an outside consultant. This specialist collects data, assesses stakeholder interest, and mediates among the operating divisions and the external stakeholders. His role is to crystallize the issue for top management.

Middle managers may still balk at implementation because they support their senior line executives rather than the staff member. They know the CEO usually supports senior line executives before staff members, regardless of the issue.

- Stage 3. Organizational involvement is the third stage of implementation. The CEO recognizes that if the social goal is to be implemented, she must involve the whole organization and institutionalize policy. A critical task is to work the issue into the company's resource allocation and reward systems.

---

[43] R. W. Ackerman, "How Companies Respond to Social Demands," *Harvard Business Review,* July–August 1973, pp. 88–98.

The Social Audit

The concept of a social audit began in the United Kingdom in the early 1960s. In *The Responsible Company,* published in 1961, Goyder proposed that companies publish regular accounts of their social impacts well as their financial performance.[44] In the early 1970s, the Public Interest Research Centre established Social Audit, Ltd., an organization designed to document a company's social performance.

In the early to mid-1970s, American managers and academics began to develop and amplify the concept of the corporate social audit. They called it a report card of the company's social performance. Using material from their 1972 book *The Corporate Social Audit,* Raymond A. Bauer and Dan H. Fenn, Jr., wrote a seminal article in the *Harvard Business Review* the following year. They defined a social audit as "a commitment to systematic assessment of and reporting on some meaningful, definable domain of a company's activities that have social impact."[45]

The article's purpose was to help managers answer questions about what activities they should audit, what measures they should use, and against what standards they should measure performance. The authors were quick to point out that any audit must be an ongoing process of collecting data on issues that have been defined as an "explicit corporate policy involving a meaningful level of resource commitment."[46]

John J. Corson and George A. Steiner discussed major issues related to the social audit. In their article "Measuring Business's Social Performance: The Corporate Social Audit," they asked whether the social audit was simply a fad that would be abandoned. They concluded that if companies used the proper model in conducting the audit, the resulting social report could be a credible measure of a corporation's commitment to social goals.[47]

The most difficult problem for managers was not data collection but developing methods to measure accomplishment. The early efforts to develop measurement techniques drew heavily on traditional accounting tools. The concepts of the social balance sheet and social income statement[48] and the Socioeconomic Operating Statement[49] appealed to some managers but were not widely adopted.

---

[44] S. Zadek, "Social Auditing for the Voluntary Sector," from Internet, July 18, 1996 [http://sosig.ac.uk/NewEconomics/volvoice.html/].

[45] R. A. Bauer and D. H. Fenn, Jr., "What *Is* a Corporate Audit," *Harvard Business Review,* January–February 1973, p. 38.

[46] Ibid., p. 44.

[47] J. J. Corson and G. A. Steiner, "Measuring Business's Social Performance: The Corporate Social Audit," (New York: Committee for Economic Development, 1974), pp. 18–20, 40–41, 49–52, 59–63.

[48] Abt Associates, Inc., was the major advocate of this approach.

[49] D. F. Linowes, *Strategies for Survival* (New York: AMACOM, 1973), pp. 166–78.

It is clear that relatively few companies found conventional accounting theory to be an adequate base for developing a social audit. Even Abt Associates, one of the most enthusiastic proponents of the social audit, dropped the procedure in the early 1980s.

Daniel H. Gray of Arthur D. Little, Inc. (ADL), explained that ADL examined and rejected the notion. Gray said, "Those social problems that disturb us most lie outside the realm of transactions. . . . Accounting . . . owes its rigor to what it excludes. To try to stretch it to measure all social costs and benefits is to violate its very foundation."[50]

By the 1980s, the British had developed and formalized the concept of the social audit. The corporate sector took the initiative in developing institutions such as Business in the Community, New Consumers, and the Fair Trade Movement through which corporations could develop more socially aware activities.

Simon Zadek, research director of the New Economics Forum, a London-based think tank, ties social auditing to strategic planning. He notes that social auditing is more than verification and accountability. "Social auditing allows corporations to become more responsive to social dimensions of [their] actitivities. . . . It recognizes the intimate relationship between allowing stakeholders' voices to be heard and taken into account, and the effectiveness of decisions made and actions taken. In general, it is therefore not surprising that social auditing has in this context been called *ethical strategic planning.*"[51] The New Economics Forum designed the key principles of social auditing in Exhibit 3–10.

Ostapski and Isaacs suggest a variation on the social audit. They say that corporations must consciously try to discharge a moral responsibility to avoid, minimize, eliminate, and compensate for a potential or actual harm they might cause. They propose that corporations establish a moral audit committee, internal to the corporation but independent of management. This committee should report directly to the company's board of directors, an independent member of the management team, and stakeholders in the community. The moral audit committee would base its actions on the company's mission statement and/or code of ethics. The authors note that management's establishment and support of this committee is likely to increase the public's respect for the company which will, in turn, increase profits.[52]

---

[50] D. H. Gray, "Methodology: One Approach to the Corporate Social Audit," in *The Unstable Ground: Corporate Policy in a Dynamic Society* (Los Angeles: Melville Publishing, 1974), pp. 92–93.

[51] S. Zadek, "Ethical Accountability & Strategic Planning: The Social Audit Approach," Internet [http://sosig.ac.uk/New Economics/corpcit.html/].

[52] S. A. Ostapski and C. N. Isaacs, "Corporate Moral Responsibility and the Moral Audit: Challenges for Refuse Relief Inc.," *Journal of Business Ethics* 11, 1992, pp. 213–39.

Exhibit 3–10 Principles of Social Auditing

Multiple Perspectives: accounts are based on the views of all stakeholders, as well as the mission statement and the organization's wider interest. People without direct authority can be heard.

Comprehensive: accounts are comprehensive assessments of an organization's social impact and ethical behavior. Accounts cover the interests of staff and volunteers as well as clients and other benficiaries. This principle strives to avoid biased reporting of the organization's activities.

Regular: accounts are produced annually. Social and ethical accounting becomes an integral part of the organization's information system.

Systematic Social Bookkeeping: the organization is required to systematize information collection relevant to the social accounts.

External Validation: a two-stage external validation process is central to social auditing. First, an external auditor and the organization agree on a methodology and the auditor monitors the preparation of social accounts. Next, the auditor establishes an audit group composed of stakeholder representatives. The audit group assesses and comments on a draft of the accounts.

Disclosure: audited accounts are disclosed to stakeholders and the public.

Source: S. Zadek, "Social Auditing for the Voluntary Sector," p. 3, from the Internet, July 18, 1996 [http://sosing.ac.uk/NewEconomics/volvoice.html/].

In recent years, Ben & Jerry's, The Body Shop, and Aveda Ecological Products have conducted social audits. Ben & Jerry hired an outsider to write a personal report on the company's social activities and began a full-scale social audit in 1996. Commenting on The Body Shop's audit, Anita Roddick said, "Consumers are increasingly vigilant about all sorts of businesses and they want to feel sympathetic with the company they deal with."

The New Economics Forum has worked with Traidcraft, a U.K.-based ethical trading company to develop a more systematic social audit. Zadek expects that "social audits of the future will include more detailed analysis of the financial impact of social and employee policies, but that concept is not yet well advanced."[53]

KPMG Peat Marwick's London office reported that two-thirds of the U.K.'s top 100 companies in 1994 included some kind of environmental evaluation in their annual reports. In the United States, Peat Marwick has started to offer ethical audits along with financial audits.

---

[53] M. Suzman, "The Audit with a Social Conscience," *Financial Times,* January 27–28, 1996, p. 9.

Summary

Clearly, implementation of social issues is a difficult and complex process. An effective evaluation and reward process for middle managers may not fall within tidy, quantifiable borders. However, Ackerman observes that "through the creative and persistent leadership of top management, the barriers to incorporating social change in the decentralized company can be overcome."[54]

This chapter deals with stakeholder identification, strategy implementation, and evaluation. The degree of social responsiveness and the company's ability to incorporate it into everyday operations depend to a great extent on the power various stakeholders have in the outcome. The stakeholder influence map (SIM) furnishes a model for identifying stakeholders and their importance to the firm. Companies that manage stakeholder demands effectively have common attributes. Their major strength is their ability to build a coalition of diverse stakeholders. Top managers cannot deal with all stakeholder issues and therefore must devise a classification and evaluation scheme.

One alternative is the social assessment system (SAS), a form of management information system that organizes social issues into major categories. Using this scheme, managers determine priorities and collect data. Then they select a policy of corrective action and develop measures of actual performance. After the company has taken action to correct the problem, managers evaluate and measure its performance.

Social implementation proceeds in corporations in a distinct pattern. In stage 1, the top executive selects an issue. In stage 2, a specialist assumes the burden of transmitting the message to middle managers. In stage 3, the whole organization becomes involved in implementation.

Nearly all companies find implementation of social goals a very difficult task. For the most part, the usual reward and evaluation procedures are not designed to deal with social issues. Companies are beginning to assess their own performance through development and application of the social audit.

---

[54] Ackerman, p. 97.

Projects

1. Choose a social issue and use the stakeholder influence map to identify stakeholders.
2. Using the stakeholder influence map, implement the social assessment system for setting social goals for a company of your choice.
3. The class divides into groups or task forces. Each task force is assigned to a particular stakeholder concern. Each group must argue for resources to implement a program to deal with that social goal. Make sure financial issues are taken into account.
4. Examine the annual reports of several publicly owned companies. To what extent does each report mention social issues or describe the company's response to social issues? What issues does each report mention? What do you conclude from your examination?

Questions

1. Give several examples of current social issues that could be classified within each element of the social assessment system.
2. Why is consumer welfare an especially difficult area in which to develop reliable measures of corporate performance?
3. What is the relationship among industry/competitor analysis, social issues analysis, and the management of corporate social responsiveness?

BETA CASE 2
STRATEGY IMPLEMENTATION AND EVALUATION

Brian Madison's E-mail was the first thing that came up on his computer screen in the morning. Today's message from Simon Owens, manager of Beta's British subsidiary, was not particularly welcome. Madison knew that because of the time difference, Owens's day started six hours earlier than his. Owens had already received reports of International Laboratory Animal Day activities in London and on the Continent. It was still too early in the morning for the U.S. picketers and activists to begin their confrontation, but Madison had no doubt, that they would appear at the company's gates by 8:00 AM.

Today marked the beginning of a week of protests and discussions by transatlantic alliances of animal-welfare groups. They were militantly opposed to scientific testing on animals and felt that animals deserved the same rights to life and safety as people. Owens told Madison that the British protestors were claiming that British research employed nearly 3 million animals in 1995 and that U.S. companies used more than 30 million. Even though the number of animals used in experiments had dropped significantly in the past several years, the activists were claiming that Beta and other pharmaceutical companies were creating a holocaust.

In principle, Madison felt somewhat queasy about using animals in experiments to test the efficacy of new drugs. On the other hand, he felt far more concerned about curing people than worrying about mice and rats that were bred specifically for laboratory testing. Nevertheless, no one in the company enjoyed the image of Beta as a company of killers rather than healers. As soon as the other top managers came in, he was going to begin a dialog focused on animal experimentation. They were going to identify the stakeholders in this controversy, decide what issues were key to the company, what policies they already had in place to deal with animal experimentation, and how they should implement a policy that would make them less vulnerable in the future. For sure, Madison decided, they were going to have an outside social audit to be certain the company was complying with the best and most humane practices consistent with developing and distributing top-quality pharmaceuticals.

CHAPTER 4
CRISIS MANAGEMENT

The preceding three chapters discuss how companies manage the routine issues of strategy formulation and implementation and how they assess a variety of economic, technological, social, and political issues. The Dow Corning case presented in this chapter demonstrates the difficulties companies face when unexpected and nonroutine events trigger a crisis.

Issues management and crisis management are related activities that require different management skills to be handled effectively. Archie B. Carroll defines issues management as "a process by which organizations identify issues in the environment, analyze and prioritize these issues in terms of their relevance to the organization, plan responses to these issues, and then evaluate and monitor the results."[1] Effective issues management contributes to strategic planning and helps avoid the need for crisis management.

However, even the most farsighted firms confront crises. According to *Webster's Ninth New Collegiate Dictionary,* a *crisis* is "an unstable or crucial time or state of affairs whose outcome will make a decisive difference for better or worse." For corporations, *crisis management* is the process by which firms manage "disasters precipitated by people, organizations, organizational structures, economics, and/or technology that cause extensive damage to human life, and natural and social environments."[2]

---

[1] A. B. Carroll, *Business & Society; Ethics & Stakeholder Management* (Cincinnati: South Western Publishing, 1989), p. 476.

[2] I. Mitroff, P. Shrivastava, and F. Udwadia, "Effective Crisis Management," *Academy of Management Executive* 1, no. 3 (1987), p. 283.

Case: Dow Corning and Breast Implants

On January 7, 1992, the Food and Drug Administration (FDA) called on manufacturers to halt the sale of breast implants pending review of new data. FDA Commissioner David Kessler requested that all plastic surgeons stop using silicone implants. The FDA noted that it had obtained many documents that raised substantial concerns about the safety of Dow Corning silicone implants manufactured between 1975 and 1985. The FDA's concerns were exacerbated by a federal court decision in December 1991 that ordered Dow Corning to pay a woman $7.3 million in damages because the firm concealed evidence linking implant ruptures to immune system disorders. Additional suits were pending.

The FDA's announcement focused the nation's attention on Dow Corning and added fuel to the already blazing controversy over the safety of breast implants. Dow Corning faced a potentially devastating crisis. Crisis management experts compared Dow Corning's situation to Exxon's dilemma with the *Valdez* oil spill and A. H. Robins' tribulations with the Dalkon Shield IUD. Would Dow Corning's top executives be more effective crisis managers?

Two weeks after announcing the ban, the FDA ordered Dow Corning to release 90 company documents to public scrutiny. The chief FDA official in charge of medical devices wrote a letter to Lawrence A. Reed, president of Dow Corning, declaring "these memoranda reflect a lack of appropriate safety and performance data." Dow Corning's spokesperson replied that "this is a true travesty, a media circus instead of a true and impartial scientific review."[3]

On March 19, 1992, Dow Corning announced it would stop making breast implants. Barbara Carmichael, vice president of corporate communications, said the decision was business-driven and not tied to the public controversy or pending litigation. In any event, she added, the business had not been profitable since 1986.[4]

What chronology of events led Dow Corning to abandon the product? Could Dow Corning have avoided the crisis? The firm had manufactured the implants for more than 30 years and had had ample warning that a crisis might occur.

Silicone is a long, flexible polymer made up of repeating molecules of oxygen and silicon that was discovered in the 1930s. Silicone was not used commercially until the 1940s, when the U.S. military asked Dow Chemical Company and Corning Glass Works to form a joint company to develop products using the material. Because silicone is not altered by extremes of temperature, it made an excellent coolant, sealant, and lubricant for Navy ships.

Silicone was first used to augment breast tissue soon after World War II. Japanese cosmetologists, concluding that large-breasted prostitutes were more attractive to American soldiers occupying Japan, injected the substance directly into the women's breasts. The American medical community heard rumors of this practice but declined to follow the Japanese example of direct injection.

In the 1960s, Dow Corning scientists developed a product that seemed to offer a much safer method of breast enlargement. Although Japanese researchers warned that silicone might cause inflammatory immune diseases, Dow Corning paid little heed. Its scientists, intrigued with silicone's potential, manufactured implants of liquid silicone enclosed in a silicone envelope. The implants appeared to be inert and nonreactive to acids or alkalis. In addition, they were both soft and flexible.

In 1972, McGhan Medical Corporation, a Dow Corning competitor, began to market a silicone-gel implant that was much softer than the Dow Corning product. McGhan quickly gained a substantial share of the breast implant market, putting Dow Corning under pressure to develop its own gel product.

In January 1975, Dow Corning officials formed a Mammary Task Force. The task force was in charge of making the gel; filling the silicone envelopes; and carrying out the engineering, chemical, medical, and quality control tasks necessary to get the product onto the market. Dow Corning officials estimated worldwide demand at 52,000 implants a year.

---

[3] P. J. Hilts, "FDA Tells Company to Release Implant Data," *New York Times*, January 21, 1992, p. C7.

[4] "Dow Corning Charts Communications after Leaving Implant Business," *PR News*, March 30, 1992, p. 3.

Although no initial data indicated potential dangers, the chairperson of the task force was concerned about potential "bleeding" of the silicone envelope. The technical staff assured him that tests showed this was not a problem. Clinical testing on women began in February 1975, even before animal testing results were reported. Within a week after the first human implants, tests on rabbits showed the animals had a "mild to acute inflammatory reaction." Evidence mounted that the new gel caused further inflammation as it migrated through the rabbits' bodies.

Within the first year after humans received the implants, Dow Corning received complaints from doctors who saw acute inflammatory reactions in their patients. Doctors also reported instances of granulomas and siliconmae, masses associated with leaking implants. As with the rabbits, escaping gel migrated through the patients' bodies.

In 1976, Congress passed a law requiring the FDA to approve the safety and effectiveness of medical devices. Silicone implants were exempted because they were already on the market. Two years later, the FDA staff proposed putting breast implants into a category requiring very rigorous safety tests. Plastic surgeons and manufacturers opposed the measure and finally won when the FDA commissioner overrode his staff's recommendation. In 1982, the FDA again tried to reclassify implants and again failed.

In 1985, Dow Corning became concerned about what one executive called an ominous shift in the FDA to require more and stricter lifetime animal tests. In an internal memo, he acknowledged that the company could be in trouble because all its data were based on two-year studies of dogs. Now lifetime dog studies had to be of seven years' duration.

Dow Corning began to warn women and doctors about two major problems with the implants: scar tissue could form around the implants, and whenever the implants leaked, women could suffer inflammatory reactions. In 1988, the FDA finally reclassified implants and notified implant makers that they would be required to provide safety data within 30 months.[5]

In April 1991, the FDA responded to inquiries from women worried about the safety of their implants. It asked all manufacturers to submit scientific data demonstrating their products' safety and effectiveness. The FDA refused to evaluate the safety and effectiveness of silicone-gel implants made by Bristol-Myers Squibb, Bioplasty, and a private physician in California. The FDA asserted the companies had not submitted sufficient evidence to conduct a review.

However, the FDA agreed to review seven other types of implants made by McGhan Medical, Mentor, and Dow Corning, as well as an alternative model made by Bioplasty. In late July, the FDA ordered U.S. marshals to seize 800 Bioplasty inflatable implant kits. The agency said the company lacked FDA marketing authorization and had made false and misleading claims about the product.[6]

Shortly thereafter, the FDA began to consider banning most or all use of silicone breast implants, noting that the makers had not submitted adequate safety data. As Commissioner David Kessler remarked, "It is as hard, as complicated, as emotional as any issue we've faced since I got here."[7]

Breast implant recipients were divided. Of the 2 million cases of breast implants since the early 1960s, about 80 percent were done for cosmetic reasons and the remaining 20 percent for reconstructive surgery following mastectomies. Some women believed breast implants had changed their lives for the better; others claimed their health had been permanently impaired. In November 1991, the FDA convened a panel to determine whether implants were safe. Two days later, the panel voted to keep breast implants on the market and urged the FDA to set strict rules for continued marketing. It also voted unanimously to reject Dow Corning's safety data.

Managing the Crisis

From the perspectives of Dow Chemical and Corning Glass Works, the FDA ruling was a disaster. Their businesses and managerial responsibilities clearly

---

[5] P. J. Hilts, "Maker of Implants Balked at Tests, Its Records Show," *New York Times,* January 13, 1992, p. A1.

[6] B. Ingersoll, "FDA Refuses to Evaluate Data Submitted by Three Manufacturers of Breast Implants," *The Wall Street Journal,* August 26, 1991, p. B3.

[7] P. J. Hilts, "Amid Heavy Lobbying, U.S. Weighs Breast Implant Ban," *New York Times,* October 21, 1991, p. A1.

overlapped in the joint venture association. Officers of both companies sat on Dow Corning's board of directors. Five Corning representatives, including Corning's chairperson, were members of Dow Corning's 14-member board. Dow Chemical also had five representatives on the board. The remaining four directors were Dow Corning managers. Even though the parent companies, Corning and Dow, were not involved in implant research and were not liable for potential damages, they stood to lose a large portion of earnings if Dow Corning's revenues suffered.[8]

Dow Corning and other implant manufacturers took a series of steps between early February and May 1992.

- February 18: Dow Corning continued to withhold hundreds of internal documents addressing safety issues.
- February 20: Dow Corning promised to carry out 15 more safety tests on implants and establish a patient tracking registry.
- March 2: Dow Corning explored the possibility of seeking bankruptcy under Chapter 11. This action could temporarily halt private litigation and resolve all claims simultaneously.
- March 19: Dow Corning, followed the lead of Bristol-Myers Squibb and Bioplasty, announcing it would get out of the implant business.
- November 4: Five hundred plastic surgeons signed up to take part in clinical studies of silicone breast implants. Under FDA rules, implants would only be available to women enrolled in the study.[9]

---

[8] J. E. Rigdon, "Corning Is Feeling the Heat in Breast Implant Debacle," *The Wall Street Journal,* January 29, 1992, p. B4.

[9] "Silicone-Gel Breast Implants Resume with Restrictions," *Boston Globe,* November 4, 1992, p. 17.

In September 1993, Dow Corning and four other manufacturers proposed a $4.2 billion worldwide settlement for 435,000 women. Judge Sam C. Pointer, Jr., initially approved the settlement in April 1994. Faced with angry creditors, bondholders, and suppliers who also lined up to compete for the company's assets, Dow Corning filed for bankruptcy under Chapter 11 in May 1995. Bankruptcy experts predicted that $3 billion more would be needed to pay all initial claims. CEO Richard A. Hazelton said the decision to file bankruptcy was difficult but "we had to take this action now to preserve both the fundamental strength of our business operations and our ability to fairly compensate all women with breast implant claims."[10]

By September, the breast implant accord was near collapse. Judge Pointer admitted the whole deal was off since the defendants and plaintiffs could not agree on the monetary offer. A month earlier lawyers failed to meet a court-imposed deadline for renegotiation of the fund. One of the manufacturers, Baxter Healthcare Corporation, walked out on the talks saying the plaintiffs wanted too much money. Union Carbide, a marginal participant, refused to budge on its original offer.[11]

Three major manufacturers, excluding Dow Corning, proposed a new settlement that significantly reduced the previous offer. Some observers thought Dow Corning had miscalculated the situation in refusing to take part in the new agreement. While other producers agreed to pay huge amounts to

---

[10] J. Mathews, "Silicone Firm Seeks Protection," *Boston Globe,* May 16, 1995, p. 1.

[11] B. Meier, "Risks in Separate Deals on Breast-Implant Suits," *New York Times,* September 1, 1995, p. D3.

put the implant controversy behind them, Dow Corning faced chronic sapping of its resources. Dow Corning had assumed Judge Pointer would support its position, but the judge declared it was the lawyers' role to forge a settlement.

In October 1995, a state jury in Nevada found parent company Dow Chemical solely responsible in for injuring a plaintiff's immune system. The jury decided to award the woman $14.1 million in compensatory and punitive damages. The plaintiff's lawyer declared, "Dow Chemical has been arrogant throughout all of the breast implant litigation." He noted that Dow Chemical scientists were aware of the potential dangers of silicone.[12]

In December, Canada's Supreme Court ruled in favor of a woman who alleged Dow Corning was negligent in manufacturing implants. The decision—the first of its kind in Canada—supported an earlier British Columbia court award of $70,000.[13]

In 1996, the breast implant controversy became even more complicated. Dow received support from court decisions and scientific studies. A Michigan state jury found 30 insurers liable for about $400 million in potential damages because of the policies they wrote covering Dow Corning. The company was pleased because the verdict helped it move through the Chapter 11 process of financial reorganization. Implant plaintiffs were also happy, because it was likely that even more money would be available to resolve claims.[14]

In June, a study of 87,501 nurses, 1,183 of whom had implants, found no link between implants and illness. Some leading rheumatologists urged the FDA to lift the 1992 voluntary moratorium on implants. Other doctors said the study was flawed because the women had symptoms that were vague and attributable to other causes. The FDA said it was not ready to make a decision but was encouraged by the high quality of the study.[15]

Questions

1. Did Dow Corning handle the early stages of the crisis effectively? Should top managers have made different decisions?
2. Should management have been more outspoken earlier? Some newspaper and magazine articles compared Dow Corning's performance to Exxon Corporation's response to the *Exxon Valdez* disaster and A. H. Robins' handling of the Dalkon Shield IUD controversy. Is that comparison fair?
3. Should Dow Corning have stopped making implants?
4. Develop a plan for resolving this crisis. What choices would you make? What should the FDA do with the new information?

---

[12] T. M. Burton, "Jury in Breast-Implant Case Finds Dow Chemical Co. Solely Liable," *The Wall Street Journal,* October 30, 1995, p. B5.

[13] "Dow Is Ruled Negligent on Breast Implants," *Boston Globe,* December 22, 1995, p. 46.

[14] T. M. Burton, "Insurers Are Found Liable in Implant Cases," *The Wall Street Journal,* February 15, 1996, p. B3.

[15] G. Kolata, "New Study Finds No Link between Implants and Illness," *New York Times,* June 22, 1996, p. A18.

Crisis Classification

Some crises are foreseeable; some are not; some are generated internally, some externally. Internal crises may develop because companies do not sufficiently monitor or manage internal activities. Even when crises are internally generated, they can affect the firm's external stakeholders as well as its internal stakeholders. Crises sparked externally by unforeseen events in the social or physical environment also may affect both internal and external stakeholders. Exhibit 4–1 offers a way of classifying crises into categories.

Internally Generated Crises

Internally generated crises are crises that affect a company or even an industry but have no direct impact on the external physical environment. Stakeholders in the internal- and external-direct quadrants of the stakeholder influence map may suffer, but there is no threat to water, air, or land. Internal crises stem from a variety of organizational problems related to management's inadequate organizational structures and controls.

Organizational problems include poor company culture, ineffective information dissemination systems, and unclear punishments and rewards. Additional organizational difficulties arise when planning procedures do not respond to events or when employees make errors that are not identified and corrected. These inadequacies may lead to production and control problems that go undetected or unanalyzed. They also may be responsible for faulty design and product defects that exacerbate the problem.

Prudential Securities, Inc., and Manville Corporation are two companies whose inadequate internal monitoring systems resulted in devastating crises that affected a wide range of direct and indirect stakeholders.

Prudential Securities, Inc., a unit of Prudential Insurance Company of America, tolerated widespread securities law violations and fraud for more than a decade. The parent company received royalties and large up-front partnership fees totaling at least $777 million from 1983 through 1990.

EXHIBIT 4–1 Crisis Classification Map

	Foreseeable	*Not Foreseeable*
Internally generated	Product design defect Improper manufacture Improper storage Unsafe products	Employee sabotage Employee ethics violations
Externally generated	Product tampering After sale misuse of product	Acts of God and nature domestic and international

Prudential Insurance and Prudential Securities continued to seek commissions and other fees long after they knew the partnerships were in trouble.

In October 1993, Prudential agreed to pay hundreds of thousands of customers $371 million for the enormous losses they suffered. Among Prudential Securities' practices were

- *Lying about risk.* Prudential brokers sold risky real-estate and energy (oil and gas) partnerships to pension funds, retirees, and others who were told the investments were safe.
- *Lying about return.* Prudential published promotional material that misled investors about the return they could expect on their money.
- *Ignoring a subsidiary's activities.* Prudential Insurance inadequately supervised the subsidiary that advertised and sold limited partnerships.
- *Ignoring employee practices.* Prudential inadequately supervised employees in nine branch offices where fraudulent practices were carried out.
- *Churning.* Prudential allowed excessive trading in clients' accounts to increase brokers' commissions without authorization.
- *Abusing client trust.* Prudential persuaded clients to sign agreements that gave Prudential employees freedoms such as margin trading with client accounts even when clients did not understand what they were signing.
- *Ignoring promises to regulators.* Prudential failed to follow the terms of a 1986 securities fraud settlement that required Prudential to adopt compliance procedures.
- *Lying.* Prudential employees told clients concerned about losses noted on their accounts that they resulted from a back-office error.[16]

We discuss the Prudential Securities situation in detail later in this chapter.

Manville's problems with asbestos-related claims is another example of an internally generated crisis. For decades, Manville's top management deliberately concealed data documenting asbestos-related deaths and disabilities. The situation became a crisis when stakeholders brought legal action.

In 1986, Manville filed for bankruptcy under Chapter 11 to protect itself from claims. In 1988, the company agreed to set up Manville Personal Injury Settlement Trust, a $2.5 billion trust to pay health claims from victims of asbestos-related diseases. Manville emerged from bankruptcy court protection in November 1988. However, litigation dragged on as the trust fund repeatedly ran out of money and fund overseers were charged with mismanagement.

---

[16] K. Eichenwald, "Prudential Agrees to a Settlement in Securities Fraud," *New York Times,* October 22, 1993, p. A1.

In the early 1990s, Manville's management struggled to overcome the constant drain on the firm's financial resources and to create a new, environmentally friendly image. According to image makers, "this kind of aggressive environmental makeover is the only way to reinvent a company whose name has become synonymous with health problems." Manville's troubles were not over. Payments to claimants dragged on and on. Observers did not expect the fund to complete payments until after the year 2000.[17] In December 1992, a federal appeals court overturned a two-year-old reorganization plan of the Manville Personal Injury Trust, putting the issue back in the lower courts and stalling settlement once again. Finally in March 1996, Manville announced it completed a settlement that gave the Manville Personal Injury Settlement Trust enough cash to continue meeting asbestos victims' claims. The company said it would give the trust 20 percent of Manville's stock and pay a special $772 million dividend in exchange for the trust's giving up its right to receive 20 percent of Manville's profits.

Environmental Crises: A Special Situation

Environmental crises affect the external physical environment as well as specific stakeholder groups. These crises include such events as nuclear accidents, chemical or oil spills, and other industrial catastrophes. Like internal crises, they often have their genesis in the firm's managerial systems. Unless the crisis is caused by uncontrollable external forces, such as actions by terrorists, criminals, or saboteurs, corporate policies and procedures often are responsible. Inadequate or poorly designed technical monitoring and backup systems precipitate crises. Employees who are not properly trained and systems that are not in place to catch mistakes also cause crises.

Occasionally a company is plunged into a crisis through no fault of its own. This kind of crisis is generated by external, uncontrollable events. Johnson & Johnson's management of the 1982 Tylenol poisonings illustrates how effective crisis management can minimize the negative consequences, especially when the company is clearly not culpable.

The crisis at Johnson & Johnson erupted in September 1982, when several Chicago-area residents died after taking cyanide-laced Tylenol. Tylenol was a leading over-the-counter pain remedy produced by one of Johnson & Johnson's divisions. In the aftermath, top management expertly articulated Johnson & Johnson's public position and company philosophy to consumers and employees. The company convinced the public that it was as much a victim as the people who died. Johnson & Johnson also demonstrated concern for its customers by immediately recalling the product and quickly taking

---

[17] J. M. Moses, "Manville Dispute with U.S. May Force Asbestos Claimants to Compete for Funds," *The Wall Street Journal,* November 14, 1991, p. B6.

steps to make the Tylenol package tamperproof. Its actions often are cited as a model of effective crisis management. Even more than a decade later, the company's expert handling of the Tylenol crisis continues to enhance Johnson & Johnson's image.

Increasingly, industrial disasters such as Union Carbide's Bhopal incident, the *Exxon Valdez* oil spill, and the ValuJet crash into the Florida Everglades focus national and international attention on company responses. It is very difficult for a company to manage external disasters because media attention is so intense and so many stakeholders are involved. The public's perception of the company's contribution to the crisis often rests on the severity of the crisis and the degree to which innocent stakeholders suffer. Prompt and appropriate responses by management can mitigate public perceptions of culpability. Delayed or inappropriate responses can exacerbate such perceptions.

When the *Exxon Valdez* spilled oil into pristine Alaskan waters, the company's reaction was slow, confused, and some charged, deliberately obtuse. Exxon's top management appeared so disorganized that *The Wall Street Journal* ran the following subheading a week after the spill: "Out of Control: How Lack of Readiness by Exxon and Others Turned Oil Spill into Ecological Debacle."[18] We discuss the details of the Exxon spill later in this chapter.

A Model for Crisis Management

Regardless of whether a situation is generated internally or externally, top management often can identify an impending crisis by the symptoms before the crisis erupts; moreover, it can predict the likelihood that the issue will become a crisis. Models for assessing the potential severity of crises and devising strategies to limit damage to the firm and its reputation can be helpful to firms. Even the worst catastrophes can be managed to minimize negative consequences.

Mitroff, Shrivastava, and Udwadia present a useful and creative crisis management model (see Exhibit 4–2).[19] The model can be entered and exited at any point and the company can take action either clockwise or counterclockwise. The model uses the following sequence:

Point I: Detection. The company's early warning systems detect a crisis. The systems include computerized process control systems, plant monitoring systems, management information systems, and internal and external environmental scans. Between the detection (point I) and crisis periods (point II),

---
[18] K. Wells, "How Unpreparedness Turned the Alaska Spill into Ecological Debacle," *The Wall Street Journal,* April 3, 1989, p. A1.
[19] Mitroff, et al., "Effective Crisis Management," p. 284.

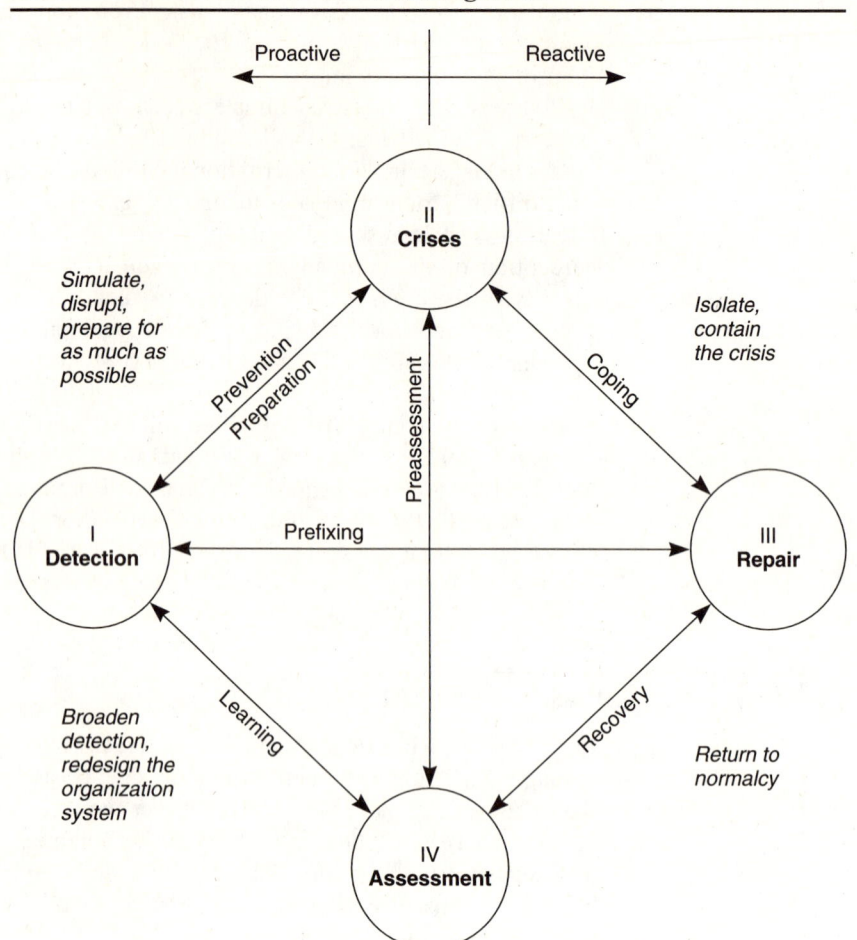

Exhibit 4–2 A Model of Crisis Management

```
                        Proactive    |    Reactive

                                   II
                                 Crises

    Simulate,                                          Isolate,
    disrupt,                                           contain
    prepare for      Prevention            Coping      the crisis
    as much as       Preparation
    possible                   Preassessment

         I        ← — — — Prefixing — — — →        III
      Detection                                    Repair

    Broaden            Learning            Recovery    Return to
    detection,                                         normalcy
    redesign the
    organization
    system
                                   IV
                                Assessment
```

the company can use simulations and mock crisis exercises to prepare for the real thing as effectively as possible.

Point II: Crisis. No organization can always escape the circumstances that cause crises. If the company has done its proactive prevention and preparation well, it can deal more effectively with actual crises when they occur. Prevention and preparation entail developing such items as safety policies, maintenance procedures, environmental-impact plans, crisis audits, and worker-training programs.

Point III: Repair. The company must isolate and contain crises before it can repair the damage. The specific strategies for repairing a crisis depend on the nature and scope of the problem. For example, Johnson & Johnson immediately recalled Tylenol, changed the seal on the package, and embarked on an expertly devised remedial advertising campaign. A company that does not have such repair mechanisms in place may never recover from the aftereffects.

Point IV: Assessment. In the final step of the crisis cycle model, the company evaluates what it has learned from the crisis. A new cycle begins as the firm develops better crisis prevention and detection systems as a result of its crisis experience.

For example, in the post-Bhopal period, Union Carbide should have examined points I through III step-by-step to put in place policies to prevent a similar accident from occurring in its factories elsewhere in the world. This process would have enabled Union Carbide to heed early warning signs in the detection stage and would have allowed the company to behave proactively. Effective routine company procedures often can pick up safety problems before they become crises and before the company loses control of events.

Norman R. Augustine, president of Lockheed Martin Corporation, observes that every crisis "contains within itself the seeds of success as well as the roots of failure." He says that the essence of crisis management is "finding, cultivating, and harvesting the potential success."[20] Augustine presents a six stages of crisis management, some aspects of which overlap with the Mitroff, Shrisvastava, and Udwadia model.

Augustine's *Stage 1: Avoiding the Crisis* often is neglected in crisis management literature even though it is the least expensive and easiest way to control events. He speculates that executives accept as a given that crises are unavoidable and that they can control crises when they occur. Augustine asks us to accept one of his homegrown basic laws of management: *Tornadoes are caused by trailer parks.* He notes, tongue in cheek, that we have ample empirical evidence of the link between trailer parks and tornadoes. He suggests that executives would do well to survey the landscape continuously for trailer parks. Executives should make lists of everything that could possibly attract trouble to the business. Next, they should consider possible consequences and estimate the cost of prevention. As he points out, this exercise is not much fun which is why it is not a popular pastime with corporate officers. Nevertheless, he comments, "Lacking control over the origin of a problem does not exempt you from living with its consequences." The real problem, Augustine posits, is that "perfect prevention in perfectly unattainable."[21]

---

[20] N. R. Augustine, "Managing the Crisis You Tried to Prevent," *Harvard Business Review,* November–December 1995, pp. 147–58.

[21] Ibid., p. 150.

Anatomy of a Major Crisis

Most crisis management scholars note than crises erupt in stages. Gerald C. Meyers identifies three specific periods in the course of a crisis: precrisis, crisis, and postcrisis.[22] These stages correspond to Mitroff et al.'s model in Exhibit 4-2.

The Precrisis or Prodromal Stage

The term *prodromal* means a crisis is looming. This phase is a warning stage. Augustine says this stage is often the most challenging and reminds us of the chemistry student who warned, "When you smell an odorless gas, it's probably carbon monoxide."[23] The prodromal stage fits in the upper-left quadrant of Exhibit 4-2. Something is wrong, but the company is unable to pin it down. The symptom is that some person or group within the company is not performing. For example, production quotas that are not being met create customer delivery problems. Perhaps intermediate goods are not being delivered on time to manufacturers, the product defect rate is increasing, or budgets are missing their targets. Every company experiences one or more of these situations, but many fail to take them as warning signs of an impending crisis.

Typically, as the problem grows, management realizes employees are becoming increasingly uncertain about what actions they should take. Relationships with one another and with top management become dysfunctional.

For example, in the early 1990s, high-technology companies suffered huge losses that threw them into internal turmoil. Yet the public had very little warning of the devastating layoff and downsizing announcements that were to come. At Union Carbide, managers discussed safety problems in the Bhopal plant two years before the crisis; they could not decide who should be responsible for instituting safety measures.

A company can determine whether it is in a precrisis or prodromal stage by assessing five specific risks:

1. The likelihood that the situation or issue will escalate in intensity.
2. The likelihood that the situation or issue will come under intense scrutiny by government or the media.
3. The likelihood that the situation or issue will interfere with the company's normal business operations.
4. The likelihood that the situation or issue will harm the company's or management's positive image.
5. The likelihood that the company's bottom line will be damaged.[24]

---

[22] G. C. Meyers with J. Holusha, *When It Hits the Fan: Managing the Nine Crises of Business* (Boston: Houghton Mifflin, 1986), pp. 4–22.
[23] Augustine, "Managing the Crisis," p. 152.
[24] S. Fink, *Crisis Management* (New York: AMACOM, 1986), pp. 15–16.

If any or all of these risks escalate into developments, the situation is likely to worsen. In looking for prodromes, or symptoms, a company should base its strategy on the old dictum that it is easier and far less expensive to treat a cold than to tackle pneumonia. The important thing is to treat the symptoms early. A good detection system will permit the firm to assess all of these risks. Augustine recommends using outsiders as well as insiders to help assess the situation. He points out that "asking the people who were responsible for preventing a problem whether there is a problem is like delivering lettuce by rabbit."[25]

The Crisis Stage

In the crisis period, the world caves in. This period is depicted in the top-center portion of Exhibit 4–2. It is an extremely painful time for a company. Managers are blamed, the company may lose money, and the problems consume executives' energies. Stakeholders in all quadrants of the stakeholder influence map may be deeply affected. Meyers declares that the harshest reactions to a company's crisis often come from creditors and lending institutions worried about financial uncertainty. He also notes that the attention the company wants least comes from the government and regulators. If the company cannot manage a major crisis effectively, there is a real possibility that the firm will eventually collapse.[26] Both Manville and Prudential Securities are examples of companies that suffered badly while trying to deal with almost unmanageable crises.

The Postcrisis Stage

The postcrisis stage, the bottom-right quadrant of Exhibit 4–2, is marked by radical changes that affect the entire company or even other companies in the same industry. During the postcrisis repair process, new players may gain control of the firm. Huge amounts of money may have to be allocated to battling lawsuits, fines, or remedial publicity. Crisis management experts agree that the bottom line always is adversely affected. Inevitably the news media make invidious comparisons between a company that has suffered through a crisis and subsequent situations with any degree of similarity. As Fink points out, "The sad and frightening truth is, the only thing that will make the media stop comparing chemical plant accidents to Union Carbide's is to have a worse accident take place."[27]

The public measures all nuclear accidents against Three Mile Island and Chernobyl. Dow and dioxin are linked in the Times Beach contamination, Beech-Nut is associated with adulterated baby food, and Morton Thiakol always brings to mind the crash of the *Challenger* spacecraft.

---

[25] Augustine, "Managing the Crisis," p. 154.
[26] Meyers, *When It Hits the Fan,* p. 20.
[27] Fink, *Crisis Management,* pp. 89–90.

Augustine paints a somewhat rosier picture. He observes that the final stage of crisis management is "making lemonade from the abundance of lemons." This stage offers the opportunity to begin the repair process. He quotes playwright Oscar Wilde who wrote, "Experience is the name everyone gives to their mistakes."[28]

Prudential Securities, Inc.: An Internally Generated Crisis

In October 1993, Arthur Leavitt, Jr., the chairman of the Securities and Exchange Commission (SEC) called the settlement against Prudential, "by far the largest monetary settlement in a retail securities fraud case. . . . The allegations set forth in the commission's proceedings today portray extremely serious misconduct which violates that commitment."[29] Only Drexel Burnham Lambert Inc.'s 1989 settlement of $650 million exceeded Prudential's initial down payment. Could Prudential have better anticipated this crisis and managed it more effectively? Did Prudential go through the stages of the crisis, and were the five risk factors apparent? How well did the company fit into the model of crisis management?

Precrisis or Prodromal Stage

If we look at events at Prudential, we can readily see that the company was in a prodromal situation for some time before the crisis erupted. The company was embroiled in scandal as early as 1986. At that time the company settled charges of widespread compliance failures with the SEC and agreed to adopt an effective compliance system. SEC sources reported that Prudential adopted a rule stating that the general counsel had "final responsibility for all compliance decisions."[30]

The activities of the office of general counsel appeared to be at the heart of the new crisis and a key institution in the prodromal stage. In 1982, George L. Ball, Prudential's chairman, CEO, and former president of E. F. Hutton, hired Loren Schechter who had been Hutton's deputy legal counsel. Schechter was, as noted above, responsible for compliance decisions after 1986. Seven years later, the SEC cited Prudential for still failing to meet the 1986 order.

Employees reported that the legal department was supposed to review sales material distributed to brokers. This oversight responsibility included the limited partnership division that continued to supply fraudulent information to investors. In 1990, the firm was faced with a trickle of litigation that widened into a torrent three years later.

---

[28] Augustine, "Managing the Crisis," p. 156.
[29] Eichenwald, "Prudential Agrees," p. D2.
[30] J. Mills, "Despite SEC Accord, Prudential Fights on," *New York Times,* November 4, 1993, p. D1.

In 1990, many investors in VMS Mortgage, a failed partnership, were told by their brokers to send claims to Prudential's legal department in New York. Brochures and promotional material had assured investors that they would get a 12 percent return and full return of their principal. Instead of a check covering their losses, most investors received a letter from the legal department informing them of the name, case number, and court where a class-action suit was filed against VMS Mortgage. The letter did not tell investors that the traditional settlement in class-actions suits was minuscule and that they would receive far less than if they took Prudential to binding arbitration for a full return of their money.

Internal Prudential documents showed that some brokers were told by their managers to tell clients that the class action was their only legal option. Investors and their lawyers found that Prudential's legal department dragged the battle on and on. Even when Prudential lost arbitration hearings, it continued to raise legal obstacles to settlement. The firm adopted the same contentious stand toward release of documents relevant to consumer complaints. Plaintiffs' lawyers often would receive different documents in response to the same request.[31]

In 1989, Theodore Rains filed an arbitration case. He had bought $12 million of partnership interests from Prudential broker, J. Frederic Storaska. Rains sought $3 million in lost principal and interest. The case was still in litigation when the 1993 SEC settlement was reached. Prudential's main outside attorney, Samuel A. Keesal, defended Storaska, arguing on October 25 that "the claims against Mr. Storaska include transactions where no money was lost, or even transactions where profits were made." An expert witness said that Keesal called the SEC settlement meaningless and said it was filled with unproven accusations. An attorney for more than 50 Prudential investors said, "They . . . are fighting investors tooth and nail."[32]

Perhaps Prudential's top management should have been more wary of supporting policies that ignored the 1986 order and approved vast expenditures to fight every claim regardless of size. Although George Ball was pressured to resign in 1991, his legal team remained and continued its confrontational strategy. In retrospect, all the risk factors were present, making a full-blown crisis virtually inevitable.

Risk 1. The first risk—the likelihood that the issue would escalate in intensity—was extremely high at Prudential. The firm's intransigent response to the SEC and investors did not bode well for settlement or resolution of the issues.

Risk 2. Prudential clearly faced the second risk—that it would come under intense media and government scrutiny. *The Wall Street Journal* noted that

---

[31] Ibid.

[32] M. Schroeder and L. H. Spiro, "Is Prudential Playing Hardball?" *Business Week,* November 15, 1993, p. 159.

George Ball had been aware of trouble as far back as 1984. According to the newspaper, Ball who was then Pru-Bache chairman and a member of Prudential Insurance's executive committee, warned of potential "flops, follies, and failures," among the partnerships. This memo came out at exactly the same time that brokers were aggressively promoting the partnerships as safe investments. The Securities and Exchange Commission (SEC) had been involved since 1986 and the media pounced on the new allegations in 1993.

Prudential promotional material continued to tout the safety of the partnerships, greatly increasing the chances the SEC would intervene and the media would use the material against them. A sales script for energy partnerships declared: "Your $10,000 is safe. Why? . . . Prudential Life Insurance Company is the largest investor in their own program. They are putting their money where their mouth is. . . . Wouldn't you agree that's a commitment from Prudential?"[33]

Risk 3. The third risk—that the crisis would interfere with the company's normal operations—quickly became a reality. The company and outside observers were stunned when, in December 1993, Prudential Securities, Inc., relieved Loren Schechter of his responsibilities. An internal memo said he was relieved of his duties "because of the unfortunate and unfair publicity and innuendo in the recent press." Prosecutors advised the following current and former top executives to retain counsel: Loren Schechter; George Ball; Frank Giordano, a former chief of the firm's partnership group and current chief counsel for Prudential's mutual fund operations; and James Kelso, current chief of the partnership group.[34]

In June 1994, some of Prudential's most senior executives were dismissed along with managers of retail branches. CEO Hardwick Simmons sent a memo to Prudential Securities employees announcing the departure of Woody Knight, president of investment banking, equity transactions, and corporate strategy. Although Knight did not have another job, Simmons denied the departure was linked to the recent problems in the company. J. Barron Clancy, director of national sales in the firm's retail division, was moved to a new post that significantly cut his authority. In addition to these changes, the managers of the Dallas, Texas; Chesterfield, Missouri; and Atlanta, Georgia, offices were dismissed.[35]

Risk 4. The fourth risk was that the company's image was at stake. In March 1994, *Fortune* magazine featured an article entitled, "Scandal Isn't

---

[33] G. Steinmetz, "Partnership Problems Embroil Insurance Business, Too," *The Wall Street Journal,* December 1, 1993, p. A.1.

[34] M. Siconolfi, "Prudential Unit Strips Schecter of Legal Duties," *The Wall Street Journal,* December 31, 1993, p. A1.

[35] K. Eichenwald, "Shake-Up under Way at Prudential," *New York Times,* June 6, 1994, p. D1.

All That Ails the Pru." The magazine noted the Pru was "in the midst of a firestorm of bad news."[36] Newspapers and magazines continued to feature stories about Pru troubles. By May 1994, criminal investigations were underway. The same question arose time after time: Did senior executives ignore warnings 14 years earlier about high-level corruption in the firm's partnership division? Prosecutors with the United States Attorney's office in Manhattan tried to determine whether Prudential tolerated wrongdoing by James J. Darr, the former partnership head at Prudential. Darr, who had been the partnership head at Josephthal & Company before joining Prudential, had received questionable payments in 1978. The money, which came from a developer who was selling a partnership through Josephthal, was deposited directly into Darr's bank account. Weeks later, Darr used the same amount of money to buy a new house. Media sources noted that establishing the firm's knowledge could raise the potential criminal liability for events that happened more recently.[37]

Risk 5. The fifth risk was corporate solvency. In 1993 and early 1994 the company was still financially solid with assets of about $163 billion; however, its portfolio was in worse shape than many of its competitors. By June 1994, Prudential Securities was facing costs of more than $1.1 billion. In October 1994, Prudential Securities reached a preliminary agreement with the U.S. Attorney's office. Under the agreement, Prudential Securities escaped criminal charges if it did not commit any future wrongdoing. Experts noted that Prudential had lost a core of investors who vowed never to return. Hardwick Simmons continued to be optimistic about Prudential's future but other observers did not share his view, noting the intense competition in the industry.

By April 1995, Prudential Securities projected costs topped $1.4 billion. Court records showed the firm had made offers to settle tens of thousands of claims from funds in a compensation fund containing almost $750 million. The administrator for the regulatory compensation fund said that as of the third week in April he had received 192,889 claims.[38]

Prudential's woes dragged on into 1996. In May, the New York Stock Exchange arbitration panel recommended that the Big Board's enforcement division investigate whether Prudential had created improper commission-splitting arrangements.[39] Prudential's problems, while not likely to put the company into bankruptcy in the near term, were sure to drag on indefinitely.

---

[36] T. P. Pare, "Scandal Isn't All That Ails the Pru," *Fortune,* March 21, 1994, p. 52.

[37] K. Eichenwald, "An Early Warning Haunts Prudential," *New York Times,* May 2, 1994, p. D1.

[38] K. Eichenwald, "Scandal's Cost for Prudential Tops $1.4 Billion," *New York Times,* April 22, 1995, p. 37.

[39] M. Santoli, "Big Board Panel Calls for Probe of Prudential Securities' Practices," *The Wall Street Journal,* May 14, 1996, p. B4.

Whatever the outcome of litigation, Prudential Securities' reputation had been irrevocably tarnished.

If we examine the model of crisis management, we see that Prudential did too little about point I: detecting, preparing, and preventing the crisis. During its heyday, Prudential Securities and its parent, Prudential Insurance, allowed certain practices that made it vulnerable to criticism when the investigations began. Had Prudential been more sensitive to stakeholders' perceptions earlier, it might have lessened public criticism. It appears that Prudential drastically underestimated the magnitude of the crisis and its potentially devastating effects.

Crisis Stage

At the moment the government filed charges in 1993, Prudential was plunged into a full-blown crisis. The company's determination to play hard ball and ignore problems may have exacerbated the crisis. Instead of taking action when the red flags were raised, complaints were dismissed or brushed off. Employees with questionable ethics were kept in high positions. Prudential continued to reject allegations of wrongdoing.

As late as the end of 1995, Prudential executives maintained they had done nothing improper or unethical. Critics noted that Prudential had a long-term legal strategy of aggressively fighting claims filed by people who said they were defrauded by Prudential's sale of limited partnerships. Seth Lipner, a securities lawyer who brought a number of claims against the company noted that "It's the same scorched-earth tactics that they have been using for years. Despite all their talk about being a new Prudential, they still won't deal honorably with the victims of their fraud."[40]

Postcrisis Stage

Many of Prudential Securities' problems continue; its fines, legal fees, and restitution exceed $1.5 billion. It appears that Prudential intends to maintain its intransigence and reject most charges of culpability. At the end of 1995, Prudential used a legal technicality to avoid settling a class-action suit. The company informed people who were suing that their cases had been settled in a class action of which they had never heard. In a letter to plaintiffs' lawyers, the company said the investors and brokers had failed to mail a note stating they did not want to be included in the settlement of the case.

---

[40] K. Eichenwald, "Class-Action Suit Deadlines Expired, Prudential Argues," *New York Times*, December 11, 1995. p. D2.

Regardless of the fact that many had never received the notice, Prudential stated the deadline for returning the opt-out notice was October 30, 1995. Therefore, if the plaintiffs continued to pursue their individual cases, Prudential would ask the federal judge in Manhattan to impose contempt charges against them. If successful, this tactic would allow Prudential to avoid millions of dollars of claims stemming from its fraudulent 1980s sales. The plaintiffs would be added to a settlement pool with $110 million that would not even cover their legal expenses. Lawyers for the plaintiffs charged that Prudential was trying to sweep plaintiffs into a class action without notifying them. Former Prudential brokers, who sued saying the firm's fraud destroyed their ability to do business, were told their claims also had been settled in the class action for investors. Prudential even declared arbitration cases to be over and threatened to seek contempt charges if the plaintiff's lawyers tried to proceed.[41]

By summer 1996, the company had settled charges with state and federal securities regulators and had admitted committing some crimes as part of a deal with federal prosecutors to avoid indictment. Nevertheless, it was clear that Prudential intended to pursue every legal, or even questionably legal avenue, to prevent plaintiffs from getting compensation.

In August, lawyers for a group of former Prudential clients filed a motion in federal court to allow a lawsuit contending Prudential cheated investors out of full compensation they should have gotten from the fund. The motion said that when Prudential calculated the maximum possible award, it subtracted the value of tax deductions taken by investors, even when the investors deferred the tax obligation to a later year. In one case, Carroll Glaser invested $153,000 in an airplane partnership. After he submitted a claim form to the settlement fund, Prudential told Glaser he would not receive compensation because he had earned a $104,723 profit on the investment. Glaser's lawyer hired an outside accountant who proved Prudential miscalculated the tax benefits. Prudential subsequently agreed that Glaser had a loss of $36,288.[42] It was clear that charges and countercharges were far from over.

The Prudential crisis affected all quadrants of the stakeholder influence map (see Exhibit 4–3). The media concentrated on the plight of the thousands of small shareholders in the internal-indirect quadrant who lost their entire investments. The media also reported on the role of federal authorities, all levels of management, and even stakeholders such as the New York Stock Exchange regulators and legal firms representing a variety of plaintiffs.

---

[41] Ibid.

[42] K. Eichenwald, "Investors Say Prudential Unit Cheated Them on Restitution," *New York Times,* August 2, 1996, p. D2.

EXHIBIT 4–3   Stakeholder Influence MAP: Prudential Securities

	Direct	Indirect
External	Competitors Government Regulators	Media The public S&Ls Other institutional shareholders
Internal	Employees Top managers Board of directors	Shareholders

The *Exxon Valdez:* A Major External Environmental Accident

The potential for industrially caused environmental disasters increased dramatically in the second half of the 20th century. As African, Asian, Middle Eastern, and Latin American nations developed economically after World War II, multinationals set up local factories, raw material processing plants, and low-cost labor operations. Indigenous companies acquired industrialized-country technology that they often used under less than ideal conditions.

When companies use potentially dangerous substances and adopt new technologies, environmental crises are inevitable. Critics of multinationals frequently point to the Bhopal incident as an example of a crisis that developed when poorly trained workers operated inadequately safeguarded technology. It is true that Union Carbide might have averted the Bhopal accident by correcting safety violations identified two years earlier. It also might have managed the aftermath of Bhopal differently or perhaps better. Everyone agrees that companies should adopt systems to diminish the likelihood of disasters. Of course, there is no way for companies to guard against every environmental accident. Once an accident occurs, however, a company should have a strategy for dealing with it and should develop its own internal systems to avoid similar occurrences in the future.

A broad coalition of environmentalists, government officials, regulators, and industry officials point to the grounding of the *Exxon Valdez* oil tanker as an example of an avoidable environmental disaster (see Exhibit 4–4).

Should Exxon have acted proactively, that is, developed systems that identified and eliminated the particular problems that led to this crisis? Did Exxon manage the crisis as effectively as possible?

Chapter 4 Crisis Management

EXHIBIT 4–4 Model of Crisis Management: The Exxon Valdez

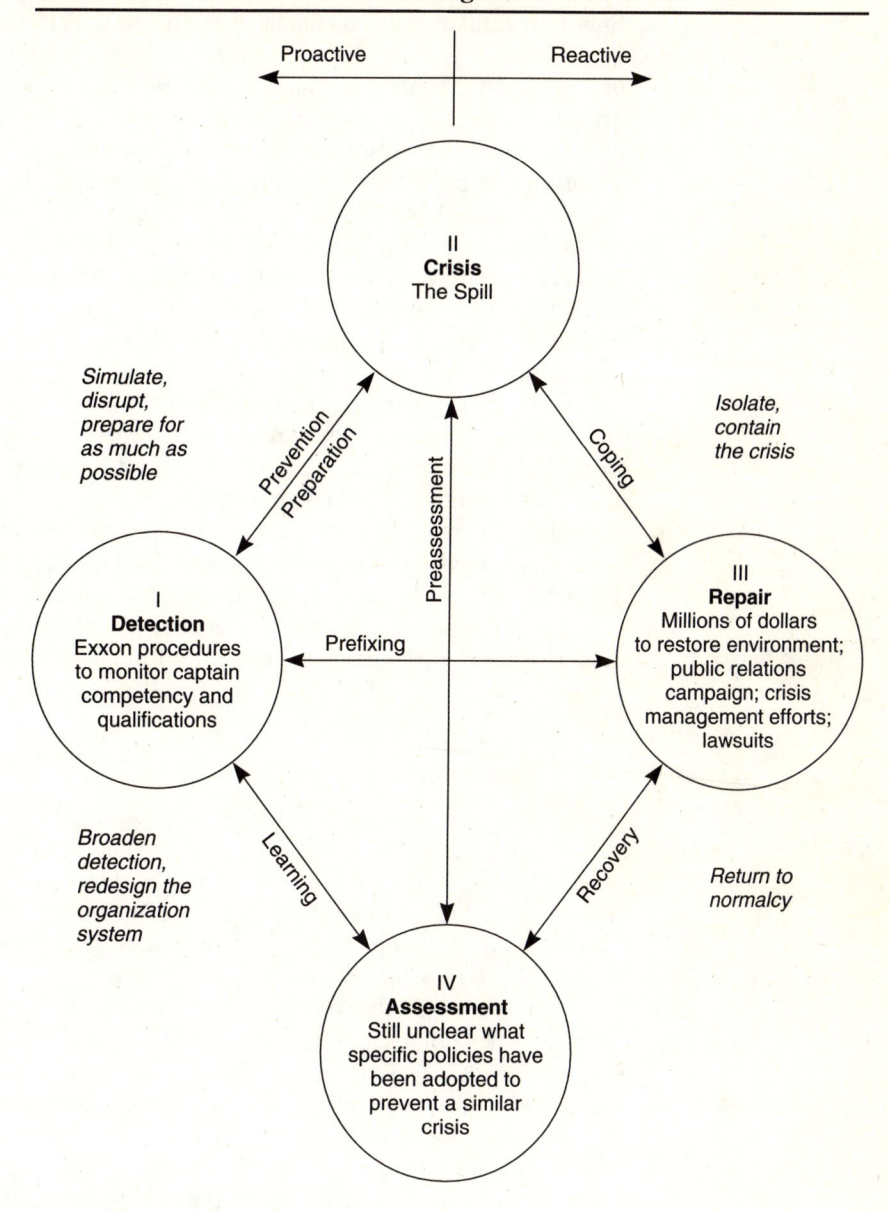

Proactive ← | → Reactive

II Crisis
The Spill

Simulate, disrupt, prepare for as much as possible

Prevention / Preparation

Preassessment

Coping

Isolate, contain the crisis

I Detection
Exxon procedures to monitor captain competency and qualifications

Prefixing

III Repair
Millions of dollars to restore environment; public relations campaign; crisis management efforts; lawsuits

Broaden detection, redesign the organization system

Learning

Recovery

Return to normalcy

IV Assessment
Still unclear what specific policies have been adopted to prevent a similar crisis

The Precrisis or Prodromal Stage

Environmental disasters do not necessarily present clear warning signs. However, major oil companies *always* face the five major risk factors. Their products and technologies make them ripe for ecological accidents. Some external indirect stakeholders, such as environmental lobbying groups, neighboring community groups, and even foreign country nationals, are skeptical about oil companies' commitment to corporate social responsibility.

These stakeholders note that oil companies are vast corporations with worldwide operations. The companies deal in a nonrenewable resource and, some critics say, have a history of exploitation and arrogance. These characteristics make them particularly vulnerable to media attention. In this age of instant communication and satellite surveillance, it is virtually impossible to hide information about an oil spill, fire, or other accident.

In the case of the *Exxon Valdez,* Captain Joseph Hazelwood's history of drunkenness was a clear prodrome. Hazelwood was convicted of drunken driving only six months before the spill, and his driver's license had been revoked three times in the previous five years. In 1985, Exxon put Hazelwood through an alcohol detoxification program but did not follow up to ascertain whether it succeeded. In hindsight, had Exxon had a system in place to track known substance abusers, it might have averted the spill. At least, Exxon could have removed Captain Hazelwood from command of the tanker, thereby reducing the chances that a prodromal situation would turn into a crisis.

The Crisis Stage

When events trigger a full-blown crisis, it is already too late to avoid public scrutiny; but even at this stage, the company has some control over how, and under what conditions, the crisis develops. Once the oil spilled from the *Exxon Valdez* into Prince William Sound in March 1989, the company lost the option of deciding *whether* to respond. Nevertheless, it still had choices concerning *how* to respond.

Critics charged that Exxon should have prepared more effectively for a disaster. They pointed out that it took Alyeska Pipeline Service Company, the consortium that was supposed to handle oil spills, 35 hours to encircle the tanker with barrier booms. Exxon had a crisis management plan designed to contain an oil spill in five hours, but the plan had never been tested. Oil dispersants were inadequate, personnel were disorganized, and radio systems lacked the power to reach some of the containment vessels. Exxon rejected the criticisms, however, maintaining that its efforts to handle the spill were impeded by state and Coast Guard meddling.

Initially Exxon's top managers refused to comment on the spill; then they attempted to shift responsibility for the slow response to others. Chairperson and CEO Lawrence G. Rawl told the media that his company got a bad rap for delays in dealing with the spill, and President Lee Raymond blamed the Coast Guard for reacting slowly.[43] Exxon did little or nothing to mollify angry fishers who saw their livelihoods threatened. Nor did the company immediately respond to the concerns of environmentalists who struggled to save thousands of oil-covered marine animals, birds, and fish.

Critics further charged that Exxon deliberately misled the press and local residents in the early days of the spill when it assured them that beach cleanups and containment were under way. In fact, an Exxon spokesperson later admitted that beach cleanup had not begun and only one boat had been sent out to assess the problem.[44]

Crisis management experts agreed that Exxon's mishandling of the acute stage of the crisis heightened public outrage. When Rawl sent lower-level executives to Alaska to observe the spill rather than going himself, he created the impression that the company thought the pollution problem was trivial. Exxon's reaction, or lack thereof, heightened the public's perception that Exxon was not responding fully to the disaster.

Experts also criticized Exxon's handling of public relations. Valdez, Alaska, the town where news briefings were held, had limited communications facilities. Complaining reporters were told they had to go to Valdez or they would get no information at all. In addition, the company often gave conflicting information in its public statements. One Exxon spokesperson told the media the spill was minor, while another acknowledged it was massive. Crisis management experts concluded that Exxon had made a mistake by refusing to take responsibility for the spill in the advertisement it ran in national newspapers.

Management consultant Gerald C. Meyers remarked that "what we have here, in my opinion, is a classic unmanaged crisis . . . As phony as it sounds, sending the chairman to the scene would have shown genuine concern for what happened there."[45]

The Postcrisis Stage

Fink calls the postcrisis stage the stage in which "the carcass gets picked clean."[46] Hundreds of lawsuits were filed in the aftermath of the Valdez oil spill. The conflicts among local residents, Native Americans, environmentalists, state and government officials, and Exxon dragged on and on.

External indirect stakeholders called for action. For example, consumer and environmental groups demanded a national boycott of all Exxon

---

[43] Wells, "How Unpreparedness Turned the Alaska Spill," p. A1.

[44] "The Big Spill," *Time,* April 10, 1989, pp. 37–41.

[45] J. Holusha, "Exxon's Public-Relations Problem," *New York Times,* April 21, 1989, p. D1.

[46] Fink, *Crisis Management,* p. 23.

products, asserting the company was "a polluter without equal."[47] Residents of an Aleut fishing village charged that fish and wildlife pollution threatened their entire cash income. Internal direct and indirect stakeholders became intensely involved. Exxon union leaders objected to changes the company made to its alcohol and drug abuse rehabilitation policies after the spill. Two thousand Exxon shareholders bombarded Chairperson Rawl with questions at the company's annual meeting. For four and one-half hours they discussed the spill. Some even demanded Rawl's resignation. At the end of the meeting, however, it became clear that management's control prevailed. Rawl was reelected.[48]

In October 1991, a federal judge accepted a $1 billion package of criminal and civil settlements to end the state and federal cases against Exxon. The criminal penalty was set at $125 million, $100 million of which was designated for restitution of the polluted area. Chairperson Rawl personally pleaded guilty to one misdemeanor charge of killing migratory waterfowl. The Justice Department reported that with this settlement, Exxon had paid $3.5 billion for cleanup, claims, and the settlement.[49] The criminal charges against Captain Hazelwood were overturned in July 1992, when he was cleared of all criminal responsibility. The only charge that remained against him was a misdemeanor for negligently discharging oil. Hazelwood's license was restored, and he took a new job as an instructor at the New York State University Maritime College.[50]

In fall 1994, a federal court judge in Anchorage ordered Exxon to pay $5 billion to fishers and other Alaskans as punishment for the spill. This was the largest punitive award ever against a corporation. The decision capped a four-month trial during which the plaintiff's lawyer characterized Exxon as "an arrogant, uncaring, and duplicitous giant with faulty operations." Exxon called the verdict "totally unwarranted and unfair . . . and excessive by any legal or practical measure." Both sides acknowledged that the award was the point at which both sides would begin bargaining.[51]

Negotiations over the verdict dragged on. In June 1996, U.S. Judge H. Russel Holland of Anchorage ruled that Exxon had designed a secret arrangement through which the company tried to redirect back to itself hundreds of millions of dollars from the $5 billion in the punitive damage verdict. The judge found that Exxon had entered a secret agreement with seven Seattle

---

[47] P. Shabecoff, "Six Groups Urge Boycott of Exxon," *New York Times,* May 3, 1989, p. A17.

[48] A. Sullivan, "Exxon's Holders Assail Chairman Rawl over Firm's Handling of Alaska Oil Spill," *The Wall Street Journal,* May 19, 1989, p. A3.

[49] "Judge Accepts Exxon Pact, Ending Suits on Valdez Spill," *New York Times,* October 9, 1991, p. A14.

[50] C. McCoy, "Criminal Charges in Exxon *Valdez* Spill Are Reversed," *The Wall Street Journal,* July 13, 1992, p. A4.

[51] C. Solomon, "Exxon Is Told to Pay $5 Billion for Valdez Spill," *The Wall Street Journal,* September 18, 1994, p. A7.

fish processors in 1991. Under the arrangement, Exxon agreed to pay $70 million to settle the processors' oil-spill claims. In return for the settlement, the processors agreed to return to Exxon most of the punitive damages they might later be awarded. In 1991, the processors could not have anticipated that the Alaska jury would award as much as $5 billion. Exxon then encouraged the processors to claim they were entitled to $745 million, almost all of which would go back to Exxon. Judge Holland called the processors' secret agreement an astonishing ruse meant to manipulate the jury and threw out their claim. An Exxon spokesperson said the company believed the "court's analysis is legally incorrect," and declared Exxon would probably appeal the ruling.[52]

It is still impossible to assess the total cost of the *Exxon Valdez* oil spill. Although years of cleanup and millions of dollars have helped restore Prince William Sound, some damage remains. Marine scientists and environmentalists disagree on how best to safeguard the coast. Five years after the spill, some environmentalists were calling for money to be spent on forests. They argued that preserving the forests from logging was the best way to protect salmon streams and wildlife breeding grounds. Marine scientists wanted the money to go for marine research on the long-term effects of the oil spill. More than 30 separate marine projects were underway in southern Alaska. Hundreds of scientists and technicians worked on projects to clean and monitor shellfish beds, and rehabilitate other natural resources. The General Accounting Office, Congress's investigative arm, reported that of the $240 million paid into a rehabilitation fund by Exxon, only $11.4 million had been spent on rehabilitation. The fund even gave Exxon $40 million for cleanup expenses.[53]

Although Exxon's profits were depressed in the fourth quarter after the spill, the company's resources were so vast that the penalty was merely an annoyance. There is no way to estimate Exxon's opportunity costs of top management's complete preoccupation with crisis management.

In *The First 24 Hours,* Dieudonneé ten Berge analyzes Exxon's handling of the crisis and concludes that Exxon was completely surprised by the disaster. Top management panicked and became paranoid. Finally, he says, "If Exxon did anything efficiently, it was to keep things covered up."[54]

While other observers are less critical, they point out that at the very least Exxon might well have spent the equivalent of cleanup costs on prevention. Although Exxon absorbed the monetary losses with little trouble, its credibility remains in question. If Exxon encounters any new environmental

---

[52] C. McCoy, "Exxon's Secret Valdez Deals Anger Judge," *The Wall Street Journal,* June 13, 1996, p. A3.

[53] K. Schneider, "Dispute Erupts on Settlement in Valdez Spill," *New York Times,* October 16, 1994, p. 22.

[54] Dieudonneé ten Berge, *The First 24 Hours* (Cambridge, MN: Basil Blackwell, 1990), p. 186.

problems, public opinion will turn against the company much more quickly than it did before the spill.

Routine Crises

Every day companies deal with crises that have the potential to be catastrophic but, for a variety of reasons, do not cause serious, long-term damage. Earnings may be affected in the short run, the media may pay attention for a while and then lose interest, or a simple mistake may be rectified. In any event, these cases are far more common than the crises we already discussed. Many companies routinely handle and resolve crises that never become catastrophes. Some companies do not develop the proactive policies necessary to avoid a public relations embarrassment. Other companies are not particularly effective in dealing with the crisis but certain aspects of the situation work against a catastrophe. As long as no one is physically harmed, companies may escape major financial consequences and damage to their corporate image.

Crisis management consultants unanimously agree that this view is shortsighted and wrongheaded. They advise companies in every industry to have teams and systems that are prepared to deal with the unexpected. They note that companies can never predict every outcome and may be far more vulnerable than they think.

Effective Crisis Management

As we have seen, effective crisis management is a skill that companies can and should acquire. All companies, regardless of size, eventually face unanticipated events. A company's survival may well depend on how effectively a particular crisis is managed. Sometimes poor or inadequate managerial oversight leads to a crisis. When events within the firm are not adequately monitored, internal problems may smolder for a long time before they explode into crises. Manville's asbestos crisis and Prudential's investment scandal are examples of these kinds of crises.

The Team Approach

Crisis consultant Robert Littlejohn suggests that effective crisis management "provides an organization with a systematic, orderly response to crisis situations"[55] This means companies should have mechanisms in place that audit or identify risk factors and prodromes. He recommends the six-step process in Exhibit 4–5.

---

[55] R. F. Littlejohn, *Crisis Management: A Team Approach* (New York: American Management Association, 1983), p. 14.

EXHIBIT 4–5   Crisis Management Model

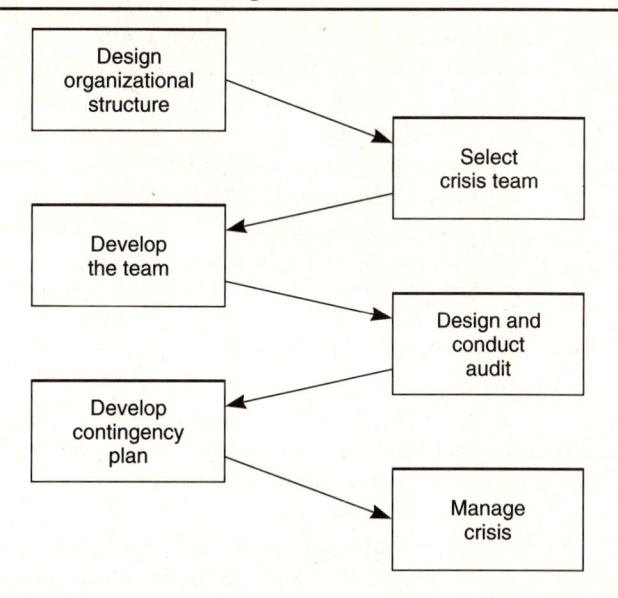

```
┌──────────────┐
│   Design     │
│ organizational│
│  structure   │
└──────┬───────┘
       │           ┌──────────────┐
       └──────────►│   Select     │
                   │  crisis team │
┌──────────────┐   └──────┬───────┘
│   Develop    │◄─────────┘
│   the team   │
└──────┬───────┘   ┌──────────────┐
       └──────────►│  Design and  │
                   │   conduct    │
                   │    audit     │
┌──────────────┐   └──────┬───────┘
│   Develop    │◄─────────┘
│  contingency │
│     plan     │
└──────┬───────┘   ┌──────────────┐
       └──────────►│   Manage     │
                   │   crisis     │
                   └──────────────┘
```

Step 1. Design the organizational structure. In many cases, an effective crisis management system should adopt a matrix structure. This multiple reporting system allows a permanent crisis unit to quickly call on the expertise of different functional divisions. Its managers can tap the corporate skills most appropriate for handling a particular situation.

Step 2. Select the crisis team. In choosing personnel, the company should decide whether to compose the team of full-time or part-time participants. The team should be made up of senior executives, led by the CEO. The heads of the functional company divisions, including legal, financial, personnel, and operations, should participate.[56] The company should also consider whether a problem requires top-, middle-, or lower-level managerial expertise. Finally, it should decide which additional functional divisions should be represented on a case-by-case basis.

Step 3. Develop the team. The crisis unit manager's task is to develop the unit into a cohesive and effective team. The team's major task is to handle the crisis so that day-to-day operations go on undisturbed. Augustine makes some suggestions for corporate behavior in this stage. He says it is useful to have a group working on the crisis full-time so that others can get on with the normal business tasks. While this advice is useful, it does not always guarantee success.

Fred Joseph, CEO of Drexel Burnham Lambert, adopted this model in 1988 when the government charged the company with insider trading and

---

[56] J. Bernstein, "The Ten Steps of Crisis Management," *Security Magazine,* March 1990, p. 75.

mismanagement of junk bonds. Drexel divided its activities into two distinct components: One part tried to conduct business as usual; the other was devoted entirely to fighting government charges. The committee assigned to work on the government charges grew from 4 to 20 members. Executive committees were organized to plan and implement crisis strategy. Despite Drexel's efforts, regulators and lawyers took control of events. The crisis was so overwhelming that daily operations were eventually paralyzed.

In most cases, such as the Tylenol incident, this model works well. The team leader should help the team analyze its goals, decide what role each member will take, and organize the process of handling the crisis.

Step 4. Design and conduct a crisis audit. The crisis audit is a data gathering process that begins with considering the probability a particular event will occur. It is imperative that the data be comprehensive and reliable. The audit also assesses the impact the event would have on the company.

Next, the team formulates priorities in the event of a crisis and integrates them into the organizational objectives. The company's goal is to integrate issues management and crisis management systems before a crisis actually occurs. The team must make sure crisis objectives facilitate the organization's goals at a minimum cost. Bottom-line considerations are extremely important but should not be the overriding factor in determining crisis objectives. The CEO or top manager must approve the objectives and be ready to implement them if necessary.

Step 5. Develop a contingency plan. The contingency plan for managing the crisis consists of five parts:

1. *Introduction:* This is the overview of the situation. In the Exxon crisis, the introduction would have been a company statement announcing that the spill occurred and assessing its magnitude. The statement should identify the concerned parties and the major issues.
2. *Objectives:* The team manager articulates the plan's objectives as clearly and specifically as possible.
3. *Basic assumptions:* The team generates a list of realistic situations the company cannot control that could cause major problems if they occurred.
4. *Trigger for action:* The trigger is an alarm mechanism that activates the plan. The mechanism should be carefully considered ahead of time so that once the plan swings into action, the corporate response is measured and incremental. The plan should be tested to ensure that it really works. Had Exxon tested its containment plan prior to the spill, the incident might have been trivial.
5. *Action:* The team implements the plan.

Step 6: Managing the crisis. Should the CEO always take over crisis management? That depends on the seriousness of the situation and the importance the crisis team attaches to events. It is useful for the team to place priorities on the crisis issues. The team should work toward determining whether the crisis represents a significant threat to the organization as a whole. If a threat to the organization exists, the CEO must participate fully in resolving the situation.[57] If not, lower-level executives can handle the problem.

Augustine recommends three additional actions a company should take: (1) One person should talk for the company to keep the message consistent; (2) a company should not let the public media become the sole source of information for customers, suppliers, and communities since these stakeholders have a special need to know what is happening; (3) a devil's advocate should be part of the crisis management team. This should be "someone who can tell the emperor in no uncertain terms when he is wearing no clothes."[58]

Crises and the Media

Throughout this chapter, we have discussed the dangers media attention poses to a company in crisis. The Dow Corning, Manville, Prudential, and Exxon cases demonstrate the importance of the media to the outcome of a crisis. Media often become the most important players in the external-indirect quadrant of the stakeholder influence map and can greatly influence other stakeholder groups' perceptions of crisis events.

As we pointed out, major crises nearly always require the involvement of the CEO or a high-level spokesperson. Perceptions of the company are determined by the dexterity and expertise with which this person handles the press and television reporters; a company spokesperson can count on facing television reporters within minutes of a breaking story.

Few people will forget the televised spectacle of Warren Anderson, chairperson of Union Carbide, dashing to India to handle the Bhopal tragedy. He was mobbed, arrested, and put in jail at a time when the company needed him to assert control. Crisis management experts agree that Anderson would have been far more effective by controlling events at headquarters until he had carefully assessed the magnitude of the tragedy. He would have avoided being seen as undignified, out of touch with headquarters, and a hostage to foreign interests.

Exxon's Lawrence Rawl, on the other hand, might have been more effective had he spoken from the scene in Alaska. Many people recall Exxon's

---
[57] Ibid., pp. 7–54.
[58] Augustine, "Managing the Crisis," p. 156.

April 3, 1988, belated advertisement responding to the disaster. Rawl signed a paid statement, titled An Open Letter to the Public, in which he noted that the tanker had lost 240,000 barrels of oil, but asserted:

> We believe that Exxon has moved swiftly and competently to minimize the effect this oil will have on the environment, fish, and other wildlife. Further, I hope you know we have already committed several hundred people to work on the cleanup.... Finally, and most importantly, I want to tell you how sorry I am that this accident took place. We at Exxon are especially sympathetic to the residents of Valdez and the people of the State of Alaska ... I can assure you that since March 24, the accident has been receiving our full attention and will continue to do so.[59]

The ad appeared on the same day television broadcasts showed the death struggles of birds and baby sea otters. Slicker-clad people roamed the beaches using rags to wipe oil off endless numbers of rocks. Rawl later appeared on "CBS This Morning" to tell the public it was not his job to know the technical aspects of the cleanup, and furthermore the Coast Guard and the government—not Exxon—were causing the delays. Most important, Rawl refused to take responsibility and admit Exxon had made mistakes that led to the disaster.

Stratford P. Sherman suggests that CEOs and other spokespersons develop and stick to guidelines for handling the press. He observes that in many cases, the CEO should be responsible for press relations and should speak for the corporation. A CEO who does not speak should delegate real authority to the public relations spokesperson. The cardinal rule of press relations is that the CEO or surrogate should be truthful. Sherman says if the company has made a mistake, it should not try to hide it and should never lie.

Jonathan Bernstein recommends that every spokesperson be professionally trained in media relations. He suggests that companies contact their local chapter of the Public Relations Society of America or the International Association of Business Communicators.[60] These organizations offer expertise and training.

In advance of crisis, Sherman advises companies to get to know reporters who write stories about them. They should educate the reporters and give them reasons to respect the company and its management. Robert Dilenschneider, CEO of Hill and Knowlton, concurs. He advises companies to talk to the press after a crisis is over and ask how they could have handled it better.[61]

Michael W. Kempner, CEO of MWW/Strategic Communications, advises companies to develop a media crisis plan as part of a crisis management

---

[59] L. Rawl, "An Open Letter to the Public," *Boston Globe,* April 3, 1988, p. 18.
[60] Bernstein, "The Ten Steps," p. 75.
[61] "The King of Public Relations Talks Damage Control," *Business Marketing,* September 1990, pp. 86–87.

package. He points out that a strategy of withholding comment from the press is potentially more damaging than speaking to the press. A company that does not offer information in a crisis may be perceived of as being guilty of wrongdoing regardless of the facts. Reporters know that full information is not always available immediately after a crisis but they become unnecessarily antagonized if they sense information is being deliberately withheld. In principle, company spokespeople should never offer "No comment," as a response to an inquiry. If the answer to a question in not yet known, the spokesperson should reply that the company is still investigating.[62]

TWA and federal authorities used this tactic fairly successfully in the aftermath of the TWA Flight 800 crash in July 1996. The media and the nation waited patiently while authorities painstakingly tried to determine the cause of the disaster. State, city, and elected officials would have done well to heed Augustine's admonition to let a single spokesperson handle questions. Governor George Pataki, Mayor Rudolph Giuliani, and Congressman Alphonse D'Amato were roundly criticized by victims' families for releasing information incorrectly and prematurely.

In general, the spokesperson should be very wary of presenting views on television unless the presentation can be done in organized, carefully worded, 10-second sound bites. There have been a few notable exceptions to this rule. Johnson & Johnson used television brilliantly in the Tylenol situation. CEO Jim Burke appeared on the "Phil Donahue Show" and also allowed Mike Wallace's "60 Minutes" team to tape a strategy session. When the "60 Minutes" segment aired in December 1982, the public's response was overwhelmingly positive.[63] Burke's message was clear. He emphasized two critical points: (1) If you run a public company you can't ignore the public; (2) institutional trust is very important. Companies have to build trust over time so when a crisis occurs people have confidence in the firm's version of events.

Companies should ensure that their side of the story gets reported. They should not appear before the media and then stonewall them. That tactic forces reporters to go to less sympathetic sources for their information. It is wise to make distinctions among the different media and among publications within one medium. Some newspaper, magazine, and television reporters have particular biases, and a small number of reporters should not be cultivated or trusted. Most reporters, however, are neither friends nor enemies; they simply convey information to the public. Sometimes the company will be portrayed favorably, and sometimes it won't.[64]

---

[62] M. W. Kempner, "How to Handle the Media during a Crisis," *Risk Management,* March 1995, pp. 43–48.

[63] Mitchell Leen, "Tylenol Fights Back," *Public Relations Journal,* March 1989, pp. 10–12.

[64] S. P. Sherman, "Smart Ways to Handle the Press," *Fortune,* June 19, 1989, pp. 69–75.

Kempner suggests companies set up a system to handle the media. A company should have a communications team that creates lists of the reporters who cover a story for local, regional, national newspapers, television, and radio stations. The team should create and nurture a positive relationship with these reporters. When a crisis occurs, the company already knows how to reach them quickly.

The physical conditions in which a news conference is staged should be set up within the first 48 hours. A communications professional should oversee all logistics including lighting, loudspeaker systems, facilities for television cameras, a press room with fax machines, telephones, and outlets for reporters' laptop computers. Sometimes a nearby conference center or hotel has facilities that are useful in an emergency. The company should have ready a crisis media kit that may include videotaped clips of company operations. Often it is not the crisis that causes the company to suffer, it is poor handling of the crisis.[65]

Summary

More and more frequently, companies have to deal with crises that can have catastrophic consequences for them and their stakeholders. The eventual outcome of a crisis may rest heavily on stakeholders' perceptions of the company's culpability and on the public response by its top management. Exxon management's inept response to the grounding of the *Valdez* points out the importance of implementing crisis management systems before the problem occurs.

Crises evolve through three basic stages: During the first period, the precrisis or prodromal stage, companies should be aware of the five major risks. Often potential crises can be avoided if these warnings are heeded. If the situation goes unremedied, the second stage, the crisis stage, occurs. At this point it is too late to avoid public scrutiny. In the third, or postcrisis stage, lawsuits, government intervention, and monetary losses may threaten the company's survival. In all these stages, management has some control over how events will unfold. The degree of control is tied to the strength of stakeholders in each quadrant of the stakeholder influence map.

Companies can put in place systems to enhance their chances of recovering from their crises and minimizing financial consequences. A six-step team approach helps a company meet a crisis in an orderly and systematic way. Expert media management often makes the difference between a successful presentation of the company's position and a bumbling, damaging interaction. All companies should train spokespeople to discriminate among media, learn presentation techniques, and maximize the likelihood that the company's activities are shown in the best possible light.

---

[65] Kempner, "How to Handle," p. 48.

Questions

1. What are differences between issues management and crisis management?
2. What are the three stages of a crisis?
3. Discuss the five risk factors that signal a potential crisis.
4. What steps can companies take to handle potential crises? Which organizational structures are most effective in dealing with crisis management?
5. Should companies deliberately foster relationships with media representatives? If so, what kinds of interactions are most appropriate?

Project

1. Get into the Internet and go to this URL site: http:www.panact.com. PANACT is a consulting firm specializing in crisis management. It recommends publications and useful material on crisis management.
2. Using a search engine such as Alta Vista or Hotbot, type in "Crisis Management." You will get thousands of sources to explore.

BETA CASE 4
CRISIS MANAGEMENT

Don Drees and Brian Madison stowed their garment bags in the airplane's overhead compartment, buckled their seat belts, and gratefully accepted the flight attendant's offer of orange juice. They were on their way to a meeting of top managers of major pharmaceutical firms in Seattle. As the plane sat on the runway, heat shimmered off the cement, making the cabin uncomfortably warm. Drees and Madison agreed they would rather have been almost anywhere else on this sticky July morning.

Yesterday's events had put them both into a thoroughly irritable frame of mind. Their moods did not improve as they scanned *The Wall Street Journal*. The lead article in the second section reported on a consumer advocate group's charges yesterday. Dr. Hayes Adams, president of Citizens for Informed Healthcare (CFIH), asked Dr. David Kessler, the commissioner of the Food and Drug Administration (FDA), to open an immediate investigation of Beta Pharmaceuticals.

Adams charged that Beta had criminally withheld crucial safety data about its anesthetic drug, Beltane. Adams told *The Wall Street Journal,* "If justice prevails, the investigation will result in the criminal conviction of Beta for violation of the laws concerning the timely reporting to the FDA of drug safety problems."

He referred to a memorandum from two doctors in Wisconsin who wrote they were no longer using the drug because they could not easily control the dose they gave their patients. "In some cases," they wrote, "we have found that the initial strength allowed oversedation too easily."

Beltane had been approved for marketing in 1987 as an injectable anesthetic. Surgeons and dentists used Beltane for uncomfortable procedures like gum surgery and bronchoscopy. Patients under the anesthetic were not really unconscious; rather, they were in a sort of twilight sleep.

Drees and Madison were aware that some doctors saw problems in Beltane's concentration levels. Because the drug was used for conscious sedation in the doctor's office, usually an anesthesiologist was not present. In a few cases, doctors and dentists reported that patients had gone into cardiac arrest and could not be resuscitated.

When these reports started coming in a year earlier, Joan McCarthy had issued a statement that Beta had every reason to believe the drug was safe and that its concentration levels were appropriate for its use. McCarthy denied any direct causality links between Beltane and the deaths. She noted that the drug had passed all of the FDA's clinical and safety tests.

Today's headlines presented a different and much more serious problem, Drees and Madison concluded. The newspaper attention was potentially very harmful. Even worse was Adams' assertion that Beta had suppressed internal documents acknowledging the problem. Although they knew the leaked memo had come from a disgruntled employee who had been fired for incompetence, they were really worried. What response should Beta make to this latest charge? Drees and Madison had to have their strategy in place when they arrived in Seattle.

CHAPTER 5 ETHICS

Managers often find it difficult to make decisions about ethical issues. Ethical standards and norms vary widely among individuals, organizations, and cultures. As we noted in Chapter 2, firms are organizational microcultures operating within industrial, local, regional, national, and even global macrocultures. Microcultures and macrocultures are likely to be based on and follow different ethical standards.

For example, in some countries the highest ethical imperative is to ensure that every member of one's extended family has a job, regardless of the individuals' abilities. In other countries, hiring one's relatives is considered nepotism and is unethical, if not illegal. Religion, family tradition, and ethnic origin further define an individual's values, beliefs, and behavior.

Each firm or organization has its own distinctive internal microculture. In one country, and even in one city, companies in the same industry have different ideas of what constitutes ethical behavior. One firm may allow its buyers to accept personal gifts from suppliers, while another strongly prohibits such behavior.

Some companies do not think ethics are a relevant consideration in making products as long as the products are profitable and meet legal requirements. Other companies refuse to manufacture products they deem shoddy or potentially harmful, even if legally permitted. In the personal care products industry, for example, some companies allow testing on animals; other companies consider animal testing unethical, even though it is legal.

Macro- and microcultures, combined with various managers' unique sets of values, create the ethical and legal contexts for decision making. Each macroculture has its own norms and values concerning right and wrong. The concepts of fairness, honesty, truth, and proper behavior vary from region to region and from country to country. Likewise, various cultures impose different legal sanctions and penalties on companies that violate ethical standards.

CASE: BARINGS PLC

On February 25, 1995, the Bank of England put Barings PLC, Britain's oldest merchant bank, into bankruptcy. Barings' collapse shocked the financial world. Nick Leeson, a 28-year-old futures trader in Barings' Singapore office was on the run. What caused the collapse and to what extent were ethical issues involved?

Barings PLC was a merchant house founded in 1763 by John and Francis Baring, descendants of a Dutch wool trader. The bank financed the British Army during the American Revolutionary War and Napoleonic Wars. It provided the money for the Louisiana Purchase and, in the Victorian era, became Britain's dominant financial power. Barings also became the bank of the royal family and hereditary peerage; for many years it informally advised Britain's central bank, the Bank of England.

In 1986, Britain deregulated its financial institutions overnight in what was called The Big Bang. Using the latest technology, United States, Japanese, and European banks challenged Britain's hitherto staid, highly protected institutions. Despite some misgivings, Barings' conservative, extremely risk averse senior managers created Barings Securities to handle the risky ventures into Asian emerging market equities. Christopher Heath, who managed the securities subsidiary, quickly became Britain's highest paid executive. Barings Securities contributed as much as 80 percent to the bank's overall profit. In March 1993, Heath resigned after a dispute over the bank's strategy and direction. His resignation pointed up the conflict between the old traditional business and emerging new opportunities.

Culture clashes were occurring in banks and investment houses across Britain. Leeson and his colleagues were the antithesis of the dark-suited, bowler-hatted, furled-umbrella-toting investment bankers. The newcomers were aggressive and energetic. The old guard, regarding them as flashy and minimally educated by traditional standards, referred to them disparagingly as *barrow boys,* the term used for street vendors selling cheap goods from wheelbarrows.

Nicholas Leeson was the son of a plasterer; he grew up in the London working-class suburb of Watford, and at the age of 18, went to work for Coutts & Company, an exclusive London bank. In 1989 he joined Barings and was very successful in the rough and tumble trading world. In 1992, Leeson was transferred to Singapore where he quickly became head of futures trading and made huge profits for the bank.[1] These enormous profits, however, went hand in hand with great risk.

Leeson's job dealt with derivatives. A derivative is a contract written between two parties called counterparties. The contract's value is derived from the value of some underlying assets, such as currencies, equities, or commodities; from an indicator such as interest rates; or from a stock market or other index. Derivative contracts are the options and futures traded on exchanges. Futures contracts are agreements to buy or sell an asset at a fixed price on a defined date. Options contracts give the right, but not the obligation, to buy or sell an asset. *Put options* confer the right to sell; *call options* confer the right to buy.

Derivative contracts are also over-the-counter operations and forwards sold by dealers and bought by end users. Giant U.S. dealers include Chemical Bank, Citicorp, J. P. Morgan, Bankers Trust Chase Manhattan, and Merrill Lynch. The term *derivatives* had been extended to a variety of transactions by 1995. "In short, if it's complex, it's apt to get the name."[2]

Lesson traded contracts on Japanese bonds and interest rates. Most of Leeson's losses, however, came from trading on two derivative instruments based on Japan's Nikkei stock and bond market. He sold *put* and *call* options simultaneously that made huge profits as long as the market continued to be less volatile than the option prices predicted.

Leeson was supposed to *arbitrage* or to seek the profit from differences in the price of Nikkei-225 futures contracts listed on the Osaka (Japan) Securities Exchange and the Singapore Monetary Exchange

---

[1] P. Dwyer, W. Glasgall, D. Foust, and G. Burns, "Untangling the Derivatives Mess," *Fortune,* March 20, 1995, pp. 50–68; J. Darnton, "Inside Barings, a Clash of Two Banking Eras," *New York Times,* March 6, 1995, p. A1.

[2] Dwyer et al., "Untangling" pp. 53–54.

(Simex). He bought in one market and sold simultaneously on the other. In this sort of arbitrage, because the margins are small, the volume of the transactions is usually very large. Most experts agree that these transactions are not very risky and certainly should not have resulted in Barings' demise.[3]

Leeson, however, appeared to have gone well beyond simple arbitrage. At some point in the autumn of 1994, he began to gamble that the Nikkei market would continue to rise. In November or December he decided to bet that the Nikkei index would not drop below 19,000 on March 10, 1995. The January 17, 1995, the Kobe earthquake rattled the Tokyo stock market and Leeson's strategy. On January 23, the Tokyo stock market fell 1,000 points. Leeson bought huge amounts of Nikkei futures hoping to push the index up to 19,000. By February 23, he had bought $7 billion worth of stock-index futures and sold $20 billion worth of bond and interest-rate futures contracts. When he was unable to force the market up, the huge losses he incurred were sufficient to sink Barings. Realizing what he had done, Leeson fled Singapore. By February 25, the day of the collapse, Barings had lost an estimated $1 billion.[4]

How could Barings have allowed a 28-year-old trader to get the bank into such a predicament? One reason, according to observers, was that no one was watching him closely. He had almost complete control over Barings' Singapore futures trading. As the head of both trading and settlements, Leeson could, therefore, settle his own deals without oversight. Barings had no independent risk management unit that would have provided an independent check. As a former colleague said, "There was no control system. Nick was the system." A Singapore floor trader observed that Leeson had long been considered a hero at Barings and faulted the bank because "he [Leeson] was given so many responsibilities; he watched the warehouse, the cash register, the whole thing."[5] A former Barings' executive agreed adding, "The bank was devoured by the monster that [its management] helped create."

The media could not agree whether Barings knew there was a problem before the crash. A Singapore-based Barings executive had written a letter to the head of Barings' equities department in London in March 1992 saying, "My concern is that once again we are in danger of setting up a structure which will subsequently prove disastrous and with which we will succeed in losing either a lot of money or client goodwill or probably both." He urged the bank to set up a structure in which Leeson would report to the head of Singapore's operations department, not London's derivatives department.

On January 26, 1995, Barings' eight-person Asset and Liability Committee met in London. The minutes of the meeting showed actions to be taken included, "Leeson to be advised that position should not be increased, and when possible, reduced."[6]

Reports of a February 8, 1995, meeting confirm that Barings knew about the bank's huge exposure but assured Simex regulators that the bank could support it. After the meeting, Anthony Hawes, the group treasurer, flew to Singapore to talk to Leeson and his team. At that time, Barings held $22 billion in Japanese government bond futures contracts and yen-denominated interest-rate futures in addition to $7 billion in Nikkei stock index futures. Barings officers assured Simex officials that they knew about this financial commitment and would arrange additional credit. In fact, Barings did transfer $890 million to Singapore in January and February.

Lisa and Nick Leeson apparently began preparations to leave Singapore shortly after the February 8 meeting. They made arrangements with a moving company to send their belongings to Kent in southeast England. Lisa left Singapore first, going to the resort of Kota Kinabalu in Malaysia where she later met her husband. Early in the morning of February 22, the couple took a Royal Brunei plane to Frankfurt, Germany, where Leeson was arrested.[7]

Within days, Barings' administrators Ernst & Young began selling off pieces of the now defunct bank. In March 1995, Barings was acquired by

---

[3] "The Collapse of Barings," *Economist*, March 4, 1995, p. 19.

[4] Ibid.

[5] J. Mark and D. McDermott, "Barings PLC Officials May Have Been Aware of Trader's Position," *The Wall Street Journal*, March 6, 1995, p. A1.

[6] N. Denton, K. Campbell, and N. Tait, "Barings told Leeson to Cut Futures Contracts Holdings," *Financial Times*, March 6, 1995, p. 1

[7] Internet: H. G. Chua-Eoan, "Going for Broke," *Time* 145, no. 10 (March 13, 1995), access through [http://pathfinder.com].

Internationale Nederlanden Groep (ING) of the Netherlands in a deal that specifically excluded Barings Futures. British and Singaporean government and regulatory authorities began to assess blame. Each conducted its own independent inquiry.

In July 1995, Kenneth Clarke, the U.K. Chancellor of the Exchequer presented a 337-page report to Parliament. The report blamed Barings' managers for failing to do their job properly but defended the Bank of England's decision not to interfere. Clarke maintained that no regulatory system could have prevented the failure. Parliament members furiously debated the role of the Bank of England and questioned the effectiveness of external auditing by Coopers & Lybrand in London and Singapore.[8]

The Singapore government blasted Barings' management and its outside auditors in its own report issued in October. Investigators charged that Barings' management did not understand the futures industry and did not develop internal controls. The report charged that Barings' failure to supervise Leeson gave rise to "a strong inference that key individuals of the Barings Group's management were grossly negligent, or willfully blind and reckless to the truth."[9]

On October 16, 1995, *Time* magazine reported that Leeson readily admitted committing the criminal fraud and forgery that destroyed Barings Bank. He was still in a German prison fighting a losing battle to stay in Germany. A week earlier the German Higher Regional Court ruled that he could be extradited on 11 of the 12 charges brought by the Singaporean authorities. Although Leeson offered to plead guilty to charges in Britain, the British government refused to let him return, concluding that Singapore was where most of the criminal activity had taken place.[10]

Having exhausted his legal right to stay in Germany, Leeson was sent back to Singapore to face fraud charges. He agreed to trade details implicating former Barings colleagues in return for dismissal of nine outstanding charges. Pleading guilty to two counts of fraud and forgery, he admitted he had falsified a funds-transfer statement to Coopers & Lybrand and he had lied to Simex about $115 million in market positions. The judge sentenced Leeson to six and one-half years in Singapore's Changi prison.[11]

The court battles over Barings and its assets continue. In August 1996, the *Financial Times* reported that the British High Court ruled ING Barings did not have primary claim on $47 million returned by Simex to Barings Futures. It ruled that accounting firm Ernst & Young, which employed Barings' administrators, was first in line for the cash. As noted earlier, ING Barings was specifically prevented from acquiring Barings Futures after the collapse and, therefore, was not what Ernst & Young called a conventional creditor.[12]

---

[8] J. Gapper and J. Blitz, "Controls Failure Sank Barings," *Financial Times,* July 19, 1995, p. 1.

[9] J. Mark, "Singapore Blasts Barings Management," *The Wall Street Journal,* October 18, 1995, p. A16.

[10] Internet: B. Hillenbrand "Losing One's Barings," *Time* 146, no. 16 (October 16, 1995), access through [http://pathfinder.com].

[11] Internet: F. Gibney, Jr.,"Leeson's Last Deal," *Time* 146, no. 24 (December 11, 1995), access through [http://pathfinder.com].

[12] J. Gapper, "Barings Creditors Row over Cash," *Financial Times,* August 2, 1996, p. 7.

Questions

1. What responsibility did Barings' managers have to assess and monitor Leeson's ethics?

2. What responsibility, if any, did outside auditors such as Coopers & Lybrand have in uncovering the fraud? What was Ernst and Young's responsibility?

3. Could Barings have drawn up an ethical code to prevent the collapse?

4. Why do you think Barings, Sumitomo, and Daiwa have had these ethics problems? Are there issues particular to the banking and securities industries?

The Background of the Ethics Debate

Business ethics became a major issue in the mid-1960s after the publication of Ralph Nader's *Unsafe at Any Speed*. Nader, a self-appointed consumer activist, accused General Motors of knowingly developing and selling a poorly designed and dangerous car. Traditional economic-based discussions of free market ideology, supply and demand, and profit maximization did not address stakeholder concerns about this kind of ethical issue.

The 1970s brought new scrutiny of U.S. corporate activities. Foreign bribery, employment discrimination, false advertising, and pollution were the decade's dominant issues. When American companies were caught paying huge bribes to foreign political parties and officials, Congress passed the Foreign Corrupt Practices Act (1977). In the same year, Congress also responded to the Arab boycott of U.S. firms doing business with Israel by passing the Antiboycott Bill.

Environmental issues also came to the fore in the 1970s with the Love Canal problem in New York State. For a decade, beginning in the mid-1940s, Hooker Chemical Company had dumped its toxic waste into Love Canal. The City of Niagara Falls purchased the land from Hooker for $1 in 1953. Despite Hooker's warning about chemical contamination, the city built a school and subdivided the rest of the land into housing and shopping center plots. Throughout the 1970s, unusually heavy rains accelerated erosion and brought chemicals oozing to the surface. By 1979, the community was suffering an exceptionally high percentage of health problems. On May 21, 1980, President Jimmy Carter signed an emergency order that forced families living on the Love Canal to abandon their homes.

Who was responsible for telling residents the area was contaminated? Did Hooker Chemical Company do everything possible to warn residents and developers? Did the Niagara Falls board of education act ethically in building a school on the land despite warnings of contamination?

In the early 1980s, Ford Motor Company came under attack for its handling of the Pinto issue. Pinto gas tanks exploded when the cars were hit from behind. Ford denied any wrongdoing, but there was compelling evidence that the company knew of the problem and did nothing to remedy it. In addition to product safety, occupational health and safety and corporate governance were added to the list of the decade's ethical issues.

In the 1990s, issues concerning business ethics centered around the environment, privacy, and financial governance. Although no data supported an increased incidence of corporate crime in the 1980s, the public outcry was dramatically louder. People were intensely skeptical of the efficacy of corporate ethical standards and behavior of corporations and their managers.

In 1991, at least 20 companies whose stock was traded on national exchanges disclosed serious problems in their past financial statements. The research service, Securities Class Action Alert, reported it had seen a substantial rise in lawsuits charging "significant fraud and failures to disclose losses or poor earnings." Fraud cases seemed to increase when a strong stock market was accompanied by a weak economy. Investors, especially institutional investors, bid up the stock of those companies that appeared financially sound and predicted strong performance. It was therefore very tempting for a financially shaky or poorly performing company to hide its weaknesses.

In the aftermath of the S&L debacle, the Drexel Burnham Lambert insider trading scandal, and the Prudential fraud situation, stakeholders questioned the ethical underpinnings of America's most powerful corporations and industries and raised questions about corporate ethical performance. Each group of stakeholders had a different perspective and agenda.

For example, in the early 1990s, medical and pharmaceutical companies came under attack for exploiting the public by charging exorbitant prices for drugs. The companies defended their pricing structures, declaring they needed the profits to plow back into research. Patients blamed health care providers, drug companies, and the government for an inadequate safety net and high drug prices.

In another case, environmental stakeholders argued that uncontrolled logging of Pacific Northwest forests was unethical. One group was concerned about the survival of the spotted owl. Another group railed against cutting down yew trees just for their bark, the main ingredient in the ovarian cancer drug Taxol. In the 1992 election campaign, Republican party pundits and forest industry stakeholders stressed the need to protect logging jobs at virtually any cost. President George Bush told Northwest loggers that if Governor Bill Clinton were elected president, they would be up to their necks in owls but would have no jobs. Despite Bush's prediction, Clinton carried the states of Washington and Oregon in the November election.

Although there was no resolution to the owl controversy, the Taxol situation was solved satisfactorily. Between 1992 and 1993, drug makers and lumber companies collaborated to study the drug's properties. They found that a hybrid of European and Japanese yews could produce a semisynthetic version of Taxol; moreover, manufacturers could use the entire tree, not just the bark.

In 1993, Weyerhaeuser harvested the first batch of nursery-grown yews. Late in 1995, the company harvested 12 million two-foot-high yews, ground them into sawdust, and sent them off to Bristol-Myers Squibb to be made into Taxol. At first the price of the drug was extremely high because there was no competition. The U.S. government gave Bristol-Myers Squibb exclusive access to the National Cancer Institute Taxol research program, the rights to harvest yews on federal lands, and exclusive marketing rights for the drug. In return, Bristol-Myers Squibb did all the initial commercial development of the drug. With the end of this exclusive arrangement in 1997, market forces and competition are expected to drive the price down and the supply up.[13]

---

[13] E. A. Robinson, "Owls, Trees, and Ovarian Cancer," *Fortune*, February 5, 1996, p. 49.

When economic times are turbulent, as they have been since the mid-1980s, stakeholders ask whether society's basic institutions, such as business and government, are working as well as they should be. People are deploring the decline in moral and social standards in all societal institutions but seem to have adjusted their behavior to standards that seem quite different than in earlier decades.

A 1995 national survey of 4,035 workers revealed that employees observed a significant amount of ethical misconduct on the job. A Washington-based Ethics Resource Center survey reported that nearly one-third of employees had witnessed misconduct they thought violated company policy or the law. One-third of the employees also reported they believed management pressured them to violate company policy to achieve business objectives. Fewer than half reported the transgressions to the company saying they feared retaliation.[14] Had employee behavior and expectations really changed from earlier years?

Craig P. Dunn asks whether moral standards really have changed over time. Was once acceptable corporate behavior now unacceptable or even criminal? Do stakeholders believe corporate behavior today is fundamentally different from earlier times?[15]

Dunn concludes that the answers to these questions are found in analyzing the behavior of managers. He asserts that corporations themselves are morally neutral, but their structures may entice managers to set aside moral and ethical considerations. Dunn turns the ethics debate on the following observations:

> Because corporate [managers] have no clear burden for actions taken on behalf of the firm, corporate decision making seems to be devoid of any moral "flavor." . . . A radical rethinking of the basic charter of corporate governance is afoot . . . Corporations failing to institutionalize . . . changes, though hardly wicked in principle will nonetheless continue to promote wickedness in practice.[16]

Clearly stakeholders do have different expectations than in decades past. They receive more information about corporate activities and are more skeptical about corporate actions. All the major television networks produce investigative reporting shows for prime-time viewing. For example, in December 1992, NBC's "Prime Time Live" reported that Wal-Mart's Made in America campaign was a sham. Most of its clothing, although advertised as American made, actually came from Asia. To make matters worse, child labor was used to sew many of the garments. Viewer response was so immediate and overwhelmingly negative that Wal-Mart issued an immediate public apology and vowed to make its advertising more accurate.

---

[14] "Workers Pressured to Ignore Violations," *USA Today,* August 22, 1995, p. 4.

[15] C. P. Dunn, "Are Corporations Inherently Wicked," *Business Horizons,* July–August 1991, pp. 3–8.

[16] Ibid., p. 8.

Wal-Mart reassurances seemed hollow in April 1996, when talk show host Kathie Lee Gifford was attacked by the National Labor Committee (NLC), a human-rights monitoring group. Charles Kernaghan, the NLC's executive director, charged that child labor in Honduras and in U.S.-based sweatshops produced Kathie Lee's line of garments that was sold by Wal-Mart nationwide.

Ms. Gifford was enraged at the implication that she condoned the situation. Noting that she had donated about $1 million of her $9 million profit to the New York-based Association to Benefit Children, Kathie Lee asserted that her goal in signing on with Wal-Mart was to provide funding for child-centered charitable causes.

Kathie Lee Gifford received far more media attention than Wal-Mart even though she disclaimed any knowledge of the manufacturing process. The media jumped on the suggestion that a celebrity profited from unethical practices but seemed much less concerned about Wal-Mart's involvement.

Wal-Mart, which claimed it did not accept garments from sweatshops, nevertheless ended its relations with the middleman who had brokered the contract. The company also promised quarterly inspections of all Kathie Lee brand manufacturers. Jay Allen, a Wal-Mart vice president asserted that the problem of sweatshops was industrywide. Pointing out that vendors in the United States, Mexico, Nicaragua, and parts of Asia used multiple subcontractors, Allen argued it was very difficult to discover which used sweatshops. A spokesperson for the needle-trades union UNITE, rejected his argument. He maintained that when a job is bid at an extremely low price, that work is going to a sweatshop.[17]

Fortune finds that the public is extremely cynical concerning the ethics of corporations. Echoing these findings and noting that corporations are facing a new crisis in business ethics, Kenneth Labich attributes the eruption of questionable and even criminal corporate behavior to several factors. In his view, the causes of unethical behavior in the 1990s differ from those in the 1980s. Today's managers are not merely greedy; they fear losing their jobs in an economic recession or corporate downsizing. They face a climate of increasing pressure to perform. For many managers, Labich says, inflating figures or fudging reports seems the only route to personal survival.[18]

Daniel Yankelovich, the marketing and opinion researcher, observes that workers' commitment to employers has dropped dramatically since the early 1990s. As the social contract between companies and their employees disappears, employees look out for their own careers and job opportunities. A young manager declared, "We're cold and calculating and looking out for ourselves. If the economy picked up, I'd consider a job elsewhere much sooner than before. I wouldn't bat an eye."[19]

---

[17] Internet: R. Howe, "Labor Pains," *People*, access through [http://pathfinder.com/@@S6tLZgcATwTZt504/people/960610/features/kathie.html].

[18] K. Labich, "The New Crisis in Business Ethics," *Fortune*, April 20, 1992, p. 167.

Ethics consultant Barbara Ley Toffler says the present corporate climate is extremely destructive. Because the effects of ethical lapses are not immediately obvious, people rationalize their behavior. Eventually, however, "a kind of moral rot can set in."[20] When that happens, people become frightened and corporate innovation is stifled.

Ethics and the elements that create an ethical corporate climate are hotly debated. As the following section illustrates, the current business ethics discussion rests on a variety of ideological arguments that has evolved over the past two decades.

Ideological Arguments

Stakeholders and managers have long debated what elements constitute corporate ethical behavior. All agree that business is an economic transaction, but they differ on the roles values and ethics play in this transaction. This section explores some of the conflicting viewpoints.

Milton Friedman's perspective lies at one end of the spectrum. In his essay, "The Social Responsibility of Business Is to Increase Its Profits," Friedman asserts that executives have only to make a profit and to obey the law.[21]

Douglas S. Sherwin acknowledges Friedman's perspective, but his view is more subtle and complex. He says owners, employees, and customers together form an interdependent system. Each of the three groups is essential to an enterprise's survival. Sherwin concludes that ensuring economic survival and profit in the short run is not management's only function, because long-run economic performance requires attention to the needs of all three groups.

Sherwin acknowledges that business is an economic transaction but points out that it cannot operate without values. Its values come from top managers who must understand the concept of business as "a system of equal, necessary, and interdependent members." Profit, he says, is not the sole purpose of business. Rather, the purpose of business is equitable distribution of benefits and rewards to all stakeholders, because "if managers do not manage business as a system, some members of the system will reduce the values of their contributions, economic performance will suffer, and society's purpose for the business institution will be compromised."[22]

---

[19] B. O'Reilly, "New Deal: What Companies and Employees Owe One Another," *Fortune,* June 13, 1994, pp. 44–47, 50, 52.

[20] Labich, "The New Business Crisis," p. 172.

[21] W. D. Litzinger and T. E. Schaefer, "Business Ethics Bogeyman: The Perpetual Paradox," *Business Horizons,* March–April 1987, p. 18.

[22] D. S. Sherwin, "The Ethical Roots of the Business System," in *Contemporary Moral Controversies in Business,* ed. A. P. Iannone (New York: Oxford University Press, 1989), pp. 35–43.

Ethics or moral principles help managers connect the purpose of business to the values business leaders should adopt. A top manager's individual cultural values and society's cultural values sometimes support and sometimes oppose each other. The underlying ethical duty of top management, according to Sherwin, is to join with other stakeholder leaders "to make public policy affecting business more reflective of the needs and desires of American society."[23]

In making a case for corporate social responsibility, Henry Mintzberg calls the Friedman argument utterly false. In his view, one cannot make a tidy distinction between private economic goals and public social goals. When a large corporation makes an important decision to introduce a new product line or close a division, it generates myriad social consequences. There is no such thing as a purely economic strategic decision in a large, divisionalized corporation.

Mintzberg warns that socially responsible behavior by business is not a solution to society's ills. Social responsibility has an important place alongside public policy to "tilt the efforts of a corporation toward what is useful to society, instead of what is useless or destructive." Commitment and personal ethics are the bases for true corporate responsibility. Managerial ethics can raise the level of corporate responsibility and galvanize the energy and ethics of the critical group of stakeholders, the employees.

John Dobson tries to reconcile the two apparently opposing views of the primary objective of a business organization. He points out corporate managers are taught that their first task is to maximize shareholder profit. At the same time, they are encouraged to adhere to company ethics policies. These objectives are not necessarily in conflict. The two motivations can be reconciled by a company's desire to build and maintain its reputation. According to Dobson, a company's reputation is an implicit contractual enforcement mechanism built on four key characteristics:

1. A firm can have several reputations for different attributes.
2. A firm builds a reputation by demonstrating a consistent mode of behavior to its stakeholders (e.g., customers, creditors, or shareholders).
3. The building or maintaining of a reputation can require net expenditures in the short run, presumably in the expectation of net revenues in the long run. Thus, the decision whether to build or maintain a reputation at any time can essentially be a capital budgeting decision.

---

[23] Ibid., pp. 35–43.

4. A firm's reputation can act as an implicit contractual enforcement mechanism: individuals may reject short-term opportunistic behavior in favor of actions that, albeit costly in the short run, will be perceived as maximizing long-run wealth through maintenance of their reputations.[24]

Other perspectives on ethics run the gamut from purely economic to purely social to purely individual concerns. For example, Peter Drucker observes that ethics is a private issue for each manager; each must make personal judgments.[25]

Vernon R. Loucks, Jr., CEO of Baxter Travenol, says ethics is a matter of trust related to the law and to moral codes of conduct. These moral codes affect all stakeholders of the firm, internal and external, direct and indirect.[26]

Professors at Tulane University's Freeman School of Business conducted a 1996 study in which 400 businesspeople and graduate students were asked to play the role of a fictitious executive. They faced the opportunity to enhance company profits by understating write-offs on a deteriorating real-estate-loan portfolio. One of the investigators, Arthur Brief, found that 47 percent of top executives, 41 percent of controllers, and 75 percent of graduate-level business students were willing to commit fraud to make the bottom line look better.

Brief expressed his disappointment in the findings. Prior to undertaking the research, he believed that individual values made a big difference in how people behaved in the workplace but, as a result of the study, concluded they had very little effect. Brief and his colleagues also found that when a company adopted a code of ethics, there was little, if any, impact on managerial behavior. The study's authors agreed that implementing a code of ethics was an inadequate response to fostering ethical behavior. The entire business climate had to change. Ray Hilgert, a management professor at the Olin School of Business at Washington University concluded, "It is very difficult to show bottom line that you are better off making an ethical decision."[27]

What guidelines, then, help managers make daily ethical decisions and create environments that are productive and understandable to employees and society? How does a corporation create and reinforce an ethical culture with clear standards? Who takes responsibility for creating the standards, culture, and environment? In the next section, we explore these questions.

---

[24] J. Dobson, "Management Reputation: An Economic Solution to the Ethics Dilemma," *Business & Society,* Spring 1991, pp. 13–20.

[25] Ibid., p. 19.

[26] V. R. Loucks, Jr., "A CEO Looks at Ethics," *Business Horizons,* March–April 1987, pp. 3, 5.

[27] D. Blalock, "For Many Executives, Ethics Appear to Be a Write-Off," *The Wall Street Journal,* March 26, 1996, p. C1.

Ethics: Whose Responsibility?

We pointed out earlier that macrocultures help create the climate in which corporate microcultures operate. As people looked at the actions of some of the nation's most influential political, corporate, and spiritual leaders during the late 1980s and early 1990s, many believed direction and purpose had been lost.

Public opinion polls suggested the national character was "wallowing in a moral morass."[28] More than 100 members of the Reagan administration had ethical or legal charges filed against them under the 1978 Ethics in Government Act. Responsibility for ethical standards in business and government was shuffled among schools, government, and business. In a 1987 interview, President Ronald Reagan protested that he was not to blame. "I am for morality," he declared. "In fact, I wish there was more of it taught in our schools."[29]

But a Time/CNN poll conducted at the end of September 1992 found Americans had little faith in their leaders' morality and ethics. Seventy-five percent of those polled thought less honesty existed in government than a decade earlier.[30] Some commentators said the central concern of the 1992 presidential election was to determine which candidate was telling the fewest lies.

Sissela Bok, author of *Lying: Moral Choice in Public and Private Life,* observes that "now there is something strange and peculiar; people take for granted that they can't trust the government."[31] In May 1996, acknowledging public mistrust in government, corporations, and their management, President Clinton asked the heads of 60 companies to come to Washington for a Corporate Citizenship Conference. The underlying message was that companies could do the right thing and make money. The president invited companies that addressed social problems and, in his view, had high ethical standards. In the opening address he said, "What I want to see us do is to elevate the good practices . . . show how they are consistent with making money and succeeding in the free enterprise system, and hope that we can reinforce that kind of conduct that so many of you have brought to bear in your own companies and with your own employees."[32]

Critics were quick to point out that the 1996 election was approaching. Milton Friedman said although the conference was fashionable, it was nothing more than rhetoric. Republican politicians scoffed at the conference's

---

[28] "Ethics: What's Wrong," *Time,* May, 1987, p. 14.
[29] Ibid., p. 17.
[30] *Time,* October 5, 1992, p. 35.
[31] S. Bok, *Lying: Moral Choice in Public and Private Life* (New York: Vintage Books, 1979).
[32] A. Mitchell, "Clinton Prods Executives to Do the Right Thing," *New York Times,* May 17, 1996, p. D1.

usefulness. Candidate Robert Dole's press secretary said President Clinton's advice to companies "made about as much sense as throwing a drowning man a brick."[33] Although there is no way to measure or assess the impact of the conference, it brought national attention to the issue of corporate responsibility and which elements constitute corporate ethical behavior.

Educating Managers in Business Ethics

Terence R. Mitchell and William G. Scott conclude that the most serious threat to American society comes when corporate and political leaders abrogate their moral stewardship. The authors chronicle a litany of corporate debacles that illustrate the problem. The solution, they propose, lies in intensive education programs. They note that schools, universities, and in-company training programs treat ethical and moral issues as problems to be solved. Students are presented with ethical quandaries to be resolved through case analysis or role-playing exercises. In addition, faculty give lectures, guest speakers are invited to give their insights, and readings are assigned.

Mitchell and Scott note this approach, though familiar to students and faculty, is ultimately unsatisfactory. The incorporation of ethics courses or modules in an educational program is only a starting point, albeit an important one. Reform of business education must involve a larger academic community. Major professional journals and professional associations should deal with moral philosophy. The function of ethics education should be "to instill an open, moral, loving, humane, and broadly informed mentality, so that students may come to see life's trials and business's ethical challenges as occasions to live through with integrity and courage."[34]

Traditionally, family, clergy, schools, and increasingly corporations have been charged with imparting a national ethical code. As more parents work longer hours, schools and the workplace bear a heavier burden as the primary transmitters of the nation's ethical values.

What happens to values and ethics when young managers join firms? Does the workplace reinforce ethical behavior? The Tulane study mentioned earlier suggests it does not. This view is reinforced by Joseph L. Badaracco, Jr., and Allen P. Webb who conducted in-depth interviews of 30 recent graduates of Harvard Business School. All the interviewees had taken a course on business ethics in their MBA program and had written papers on ethical dilemmas they had encountered in their first jobs. The researchers wanted to discover whether the following conventional wisdom had any relevance in today's corporate environment.

---

[33] Ibid., p. D8.
[34] T. R. Mitchell and W. G. Scott, "America's Problems and Needed Reform: Confronting the Ethic of Personal Advantage," *Academy of Management Executive* 4, no. 3 (1990), pp. 23–35.

Well-intentioned business executives rely on some mix of corporate credos, statements of their own convictions, ethics, hotlines, ombudsmen, and training programs to set the ethical standards for their organizations. Scholars study deviance, corporate crime, and the effectiveness of efforts to shape a company's ethical climate. In business ethics classrooms, students learn the basic principles of utilitarianism and deontology[35] and practice applying them to contemporary management dilemmas such as affirmative action, pollution, layoffs, and takeover battles.[36]

The young managers reported they were constantly exposed to organizational pressures to act unethically. Most said they believed the pressure to act unethically came from organizational pressure, not character flaws in their superiors. They believed their superiors were responding to these four organizational commandments.

1. *Performance is what really counts:* The interviewees noted that intense competition created overriding pressure. Stress was constant and debilitating. Interviewees commented that their bosses were desperate to keep their jobs, especially if they had families. One respondent said, "I felt that the code was you do what you have to in order to satisfy client needs. Period. If it was illegal, not just unethical, they wouldn't tolerate it."

2. *Be loyal and show us you're a team player:* Less than a third of the interviewees believed their organizations respected or encouraged whistle-blowers. One-third believed whistle-blowing was dangerous. A young manager noted, "People always encouraged them to do it [blow the whistle]. But in every case they were hung out to dry. Then the people who encouraged them backed off. The whistle-blowers were devastated by the experience."

3. *Don't break the law:* All agreed they should avoid stealing, lying, or drinking on the job. Sleazy behavior wouldn't hurt their careers but breaking the law would.

4. *Don't overinvest in ethical behavior:* Few of the managers believed that sleazy behavior hurt their careers. A large number were firmly convinced that sleazy people got ahead faster as long as they were smart.

How important were corporate codes of conduct or formal ethics programs? According to the authors, they made very little difference except when the young managers believed their corporate cultures were ethical. The young managers resolved ethical dilemmas by applying the sleep test. They asked themselves: "If I do this, can I sleep at night?" Religion, corporate credos, or philosophical principles had little to do with their decisions.

---

[35] Note: Deontology presumes the moral worth of an action cannot depend on the outcome because outcomes are indefinite and uncertain at the time at which the decision is made. The moral worth of an action must depend on the intention of the person making the decision. Utilitarianism considers that in any circumstances, the ethically right action is the one expected to produce the greatest net good or to prevent the greatest net harm.

[36] J. L. Badaracco, Jr., and A. P. Webb, "Business Ethics: A View from the Trenches," *California Management Review* 37, no. 2 (Winter 1995), pp. 8–25.

Badaracco and Webb draw some important implications from their study:

- It is extremely difficult to establish sound ethical norms for an organization, especially a large one. The task requires constant effort.
- Many people, perhaps most, are intensely concerned about their own careers and job performance. This creates strong pressures to choose the easier wrong than the tougher right.
- Ethics codes can be helpful, although not decisive, if they are specific about acceptable and unacceptable behavior and provide advice about handling gray-area matters.
- The grapevine quickly communicates situations in which executives have chosen expedient action over the right action. This undermines the credibility of subsequent pronouncements by senior executives.
- Young managers are much more likely to believe that a code means what it says if the code is enforced.
- Ethical actions of senior executives matter far more than what they say.
- It is better for senior managers to say and do nothing about ethics codes if they are not prepared to act on them.[37]

As noted earlier, undergraduate and graduate business schools are taking more responsibility for teaching business ethics to the country's prospective managers. However, educators and executives alike are realizing that to be effective, ethics education must be an ongoing process that continues after managers receive their academic degrees. Ethics education can and should become part of a corporate culture that enhances a company's strategic advantage.

Although most corporate officers and business schools agree that ethics can and should be taught, they disagree about what the content of curriculum should be and who should teach it. In 1989, John S. R. Shad, former ambassador to The Netherlands and former chairperson of the Securities & Exchange Commission, made some general observations about ethical attitudes and how business schools should respond. Shad noted it was not enough for professional schools to impart the fundamentals of law, business, medicine, and government: "The schools must hone their ability to certify that their graduates have the character and integrity to use the knowledge gained for the benefit—rather than the abuse—of society."[38]

Shad made some specific suggestions for business schools. First, schools should use the admission process to keep out students who are ethical misfits.

---
[37] Ibid., pp. 23–24.
[38] J. S. R. Shad, "Business's Bottom Line," *The Wall Street Journal,* July 27, 1989, p. A19.

He did not specify what actions schools should take to screen for morality. Second, schools should develop cases with ethical components for use in every functional area, not for just a single course in ethics. The message Shad wanted to convey to students is: "Those who go for edges—like high rollers in Las Vegas—are eventually wiped out financially."

Shad's advice seems inadequate if we are to believe the results of the most recent studies. In fact, the Badaracco and Webb study seems to conclude there is very little financial penalty in going for the edges. The critical decision is to ascertain exactly where the edge of the precipice is located just before you take the final step.

Badaracco and Webb suggest that courses should focus more closely on issues of right versus wrong rather than right versus right. It is valuable to discuss moral dilemmas in which one genuine claim conflicts with another. Students are more likely to face situations in which they are pressured to do something sleazy than downright illegal. Faculty should advise students how to defend themselves in these situations, explain various ways of blowing the whistle, and make clear the hazards of their actions.

The authors speculate that the business of teaching ethics is going to become even more difficult. Teachers have to draw a fine line between being realistic and encouraging cynical, pessimistic, and expedient behavior. It is still valuable to teach the concepts of deontology and utilitarianism. These principles can help students understand the broader outcomes of their actions and serve as a counterbalance to the sleep test.

Setting Standards for Ethical Behavior in Corporations

Business ethics are based on individual and collective moral decision making at every level in the corporation—from janitor to president. Standards for moral behavior are sometimes informal, but more often they are explicit and embodied in a written document. Before a company can draw up a credo, design a code of ethics, or institute an ethics program, its managers must decide which ethical issues are important to them and how to identify and manage them. Recent scholarship supports the importance of credos and codes if the entire corporation from top to bottom really adheres to these principles.

In her widely read *Harvard Business Review* article, Laura L. Nash suggests 12 questions top managers should pose in examining the ethics of a business decision.[39] She argues that these guidelines are a practical approach to considering the ethical dimensions of a decision. Although this article was written in 1981, it is still meaningful and useful to practicing managers.

---

[39] L. L. Nash, "Ethics without the Sermon," *Harvard Business Review,* November–December 1981, pp. 79–80.

Have You Defined the Problem Accurately? Make sure you have a clear understanding of the problem. The more facts you collect and the more precise your use of those facts, the less emotional your approach will be.

How Would You Define the Problem if You Stood on the Other Side of the Fence? This question demands that you look at the issue from the perspective of those who may question your ethics or those who are most likely to be adversely affected by your decision. Are you being objective?

How Did This Situation Occur? Look into the history of the situation, and make certain you are dealing with the real problem rather than just a symptom. Doing so will help you gain perspective and contribute to your understanding of the views of others.

To Whom or What Do You Give Your Loyalties as a Person and as a Member of the Corporation? Nash points out that "every executive faces conflicts of loyalty. The most familiar occasions pit private conscience and sense of duty against corporate policy. Equally frequent are situations in which one's close colleagues demand participation (tacit or implicit) in an operation or decision that runs counter to company policy."[40] Managers must ask themselves to whom or what they owe the greater loyalty.

What Is Your Intention in Making This Decision? Ask yourself the simple question "Why am I really doing this?" If you are not comfortable with the answer, don't make the decision.

How Does This Intention Compare with the Likely Results? Sometimes, despite the goodness of the intention, the results are likely to be harmful. Therefore, it is important to think through the probable outcome.

Whom Could Your Decision or Action Injure? Even if a product has a legitimate use, if it is likely to harm the consumer by falling into the wrong hands or being incorrectly used, managers should reconsider whether to produce and distribute the product. This issue is particularly difficult. Drain cleaner in the hands of a child can be lethal, while a childproof cap on an aspirin bottle can prevent injury. An assault rifle, on the other hand, could theoretically be used for hunting, but it is more likely to be used by criminals. Thus, is it ethical to sell that rifle even if it is legal to do so?

Can You Discuss the Problem with Affected Stakeholders Before You Make a Decision? If you are planning to close a plant, should you talk with affected workers and the community beforehand to help assess the conse-

---

[40] Ibid., p. 84.

quences? If you are changing benefits packages, should you hold meetings to discuss the changes?

Are You Confident That Your Position Will Hold Up in the Long Run? Can you sustain the commitment you have made? Can you foresee conditions that are likely to make you change your mind? Will today's good decision be tomorrow's mistake?

Could You Disclose, without Qualm, Your Decision or Action to Your Boss, Your CEO, the Board of Directors, Your Family, or Society as a Whole? Arjay Miller, former president of Ford Motor Company and later dean of Stanford Business School, used to suggest the following public opinion test: "Ask yourself, would I feel comfortable in reporting my action on TV?" This can be called the CNN test. Would I be comfortable having Larry King interview me on the implications of my decision? As we have seen repeatedly, decisions that seem very private and confidential often end up receiving full public disclosure.

What Is the Symbolic Potential of Your Action if Misunderstood? The essence of this question is the issue of sincerity and others' perceptions of your action. Politicians campaigning for office engage in many symbolic acts to attract various voter groups. In July 1996, President Clinton went to Long Island to meet with the families of TWA Flight 800 victims. A few days later, he went to Atlanta to open the Olympic Games and later posed with the gold-medal-winning American gymnastics team.

Sometimes symbolic acts backfire and create more skepticism than goodwill. Corporate managers face the same problem; for instance, a CEO may hire a minority member to "sit near the door." When the CEO has not made a real commitment to providing opportunities for minorities, managers and stakeholders are likely to greet the effort with cynicism.

Under What Conditions Would You Allow Exceptions to Your Stand? Nash asks, What conflicting principles, circumstances, or time constraints provide a morally acceptable basis for making an exception to one's normal institutional ethos? For example, suppose you learn that a highly productive and loyal office manager borrowed $250 and subsequently repaid that amount to a petty cash fund. The company has a very strict policy against personal use of company funds. The employee manual states clearly that such actions will lead to immediate termination, without exception. What would you do had the money been borrowed to pay emergency medical bills? Would you act differently had the money been used to pay gambling debts? What if the employee had been with the company only 18 months instead of 12 years?

Benefits of Guidelines

The questions just raised help managers sort out their own perceptions of ethical problems and provide various ways of thinking about them. The process of asking these questions facilitates group discussions about subjects that have traditionally been left to the individual. As we discussed earlier, when these questions are raised and top management does not implement clear policies to instill ethical behavior through the firm, managers are likely to become even more cynical than if the issues had never been articulated at all. If done well and thoroughly, this process:

- Builds understanding and consensus among managers. People from different functional areas discover they share common problems. Raising questions makes the company's values and goals explicit and an integral part of determining corporate strategy.
- Encourages information sharing. Senior managers learn about other parts of the company with which they may have little contact.
- Helps uncover ethical inconsistencies in the company's mission or values statement or between those values and the company's strategy.
- Helps reveal sometimes dramatic disparities between the company's values and their implementation. It helps the CEO understand how senior managers think about and handle ethical problems. It helps the CEO assess how willing and able senior managers are to deal with complexities. It also reveals how individual managers' ethics and values interact with corporate activity.
- Draws out individual managers' ethics and illuminates how they fit into the corporate ethics system.
- Helps top management improve the nature and scope of alternative strategies.
- Gives managers a chance to reduce stress and unload troublesome problems.[41]

Ethics Credos, Programs, and Codes

In recent years, companies have developed credos, instituted corporate codes of conduct, and implemented ethics programs throughout their organizations. Companies are writing ethics codes so they do not find themselves in ethical misconduct situations similar to those described in this and earlier chapters.

---
[41] Ibid., p. 88.

The Wall Street Journal reported in August 1996 that ethics training initiatives have skyrocketed. It is estimated that training is now a $1 billion industry. Hundreds of lawyers, accounting firms, academics, and management consultants have found new employment opportunities and charge fees ranging between $50 and $2,000 per hour. So-called experts conduct seminars in sensitivity and awareness training on a variety of topics, help companies develop ethics codes, and offer experiential seminars. Barbara Ley Toffler, director of Arthur Andersen's ethics and responsible business practices consulting services voiced concern about the ethics of the ethicists. "There are a lot of people out there selling services. Hopefully we're all going to be doing a responsible job and not reinforcing a checklist mentality."

Clinical psychologist Craig Dellinger who helps companies package ethics programs to employees put it more bluntly. "My only hope is that as more players come in, we don't start to prostitute the business." Like Badaracco, Webb, and others, Dellinger stresses the importance of making ethics personally relevant and beneficial. He concludes, "If you only say 'This is going to help the company,' it will crash and burn."[42]

Companies that already have run afoul of regulations and laws or have been caught in unethical behavior, often hire ethics consultants to help clean up their images. *Business Week* outlined this step-by-step procedure many consultants follow in restoring a company's image.[43]

Step One. Hire an independent investigator to issue a report on the misconduct. A credible former government official is a good choice. Of course, an independent investigator may have a conflict of interest because he is being paid by the company under scrutiny. The investigator, not surprisingly, usually tries to put the best face on the situation.

Step Two. Write a new ethics policy. Deliver the document to all company employees with a memo from the CEO instructing employees to comply. As we discussed earlier, employees are cynical about statements from top management when they are not accompanied by rewards for ethical behavior and, even more important, punishment for unethical behavior.

Step Three. Expand training. Hire consultants, buy videotapes on ethics, schedule regular sessions on topics such as sexual harassment, bribery, and other unethical practices. There is no question that companywide training informs employees about what the law requires. A 1995 study by the Ethics Resource Center showed that employees at companies with comprehensive ethics programs knew the law better than workers without the programs.

---

[42] L. Khalfani, "As Employers Focus on Ethics Training, Cottage Industry for Consultants Grows," *The Wall Street Journal,* August 12, 1996, p. 5A.

[43] P. C. Judge and I. Sager, "Ethics for Hire," *Business Week,* July 15, 1996, pp. 26, 27.

However, they reported they felt just as much pressure to compromise standards to meet business objectives. They also reported they witnessed just as much misconduct, a finding entirely consistent with our previous discussion.[44]

Step Four. Install a whistle-blowers' hotline. Make sure employees have the phone number and details of a systematic complaint procedure.

Step Five. Hire a full-time ethics officer. This person's job is to investigate whistle-blower complaints, supervise ethics training programs, and update ethics policies. The 1991 federal sentencing guidelines issued by the U.S. Sentencing Commission suggests that the corporate ethics officer have training in business management, law, accounting, or human resources. She is likely to be picked by the CEO to both develop and communicate the corporation's ethics code. Michael Hoffman, executive director of Bentley College's Center for Business Ethics, observes that an ethics officer should be a person who "avoids harmful extremes and tries to achieve some sort of balance between ethical principles and corporate survival."[45]

Ethics Credos

A corporate credo is a short statement that delineates a company's values. Its objective is to provide a general set of principles and beliefs that give the company guidance. Gulf Oil's Statement of Business Principles in Exhibit 5–1 is one example of a credo or general approach to managing corporate ethics.

The Johnson & Johnson (J&J) credo in Exhibit 2–3 covers the essential issues for that company. When the Tylenol tragedy occurred, J&J managers based their response on the credo. The credo evolved from, and continues to influence, the J&J corporate culture. For 40 years the credo has been, as chairperson James Burke says, "the unifying force for our corporation . . . The Credo is our common denominator. It guides us in everything we do. It represents an attempt to codify what we can all agree upon since we have highly independent managers."[46]

In 1932 General Robert Wood Johnson, the son of J&J's founder, became the head of the company. He was convinced the company's highly centralized structure was counterproductive and broke the company into several independent operating companies. The issue of independence is still very important at J&J. The company continues to be highly decentralized, and top management emphasizes individual autonomy and initiative. As this example

---

[44] Ibid., pp. 27.

[45] S. Gaines, "Who Are These Ethics Experts Anyway?" *Business Ethics,* March–April 1996, pp. 26–28, 30.

[46] Johnson & Johnson Mission Statement, *Johnson & Johnson 1982 Annual Report.*

Exhibit 5–1 Gulf Oil's Company Credo
Statement of Business Principles

Gulf will adhere rigorously to the highest ethical standards of business conduct. To this end the following specific principles are hereby confirmed as corporate policy, effective immediately, binding on all Gulf employees wherever located:

1. Gulf's business will be conducted in strict observance of both the letter and the spirit of the applicable law of the land wherever we operate.
2. Where a situation is not governed by statute—or where the law is unclear of conflicting—Gulf's business will be conducted in such a manner that we would be proud to have the full facts disclosed.
3. In case of doubt, employees should seek competent legal and other advice, which the Company is prepared to make available through regular channels.
4. Gulf reaffirms its conviction that in any democratic society proper and constructive participation in the political process is a continuing responsibility of individual citizens and groups of citizens, including Gulf employees and the Company itself. Such participation, however, must be in full accord with the regulations, laws, and generally accepted practice of the jurisdiction involved.

Strict adherence to the foregoing principles is hereby made a condition of continued employment.

---

shows, the concepts of decentralization and a strong set of commonly held values can be compatible rather than contradictory.

General Johnson's personal belief in fair employee treatment, decentralization, and product quality were the essence of the document he formalized in 1945. The four central responsibilities of what was then called An Industrial Credo were (1) customers, (2) employees, (3) communities in which they work and live, and (4) stockholders.

The J&J credo integrates profit and ethics. When reports of corporate misconduct proliferated in the 1970s, J&J's top managers discussed and rejected the idea of drawing up a more detailed code of ethics. Today most J&J managers report that the credo has a powerful influence on their decision making. It stands for day-to-day values.[47]

Ethics Codes

Almost all Fortune 500 firms and more than half of smaller firms have ethical codes or codes of conduct that provide specific guidance to employees in functional business areas. These documents clarify company expectations for employee conduct in a variety of situations. They also make clear that the company expects its employees to recognize ethical issues in company policies and actions. Generally codes are the most effective way to encourage

---

[47] J. Keough, ed., *Corporate Ethics: A Prime Business Asset* (New York: The Business Roundtable, 1988), pp. 1–138.

ethical conduct; to work as their framers intend, however, they must be specifically tailored to the company's activities. The corporate culture and the specific nature of the company's business determine the exact statements to be included.

Gary R. Weaver writes that managers have a variety of reasons for advocating the development of codes.[48]

- *Codes may be drawn up to manage or respond to stakeholders' demands or expectations in order to benefit, or avoid harm, to the firm.* He notes that the U.S. government's federal corporate sentencing guidelines make ethics codes financially important to any company that may intentionally or accidentally violate federal law. Regulators may be less inclined to supervise a company whose code of ethics includes guidelines more stringent than the regulation itself.
- *Codes may constitute a response to nonspecific elements or issues in the broader business environment.* For example, a code may provide an opportunity for a firm to symbolically address a general social issue such as discrimination or social welfare. The firm's stated position may positively affect external direct and indirect stakeholders' perceptions and expectations. Government agencies, activist groups, customers, and suppliers may be more sympathetic to the firm's activities.
- *Codes may be used to manage or respond to internal organizational dynamics.* Weaver points out that corporate restructurings, total quality management programs, and downsizing may help reinforce company obligations to employees, thereby raising morale. Weaver cautions that when a company includes an issue in an ethics code, the issue becomes more legitimate and important, hence more visible and subject to criticism.[49]

Lockheed Martin Corporation's Code of Ethics and Business Conduct. Lockheed Martin developed a booklet, *Setting the Standard,* that "summarizes the virtues and principles that are to guide our actions in business." The booklet sets the firm's standard for ethical business conduct by explicitly furnishing the guidelines for Lockheed Martin's agents, contractors, representatives, and suppliers. Because the firm operates globally, the code is available in 12 languages in addition to English.

The June 1996 version of the code includes the usual, predictable statements about the company's commitment to ethical treatment of employees, customers, the communities in which it is located, shareholders, and suppliers. It stresses that compliance with the law is a "minimum absolutely essen-

---

[48] G. R. Weaver, "Corporate Codes of Ethics: Purpose, Process, and Content Issues," *Business & Society* 32, no. 1 (Spring 1993), pp. 44–58.

[49] Ibid., pp. 54–56.

tial condition for performance of our duties." It goes on to make a statement about the unacceptability of any kind of discrimination based on race, color, religion, gender, age, national origin, disability, or marital status.

Gulf Oil has explicitly included some areas because so much of the company's business is with governments. One example is a clear admonition to obey the Foreign Corrupt Practices Act, a law we discuss in detail later in the chapter. There are also numerous guidelines for dealing with former U.S. government personnel, making political contributions, negotiating and performing contracts, and giving and receiving gifts or favors.

One of the unique aspects of this code is the care taken to make sure employees understand exactly what they may and may not do and what warning signs to look for (see Exhibits 5–2 and 5–3).

Exhibit 5–2

You're on Thin Ethical Ice When You Hear . . .

"Well, maybe just this once . . ."
"No one will ever know . . ."
"It doesn't matter how it gets done as long as it gets done."
"It sounds too good to be true."
"Everyone does it."
"Shred that document."
"We can hide it."
"No one will get hurt."
"What's in it for me?"
"This will destroy the competition."
"We didn't have this conversation."

Exhibit 5–3 Quick Quiz

When in Doubt, Ask Yourself . . .

◊ Are my actions legal?
◊ Am I being fair and honest?
◊ Will my actions stand the test of time?
◊ How will I feel about myself afterwards?
◊ How will it look in the newspaper?
◊ Will I sleep soundly tonight?
◊ What would I tell my child?

If you are still not sure what to do, ask . . . and keep asking until you are certain you are doing the right thing.

Source: Reproduced with permission of Lockheed Martin's Office of Ethics and Business Conduct.

General Code Contents

Ethics researchers examined 84 codes and clustered the categories of issues covered; see the results in Exhibit 5–4.[50] The majority of the issues fell into three major clusters. The first cluster, "Be a dependable organization citizen," usually has very little to do with ethical conduct. Instead, statements from categories in this cluster exhort employees to be dependable and law abiding. An example from the Bank of Boston's code tells employees, "Demonstrate courtesy, fairness, honesty, and decency in all relationships with customers, competitors, the general public, and with other employees." Codes of service organizations such as banks and utilities are represented heavily in this category.

Cluster 2 is "Don't do anything unlawful or improper that will harm the organization." More than 50 of the 84 companies' codes include statements in these categories. Statements in this cluster deal with obeying the law but go beyond it in categories dealing with bribery, confidentiality, and outside activities. Exxon Corporation's statement, for example, declares, "It is the policy of Exxon Corporation that all of its directors and employees shall, in carrying out their duties to the Corporation, rigidly comply with the antitrust laws of the United States and those of any other country or group of countries which are applicable to the Corporation's business."

AT&T's code of ethics contains overriding principles to which employees must adhere, Employees are told:

- Don't participate in any dishonest, destructive, or illegal acts of any kind.
- Don't use employment with AT&T . . . to further personal interests.
- Don't attempt to justify an illegal or dishonest act by claiming it was directed by a superior, and don't direct fellow AT&T employees to commit such acts in performing their duties.
- Observe all laws and regulations that apply to AT&T's business.
- Don't deviate from Company policies, rules, or procedures even if doing so might appear to be to AT&T's advantage.
- Promptly alert the AT&T Corporate Security Organization whenever any dishonest, destructive, or illegal act is observed, learned of, or even suspected.
- Cooperate with AT&T Corporate Security when alleged conduct is being investigated.[51]

The third cluster, "Be good to our customers," deals with ethical and legal behavior toward direct external stakeholders, namely customers. J. C.

---

[50] D. Robin, M. Giallourakis, F. R. David, and T. E. Moritz, "A Different Look at Codes of Ethics," *Business Horizons,* January–February 1989, pp. 66–73.

[51] AT&T International Code of Ethics.

EXHIBIT 5–4 Clusters of Categories Found in Corporate Codes of Ethics

Cluster 1
"Be a dependable organization citizen."

1. Demonstrate courtesy, respect, honesty, and fairness in relationships with customers, suppliers, competitors, and other employees.
2. Comply with safety, health, and security regulations.
3. Do not use abusive language or actions.
4. Dress in businesslike attire.
5. Possession of firearms on company premises is prohibited.
6. Use of illegal drugs or alcohol on company premises is prohibited.
7. Follow directives from supervisors.
8. Be reliable in attendance and punctuality.
9. Manage personal finances in a manner consistent with employment by a fiduciary institution.

Cluster 2
"Don't do anything unlawful or improper that will harm the organization."

1. Maintain confidentiality of customer, employee, and corporate records and information.
2. Avoid outside activities that conflict with or impair the performance of duties.
3. Make decisions objectively without regard for friendship or personal gain.
4. The acceptance of any form of bribe is prohibited.
5. Payment to any person, business, political organization, or public official for unlawful or unauthorized purposes is prohibited.
6. Conduct personal and business dealings in compliance with all relevant laws, regulations, and policies.
7. Comply fully with antitrust laws and trade regulations.
8. Comply fully with accepted accounting rules and controls.
9. Do not provide false or misleading information to the corporation, its auditors, or a government agency.
10. Do not use company property or resources for personal benefit or any other improper purpose.
11. Each employee is personally accountable for company funds over which he or she has control.
12. Staff members should not have any interest in any competitor or supplier of the company unless such interest has been fully disclosed to the company.

Cluster 3
"Be good to our customers."

1. Strive to provide products and services of the highest quality.
2. Perform assigned duties to the best of your ability and in the best interest of the corporation, its shareholders, and its customers.
3. Convey true claims for products.

Unclustered Items

1. Exhibit standards of personal integrity and professional conduct.
2. Racial, ethnic, religious, or sexual harassment is prohibited.
3. Report questionable, unethical, or illegal activities to your manager.
4. Seek opportunities to participate in community services and political activities.
5. Conserve resources and protect the quality of the environment in areas where the company operates.
6. Members of the corporation are not to recommend attorneys, accountants, insurance agents, stockbrokers, real estate agents, or similar individuals to customers.

Penney Company, for example, states, "Advertising used by the Company is legally required to be true and not deceptive in any manner." The Body Shop notes, "We make a difference to our customers. The Body Shop does not promote idealized notions of beauty nor do we claim that our products will perform cosmetic miracles."

Employee Issues

Employees are expected to adhere to ethical standards and company ideals embodied in credos and codes and reinforced through programs. As we have noted earlier, the degree to which employees do so depends largely on how they perceive the company treats them. Management creates a culture that represents an unwritten contract between the company and its employees. That unwritten contract, along with the written rules, indicates the company's values, beliefs, behavior, and practices. In written documents and informal norms, it states management's expectations about the mutual obligations of employer and employee. When an employee is hired, he enters into a contract containing these mutual obligations.[52] For such contracts to be ethical, the company must meet four major requirements:

    1. Both parties to the contract must have full knowledge of the nature of the agreement they are entering. Often gaps exist between what a company says in its policy and what it does on a daily basis. Despite good intentions, corporations may be unrealistic about their ability to deliver on their own expectations. In an economic downturn, they may be financially unable to carry out their stated policies. When companies change owners, as is now happening frequently, managers may have to deal with conflicting cultures that temporarily preclude full knowledge. Particularly in times of transition, managers may rely on their own imperfect interpretations of company values. Managers' assumptions about the new values may lead to situations in which actions are inconsistent with stated policies or are inequitable to employees.

    2. Neither party to a contract may intentionally misrepresent the facts of the contractual situation to the other party.

    3. Neither party to the contract can be forced to enter the contract under duress or coercion. This stipulation includes manipulation as well as threat. When employees are skeptical about corporate values and the value of a contract, they are likely to be susceptible to manipulation. Other employees have a strong need to belong and thus can be intimidated into behaving in a particular way. According to Manuel Velasquez, "Deception and manipulation are both attempts to get a person to do (or believe) something that the

---

[52] B. H. Drake and E. Drake, "Ethical and Legal Aspects of Managing Corporate Cultures," *Business & Society,* Winter 1988, pp. 109–10.

person would not do (or believe) if he or she knew what was going on."[53] Such agreements are not voluntary.

4. The contract must not bind the parties to an immoral act. Any company that punishes an employee for whistle-blowing or for voicing concerns over unethical practices acts unethically. In general, managers may not require employees to engage in immoral or unethical acts. On some occasions, however, employees go outside the company and expose issues that management has deliberately covered up.

Whistle-Blowing

Whistle-blowing is "the disclosure by organization members (former or current) of illegal, immoral, or illegitimate practices under the control of their employers, to persons or organizations that may be able to effect action."[54] We noted earlier that companies often retaliate against whistle-blowers and many pay a very high price for the decision to tattle on their companies. Some assume that a whistle-blower is a disgruntled employee who, out of a desire for revenge or satisfaction, vents her frustration or anger by accusing the firm or superiors of wrongdoing.[55] A *Fortune* magazine article noted that "nobody loves a fink. A snitch. A rat."[56] A second school of thought views a whistle-blower as an individual concerned about the organization and society. In fact, most whistle-blowers consider themselves to be highly loyal employees in need of legal protection against the companies they are accusing of wrongdoing.

The first legislation to protect whistle-blowers was passed by the state of Michigan in 1981. The Whistle-Blowers Protection Act covered any employee in private industry who was fired or disciplined for reporting to public authorities alleged violations of federal, state, or local law. If the employer could not show that treatment of the employee was based on proper personnel standards, the court had the power to award back pay, the costs of litigation, and attorneys' fees.[57]

This law came out of Michigan's PBB (polybrominated biphenyl) tragedy in the 1970s. Michigan Chemical Company accidently shipped poisonous fire retardant to a state feed grain cooperative. The PBBs fed to livestock contaminated their milk and meat. When farm animals began dying

---

[53] M. G. Valasquez, *Business Ethics: Concepts and Cases* (Englewood Cliffs, NJ: Prentice Hall, 1982), p. 332.

[54] J. P. Near and M. P. Miceli, "Effective Whistle-Blowing," *Academy of Management Review* 20, no. 3 (1995), p. 697.

[55] M. D. Street, "Cognitive Moral Development and Organizational Commitment: Two Potential Predictors of Whistle-Blowing," *Journal of Applied Business Research* 11, no. 4 (Fall 1995), p. 105.

[56] M. Jaynes, "When to Rat on the Boss," *Fortune,* October 2, 1995, p. 83.

[57] A. F. Westin, "Michigan's Law to Protect Whistle-Blowers," *The Wall Street Journal,* April 13, 1981.

in large numbers, Michigan Chemical employees were warned not to tell investigators about the accident or they would be fired.

The number of instances of whistle-blowing in both government and the private sector grew throughout the 1980s, and as it did, pressure for employee protection increased as well. Much of this pressure focused on new corporate grievance procedures and implementation of new internal policies. Historically courts were reluctant to meddle in what they saw as private contracts between employers and employees. With the precedence of the Michigan law, companies tried to ward off further legislation by voluntarily instituting due process for employees.

Lincoln Electric, Donnelley Mirrors, Pitney Bowes, Polaroid, and IBM pioneered this trend. By 1983, they had due process procedures in place. IBM, for example, created an open-door program for employees unhappy about their bosses. An employee initiated the process by sending a message to the CEO. Within a week, a trained investigator interviewed those involved, operating on the assumption that the employee was right. Polaroid created an employee-elected committee to hear workers' complaints. The committee members served for three years. Although their decisions were not binding, management usually adopted their recommendations.[58]

Some organizations still questioned employees' right to publicly identify wrongdoers. In 1983, the National Association of Accountants drew up the first code of ethics for companies' internal accountants. The association urged employees to report improper behavior to their superiors in the company. If the employee is legally required to report a practice to outside authorities, she should do so. However, the code suggested that if the law did not require whistle-blowing and the wrongdoing was not corrected, the employee should resign. The president of the association, Charles T. Smith, observed that "we cannot allow the minds of the public to be poisoned against business because a few businessmen are unethical."[59] In other words, the association believed its members' only obligation was that which the law required.

In 1986, Congress revised a Civil War era statute known as the False Claims Act. This law requires the Justice Department to investigate employee claims of fraud against the government. If the Justice Department finds substantial evidence of actions such as inflated billing or shifting cost overruns from one contract to another, an employee can earn as much as 30 percent of any damages awarded. Between 1986 and 1988, individuals filed more than 75 suits, mostly against defense contractors. In contrast, in the 1970s only 20 cases were filed.

---

[58] D. Warsh, "Employee Dissidents: Once a Rag-Tag Band, Now a Growing Army," *Boston Globe,* January 4, 1983, pp. 45, 49.

[59] D. B. Hilder, "Accountants Code Calls Whistle-Blowing Inappropriate Unless the Law Requires It," *The Wall Street Journal,* July 21, 1983, p. 6.

Some companies questioned the legality of the act. Northrup, for example, asserted that Congress had violated the separation of powers provision of the Constitution by giving individuals the right to sue for fraud against the government. In 1987, two Northrup employees charged the company had falsified tests on its air-launched cruise missile. In July 1989, the government suspended its business with Northrup's Precision Products Division and agreed to help the plaintiffs litigate. In June 1991, Northrup finally agreed to pay about $9 million to the two former employees.

Use of the False Claims Act spread quickly to other industries. By 1991, suits alleging falsification of Medicare bills and environmental permits had been filed. Some likened the law to the Racketeer-Influenced and Corrupt Organizations Act (RICO) that acted as a sword of Damocles over Wall Street. *Business Week* speculated that unless the Supreme Court ruled otherwise, the False Claims Act "would be to the 1990s what private securities cases were to the 1970s and RICO was to the 1980s."

Marcia P. Miceli and Janet P. Near recommend companies adopt proactive policies to deal with whistle-blowers. They say that even if management believes the whistle-blower is incorrect or a chronic complainer, doing nothing is as risky as retaliating. Preventing wrongdoing, or at least reducing it, may be the most effective strategy for avoiding whistle-blowing. They recommend many of the measures we have already discussed in this chapter to implement meaningful ethics codes. In addition, they recommend that companies encourage internal whistle-blowing.

Everyone in the company must understand clearly what activities are right or wrong and what each employee should do when observing wrongdoing. Nearly all external whistle-blowing is first reported internally. This suggests the corporate responsiveness to an initial complaint is key to avoiding external reporting. When employees know that internal channels are effective, they are more likely to engage in internal whistle-blowing. Hot lines, open-door policies, arbitration, and in-house review panels are all effective settlement mechanisms. Above all, management responsiveness is the key to successful internal resolution. Miceli and Near's research shows that the most powerful incentive a company can offer potential whistle-blowers is the willingness to correct wrongdoing.[60]

International Ethics

As noted earlier, countries and cultures have different standards of ethics and business practices. In fact, business ethics are becoming globalized very slowly. Unlike the United States, few countries impose their own cultures' ethical standards and practices on their corporations wherever their companies operate.

---

[60] M. P. Miceli and J. P. Near, "Whistle-Blowing: Reaping the Benefits," *Academy of Management Executive* 8, no. 3 (1994), pp. 65–72.

David Vogel notes, "The unusual visibility of issues of business ethics in the United States lies in the distinctive institutional, legal, social, and cultural context of the American business system. Moreover, the American approach to business ethics is also unique: it is more individualistic, legalistic, and universalistic than in other capitalist societies."[61]

In 1977, the U.S. Congress passed the Foreign Corrupt Practices Act (FCPA). In effect, this act requires all publicly held U.S. corporations to report to the Securities & Exchange Commission all payments of a substantial nature. This act specifically forbids American companies to make payments to foreign officials or political parties. It does allow small payments to individuals if such payments are a normal part of doing business. For example, a company may make an extra payment to a nighttime security guard above and beyond the person's salary if the salary structure for the position in that country is inadequate. This extra payment is a normal part of doing business in developing countries and is permissible under the FCPA.

U.S. companies that violate the FCPA can be fined as much as $1 million. Executives may be sentenced to up to five years in jail and fined. Since the act was passed, U.S. managers have complained bitterly that it places them at a competitive disadvantage in doing business abroad, where standards differ and bribery is commonplace. The reality is that the United States is the only country that forbids its companies from making payments to secure contracts outside its borders.

Transparency International is a multinational organization dedicated to curbing corruption in international business. After assessing the degree to which public officials and politicians were involved in accepting bribes, taking illicit payments in public procurement, and embezzling public funds, it ranked 41 countries. The rankings in Exhibit 5–5 were based on the perception of businesspeople who participated in the surveys. A ranking of 10.00 signifies a totally corruption-free country.[62]

John Strauchs analyzed economic crime in *The Hallcrest Report*. He estimates that U.S. companies lose between $100 billion and $150 billion annually. Bribery, he says, accounts for most of the loss. Secretary of the Interior and former U.S. Trade Representative Mickey Kantor claimed that in 1994 foreign companies paid bribes to win contracts away from American firms bidding for $45 billion worth of international contracts.

Although British law forbids bribery to win foreign contracts, other European countries put winning a contract far ahead of any ethical considerations. The European Union (EU) Court of Auditors estimates that the EU squandered $1.2 billion on fraudulent infrastructure projects in 1994.[63]

---

[61] D. Vogel, "The Globalization of Business Ethics: Why America Remains Distinctive," *California Management Review,* Fall 1992, p. 30.

[62] P. Norman, "New Zealand 'Least Corrupt Country'," *Financial Times,* June 3, 1996, p. 5.

[63] G. L. Miles, "Crime, Corruption, and Multinational Business," *International Business,* July 1995, pp. 34–45.

Exhibit 5–5

International Corruption: A Survey of Business Perceptions (1996)

1. New Zealand	9.43	15. United States	7.66	29. Taiwan	4.98
2. Denmark	9.33	16. Austria	7.59	30. Jordan	4.89
3. Sweden	9.08	17. Japan	7.09	31. Hungary	4.86
4. Finland	9.05	18. Hong Kong	7.01	32. Spain	4.31
5. Canada	8.96	19. France	6.96	33. Turkey	3.54
6. Norway	8.87	20. Belgium	6.84	34. Italy	3.42
7. Singapore	8.80	21. Chile	6.80	35. Argentina	3.41
8. Switzerland	8.76	22. Portugal	6.53	36. Bolivia	3.40
9. Netherlands	8.71	23. South Africa	5.68	37. Thailand	3.33
10. Australia	8.60	24. Poland	5.57	38. Mexico	3.30
11. Ireland	8.45	25. Czech Rep.	5.37	39. Ecuador	3.19
12. United Kingdom	8.44	26. Malaysia	5.32	40. Brazil	2.96
13. Germany	8.27	27. South Korea	5.02	41. Egypt	2.84
14. Israel	7.71	28. Greece	5.01	44. Philippines	2.69

The four most corrupt countries were Bangladesh at 2.29, Kenya at 2.21, Pakistan at 1.00, and Nigeria at 0.69.

Source: P. Norman, "New Zealand 'least corrupt country'," *Financial Times,* June 3, 1996, p. 5.

According to a study of French executives, the French tax authorities have a sliding scale of acceptable commissions paid to win business in other countries.[64] Stories abound about institutionalized corruption in Italy, Greece, Spain, and Germany.

As companies become more global, newspapers and business presses focus worldwide on instances of corporate crime and corruption in Asia. In 1993, *Asian Business's* cover story, "How Ethics Helps the Bottom Line," reported on rampant corruption that it said pervaded business and politics in the region. The magazine noted that companies were coming under fierce public scrutiny and ordinary people were getting tired of the way customers were being shortchanged, workers were being abused, and the environment was being polluted. "Now, as at no time before in Asia, business ethics is an issue that goes straight to the bottom line. Companies that read the handwriting on the wall and take ethical codes on board will improve their revenues over those which don't."[65]

What were the foci behind this new attention to ethical behavior? The most important reason was political upheaval. For example, pro-democracy movements in Thailand protested against power by the military. The

---

[64] Ibid., p. 37.

[65] N. McGrath, "How Ethics Helps the Bottom Line," *Asian Business,* December 1993, p. 20.

Japanese government reeled under revelations of corruption and deal making. Japan's Liberal Democratic Party, which had ruled unopposed since 1955, was defeated. In Taiwan, a Gallup poll showed that 65 percent of respondents believed that corruption was a major problem. New political forces, focusing on clean politics, emerged to contest the entrenched Kuomintang. In Jakarta, Indonesia, protests rocked the capital city in mid-1996. Much of the protest focused on the vast power, money, and corporate control held by President Suharto's immediate family.

Andrei Shleifer and Robert Vishny explored the issue of corruption and its connection to economic growth in Russia's post-communist era. They concluded the big problem came when officials had monopoly power over a government service. In the absence of a monopoly, there was much less need to pay the bribe. A prospective entrepreneur or investor was free to shop for an official willing to settle for less money or one who did not accept bribes at all. Shleifer and Vishny pointed out corruption is still harmful. Because it is wrong, people do it as secretly as possible. Even if a corrupt government is strong, it favors activities that allow bribes to be taken secretly—at the expense of economically superior alternatives.[66]

Corruption hurts more than the morals of those involved. When a prospective investor or a local enterprise pays a bribe to a government official to gain a contract, the action begins a cycle. Initially, a company that pays a bribe has an advantage over its competitors. However, other officials from other departments also may want payments for their help in making the enterprise continue. Red tape proliferates because there is every incentive to create a bureaucracy to put the squeeze on the investor and no incentive to make things simpler.[67]

How do U.S. companies, bound by the Foreign Corrupt Practices Act, compete in countries where bribery flourishes? They find ways to bestow favors. One of the most sought after favors is the trip to the United States. A U.S.-China Business Council employee mused, "You'd think Disney World was a training site." Other regular visiting sites include gambling meccas Las Vegas and Atlantic City. For Chinese officials, the small daily allowances given them by their hosts are the equivalent of a week's pay.

The U.S. government allows and even encourages paid travel for foreign businesspeople. Other favors include the allocation of corporate scholarships for children of officials with whom U.S. companies want to do business. Computer companies donate hardware and software to schools and universities abroad. Still other companies work through networks of wholesalers. As Wal-Mart and other mass merchandisers admit, they don't know with whom the wholesalers deal.

---

[66] "Brionomics," *Economist,* March 19, 1994, p. 86.
[67] Ibid.

Multinational Corporations

Multinational corporations are a tremendously powerful force in today's global business environment. The 100 largest companies in the world are multinationals; some have yearly earnings that surpass the GNPs of developing countries. Multinationals diversify their political and economic risk by expanding operations across the globe. They facilitate their search for lower-cost labor and natural resources by linking their subsidiaries with highly sophisticated technology and communications. Environmentalists and ethicists are paying increasing attention to the immense market power of these corporations.

Stakeholders and others acknowledge that different countries have their own laws and customs that create unique national ethical environments for business. Nevertheless, they conclude that ethics transcend national boundaries and that managers in multinational corporations must try to develop and adhere to a global norm.

During the 1980s, U.S. multinationals began to adopt the view that their ethics programs should cover corporate activities wherever those activities took place. The Bhopal incident, insider trading scandals, the controversy surrounding South African investment, toxic waste dumping in developing countries, and a host of other ethical issues all drew media attention. The impetus grew to develop global codes of ethics that addressed the rights of host country nationals.

Thomas Donaldson looks at international ethics from this perspective and argues that multinational corporations operating in other countries must honor certain fundamental rights of their citizens even if they are not required to do so (see Exhibit 5–6).

Who bears the responsibility for developing and implementing these basic rights? Is it the responsibility of corporate managers, shareholders, environmental activists, the U.S. government, or multinational agreements such as the World Trade Organization?

Karen Springen notes that codes are being developed to cover an increasing number of activities. Between 1989 and 1992, new codes were developed to cover everything from the environment to Mexican factories called maquiladoras. Springen suggests this proliferation reflects business's desire to police itself before the government gets involved. As we see in the chapters on regulation, this view is consistent with corporate involvement in developing regulation.

These codes must take a carrot-and-stick approach. Because compliance is voluntary, companies must see that codes bring them benefits. There must also be a stiff public relations penalty for failure to observe a particular code.[68]

---

[68] K. Springen, "Codes to Live by," *Business Ethics,* January–February 1992, pp. 883–90.

Exhibit 5–6 Citizens' International Rights

1. **The right to nondiscriminatory treatment.** Multinational corporations (MNCs) have a double obligation. It is not sufficient to refrain from discrimination in hiring or firing on the basis of sex, race, caste, or religion, or family affiliation. MNCs should go beyond that to establish procedures that protect the right to nondiscriminatory treatment and should make sure that lower-level managers adhere to reward or penalty systems based only on performance.
2. **The right to physical security.** Multinational corporations should provide safety equipment and safe procedures regardless of the stipulations of local law.
3. **The right to free speech and association.** Multinationals have an obligation to allow discussion about labor organization and association.
4. **The right of education.** Children are entitled to minimal education. In countries where MNCs use child labor, the company should not hinder a child's access to learning how to read and write.
5. **The right to subsistence.** An MNC should not become involved in activities that would result in people leaving land they need for growing food.

Source: T. Donaldson, *The Ethics of International Business* (New York: Oxford University Press, 1989), pp. 81–89.

The Caux Round Table Principles for Business (CRT) In 1986, corporate leaders from the United States, Japan, and Europe met in Caux-sur-Montreux, Switzerland, to develop an international code of ethics. The goal of the CRT Principles was to set "a world standard against which business behavior can be measured." The American, Japanese, and European delegations each worked out individual versions of the code. The final version was hammered out at a conference at the Minnesota Center for Corporate Responsibility in January 1994. Senior executives from companies such as Philips Electronics, Ciba-Geigy, Cummins, Matsushita, 3M, and Honeywell launched the CRT Principles (see Exhibit 5–7).

As international ethics codes and principles become more numerous, companies may feel overly constrained by multiple, possibly conflicting demands. Multinationals are bound to think their degrees of freedom are reduced and the attractions of foreign markets, labor, and resources are diminished by the need to adhere to multiple, economically unrealistic codes. Yet stakeholder demands for ethical behavior are likely to keep increasing.

EXHIBIT 5-7   Caux Round Table

Principles for Business

These principles are rooted in two basic ethical ideals: Kyosei and human dignity.

The Japanese concept of kyosei means living and working together for the common good—enabling cooperation and mutual prosperity to coexist with healthy and fair competition. "Human Dignity" refers to the sacredness or value of each person as an end, not simply as a means to the fulfillment of other's purposes or even majority prescription.

The General Principles in Section 2 seek to clarify the spirit of kyosei and "human dignity," while the specific Stakeholder Principles in Section 3 are concerned with their practical application.

Section 1. Preamble

The mobility of employment, capital, products, and technology is making business increasingly global in its transactions and its effects.

Laws and market forces are necessary but insufficient guides for conduct.

Responsibility of the policies and actions of business and respect for the dignity and interests of its stakeholders are fundamental.

Shared values, including a commitment to shared prosperity, are as important for a global community as for communities of smaller scale.

For these reasons, and because business can be a powerful agent of positive social change, we offer the following principles as a foundation for dialogue and action by business leaders in search of business responsibility. In so doing, we affirm the necessity for moral values in business decision making. Without them, stable business relationships and a sustainable world community are impossible

Section 2. General Principles

Principle 1. *The Responsibilities of Businesses: Beyond Shareholders toward Stakeholders*

The value of a business to society is the wealth and employment it creates and the marketable products and services it provides to consumers at a reasonable price commensurate with quality. To create such value, a business must maintain its own economic health and viability, but survival is not a sufficient goal.

Businesses have a role to play in improving the lives of all their customers, employees, and shareholders by sharing with them the wealth they have created. Suppliers and competitors as well should expect businesses to honor their obligations in a spirit of honesty and fairness. As responsible citizens of the local, national, regional, and global communities in which they operate, businesses share a part in shaping the future of those communities.

Principle 2. *The Economic and Social Impact of Business: Toward Innovation, Justice, and World Community*

Business established in foreign countries to develop, produce, or sell should also contribute to the social advancement of those countries by creating productive employment and helping to raise the purchasing power of their citizens. Businesses also should contribute to human rights, education, welfare, and vitalization of the countries in which they operate.

Businesses should contribute to economic and social development not only in the countries in which they operate, but also in the world community at large, through effective and prudent use of resources, free and fair competition, and emphasis upon innovation in technology, production methods, marketing, and communications.

Principle 3. *Business Behavior: Beyond the Letter of Law toward a Spirit of Trust*

While accepting the legitimacy of trade secrets, businesses should recognize that sincerity, candor, truthfulness, the keeping of promises, and transparency contribute not only to their own credibility and stability particularly on the international level.

Principle 4. *Respect for Rules*

To avoid trade frictions and to promote freer trade, equal conditions for competition, and fair and equitable treatment for all participants, businesses should respect international and domestic rules. In addition, they should recognize that some behavior, although legal, may still have adverse consequences.

Principle 5. *Support for Multilateral Trade*

Businesses should support the multilateral trade systems of the GATT World Trade Organization and similar international agreements. They should cooperate in efforts to promote the progressive and judicious liberalization of trade, and to relax those domestic measures that unreasonably hinder global commerce, while giving due respect to national policy objectives.

Principle 6. *Respect for the Environment*

A business should protect and, where possible, improve the environment, promote sustainable development, and prevent the wasteful use of natural resources.

(continued)

EXHIBIT 5–7 (Continued)

Principles for Business

PRINCIPLE 7. *Avoidance of Illicit Operations*

A business should not participate in or condone bribery, money laundering, or other corrupt practices: indeed, it should seek cooperation with others to eliminate them. It should not trade in arms or other materials used for terrorist activities, drug traffic, or other organized crime.

SECTION 3. STAKEHOLDER PRINCIPLES

Customers

We believe in treating all customers with dignity, irrespective of whether they purchase our products and service directly from us or otherwise acquire them in the market. We therefore have a responsibility to:

- provide our customers with the highest quality products and services consistent with their requirements;
- treat our customers fairly in all aspects of our business transactions, including a high level of service and remedies for their dissatisfaction;
- make every effort to ensure that the health and safety of our customers, as well as the quality of their environment, will be sustained or enhanced by our products and services;
- assure respect for human dignity in product offered, marketing, and advertising; and
- respect the integrity of the culture of our customers.

Employees

We believe in the dignity of every employee and in taking employee interest seriously. We therefore have a responsibility to:

- provide jobs and compensation that improve workers' living conditions;
- provide working conditions that respect each employees's health and dignity;
- be honest in communications with employees and open in sharing information, limited only by legal and competitive restraints;
- listen to and, where possible, act on employee suggestions, ideas, requests, and complaints;
- engage in good-faith negotiations when conflict arises;
- avoid discriminatory practices and guarantee equal treatment and opportunity in areas such as gender, age, race, and religion;
- promote in the business itself the employment of differently abled people in places of work where they can be genuinely useful;
- protect employees from avoidable injury and illness in the workplace;
- encourage and assist employees in developing relevant and transferable skills and knowledge; and
- be sensitive to serious unemployment problems frequently associated with business decisions, and work with governments, employee groups, other agencies and each other in addressing these dislocations.

Owners/Investors

We believe in honoring the trust our investors place in us. We therefore have a responsibility to:

- apply professional and diligent management in order to secure a fair and competitive return on our owners' investment;
- disclose relevant information to owners/investors subject only to legal requirements and competitive constraints;
- conserve, protect, and increase the owners/investors' assets; and
- respect owners/investors' requests, suggestions, complaints, and formal resolutions.

Suppliers

Our relationship with suppliers and subcontractors must be based on mutual respect. We therefore have a responsibility to:

- seek fairness and truthfulness in all of our activities, including pricing, licensing, and rights to sell;
- ensure that our business activities are free from coercion and unnecessary litigation;
- foster long-term stability in the supplier relationship in return for value, quality, competitiveness, and reliability;
- share information with suppliers and integrate them into our planning processes;
- pay suppliers on time and in accordance with agreed terms of trade;
- seek, encourage, and prefer suppliers and subcontractors whose employment practices respect human dignity.

Competitors

We believe that fair economic competition is one of the basic requirements for increasing the wealth of nations and, ultimately, for making possible for just distribution of goods and services. We therefore have a responsibility to:

- foster open markets for trade and investment;
- promote competitive behavior that is socially and environmentally beneficial and demonstrates mutual respect among competitors;
- refrain from either seeking or participating in questionable payments or favors to secure competitive advantage;

(continued)

Exhibit 5–7 (Concluded)

Principles for Business

- respect both tangible and intellectual property right; and
- refuse to acquire commercial information by dishonest or unethical means, such as industrial espionage.

Communities

We believe that as global corporate citizens, we can contribute to such forces of reform and human rights a are at work in the communities in which we operate. We therefore have a responsibility in those communities to:

- respect human rights and democratic institutions, and promote them wherever practicable;
- recognize government's legitimate obligation to the society at large and support public policies and practices that promote human development through harmonious relations between business and other segments of society;
- collaborate with those forces in the community dedicated to raising standards of health, education, workplace safety, and economic well-being;
- promote and stimulate sustainable development and play a leading role in preserving and enhancing the physical environment and conserving the earth's resources;
- support peace, security, diversity, and social integration;
- respect the integrity of local cultures; and
- be a good corporate citizen through charitable donations, educational and cultural contributions, and employee participation in community civic affairs.

Summary

Business ethics are part of a country's social environment. Both macro- and microcultures determine the form ethical behavior takes. In the United States, there is an ongoing debate about what constitutes ethical behavior. Opinions range from solely economic to purely noneconomic concerns.

Increasingly, the transmittal of ethics and ethical behavior is being done by academic institutions and companies. However, academics agree very little on how to carry out this effort or even on what guidelines they themselves should follow.

Managers should address several important questions before they try to design ethical credos, codes, or programs. These questions include defining a problem, determining how the problem occurred, examining internal company loyalties, finding out who will be affected by decisions, and assessing whether management can stick to a decision once it is made.

Each company selects its own approach to dealing with ethics. Most companies select some form of credo, code, or program to give structure to the firm's ethical climate. Each firm should rely on its own corporate history, leadership, and culture as it undertakes this task.

The employee is perhaps the most important stakeholder in the ethics implementation process. A company must treat its employees in an ethical manner on a daily basis or its ethics programs will fail. In some cases, the implicit contract between firm and employee is broken and the employee becomes a whistle-blower. Although whistle-blowers are legally protected, they often lose their jobs and suffer other personal losses.

International business ethics are impossible to define. Each company operates on some internal ethical principle that it communicates to its foreign subsidiaries. Different national cultures and legal requirements are confusing and sometimes ethically contradictory. International managers have a particularly important role to play in transferring and rationalizing ethics throughout the corporation. Increasingly, international codes and principles are being developed and applied to the actions of multinational companies wherever they operate.

Projects

1. You are manager of a large computer manufacturing company that operates in the United States, Europe, and Japan. Research the efforts of the European Economic Community (EC) and Japan in dealing with ethics. Check the Internet site of the EU [http://www.cec.lu]. Do an Internet search using Japan and ethics as key words. Write an executive memo to your CEO that compares U.S., EC, and Japanese business ethics.
2. Your company is considering building a small assembly plant in Russia. Your board of directors is concerned that the company will be expected to comply with a different set of ethics. The board has heard that organized crime is prevalent. What do U.S. law and your own conscience require? Prepare a report for your board on this topic.
3. Your mother has been president of a regional apple and pear growers' association and is now retiring. Members have chosen you to succeed her and have given you a major task. Your association has no statement on ethics. Stakeholders are pressuring you to commit the association to a stand on the use of pesticides and conditions for migrant workers. You decide you have to draw up a more comprehensive code that addresses issues important to your members. Write a complete ethics statement, including all the major issues that involve your association.

Questions

1. Review the 12 questions posed by Laura Nash. Which do you consider most helpful in assessing the ethics of a business decision? Why?
2. How large a role do you think business schools should play in teaching ethics?
3. What approach to teaching ethics do you think would be most helpful? Should faculty members provide the frameworks? Use cases to illustrate various decisions? Lecture on what ethical stand you should take? Why?
4. What do you think of whistle-blowers? Would you ever blow the whistle on a company for which you worked? How would you deal with a situation in which you knew of a wrongdoing, reported it to your boss, and were subsequently ignored?
5. What is the future for international codes of conduct and principles of behavior for multinational corporations?

BETA CASE 5
ETHICS

One morning in June 1997, Ken Braddock, vice president and general manager of ethical products, picked up his morning *New York Times*. A front-page article immediately seized his attention. It reported on an article in the *Annals of Internal Medicine,* written by researchers at the University of California at Los Angeles, that described a study of advertisements of prescription drugs carried in medical journals. The researchers had asked a group of 150 doctors and clinical pharmacists to study all of the 109 full-page advertisements in the first 1990 issues of 10 leading medical journals. The study concluded that advertisements often mislead doctors about the safety and effectiveness of the drugs being promoted.

Braddock was well aware that physicians got much of their information about new drugs from those advertisements. He also knew Beta spent a considerable amount of money promoting its own ethical drugs through those ads. In fact, Braddock had just looked at the industry data of advertising expenditures. In 1994, drug companies had spent $351 million on advertisements in medical journals.

Beta had safeguards in place to ensure the accuracy of its ads, Braddock reassured himself. Beta's medical director, Dr. Abigail Thompson, screened all of Beta's ads. In addition, Beta followed Food and Drug Administration (FDA) regulations and guidelines for advertising. It was company policy to adhere to FDA requirements that drug companies include only those data approved by the FDA and placed in the drug package insert.

However, Braddock still worried about the study's findings. The *New York Times* reported that the journals in which the ads were carried also published academic research papers. Although the papers were carefully reviewed and evaluated by medical experts, no one subjected the advertisements to the same standards of scientific rigor. The 150 expert reviewers concluded that many of the ads failed to highlight potentially dangerous side effects. Other ads had misleading information, inadequately referenced or distorted graphs, and generally inadequate scientific documentation.

Apparently not only those researchers found drug advertisements misleading. The director of the FDA's own drug marketing division had analyzed the same ads and found that half of them violated FDA guidelines. Her boss, Dr. David Kessler, FDA commissioner, wrote an editorial in the *Annals* claiming that "the problem of misleading drug advertisements is real" and the number of these ads disturbingly high.

Braddock wondered whether Beta had unintentionally misled physicians with its ads and what, if anything, he should do. Perhaps, he mused, he should not do anything at all, since the company had followed FDA guidelines to the best of its knowledge. After all, the Pharmaceutical Manufacturers Association, the industry's Washington-based trade group, had disparaged the study, noting "Prescription drug advertising is the most regulated form of advertising in the United States."

CHAPTER 6
THE ORIGINS OF BIG BUSINESS

The first five chapters of this book emphasize how important it is for managers to develop and maintain a strategic perspective. Whether embarking on the strategic planning and implementation process or coping with crises, managers are always influenced by the historical background of their particular enterprise and the way the company evolved in its cultural environment.

Managers can profit from understanding and incorporating the positive attributes of their corporate histories. Corporate character, culture, and long-term success are not static but the result of a historical process. Astute managers recognize that "the present is a monument in the past's trajectory into the future. Corporate history can be a way of thinking about the company, a way of comprehending why the present is what it is and what might be possible for the future."[1]

In this chapter, we survey the major components of the history of American business. We look at basic historical trends over time and the interrelationships between business and major stakeholders in society. We discuss the dramatic rise of big business as an American institution in the 19th century. We go on to consider the dynamic interaction that characterizes business and society in the 20th century. The first half of the chapter focuses on the environmental conditions that supported business growth. The second half reviews the later stages of capitalism and periods of business expansion that depended on that infrastructure.

In many respects, America was first and foremost a business venture. In the 17th century, mercantilist economic doctrine so heavily dominated European thought that it became the guiding ideology of the early colonists. Mercantilism called for the establishment of colonies to provide sources for

---
[1] G. D. Smith and L. E. Steadman, "Present Value of Corporate History," *Harvard Business Review* 59, November–December 1981, pp. 164–73.

raw materials and markets for finished goods. British mercantilists advocated extensive trade with other countries as well; a major objective was to create an excess of exports over imports so that Britain's treasury would swell with gold. To protect its markets, Britain imposed high duties on imports and strengthened its merchant fleet. According to historians Harry Carman and Harold Syrett,

> Four colonies subsequently part of the United States—not to mention others in Canada and the West Indies—were, in part at least, the work of trading corporations: Virginia, founded in 1607 by the Virginia Company of London; New Netherlands, planted by the Dutch at Fort Nassau in 1614; Massachusetts, established by the Massachusetts Bay Company in 1630; and Delaware, begun by a Swedish commercial company in 1638. Even the Pilgrims, who founded Plymouth in 1620, were financed by an English merchant, Thomas Weston, and his associates.[2]

Therefore, an American business system evolved over many years prior to the American Revolution.[3]

Although business and economic matters played a central role in the processes of colonization, the revolution, and the shaping of the new republic, the origins of big business were rooted in the period between the 1820s and the outbreak of the Civil War in 1861. As manufacturing and trade increased, financial institutions expanded to supply credit and banking services and transportation facilities to move goods from one place to another.

Dramatic growth in the business sector had a profound impact on the American way of life. Historian Thomas C. Cochran notes, "No culture can be satisfactorily characterized by a single phrase. Yet businesslike values and respect for them seemed the most pervasive common element in American culture, more so than religion, world mission, the democratic spirit, or similar formulations of American ideals."[4] Most observers agree that business was the dominant American institution and that the culture of the United States was shaped in part by its business institutions.

Conditions Supporting Business Development in the United States

The United States began the 19th century as an agrarian society of 5 million people. By 1900, 76 million people were producing twice the economic output of Britain.[5] Abundant natural resources, favorable social and political environments, rapid population growth and urban migration, the transporta-

---

[2] H. J. Carman and H. C. Syrett, *A History of the American People,* vol. 1 (New York: Alfred A. Knopf, 1957), p. 24.

[3] B. Bailyn, The New England Merchants in the Seventeenth Century (Cambridge, MA: Harvard University Press, 1955).

[4] T. C. Cochran, *American Business in the Twentieth Century* (Cambridge, MA: Harvard University Press, 1972), p. 7.

[5] H. E. Krooss and C. Gilbert, *American Business History* (Englewood Cliffs, NJ: Prentice Hall, 1972), p. 145.

tion revolution, and innovations in communication were among the factors contributing to the development of a strong U.S. business system. Technological developments, especially the development of mass production techniques, also were critical to the growth of big business.

Companies integrated technologically and synchronized stages of production using machinery in mass production techniques. At each stage of operation, their output became much faster and greater in volume. Managers using the new processes of production considered a high throughput—usually units processed per day—a critical criterion of performance.[6]

Plentiful Natural Resources

Abundant natural resources were critically important to economic growth in the pre- and post-industrial United States. From the beginning, the United States possessed "a vast continent, irrigated by numberless rivers sweeping down the sides of the mountains fabulously rich in precious metals and inexhaustible supplies of fuel. America's soil was the richest in the world, her forests thick and varied. Deep harbors indented her coasts; her rivers and lakes beckoned trade."[7]

Agricultural output rose rapidly in the rich virgin soil. The many rivers facilitated power generation and transportation, and the timber and minerals provided the inputs to industrial processes. Other nations claimed a similar abundance of resources, but only the United States promised the opportunity for individuals to become owners of rich farmland. Land was given to early settlers in colonial New England.

According to Herman Krooss, "Most colonies . . . used the system of headrights to encourage settlement. Proprietors granted 50 acres of land to every settler who came over at his own expense and 50 more to every person who brought over another settler. Virginia supplied every family with 12 acres, a four-room house, and tools and provisions."[8] During the Civil War, the Homestead Act of 1862 promised 160 acres of unoccupied public land to anyone who would cultivate it for five consecutive years. Even though much of the land was of poor quality, by 1882 the government had distributed 50 million acres to farmers and would-be entrepreneurs.

Various legislative acts granted railroad companies ownership of approximately 200 million acres of prime land, which comprised nearly 10 percent of the continental land mass. Much of this land was sold to settlers at reasonable rates. Immigrants, attracted to the United States by the opportunity to

---

[6] A. D. Chandler, Jr., *The Visible Hand* (Cambridge, MA: Belknap Press, 1977), pp. 240–41.

[7] T. C. Cochran and W. Miller, The Age of Enterprise: A Social History of Industrial America (New York: Macmillan Publishing Co.)© renewed 1970 by Thomas C. Cochran and William Miller.

[8] H. Krooss, *American Economic Development: The Process of Business Civilization*, 3rd ed. (Englewood Cliffs, NJ: Prentice Hall, 1974), p. 87.

share in the plentiful natural resources, quickly found that entrepreneurship, whether in farming or in business, was a prevalent social value.

Favorable Social and Political Environments

Social Values. In contrast to many Western European nations, the United States had no strong aristocratic class. Even the descendants of early settlers in Massachusetts and Virginia and of plantation owners in the southern states rejected a rigid aristocratic social structure and its values. Personal achievement was considered far more important than family name or birth order. Most Americans respected and emulated business leaders, particularly those who were self-made. William Letwin notes, "Businessmen rose prior to the Civil War in the United States because they embodied the common aspirations and symbolized the working life of most Americans."[9] The unifying social ethic was individualism, hard work, and diligence—all prized virtues and all virtues of the successful businessperson. Economist John E. Sawyer comments on the unique social environment enjoyed by American entrepreneurs:

> In the classic era of the 19th and early 20th centuries American entrepreneurship grew and prospered in a society whose institutions and goals were as uniquely favorable to the individual entrepreneur as were its physical conditions. By inheritance and diffusion, America is, of course, part of a common Western civilization. But the historical timing of the American settlement and the extremely uneven weighting involved in the social and cultural transfer gave the United States a highly selective extraction of the European heritage.[10]

Sawyer referred to the transfer of values that supported individual growth and development. Perhaps the best examples of such values are those immortalized in Horatio Alger's success stories. Although they were not regarded as a high literary form, Alger's books were widely read in the post-Civil War era. Readers bought more than 20 million copies of such books as *Luck and Pluck, Tom the Bootblack,* and *Bound to Rise.*[11] Many people believed that by working hard and getting a few lucky breaks, they could achieve respectable middle-class membership. Although we now think of Alger's heroes as epitomizing the rise from rags to riches, in fact they usually became small-town businesspeople.

---

[9] W. Letwin, "The Past and Future of the American Businessman," *Daedalus,* Winter 1969, p. 8.

[10] J. E. Sawyer, "The Entrepreneur and the Social Order," *Men in Business: Essays on the Historical Role of the Entrepreneur,* ed. W. Miller (New York: Harper & Row, 1962), p. 20.

[11] F. L. Allen, *The Big Change: America Transforms Itself, 1900–1950* (New York: Harper & Row), p. 63.

It was possible to get a start in business with extremely small amounts of capital. For instance, Andrew Carnegie's first major investment was $217.50 (borrowed without collateral) to buy a one-eighth interest in Woodruff's Palace Car Company. In two years the investment yielded an annual return of $5,000.[12] Many other entrepreneurs were able to start businesses with even smaller sums. In 1850, I. M. Singer borrowed $40 from a friend to build a model sewing machine. By the 1880s, Singer Manufacturing Company was the preeminent sewing machine company in the world. It had a huge sales network and giant factories abroad as well as in the United States.[13]

The Role of Government. Throughout the 19th century, the government and the courts pursued policies and programs that supported business needs. As early as 1816, the government enacted tariffs to protect American textile interests from foreign competition. The government provided massive support for the railroad industry through grants, first-mortgage bonds, guaranteed loans, and remitted taxes. By and large, it left the industry free from regulation.[14] Although the Supreme Court had clearly established the right of the federal government to regulate interstate commerce by 1827, the government did not exercise that right until 50 years later.

As we shall see, the role of transportation was critical to business development. Business leaders quickly became acquainted with the dictum, "There's no such thing as a free lunch." It became apparent that there was a price to the advantages enjoyed by railroad magnates and other industrialists. According to Thomas Cochran and William Miller, "The politicians were eager to do business with Big Businessmen only because the latter offered the largest fees; in an age of fearful competition, such businessmen vied with one another in bribing legislatures, administrators, and judges to gain any advantage over their rivals."[15]

The same comment could have applied to other industries and their government relations. For instance, Henry Demarest Lloyd, then financial editor of the *Chicago Tribune,* said of John D. Rockefeller that "the Standard [Oil Company] has done everything with the Pennsylvania legislature except to refine it."[16] Because U.S. senators were appointed by state legislatures until the Seventeenth Amendment was passed in 1910, there was a strong incentive for big-business interests to attempt to control state senatorial votes. So many business leaders became U.S. senators that the Senate was widely referred to as the Millionaire's Club.

---

[12] J. R. Hughes, *The Vital Few* (Boston: Houghton Mifflin, 1966), pp. 227–28.

[13] M. Wilkins, *The Emergence of Multinational Enterprise: American Business Abroad from the Colonial Era to 1914* (Cambridge, MA: Harvard University Press, 1970), pp. 37–45.

[14] S. H. Holbrook, *The Story of the American Railroads* (New York: Crown Publishers, 1947).

[15] Cochran and Miller, *The Age of Enterprise,* p. 158.

[16] H. D. Lloyd, *Wealth Against Commonwealth* (New York: Harper & Row, 1894).

As might be expected, the Senate protected business interests during the last quarter of the 19th century. As a reaction to the excesses in the railroad industry between 1874 and 1885, the House of Representatives considered more than 30 bills to provide greater control over interstate commerce. The Senate, however, prevented the passage of any such bill until 1887, when the Interstate Commerce Act, which created the Interstate Commerce Commission, became law. (That law and subsequent legislation that strengthened its provisions are discussed in Chapter 8.) The Sherman Antitrust Act, designed to prevent monopolies and restraint of trade, was passed in 1890. Like the Interstate Commerce Act, it was a weak act also strengthened by subsequent legislation. (The Sherman Act is discussed in detail in Chapter 8.)

In 1900, the federal government operated on a budget of approximately $500 million, supported mainly by tax revenues from tariffs and excise taxes. There was no income tax at all. The Federal Trade Commission, the Department of Commerce, the Food and Drug Administration, the Department of Labor, and the Federal Reserve System had not yet been created.

Thus, business was virtually unfettered and it was widely believed the federal government should not get involved in issues that were none of its concern. In fact, as David Vogel notes, measures to ameliorate dangerous or unfair business practices "tended to be strongly opposed . . . and often were significantly weakened as a result of political pressure from industrialists."[17] However, as the country grew in population and became heavily urbanized, the role of the federal government expanded beyond merely increasing regulation.

Population Growth and Urbanism

Immigration fueled population growth. While such growth was slow during economic declines, it was heavy in prosperous periods, reaching an all-time peak of 1,285,000 in 1907.[18] Most immigrants, particularly toward the end of the 19th century, settled in industrial centers, such as New York, Boston, Philadelphia, and Chicago, where they were joined by migrants from rural America.[19] The number of Americans living in cities grew from 6 percent in the year 1800 to 33 percent in 1900. As 18th- and 19th-century migration to the West Coast continued and open areas were settled, the only remaining frontier was the city. Foreign-born Americans, who comprised 14 percent of the population, were twice as likely as native-born Americans to live in cities.[20]

---

[17] D. Vogel, *National Styles of Regulation: Environmental Policy in Great Britain and the United States* (Ithaca, NY: Cornell University Press, 1986), p. 230.

[18] R. Hofstadter, *The Age of Reform: From Bryan to F.D.R.* (New York: Vantage Books, 1955), p. 177.

[19] A. M. Schlesinger, "The Rise of the City: 1898–1898," in A History of American Life, vol. 10, ed. A. M. Schlesinger and D. R. Fox (New York: Macmillan, 1933), pp. 53–57.

[20] Krooss, *American Economic Development,* pp. 105–11.

The massive influx of workers to the cities created low-wage labor markets. However, the scarcity of skilled labor characteristic of the American workforce since colonial times persisted. Raymond Vernon observes that "labor in the United States has always been scarce, especially labor skilled in production techniques."[21] As a result, industrialists used the ample raw materials and capital available to generate large quantities of goods that used low-skilled labor.

Although most of the workers were unskilled, they earned comparatively high incomes. Wages earned by both low-wage workers and the smaller pool of skilled workers led to the development of even larger markets for all types of consumer goods. Cochran and Miller note,

> It is impossible to exaggerate the role of business in developing great cities in America, and it is impossible to exaggerate the role of the cities in creating our business culture. The cities subjected hundreds of thousands of people to identical pressures, at the same time exporting to every rural river valley, plain and plateau uniform factory products. Creating a national market for standardized goods, they also created a national model of the successful man: the thrifty, shrewd, and practical clerk or mechanic who rose from the ranks to leadership.[22]

The Transportation Revolution

Shipping costs were high in the early 19th century. Toll roads and post roads were used to ship wagon loads of goods. The Erie Canal was only one of a network of canals and rivers, totaling more than 4,200 miles in length. Although surface and water routes led to a major reduction in shipping costs between 1825 and 1860, the railroads revolutionized shipping. On August 8, 1829, John B. Jervis ran the first steam locomotive in the United States.[23] The massive, eight-ton Stourbridge Lion ran less than 200 yards before it crushed the wooden rails. Lighter engines, iron rails, and countless other innovations led to a rapid expansion of railroads after 1830. By 1865, 35,085 miles of track were in use. Another 165,000 miles were laid by 1890.[24]

The railroads were the nation's first big business. Unprecedented amounts of capital were required to build railways and maintain equipment. For instance, in the 1850s, a major textile mill might have cost $500,000 to build and as much as $300,000 per year to run with a workforce of fewer than 800 workers. In contrast, railroad construction cost a minimum of $30,000 per mile. The New York Central cost more than $30 million to build, $3 million per year to operate, and employed 4,000 workers.[25]

---

[21] R. Vernon, *Sovereignty at Bay* (New York: Basic Books, 1971), p. 66.
[22] Cochran and Miller, *The Age of Enterprise,* p. 153.
[23] E. E. Morison, *From Know-How to Nowhere: The Development of American Technology* (New York: Basic Books, 1974), p. 52.
[24] D. J. Boorstin, *The Americans: The Democratic Experience* (New York: Random House, 1974), p. 120.
[25] Krooss and Gilbert, *American Business History,* p. 123.

The railroads generated massive requirements for steel rails and bridges, thus fostering the growth of a steel industry. Iron rails, which could be forged in small shops, were used only until the processes for producing steel were commercially perfected in the mid-1860s. Much more capital and equipment were required to produce the stronger and lighter steel rails, giving further impetus to the development of big business.

Many financiers made fortunes in the railroad industry, although they were rarely competent in railroad management. Alfred Chandler notes that "large sums of money were essential if the road was to be built at all, if it was to expand its physical equipment as the traffic grew, if it was to build feeders and branches necessitated by competition, or if it was to survive sudden contractions of the money market."[26] An executive who could command large sums of money was therefore a valuable asset to a railroad company.

Railroads were the first businesses in which a definite separation between ownership and management existed. There were exceptions, however; most notably the Pennsylvania Railroad that was successfully managed and financed by wealthy engineer J. Edgar Thomson. The need for sound operations management for the nation's railroads was apparent as early as 1850.

The most basic needs, however, were difficult to implement. For example, although standardization of time zones was essential, it took 11 years to reach a consensus to consolidate. Prior to 1883, a train crossing the continental United States might have gone through as many as 54 time zones instead of the present 4. Similarly, railroads adopted standardized rail widths, car couplings, and air brakes only after protracted delays.[27] One can imagine the delays and other difficulties passengers and shippers encountered as railroad workers switched trains from wide-gauge to narrow-gauge tracks and then back again.

Innovations in Communication

As businesses proliferated, they increasingly needed quick and easy communication. In 1844, Samuel F. B. Morse constructed a telegraph line from Baltimore to Washington that "hastened the pace of business . . . speeding news to the papers within a day after it happened."[28] By 1860, there were 50,000 miles of telegraph lines.

The real boom came after Western Union achieved a monopoly in telegraphy. The company entered agreements with the railroads to use rights of way and station houses in exchange for free telegraph service. By 1878, there

---

[26] A. D. Chandler, Jr., "Henry Varnum Poor: Philosopher of Management, 1812–1905," in *Men In Business,* ed., W. Miller (New York: Harper & Row, 1952), p. 283.

[27] E. C. Kirkland, "Industry Comes of Age: Business, Labor and Public Policy, 1860–1887" in *The Economic History of the United States,* vol. 6, ed. Henry Davis (New York: Holt, Rinehart & Winston, 1961), pp. 46–52.

[28] Boorstin, *The Americans,* p. 390.

EXHIBIT 6–1 Selected Innovations in Mass Communications

1833	First penny paper, *The New York Sun*.
1839	Daguerre developed practical method of photography.
1844	Morse transmitted first telegraph message.
1853	Paper made from wood pulp.
1857	First trans-Atlantic cable.
1867	First practical typewriter.
1872	Process of photoengraving developed.
1873	First daily illustrated paper.
1876	Bell transmitted the first telephone message.
1877	Edison invented the phonograph.
1894	Motion picture projection perfected.
1895	Marconi sent and received a wireless message.
1904	Telephone wirephoto sent from Munich to Nuremberg.
1906	Human voice transmitted by radio.
1920	Beginning of regularly scheduled radio broadcasting.
1923	Picture televised from New York to Philadelphia.
1924	Tabloid newspaper.
1926	Beginning of book clubs.
1928	Beginning of regular, scheduled television broadcasting.

Source: W. Schramm, ed., *Mass Communications,* 2nd ed. (Urbana: University of Illinois Press, 1960), pp. 6–7.

were 200,000 miles of telegraph.[29] In that same year, Theodore N. Vail took over the management of the recently organized Bell Telephone Company. Over the next 34 years, under his skillful management, the telephone became an indispensable part of American life.

Many other developments further improved the ability of Americans to communicate with one another. Exhibit 6–1 briefly summarizes major innovations in communication. Each innovation provided opportunities for businesses to build and distribute needed equipment. Efficient communication was extremely important to the growth of business. For instance, the development of carbon paper in the 1880s was one immeasurable improvement. Now businesspeople could create duplicates of memos and letters without cumbersome letter presses and gallons of iron-based ink.

Technological Developments

Technological advances in transportation and communications were, of course, not isolated events. Technological change played a central role in the development of many industries. But technology was not limited to the creation of mechanical objects and machines. Management scientist Herbert H. Simon observes that "technology is not things; it is knowledge—knowledge that is stored in hundreds of millions of books, in hundreds of millions or billions of human heads, and, to an important extent, in the artifacts themselves. Technology is knowledge of how to do things, how to accomplish human goals."[30] Future historians will doubtless add that computerization constituted nothing less than a transformation of and revolution in the storage and dissemination of technological knowledge.

It was difficult to develop or apply knowledge in the early 19th century. Engineers generally passed their knowledge on to apprentices. Prior to 1830, companies recorded very little in print about such subjects as canal building, steam engines, and textile machinery. The British deliberately withheld plans for textile machinery from American manufacturers. Indeed, the British had legislated against transporting machinery or even drawings of machines to the colonies. Thus, although steam engines and textile machines were introduced in Great Britain in the late 18th century, innovations appeared in the United States only after such engineers as Samuel Slater and Francis Cabot Lowell memorized and re-created British designs.

In the early 1800s, Britain imposed an embargo on British textile technology. British ships prowled the high seas, blockading American ports. For more than a decade, British sailors successfully confiscated plans American entrepreneurs tried to smuggle into the United States.

Francis Cabot Lowell, however, was not deterred. He and financier Nathan Appleton traveled through Scotland and Britain, memorizing the various configurations of textile machinery. During the return trip to Boston, British sailors boarded their ship on the high seas several times to search for textile machinery plans. After coming up empty-handed, they finally let the ship proceed. Within several weeks of returning to Boston, Lowell and mechanic Paul Moody had built a prototype that became the foundation of the New England textile industry.[31]

The major innovations that sparked the business revolution included the Bessemer process for manufacturing steel, which was commercially implemented in the United States in 1872. The harnessing of electricity gave rise to the electrical equipment industry and the electric utilities. The refrigerated railroad car, introduced in 1875, led to the development of the meatpacking industry. The influence of technology was so great between 1850 and 1900 that historians deemed it "the precipitating factor in whatever transformation occurred in American society."[32]

---

[29] Krooss, *American Economic Development,* p. 387.

[30] H. A. Simon, "Technology and Environment," *Management Science* 19, June 1973, p. 1–10.

[31] H. Vernon-Wortzel, *Lowell: The Corporations and the City* (New York: Garland Publishing, 1992), pp.4–5.

[32] Krooss and Gilbert, *American Business History,* p. 145.

Stages of Capitalism

One might adopt several frameworks to describe the stages of development in a business-oriented society. One approach is to consider the common stages of growth in a society that recognized private property. The late business historian N. S. B. Gras delineates six stages of capitalism: prebusiness capitalism, petty capitalism, mercantile capitalism, industrial capitalism, finance capitalism, and national capitalism.[33] Although Gras's stages and labels are somewhat rigid and arbitrary, they are useful for dividing the capitalist orientation into chronological order. Capitalism was and is today the ideological basis of U.S. development. However, other countries have evolved under different systems that fall along a continuum from total central planning to totally free enterprise. Most countries combine some elements of government and business control.

The rigid central planning model has virtually disappeared. Only Cuba, North Korea, and a few other countries still cling to this model, and none of them has a thriving economy. The former Soviet Union, Eastern Europe, and many African and Latin American countries have abandoned central planning in favor of private enterprise. Even China has moved toward free enterprise and is rapidly loosening government control over most industrial sectors. Divestment programs have put state-owned industries around the world back into the private sector.

Many European countries combine aspects of capitalism and government control. Some countries still retain control over airlines, telecommunications, and other critical industries but their number is shrinking rapidly. Even those with some aspects of central planning encourage free enterprise in consumer goods and other nonstrategic enterprises. Government responsibility for social programs and industrial relations also varies across cultures and countries. One should be wary of applying labels such as communist, socialist, capitalist, and so on to national policies. Most countries combine policies as they define and redefine the roles of government and the private sector.

Although real-life situations cannot be neatly classified and compartmentalized, categorizations such as the following provide a structure for discussion purposes.

Prebusiness and Petty Capitalism

Gras's stage, *prebusiness capitalism,* was rooted in the manorial estates and settled villages of Western Europe during the medieval period. Social mobility during this period was very low. A person born into a farming family was

---

[33] N. S. B. Gras, *Business and Capitalism: An Introduction to Business History* (New York: F. S. Crofts, 1930).

destined to be a farmer. Lords and ladies of the manors and peasants and artisans in the villages worked and shared under a barter exchange system. They achieved a condition approximating self-sufficiency by trading goods and services. Society in rural colonial America had some of these elements, but even in those early days Americans were far more socially and geographically mobile.

The second stage, *petty capitalism,* prevailed in the North American British colonies in the 17th century and the first half of the 18th century. The petty capitalist was a shopkeeper or a traveling merchant. His enterprises were small, seldom extending beyond the town in which the store was located or the route the merchant followed. Businesses started and failed with great regularity. Because entrepreneurs required little capital to set up shop, the system encouraged "over competition, which would sooner or later be ruinous to all."[34] Of course, many petty capitalists survived and thrived. As the dominant form of business, however, the petty capitalist yielded to the mercantile capitalist around 1750.

Mercantile Capitalism

In the American experience, the third stage, *mercantile capitalism,* consisted of two parts. The first period was that of the colonial merchant, who, as Chandler noted, was "an all-purpose, nonspecialized man of business. He was a wholesaler and a retailer, an importer and an exporter. In associations with other merchants he built and owned the ships that carried goods to and from his town. He financed and insured the transportation and distribution of these goods. At the same time, he provided the funds needed by planters and artisans to finance the production of crops and goods."[35]

By providing a market for agricultural and consumer goods, the merchant became the dominant business leader in the second half of the 1700s. Specialized intermediaries, such as importers, insurers, bankers, and wholesalers, had taken over by 1800.

Thus, in the second period of mercantile capitalism, intermediaries replaced merchants as the integrating force in the economy. Between 1800 and 1850, wholesalers directed the flow of goods from producers to consumers; financed the canals, turnpikes, and early railroads; and supplied the funds for the early steel and textile factories. Chandler says, "They not only raised the funds for plants and machinery, but also supplied a large amount of the cash and credit that the new manufacturers needed as working capital to pay for supplies and labor."[36] As manufacturing grew in importance, the role of the mercantile capitalist intermediaries became less and less critical.

---

[34] Ibid., p. 61.

[35] A. D. Chandler, Jr., "The Role of Business in the United States: A Historical Survey," *Daedalus,* Winter 1969, p. 24.

[36] Ibid., p. 26.

Industrial Capitalism

The era of industrial capitalism and the rise of factory-based manufacturing followed mercantile capitalism. The first fully integrated factory in the United States, a textile plant in Waltham, Massachusetts, was owned by Boston Manufacturing Company, a group of Boston merchants who opened it in 1814. This company, led by Nathan Appleton and Francis Cabot Lowell, was the first to process raw materials into finished goods and market the output. Until that time, home looms turned out goods that were sold in local markets. The expansion of the highly profitable textile factories into Lowell and Lawrence, Massachusetts, was followed by the development of the iron and agricultural implement industries. However, most manufacturers continued to rely on wholesalers for marketing and financial support. Once the railroads provided access to larger markets and technological progress provided economies to larger firms, many companies assumed their own marketing and financing functions.

Some characterized the leaders of big business as *captains of industry;* others called them *robber barons.* Both terms were appropriate for these complex individuals. Although the Industrial Revolution was in full swing before the Civil War, industrialists did not make their mark until the conflict was over. In 1861, John D. Rockefeller had a thriving wholesale business in Cleveland, and Andrew Carnegie was the personal secretary to the powerful Thomas Scott, general superintendent of the Pennsylvania Railroad. Jay Gould operated a tannery in eastern Pennsylvania, J. Pierpont Morgan had just opened an investment office in New York, James Hill (later president of Northern Pacific Railroad) was a merchant in what is now St. Paul, Missouri, and Edward Harriman (later president of Union Pacific Railroad) was a 14-year-old errand boy on Wall Street. In the West, members of the Pacific Associates—Collis Huntington, Leland Stanford, Mark Hopkins, and Charles Crocker—were merchants who would soon acquire the rights to build the western part (Union Pacific) of the transcontinental railroad.

With the exception of members of the Pacific Associates, none of these industrialists was more than 26 years old, and only Morgan and Stanford had gone to college. In fact, most of them had left home by age 16 to make their way in the world. Historian Stewart H. Holbrook describes the future robber barons or captains of industry as having had "a splendid audacity and a vital energy that erupted in astonishing ways . . . all were men of devout individualism . . . each had an overpowering sense of acquisitiveness . . . [each] held stoutly to the proposition that what is and shall be is determined by the forces at work."[37] With few exceptions, these self-made individuals came from poor families, were relatively uneducated, and entered the business world before age 16.

---

[37] S. H. Holbrook, *The Ago of the Moguls* (Garden City, NY: Doubleday, 1953), p. viii.

This generation of leaders was determined to dominate in all their endeavors. The stories about Rockefeller's ascent to the position of monopolist in the oil industry are legion. "Reckafellow," as Carnegie called Rockefeller, was known for such tactics as offering to buy a competitor's business at about 40 percent of its asset value. If the competitor refused, Rockefeller would proceed to bankrupt the company through various ploys such as selling below cost or suggesting that railroads not handle shipments (or that they charge double or quadruple the normal rate). However, Rockefeller was unique only in his level of success, for his colleagues used similar strategies.

Additional factors often were involved in the emergence of big business. The diligence and attention to detail that characterized the business conduct of such business leaders as Rockefeller, Cornelius Vanderbilt, and J. Pierpont Morgan helped them dominate others in business transactions. Rockefeller's most thorough biographer, Allen Nevins, offers an example that supports Rockefeller's quest for efficiency:

> He watched a machine for filling the tin cans. One dozen cans stood on a wooden platform beneath a dozen pipes. A man pulled a lever, and each pipe discharged exactly five gallons of kerosene into a can. Still on a wooden carrier, the dozen cans were pushed along to another machine where 12 tops were swiftly clamped fast on the cans. Thence they were pushed to the last machine in which just enough solder to fasten and seal the lid was dropped on each can.
>
> Mr. Rockefeller listened in silence while an expert told all about the various machines used to save labor and time and expense in the process. At last Mr. Rockefeller asked:
>
> "How many drops of solder do you use on each can?" "Forty."
>
> "Have you ever tried 38? No? Would you mind having some sealed with 38 and let me know?"
>
> Six or 7 percent of these cans leaked. Then 39 drops were used. None leaked. It was tried with 100, 500, 1,000 cans. None leaked. Thereafter every can was sealed with 39 drops.[38]

Nevins explains that "Rockefeller grasped early the great truth that inefficiency and waste are a form of dishonesty, a theft of wealth which might be used for the general good."[39] Nevins further notes that the savings from the use of less solder amounted to $2,500 in the first year, and as the business grew, "the savings accumulated into a fund of hundreds of thousands of dollars."[40]

Even the closest attention to detail could not help companies whose management was unable to ensure continuous sources of supply, transportation at competitive rates, and markets in which the output could be sold at equitable prices. The same free marketplace that allowed all firms to compete

---

[38] A. Nevins, *Study in Power: John D. Rockefeller, Industrialist and Philanthropist.* vol. 1 (New York: Charles Scribner's Sons, 1953), pp. 280–81.

[39] Ibid., p. 281.

[40] Ibid., p. 428.

unhampered by restrictive taxes and government regulations also permitted financially strong and aggressive entrepreneurs to engage in predatory price cutting, gain rate concessions from railroads, and otherwise wreak havoc with highly competitive markets. The difficulty was compounded whenever a firm had a high investment in capital, as economist Alfred Eichner noted:

> The same force of technology which so greatly reduced the costs of production and made it possible to turn out goods of uniform quality in large numbers also required a substantial investment in fixed assets, thereby making the capital output ratio significantly high. This meant that whenever the demand for a firm's produce fell, it was under considerable economic pressure to try to expand its sales by cutting its price and in this way spread its overhead costs over a larger volume."[41]

The typical response to price cutting in the 1870s and 1880s involved informal alliances, known as pooling, among competitors. Rival firms got together to agree on common prices for the various classes of products, establish output quotas, and divide market territories. Voting power in the pool was allocated on the basis of market power, with larger competitors having more votes. The pool also established fines for members that cut prices. The fines were often ineffective, however, because excess capacity in most industries encouraged companies to undercut the legally unenforceable prices and quotas.

A successful pooling arrangement in the oil industry, the South Improvement Company, was set up in 1872. But the Gunpowder Trade Association, established in the same year by Colonel Henry DuPont, served as the model for pooling arrangements.[42] Seven competitors met to agree on prices for black gunpowder and set a $1-per-keg fine for price cutting. There were 48 votes, with DuPont and two other large companies having 10 votes each. By 1877, Henry DuPont had bought interest in several other pool members, thus obtaining control of more than 50 percent of the votes.[43] However, many members violated the pooling agreements. Between 1881 and 1883 alone, there were 230 separate, short-lived incidents of price cutting by members of the pool.[44] The Gunpowder Trade Association continued in operation until 1907, when the federal government successfully brought suit against DuPont for violation of the Sherman Antitrust Act. The suit, which was resolved in 1911, divided DuPont into three companies: DuPont, Hercules Powder, and Atlas Powder.

---

[41] A. S. Eichner, *The Emergence of Oligopoly: Sugar Refining as a Case Study* (Baltimore: Johns Hopkins University Press, 1969), p. 13.
[42] G. C. Zilg, *DuPont: Behind the Nylon Curtain* (Englewood Cliffs, NJ: Prentice Hall, 1974), p. 66.
[43] Ibid., p. 67.
[44] Ibid., p. 89.

Industrialists quickly found a solution to the price cutting in pooling arrangements: Competitors joined into one organization. The trust, as this form of business organization was called, is discussed in Chapter 8. Cochran and Miller observe, "Trusts could appear only in a society in which the corporation had become the dominant type of business organization, in which property rights were represented not by land or other physical assets, but by negotiable paper easily convertible into other types of negotiable paper."[45]

Soon the whiskey, salt, leather, cottonseed oil, sugar, and many other industries created trusts. Several states challenged the charters of companies that had become trusts, questioning whether such an "agreement tends to stifle competition and enhance prices, and therefore to work an injury to trade and commerce."[46] By 1889, cases had been successfully prosecuted against the Sugar Trust in New York, the Gas Trust in Illinois, and the Cottonseed Oil Trust in Louisiana.[47] The passage of the Sherman Antitrust Act in 1890 did little to dissolve trusts, partly due to vague wording and partly because the government was rather lax in its enforcement. Indeed, business leaders, realizing that some antitrust legislation was inevitable, worked diligently to ensure that the wording of the act made the law as weak as possible. Only one case was successfully prosecuted against a trust in the first 14 years of the Sherman Act.[48]

Horizontal combinations continued under a state law enacted in New Jersey in 1889. The New Jersey Holding Company Act allowed companies to achieve the price control purpose of trusts by buying controlling interests in competing firms. By 1904, the seven largest industrial companies in the country were chartered in New Jersey.[49] The strategy for many of the combinations was defensive. The primary concern was preservation of capital. However, the financial resources and expertise required to create trusts and holding companies resided not with the owner-managers of industrial capitalism but with the investment bankers who came to dominate business during the mid-1890s to the depth of the Great Depression in 1933.

Finance Capitalism

The period from 1893 to 1933 marked the fifth stage of capitalism, finance capitalism. Bankers and investment brokers became the prevailing force in American business during this period. A major reason for their dominance was their ability to effect industrial combinations and subsequently gain important directorships. Alfred Chandler observes that the railroad system most closely exemplified financial capitalism in the United States. The

---

[45] Cochran and Miller, *The Age of Enterprise*, p. 142.
[46] Eichner, *The Emergence of Oligopoly*, p. 137.
[47] Ibid., p. 141.
[48] *United States v. Addystone Pipe and Steel Co., et al.*, 175 U.S. 211(1899).
[49] Cochran and Miller, *The Age of Enterprise*, p. 190.

bankers, who sometimes outnumbered shareholders, were not strategists or operating managers but nevertheless had tremendous influence over board decisions.[50]

By 1893, it was apparent in many industries that economies of scale were being achieved through merger. The national railroad system was essentially complete, providing access to vital markets. High tariffs protected nearly all major industries. The federal government failed to use the Sherman Act to aggressively prosecute trusts and holding companies. In addition, the financial capitalists often were able to produce enormous profits for stock owners who entered into trusts and holding companies. The device used was to overcapitalize assets by offering the shares of the new corporation to the public at a much higher price than the par, or stated value, of existing assets. The public, perhaps believing large trusts and holding companies could earn more profits than the individual components would have earned, seldom disappointed the financiers.

By 1904, at the height of the merger movement, there were 318 industrial trusts involving 5,288 separate plants, 75 percent of which had been incorporated since 1897.[51]

The most visible example of the financial capitalist's dominance in business during this period was the formation of U.S. Steel in 1901. The first billion-dollar corporation, U.S. Steel was capitalized at $1,402,846,000, although its constituent parts had assets of only $626 million.[52] The major components were Federal Steel (a trust organized in 1898), Carnegie Steel, and the Mesabi Range iron ore interests of John D. Rockefeller. The combine brought together more than 60 plants, including mines, railroads, shipping companies, and steel mills with 60 percent of the nation's steel-producing capacity.

Andrew Carnegie was the major stumbling block to creating U.S. Steel. He had neither joined nor participated in any of the trusts and was not dominated by financial interests because he had financed the growth of his $400 million enterprise through retained earnings. When the various smaller steel and iron trusts (wire, tin plate, nails, tube, and others) had been formed and threatened to discontinue purchase of Carnegie Steel, his response was to begin manufacture of the products made by the trusts. Not only could he make the products but, in his well-known quest for efficiency, could probably do so at lower cost than the trusts. Financier J. Pierpont Morgan, whose syndicate would clear $57 million for assembling U.S. Steel, approached Charles Schwab, one of Carnegie's closest associates.[53] Carnegie recounted the story in his autobiography:

---

[50] Chandler, *Visible Hand,* p. 187.

[51] M. Josephson, *The Robber Barons* (New York: Harcourt Brace Jovanovich, 1962), p. 387.

[52] F. L. Allen, *The Great Pierpoint* (New York: Harper & Row, 1949), p. 144.

[53] Ibid., p. 147.

> Mr. Schwab told me Mr. Morgan had said to him he should really like to know if I wished to retire from business; if so he thought he could arrange it . . . I considered what was fair and that is the option Morgan got. Schwab went down and arranged it. I never saw Morgan on the subject or any man connected with him. Never a word passed between him and me. I gave my memorandum and Morgan saw it was eminently fair. I have been told many times since by insiders that I should have asked $100 million more and could have got it easily.[54]

Morgan's power was unequaled. Journalist Lincoln Steffans said of him, "In all my time, J. P. Morgan sat on the American throne as the boss of bosses, as the ultimate American sovereign."[55] N. S. B. Gras wrote of Morgan, "For nearly a generation, Morgan rivalled kings and presidents as an object of interest, respect, and hate."[56] Among Morgan's achievements were the rescue of the U.S. monetary system in 1895 and the prevention of a banking collapse of 1907. On both occasions, U.S. presidents sought his counsel and followed his directions explicitly. Morgan was also responsible for the creation of such industrial giants as General Electric, International Harvester, and American Telephone and Telegraph. Morgan, however, nearly destroyed the financial structure of the country in an incident that led to the first antitrust dissolution decision of the U.S. Supreme Court. The following account describes the methods of finance capitalism.

In 1900, the two major railroads in the Pacific Northwest were the Great Northern, owned and operated by James J. Hill, and the Northern Pacific, controlled by Hill with the backing of Morgan. Hill and Morgan wanted to extend the line eastward to Chicago by purchasing the Chicago, Burlington, and Quincy line and operating as a subsidiary of the Northern Pacific. However, Edward H. Harriman, then president of the Union Pacific, also coveted the Chicago, Burlington, and Quincy line. His approach, which was totally unexpected, was to buy the operating control of the parent, Northern Pacific. He did so quietly on the open market, supported by the Rockefeller-controlled investment house of Kuhn and Loeb. By the time Morgan (who was on an extended vacation in Europe) found out, Harriman had nearly 50 percent of the Northern Pacific stock, at a cost of more than $78 million. When Morgan and Harriman each made a last effort to obtain over half of the stock, they drove the price from $120 to $1,000 per share in less than two days. Those who had sold the stock scrambled to buy the extremely scarce shares to be able to participate in the price rise.

As a result of these and other machinations, the vast majority of stocks on the New York Stock Exchange declined precipitously, and many fortunes were lost. Morgan and Harriman quickly made peace and prevented a total

---

[54] A. Carnegie, *Autobiography of Andrew Carnegie* (Boston: Houghton Mifflin, 1920), p. 246.

[55] L. Steffans, *Autobiography of Lincoln Steffans* (New York: Harcourt Brace Jovanovich, 1931), p. 587.

[56] Gras, *Business and Capitalism,* p. 247.

market collapse by offering to buy Northern Pacific shares at $150 per share. The Morgan and Harriman forces then created Northern Securities Holding Company to merge the assets of the Great Northern, Northern Pacific, and Chicago, Burlington, and Quincy railroads.

Shortly thereafter, Theodore Roosevelt, who had become president after McKinley was assassinated, brought suit against the Northern Securities combine under the Sherman Act. President Roosevelt differentiated between the good trusts, which had acquired assets through efficient operation, and bad trusts, which represented financial manipulation. These latter combinations, which he called malefactors of great wealth, were represented by Northern Securities Company.

When he heard of the antitrust suit, Morgan was amazed he had received no previous warning. According to Frederick Allen, "He went to Washington and saw the President. 'If we have done anything wrong,' said he, 'send your man to my man and they can fix it up.'"[57] The president refused to withdraw the suit, and in 1904, by a five-to-four vote, the U.S. Supreme Court ordered the dissolution of Northern Securities Company. Other antitrust cases followed, and by 1911 Standard Oil, American Tobacco, and DuPont all were ordered to divide into smaller companies.

The American public was informed of the excesses of the money trust during the 1912 hearings conducted by Senator Pujo of Louisiana. The widely chronicled testimony of J. Pierpont Morgan and other New York bankers and investment brokers produced some astounding revelations. Although the then 75-year-old Morgan denied he had any power at all, he gave an insight into his methods when he insisted that what ruled the financial world was not money but character:

> "Is not commercial credit based primarily upon money or property?" asked [committee counsel] Untermayer.
> "No, sir," said Morgan, "the first thing is character."
> "Before money or property?"
> "Before money or anything else. Money cannot buy it . . . Because a man I do not trust could not get money from me on all the bonds in Christendom."[58]

The Pujo committee revealed to a shocked nation that Morgan and two other New York bankers and their associates controlled 341 directorships in 112 corporations having a combined capitalization of $22 billion.[59]

The criticisms of the finance capitalists revealed by the Pujo committee were subsequently incorporated into the New Freedom program of Woodrow Wilson through the passage of the Federal Reserve Act and the Clayton Antitrust Act, which were intended to limit the powers of the private bankers.

---

[57] F. L. Allen, *The Lords of Creation* (New York: Harper & Row, 1935), p. 68.
[58] Allen, *The Great Pierpoint Morgan*, p. 8.
[59] R. Hofstadter, ed., *The Progressive Movement, 1900–1915* (Englewood Cliffs, NJ: Prentice Hall, 1963), p. 160.

However, these acts had little immediate impact as the nation prepared to enter World War I. The War Industries Board was established under the direction of financier Bernard Baruch to mobilize production capacity. During World War I, the performance of large industrial firms was generally well regarded by the populace.

Business-government relations hit a new high during the 1920s, particularly with Herbert Hoover as secretary of commerce. Hoover openly encouraged trade association activity and was so strongly probusiness that he once acted as intermediary for a company inquiry about possible antitrust consequences of a proposed acquisition. During this period, Judge Elbert H. Gary, as chief executive officer of U.S. Steel, could announce price rises honored throughout the industry at quasi-public dinners, with no government action.

Also during the 1920s, holding companies became so widespread that by 1928 only 86 out of 573 firms listed on the New York Stock Exchange were nonholding companies.[60] The holding company, particularly as it functioned in public utilities, became so "complicated that it was difficult to arrive at even the vaguest idea of the actual worth of their soaring stocks."[61] There was no strong movement to change the holding company, since its stock prices were steadily rising.

Calvin Coolidge became president following Warren Harding's sudden death in 1923. The years that followed have been referred to often as the period of Coolidge prosperity because the nation enjoyed unprecedented economic growth. There were many reasons for the tremendous growth. First, the automobile became a necessity for many Americans; 23,121,000 cars were in service by 1929, compared to 6,771,000 in 1919. Second, the nation fell in love with the wireless phoney as the radio, commercially introduced in 1921, was called. Third, sales of cigarettes doubled in the 1920s. Fourth, demand for such products as rayon, telephones, refrigerators, and cosmetics increased dramatically. Fifth, urbanites went to the movies at an average rate of more than once per week. Finally, chain drug, grocery, and five-and-dime stores doubled and then tripled sales in the 1920s.[62] All these factors added to the ever-increasing demand for the products of business.

Coolidge prosperity owed its success to several factors. The nation emerged from World War I intact both economically and physically, while most of Europe was devastated. As a result, the United States became the world economic superpower. Engineers such as Frederick W. Taylor and Frank B. Gilbreth developed and applied mass production methods widely and with considerable success. In addition, demand for new products such as

---

[60] A. Rochester, *Rulers of America: A Study of Financial Capital* (New York: Harper & Row, 1949), p. 87.

[61] Allen, *The Lords of Creation,* p. 244.

[62] F. L. Allen, *Only Yesterday: An Informal History of the 1920s* (New York: Harper & Row, 1931), pp. 109, 163, 165, 166–68.

Exhibit 6–2 Selected Stock Prices, 1929 High versus 1932 Low

	1929 High	1932 Low
Consolidated Cigar	$115	$ 2½
Erie Railroad	93½	2
General Foods	82	20
General Motors	91	8
New York Central	256	9
Radio Corporation of America	115	2½
Southern Railway	165	2½
U.S. Steel	261	21
Wright Aeronautical	150	4

Source: G. V. Axon, *The Stock Market Crash of 1929* (New York: Mason and Lipscomb, 1974), pp. 93–94.

the automobile, created many jobs. For instance, out of a workforce numbering just over 30 million, nearly 4 million workers were either directly or indirectly involved in auto production. On the demand side, installment buying became popular; more than 15 percent of retail purchases were made on credit by 1929. There was a widespread rise in advertising and sales techniques. These marketing tools became very important ingredients in the success formula for consumer goods companies.

Yet another factor contributing to Coolidge prosperity came from profits made in stock market speculation. Everyone seemed to be putting money into the stock market, often on credit by buying stock and using it as collateral to obtain a loan to buy more stock. Such methods created leverage that worked beautifully when stock prices were rising rapidly. The same methods produced very different results when stock prices tumbled precipitously and the bottom fell out of the stock market in the period following Black Monday, October 29, 1929. Exhibit 6–2 shows the dramatic fall in selected stock prices from 1929 to 1932. Hearings held by the Senate Committee on Banking and Currency in 1933 did much to discredit the bankers who dominated the era of finance capitalism. The findings showed widespread manipulation of stock prices, misuse of the holding company approach to business organizations, and tax dodges such as sales of stock (at a loss) to family members to eliminate income tax liability. Allen noted about the hearings, "Again and again, it showed how men occupying fiduciary positions in the financial world had been false to their trust."[63] Such revelations, coupled with the inability of big business to lift the country out of the Great Depression, lowered public confidence in big business and thus set the stage for the reform programs of the New Deal.

---

[63] Allen, *The Lords of Creation,* p. 244.

National Capitalism

Gras's sixth and final stage of capitalism is *national capitalism.* At this stage proponents rejected the strict application of the laissez-faire theory of government nonintervention in the economy.[64] However, they also differed on the extent and content of a broadened government role.

Gras identifies four major movements advocating the expanded use of government fiscal, monetary, and regulatory capability: the Progressive movement of the early 20th century, the New Deal of the Great Depression, the Fair Deal of the late 1940s and early 1950s, and the New Frontier-Great Society programs of the 1960s. These movements "were essentially pragmatic in their approach to the use of state power and were inclined to decide whether or not to invoke the aid of the state in coping with any particular problem on the merits of the case rather than in accordance with some preconceived plan or idea."[65] However, these social movements differed with respect to particular objectives and programs.

The Progressive Movement. The Progressive movement came out of the Populist and Grange movements of the 1880s that advocated equal opportunity for farmers, workers, and small-business owners. However, the national Progressive movement leadership was mostly urban and middle class. The Progressive party, which developed its formal program in 1910, sponsored Theodore Roosevelt as a third-party candidate for president of the United States. The party's platform rested on restoring competition and equal opportunity for all.

Progressives had several goals. The first was to provide the underprivileged with a larger share of the nation's benefits. The second was to make government more responsive to voters' wishes and to regulate the economy for the public good. Progressives promoted the concept of the *living wage,* an income sufficient for basic family needs such as education, recreation, health, and retirement.

Progressives also were strongly concerned with the preservation and sound use of natural resources. They called for conservation of forests and other public lands and for the orderly development of the nation's river basins. They pushed for reform in state and municipal governments to control utilities and business more efficiently and to better manage the functions of government. With respect to big business, the Progressives pressed for repeal of protective tariffs and for the establishment of the National Industrial Commission that would "compel publicity for the acts of corporations that it supervised, ensure honest capitalization, and check unwarranted price boosts, restrictions on production, and any other unfair practices."[66]

---

[64] Gras, *Business and Capitalism,* p. 323.

[65] S. Fine, *Laissez-Faire and the General-Welfare State: A Study of Conflict in America Thought, 1865–1901* (Ann Arbor: University of Michigan Press, 1956), p. 380.

[66] Fine, *Laissez-Faire,* p. 390.

The Progressive movement ended in 1916 with the return of Theodore Roosevelt to the Republican party. President Woodrow Wilson enacted the major proposals of the Progressives in 1913 and 1914 under his New Freedom program but major social and business reform movements remained dormant until 1932. When Franklin D. Roosevelt was sworn into office as president on March 4, 1933, he began what he had earlier called "bold, persistent experimentation."

The New Deal. In his inaugural address, President Roosevelt blamed bankers for the country's troubles, declaring that "the money changers have fled from their high seats in the temples of our civilization."[67] Roosevelt closed the nation's banks for several days to prevent mass withdrawals. The banking system was not the only part of the economy in disrepair; 25 percent of the workforce was unemployed, and low commodities prices had made farmers destitute. Two days later, in the first of many fireside chats broadcast over the radio, the president explained calmly and reassuringly how the banks would be reopened. Aided by his brain trust of economic advisers, his legislative program rapidly took shape. Its major thrust was "to gain a greater social justice" for the working class.

The National Industrial Recovery Act (NIRA), enacted in 1933, was to restore the business sector to full productivity. The act suspended the antitrust laws to allow trade associations to draw up codes of conduct governing prices, hours, and output to encourage production at fair rates of profit.

The NIRA included a clause that gave employees the right to choose their own representatives to organize and bargain for them, free from employer interference, restraint, or coercion. This clause encouraged labor to accept the act. Manufacturers, however, opposed the legislated right of labor to bargain collectively. Indeed, when Henry Ford refused to join the automobile industry's effort to develop a code of conduct, his company suffered lengthy strikes at two plants. Ford fired many of the strikers following the strikes.

After the Supreme Court declared the NIRA unconstitutional in 1935, Roosevelt reintroduced collective bargaining legislation under the Wagner Act. This act created the National Labor Relations Board to supervise the rights of employees to select a bargaining agent. Congress also enacted the Fair Labor Standards Act that specified rights for employees not covered by collective bargaining agreements.

Under the New Deal, the federal government introduced regulatory controls over banks, issues of securities, securities exchanges, public utility holding companies, and motor carriers. The New Deal also provided relief and jobs for the needy and the unemployed, constructed public housing, and provided electrical power for farmers and others. It extended low-interest loans to a wide variety of individuals and institutions, generally expanding the

---

[67] A. Schlesinger, Jr., *The Coming of the New Deal* (Boston: Houghton Mifflin, 1958), p. 303.

entire program of natural resource conservation. The national Social Security program was yet another innovation. Despite all the programs and successes of the Keynesian-oriented New Deal, President Roosevelt told the nation in his second inaugural address in 1937, "I see one-third of the nation ill-housed, ill-clad, ill-nourished."

By the close of the decade, the New Deal had effectively run its course. According to Cochran, "In spite of loud protests and mutual mistrust, the New Deal and World War II forced government and business to work more closely together, a relationship which grew in importance in later years."[68] After Roosevelt's death, the nation entered a new stage of national capitalism under the presidency of Harry S. Truman.

The Fair Deal. President Truman supported the basic concepts of the New Deal. His Fair Deal institutionalized the role of government as the stabilizing force in the economy. The Employment Act of 1946 established the three-member Council of Economic Advisers, whose role included assisting the president in formulating economic policy and publishing an annual economic report.

The remainder of the Fair Deal, outlined in a State of the Union Address in 1949, pledged, "Every segment of our population and every individual has a right to expect from his government a fair deal."[69] Specifically, this program included measures to improve the collective bargaining process while prohibiting certain types of strikes. It strengthened the antitrust laws, improved farm output and prices, and expanded Social Security, medical insurance, and public housing. While some major features of this program were enacted (notably in public housing and Social Security), much of the Fair Deal wallowed in the do-nothing 80th Congress of 1947-1948[70] and the ho-hum 81st Congress of 1949-1950.[71]

Much of the legislation sought by President Truman was enacted during Dwight D. Eisenhower's presidency. The Eisenhower years, from 1953 to 1960, featured a middle-of-the-road domestic policy, preserving the social gains of the earlier reform movements while stressing the need for a balanced federal budget. From 1955 to 1960, President Eisenhower worked with an active Democratic Congress. The combination yielded noteworthy achievements in civil rights, air and water pollution control, aid to education, Social Security, highway construction, and agricultural support.[72]

---

[68] Cochran, *American Business,* p. 176.

[69] Quoted in L. W. Koenig, ed., *The Truman Administration: Its Principles and Practices* (New York: New York University Press, 1956), p. 93.

[70] *Politics in America: The Politics and Issues of the Post-War Years,* 3rd. ed. (Washington, DC: Congressional Quarterly Service, 1969), p. 9.

[71] E. F. Goldman, *The Crucial Decade—And After: America, 1945–1960* (New York: Vantage Books, 1960), p. 95.

[72] J. L. Sundquist, *Politics and Policy: The Eisenhower, Kennedy, and Johnson Years* (Washington, DC: Brookings Institution, 1968), pp. 390–91.

President Eisenhower's cabinet included several business leaders. Indeed, the cabinet was known as eight millionaires and a plumber. The former term referred to the large number of business leaders who served in the cabinet. The plumber was Secretary of Labor Martin Durkin, president of the Journeyman Plumbers and Steamfitters Union.

The New Frontier. John F. Kennedy continued the social progress begun under Presidents Truman and Eisenhower. He supported programs to deal with structural unemployment through retraining and area redevelopment.[73] Additional social legislation included a housing bill, a minimum-wage increase and extension of the minimum wage to additional groups, and an increase in Social Security benefits.

President Kennedy spoke of a New Frontier in economics under which the nation would experience unprecedented economic growth.[74] A major element of the New Frontier concept was the idea of a personal income tax cut to stimulate investment, consumption, and employment at a time when the federal budget was balanced and inflation, production increases, and unemployment were all at tolerable levels.[75]

Under the New Frontier, business was asked to voluntarily maintain price and wage levels in accordance with demonstrated increases in productivity gains. In 1962, an incident occurred that tested President Kennedy's power of persuasion to hold down inflation. Roger Blough, chairperson of the board of U.S. Steel, announced a $6-per-ton price increase for steel shortly after signing a noninflationary wage settlement with the Steelworkers Union. Other major steel producers also increased prices. Kennedy responded immediately, bringing the full fiscal power of the federal government to bear by threatening to transfer government steel purchases to companies that had not raised prices. Three days after the announcements of increased prices, the major companies returned to the earlier prices. Many businesspeople saw Kennedy's effort as a major example of an antibusiness administration. The incident may have contributed to the remarkable price stability experienced from 1961 to 1965, a period during which consumer prices advanced at approximately 1 percent per year.

At the time President Kennedy was assassinated, the Tax Reform Act, the Equal Opportunity Act, and the Civil Rights Act had not yet been passed. All were passed in the year following his death. However, President Kennedy clearly initiated the basic ideas in the three measures.

---

[73] *Structural unemployment* refers to unemployment brought about by the displacement of workers due to changes in the means of production, most notably through automation of manual work.

[74] E. R. Canterbery, *Economics on a New Frontier* (Belmont, CA: Wadsworth, 1986), p. 6.

[75] *Politics in America,* pp. 49–50.

The Great Society. President Lyndon B. Johnson's Great Society extended national capitalism. From 1964 to 1968, Congress enacted programs to support medical aid for older Americans, improve consumer information and product safety, improve housing, and create the Office of Economic Opportunity to administer the War on Poverty program. Johnson also created the cabinet-level Department of Housing and Urban Development in 1965 and the Department of Transportation in 1966. The role of government continually expanded in the Great Society years. Fine concluded,

> Americans would appear to have rejected the admonition that the government is best which governs least and to have endorsed the view that in the interests of the general welfare the state should restrain the strong and protect the weak, should provide such services to the people as private enterprise is unable or unwilling to supply, should seek to stabilize the economy and to counteract the cycle of boom and bust, and should provide the citizen with some degree of economic stability.[76]

The 1970s. On the domestic front, the administrations of Presidents Nixon, Ford, and Carter called for less government involvement in the private sector and less regulation of business. Nevertheless, federal legislation continued to influence nearly every aspect of business management.

By the late 1970s, the distribution of wealth in the United States was changing. The rich were getting richer and the poor poorer. The very rich had made up the smallest segment of the American public since the 1830s, and the middle class was suffering an increasing tax burden.

The overhaul of the United States Bankruptcy Code in 1978 set the stage for the explosion of corporate debt that lasted throughout the 1980s. For the first time, companies were permitted to stay in business while they resolved their financial problems.

The 1970s marked the proliferation and growth of international business as technologically sophisticated multinationals produced large volumes of chemicals, machinery, automobiles, and electronics. As international trade in these products and in developing-country raw materials expanded rapidly during the 1970s, the United States grew increasingly dependent on foreign markets. The control of the Organization of Petroleum Exporting Countries (OPEC) over world oil prices brought home the consequences of such interdependence. We discuss the emergence and operations of multinationals in Chapter 18.

The Reagan and Bush Administrations. As restructuring through takeovers, diversification, and consolidations became rampant, corporations changed in size, scope, and shape. In April and May 1988 alone, the Campeau Company bought Federated Department Stores for $6.6 billion and

---

[76] Fine, *Laissez-Faire,* pp. 399–400.

sold $1.1 billion of Federated assets to R. H. Macy & Company; West Point-Pepperell, Inc., agreed to buy J. P. Stevens & Company for $1.2 billion and sold nearly half of it to the rival bidder, Odyssey Partners; and General Electric and Whirlpool made a deal over the acquisition of Roper Corporation. Tax law changes in the late 1980s made it more attractive to carve up newly acquired assets among takeover bidders.[77]

Employees of these companies faced an uncertain future in the 1980s. In the late 1980s, middle management and even top-level ranks were slashed along with unprofitable divisions. The crash of the stock market on October 19, 1987, threw thousands of investment bankers and financial institution managers into the ranks of the unemployed. Fewer and fewer companies offered lifetime career opportunities.

Public concern about ethics was aired more frequently during the second Reagan term. On the corporate side, Ivan Boesky's conviction and the indictment and conviction of others who took part in insider trading rocked Wall Street. Heroes turned into villains almost overnight. As a result of the crash and the scandals, business schools began to examine their curricula. The study of ethics, long considered irrelevant or unteachable, became a mandatory part of undergraduate and graduate programs in business.

Ethics in government came under closer scrutiny as members of President Reagan's staff and cabinet became involved in scandals ranging from military procurement to illegal lobbying to trading of arms for hostages. The scandals that rocked the administration often were linked to corporations and to the process through which corporations received government contracts.

Women made major inroads into lower- and middle-management ranks of American companies throughout the 1980s. However, they continued to hit the glass ceiling of top management and to earn less than their male counterparts. Minorities and people with disabilities fared even worse. The three Reagan appointees to the Supreme Court changed the court's ideological balance and opened some of the civil rights legislation of the 1960s and 1970s to reconsideration.

Concerns about the environment proliferated in the 1980s. During the last year of the Reagan administration, the hazards of acid rain, increased levels of atmospheric ozone, and ocean pollution became all too apparent. During the summer of 1988, as scorching temperatures broke records across the United States, bathers on Atlantic Ocean beaches had to dodge illegally dumped vials of contaminated blood and used hypodermic needles. Elderly people and people with respiratory or allergy problems gasped in smoggy cities from coast to coast, and farmers wondered whether the drought that stunted their crops was due to the greenhouse effect.

---

[77] E. D. Lee, "Takeover Predators Now Share the Prey," *The Wall Street Journal*, April 29, 1988, p. 6.

Consumers continued to lobby for safer products and to sue when products failed to fulfill expectations or caused injury. Administration-sponsored legislation to limit damages and preempt state laws that were inconsistent with federal laws slowly worked its way through Congress.

By the 1992 election campaign, the public demanded a change. In mid-August, a Gallup poll asked voters how President Bush was doing. Only 30 percent approved of his performance. The country was mired in a recession that put millions of Americans onto the unemployment rolls. Most Americans no longer believed in unfettered upward mobility or in the American Dream of the 19th century. Clinton's election can be attributed as much to disenchantment with Reaganomics and the recession of the Bush administration as to enthusiasm for the young president. But Clinton's call to change was a promise voters could not ignore.

The Clinton Presidency, 1992–96. Clinton's election and subsequent initiatives accentuated the nation's ideological divisions. In the summer of 1993, Clinton pushed for a budget to reduce the deficit. He told the American people, "We're on the verge of breaking out of the old false choice between tax-and-spend and trickle-down, between abandonment and entitlement." He promised to overhaul the health care and welfare systems.[78] Senate Democrats narrowly passed the $496 billion deficit-reduction package on August 6. Senate Republican leader Bob Dole ridiculed the measure urging Americans to "put down their remote control and grab their wallet . . . because your taxes are about to go up."[79]

Controversy roiled as Clinton's budget, health care, and regulatory proposals came under Republican fire. National malaise and uncertainty over the economy swept House Republicans to victory in the November 1994 congressional elections. At the end of December, House Republicans prepared to push for legislation that would radically restrict the government's ability to regulate everything from wilderness to product safety. During the first 100 days, they vowed to push to a vote legislative proposals that would create a regulatory budget or a specific ceiling on the cost of complying with all federal regulations. If adopted, the proposals would radically alter the operations of the Environmental Protection Agency, the Transportation Department, and the Forest Service.

A Republican draft bill was called the Job Creation and Wage Enhancement Act of 1995. Its approach was to limit the scope of regulation by imposing limits on the rule makers. Interest groups on both sides of the issues agreed that the proposals would create the most bitter political struggles in

---

[78] G. Ifill, "Clinton Pushes for Budget, Reassuring Public on Taxes and Vowing Economic Gains," *New York Times,* August 4, 1993, p. A1.

[79] J. A. Farrell, "Senate Gives Final Nod to Deficit Plan," *Boston Globe,* August 7, 1993, p. 1.

recent memory.[80] The job creation bill and the Contract with America are discussed in detail in Chapter 1. Despite the fervor of the newly elected House members, the balance of powers developed by the Founding Fathers stymied rapid adoption of new rules and regulations.

As the November 1996 election approached, the national mood was quite different from two years earlier. The economy was stable, the budget deficit reduced, and there were no foreign policy disasters involving American troops. The Clinton administration moved toward the center of the political spectrum, reducing the impact of Candidate Bob Dole's apocalyptic predictions of economic and moral disaster. The Dole–Kemp campaign's economic plan proposed $548 billion in tax cuts while promising to balance the budget by 2002. Analysts figured that as president, Dole would have to come up with $832 billion in savings over six years. The proposal was a 10 percent cut in administrative costs from all nondefense federal agencies; abolition of the Energy and Commerce Departments; reduction of discretionary spending on parks, highways, and mass transit and the environment; and a sell-off of broadcast frequencies.[81]

A Louis Harris poll of 1,007 adults conducted July 26–31, 1996, asked whether it was possible for Dole to both cut taxes and balance the budget. Sixty-nine percent of respondents answered it was not possible, 28 percent thought it was possible, and 3 percent didn't know. Forty-five percent of those polled said they would be most likely to vote for Clinton, 24 percent for Dole, 11 percent for Perot.[82] These percentages changed daily as the campaign season progressed but voters remained intensely skeptical of the Republicans' ability to deliver on its economic promises.

Clinton's approval ratings rose just before the Democratic convention with his signing of a bipartisan welfare reform bill, a health care reform bill, and an antismoking bill. There was no doubt that the bully pulpit strongly helped the incumbent president.

Summary

This chapter examines the development of business as the dominant institution in American society. It traces the factors leading to the development of big business and the major stages of business growth. Plentiful natural resources and favorable social and political environments were contributory factors.

The workforce, although growing and capable, was characterized by a shortage of skilled labor. As workers migrated to cities, they received relatively high wages and spent their discretionary income on a wide variety of consumer goods. Additional factors fostering the growth of big business included the

---

[80] J. H. Cushman, Jr., "Republicans Plan Sweeping Barriers to New U.S. Rules," *New York Times,* December 24, 1994, p. 1.

[81] K. Q. Seelye, "Dole Offers Economic Plan Calling for Broad Tax Cut Aimed at Spurring Growth," *New York Times,* August 6, 1996, p. A1.

[82] "*Business Week/*Harris Poll," *Business Week,* August 19, 1996, p. 38.

development of affordable and widely available transportation and the expansion of knowledge and know-how. No one of these factors explains the growth of big business in the United States, but together they served as a catalyst for economic and social development.

N. S. B. Gras's six stages of capitalism suggest a framework for analyzing the major trends and developments of big business. The periods of industrial capitalism and finance capitalism were dominated by relatively small numbers of individuals who created major business enterprises. The stage of national capitalism involved a larger role for government in guiding and controlling the business sector of the economy. The Progressive movement, the New Deal, the Fair Deal, the New Frontier, the Great Society, the Reagan and Bush administrations, and the Clinton administration differed in their causes and programs. Since World War II, the relationships between business and the economic environment have generally increased in complexity.

Questions

1. Are the conditions that enabled big business to grow in the United States the same as those that fostered big-business growth in Europe? Explain.
2. What are the common factors of big-business growth, if any, in the United States and Japan?
3. How has American ideology changed in the century since the passage of the Interstate Commerce and Sherman Antitrust acts?
4. Are there robber barons in the 1990s in the sense of a few business leaders who enjoy immense economic power? Do the trends of the 1990s differ from those of the 1980s?
5. What are some fundamental changes in the business-government interaction that occurred during the Clinton administration?

Beta Case 6
The Origins of Big Business

Robert Mobley, Beta's general counsel and a senior partner of Sullivan, Timberlake, and Frawley, regularly attended the firm's monthly operating committee meeting. At the October meeting, he suggested that the company institute a document retention program. It soon became apparent to the committee that Mobley was proposing a program that should have been called a document disposal program. Mobley wanted to implement a policy that would discard hard copies of most company documents after five years. He argued that if Beta were involved in litigation with the government or another company, documents could be subpoenaed. These documents, however innocent, could be twisted and used for a corporate witch hunt. Mobley even rejected the idea of transferring the data to disk, detailing several cases in which memos and telephone messages were used as evidence against a company involved in litigation regarding patent infringement, antitrust, and other violations. On several occasions, damages to the company totaled millions of dollars. He did not want a paper trail or even the possibility of retrieving electronic data. He noted that even E-mail left a trail that could be used in litigation.

Everyone on the committee seemed persuaded that the document retention program was a good idea. The only dissenter was Bill Parker, head of the company's Hospital Products Division. Parker, a history buff who enjoyed reading company chronicles, asked how Beta could hope to have any sense of its present and future if it systematically destroyed the record of its past. Parker was determined to keep original copies regardless of the technology that could copy them to disk.

As the committee debated the two points of view, Joan McCarthy remembered the process she had gone through as she set company objectives for social issues. She had rummaged through boxes and boxes of old records to find out what the company did before she made recommendations for what it should do. These boxes were still in an old storeroom next to the boiler in the basement. If Mobley's plan were adopted, they would be destroyed along with other documents. At the very least, she argued, it would be foolish not to keep an electronic copy.

PART II
POLITICAL AND COMMUNITY RESPONSIVENESS

The management of social responsiveness is tied to political and regulatory processes. An intricate web links firms to all levels of government and to the communities in which they operate. Part II establishes the ideological underpinnings of issues that we explore in much greater depth in subsequent chapters.

The four chapters that follow deal with the company's ability to conduct its affairs legally, to influence its political and regulatory environment in a forthright and positive fashion, and to act as a responsible citizen within the worldwide community.

CHAPTER 7
MANAGING THE LEGAL AND POLITICAL PROCESSES

Managers who formulate and implement social goals strategies must understand the legal structures and political processes that both provide opportunities for, and impose constraints on, their companies. The underpinnings of the U.S. legal and regulatory systems rest on a series of uniquely American events and historical antecedents. Today's corporate stakeholders shape and are shaped by legal and political processes that have evolved over more than two centuries.

In this chapter, we discuss the legal and regulatory frameworks within which corporations and their stakeholders operate. We examine the ideology that led to America's unique governmental system and the process through which legal and regulatory issues are developed and pursued.

The legal framework helps us understand the interaction between business and the political process. We examine the actions a company can take to train managers to operate effectively within the legal and political systems. We also discuss the specific managerial activities that influence the content and passage of legislation. We begin with a look at the legal system.

Case: Product Liability Law

During the 1970s and 1980s, product liability was a major issue for American companies. Business pointed to mounting numbers of lawsuits and huge judgments against them as evidence that the legal system was unfair and unbalanced. There was no nationwide, uniform law covering product liability; cases involving product liability were heard on a state-by-state basis. Huge judgments were awarded to plaintiffs in some states, while in others, awards for similar cases were relatively small. In some states, product liability cases were heard by judges; in others, juries made the decisions and allocated awards.

Trade organizations pressured Congress to pass federal legislation to eliminate aspects of product liability law their industries found particularly oppressive. In some states, for example, companies could be held liable even if their misconduct was unintentional. Business wanted the law changed to award punitive damages only if the company's wrongdoing was deliberate.

Business also wanted Congress to enact statutes of repose. A statute of repose assumes a product has a limited useful lifetime and provides an outer limit of liability for that product. After a specified time, the product's useful life is assumed to be over, and the owner or user can no longer sue the manufacturer. Industry claimed it was unreasonable to assume a product could be used forever.[1] The reform movement gathered support when litigation studies showed the number of product liability suits in federal courts increased 758 percent from 1975 to 1985.

Soaring insurance premiums were equally troublesome to companies. The genesis of the insurance crisis was complicated. Using a formula based on a company's capital and surplus, state regulations mandated how much insurance companies could write. Insurance companies collected dollars from the premiums of the firms they insured and invested those dollars to earn income. Investment income, coupled with the premiums, offset expected losses from claims.

In the early 1980s, interest rates rose dramatically, leading insurance companies to drop their premiums. They expected to write more policies to generate more money that they could then invest at the higher interest rates. In 1984 interest rates began to fall, however, and losses rose; the insurance industry lost nearly $4 billion.

When insurance companies reached the maximum number of policies permitted by state laws and were forced to reduce the amount of insurance they could write, they hiked their premiums to reduce losses. Businesses went to state legislatures, arguing that reform of tort law (civil law that allows recovery of damages) was necessary because they could no longer afford to buy sufficient insurance.

During the 1980s, some states passed reform laws covering some of the above issues and others. However, Congress repeatedly rejected any attempt to pass federal legislation despite the intensive efforts of lobbyists and other interest groups.[2]

Some consumer advocate groups argued that big business would take advantage of uniform limited-liability laws by foisting unsafe products on an unsuspecting public. They were convinced many businesses would try to save money in manufacturing if their legal liability for accidents or problems was limited. Many manufacturers and their lobbyists argued that the huge settlements and perpetual liability reduced their competitiveness and required them to pass unreasonable costs on to consumers.

In September 1992, after a decade of wrangling, the Federal Product Liability Fairness Act reached the floor of the Senate. If passed, it would supersede most state laws. It had some important provisions: Under this bill, the statute of limitations would begin to run only when claimants recognized they had suffered an injury and identified its cause. For example, an asbestos worker would have two years in which to file a claim after he was diagnosed with cancer, provided the cancer could be traced to asbestos exposure. The bill also encouraged pretrial settlement. If a claimant rejected settlement and, after a trial, received less

---

[1] F. E. Zollers and R. G. Cook, "Product Liability Reform: What Happened to the Crisis," *Business Horizons*, September–October 1990, pp. 47–52.

[2] Ibid.

than the settlement offer, the claimant would have to pay the other side's legal costs.[3]

An important provision of the bill eliminated joint liability for pain and suffering. Joint liability is the so-called deep pockets liability in which one defendant may be forced to pay for the acts of others. For example, if a plaintiff wins a $2 million lawsuit against a total of four companies, three small and one large, the three small companies are each held 30 percent responsible, and the one large company 10 percent responsible. The plaintiff can collect the entire $2 million from the one large company that was supposed to act as a collection agency for the three smaller companies.[4] Despite strong bipartisan support, the bill was defeated.

Immediately after President Bill Clinton's inauguration in January 1993, stakeholders from both sides geared up for a new fight. One major issue, left over from the defeated bill, was the passage of legislation limiting the ability of companies to conceal internal safety records in federal suits over allegedly defective products. Any new law would be especially important in ongoing litigation involving cigarettes, breast implants, and automobiles.

Pro-plaintiff stakeholders, including Ralph Nader's Public Citizen organization, planned to introduce legislation to require public disclosure of internal company documents. These same groups prepared to pressure Congress to expand the law to allow injured victims to sue polluters for personal injuries related to toxic dumping. (Current federal law allows recovery for cleanup but not for personal injury.) Another legal issue of concern was whether injured workers would be allowed to sue employers for damages in addition to civil penalties.[5]

By mid-1994, it was apparent that juries were getting tougher on plaintiffs. Jury Verdict Research, a court-watching group, reported the results of a survey of 3,300 product-liability cases. In 1987 individuals suing companies won 54 percent of product-defect cases; in 1994, they won 41 percent. The group attributed the change to lobbying and advertising efforts of the insurance industry. A lobbyist for the Consumer Products Coordinating Committee, a consortium of businesses and manufacturers that had pushed for changes in federal litigation law, said, "I do believe that some of our efforts to try to reform product-liability laws have had an impact, not only in terms of jury decisions, but judges' decisions on appeal."[6]

In February 1995, the new Republican House of Representatives prepared to move legislation through Congress that would dramatically change the way courts handled negligence and product-liability lawsuits. The House Judiciary Committee approved a measure that put a significant portion of torts under federal law. The effect would be to provide greater protection to businesses that asserted they had become unfair targets of consumer and securities lawsuits.

A bill sponsored by Representative Henry J. Hyde of Illinois, the new Republican chairperson of the Judiciary Committee, proposed to sharply limit punitive damages, make it more difficult to sue sellers of products, and to restrict the ability of plaintiffs to recover damages from some defendants. The legislation specified that sellers could not be held liable unless they acted with negligence. If the consumer was intoxicated when using the product and an accident occurred, the defense could cite intoxication as the cause. Under this legislation, defendants no longer would be jointly liable for noncompensatory damages such as pain and suffering. They would be responsible only for their own role in the harm done. The statute of repose would be implemented so that 15 years after a product was sold, a manufacturer would be immune from injuries arising out of the use of the product. The proposal would not include asbestos or other products causing serious illness.

The new Republican chairperson of the Commerce Committee, Thomas J. Bliley, Jr., proposed a second measure. This bill would protect all drug and medical companies from lawsuits if the products that caused injuries had been approved by the Food and Drug Administration (FDA).[7]

The Clinton Administration, which had been conspicuously quiet during the drafting of the legislation,

---

[3] V. E. Schwartz, "Finally, a Chance to Reform Product Liability Law," *The Wall Street Journal*, September 9, 1992, p. A15.

[4] D. Frum, "High Noon," *Forbes*, September 14, 1992, p. 478.

[5] M. Geyelin, "Product-Liability Groups Take Up Arms," *The Wall Street Journal*, January 29, 1993, p. B1.

[6] M. Geyelin, "Product-Liability Suits Fare Worse Now," *The Wall Street Journal*, July 12, 1994, p. B9.

[7] S. Labaton, "G.O.P. Preparing Bill to Overhaul Negligence Law," *New York Times*, February 19, 1995, p. 1.

issued a statement shortly before the bill went to the floor of the House. In a letter to Speaker Newt Gingrich, the administration warned that central provisions in the legislation were too extreme and would "tilt the legal playing field dramatically to the disadvantage of consumers and middle-class citizens." Abner J. Mikva, the White House counsel, said the proposal would work a "significant injustice, particularly against parties that have fewer resources."[8]

Despite administration opposition, the House passed the Attorneys Accountability Act, the first of three legal reform bills. This act exposed both parties to paying their opponent's legal costs; proponents said this would curtail the number of cases in federal courts. The Hyde and Bliley bills also passed easily, with voting along party lines.

In April 1995, a bipartisan group of senators unveiled the Gorton–Rockefeller compromise bill that limited old legislation to product-liability cases. The senators hoped to find a middle ground on the question of limiting punitive damages. This proposal would set a limit on punitive damages while allowing judges to make higher awards when they believed a defendant had acted egregiously. The provision was a major concession to President Clinton who strongly opposed the idea of a federal limit on damage awards.

The compromise initially would limit punitive-damage awards in product cases to two times compensatory damages, or $250,000, whichever was greater. Compensatory damages included wage loss, medical bills, and pain and suffering. Judges would have the discretion to increase the awards and defendants would then have the right to seek a new trial.

Consumer groups criticized the proposal asserting judges would hesitate to make large punitive awards if the action automatically triggered the possibility of a new trial. Manufacturers, who had wanted a cap on punitive damages, were not much happier.[9]

After substantial jockeying between Senate Republicans and Democrats, the Senate voted 61–37 to pass a measure restricting the amount of punitive damages. The measure covered lawsuits in both federal and state courts in cases involving faulty products such as toasters, hospital equipment, and car parts. Like many other contentious measures, the bill languished. In May 1996, it still had not been signed into law and President Clinton promised to veto the newest version of the bill. The White House issued a statement saying, "The president believes the product liability legislation passed by Congress does not adequately protect consumers and does not address the need to protect the American people from faulty products that could cause damage to American families."[10] On May 3, President Clinton carried out his threat to veto saying the bill "tilts the playing field against consumers inappropriately intrudes on state authority." There was no chance that supporters of the bill could garner the two-thirds majority in both houses of Congress to override the veto.[11]

---

[8] D. Jehl, "Clinton to Fight Measure Revising Rules on Lawsuits," *New York Times,* March 6, 1995, p. 1.

[9] R. B. Schmitt, "Supporters of Product Bill in Senate Abandon Cap on Punitive Damages," *The Wall Street Journal,* May 9, 1995, p. A3.

[10] "Bill to Limit Product Liability Sent to Clinton Despite Veto Promise," *Boston Globe,* May 1, 1996, p. 75.

[11] N. A. Lewis, "President Vetoes Limits on Liability," *New York Times,* May 3, 1996, p. A1.

Questions

1. Should Congress pass a federal law that covers product liability law nationwide? Why or why not?
2. If new federal legislation is passed, are plaintiffs likely to prevail against big business?
3. What are the relevant arguments big business should use to justify limiting damages?
4. Is it reasonable and just to have product liability awards differ vastly from state to state? Why or why not?
5. Why is it so difficult to pass a product-liability law? Are there issues that make this law more contentious than others?

The Legal Framework

The US Constitution

The ideology and value system of a society both shape and are shaped by that society's legal framework. The U.S. common law system evolved from British colonial laws. However, Britain had no written constitution and no written fundamental law. Final power was vested in the Parliament.

The founders of the new United States were determined to create a stable system that limited the power of the people, prescribed rules of decisions that were binding on a nationwide court system, and set up a framework within which all government acts must be "subject to law, as interpreted by its traditional custodians, the judges."[12]

The U.S. Constitution is the written foundation on which the nation's legal framework rests; it provides the guiding principles by which the United States is governed. At the end of the 18th century, a Supreme Court justice defined a constitution as "the form of government, delineated by the mighty hand of the people, in which certain fundamental laws are established."[13]

The framers of the Constitution were determined to remedy what they perceived as major weaknesses of the colonial period's Articles of Confederation. The Articles of Confederation placed all authority with the state legislatures, leaving the Union with no coercive power over individuals unless specifically granted by the state. The framers were particularly troubled by government's inability to regulate commerce. What would happen, they mused, if Pennsylvania levied tariffs against goods coming from New Jersey? It was imperative to put enough power in the hands of the federal government to prevent what some called a drift toward anarchy.

The framers of the Constitution were acutely aware they could provide no more than a framework for government. They could not possibly cover every contingency that would occur over time. The result was a constitution that generally rested on the authority of the nation over the people. It established a tripartite central government consisting of separate legislative, executive, and judicial branches, each of which had checks and balances on the other two. Above all, the Constitution created a rule of law over every private or public individual, no matter how highly placed.

The great power of the U.S. common law system is that laws change over time and are based on previous decisions (precedents). Common law tends to be closely connected to the prevailing value system. Over the lifetimes of most American adults, values and laws have changed regarding such fundamental

---

[12] B. Schwartz, *A Commentary on the Constitution of the United States, Part I: The Powers of Government* (New York: Macmillan, 1963), p. 21.

[13] Ibid., p. 1.

Exhibit 7-1 Legal Classifications

Private and Public Law
Private law establishes rights among private companies and individuals, as distinct from those in which society is involved. This classification includes contract and property law.

Public law is usually established by administrative regulations and statutes. The interests of society as a whole or protected classes of people are directly involved. They are usually represented by a government agency or its officer. These rules cover environmental law, securities law, antitrust law, and labor law. The issues may be constitutional, administrative, or criminal in nature.

Procedural Law and Substantive Law
Procedural law pertains to the operation of the court system and the conduct of trials. In other words, it is the mechanism by which rights and duties are enforced.

Substantive law establishes rights and duties. It defines the legal relationships among people and between people and the state.

Criminal and Civil Law
Criminal law covers violations of the public rules of behavior. It is divided into felonies and misdemeanors. Corporations can and do commit felonies for which their officers may be held criminally accountable.

Civil law covers lawsuits brought by one party to assert a private right. In a civil suit, the plaintiff may be a person, a corporation, or a government entity. Civil law covers many areas:

1. *Breach of contract* covers the legal relationships that individuals create by their own agreement.
2. A *tort* is a civil wrong other than breach of contract. The law gives the plaintiff the right to recover damages. Malpractice suits are a major area in today's society. A plaintiff seeks dollar damages but not punishment of the defendant.
3. *Law of property* concerns ownership and possession of real estate and personal property. A fundamental concept of property ownership is the right to exclude others from possession and use.

Source: R. N. Corley, R. L. Black, and O. L. Reed, *The Legal Environment of Business,* 5th ed. (New York: McGraw-Hill, 1981), pp. 1–8; T. W. Dunfee, J. R. Bellace, and A. J. Rosoff, *Business and Its Legal Environment* (Englewood Cliffs, NJ: Prentice-Hall, 1983), pp. 5–6.

societal issues as abortion, minority rights, capital punishment, religious observance in schools, and affirmative action. Exhibit 7–1 shows the categories of legal issues.

Informal Societal Rules

Politicians routinely declare that the United States is a nation of laws, and almost all citizens agree that no society can exist without a set of strongly enforced rules. But we know from experience that the formal legal apparatus determines only part of our behavior. In our society as well as others, complex written and unwritten rules guide individuals and organizations.

All communities, whether primitive or highly industrialized, develop social environments that dictate behavior the group considers vital to its welfare. When an individual or an institution violates these customs, mores, or norms, society may levy penalties as severe or even more severe than those for violating formally passed laws.

In simple societies without written law, customs are de facto laws and the community informally enforces them. As communities become increasingly complex, they generally formalize their bodies of norms into laws.

Many new laws affecting the conduct of American businesses have been passed in the last two decades. Altering the business environment, however, does not necessarily require the passage of new laws. In the United States, for example, a conservative president may appoint an attorney general who is less aggressive than her predecessor in enforcing antitrust laws. Or the president may issue executive orders that intensify or diminish equal employment efforts. In such instances, although Congress has not passed new laws, the effect on business may be profound.

Highly partisan political campaigns invoke their own interpretation of the opposing party's ideology even in absence of evidence that the interpretation is supportable. In the 1996 election for example, the Republicans talked about the tax-and-spend Democrats. The Democrats implied that Dole, Kemp, and Gingrich were all running on the Republican ticket. Both sides issued dire warnings about how each other's policies would affect business.

When the chief executive's political philosophy differs from that of his predecessor, the government's administrative apparatus reflects different levels of commitment to the enforcement of legislation. When a Republican House of Representatives was elected in 1994, the legislation that emerged from the House was vastly different in tone and substance from measures considered by a Democratic House two years earlier. By 1996 even though most of the Republican Contract with America had stalled, President Clinton and his administration's position had moved closer to the center of the political spectrum.

Corporations and the Law

Before the 1960s, executives were rarely held criminally responsible for actions of their corporations; by the 1990s, the legal climate had changed. Holcomb and Sethi have explored the topic of corporate and executive criminal liability.[14] They suggest standards, remedies, and managerial responses. Since the early 1980s, society has become more determined to further define and curb corporate crime. The major task is to protect social welfare and balance that protection against corporate rights and power.

Holcomb and Sethi caution that criminal liability is difficult to assess when applied to corporations and executives. It is equally difficult to determine penalties and evaluate the deterrent effect of a punishment. For

---

[14] J. M. Holcomb and S. P. Sethi, "Corporate and Executive Criminal Liability: Appropriate Standards, Remedies and Managerial Responses," *Business and the Contemporary World,* Summer 1992, p. 92.

executives to be found guilty, three elements must be considered:

- Did the individual make a choice to commit a wrongful act?
- Was this choice freely made?
- Did the individual know, or could she have recognized, the wrongfulness of this act?[15]

Similar determinations must be made about corporate intent. For example,

- Did a corporate practice or policy violate the law?
- Was it reasonably foreseeable that a corporate practice or policy would result in a corporate agent's violation of the law?
- Did the corporation adopt a corporate agent's violation of the law?[16]

Holcomb and Sethi suggest that a "corporate ethos test" be applied requiring the government to prove that a corporate agent or executive engaged in criminal conduct and that a preexisting corporate ethos, or set of values, encouraged the conduct. In the absence of such an ethos, the corporation could not be found guilty.

Once guilt has been established in so-called white-collar crimes, a number of laws dictating the severity of punishments can be applied. For example, in recent years the Racketeer Influenced and Corrupt Practices Act (RICO) has been used against businesses to combat fraud. Originally RICO was passed to fight organized crime, but the court now interprets it to cover a wide range of business activities that can be loosely construed as racketeering. The government used the threat of RICO to persuade Drexel Burnham Lambert's Michael Milken to plead guilty and pay a huge fine. RICO allows the government to impose compensatory and punitive damages, court costs, attorneys' fees, and to freeze corporate assets.

Other laws applying to corporate crime include the following:

- The Mail and Wire Fraud statutes cover situations in which individuals have used the postal or telephone systems for illegal activities. Mail-order companies and telemarketers have been prosecuted under these statutes.
- The Insider Trading Sanctions Act increased penalties for insider trading to $1 million for individuals and $2.5 million for corporations. The act also included bounty payments to informers.
- Penalties for violating the 1977 Foreign Corrupt Practices Act were raised in 1988 to $2 million for corporations and $100,000 for individuals. Individuals can be imprisoned for as long as five years.[17] Larger fines have been imposed in recent years commensurate with the severity of the violation.

---

[15] Ibid., p. 92.
[16] Ibid., p. 93.
[17] M. T. Tucker, "Corporate Crime and Punishment," *Business and the Contemporary World,* Summer 1992, pp. 160–62.

It is still unclear whether stiffer penalties will deter corporate crime. The U.S. Sentencing Commission has established penalty guidelines for white-collar crime and encourages firms to institute steps to deter crime. As we discussed in the previous chapter, the commission recommends that companies develop comprehensive ethics codes and implement policies to persuade employees that ethical conduct codes can have economic rewards.

The Political and Legal Frameworks

The political and legal frameworks of business are inseparable. The political framework has both legal and quasi-legal components. The legal framework includes acts lawmaking bodies pass at all levels of government. Quasi-legal influences on decision making often can have the same force as laws. For example, when the executive branch of the government establishes price and wage guidelines, those guidelines are not legally enforceable. However, an executive who makes a decision to raise prices beyond the guidelines must carefully consider the possible consequences of incurring presidential wrath.

It is clearly illegal for companies to participate in an explicit agreement among themselves to divide the nation into exclusive territories to restrain competition. However, trade practice statements and trade association agreements, combined with sanctions such as "violators will be subject to reprisals from other members of the group," may influence companies more than does the law itself. Therefore, quasi-legal devices, coupled with implied sanctions for violators, often restrain business executives from taking certain actions whether or not those actions violate the law.

The underlying purpose of most legal and quasi-legal regulation of business is simply to encourage and maintain a desirable level of competition. Different groups of stakeholders, such as industry competitors and customers, may have significantly different views about what constitutes a desirable level.

Corporate Political Stakeholders

Business, one of the most central institutions in U.S. society, is deeply involved in and affected by the political and legal processes. In the view of Jeffrey Pfeffer and Gerald Salancik, a business organization is one part of the larger social and political system. Firms survive and prosper to the extent that they effectively deal with the other organizations that make up that larger system.[18] Pfeffer and Salancik observe that "effectiveness derives from the management of demands, particularly the demands of interest groups upon

---

[18] J. Pfeffer and G. R. Salancik, *The External Control of Organizations* (New York: Harper & Row, 1978), p. 11.

which the organizations depend for resources and support."[19] Chrysler Corporation might well have gone bankrupt had it not built an effective coalition of stakeholders to influence the White House and pressure Congress to secure a bailout.

Stakeholder groups disagree over the role business plays or should play in the political process. Consumer activists may object to power companies' advocacy of nuclear energy because they are concerned about safety. On the other hand, shareholders in power companies may support nuclear energy because they want a good return on their investment. Both sides apply political and legal pressure to achieve their own group's goals. To understand this conflict, we need to look more closely at the question of corporate political power.

A large number of books and articles discuss various aspects of corporate political power; some are examples of sensationalistic journalism. Kenneth D. Meyers' *False Security: Greed & Deception in America's Multibillion Dollar Insurance Industry* (1995) is an example of this genre. Meyers, an investigative reporter, tells story after story about graft in the insurance business.

Ralph Estes takes on the question of corporate accountability in *Tyranny of the Bottom Line* (1995). He espouses the view that America's largest corporations are no longer accountable to anyone except the interests of shareholders. Other stakeholders such as employees, the local community, state, and even the nation, suffer as a result. Estes asserts that companies are judged by their profit-and-loss statements, a measure he says is far too narrow. He proposes that each company issue a comprehensive Corporate Report including data on the environment, plant closings, job safety, and job discrimination. If the company does not issue the report voluntarily, legislation should make it mandatory.

In a scholarly treatise, Ira Millstein and Salem M. Katsh observe that many people are concerned about corporations having virtually unlimited ability to exercise power in a wide spectrum of economic, social, and political issues.[20] While corporations do have considerable influence in shaping their environment, stakeholders can bring countervailing pressure to bear on firms' autonomy. Increasingly, companies are choosing to avoid adverse publicity by acknowledging the legitimacy of stakeholder concerns.

Major Stakeholders Groups

Exhibit 7–2 shows the stakeholder influence map for seven major groups of stakeholders.

---

[19] Ibid., p. 2.

[20] I. Millstein and S. M. Katsh, *The Limits of Corporate Power* (New York: Macmillan, 1981), p. xvii.

EXHIBIT 7–2
Stakeholders Influence Map for Major Political Stakeholders

	Direct	Indirect
External	Institutional investors: Banks and insurance companies Government	Broadcast media: Television and radio Press: Newspapers and magazines Industry associations Intellectual community Public-interest groups Government
Internal	Employees: Management level and lower level	Labor unions

News and Broadcast Media. The media provide information that shapes public opinion. Public opinion "establishes the intellectual and moral environment within which corporate managers formulate their own views of corporate responsibility; it establishes . . . the likely expectations of shareholders . . . and it defines the public will to which government officials must be responsive."[21] The media affect corporate power by the way they report corporate policy issues, either positively or negatively. Sophisticated television and Internet applications have become powerful media tools.

Industry Associations. Some associations set industry standards to allow corporations to regulate their own behavior. Other associations promote product quality and safety guidelines that industry participants can treat as minimally acceptable standards. Still other associations, such as the U.S. Chamber of Commerce, the Business Roundtable, and the National Association of Manufacturers, serve as informational conduits between industry and government. They also develop responses to the demands of other stakeholders. For example, nearly 100 companies contributed information on corporate ethics to the Business Roundtable's report on policy and practice in company conduct.

Employees. Management-level employees express convictions about the social and ethical role of their corporations. Lower-level employees exert influence on their companies through their own and union demands for better

---

[21] Ibid., p. 231.

working conditions and social responsiveness. Every employee influences corporate behavior through the way she votes in local, state, and federal elections.

Shareholders and Institutional Investors. Shareholders elect the board of directors that makes basic decisions regarding corporate structure. They also constrain corporate decisions to merge, acquire, or be acquired. Labor unions, banks, insurance companies, churches, universities, and other institutions can and do use their stock holdings to influence corporate behavior.

The Intellectual Community. Academics, students, professionals, and others who influence what many members of society think and do comprise this group of stakeholders. Intellectuals write articles and books to raise issues concerning the corporate, legal, and political environments. Conservatives and liberals alike continue to debate the degree of influence of the written medium.

Public-Interest Groups. Various public-interest associations advocate special perspectives on certain issues. Some have become very adept at soliciting funds from foundations and grassroots supporters. They also have learned how to use the political process, the media, and the courts to further their causes. As we pointed out earlier in the nuclear energy debate, different groups espouse conflicting goals. Corporate managers confronted by the demands of organized public-interest groups must determine how each group's demands fit the economic, social, or legal constraints their companies face.

Government. Government officials can apply subtle or even overt pressure on corporations to make them behave in a particular way. Ronald Reagan tried unsuccessfully to prevent Dresser Industries from selling its French-made turbines to the Soviet Union. John F. Kennedy was more successful in his attempt to make U.S. Steel roll back a price hike. Legislators can affect corporate policy by threatening to take legislative action if such policy does not change.[22]

Corporate Political Power

Edwin Epstein makes the critical point that power—the capacity to control or determine the behavior of others—should not be confused with potential power.[23] Epstein points out that both a base of power and the means of power

---

[22] Ibid., pp. 229–55.
[23] E. Epstein, *The Corporation in American Politics* (Englewood Cliffs, NJ: Prentice Hall, 1969), p. 197.

may exist without power ever being exercised. For example, some interest groups have expressed concern about corporations' tremendous wealth. These groups point out that if even a small percentage of this money were used to pursue a political cause, the effect on society could be profound.

E. I. DuPont de Nemours, the number one chemical company in the Fortune 500 in 1987, had sales income of more than $30 billion. Only 2 percent of that total would put $15 million at the company's disposal for political purposes. However, Epstein notes, "Because there are so many internal demands on company monies, only a very small—one might even say minuscule—percentage of corporate assets or revenues is used for political purposes."[24]

A few companies have used large amounts of money to curry favor, typically in operations outside the United States. Prior to the passage of the Foreign Corrupt Practices Act in 1977, American corporations were party to numerous cases of bribery. For example, McDonnell Douglas admitted making payments on aircraft sales to Pakistan, Zaire, South Korea, the Philippines, and Venezuela between 1972 and 1977. General Tire and Rubber made payments of $500,000 in Morocco in 1969 to get approval of plant expansion. Burroughs admitted that $1.5 million in corporate funds might have been used to pay bribes to foreign officials.[25] In a much less dramatic case, Kenny International Corporation, a small stamp distributor, pleaded guilty to paying a $337,000 bribe to the prime minister of the Cook Islands in the South Pacific to keep the company's exclusive rights to distribute the island's postage stamps.[26]

More recently, the Lockheed Corporation pleaded guilty to bribing an Egyptian legislator in the $79 million sale of three transport planes. The indictment said the payments, or commissions, came to $600,000 per plane. Under the Foreign Corrupt Practices Act, the penalty included a fine of $21.8 million and a $3 million civil settlement with the U.S. government. The fine, twice Lockheed's profit from the planes, was the maximum allowed by law.[27]

Epstein assesses corporate political resources such as organization, access, and patronage.[28] *Organizationally,* corporations can draw on their own public or government relations staff to pursue their political agendas. They also can use employees, shareholders, suppliers, and customers to help them create a favorable corporate political identity.

Access means corporations have the opportunity to get a hearing and to make their case at a crucial time. Top executives of large corporations can easily make social as well as formal contacts with government officials.

---

[24] *Fortune,* April 25, 1988, pp. D33–D39.

[25] *U.S. News & World Report,* June 27, 1988, p. 46.

[26] B. Jackson, "Overseas Bribery Gets a Lot Less Attention," *The Wall Street Journal,* February 23, 1983, p. B1.

[27] "$24.8 Million Penalty Paid by Lockheed," *New York Times,* January 28, 1995, p. 28.

[28] Epstein, *The Corporation,* pp. 192–208.

Bill Gates of Microsoft, Jack Welch of General Electric, and CEOs of other top firms are likely to be invited to social and business functions that bring them into contact with members of the administration or Congress. Finally, large companies use *patronage to* obtain leverage with their employees, suppliers, subcontractors, state and local governments, and present and even former government officials. Sometimes former government officials end up on the payroll of a major company or trade association.

Prior to Clinton's election in 1992, private companies had hired many former Pentagon officials to work on the same weapons projects they supervised while still government employees. Even before President Clinton's inauguration, the incoming administration announced more stringent legal guidelines covering former government officials who wished to become lobbyists. The new administration clearly hoped to avoid situations like that created by Michael K. Dever. Dever, former director of the White House Office of Management and Budget in the Reagan years, resigned to form a lobbying firm that represented the governments of Canada, Singapore, South Korea, Mexico, and Saudi Arabia, as well as domestic and foreign companies.[29]

Notwithstanding the fact that corporations have considerable political resources, business firms do not constitute a threat to political democracy in the United States. Epstein argues that (1) political resources are not synonymous with political power; (2) corporations do not have a monopoly over political resources (he points to countervailing special-interest groups such as farm groups, organized labor, and others); (3) the public is too deeply committed to social pluralism to allow business to become politically dominant; and (4) major constraints within the business system are played out in intercorporate competition.[30]

The Corporate Political Program

Carl P. Zeithaml and Gerald D. Keim propose a five-phase framework for planning, evaluation, and integration of a corporate political program.[31]

- In *Phase I*, the planning phase, it is critical that management at all levels understand and support the political program. Management should implement a program evaluation process that incorporates qualitative and quantitative measures of the political activity.

---

[29] M. Tolchin, "Democrats Press Meese for Inquiry on Dever Ethics," *New York Times,* April 25, 1986, pp. A1, 11.
[30] Epstein, *The Corporation,* p. 227.
[31] C. P. Zeithaml and G. D. Keim, "How to Implement a Corporate Political Action Program," *Sloan Management Review* (Winter 1985), pp. 23–31.

- *Phase II* is the program assessment phase. The company should ask itself two questions: First, why did the corporation develop a political action program? Even the process of asking this question helps the company assess the personal commitment of the CEO and focus on operating problems that might be due to regulation. The second question is what are the objectives and strategies of the corporation's political program? As the manager identifies issues, he should apply the framework for strategy formulation discussed in Chapter 2. The corporation should take care to identify past, current, and potential issues. The product of this step should be a document that outlines each issue and its effect on the corporation.
- During *Phase III*, managers develop an issue database and a document that analyzes the effect each issue is likely to have on the corporation. Then, senior managers from line and staff should prioritize the impact of each issue on the corporation.
- In *Phase IV*, managers select a specific strategy and carry it out. They should appraise the probability of success realistically.
- *Phase V*, program implementation and evaluation, should follow the guidelines in Chapter 3. During the implementation phase, managers should monitor costs and returns relative to the objectives they have set.

These Zeithaml and Keim recommendations assume the manager understands the political process. However, most managers admit they know very little about the inner workings of the political process on the national level. Indeed, many do not even understand the process by which a bill becomes an Act of Congress or the process of rule making in regulatory agencies. In the remainder of this chapter, we discuss the skills a political manager must possess, the basic steps in the passage of bills through Congress, and the means by which laws and rules are administered.

Skills of the Political Manager

Formulation and implementation of social goals is a managerial skill that is becoming increasingly important in American companies. Michael Useem recommends the development of in-house programs to help middle managers understand the legislative process and each stakeholders' power to affect the firm.[32] As he notes, social goals must be implemented throughout the

---

[32] M. Useem, "The Rise of the Political Manager," *Sloan Management Review,* Fall 1985, pp. 15–26.

company; firms can no longer relegate them to a public affairs office. Useem observes that various levels of management require different political skills.

Entry-level managers often come into a large company with little or no interest in a political agenda. Their job is to gain control over functional area tasks and to learn the culture of the company. Although they rarely serve as formal spokespeople, they may be informally identified with their firms if they become involved in community activities.

Middle-level managers, the implementers of social issues, must participate if the company is to realize its goals. Some companies undertake a variety of activities to heighten political awareness and activity in the achievement of social goals. To foster participation, firms encourage middle managers to get involved in community activities as company representatives. Some even give employees time off for this work. Company publications often feature articles about employees who meet fund-raising goals or serve on community boards of directors. To heighten awareness of social and legal issues, some companies conduct public affairs courses, both inside and outside the firm.

Senior managers must go beyond this. They should become directly involved in public affairs through service on the boards of directors of other companies. They should take part in the deliberations of business associations such as the Business Roundtable, serve on boards of trustees of nonprofit organizations, or meet with high-ranking government officials. They must also actively support programs and legislation on the national level.

In sum, the more involved managers at all levels are in the political process, the better able they are to influence the issues that affect their firms. Participation in the political process is more effective and more relevant to the firm if managers understand how laws and regulations are passed.

Some large, politically active firms establish offices in Washington. The Washington-based staff usually consists of lawyers or public affairs specialists who have experience in government. Often the office maintains close relations with trade organizations or lobbyists in the firm's industry. As we will see, relationships with PACs and interest groups have proliferated enormously in recent years. To be most effective, the Washington office staff works with all three branches of the federal government: the executive, the legislative, and the judicial. Its primary responsibility is to keep corporate headquarters informed about issues that have potential impact on the firm's strategy and to promote the interests of the firm to government officials. As in any policy-setting matter, the CEO's commitment and involvement are critical.[33]

---

[33] R. A. Buchholz, *Essentials of Public Policy for Management* (Englewood Cliffs, NJ: Prentice Hall, 1985), pp. 209–14.

Political and Legal Stakeholder Groups

Stakeholder groups spend a great deal of time and money attempting to influence the political and legal processes. Many of the groups that fall into the external indirect quadrant of the stakeholder influence map include business associations, political action committees (PACs), other lobbies, and industry groups. In addition to these external stakeholders, managers within the corporation can affect the drafting of laws and passage of legislation by forming their own PACs or other stakeholder groups. In this section, we begin by looking at the structure and the role of business associations. Next, we examine PACs and the ways they affect political and legal processes. Finally in this section we look at how the federal and legislative process worked to try to pass a lobbying reform bill.

Business Associations

A variety of business associations have political agendas. The National Association of Manufacturers (NAM), a group of 13,500 manufacturing firms, is one of the oldest and best known. The NAM's Public Policy Internet Network address can be found at [http://www.intervisage.com:80./issuesnews/pending.html]. Readers are informed about pending legislation and deadlines for hearings. The NAM follows issues that manufacturers consider important and disseminates information to its membership. Lobbyists who work for the NAM represent many companies that cannot afford to have their own Washington-based staffs. Some areas such as international economic affairs, government regulation, and taxation policy are particularly important to the NAM.

The U.S. Chamber of Commerce is the world's largest federation of business chambers of commerce, American chambers overseas, and trade and professional organizations. Its 215,000 members share a mission to "advance human progress through an economic, political, and social system based on individual freedom, incentive, initiative, opportunity and responsibility."[34] The agenda of the U.S. Chamber of Commerce is very broad. Its tasks include helping members testify before Congress and disseminating information about pending legislation. It has an extensive communications outreach program that has been greatly enhanced by members' access to the Internet. For example, its August 29, 1996, Internet update introduced a new book being written about how to help businesses become more profitable. Developed especially for the chamber, the book features interviews and case studies of successful businesspeople.

The chamber works closely with its affiliated organizations to advocate U.S. business. The Center for International Private Enterprise (CIPE)

---

[34] See the U.S. Chamber of Commerce home page at Internet [http://www.uschamber.org/groupabo.htm].

sponsors programs promoting economic growth and democratic development in more than 40 countries worldwide. The Center for Workforce Preparation and Quality Education is an employer-based organization focusing on education restructuring and workforce preparation. The National Chamber Foundation (NCF), a public policy research organization, analyzes and conducts training for chamber association managers and business executives. The National Chamber Litigation Center, Inc., is a public policy law firm that represents business before the courts and regulatory agencies.

The International Division of the U.S. Chamber of Commerce provides an umbrella for American Chambers of Commerce (AMCHAMs) abroad. The AMCHAMs are extremely active in a variety of endeavors. They offer networking opportunities for U.S. companies abroad, organize programs on local conditions, and assess market potential. The AMCHAM in Australia, for example, produced *More Business Down Under: A Guide to American Business in Australia.* The book includes an overview of Australia's political and economic environment, banking system, infrastructure, and best trade prospects.[35]

The Business Roundtable, an association made up of nearly 200 CEOs of the top U.S. corporations, was created in 1972 during the Nixon administration. The underlying concept of the Business Roundtable is that business and government have mutual interests that can affect corporate profits. The Roundtable prefers to deal with relatively apolitical issues such as American competitiveness, the budget deficit, and global trade.[36] From time to time, it publishes reports on various issues. In 1994, the organization published a position paper on pollution prevention. It conducted a detailed benchmarking study of six industrial manufacturing facilities that met its criteria for having best-in-class pollution prevention programs.[37]

Political Action Committees

More than a decade ago Gerald D. Keim, Carl P. Zeithaml, and Barry D. Baysinger observed, "One of the most visible changes in the U.S. political landscape over the past ten years has been the increased participation of corporations in electoral and legislative processes."[38] Political action committees (PACs) are fund-raising organizations that solicit money from employees and shareholders to use as political campaign contributions. While not all lobbyists belong to PACs, all PACs are lobbyists.

---

[35] Internet [http://www.uschamber.org/international/bluetrad.htm]

[36] "Knights of the Roundtable," *Business Week,* October 21, 1988, pp. 39–44.

[37] Internet [http://es.incl.gov/new/groups/business/rondtabl.html]

[38] G. D. Keim, C. P. Zeithaml, and B. D. Baysinger, "SMR Forum: New Directions for Corporate Political Strategy," *Sloan Management Review,* Spring 1984, p. 53.

Labor unions invented PACs in the 1940s as a means of supporting prounion political candidates. The business community was upset by what it saw as union efforts to affect legislation, but it did not immediately retaliate by forming its own PACs on a large scale. Until the 1960s, the more usual pattern was for business leaders to give large personal contributions to like-minded political candidates.

Corporate PACs proliferated in the 1970s for two major reasons: First, federal election laws restricted the amount of money individuals could contribute to a candidate. Second, the Federal Campaign Act of 1971 officially sanctioned corporate PACs. In 1974, the last barrier to PAC activity was removed when the 1971 act was amended to allow corporations with government contracts to form PACs.[39]

PACs of all kinds began to proliferate in the early 1980s, but corporate PACs were the fastest-growing single segment. These PACs, which were set up by individual companies, numbered 89 in 1974, 1,682 in 1986, and 4,172 in 1990.[40] During the 1990 congressional elections, PAC money accounted for one-quarter of the campaign funds of winning senators and one-half of the funds of representatives who were elected.

Lobbying and Legislation

The following discussion of the PAC bill's passage illustrates the tortuous process controversial legislation goes through before it becomes law. Multiple stakeholder interests wax and wane. In almost every case, when contentious legislation is finally passed, it represents a "satisfying" compromise for both sides but no one can declare a clear victory.

In May 1993, President Clinton proposed a bill that would affect PACS and other lobbyists. In his campaign, Clinton promised to reduce the amount a PAC could give to an individual candidate from $5,000 to $1,000. Congressional Democrats, fearing their chances for a 1994 victory would be jeopardized if he adhered to his pledge, pressured him to drop this stipulation. Clinton's proposal, if passed, would prohibit lobbyists from contributing to or raising money for anyone they had lobbied in the previous 12 months. House candidates could receive no more than one-third of their donations from PACS. Senate candidates could collect only 20 percent of their money from PACs. Registered lobbyists could not contribute or solicit money for any member of Congress, the president, or vice president if they had lobbied the lawmaker in the previous year. When this bill was proposed, there were no

---

[39] A. L. Fritschler and B. H. Ross, *How Washington Works: The Executive's Guide to Government* (Cambridge, MA: Ballinger Publishing, 1987), p. 87.

[40] "Buying Attention But Not Votes," *Washington Post Weekly,* April 14, 1986, p. 33; "Small Dog Bites PAC," *Economist,* May 9, 1992, p. 27.

special limits on the amount of money candidates could receive from PACs and lobbyists.[41]

The PAC provisions of the bill, which passed the Senate in June 1993, were strongly opposed by House Democrats and organized labor. After the vote, the bill went to the House where it faced difficult conference committee negotiations. By August the lobbyists had switched into high gear. They churned out position papers and staged intricate legal seminars as they moaned about another stipulation of the Clinton bill. They would no longer be able to write off the costs of their efforts to influence legislation in the federal and state governments. Since 1962, they had been able to take a tax deduction for lobbying as an ordinary or necessary business expense. Despite numerous loopholes in the proposed law, the lobbyists asserted they had been singled out unfairly. The Society of Association Executives enlisted support from the 15,500 groups its membership represented. Trade groups were angry because their members could no longer deduct the share of the dues that was spent on lobbying. Major industry groups like the Tobacco Institute, the Pharmaceutical Manufacturers, and Fortune 500 firms complained bitterly that it would be a hardship to break out lobbying costs from other expenses of dealing with the government.[42]

As legislators and lobbyists debated the merits of the Clinton bill, the Treasury Department issued a 30-page definition of lobbying. Despite microscopic analysis of lobbying activities, its definition left many issues unresolved or mired in confusion. For example, the Treasury Department specified that the cost of an activity conducted for both lobbying and nonlobbying reasons should be allocated in a reasonable manner but did not define "reasonable."[43]

As expected, debate sharpened as the bill moved through Congress. At the end of September 1994, it passed the House but immediately ran into trouble with groups as disparate as the Christian Coalition, the U.S. Chamber of Commerce, and the American Civil Liberties Union. The Christian Coalition, led by Pat Robertson, said the bill could require his group to print and provide a membership list to a federal bureaucrat every time a member of Congress was asked for help on a legislative issue. The other groups had the same objection.[44]

A GOP filibuster appeared to doom the measure. The main objection appeared to be the stipulations that prohibited members of Congress from receiving gifts. The effect, however, was to scuttle a larger measure including

---

[41] R. L. Berke, "Clinton Unveils Plan to Restrict PAC Influence," *New York Times*, May 8, 1993, p. 1.

[42] M. Wines, "Lobbyists Scrambling to Kill a Clause That's about Them," *New York Times*, August 27, 1993, p. A1.

[43] R. D. Hershey, Jr., "What Is a Lobbyist? Read the Fine Print," *New York Times*, May 11, 1994, p. A16.

[44] A. Clymer, "Lobbying Bill Caught in a Partisan Wrangle," *New York Times*, October 6, 1994, p. A22.

stricter reporting rules and broader definitions of lobbyists that—for the first time—covered lawyers. It also added lobbyists who sought help from the executive branch.

The Christian Coalition used what it called a state-of-the-art network to mobilize 250,000 people expressing opposition to the bill. The message of the coalition was that the lobbying bill was a gag order on grassroots advocates. The group also asserted that it was "a direct attempt to suppress organizations like the Christian Coalition." Other religious groups like the U.S. Catholic Conference and American Hebrew Congregation said the bill was harmless to their interests.[45]

House Speaker Newt Gingrich and his supporters began to conduct background checks on lobbyists and ask their political affiliation. They also examined lobbyists' contribution histories and cut off those they did not perceive as loyal. They bluntly told PACS to hire more Republicans and get rid of Democrats in their employ. Steven F. Stockmeyer, executive vice president of the National Association of Business Political Action Committees said, "The hard-liners in Congress want to put the business community or the PAC community out of business for their decades of paying tribute to leading Democrats who had power over their issues."[46]

PACs quickly switched their donations to the GOP. *Business Week* analyzed campaign contributions by the top 20 corporate PACs during the 1993–94 election cycle. It showed big business gave to both parties but contributed more than before to GOP candidates and reduced contributions to Democratic challengers. After the November 1994 election, GOP House members received $170,000 from the top 20 PACs, compared with the Democrats' $22,000. Between January and April 1995, the National Republican Senatorial Committee raised $6.5 million from business. By contrast the Democratic Senatorial Campaign Committee received just $1.7 million and was $1.5 million in debt.[47]

By the end of July 1995, the bill was back in the Senate in altered form. On July 29 the Senate voted 98-0 to adopt new rules that would forbid senators, their aides, and other Senate officers from accepting any privately paid travel to recreational events, from accepting any gifts or meals worth more than $50, and more than $100 worth of gifts and meals from any person in a year. The rules demanded only a good faith effort to comply.[48]

---

[45] A. Clymer, "GOP Filibuster Deals a Setback to Lobbying Bill," *New York Times*, October 7, 1994, p. A1; K. Q. Seelye, "Hobbling of Lobbying Bill Shows Muscle Power of 'Grass Roots' Conservative Network," *New York Times*, October 7, 1994, p. A22.

[46] R. L. Berke, "Republicans Rule Lobbyists' World with Strong Arm," *New York Times*, March 20, 1995, p. A1.

[47] M. B. Regan and S. H. Wildstrom, "PACs Cross the Street," *Business Week*, April 10, 1995, pp. 94–98.

[48] A. Clymer, "Senate Votes 98-0 for Strict Limits on Lobbyist Gifts," *New York Times*, July 29, 1995, p. 1.

The loopholes protecting lobbying disclosure remained because Senate Republicans insisted on removing all disclosure requirements for grassroots lobbying (money spent on sophisticated ad campaigns, direct-mail drives, phone banks, and constituent appearances to encourage citizens to pressure government officials).[49]

Congress finally passed the bill to disclose lobbyists' roles. By a vote of 421-0 in the House and a vote of 98-0 in the Senate, lawmakers ruled that lobbyists must register with the Clerk of the House and Secretary of the Senate. Also, they must report their clients, issues, the agencies and house they lobbied, as well as the amount they were paid. Violators could be punished by civil fines of up to $50,000. Lobbyists were defined as those who (1) spend at least 20 percent of their time lobbying members, their staffs, or executive branch officials; (2) are compensated for more than one lobbying contact in six months; and (3) lobby on behalf of foreign interests. Lawyers were no longer exempt.[50]

The issue of grassroots lobbying was not included. Republican opposition was so strong that the bill would not have passed if the measure were included. For more than two weeks after the bill's passage it was held up in the office of the Senate enrolling clerk. The clerk's duty was to make a fancy copy to be sent to the White House for the president's signature. The ostensible reason for the delay was that typographical errors needed to be fixed. In reality, Senators Alan K. Simpson of Wyoming and Larry E. Craig of Idaho were trying to change words that might cause a problem for Blue Cross and Blue Shield lobbyists. The House refused to change the wording and the bill went to President Clinton who signed it. The bill took effect on January 1, 1996.[51]

As the 1996 election drew near, more interest groups and PACs than ever before became involved in politics. The *New York Times* reported that the battle for control of the House was not between the Democrats and Republicans; it was a struggle between the "AFL–CIO and the United States Chamber of Commerce, the League of Conservation Voters and the National Federation of Independent Business, the National Abortion Rights League and the Christian Coalition." Interest groups ran their own campaigns, picked congressional districts where they thought they could win, framed their own agendas, and developed their own advertisements. They no longer just handed out endorsements and political contributions to selected candidates.[52]

---

[49] P. Kuntz, "Attempt to Toughen Lobbyist Disclosure Law Leaves Huge Loophole for Grassroots' Money," *The Wall Street Journal,* September 6, 1995, p. A20.

[50] A. Clymer, "Congress Passes Bill to Disclose Lobbyists' Roles," *New York Times,* November 30, 1995, p. A1.

[51] A. Clymer, "Congress Sends Lobbying Overhaul to Clinton," *New York Times,* December 17, 1995, p. 36.

[52] R. Toner, "Interest Groups Take New Route to Congressional Election Arena," *New York Times,* August 20, 1996, p. A1.

Passage of Legislation

As we have seen, the legislative process in the United States works slowly and involves multiple stakeholders at each stage. Throughout the history of the United States, managers and owners of corporations have been remarkably successful in influencing the design and content of legislation. Legislation goes through a series of steps before it is finally signed into law. The degree of contention we observed over the passage of the lobbying bill is not unusual. There are benefits to having an elaborate process where bills can be changed and amended until a compromise is reached. Part of this process includes the participation of companies whose managers are involved in every step from the identification of issues to the passage and implementation of legislation.

Prelegislative Phase

Even before legislation begins to be formulated, it goes through a prelegislative phase. Politically astute managers realize that public expectations of corporate behavior changes. Managers note that certain issues are beginning to attract the attention of community action groups or lobbies. Newspapers, television, and other media report on the particulars of the issues, and citizens may initiate petitions to get the issues on local or statewide ballots.

In the 1992 presidential election, we saw how important television and radio talk shows became in developing public awareness of a wide range of issues. The Ross Perot candidacy was fertilized by a new, grassroots involvement of people formerly estranged from the political process. The Clinton campaign, and later the Clinton administration, continued to air and build consensus around issues through a televised town meeting forum. Sophisticated polling techniques gave political leaders on both sides of the aisle instant feedback about constituents' views. This information made it easier for lawmakers to anticipate the issues that might be politicized.

Technology changed the process by which citizens acquired information in the mid-1990s. During the 1996 election, each of the candidates had a home page on the Internet. Users shared information and set up political hotlines. Interest groups and PACs also set up home pages that gave users a particular perspective on events and candidates' views. Major newspapers, news magazines, and even television channels provided Internet news up to the minute and developed interactive capability.

Instant polling of the electorate was a new phenomenon. Sample groups watched President Clinton and Bob Dole make their acceptance speeches at the presidential conventions. Group members held meters and recorded their interest levels for nearly every word and concept. Meanwhile, computers analyzed the responses of the sample population, noting interest or lack thereof in key words and phrases. Feedback to the pollsters was instantaneous. Within one minute of the end of President Clinton's acceptance speech, analysts at CNN could ascertain how much his approval rating had gone up and which ideas had been most and least appealing.

The Legislative Process

Firms find that nonprofit organizations, lobbies, and even individuals heighten public awareness of potentially harmful products or situations. In 1907, the Federal Meat Inspection Act set up the first standards to certify that beef was fit to eat. For the next 90 years, as carcasses passed by on the conveyor belt, inspectors relied on a sniff-and-poke method to certify they were disease-free. Repeatedly consumers pressed for new legislation, pointing out that 4,000 people died each year and 5 million became ill from salmonella poisoning. *E. coli* bacteria was another hazard associated with beef. In 1993 *E. coli* was traced to undercooked hamburgers sold at Jack in the Box Restaurants. Several children who ate the meat died. Consumer groups such as the Safe Food Coalition, representatives of the National Cattlemen's Beef Association, Agriculture Department representatives, and corporations all backed sweeping changes in regulations. It took two years of negotiation to pass a new bill in 1996.

To turn a concern into a law, legislators must follow the series of steps depicted in Exhibit 7–3.

Step 1: Introduction of the Bill. The *introduction of the bill* is the first step in the legislative process. Although the procedure Senate and House members use to introduce bills differs slightly, once the bill has been introduced in either house of Congress, it is given a number prefixed with HR for the House and S for the Senate. Then the bill is labeled with the sponsor's name and sent to the U.S. Government Printing Office to be copied.

Step 2: Committee Action. The next step in both the House and the Senate is *committee action*—referring the bill to an appropriate committee. Then the bill is placed on the committee's calendar. At this point, the committee makes its first major decision about whether to pursue the issue. When the designated committee does not act on the bill, it dies. When the committee decides to proceed, it refers the bill to a subcommittee and asks relevant federal agencies to comment.

The subcommittee holds hearings that may be public, private, or both. Once it completes its hearings, the subcommittee recommends actions and proposed amendments to the full committee. The full committee votes on recommendations that are sent to the House or the Senate. The committee sends the bill and its amendments to the chamber floor. The chamber must approve, alter, or reject the committee amendments before the bill can be put to a vote.

Step 3: Floor Action. *Floor action* is the step that places the bill on the calendar, where it is debated and subsequently put to a vote. Senators and members of the House can use a variety of procedures to bring a bill to debate; the speed of the process lies in their hands. They vote on the amendments and

EXHIBIT 7–3 How a bill becomes law.

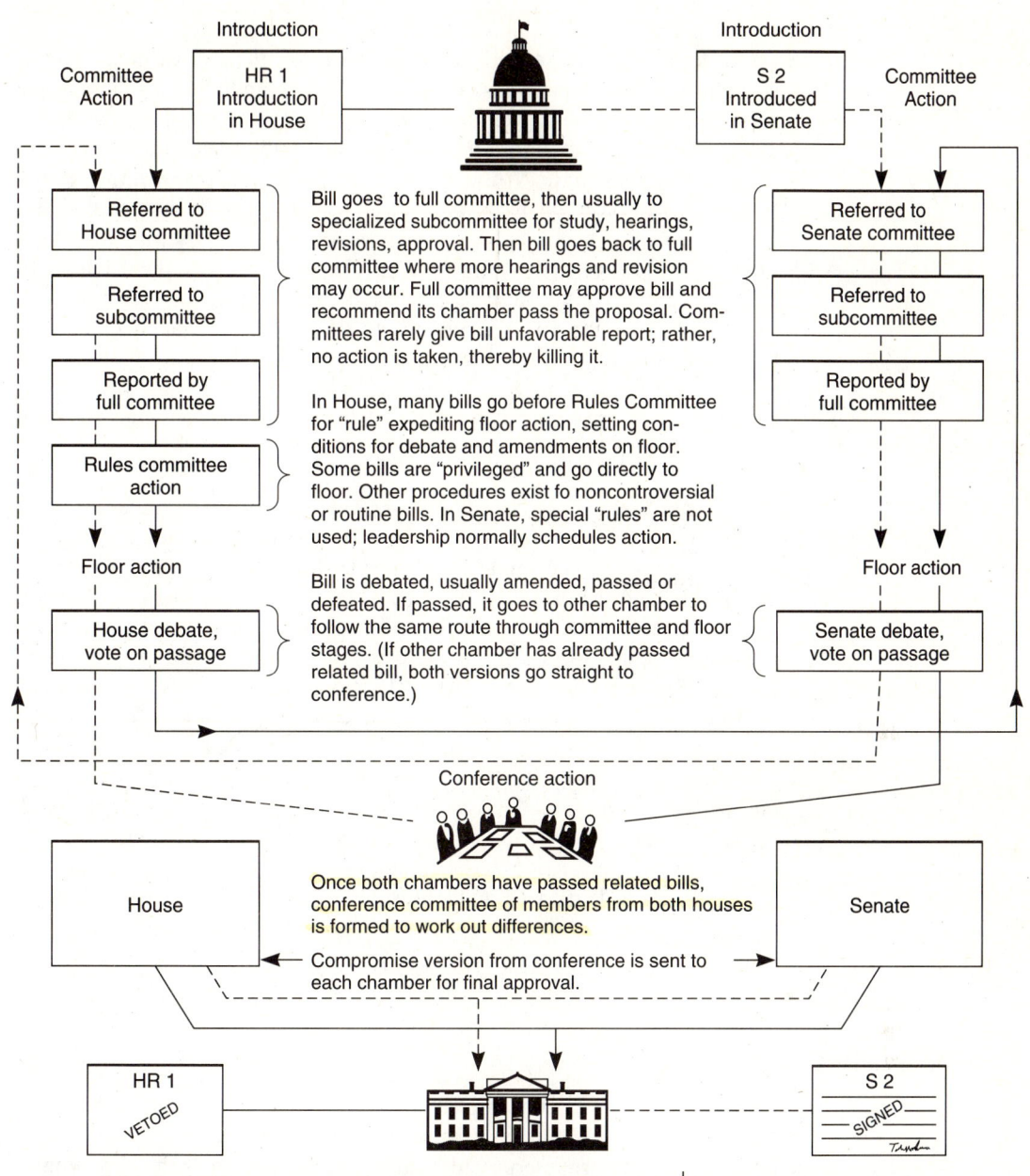

Introduction
HR 1 Introduction in House

S 2 Introduced in Senate

Committee Action

- Referred to House committee
- Referred to subcommittee
- Reported by full committee
- Rules committee action

- Referred to Senate committee
- Referred to subcommittee
- Reported by full committee

Bill goes to full committee, then usually to specialized subcommittee for study, hearings, revisions, approval. Then bill goes back to full committee where more hearings and revision may occur. Full committee may approve bill and recommend its chamber pass the proposal. Committees rarely give bill unfavorable report; rather, no action is taken, thereby killing it.

In House, many bills go before Rules Committee for "rule" expediting floor action, setting conditions for debate and amendments on floor. Some bills are "privileged" and go directly to floor. Other procedures exist fo noncontroversial or routine bills. In Senate, special "rules" are not used; leadership normally schedules action.

Floor action

- House debate, vote on passage
- Senate debate, vote on passage

Bill is debated, usually amended, passed or defeated. If passed, it goes to other chamber to follow the same route through committee and floor stages. (If other chamber has already passed related bill, both versions go straight to conference.)

Conference action

Once both chambers have passed related bills, conference committee of members from both houses is formed to work out differences.

House ← Compromise version from conference is sent to each chamber for final approval. → Senate

HR 1 VETOED

S 2 SIGNED

Compromise version approved by both houses is sent to president who can either sign it into law or veto it and return it to Congress. Congress may override veto by a two-thirds majority vote in both houses; bill then becomes law without president's signature.

the body of the bill separately. After all the votes are taken, the bill proceeds to the next step.

Step 4: Action in the Second House. *Action in the second house* means that a bill initiated in the House goes to the Senate and a bill initiated in the Senate goes to the House. Members have three alternatives: They can either pass the bill as is, reject it, or alter it. If the bill is not substantially reworded and passed, it goes to the White House for signing. If, however, the second chamber makes basic changes, the bill is sent to a conference committee.

Step 5: Conference. In *conference,* senior members of the House and Senate conference committee try to reconcile their conflicting versions. Conferees try to forge language acceptable to their own colleagues. Once they reach an agreement, conferees prepare a report and, along with their recommendations, submit it to each house. If both the Senate and the House approve the compromise bill in identical form, the bill goes into the final legislative stages.

Step 6: Final Stages. In the *final stages,* the clerk of the chamber prepares the bill on parchment paper, a process called enrollment. The clerk of the house in which the bill originated certifies that it is correct, and the speaker of the House and the president of the Senate sign it. Next, the bill is sent to the White House. Upon receiving the bill, the president has several options. The president can approve the bill and sign it, in which case it becomes law. If the president does not sign it within 10 days and Congress is in session, the bill becomes law. If Congress has adjourned and the president does not sign the bill, a pocket veto results and the bill does not become law. If the president refuses to sign the bill within the 10-day period and returns it to Congress along with reasons for the refusal, the bill is vetoed. The chamber in which the bill originated can let the bill die by refusing to take action. However, Congress can try to override the president's veto and pass the bill into law. For Congress to override the veto, there must be a quorum, the vote must be taken by roll call, and two-thirds of the members of both houses must vote in the bill's favor.

Administrative Agencies

Obviously Congress cannot implement every law it passes and cannot write all the rules needed to run the programs it creates. As we noted earlier in the chapter, U.S. laws are interpreted, refined, and rewritten as they are administered. Despite the attention to wording both houses of Congress give to bills, many bills that become law are ambiguous when applied to specific situations. All bills need to be fine-tuned as they are applied. Congress delegates much of its rule-making and writing authority to administrative agencies.

Agencies receive and sift detailed information, set priorities on issues, solicit advice, and have wide discretion over actions they may take. Some agencies are part of departments in the executive branch of government, while others are independent of any government branch. In nearly every case, the degree to which agencies enforce rules and laws depends on funding and support from both Congress and the White House. A full list of regulatory agencies appears in the appendix to Chapter 9.

All agencies have career staff who run them regardless of the politics of the administration in power. Political appointees who hold the top jobs in federal agencies can set the tone for the agencies' activities. Sometimes an administration's political agenda comes into conflict with that of the permanent staff, but on those occasions the differences usually are resolved. Exceptions occur, of course, when career bureaucrats and others raise so much opposition to the agenda of the political appointee that a new appointment must be made.

Working with Agencies

Astute, politically aware managers understand they can have substantial input into agencies' processes for defining and writing the rules that affect their companies. Three major opportunities exist for managers, or people who represent their interests, to affect legislation. The first, as we already discussed, is during the passage of a bill. After the bill has been passed, agencies solicit public opinion twice, both before and after the rule has been made.

Any time an administrative agency passes a new rule or alters an existing one, it must publish that change in the *Federal Register*. This newspaper, in which the government publishes regulations, orders, and other documents, can be ordered from the Office of the Federal Register in Washington. It is also in the collections of most public, university, and even corporate libraries.

Many corporations monitor the *Federal Register* and notify their managers of proposed new rules or changes in existing rules. If a company wants input into the substance of a rule, it can comment by either writing to the agency or attending hearings held by the agency. Many of the *Federal Register's* notices are on the Internet and can be located through the Alta Vista search engine. In September 1996, there were 40,000 entries under the words *U.S. Federal Register*. For example, the U.S. Department of Labor's Mine Safety and Health posts new rules at [http://www.msha.gov/REGSMISC.htm]. The Employment and Training Administration of the Department of Labor can be accessed at [http://www.doleta.gov/regs/fedregs/]. A proactive, politically astute manager who influences legislation prior to passage has fewer surprises than one who simply reacts to legislation after the fact.

Washington-based corporate offices know administrative agencies have wide discretion over their own actions. Agencies are also a source of information for legislators and government decision makers. Increasingly lobbyists,

PAC members, and managers are spending more time trying to influence the agencies than individual members of Congress. Well-prepared managers and lobbying organizations often can alter the substance of rules and regulations through their participation with administrative agencies.[53]

Most experienced lobbyists are scrupulous about giving accurate and truthful information to regulators and agency staff. The manager or lobbyist who deliberately disseminates slanted or false information seriously damages her personal credibility and the credibility of the industry represented. However, managers should recognize that agency staffs also have political agendas. The political appointees who head the agencies often have goals very different from those of the career bureaucrats who carry out the work as apolitically as possible.

Summary

The U.S. legal system is based on precedents and on interpretation of laws. Because laws change in response to the prevailing value system, managers have considerable opportunity to influence the political and legal processes. Laws are classified according to whether they are public or private, procedural or substantive, and criminal or civil. Instances of white-collar crime are rising, and the legal system is adjusting to cover those cases.

For legal and regulatory matters, managers should be aware of seven basic stakeholder groups: (1) news and broadcast media, (2) industry associations, (3) employees, (4) shareholders and institutional investors, (5) the intellectual community, (6) public-interest groups, and (7) government.

Managers use a variety of methods to make their influence felt in the political and legal processes. Participation in political action committees (PACs) helps companies concentrate and focus on specific industry concerns. Therefore, companies should consider designing a political action process and enhancing the political skills of managers at all levels.

It is critical for managers to understand the steps an issue goes through to become legislation and the points at which it is possible to influence that legislation. It is also important that managers know what administrative agencies do and how their companies can work with those agencies.

Projects

1. From your own observation, what role does your local media play in defining social issues in your community?
2. Choose a specific industry association, write or telephone its headquarters, and assess its role in influencing legislation.
3. Contact a public-interest group such as a state Public Interest Research Group (PIRG), Common Cause, Consumers Union, Greenpeace, any of the scores of organizations you are likely to find in your community. Ask a representative to address your class. Evaluate this spokesperson's message for objectivity, accuracy, and expertise.
4. In a memo to the CEO of your company, propose a detailed plan for using state or local legislators to promote your company's social goals.

---

[53] J. R. Fox, *Managing Business-Government Relations: Cases and Notes on Business-Government Problems* (Homewood, IL: Richard D. Irwin, 1982), pp. 482–86.

5. Visit a municipal, state, or federal lawmaking body to observe a legislature or town government at work.

6. Choose a social issue and use the *Federal Register* to track its progress.

Questions

1. What are the seven major groups of stakeholders that exercise social and political influence?
2. What role do business associations and their PACs play in influencing legislation?
3. Describe the evolution of PACs, and discuss whether politicians should accept their donations.
4. Discuss the five-phase framework for planning, evaluation, and integration of a corporate political program.
5. Describe the six stages through which a bill passes before it becomes law.
6. Discuss the importance of administrative agencies in formulating public policy.
7. What are the different classifications of law?

Beta Case 7
The Legal and Political Arenas

Joan McCarthy had been struggling with the issue of PAC contributions since 1990 when she convened a committee to deal with the issue of PAC donations. That committee's deliberations had been inconclusive and disappointing.

Part of the social issues formulation and implementation process in 1990 had been to develop an explicit policy toward political stakeholders. In 1976, Beta formed its own political action committee and, until 1990, had regularly donated to all incumbent members of the U.S. House and Senate from Michigan. Although the company had not really asked itself why it followed this policy, the board of directors and top management hoped PAC money would foster good relations between Beta and the state legislators. Beta complied with the Federal Election Campaign Act by giving no more than the maximum allowable amount of $5,000 to each political candidate.

William G. Flanders, the junior senator from Michigan, had received his share of Beta PAC money six years earlier. In his bid for a second term, PACs, including Beta, gave generously and Flanders was easily reelected.

During the six years of his first term, Flanders repeatedly and vehemently criticized the pharmaceutical industry. From time to time, he gave speeches deriding pharmaceutical companies for selling unsafe products to developing countries. He accused the firms of inadequate testing procedures and making outrageous profits.

Flanders's opponent, Richard Devens, was far more conservative and generally very supportive of the pharmaceutical industry. He spoke often about the prosperity the industry had brought to Michigan and from time to time singled out Beta as an example of a good corporate citizen. Devens's campaign received a great deal of PAC money from other pharmaceutical firms and trade organizations around the country.

This year, as McCarthy quickly discovered, Beta's PAC policy came under closer scrutiny. Federal rules had changed and documentation had to be monitored much more closely. Frequent friendly lunches and dinners were no longer possible. During the campaign, committee member Bob Hodges argued for himself and several others that a contribution to Flanders constituted a "reward to the enemy." Hodges observed, "Flanders will cash the check, smile, and continue to attack us." Now that the election was over, Hodges told McCarthy and other committee members he was determined to change Beta's policy.

CHAPTER 8 REGULATION

In 1976 the Congressional Budget Office defined regulation as "all governmental activities which somehow affect the operation of private industry or the lives of private citizens." This definition encompasses all federal, state, and local government activities.

Today we are accustomed to working and living with an alphabet soup of regulatory agencies and organizations that affect nearly every aspect of our working and private lives. Despite federal, state, and local government attempts to deregulate and to return many government activities to private hands, regulation remains pervasive. The government defines the nature and scope of competition in the United States and passes regulations that constrain business activities.

The government also oversees a vast array of more personal activities. Regulations dictate how the products we use are marketed. For example, government agencies require advertising to be truthful information. Federal, state, and local government agencies also issue regulations that set standards for the food we eat and the cleanliness of the markets or restaurants in which we buy the food.

The government requires tests of the safety and effectiveness of our prescription and over-the-counter drugs, approving them only after they have been properly tested. Government agencies tell us whether children's toys are safe and specify the kind of information manufacturers must give us when we buy and use a wide variety of products.

Managers must deal with numerous regulations that affect their financial, production, marketing, and personnel decisions. They must comply with rules to make the workplace safe and must provide facilities for the physically challenged. Managers are permitted to discuss sports, politics, and a wide variety of topics with colleagues but are not permitted to inquire into matters of health, sexual preference, and other personal matters unless the employees' job performance is affected. Managers must follow strict rules dealing with hiring and firing, administering tests, and providing health care. Regulations tell companies how to store hazardous materials and where to dispose of waste by-products. Yet only a century ago, very few government regulations impacted everyday activities.

Although the past two decades have seen deregulation in some industries, managers still must formulate their strategies and operate in a regulated business environment that defines the nature of competition. This chapter and the chapter that follows trace the evolution and implementation of regulation from the 19th century to the present. Note that the purpose of regulation and society's expectations of government's role in their personal and professional lives have changed over time. Economic and social conditions, coupled with technological developments, at times create pressure for increased regulatory action, at times government inaction, or even pressure to dismantle regulatory bodies.

In this chapter, we examine the development of early regulation and the balance between producer and consumer issues achieved through Franklin D. Roosevelt's New Deal.

CASE: REGULATION IN OUR DAILY LIVES

Beverly Anderson's alarm clock jolted her out of a deep sleep. The clock, imported from China, still had its Underwriters' Laboratory (UL) tag attached. Anderson knew UL approval meant she had a safe product. Sliding off her flameproof mattress, Anderson padded into the bathroom. After taking a shower, she stood in front of the mirror and plugged in her hair dryer. The dryer had tags attached to the cord warning her not to leave it plugged in near the sink or tub and assuring her that it was free of asbestos.

Before she put on her lipstick, Anderson used a lip balm. She noticed the tube weighed .15 ounces, or 4.2 grams. It contained petrolatums, lanolin, isopropyl myristate, and cetyl alcohol. The label told her the stick would help prevent dry and chapped lips and help heal her lips if they were sun- or windburned. It also warned her not to purchase the lip balm if the cap was not sealed. This little tube contained still more information, including the manufacturer's name, product division, and address, as well as the fact that the brand name was protected by trademark. A bar code running the length of the tube provided information useful to the retailer from whom Anderson had bought it. When Anderson brought the lip balm to the cash register, the scanner read the bar code and deleted the item from inventory. It also gave the drugstore comparative data about how that item was selling. Bar codes on Anderson's deodorant, soap, and cosmetics packages also had all this information and more.

Anderson sprayed a little liquid cleanser on the sink to dissolve the soap lather. The plastic spray bottle contained twice as much information as the tube of lip balm, and even included a raised triangle on the bottom to tell her it could be recycled when empty.

Anderson settled for a quick breakfast of cold cereal. The cereal box packaging told her the ingredients of the cereal and how much fat, fiber, sodium, and cholesterol it contained. She could see how many calories a single serving contained with and without skim or regular milk. Anderson remembered that when she was traveling in Asia last year, none of this information was on the little box of cereal served in the hotel dining room. The cereal, however, tasted exactly the same.

The car in which Anderson drove to work had been built to comply with a variety of state and federal regulations. The previous week she had taken the car to her local garage, where a mechanic inspected it to make sure its emissions did not exceed state standards. A variety of safety features inside the car, such as seatbelts and dual airbags, protected her in the event of collision.

By 8:15 A.M., Anderson had encountered more than 20 federal and state regulations covering every product she used. The rest of her day would bring her into contact with many more regulations.

As the controller for a large real estate corporation, Anderson was aware of the myriad regulations that covered her own industry. She knew she had to follow certain state and locally mandated procedures. Her industry had to adhere to state and federally defined rules on competition. The banks with which she did business were continuously under intense government scrutiny.

Yet Anderson, like most of us, was only dimly aware of the degree to which regulations affected nearly every action she took and every item she used. She took all the information for granted, not realizing that most of those rules had been implemented during her lifetime. In her great-grandparents' time, none of those regulations had existed.

Questions

1. Do consumers really need so much information about the products they use?
2. Does all the information about each product add unnecessarily to its cost?
3. Write down every regulation you encounter in the first hour after you awake in the morning. How many have you found?
4. Why doesn't the same product have the same labeling requirements from country to country?

Business Regulation from the 19th Century to World War I

Before the late 19th century, people rarely encountered government intervention in their private lives. Even in business, few regulations constrained managerial decision making. Managers and other businesspeople were free to make nearly all major decisions for their companies as long as most Americans perceived that the free market was functioning smoothly and opportunities were made available to all individuals according to their abilities. Because most people believed competitive forces were working fairly and justly, there was no overwhelming public sentiment for regulatory control.

In the last two decades of the 19th century, however, large businesses began to squeeze their small competitors and dictate the terms of transactions. More and more people became convinced that huge corporations fettered competition. Large customers received more favorable rates and prices than small customers did. Suppliers became increasingly dependent on the companies they served, and in some cases became those firms' financial captives.

State legislatures and the federal government began to impose rules and regulations on specific industries that were deemed to be "clothed with the public interest."[1] These industries enjoyed large economies of scale and had the potential to exclude new entrants or force out competitors. Small businesses were prevented from entering industries in which only a handful of companies constituted a natural monopoly or oligopoly. Many small businesses also discovered they could not obtain the lower rates and rebates their large competitors enjoyed.

New regulations were particularly important to stakeholders in the upper left quadrant of the stakeholder influence map (see Exhibit 8–1). These external direct stakeholders included suppliers, customers, competitors, potential entrants, and state and federal governments.

Interstate Commerce Act of 1887

In 1887 Congress passed the Interstate Commerce Act to regulate the railroads. Historically railroads were the pioneers of big business. Beginning in the 1830s, they developed new methods of management, new interactions with organized labor, and new relationships with government. The capital for railroad expansion came from the federal government and a variety of investors, including private citizens and local and state governments. Money and investment markets that handled railroad stocks and bonds were centralized in new investment banking houses on Wall Street, close to the New York Stock Exchange building.

---

[1] A. E. Kahn, *The Economics of Regulation: Principles and Institutions,* vol. 1 (New York: John Wiley & Sons, 1970), p. 3.

EXHIBIT 8–1   Stakeholder Influence Map for the 19th Century

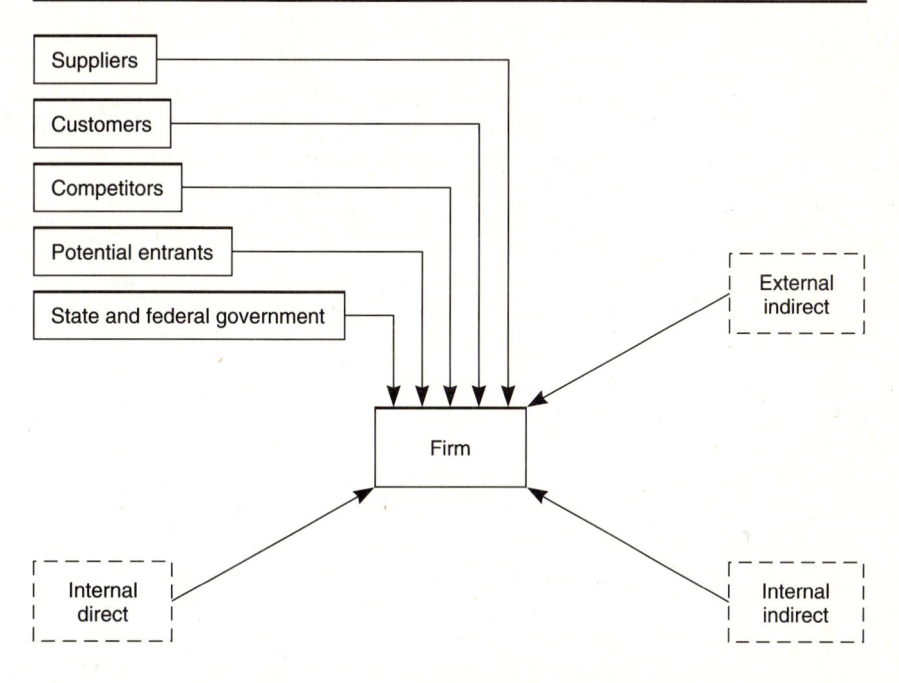

```
  ┌──────────────┐
  │  Suppliers   │──────────────────┐
  └──────────────┘                  │
  ┌──────────────┐                  │
  │  Customers   │─────────────┐    │
  └──────────────┘             │    │
  ┌──────────────┐             │    │
  │  Competitors │────────┐    │    │
  └──────────────┘        │    │    │
  ┌──────────────────┐    │    │    │          ┌─ ─ ─ ─ ─ ─┐
  │Potential entrants│───┐│    │    │          │ External  │
  └──────────────────┘   ││    │    │          │ indirect  │
  ┌──────────────────────┐│    │    │          └─ ─ ─ ─ ─ ─┘
  │State and federal     ││    │    │                │
  │government            │┤    │    │                │
  └──────────────────────┘▼ ▼ ▼▼ ▼ ▼▼               │
                        ┌──────────────┐ ◄──────────┘
                        │     Firm     │
                        └──────────────┘
                           ▲         ▲
  ┌─ ─ ─ ─ ─┐              │         │      ┌─ ─ ─ ─ ─┐
  │Internal │──────────────┘         └──────│Internal │
  │ direct  │                               │indirect │
  └─ ─ ─ ─ ─┘                               └─ ─ ─ ─ ─┘
```

As railroad growth exploded, state legislatures tried to ensure that the companies lived up to their charters by creating independent regulatory commissions. Louis Galambos and Joseph Pratt call these state commissions a curious innovation.[2] Initially established to regulate canal transportation, they were a variation on a model that already existed in Great Britain. The British developed their regulation and enforcement process as a compromise to extend government control without requiring existing agencies to assume the burden. The independent commissions "seemed to promise Americans a way to have more government without having more politics."[3]

In 1849, the state of Connecticut established the first independent special railroad commission to report to the legislature on safety inspections, land disputes, and rate discrimination. This was a fact-finding commission with very limited powers.

In 1869, Massachusetts set up a permanent advisory commission that served as a model for other states; and by 1887, 15 states had working advisory commissions.[4]

---

[2] L. Galambos and J. Pratt, *The Rise of the Corporate Commonwealth* (New York: Basic Books, 1988), p. 45.
[3] Ibid., p. 47.
[4] R. E. Cushman, *The Independent Regulatory Commissions* (New York: Oxford University Press, 1941), pp. 20–25.

As the railroads grew, they became fiercely competitive. Because fixed costs were very high, railroads tried to use as much of their carrying capacity as possible. At first they pursued the logical strategy of lowering rates, but competitive rate wars quickly followed. Railroad managers soon realized that if they did not cooperate, the combination of high fixed costs and destructive rounds of rate reductions would lead to the financial collapse of some lines. Monopolistic survivors would then be able to set rates at whatever levels they chose.

For a short time, railroad managers tried to bring order to their industry by creating cartels or pools to set rates and allocate traffic. However, these voluntary agreements broke down not only because they had no legal basis but also some railroads had offered under-the-table rebates to large customers.

Before long, external direct stakeholders, such as small-business owners, passengers, shippers, and farmers, pressured state governments to set maximum rates and prohibit the railroads' practice of charging higher rates for shorter hauls. Between 1874 and 1885, the U.S. House of Representatives considered more than 30 bills to provide greater control over interstate commerce. Railroad and other big-business interests opposed the bills, and none was passed.

State legislators, who were more responsive to their grassroots farming constituents, passed the Granger Laws regulating railroads. However, all stakeholders, big and small, soon realized railroads and interstate commerce had to come under federal law rather than a hodgepodge of individual state regulations. In 1886, the Supreme Court ruled in the Wabash case that only Congress could regulate interstate commerce.

A year later, Congress passed the Interstate Commerce Act that created the Interstate Commerce Commission (ICC).[5] The act mandated that all rates be reasonable and just while expressly forbidding certain practices. Railroads could no longer discriminate in rates, fix prices, or furnish rebates.

Although the president of the United States nominated the five commissioners and the Senate confirmed them, ICC members were deliberately selected to balance conflicting perspectives on interstate commerce. The ICC was charged with carrying out the Interstate Commerce Act. When the act was drawn up, corporate leaders worked with sympathetic members of Congress to water down its provisions.

The Supreme Court heard 16 cases under the Interstate Commerce Act between 1887 and 1905. Of these cases, justices resolved 15 in favor of the railroads. Historian Edward C. Kirkland concludes that "the court threw itself as an obstacle across the path willed by Congress and the public."[6] The

---

[5] G. Porter, *The Rise of Big Business, 1860–1910* (Arlington Heights, IL: AHM Publishing, 1973), pp. 27–39.

[6] E. C. Kirkland, "Industry Comes of Age: Business, Labor, and Public Policy, 1860–1897," in *The Economic History of the United States,* vol. 6, ed. Henry Davis (New York: Holt, Rinehart & Winston, 1961), p. 134.

sad truth was that a farmer or small supplier who appealed high railroad rates to the ICC was likely to die of old age before receiving relief.

Hepburn Act of 1906. To strengthen the provisions of the Interstate Commerce Act, Congress passed the Hepburn Act in 1906. The new legislation expanded the scope and jurisdiction of the ICC and added two more commissioners, bringing the number to seven. One important provision of the Hepburn Act gave the ICC the power to require corporations to use a unified system of accounting. Prior to 1906, companies used a wide variety of accounting systems; this made it difficult for the ICC to obtain reliable information. Yet another provision made ICC rulings binding until the courts could review them.

Sherman Antitrust Act of 1890

The Sherman Antitrust Act was the second major piece of congressional regulatory legislation. It was titled "an act to protect trade and commerce against unlawful restraints and monopolies." Like the Interstate Commerce Act, the Sherman Antitrust Act at first primarily affected external direct stakeholders.

Throughout the 1870s and 1880s, other industries followed the railroads' example of horizontal growth and increasing complexity through mergers. Manufacturers integrated vertically, either to control access to raw materials or to move closer to consumers. For example, lumber companies integrated forward into furniture making and backward into forest acquisition. Oil refineries integrated vertically into athletic footwear, chemicals, and explosives.

Although few companies actually gained total control over an entire industry, some firms' activities were so comprehensive that they constituted what many considered to be a monopoly position. These large firms attempted to control suppliers, customers, and competitors in a single industry by dictating terms of trade. As Exhibit 8–2 shows, they formed trade associations and lobbies that worked to set prices and establish production quotas among participants.

Like the railroad cartels, these industry agreements fell apart when the terms no longer suited one of the participants. Rather than lobbying Congress for legalization of cartels, owners of leading firms in a single industry purchased stock in one another's firms and in the firms of their smaller competitors. When this strategy also failed to provide the control manufacturers desired, they devised an organizational structure called a trust.

A trust was an arrangement in which companies turned over their stock certificates and voting rights to a group or board of trustees, who then became directors. Directors were vested with the power to make operating decisions and to determine investment strategies for the companies that comprised the

EXHIBIT 8–2   Stakeholder Influence Map

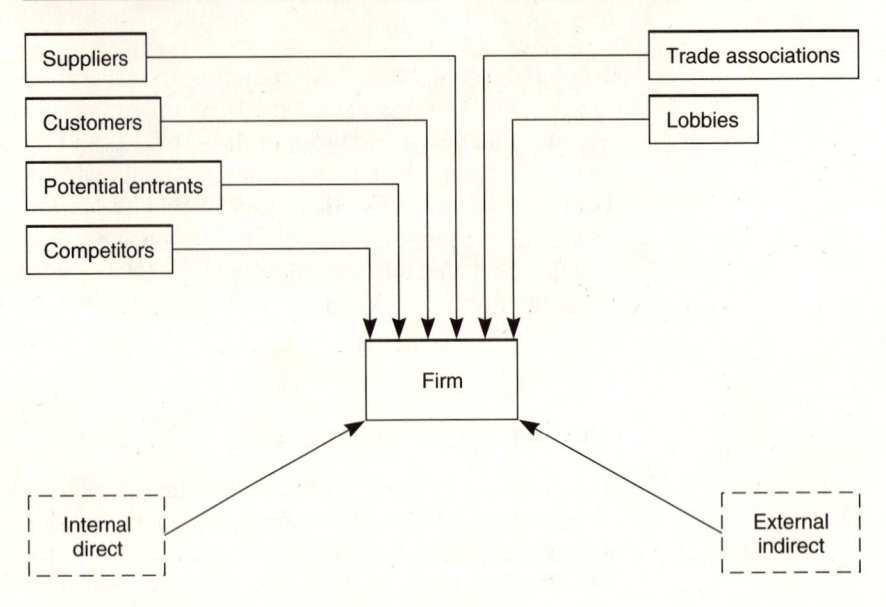

```
Suppliers ─────────────┐       ┌───── Trade associations
Customers ────────────┐│       │┌──── Lobbies
Potential entrants ──┐││       │││
Competitors ────────┐│││       │││
                    ▼▼▼▼       ▼▼▼
                    ┌─────────────┐
                    │    Firm     │
                    └─────────────┘
                      ▲         ▲
                     ╱           ╲
          ┌─────────┐             ┌─────────┐
          │Internal │             │External │
          │ direct  │             │indirect │
          └─────────┘             └─────────┘
```

trust. Directors became the new group of stakeholders in the internal direct quadrant of the stakeholder influence map.

As with legislation to control railroads, a diverse group of competitors and potential market entrants gathered together and attacked trusts in state and federal courts and in state legislatures.[7] With Populist support, the state of Kansas passed the first antitrust act in 1889. The following year, Congress passed the Sherman Antitrust Act. One of the most important stipulations of the Sherman Act appears in Section 1. It declares, "Every contract, combination in the form of trust or otherwise, or conspiracy, in restraint of trade or commerce among the several States, or with foreign nations, is hereby declared to be illegal."[8] It was left to the courts to decide what constituted combinations in restraint of trade.

In Section 7, the Sherman Antitrust Act actively encouraged competitors to sue for damages. Sec. 7 stipulates, "Any person who shall be injured in his business or property by any other person or corporation by reason of anything forbidden or declared to be unlawful by this law, may sue . . . for the amount in controversy, and shall recover threefold the damages by him sustained." Even though much of the law was vague, the prospect of realizing triple damages encouraged litigation.

---

[7] A. D. Chandler, Jr., *The Visible Hand: The Managerial Revolution in American Business* (Cambridge, MA: Belknap, 1977), pp. 317–19.

[8] R. H. Bork, *The Antitrust Paradox* (New York: Basic Books, 1978), p. 19.

Clayton Act of 1914. The Sherman Antitrust Act was so broad that it left companies uncertain as to what actions constituted violations and what did not. In 1914, Congress passed the Clayton Act to tighten and clarify the Sherman Act and address specific business practices that might lessen competition. The Clayton Act barred price discrimination if it lessened competition or created a monopoly. It prohibited *tying agreements*, in which a seller required a buyer to purchase unwanted goods to get goods the buyer *did* want. It also prohibited *exclusive dealing arrangements* in which buyers could not deal with rival sellers. In addition, the Clayton Act prohibited interlocking directorates among competing firms if those directorates would tend to create a monopoly.

Federal Trade Commission Act of 1914

Lawmakers recognized that laws prohibiting monopoly and restraint of trade needed to be enforced in a systematic way. The Federal Trade Commission Act (FTCA) created the Federal Trade Commission (FTC), which was charged with investigating unfair methods of competition among businesses. Congress directed the FTC to prohibit unfair and deceptive acts or practices and gave it broad discretion to define business practices that constituted "unfair methods of competition."

Like the Interstate Commerce Commission, the FTC was created as an independent commission with commissioners appointed by the president and confirmed by the Senate. The commission's charge was to protect consumers against "unfair methods of competition in or affecting commerce." Congress, the U.S. Chamber of Commerce, and nearly all trade associations supported the mission of the FTC. However, the commission had little real clout. Because the law did not stipulate what elements constituted unfair competition, the FTC made its own determination. Although it had the power to investigate business practices, it could not compel companies to comply with its regulations.

Wheeler-Lea Amendment (1938). One portion of the Wheeler-Lea Amendment, passed in 1938, stated that the FTC could intervene when trade practices were deemed "unfair or deceptive acts or practices in commerce." The change in wording from the original act meant the FTC did not have to prove competition was affected. The FTC generally relied on companies' voluntary compliance until the 1940s, when the courts showed more interest in pursuing violators.[9]

These early acts and commissions responded to society's widespread conviction that corporations required government oversight. The public demanded that Congress preserve a competitive business environment in

---

[9] *Federal Regulatory Directory,* 6th ed. (Washington, D.C.: Congressional Quarterly, 1990), p. 262.

which small participants were treated equitably and were not excluded from participation.

Among business leaders, antitrust legislation created great uncertainty. They fiercely resisted new legislation until they realized it was inevitable. Then they worked with Congress and other government entities to make the laws and regulatory agencies as business-friendly as possible. However, the vagueness of the resulting acts led to inconsistent court rulings that constrained executives in developing their strategic initiatives.

The legislative process reflected business's ambivalence toward government regulation. As a result, initial legislation was usually weaker than it would have been had business not gotten involved in its development. These early acts and the regulatory bodies they created focused stakeholders' attention on competition, price fixing, and deceptive business practices. Government refused to address the public policy issue of how economies of scale should be treated in a growing and more technology-based economy. According to Galambos and Pratt, "Technologically and organizationally the business system was changing in fundamental ways, but public officials had yet to work out how society could best capture the long-range economic benefits offered by modern large-scale enterprise while maintaining a satisfactory level of competition."[10]

Consumer Regulation from the 19th Century to World War I

Although the term *consumerism* was not coined until the 1960s, public concern about accurate information, product content, and product use dates from the end of the 19th century. As urban populations grew and new products and processes proliferated, industries operating without regulation often manufactured unsafe products. Reformers organized to deal with the problems created by the hazardous products of unregulated industries. In 1891, activists formed the first Consumers' League in New York City. Within a few years, a number of local groups formed a national federation, the National Consumers' League. By 1903, the League had 64 branches in 20 states. The National Consumers' League joined a variety of other organizations to alert the public to the dangers of impure, mislabeled, and misrepresented food and drugs then on the market.

Pure Food and Drug Act of 1906

Drugs. Growing markets and technological advances were a strong force for change in the delivery of medication to the public. After the Civil War, concentration of capital, labor, and control was evident in the growth of

---

[10] Galambos and Pratt, *The Rise of the Corporate Commonwealth*, p. 62.

large-scale prescription pharmaceutical manufacturers and the explosion of the patent medicine industry.

Traditionally, pharmacy schools trained pharmacists to compound drugs. Some physicians, however, prescribed and filled their own prescriptions. They routinely used substances such as morphine, quinine, iodine, chloroform, and carbolic acid in their potions. These substances had the potential to do tremendous harm as well as good. As the market for mass-produced pharmaceuticals grew, the public demanded that an oversight body ensure quality control.

The patent medicine industry garnered much of the stakeholder concern. Its misuse of toxic, narcotic, and addictive substances was nothing short of scandalous. Patent medicine makers routinely turned out substances such as Hostetter's Bitters, Radam's Microbe Killer, and Swain's Panacea. Fretful babies were given opium-laced Winslow's Soothing Syrup to stop their crying. Elixir Terpin Hydrate with heroin was a popular over-the-counter cough syrup.

Working together, pharmaceutical and medical associations pressed for passage of pure food and drug legislation. They desired, in large part, to eliminate the quackery of the patent medicine industry and remove harmful products from the marketplace.

Food. Food-processing companies also came under attack. By the turn of the century, refrigerated railroad cars carried processed food from coast to coast. Packers and canners had only rudimentary knowledge of food preservation and bacteriology. They added preservatives such as formaldehyde to canned meats and copper sulfate to vegetables to make them look and smell fresher.

Lobbying groups were particularly vocal in pressuring Congress for pure food and drug legislation. External indirect stakeholders such as the General Federation of Women's Clubs, the National Consumers' League, and chemists' organizations joined together after bills failed to pass Congress in 1892 and 1902. When Theodore Roosevelt was elected in 1904, these groups enlisted presidential support; in his annual message to Congress in 1905, Roosevelt urged the enactment of a pure food and drug law.

The law passed the Senate shortly after Upton Sinclair's *The Jungle* was published. Sinclair drew the public's attention to the meatpacking industry, writing, "Men, who worked in the tank rooms full of steam . . . fell into the vats; and when they were fished out, there was never enough of them to be worth exhibiting—sometimes they would be overlooked for days, till all but the bones of them had gone out to the world as Durham's Pure Leaf Lard."[11]

When federal inspectors confirmed Sinclair's charges, Roosevelt threw his full support behind a meat inspection bill. Packers, worried about

---

[11] U. Sinclair, *The Jungle* (New York: Doubleday, 1906), p. 117.

consumer outrage and foreign competition, realized a federal law would help them save their reputations.

Finally, in 1906, Congress sent President Theodore Roosevelt the Pure Food and Drug Act that he promptly signed. The law required manufacturers to give truthful information about the contents of their products. Dangerous substances had to be listed on labels, but there was no requirement to list other ingredients. Interpreted generously, the act meant manufacturers could not deliberately mislead the public.

The Sherley Amendment (1912). The Sherley Amendment, enacted in 1912, tightened restrictions against deceptive labeling. As with the railroads and other industries, the courts did very little to interfere with the patent medicine business. Not until 1938 did the Food and Drug Administration receive congressional authority to require proof that any new product, whether prescription or over-the-counter, was safe.

Business Regulation Summary

In the late 19th and early 20th centuries, legislators and the public were very concerned about the nature of competition. American ideology supported the notion of unfettered competition as long as that competition was fair. Fairness demanded access to the industrial environment and at least the possibility of an equitable chance. Very few legislators on the national level considered widespread consumer protection, workplace, or environmental legislation. During this early period, newly formed groups of external indirect stakeholders such as trade associations and lobbies began to exercise their power, a trend that would continue to grow. As cataclysmic events often do, World War I precipitated fundamental changes in business and government relations.

World War I to the New Deal

Before World War I, most regulatory legislation concentrated on the railroad, oil, steel, and coal industries. As we noted in the previous chapter, Secretary of Commerce Herbert Hoover pursued policies to make production more efficient and competition less destructive. Trade associations flourished. The government, backed by the U.S. Chamber of Commerce and the National Association of Manufacturers, grew more supportive of price and production agreements. But agencies like the U.S. Department of Commerce had a difficult time defining improved trade practices and the elements of criminal price fixing which came under their control. Courts ruled gingerly and narrowly on competition and trade practice cases.

Consumer-focused regulation drew new attention in the postwar era. Companies eagerly responded to pent-up demand for consumer products. Issues such as market entry and competitive practices began to take a backseat to more pressing problems dealing with selling a vast variety of goods to mass markets.[12] The FTC began to focus on eliminating deceptive trade practices such as misleading advertising. Its rulings were still once removed from direct intervention to protect consumers. Instead, it tried to prevent fraud that indirectly injured consumers.

The Great Depression led legislators and legal scholars to question the nation's economic order. The courts waffled on many issues, and neither they nor government policy produced a reasoned approach to regulation. A few Supreme Court decisions supported government price and production controls. On the other hand, when small retailers demanded protection from chain stores, several states passed fair-trade laws that restrained price cutting. Morton Keller notes that "as so often before, administrative implementation and court interpretation of the law came to be thoroughly muddled by the gulf between the public policy goal and economic realities, by the sheer complexity and multiplicity of the interests involved."[13]

Regulation in the New Deal

The administration of Franklin D. Roosevelt heralded a new era in regulation. The New Deal's major goal was to pry the economy out of the depression. A cooperative Congress created three basic types of regulatory agencies: functional, economic, and social.

Functional Agencies

Functional agencies regulated particular functions such as labor relations or financial transactions within an industry. For example, the Federal Home Loan Bank Board (FHLBB) was an independent agency organized under the executive branch. It regulated federally chartered savings and loan associations. The S&Ls were the major source of private funding for building and buying housing.

The National Labor Relations Board (NLRB) was established by the Wagner Act in 1935. This independent commission protected the rights of employees to bargain collectively and was created to prevent unfair labor practices.

---

[12] M. Keller, "The Pluralistic State: American Economic Regulation in Comparative Perspective, 1900–1930," in T. K. McCraw, ed., *Regulation in Perspective* (Cambridge, MA: Harvard University Press, 1981), p. 74.
[13] Ibid., p. 94.

The Securities and Exchange Act of 1934 created the Securities and Exchange Commission (SEC). The SEC, also an independent agency, began operations in 1934. Its job was to protect the public against fraud and deception in the securities and financial markets. For the first time, the government exercised its power in the securities industry and required companies to disclose financial information.

The Banking Act of 1933 (or the Glass-Steagall Act) created the Federal Deposit Insurance Corporation (FDIC). Operating under the executive branch, this independent agency regulated state-chartered, insured banks that were not members of the Federal Reserve System. In addition to separating commercial and investment banking functions, the FDIC protected small depositors by insuring their bank deposits.

Economic Agencies

Economic agencies regulated an entire industry. The Motor Carrier Act of 1935, for example, created an agency to regulate the trucking industry. The act also brought the entire industry under the ICC, which regulated entry, rates, and mergers. The Federal Communications Commission (FCC), formed in 1934, was charged with consolidating federal regulation of radio, telephone, and telegraph.

The Civil Aeronautics Authority (CAA), formed in 1938, lasted for two years before it was replaced by the Civil Aeronautics Board (CAB). The CAB handled the coordination of airline routes and regulations covering airlines.

Social Agencies

The Social Security system was the only major social body created during the New Deal. Like the economic regulators, it applied across industries. Social agencies did not proliferate until the 1960s.[14] We discuss them in detail in the next chapter.

The following case on antitrust discusses how antitrust legislation has evolved and is enforced by the Justice Department. The framers of the original antitrust legislation could not have anticipated the issues that arose in the 20th century. As with other laws, antitrust legislation evolved in response to a new competitive environment.

---

[14] C. M. Kerwin, "Introduction," *Federal Regulatory Directory,* 6th ed. (Washington, D.C.: Congressional Quarterly, 1990), pp. 1–5.

CASE: THE JUSTICE DEPARTMENT AND ANTITRUST LEGISLATION

In the century following 1890, various federal administrations developed their own views of how the Sherman and Clayton acts were to be interpreted. As membership on the Supreme Court changed over time, justices interpreted the acts in a variety of ways. Even the framers of the original legislation, who could not have anticipated the development of modern business firms, had made no provision in the Constitution for competitive issues created by the emergence of large, divisionalized enterprises. It was left to regulatory agencies and the courts to continue to interpret and determine the nature of competition. After World War II, the competitive environment took on global dimensions, further complicating the U.S. government's response to antitrust issues.

By the 1980s, the uniquely American practice of settling antitrust action in the courts was becoming extremely costly. No industrialized country other than the United States used the traditional court system for trade matters. Great Britain's Restrictive Trade Practices Commission settled its private antitrust suits that comprised up to 90 percent of all antitrust cases. The European Community (EC) drew up rules regarding competition that expressly prohibited price-fixing agreements and discriminatory pricing. However, the EC pragmatically avoided litigation by developing a system of block exemptions from the rules governing competition.

When the Reagan administration took office in 1981, one of its greatest concerns was the effectiveness with which American companies were competing in the global arena. Japanese and European competitors presented a serious challenge to American companies. They had captured large shares of U.S. domestic markets in autos, steel, electronics, and chemicals. Many legal scholars, economists, and politicians concluded that national boundaries were increasingly irrelevant in defining the competitive market in a number of industries.

The Reagan administration, which was committed ideologically to a laissez-faire regulatory environment, began to look for ways to enhance American corporations' international competitiveness. The administration settled on a policy that punished price fixers but approved mergers. Its view was that size was unimportant and efficiency should be encouraged. In 1984, the Justice Department gave the go-ahead to vertical integration between suppliers and customers. It also made horizontal mergers between competitors much easier. For the first time in the history of antitrust legislation, the government defined markets internationally instead of domestically.

In 1985, Secretary of Commerce Malcolm Baldrige called for a repeal of Section 7 of the Clayton Act that prohibited mergers that "may . . . substantially lessen competition . . . or may tend to create a monopoly." Baldrige insisted that foreign competition was behind his proposal and that the Clayton Act stopped "the kinds of efficiency-creating mergers we need to become internationally competitive."[15]

The administration's new attitude toward antitrust created the climate within which the biggest nonoil company merger in history took place; General Electric Company purchased RCA Corporation for $6.3 billion. This event created the nation's seventh largest industrial company. GE chairperson John F. Welch, Jr., declared this colossus would be a new breed of U.S. corporation and would be powerful enough to beat its Japanese rivals. While not everyone agreed with Welch that sheer size was a critical competitive variable, the international arena became the new venue for any discussion of competition.

In December 1988, Attorney General Richard Thornburgh and Secretary of Commerce C. William Verity debated the issue of antitrust and foreign competition on the editorial page of *The Wall Street Journal*. International antitrust law dated back to the early 20th century. In 1909, the Supreme Court had ruled that the legality of conduct must be determined by the law of the place where it occurred. This was called the presumption of territoriality. However, in 1945, the Supreme Court adopted what was called the effects test. The Court ruled the United States could impose liability on persons not within its domain for conduct

---

[15] A. Reilly, "Reagan Turns a Cold Eye on Antitrust," *Fortune,* October 14, 1985, p. 31.

that took place outside its borders if it had an effect within this country. Over time, subsequent rulings refined the law into the principle that any conduct having a direct and reasonably foreseeable effect on U.S. commerce was subject to U.S. jurisdiction.[16]

Foreign companies and governments could confound U.S. law, however, by refusing to hand over documents and refusing to compel witnesses to testify. Foreign governments also could retaliate against U.S. exports. Many were outspoken in insisting that the United States could not impose its rules on foreign soil.[17]

Thornburgh asserted that U.S. firms faced unprecedented international competition in the global marketplace. He pointed to foreign inroads in superconductors, high-definition television, robotics, and computer-aided design and manufacturing. Although U.S. firms were bringing products to market, so were its major competitors. The costs of research and development and the demand for customization were extremely high, often exceeding the resources of any single firm.

Thornburgh noted that foreign firms had entered into cooperative production ventures but American companies had failed to do so because they feared an antitrust challenge. He pointed to the Sherman Act's triple damages in private suits and to huge legal fees. He recommended two approaches: First, a company that wanted to enter a joint-production venture would apply to the government through the Commerce and Justice departments. These departments would make sure the venture did not threaten competition. They would jointly issue a certificate saying the conduct covered by the certificate could not be challenged under state or federal antitrust laws in either a government or a private suit. The second approach used the stipulations of the National Cooperative Research Act (1984), which prohibited a court from stopping a joint-research venture without considering its competitive benefits.

Verity observed that U.S. firms were losing the race in the global marketplace. He suggested protecting U.S. firms engaged in cooperative research from antitrust legislation. Two possible high-tech sectors worthy of this protection were high-definition television and flexible computer-integrated manufacturing. In his view, "permitting qualified firms jointly to finance, construct, or operate such would aid technology development and product diversity. The net result is increased competition and its benefits."[18]

The Bush administration took a much more active role in global antitrust enforcement. It used U.S. antitrust law to punish foreign competitors if they stifled American firms in the global market. The Justice Department's antitrust division looked for ways to reach beyond U.S. borders to strike at bid rigging, price fixing, and cartel-like behavior that hurt U.S. exports.

The administration pointed to several examples of this behavior. One hundred forty Japanese construction firms were suspected of rigging bids at the Yokosuka U.S. naval base near Tokyo. Allied Signal alleged it had been shut out of Japan's $100-million-a-year market for electrical transformers, because the Japanese utilities claimed Allied's transformers were too noisy, expensive, and unsafe. In yet another example, Japanese carmakers favored Japanese part suppliers in their U.S. operations.[19]

The Bush administration took yet another step in the spring of 1992. The Justice Department issued a statement extending U.S. antitrust enforcement policy to non-U.S. markets. The department announced that, when appropriate, it would take antitrust action against overseas conduct

> that interfered with U.S. exports, regardless of whether U.S. consumers were harmed when the conduct directly affected the exports of goods and services from the U.S. The Justice Department would also take action if there were anticompetitive activities violating U.S. antitrust law, or in cases in which U.S. courts had jurisdiction over foreign nationals or companies involved in anticompetitive conduct.

The *Financial Times* pointed out the complications for foreign companies whose countries' legal

---

[16] T. Calvani, "Long Arm of U.S. Regulations," *Financial Times,* October 25, 1996, p. 12.
[17] C. Yang and W. Spindle, "Commerce Cops," *Business Week,* December 13, 1993, p. 69.
[18] "U.S. Firms Get Tripped in Race to the Marketplace," *The Wall Street Journal,* December 27, 1988, p. A10.
[19] "Return of the Big Stick," *US News & World Report,* June 4, 1990, pp. 54–55.

systems differed from that of the United States. It noted that few other countries endorsed U.S. triple-damage private lawsuits. Unlike laws in most other countries, U.S. law did not distinguish between protecting a domestic market from foreign-source abuse and protecting the domestic rights of citizens abroad from abuse in the foreign market.[20]

In 1993, President Clinton appointed Anne K. Bingaman as head of the Justice Department's Antitrust Division. She adopted an activist approach immediately; foreign companies were among her first targets. Bingaman announced she would go after foreign companies that violated American antitrust laws. She declared, "Anyone who sells in U.S. markets should play by our rules."

In December 1993, the get-tough approach against foreign companies became explicit. U.S. investors continued to find that foreign local business practices and industry structures shut them out of Asian and European markets. U.S. industries, frustrated by the failure of low tariff policies to loosen overseas markets, strongly supported antitrust measures.

In October 1994, the Clinton administration published its draft Antitrust Enforcement Guidelines for International Operations. The centerpiece of this document was the extraterritoriality application of U.S. antitrust law. The new guidelines asserted U.S. jurisdiction over foreign cartels that had substantial sales in the United States.[21] The law's meaning did not change if the cartel was located totally outside the United States, if it was administered by foreign nations, or if it was legal in its home country. It did not even matter if its prices into the United States were lower than the competitive price that would benefit U.S. consumers.[22] Despite the tough rhetoric, the Clinton administration remained fairly lenient when it came to global deals.

Trustbusters began to concentrate their antitrust efforts in the computer and health care industries. Almost immediately after President Clinton took office, the Justice Department asked for documents in the Federal Trade Commission's case against Microsoft. In 15 years, Bill Gates's Microsoft had grown from a start-up to the world's largest software company. The FTC had been examining alleged unfair business practices at Microsoft for three years but commissioners could not agree whether to sue the company.

By 1995, Microsoft dominated the personal computer software market through MS-DOS and Windows. Microsoft provided the operating system software programs for 8 out of 10 of the world's personal computers. All kinds of other software from spreadsheets to word processing to games required Microsoft operating systems.

The Justice Department filed an antitrust suit charging Microsoft's proposed $1.2 billion acquisition of Intuit, Inc., would monopolize the newly burgeoning market for personal-finance software and future markets for electronic business. In the government's view, Intuit and Microsoft might have been expected to compete in the personal-finance software market and for links to financial institutions in the new market of home on-line banking services. Their merger would mean a single option in which Microsoft-owned Intuit could set prices.[23]

Gates rejected Justice Department charges. He asserted that the company achieved its dominance because it created innovative products and developed effective marketing strategies. Gates also dismissed government allegations that, in the future, competitors would be at a great disadvantage because the Intuit takeover would allow Microsoft to dominate future markets in electronic banking.[24]

Although the Justice Department blocked the Intuit deal, it continued its investigation of Microsoft. In September 1996, it began to probe Microsoft's Internet software business. The Justice Department informed the company it would issue a written request for documents focusing on the browser programs that navigated the Internet's World Wide Web. Netscape Communications, which led the browser market had asked the Justice Department to see whether Microsoft's Web marketing strategy violated the company's 1994 consent decree with the government. This decree set restrictions on Microsoft's behavior in the

---

[20] C. Hampton, "Long Arm of U.S. Antitrust Law," *Financial Times,* April 30, 1992, p. 12.

[21] A cartel is two or more companies that collude to fix prices or divide markets.

[22] Calvani, p. 12.

[23] D. Clark, "Microsoft Sticks by Its Tactics Despite Uproar," *The Wall Street Journal,* May 1, 1995, p. A1; E. L. Andrews, "A Question of Trust," *New York Times,* May 1, 1995, p. D1.

[24] Andrews, p. D1.

market for computer operating systems. Netscape charged that Microsoft was using clandestine incentives and penalties to persuade personal-computer makers and Internet-service providers to offer Microsoft's browser rather than Netscape's.[25]

Bingaman also targeted the health care industry. The Justice Department and the Federal Trade Commission took aim at fees doctors charged health maintenance organizations (HMOs). Since the early 1980s, HMOs had gradually wielded more and more power. They had recruited physicians to treat patients at sizable discounts from standard fees. The HMOs, which provided health care to groups of workers at a fixed monthly rate, relied on cut-rate doctor networks. In many specialties, HMOs were able to set their reimbursement rate more than 25 percent below standard fee schedules. In retaliation, some doctors tried to band together to protect their rates against price cutting by HMOs. In the mid-1990s antitrust regulators took aim at these doctors, alleging it was anticompetitive to engage in price fixing or a mass refusal to provide service to certain HMOs.[26] This issue was not easily or quickly resolved.

When Bingaman resigned in August 1996, some legal experts noted that she had raised morale and funding in the Antitrust Division of the Justice Department. She had taken on many more cases than her predecessors and had given the division a more international focus. William F. Baxter, the Reagan administration antitrust chief for three years summed up Bingaman's tenure. He noted that she "rattled more cages and sounded gruffer but the cases came out about the same."[27]

---

[25] S. Lohr, "Justice Dept. in New Inquiry into Microsoft," *New York Times,* September 20, 1996, p. D1.

Questions

1. Should the Sherman Act be altered to do away with private suits and triple damages?
2. Should antitrust be negotiated and resolved by committees or by arbitration as it is in many other countries?
3. What activities should exempt U.S. firms from antitrust legislation?
4. Are the issues that led to the passage of the Sherman Act irrelevant in today's world?
5. If you could construct the ideal policy on competition for U.S. corporations, what would it be? Why?
6. Should the United States (or any other country) be able to bring charges against a foreign firm for activities outside its own borders if the foreign firm's actions do not affect U.S. firms? What if the foreign firm's actions do affect U.S. firms?

---

[26] G. Anders, "Antitrust Laws Roil World of Healing," *The Wall Street Journal,* May 14, 1993, p. B1.

[27] R. W. Stevenson, "Antitrust Chief to Resign from Justice Department," *New York Times,* August 2, 1996, p. D2.

Summary

During the decade-and-a-half of the 1940s and 1950s, business, government, and other stakeholders developed expectations that fundamentally changed the nature of regulation from economically focused to socially activist. The period between the end of the New Deal and the 1960s was relatively uneventful in terms of developing regulations. Stakeholders gathered their strength and resources to face the turbulent social and environmental events of the 1960s and 1970s.

This chapter lays the foundation for the regulatory process. It discusses the major regulatory agencies created between 1887 and the New Deal. The debates that led to the passage of legislation and the role business played in developing the new regulatory agencies were peculiarly American. No other industrialized country took exactly the same approach to the interaction among business, government, and special-interest groups.

Debate continues over the nature of competition, the degree of government oversight, and the development of public policy. Issues shift with changing economic conditions and partisan politics. Groups of stakeholders coalesce around their pet issues. The activities of external indirect stakeholders continue to gain strength. Lobbyists, special-interest groups, and advocacy organizations on all sides of issues use many of the same organizational skills that made corporate interests so powerful.

The competitive international environment, coupled with the ideological predisposition of political parties and presidential appointees, challenges the courts and legislators to wrestle with evolving policy. Application of one of the most fundamental and basic pieces of legislation, the Sherman Antitrust Act, is difficult and subject to change in a global competitive environment.

Projects

1. Examine the role the courts play in the U.S. regulatory process. Does our legal framework contribute to or detract from the competitive environment?
2. Interview a top manager of, or legal counsel to, a newly merged firm to find out what impact the Sherman Act had on the merger.
3. Interview a member of the legal division of a multinational company. What does he consider the most pressing regulatory issues for the company? Would those issues be different if the company were purely domestic?

Questions

1. What were society's main concerns that led to the passage of the Interstate Commerce Act and the Sherman Antitrust Act?
2. What role do lobbying or special-interest groups play in the passage of legislation in the United States?

Beta Case 8
Regulation

CEO Donald Drees burst into attorney Robert Mobley's office. Drees was absolutely furious. He had just heard that Beta had lost its contract to administer the Maryland state employees' prescription-drug benefit program. His friend at the Maryland State House told Drees that more than half the state's pharmacies refused to fill the prescriptions of the program Beta administered. Drees' friend also hinted that Rev-Aid, one of the nation's biggest chains was behind the stores' action. In his opinion, Rev-Aid was trying to keep Beta from administering these benefit programs. Some Rev-Aid executives even claimed that Beta offered big discounts to mail-order pharmacies and managed care plans while charging retail pharmacies and drugstore chains much higher prices for the same drugs.

"That charge is ridiculous. I know that a group of Rev-Aid pharmacies has organized a boycott against Beta," he told Mobley. "This is a perfect time to complain to the Federal Trade Commission about the power of the drugstore chains. I'm sure you have heard that Rev-Aid is trying to buy out Rite-Co., Inc. Rev-Aid is trying to become the biggest drugstore chain in the country. It will be able to dictate drug prices and squeeze out competition. I'm going to get in touch with FTC Commissioner Robert Pitofsky and give him an earful about this acquisition. At the very least he's got to agree that if the deal goes through, they've got to divest themselves of stores in Maryland. They can't get away with this."

Mobley, sat back in his chair and sighed. "Calm down Don," he said, "let's take a realistic look at what the FTC is doing in antitrust. Let me explain the relationship between the Justice Department and FTC in antitrust issues. Then let's try to work through the likelihood that the FTC will make Rev-Aid give up the idea of acquiring Rite-Co. Let's also look at what power we have as stakeholders in this issue."

CHAPTER 9
REGULATION AND DEREGULATION FROM THE 1960s TO THE 1990s

The previous chapter traces the development of regulation from the end of the 19th century through the New Deal. This chapter's primary topics are deregulation in general and the consequences of economic deregulation in particular. This chapter traces the broad development of social legislation from the 1960s to the 1990s. Subsequent chapters examine specific social legislation in greater detail.

CASE: REGULATION AND THE CABLE INDUSTRY

In the 1980s, cable television service began to spread its plethora of programs across the United States. In 1984, to encourage expansion, Congress passed the Cable Communications Policy Act that allowed municipalities to regulate basic service for local broadcast channels. This act was ineffective, however, because by the late 1980s, cable television rates had doubled and even tripled in some cities and most communities continued to be served by a single cable distributor. As a practical matter, more than 95 percent of cable systems were free of regulation under the Federal Communications Commission's (FCC) definition of effective competition. Effective competition for local cable systems meant they operated in an area that had at least three broadcast television channels. This definition that covered more than 95 percent of markets meant few municipalities were allowed to regulate cable rates.

In December 1990, Congress and the FCC proposed new rules to give communities more power to limit consumer costs for cable television services. Early in 1991, the Justice Department announced it would back new standards allowing the reregulation of cable television by local governments in many communities across the United States. If the proposed rule passed, the FCC would redefine existing competition:

- Competition would exist in an area if television viewers could receive at least six broadcast channels and less than half the households subscribed to the cable system.
- Competition would exist if new rival technologies such as satellite or microwave services reached at least half the households and captured at least 10 percent of the subscribers.

In reality, relatively few cable systems were able to meet the FCC definition of competition and become subject to control. Cable systems could escape regulation by claiming they were "good actors" that provided basic services at prices comparable to those offered in cities with effective competition.

Even so, the FCC said the proposal offered a way to exercise control over cable companies without becoming involved in defining reasonable pricing. The hope was that cable companies would behave as if they faced competition to avoid the prospect of having local officials decide issues of rates of return.[1]

In March 1991, more than 600 mayors and local officials asked Congress for legislation to increase competitiveness among operators of local cable television franchises. They observed that the cable television industry now served nearly 60 percent of the 93 million households with television sets. They also noted that the 1984 Cable Communications Policy Act had taken away their authority to ensure reasonable costs to consumers. Local officials wanted a totally competitive renewal process that allowed municipalities to grant franchises to whomever they wished. They also wanted to restrict cable operators' ability to sue municipalities.[2]

In June 1991, the FCC adopted rules to give local governments more power to roll back prices for basic service. However, the new rules were substantially weaker than those proposed the previous December. Under the new rules, cable companies would have an easier time showing they faced effective competition. The FCC also dropped the stipulation about six competing broadcast signals.

Consumer groups charged the new rules were virtually useless. Even though stricter measures were pending in the Senate and House, their fate was uncertain. Critics noted that a measure passed the previous year in the House had quickly died in the Senate.[3]

In February 1992, the Senate defied the Bush Administration and powerful cable television lobbyists by voting to impose local and federal regulation on cable rates. Hoping to create more competition, they also ordered cable companies to pay for broadcasters' programming. The FCC would have to establish national guidelines for basic cable television rates and customer service standards. The FCC could either regulate rates itself or allow local authorities to do so using national guidelines.

The *Economist,* a British newsmagazine, reported that the U.S. Congress was trying to bash one of its pet hates—the cable-television business. In doing so, Congress was hindering the natural emergence of competition among broadcast, cable, telephone, and newspapers. The magazine reminded readers that technology was changing faster than government's ability to regulate. It noted that multichannel television was now coming from satellites and microwave television. Soon cable-television providers would be battling for positions with telecommunications companies on the electronic superhighway. The highway would be crowded with traffic consisting of telecommunications, databases, tailor-made television programming, and advertisements. The *Economist* declared the "impending congressional action is only too likely to rein back cable's undoubtedly large investment in providing what people increasingly want." The best policy was to encourage more investment from cable and telecom in a communications policy that "maximizes revenues for the government and lays out an open field for competition."[4]

By mid-1992, legislation was still pending in Congress but industry competition had forged ahead of the debate. Cable television providers were in pitched battle with local telephone companies. Telephone companies vigorously lobbied Congress for the freedom to offer television programs and electronic information services over their networks. Regional Bell companies argued they should be free of restrictions imposed by the AT&T breakup. At that time, Congress had barred them from the cable industry to compensate for phone companies' near monopoly over local telephone service. The phone companies said they could envision a future in which all telephone lines were optical fibers with virtually unlimited capacity to carry information on beams of light.

At the same time, cable operators began to obtain federal licenses to build experimental wireless telephone networks, using existing cable networks to link cellular telephones through a city's tiny radio relay stations. Cable industry executives stressed their net-

---

[1] E. L. Andrews, "Rules May Tighten on Cable TV Rates," *New York Times,* December 14, 1990, p. A1.

[2] M. Tolchin, "Mayors Press Congress for Control over Cable," *New York Times,* March 6, 1991, p. D2.

[3] E. L. Andrews, "F.C.C. Is Increasing Local Regulation of Cable TV Rates," *New York Times,* June 14, 1991, p. A1.

[4] "Reregulation Frenzy," *Economist,* February 15, 1992, p. 25.

works were ideal for providing the foundation for a new generation of low-cost, wireless personal communication services. Cable companies were already upgrading their coaxial cables with high-capacity optical fibers.[5]

In September 1992, the Senate passed a controversial compromise bill to reregulate the cable industry. Although cable operators lobbied furiously against the bill and President Bush threatened to veto it, a majority of the Senate's Republicans supported the measure. A few days later, President Bush vetoed the bill as promised, saying it benefited special interests and would discourage investment in telecommunications.[6] A successful congressional override set the stage for FCC intervention.

Immediately after the bill was passed, cable companies raised prices sharply. In April 1993, the FCC ordered a billion-dollar rollback in cable rates. Its action explicitly wiped out postpassage price increases of about $400 million and set a formula for establishing new ceilings in basic rates. Industry analysts figured that about two-thirds of the nation's cable systems would have to reduce their prices by 10 percent. The FCC also stopped cable operators' practice of bundling together charges for remote controls, cable boxes, and installation fees and ruled they had to devote one-third of their channel capacity to local broadcast stations.

While these provisions were implemented, Congress continued to debate the issue of telephone and cable competition and proposed a major overhaul of cable laws. Billions of dollars in business hung on the bill's details. It would have allowed regional Bells like Nynex to enter the cable television and long-distance telephone markets. In turn Nynex and the other Baby Bells would face their first serious competition for local service. In September 1994, the Senate made an unexpected shift and abandoned the effort.

Senator Ernest F. Hollings, who pronounced the bill dead, blamed its demise on opposition from some of the regional Bells, noting this was the closest Congress had ever come to passing a comprehensive overhaul of the nation's 60-year old communications law. Experts could not agree what impact the bill would have had on consumers and the industry. Phone companies already had begun to experiment with videoservices, and cable companies were entering telephone services.[7]

During 1995 cable rates began to rise again; the FCC reversed an earlier decision to limit rate hikes. In April 1996, the FCC agreed to deregulate rates within three years for most of the nation's 62 million cable-TV subscribers. Rate restrictions were lifted immediately for cable systems with fewer than 50,000 subscribers and for those competing with video providers such as local phone companies.[8] It became clear that a communications overhaul would not be a congressional priority for the foreseeable future. The industry had become so competitive and intertwined that few legislators wanted to spend their time trying to develop policy on such a complex and contentious matter.

---

[5] E. L. Andrews, "Cable TV Battling Phone Companies," *New York Times,* March 29, 1992, p. A1.

[6] E. L. Andrews, "Bush Rejects Bill That Would Limit Rates on Cable TV," *New York Times,* October 4, 1992, p. 1.

[7] E. L. Andrews, "Bill to Revamp Communications Dies in Congress," *New York Times,* September 24, 1994, p. 1.

[8] "Feds Lifting Cable-TV Rate Regulations," *USA Today,* April 10, 1996, p. A1.

Questions

1. What are the issues of competition in the cable industry?
2. How should consumers be protected? Should competition be allowed to set the price for services such as cable television or should Congress do it?
3. What is your view on the role of the Federal Communication Commission (FCC)? What role should the FCC play in regulating communications?

Regulation in the 1960s

In the decade after World War II, people had the leisure and the affluence to think about what an ideal society should be. Women entered the workforce in greater numbers, the civil rights movement shifted into high gear, and Lyndon Johnson's vision of a Great Society galvanized Congress into a frenzy of creating social programs and regulatory controls. The spate of regulation that gushed forth in the 1960s and 1970s touched nearly every aspect of American corporate and personal life.

Consumer advocate Michael Pertschuck notes that until the 1960s and early 1970s, consumer advocates could point to few successes against the "determined opposition of business." He observes that "for consumer entrepreneurial politics to succeed in the 1960s, consumer goals had to harmonize with public attitudes and the political environment."[9] He attributes stakeholders' new interest in social regulation to the liberal political agenda of the Kennedy and Johnson administrations. It is equally plausible that stakeholder interest promoted the agenda rather than the other way around.

Richard Harris and Sidney Milkis assert that social regulation was a direct result of "new conceptions about the relations among business, government, and society."[10] They point to two competing theories: First, Theodore Lowi, in *The End of Liberalism,* suggests that the social regulation of the 1970s represented a more mature phase of New Deal ideology. Second, Irving Kristol, a neoconservative spokesperson, promotes a contradictory idea. Kristol sees the push for social legislation as a betrayal of the New Deal by the New Left. The New Left, Kristol says, was hostile to and suspicious of market forces inherent in the New Deal.

Harris and Milkis contend that neither perspective is entirely accurate. The ideas of the New Deal and the New Left came together in a tense and uneasy union: "The difficulty in devising adequate responses derives from the idea of participatory democracy as being rooted in the ideals and suspicions of the New Left and as being practiced in an institutional environment established in the New Deal."[11]

Regardless of ideology and the roots of the new forces, nothing less than a social revolution swept the country. People took sides in the antiwar movement, the women's movement, civil rights activities, environmental activism, and product safety initiatives. Public demonstrations supporting all sides of nearly every issue were commonplace. Nearly every cause, from toxic-waste dumping to abortion rights, had multiple, highly vocal proponents and detractors. People joined shifting and sometimes conflicting coalitions.

---

[9] M. Pertschuck, *Revolt against Regulation: The Rise and Pause of the Consumer Movement* (Berkeley: University of California Press, 1989), pp. 12–13.

[10] R. A. Harris and S. M. Milkis, *The Politics of Regulatory Change* (New York: Oxford University Press, 1989), pp. 53–96.

[11] Ibid., pp. 53–96.

Companies found themselves in the middle of these controversies, taken to task by some for what they did do and by others for what they neglected to do. Newly implemented rules and regulations restrained their decision making and strategic options.

Susan and Martin Tolchin point out that many companies supported regulatory efforts at the same time they complained bitterly about them. Companies looked to Congress to protect them from the vagaries of the marketplace.[12] Not surprisingly, both firms and individuals were inconsistent in their demands. Products and services had proliferated dramatically in the post-World War II period. Stakeholders in every quadrant of the stakeholder influence map wanted protection from discriminatory practices and unsafe products as well as the freedom to grow and innovate (see Exhibit 9–1). These goals were sometimes in conflict.

Congress passed regulations that covered consumer products, employment discrimination, product safety, consumer finance, workplace safety, and the environment.[13] The passage of one regulation led to the need for others. Douglas Needham points out that stakeholders often make multiple, interdependent demands for corporate regulation. When regulation changes one aspect of a firm's behavior, all parts of the firm are affected. Stakeholders

---

EXHIBIT 9–1 Stockholder influence map, 1960s and 1970s

	Direct	Indirect
External	Customers Government Suppliers	Social activists Lobbies Religious institutions Environmentalists Community groups Regulators Local politicians
Internal	Employees Management	Unions Shareholders

---

[12] S. J. Tolchin and M. Tolchin, *Dismantling America: The Rush to Deregulate* (Boston: Houghton Mifflin, 1983), pp. 11–12.

[13] M. L. Weidenbaum, *Business, Government, and the Public* (Englewood, Cliffs, NJ: Prentice Hall, 1977), p. 5.

call for additional regulation to cover the new behavior and unregulated activities.[14]

From Regulation to Deregulation, 1960–1978

The surge of regulation during the Kennedy, Johnson, Nixon, and Ford administrations created vast networks of regulatory agencies and large government bureaucracies. By the late 1970s, all businesses faced new demands and constraints in a growing regulatory environment. On local, state, and federal levels, legislators responded to constituents' pressure to make working conditions free of hazards, the environment cleaner, and products safer. Murray Weidenbaum asserts there was also a widespread belief that unless the government regulated corporate activities, businesses would not voluntarily respond to public demands.[15] Some Americans, however, were increasingly skeptical about the willingness of business to implement the policies needed to achieve their vision of a proper society.

The costs associated with burgeoning regulations and enforcement agencies were substantial. According to Weidenbaum, the operating expenses of the major regulatory agencies totaled $1.9 billion in 1974 and rose 48 percent over the next two years. Regulatory agencies hired inspectors, reviewers, and rule makers to monitor and enforce rules. (See the appendix to this chapter for a list of regulatory agencies.)

The public paid directly or indirectly every time a new rule went into effect. For example, if the Equal Employment Opportunity Commission reviewed and assessed a company's affirmative action plan, the salaries of compliance officers were added to the government's payroll and the taxpayer eventually picked up the bill. When an electric appliance company added safety features to a toaster oven, the consumer paid for them directly in the purchase price. For the time being, stakeholders found the costs acceptable and paid them without much complaint.

Public enthusiasm for ever-increasing regulation was tied to the health of the economy. The liberal agendas of the Kennedy and Johnson administrations coincided with substantial economic growth. As a result, says Pertschuck, "the prevailing public mood in the mid-1960s remained buoyant, confident, generous."[16]

By the mid-1970s, the public mood, corporate interests, and the national political perspective had changed. People began to perceive some of the rules

---
[14] D. Needham, *The Economics of Regulation: A Behavioral Approach* (Boston: Little Brown, 1983), pp. 258–63.
[15] Widenbaum, *Business, Government, and the Public,* p. 16.
[16] Pertschuck, *Revolt against Regulation,* p. 13.

and constraints under which companies operated as frivolous and arbitrary. The national mood switched just as agencies were about to implement the far-reaching industrywide regulations they had developed and written over the previous decade. Businesses and professions, both large and small, faced additional government interference with their strategic decision-making powers and were forced to bear much of the cost.

Important and powerful special-interest groups gathered to oppose more social and economic legislation. Trade associations and other lobbyists called for a new assessment of the regulatory process. The so-called liberal lobbies that had pushed social legislation found their popular support waning.

Business and government not only opposed greater regulation but also sought deregulation. However, there was little agreement on what deregulation actually meant. Cornish Hitchcock, legal director for the Aviation Consumer Action Project in the late 1980s, writes,

> The word *deregulation* has been used in so many contexts to mean so many different things that the currency of the term has been devalued. I think the result has been confusing to the public, and deregulating the airlines is certainly different from deregulating the FTC or deregulating financial institutions, yet the debate on these and many other topics has come down to a question of whether you are for or against deregulation generically. That oversimplification has tended to cloud discussion of specific topics because there may be valid reasons for some types of deregulation, but not others.[17]

The Carter Administration

The Carter administration, eager to cut costs and bureaucracy, began the economic deregulatory process in 1978. At first, social legislation was left virtually untouched. President Jimmy Carter emphasized the need for greater market competition. He issued executive orders that systematically reduced the quantity of paperwork businesses were required to submit to the government. Next, he instituted a group called the Regulatory Council to oversee and monitor executive agencies' structure and activities. Carter also organized the Regulatory Analysis Review Group (RARG). Charles L. Schultze, chairperson of the President's Council of Economic Advisers, headed this top-level committee. RARG reviewed and conducted cost-benefit analyses on regulations that cost more than $100 million a year.

Carter attempted to intervene in environmental issues such as cotton dust and strip-mining standards. However, stakeholders raised such a storm of protest that he immediately backed off and focused his attention on economic deregulation of the transportation and communications industries.

---

[17] Harris and Milkis, *The Politics of Regulatory Change*, p. 280.

The Airline Industry

Prior to deregulation, most air carriers charged passengers similar fares. Airlines differentiated themselves by promising friendly service and a variety of menu offerings. Determined to open the industry to competition, President Carter actively supported the passage of the Airline Deregulation Act of 1978. The act mandated the gradual dismantling of the Civil Aeronautics Board (CAB). The Federal Aviation Administration (FAA) that was responsible for airline safety remained intact.

Carter appointed economist Alfred E. Kahn to preside over the CAB's demise. Kahn concluded the government should remove itself from making technical decisions about air routes, pricing, and services. Those duties should be left to industry managers; as Kahn put it, "I have more faith in greed than in regulation."[18]

Deregulation led to the swift proliferation—and equally rapid bankruptcy—of commuter lines. In addition to financial instability, these lines also suffered major safety problems. Between 1975 and 1980, commuter lines had eight times as many accidents per 100,000 flights as did the major carriers. Poor plane maintenance, fewer experienced pilots, and less safety equipment all contributed to the problem.

By December 1981, the CAB had given up much of its authority over domestic routes. Two years later, it relinquished control over domestic fares, domestic mergers, and interlocking relationships among airlines. Finally, on January 1, 1985, the CAB ceased operations.

The Trucking Industry

The Carter administration also supported the passage of the Motor Carrier Act of 1980. Before the act went into effect, truckers had to apply to the Interstate Commerce Commission (ICC) for operating rights. An operating right gave a trucker exclusive permission to follow a certain route carrying certain commodities. Beginning in the 1960s, the ICC began to limit operating rights. Truckers immediately created a market in operating rights, buying and selling them to one another. Like any limited commodity, rights soared in price. The rights were carried as intangible assets on truckers' balance sheets and had actual monetary value. On average, they totaled 15 percent of trucker equities.

After July 1980, the ICC began granting operating rights to nearly anyone who applied. In the first year after deregulation, the ICC processed 28,700 applications for new or expanded operations. Companies that had held operating rights before deregulation suffered major financial losses.

---

[18] E. Holdendolph, "The U.S. Drive for Deregulation," *New York Times,* October 7, 1980, pp. D1, D19.

What was the consequence of having such valuable assets become virtually worthless overnight? Major truckers simply wrote the amounts off on their balance sheets. Roadway Express, one of the nation's largest truckers, wrote off all of its $26.8 million in operating rights in its third quarter of 1980. This action, which represented a significant loss for Roadway, was catastrophic for smaller competitors. Some truckers' entire equity was literally wiped out overnight. As deregulation continued, the role of the ICC diminished.

The Communications Industry

Television. In 1978, the Federal Communications Commission (FCC) created a special staff to investigate television networks. The staff's report strongly supported deregulation. It concluded that beginning in 1952, the FCC had protected NBC, CBS, and ABC from potential competitors. The advent of cable television in the 1960s brought consumers new and original programming, but the three established major networks persuaded the FCC that cable threatened free networks. The FCC promptly imposed severe limits on the cable industry, an action that inhibited its growth for a decade.

In 1972 when the FCC began to remove some of cable's programming restrictions, the industry flourished. In 1978 the FCC's deregulatory efforts increased competition. The commission eliminated restrictions on the programs pay television was permitted to carry. It allowed cable television systems to use a wider variety of stations on channels and removed the barriers to direct satellite broadcasting. Finally, the FCC licensed hundreds of new, low-power broadcast television stations. Charles Ferris, chairperson of the FCC in 1980, declared, "The FCC is allowing new technologies and new entrepreneurs to achieve the potential that burdensome regulation denied them in a previous era."[19]

Radio. Before long, the FCC deregulated radio's nearly 9,000 stations. Stations were no longer required to poll listeners to ask what they wanted to hear, offer news or other forms of nonentertainment, or place time limits on advertising. We discuss the telecommunications industry and the impact of the Internet later in the chapter.

The Reagan Administration, 1980–1988

President Ronald Reagan's election in 1979 reflected a new conservative mood sweeping the nation. The initiatives of the Carter years were a mere trickle presaging a flood of economic and social deregulatory activity. The

---

[19] T. Schwartz, "F.C.C. Battleground: Deregulation of TV," *New York Times,* October 22, 1980, p. D1.

Tolchins assert the Reagan administration was dedicated ideologically to nothing less than what they called the dismantling of America. They note that Reagan vowed to get the government off people's backs during his campaign. In their view, "the new President initiated a crusade against government regulation and quickly laid the groundwork for the direction of regulation in the 1980s."[20]

Social and economic regulation were clearly on the wane. Barbara S. Thomas, a commissioner of the Securities and Exchange Commission, articulated the new ideology very clearly:

> We need to reform the regulatory system and lessen our reliance on regulations as a means of controlling business. In the past we thought a vastly better society could be achieved if only we could specify . . . the procedures that business had to follow. . . . In recent years, however, we have become acutely aware of the limitation of such regulatory techniques. We now understand that they have negative consequences, subtle in their operation, but devastating in their overall impact. They can stifle creativity, erode an individual's sense of responsibility, and impose societal costs that may far exceed the benefits provided.[21]

Presidents Carter and Reagan had fundamentally different ideological goals for the deregulatory process. Both presidents wanted to encourage investment, reduce inflation, and foster productivity. However, Carter's approach was far narrower in scope. He limited economic deregulation to a few industries such as airlines, trucking, communications, and financial institutions.

Using an economic rationale, the Reagan initiatives cut into social areas such as health, safety, and the environment. Reagan chose new appointees with similar ideologies and philosophies to carry out his programs. He and his appointees ignored the outcry that stymied Carter's tentative forays into social regulation reform. In indicating the differences between the two presidencies, James C. Miller, head of the Office of Management and Budget under Reagan, said Reagan was tough but "Carter folded on his first big issue, cotton dust."

Toughness, however, was not as important as planning. Miller noted the new administration did all its homework during the transition period. As soon as Reagan took office, he put the full force of his administration behind deregulation, which, with political astuteness, he called regulatory relief.[22] Exhibit 9–2 lists the major principles behind the administration's deregulation approach.

Gary Bryner points out that ideological compatibility was President Reagan's major criterion for appointing senior administrative officials.[23]

---

[20] Tolchin and Tolchin, pp. 20–22.
[21] B. S. Thomas, "Overregulating the Regulators," *New York Times,* May 1, 1981, p. B10.
[22] Tolchin and Tolchin, pp. 56–58.
[23] G.C. Bryner, *Bureaucratic Discretion: Law and Policy in Federal Regulatory Agencies* (New York: Pergamon Press, 1987), p. 66.

Exhibit 9–2 Reagan Administration Principles

- Impose regulations only if benefits exceed costs.
- Choose least expensive methods to achieve regulatory goals.
- Rely on economic incentives and penalties to encourage companies to meet standards. Eliminate rigid compliance.
- Tailor regulatory burdens to size and nature of affected companies.
- Reduce unnecessary paperwork and regulatory delays.
- Shift regulatory control from the federal government to the states.
- Support legislation requiring Congress periodically to assess the current relevance of regulation.

Source: "Deregulation: A Fast Start for the Reagan Strategy," *Business Week,* March 9, 1981, p. 63.

Reagan insisted his appointees demonstrate absolute loyalty in their pursuit of his objectives. Many business leaders applauded Reagan's initiatives and the single voice with which his administration now spoke. These leaders asserted they could safely put resources into productivity instead of facing endless paperwork.

The administration sent regulatory agencies new guidelines requiring them to conduct cost-benefit analyses of all their objectives. In June 1981, the President's Task Force on Regulation Relief praised the government's rapid movement toward deregulation. The task force predicted businesses would save more than $18 billion by not having to comply with regulations from which the administration had withdrawn support. In fact, the administration wrote very little new deregulatory legislation. Instead, it cut the budgets of existing regulatory agencies, reorganized agency leadership, and issued directives to limit enforcement.

In some cases, the consequences were fairly trivial. The Department of Education eliminated regulations that caused schools to lose federal funding if their dress codes distinguished between boys and girls. The Postal Service had to show the benefits of the nine-digit ZIP code outweighed the costs before it could implement the code. The Department of Energy eliminated paperwork demands on the private sector by 820,000 hours.[24]

Other consequences were more profound. During the first nine months of the Reagan administration, the National Highway Traffic Safety Administration opened only four investigations into automobile defects; the Carter administration had begun 15 investigations each year. The number of monthly investigations conducted by the Occupational Safety and Health Administration plummeted 17 percent between February and August 1981. Average monthly follow-up inspections dropped 68 percent.

---

[24] C. H. Farnsworth, "Reagan Group Predicts Curbs on Regulatory Agencies Will Save Billions," *New York Times,* June 14, 1981, p. 20.

Some of the most dramatic effects occurred at the Environmental Protection Agency (EPA). The agency abolished its Office of Enforcement, split its functions into several offices, and cut the number of enforcement lawyers from 400 to 40. At the regional level, lawyers were instructed to check with Washington before beginning any new initiatives. Under President Carter, the EPA had referred an average of 200 cases per year to the Justice Department. In 1981 it referred only 30. EPA administrator Anne Gorsuch asked the Justice Department to return more than 40 pending cases to the EPA, declaring they lacked sufficient evidence to go forward.[25]

The consumer protection policy of the Federal Trade Commission (FTC) was reduced to ashes according to Barry Boyer. Boyer asserted that the White House's insistence on cost effectiveness and data collection undermined any meaningful, rational analysis of its policies. He noted that FTC staff members quickly assumed the process of regulatory analysis was really a political filter. Commissioners "seemed primarily concerned with the practicalities of enforcing any rules they might adopt and finding ways to replace detailed . . . regulations with self-enforcing, market incentives."[26]

By the mid-1980s, many questioned whether deregulation was working as it should. There was no doubt prices had fallen for a variety of goods and services, but some wondered whether the rash of mergers and acquisitions had fostered such a high degree of concentration that new entrants would be unable to compete with established giants. Instead of enhanced competition and productivity, new oligopolies emerged. Even Alfred E. Kahn, former chair of the now defunct Civil Aeronautics Board, expressed reservations about the anticompetitive side effects of deregulation. Small companies often became clients and even captives of the large players in their industries.

Although the promoters of deregulation recognized their policies might have anticompetitive side effects, they maintained the benefits outweighed the liabilities. Critics charged that regulatory agencies had mishandled the transition and that if no remedial steps were taken, the pendulum could swing too far toward deregulation.

Benefits were spread unevenly across the nation. Sparsely populated and rural areas found services disappearing and prices skyrocketing. Deregulation wiped out the hidden subsidies on which rural areas had depended. For example, before the telecommunications industry was deregulated, the FCC required phone companies to charge urban and rural customers the same prices for service. This new policy meant relatively fewer customers covered the phone companies' fixed costs in rural areas. After deregulation, phone companies could pass on more of the actual cost to rural customers. One

---

[25] C. Mayer, "Reagan Gets Tough with Regulation," *Boston Globe,* November 29, 1981, p. 67.

[26] B. Boyer, "The Federal Trade Commission and Consumer Protection Policy: A Postmortem Examination," in *Making Regulatory Policy,* ed. K. Hawkins and J. M. Thomas (Pittsburgh: University of Pittsburgh Press, 1989), pp. 93–132.

customer in Nebraska saw her phone bill go up 300 percent between 1984 and 1987, from $7 to $27 per month. Although the dollar amount was fairly trivial in this case, the trend was chilling.

Transportation deregulation hit rural areas particularly hard. Many small towns that had already lost bus routes found that they were paying higher fares for airline service or that the airlines, too, had simply abandoned the routes.

After deregulation, residents of South Dakota's panhandle had to pay twice as much to fly to Denver as they had paid before. Four local airlines came and went between 1984 and 1987. Only the federal government's Essential Air Service program that subsidized commuter lines serving otherwise unprofitable rural areas guaranteed any service at all, and even that safety net was snatched away in 1988.[27]

By the end of 1986, five major industries had felt the full force of deregulation: the airlines, the trucking industry, the railroads, the telephone industry, and the bus industry.

Airlines

By 1986, six air carriers controlled 84 percent of the market, compared to 78 percent in 1978. Hub-and-spoke configurations replaced direct flights. This system allowed the airlines to dominate traffic patterns and, indirectly, to control prices in those concentrated markets. We discuss the airline industry more fully later in the chapter.

Telephone Industry

In January 1982, the Justice Department ordered the breakup of AT&T and imposed a 1984 deadline for implementation. At the time of the initial judgment, AT&T controlled $137 billion in assets, more than those of Exxon, General Motors, and U.S. Steel combined and more than the GNP of all but 20 nations. AT&T owned 24,000 buildings, 177,000 motor vehicles, 142 million telephones, and 1.7 billion miles of cable, microwave, radio, and satellite circuits.

Under the terms of the breakup, AT&T agreed to divest itself of its 22 local telephone companies. In exchange, the company would be allowed to enter the then unregulated computer and information-processing businesses. The surviving company would continue to provide most of the country's long-distance service to other nations, continue to sell and lease communications equipment manufactured by its giant Western Electric subsidiary, and retain Bell Labs, one of the world's best R&D facilities. In addition, AT&T

---

[27] B. Richards, "Deregulation Raises Prices, Cuts Services in Many Rural Areas," *The Wall Street Journal,* October 5, 1987, p. 1.

could use its newly streamlined but still integrated structure to offer computer products and services as well as new methods of voice data storage and transmission.

In 1985 and 1986, American households received ballots allowing them to choose their long-distance carriers. AT&T, MCI Communications, and GTE Sprint were the major contenders. However, AT&T's dismantling did not mean competitors flourished. By 1987, MCI and Sprint had incurred huge losses. The Justice Department added to their woes by urging the courts to allow so-called Baby Bells (former local Bell companies) to get into the game. Although the courts refused to go along with the Justice Department, the industry remained intensely competitive and increasingly complex.

The real import of the breakup was that companies and individuals could now purchase their own equipment. By 1986, large numbers of competitors were fighting for the corporate market. Even Japanese companies such as Toshiba vied for market share. In long-distance service alone, 300 companies offered lower rates than AT&T. On the local level, three dozen vendors sold hundreds of complex systems. New companies sprang up to offer confused business people telephone consulting services. One consultant assured potential clients that "there are no bargains in parachutes, brain surgery, or telephones."[28]

The Reagan-Bush Transition: The Case of the Banking Industry

The Reagan administration allowed eight years of unfettered competition to rule in the banking industry. Ralph Nader's public citizen group issued a scathing report on the effects of bank deregulation. Soon charges of criminal mismanagement rocked the industry. For many people, the savings and loan (S&L) failures epitomized the problems deregulation had brought to banking.

In 1988, the General Accounting Office (GAO) recommended more effective regulation. The GAO observed that bank deregulation had resulted in "a risky hodgepodge of banking and other functions that could imperil the safety and soundness of the banking system."[29] In fact, the GAO concluded, nearly one-third of U.S. savings and loan institutions had become insolvent due to poorly implemented deregulation.

The banking industry was in a state of flux between 1988 and 1991. The *Economist* attributed "today's [January 1991] shaky financial structure" to 60 years of haphazard legislation. Diversification was a major issue with which the banking industry had struggled for decades. Nearly everyone involved in banking agreed many banks had gotten into trouble through their

---

[28] R. L. Simison, "Wrestling with Choice," *The Wall Street Journal,* February 24, 1986, pp. 1D, 4D.

[29] R. L. Berke, "Deregulation Has Gone Too Far, Many Telling New Administration," *New York Times,* December 11, 1988, p. 1A.

own mismanagement. However, banks were constrained by regulations that prohibited diversification into new businesses such as insurance and underwriting. In addition, they could not enter markets outside their home states. To remain competitive, commercial banks engaged in high-risk loans to borrowers who defaulted. The credit crunch pushed the economy deeper into the recession.[30] Bankers, lawyers, Congress, and the Bush administration all agreed bold new reforms were overdue. However, there was little agreement on the exact details of that reform.

New Banking Regulation

It took three years for the Bush administration to propose its banking plan. In February 1991, the administration recommended a sweeping overhaul of the banking system. Treasury Secretary Nicholas F. Brady declared the legislation had two main goals: to strengthen the banking system and to make banks more competitive internationally. The bill contained five major provisions:

1. **Bank ownership.** Industrial companies would be allowed to own banks, but insured deposits would be held in a separate affiliate to reduce opportunities for speculation. These banks would be able to have affiliates that sold mutual funds and insurance and underwrote corporate securities. The administration held that banks would be able to attract more capital and diversify risk. Opponents said this provision might create another S&L debacle and would make banks more vulnerable to recession.

2. **Nationwide banking.** The bill would authorize full nationwide banking by 1994. National banks would be able to open branches in additional states more easily. The administration declared this move would result in huge financial savings, but critics maintained community-based banks would be at a competitive disadvantage.

3. **Banks and insurance.** States would decide whether to allow banks to sell insurance in the states in which they were chartered or operated. The administration said this provision would allow positive diversification. Critics noted the insurance industry was already weak and the states had been ineffective insurance regulators.

4. **Regulatory restrictions and consolidation.** S&L and bank regulation would be consolidated from four agencies into two. This consolidation would eliminate layers of regulators and conflicting directives. The Federal Reserve Board would regulate all state banking organizations. A new federal banking agency under the Treasury Department would regulate all national banking and thrift organizations. The sole function of the Federal Deposit Insurance Corporation (FDIC) would be as an insurer. While everyone agreed consolidation was a correct move, some critics wanted a single regulatory body instead of two.

---

[30] "A Brave New World for America's Banks," *Economist,* January 12, 1991, p. 69.

5. **Federal deposit insurance.** The coverage of this insurance would be scaled back by limiting the number of insured accounts an individual could hold in one bank. Bank failure standards would be changed to limit coverage in any one bank to two deposits of $100,000, one being a retirement account. Coverage would end for brokered deposits (certificates of deposit sold through brokerage houses to raise funds for banks). Institutional investors such as pension funds and securities firms that break down deposits into $100,000 increments to obtain insurance would no longer be covered. Critics pointed out most families would be able to circumvent the $100,000 limit simply by opening an account at another bank.[31]

The Bush administration plan provided the basis for media and interest group discussion about the American banking industry. In a special report on the future of banking, *Business Week* concluded the banking industry was dying and the administration's bill was far too limited in scope. Although the Brady legislation would make banking more competitive, even greater deregulation was needed. *Business Week* saw a future in which "most of today's banks will be just another set of participants in a financial services free-for-all where everyone will be able to invade rival turf."[32]

Few observers thought Congress would take the bank reform bill seriously. However, by July 1991, the House Banking Committee had passed much of the proposal. The major difference between the administration's bill and the Senate Banking Committee's draft was that in the Senate version, commercial companies would not be allowed to own banks.

The *Economist* applauded the Senate version, concurring in the decision not to let industrial companies own banks. It assessed America's record at regulating and supervising banks as lousy. In the case of thrifts, it declared, "The record is one not just of incompetence but also of political interference and outright corruption."[33]

The optimism of summer 1991 turned to gloom in autumn. Unhappy with the House and Senate banking committees' revisions, the administration and big banking stakeholders successfully pressured the House to reject the entire bill. Treasury Secretary Brady, representatives from American Express, J. P. Morgan, Citicorp, and the American Bankers Association combined forces to lobby for defeat of the altered bill. In November, the House overwhelmingly turned it down.[34]

---

[31] S. Labaton, "Administration Presents Its Plan for Broad Overhaul of Banking," *New York Times,* February 6, 1991, p. A1; K. H. Bacon, "Financial Overhaul: Big Banks Would Get Vastly Broader Powers under Treasury's Plan," *The Wall Street Journal,* February 6, 1991, p. A1.

[32] "The Future of Banking," *Business Week,* April 22, 1991, pp. 72–81.

[33] "A Needless Risk," *Economist,* July 6, 1991, p. 16.

[34] S. Labaton, "House Turns Down Banking Overhaul by 324–89 Vote," *New York Times,* November 5, 1991, p. A1.

By the end of that month, lawmakers passed a leaner and more limited banking law. Congress rejected most of the administration's proposals to expand bank functions. In fact, the new legislation approved a much tougher regulatory system. Under the new law, regulators would have to move more quickly to close banks before those banks became insolvent. After 1994, the FDIC would lose its authority to reimburse foreign deposits and uninsured deposits over $100,000 when large banks failed. However, the bill added $70 billion in borrowing authority to support deposit insurance.

Unwilling to make a commitment before the upcoming presidential election, Congress continued to debate the bill into the summer of 1992. National banking was the one aspect of the bill everyone agreed would come to fruition. President Clinton's appointment of Lloyd Bentsen as Secretary of the Treasury opened up new possibilities and the opportunity for innovative initiatives. However, no new bill would mitigate the devastating costs of the S&L fiasco.

The Clinton Years, 1992–1996

President Clinton's Executive Order 12866 "Regulatory Planning and Review" established principles guiding the development of regulations in federal agencies and the review of regulations in the White House. The executive order established 12 policies the president expected agencies to observe:

- Identification of problems to be addressed by regulation and their magnitude.
- Review of existing regulations for possible elimination or modification.
- Assessment of nonregulatory alternatives to solving problems.
- Use of risk assessment to establish regulatory priorities.
- Establishing steps to ensure that the benefits of regulation justify the costs and that regulations adopted a cost-effective approach.
- Use of the best available information when developing regulations.
- Use of performance objectives whenever possible.
- Wide consultation with state, local, and tribal governments.
- Avoidance of inconsistent, incompatible, or duplicative regulations.
- Tailoring of regulations to produce the least burden possible on society.
- Writing regulations that are simple and easy to understand.[35]

---

[35] "Federal Regulation Directory," *Congressional Quarterly,* 7th ed. (Washington, D.C.: Congressional Quarterly, 1994), p. 41.

The Republican victory in the 1994 congressional election wiped out Clinton's strategy. Although Clinton's policy relied on cost-benefit analyses (a calculation of social benefits against potential costs to business), the Republicans wanted to go well beyond the current policies. The Republican Congress created a brand new climate concerning regulatory discussion. *Business Week* noted that to the Republican Congress "regulations are like a red cape waved in front of a raging bull." Robert S. Walker (R-Pennsylvania) charged that nonsensical federal rules crippled the economy, killed jobs, and sapped innovation.[36]

Majority Leader Bob Dole called for cost-benefit analysis of all regulations and elimination of those that couldn't be justified. However, academics observed that it was hard to estimate costs and benefits. Even when attempts were made, affected industries invariably exaggerated regulatory hardships, frequently leading analysts to overestimate costs.

Even regulatory critics like Murray L. Weidenbaum suggested the adoption of flexibly written regulations so that businesses could find their own solutions to reducing costs. Experts worried that Congress would undertake reform of an enormously complex issue without understanding the ramifications. They suggested overreliance on cost-benefit analysis could make things worse instead of better for workers, business, and the environment.

In July 1995, Republican and Democratic-sponsored House and Senate bills were in trouble. Existing policy required all new rules costing more than $100 million a year be subject to cost-benefit analysis. The House bill set the threshold at $25 million, the Republican Senate bill at $50 million, and the Democratic Senate bill at $100 million. There were many additional differences among the three versions but, as usual, the checks and balances within Congress led to a legislative standoff. Senate Democrats refused to bring the matter to a vote. The legislation would have subjected hundreds of major regulations to elaborate studies of how effectively they controlled risks to public health, safety, and the environment and at what cost. It also would have given industry new legal grounds to challenge regulatory decisions. Business groups supported the legislation while environmentalists said it would roll back a generation of progress.[37]

Deregulation led to the demise of the Interstate Commerce Commission (ICC), the country's oldest regulatory body. Richard Nixon tried to eliminate the ICC in 1970 and Ronald Reagan tried to take away its budget more than a decade later. Finally, in December 1995, President Clinton signed the bill ending 108 years of operation. The last 190 employees were transferred to the Transportation Department. The ICC's purpose had been to break up huge concentrations of wealth in the hands of railroad magnates. The agency's

---

[36] J. Carey, "Are Regs Bleeding the Economy?" *Business Week,* July 17, 1995, p. 75.

[37] J. H. Cushman, "Democrats Block Vote on Anti-Regulation Measure," *New York Times,* July 21, 1995, p. A16.

original framers could not have imagined that it would have regulated the telephone industry until the creation of the Federal Communications Commission or that it would have gained control over every vehicle that crossed state lines. Representative John Kasich (R-Ohio) who led the effort to dismantle the ICC, called it the dinosaur that wouldn't die. He was wrong; on January 1, 1996, it finally expired.[38]

In March 1996, House Republicans withdrew their regulatory reform bill shortly before it was due to be brought up for debate. The move reflected a growing concern of moderate Republicans that there would be election year fallout from the campaign to dismantle regulation. Republican leaders asked the party's moderates and conservatives to work together on a less comprehensive version of the legislation. Clearly, in an election year, politics and pragmatism took precedence over ideology and zealotry.

Regulatory Issues in the Clinton Administration

Republican and Democratic legislators reached a stalemate on many issues; however, some specific regulatory issues generated heated discussion and action. The use and control of the Internet was widely discussed in the press and other media.

The Internet and Regulation. The Internet evolved from a Defense Department computer system built in the early 1970s. The idea was to enable academic and military researchers to continue to do government work even if parts of their computer network were destroyed in a nuclear attack. As time went on, AT&T Bell Laboratory researchers and graduate students at MIT and Berkeley collaborated with Apple Computer and Sun Microsystems computer designers to elaborate on the original system. By 1995, nearly 25 million computer users connected with the Internet and that number was projected to double each year for the foreseeable future.

The Internet is a system in which personal computers connect through a gateway computer belonging to a commercial bureau (America Online, Prodigy, or CompuServe), a large company, a government organization, or a university. The computers communicate with one another so that people can exchange information in the form of messages, text, pictures, sound, and movies. People can easily post news and information on electronic bulletin boards called Usenet groups. Allison and Baxter note that "the information provided on the Internet, particularly through the WWW (worldwide web) ranges across train timetables, university lecture notes, books, art exhibits, film promotions, the wisdom and ravings of individuals and, yes,

---

[38] D. E. Sanger, "A U.S. Agency Once Powerful Is Dead at 108." *New York Times,* January 1, 1996, p. 1.

pornographic pictures. . . . It is as easy to read *Playboy* as the *Magna Carta* in the privacy of your own home or office."[39]

Diamond and Bates noted the conflict over the conduct and culture of computer communications revolved about some fundamental questions:

- *How far does the Constitution go in protecting repugnant or defamatory speech on the Net?* They noted that while some Net boosters say the medium provides for the freest speech in the world, de facto monitors have appeared. Some of the commercial online services scan for dirty words in messages sent to public chat areas. The moderators of some mailing lists and Usenet groups exclude material they deem inappropriate. While this sort of interference does not seem to create a First Amendment challenge, it may be a different story if public officials try to restrict information in public schools, state universities, or government offices. Questions arise whether hate speech is protected under the Constitution. As law evolves, will the courts extend the public forum doctrine that guarantees the right to speak in public parks, streets, and sometimes shopping malls to privately owned computer bulletin boards? Will a victim of a defamatory statement be able to sue for libel a system operator (sysop) who allows a user to post the statement? Most observers agree the process of creating the boundaries of free speech online will take years as judges, network operators, and lawyers decide issues case by case.

- *Laws and mores differ worldwide. Whose rules and laws apply in cyberspace?* How are cross-cultural flows of information regarded from country to country? The Net spans the globe. Although individuals and groups can subvert government attempts to restrict information flow, some nations are trying to erect firewalls against the free flow of information. Countries as diverse as Germany, Iran, China, and Singapore see the Internet as a threat to national security, cultural decency, or religious purity.

Some Asian countries have taken strong measures to control cyberspace. Most are as concerned about political issues as about pornography. In March 1996, Association of Southeast Asian Nations (ASEAN) information ministers meeting in Singapore discussed their concerns about the spread of political criticism. Singapore, an enthusiastic user of the Net for public relations and tourism, announced it would hold both content providers and access providers responsible for banning pornographic and hate literature. Political and religious groups posting material would have to be officially registered.

---

[39] Internet: L. Allison and R. Baxter, "Protecting Our Innocents," Technical Report 95/224, Monash University, June 2, 1995 [http://www.u.au/~lloyd/internet innocent/1995/zz4.html].

Internet users quickly found they were unable to get access to *Playboy* and *Penthouse* home pages. The Socratic Circle, an informal discussion group that had held a brief political discussion the previous year, also disappeared. Instead of the Circle's home page, users received a message that technical difficulties prevented access.

Unlike the United States where First Amendment rights protect private communication, Singapore's laws allow censorship of print media. George Yeo, minister of information, announced that laws applied as much to cyberspace as to traditional print and broadcast media. The Singapore government planned to enforce its cyberspace laws by controlling content providers who would be automatically licensed and would only hear from the Singapore Broadcasting Authority if they broke the law. The exception to this rule included political or religious groups that would be required to register their online presence up front. Schools, public libraries, and cafes would be required to install filtering software such as the Canadian-developed Net Nanny.[40]

Chinese authorities also tightened control over information networks. Prime Minister Li Peng issued a decree on February 1, 1996, stipulating that:

- All computer information networks making international connections must use a channel designated by the Ministry of Post and Telecommunications. All networks would be supervised by one of the four branches of the Ministry of Post and Telecommunications (general), the Ministry of Electronics (computer companies), the State Education Commission (universities), and the Academy of Sciences (scientific research).
- An organization applying for an Internet node must have (1) legal status; (2) appropriate equipment and technical personnel; (3) perfect safety and security measures; (4) other conditions conforming to relevant laws, rules, and regulations.
- No organization or individual could engage in activities at the expense of state security. Producing, retrieving, duplicating, or spreading information that might hinder public order were forbidden. Obscene and pornographic materials were banned.[41]

China, like Singapore, tried to control the Internet rather than choke it off. At every point in which a country tried to eliminate the dissemination of material, hackers were determined to overcome barriers to information. In developing countries, limited access to computers made censorship relatively

---

[40] D. McDermott, "Singapore Restricts Access to Internet to Curb Pornography, Unwanted Ideas," *The Asian Wall Street Journal,* March 6, 1996, p. 18.

[41] S. Faison, "Chinese Tiptoe into Internet, Wary of Watchdogs," *New York Times,* February 5, 1996, p. A3.

easy. Experts agreed that as access increased, control would become more difficult.

- *How can children be protected from the Internet's sexually-explicit material?* As traffic on the Internet increased in the mid-1990s, conflicting groups of stakeholders pressured the government to set guidelines for children's use and access. Instead of less regulation, large groups of stakeholders wanted to increase control over this relatively new medium. Parents, teachers, psychologists, civil libertarians, religious groups, and a wide variety of special interest groups began to debate the scope of the First Amendment protecting free speech. Children's access to indecent material was the focus of much of the attention. Those in favor of censorship pointed out that children could gain access to smut and pornography as easily as adults. A Carnegie Mellon study found 68 commercial adult computer bulletin boards located in 32 states with 450,620 pornographic images, animations, and text files that had been downloaded by consumers over 6 million times.[42]

As part of a larger telecommunications bill, President Clinton signed the Communications Decency Act on February 8, 1996. Supporters of the bill argued that the government could and should regulate the flow of information on the Internet and other computer-based communications networks. Critics said the bill was overly broad and unconstitutional and that it eroded First Amendment protections for the press. They also said the law was unenforceable and that parents were best able to decide what their own children should see.

The new law made it a crime to transmit patently offensive material or to allow it to be transmitted over public computer networks where children might see it. The act authorized the government to restrict online speech and conduct with fines of $250,000 and jail sentences of two years for anyone who made such material available to children online.[43]

The American Civil Liberties Union, Microsoft, and other civil libertarian stakeholders immediately challenged the new law. They argued the Decency Act, proporting to protect children, criminalized everything from safe sex information to literary works such as *Catcher in the Rye.* Their viewpoint was illustrated when America Online tried special software that looked for specific words and blocked newsgroups that featured them. One of the taboo words, *breast,* blocked pornographic sites but also those belonging to breast cancer associations. The outcry from women's groups and the medical

---

[42] E. Diamond and S. Bates, "Law and Order Comes to Cyberspace," *Technology Today,* October 24, 1995, p. 24.

[43] P. H. Lewis, "Internet Courtroom Battle Gets Cyberspace Preview," *New York Times,* March 20, 1996, p. A14.

community was immediate.[44] Government officials decided not to implement the law until the courts had a chance to rule.

In June 1996, a three-judge panel in Philadelphia unanimously declared unconstitutional key parts of the Communications Decency Act. The judges called government attempts to regulate content on the Internet "a profoundly repugnant affront to the First Amendment's guarantee of free speech." The judges granted a temporary restraining order prohibiting the Justice Department from enforcing, or even investigating, violations of the act. Judge Stewart R. Dalzell of federal district court wrote: "Just as the strength of the Internet is chaos, so the strength of our liberty depends upon the chaos and cacophony of the unfettered speech the First Amendment protects."[45]

In New York, a special federal court panel struck down congressional restrictions on indecent material on the Internet as unconstitutionally overbroad because they banned protected indecent speech among adults. This ruling, coming only three weeks after the Philadelphia decision, also found the Communications Decency Act to be "an overly broad restraint on protected communication between and among adults." In addition, the court said the law would not be effective because it didn't apply to sexually explicit material originating outside the United States.[46] Observers on both sides agreed that it was unlikely the Supreme Court would rule against both federal court panels if the rulings were appealed. For the time being, at least, it appeared that the U.S. Internet industry would remain largely unregulated and would not join some European and Asian countries in determining what information and material its citizens could and should be able to receive.

The Banking Industry. The U.S. banking system, which defied rational structuring in the Bush years, continued to be the most complex financial regulatory system of any large industrial country. Five different agencies were responsible for overseeing various combinations of banks, savings and loans, and credit unions. The Clinton administration proposed combining the Federal Reserve (the Fed.), the Federal Deposit Insurance Corporation (FDIC), the Office of Thrift Supervision, and the Office of the Comptroller of the Currency into a giant federal banking commission. The National Credit Union Administration would remain as a separate entity. The Fed, reluctant to lose its regulatory powers over monetary policy made a counterproposal to combine the thrift supervision and comptroller's offices and to take over the FDIC's regulatory functions.[47] Discussions of reorganization continued without resolution.

---

[44] M. D. Lemonick, "The Net's Strange Day," *Time,* February 19, 1996, p. 55.

[45] P. H. Lewis, "Judges Turn Back Law to Regulate Internet Decency," *New York Times,* June 13, 1996, p. A1.

[46] F. A. McMorris and J. Sandberg, "Indecent-Material Curbs Are Struck Down Again," *The Wall Street Journal,* July 30, 1996, p. B6.

[47] K. Bradsher, "Deal Reported on Bank Regulation," *New York Times,* May 10, 1994, p. D2.

In the meantime, government regulators turned their attention to developing rules that would allow federally chartered banks to enter new lines of business. The proposals represented a new erosion of the Glass–Steagall Act that for 61 years had barred commercial banks from trading securities. The Glass–Steagall Act, which was passed in 1933 during the Great Depression, focused on limiting banks to more conservative practices that would be less likely to produce large losses and threaten depositors' savings.

The first major crack in support for the Glass–Steagall Act came in the late 1980s when holding companies of some big banks won permission from the Federal Reserve to set up separate subsidiaries for trading securities. The holding companies remained legally separate from the banks.[48]

In February 1995, Treasury Secretary Richard E. Rubin urged Congress to repeal the Glass–Steagall Act. Large banks with extensive retail networks supported the plan, saying competition would drive down fees for everything from checking accounts to stock trading. Opponents, such as small banks and insurance agents, claimed that giant companies were less likely to be sensitive to the needs of individuals and small businesses, making it harder for them to borrow.

A *Business Week* editorial asserted that "by eliminating the Glass–Steagall barrier, Washington actually will lessen taxpayer risk by allowing banks to expand further into a business they've shown a better penchant for managing: consumer finance. Bankers will be able to leverage their rich base of checking customers, home buyers, and credit-card holders to market insurance products, mutual funds, and other investments."[49]

Despite bipartisan enthusiasm for reform, intense lobbying by opponents and proponents led House leaders to drop the measure from the calendar. The prospects for reform in 1995 dimmed as House Republicans used the rider system that allows legislators to attach a bill to another unrelated bill. If legislators do not pass the primary bill, the rider also fails to pass. In this case, the Republican Congress abandoned a proposal for a $4.8 billion fee on three government-sponsored businesses that assisted the housing industry. The Glass–Steagall Bill repeal, which was the rider on the unrelated fee proposal, also was dropped. Newt Gingrich and other senior Republican representatives were beset by the pleas of insurance agents who feared the overhaul would put them out of business. While banks were divided on the reform measures, insurance agents cast Glass–Steagall as a life and death necessity for their industry. Under siege, newly elected House members relayed insurance agents' concerns to Speaker Gingrich who capitulated to the pressure. More than one-half million insurance agents threatened to withdraw

---

[48] K. Bradsher, "U.S. Seeks to Loosen Bank Rules," *New York Times,* November 29, 1994, p. D1.

[49] A. Barrett and D. Foust, "It's Time to Guillotine Glass–Steagall," *Business Week,* March 13, 1995, p. 33.

their political support from Republican representatives. As the *New York Times* noted, "It was too stark a show of political muscle for Mr. Gingrich to ignore."[50]

Although almost everyone agreed the Glass–Steagall Act was an anachronism in a global economy and a drag on the U.S. economy, they could not agree on how to dismantle it. In June 1996, the House Banking Committee finally abandoned its election-year effort to overhaul the financial services industry. Representative James A. Leach (R-Iowa) commented that "the committee has become entangled in partisan and interest-group wrangling." As we have seen many times before, concentrated and energetic stakeholder efforts can delay legislative reform and can impede the passage of regulatory or deregulatory measures that nearly everyone agrees are desirable. It would be up to the new Congress to take up banking reform after the 1996 elections.

The Airline Industry. Discussion of airline deregulation continued in the Clinton administration. By mid-1993, the U.S. airline industry had lost more than twice the accumulated profit it earned since it began commercial service in the 1920s. About 18 percent of the carrier industry was in Chapter 11 bankruptcy and aircraft makers continued to slash production. To be sure, the airline industry had gone through recessionary periods before the Airline Deregulation act of 1978, but companies the size of Pan American, Eastern, TWA, and Continental had never before gone into bankruptcy.[51]

Some suggested that airlines needed to be reregulated. They noted that deregulation was supposed to bring more consumer choice, more price competition, and lower fares. Although new airlines entered the market after 1978, the more established lines undercut the newcomers' cheap fares, set up the hub system to be more efficient, and used computer systems to complicate fare structures. Robert Kuttner, writing in *Business Week,* observed that airlines "dwell not in an Adam Smith world but in a world more reminiscent of economist Joseph Schumpeter's model in which 'efficiency' depends more on technical advances than on price wars." He suggested reregulating, prohibiting discriminatory pricing, and establishing zones of reasonableness that required fares to reflect distance and costs.[52]

In November 1995, a *New York Times* article examined the effect of deregulation on the airline industry. Five of the 10 largest carriers at the time of deregulation were gone. Thousands of airline workers were tired of working for troubled or bankrupt airlines and more than 100,000 had been laid off since 1989. Although profit prospects began to improve beginning in 1994, the industry had made money in only 8 of the 17 previous years.

---

[50] K. Bradsher, "No New Deal for Banking," *New York Times,* November 2, 1995, p. D1.
[51] P. S. Dempsy, "The Bitter Fruits of Airline Deregulation," *The Wall Street Journal,* April 8, 1993, p. A15.
[52] R. Kuttner, "Flying in the Face of Reason: Why the Skies Need Reregulating," *Business Week,* April 10, 1993, p. 26.

Travelers were, on balance, somewhat happier than industry employees. Fares overall dropped after deregulation although short trips grew more expensive. However, planes were fuller, making flying more physically uncomfortable. In 1970, 49.7 percent of seats were filled with paying passengers; in 1995, 66.8 percent of seats were occupied. Airlines argued that it was better to sell a seat at a deeply discounted fare than not to sell the seat at all.

Airline fares were complex and even described by some as byzantine. In 1978, 37 percent of passengers paid fares that were less or equal to the average; only 2 percent paid more than 1.5 times the average. In the mid-1990s, about 60 percent of passengers paid less or equal to the average while about 13 percent paid more than 1.5 times the average.[53]

Airline personnel were demoralized. A Delta agent in San Francisco acknowledged that air travel was like entering a pack of snarling dogs. He commented, "You're lucky we don't treat you worse, considering the way they treat us." Another agent in this airport told a passenger, "This is the new airline industry, lady. Get used to it." It appeared that customer service in the 1990s was based on overpromising and underdelivering.[54]

Mergers, acquisitions, and foreign competition became a major issue in the mid-1990s. Prior to 1996, U.S. airlines that met with foreign carriers to set prices violated the Sherman Antitrust Act. In May, United Airlines, American, and Delta asked for antitrust immunity to work with foreign marketing partners. United had a marketing partnership with German-Lufthansa, American Airlines with Canadian Airlines, and Delta with Swissair, Belgian Sabena, and Austrian Airlines. Under the rules at the time of this request, marketing partnerships allowed carriers to share some operations, thereby facilitating travelers' connections between U.S. and foreign airlines more easily. However, they could not share financial or fare data. If granted immunity, they asserted they could share more flight information and could better determine thousands of fare schedules between the United States, Canada, and Europe. Critics charged that antitrust immunity would let airlines form a cartel to set higher prices.[55]

In June 1996, British Airways and American Airlines announced their intention to enter an alliance that would create the world's largest airline network. The two giants hoped that in April 1997, operations would begin to funnel passengers from one partner to the another. They announced they would not exchange equity nor would the arrangement include any form of cross-ownership. British Airways did not intend to change its 24.6 percent ownership of USAir nor did American, which owned 25 percent of Canadian

---

[53] A. Bryant, "On a Wing and a Fare: Deregulation Decoded," *New York Times,* November 5, 1996, p. E5.

[54] B. Saporito, "Going Nowhere Fast," *Fortune,* April 3, 1995, p. 58.

[55] A. Q. Nomani, "Airlines Hope to Get around Antitrust Laws," *The Wall Street Journal,* May 8, 1996, p. B1.

Airlines, expect to change its marketing alliance. British Air, in announcing the deal, said that it was a response to President Clinton's April 1995 International Air Transportation Policy statement that generally approved of code-sharing (sharing of fare and scheduling information).[56] As deregulation of airlines continued worldwide, observers expected more and more deals like British Air and American to be negotiated and consummated. Consumers were more likely to benefit from greater convenience and lower fares. Entrepreneurial activity was likely to increase although it was not clear how many start-ups would survive in the long run.

As President Clinton began his second term, it seemed likely that deregulation would continue in a number of industries. Republicans held both the House and Senate for the next two years. The 105th Congress was likely to reintroduce legislation that had not been passed in the previous session. Competition would increase and some, but by no means all, stakeholders would benefit.

---

[56] Internet [http://www.british-airways.com/batext/aabackground.htm]

Summary

Stakeholder interaction regarding regulation became very complex after the 1960s. Economic and social regulation waxed and waned. Many new products and processes were developed during this period. As stakeholders began to use those products and as the environment was affected by them, pressure for regulatory control increased. Presidents Carter, Reagan, Bush, and Clinton each had different political and social agendas as they developed regulatory policy. Coalitions of stakeholders shifted in the external direct and indirect quadrants of the stakeholder influence map.

At the end of the 1970s, the government took major initiatives to deregulate specific industries. President Carter's view of deregulation was quite narrow, concentrating on competition in a few industries. President Reagan did very little to overturn existing regulations but substantially diminished the ability of regulatory agencies to carry out their mandates. President Bush waffled back and forth on regulation. His rhetoric supported social regulation, while his Supreme Court appointments demonstrated a more conservative view of society and interpretation of the law. Some of his cabinet appointments appeared to mollify more liberal elements of his party, whereas others toed the strict conservative line. No clear strategy emerged.

Regulation, deregulation, and reregulation overlapped and conflicted, leaving most stakeholders confused and concerned. The 1992 election of Bill Clinton signaled a sharp break with past policies. Two years later, the Republican sweep of the House of Representatives led to the first real attempt to dismantle the nation's regulatory apparatus. Despite energetic attempts on the part of the conservative House, there were relatively few major changes. The Clinton administration appeared to adopt a more centrist position on regulation as the 1996 presidential campaign heated up. With Clinton's election to a second term, Republicans predicted he would try to develop a more liberal agenda. The president, however, vowed to reduce government spending and continue deregulation, as well as to consider stakeholders' security and economic well-being.

Questions

1. What are the ideological problems a nation faces as it tries to balance regulation and free market forces?
2. What are the societal drawbacks to unregulated transportation industries? What are the benefits?
3. Are partisan politics helpful or harmful to regulatory policy? What were the major regulatory issues of the mid-1990s?

Projects

1. Interview your local member of Congress about his or her stand on banking legislation.
2. Compile a list of new technologies that are coming under the regulatory process. What kinds of regulations should be put in place to address the concerns of stakeholders?

BETA CASE 9
REGULATION AND DEREGULATION

Brian Madison drummed his fingers on his desk and rocked back and forth in his large leather swivel chair. He knew the FDA was speeding up the testing of new drugs. But would Beta be held responsible if its drugs, tested under the relaxed guidelines, developed problems later? What policy would the second Clinton administration and the new director of the FDA adopt?

Drug-testing requirements were of utmost importance to Beta. All of its operating divisions spent huge amounts on testing and meeting FDA requirements. Any substantive change in those requirements had profound strategic and monetary implications.

Back in 1990, Beta began to make generic drugs.[57] The company hired David Shapiro, the vice president of a small, successful generic company in New Jersey, to run the new division. Shapiro had spent endless hours with regulators trying to move his previous company's application process through the FDA's maze of paperwork. He had explained the problems to Madison at the time he was interviewed: "Those folks at the FDA are totally inept, especially when it comes to evaluating generic drugs. I personally know three generic drug manufacturers that have submitted phony data. I know Beta does everything by the book, but there's a risk of losing out to the company that gets quick approval."

Madison was impressed with Shapiro's candor and expertise. Everyone in the industry knew about Mylan Laboratories and the generic-drug scandal. Mylan blew the whistle on FDA procedures in 1989.

The company realized it was losing millions of dollars because the FDA sat on its applications but passed competitors' applications quickly. After complaining to the FDA about favoritism and payoffs for two years, Mylan executives hired private detectives. The detectives uncovered evidence of payoffs that they quickly delivered to the House oversight committee. After the committee investigated, the FDA withdrew its approval of several drugs that competed with Mylan products."[58] Eventually, the FDA recalled or suspended more than 150 drugs and inspected more than 20 major companies.

The FDA regulatory process continued to be a concern. Drug testing was a major topic of conversation every time pharmaceutical industry executives got together. No one really knew what the Bush administration or FDA commissioner Dr. David Kessler would do about drug testing. Early in 1991, Kessler announced he would get a lot tougher on the violators,

---

[57] Generic drugs are less expensive versions of brand-name medicines. Generics account for more than one-third of all prescription drugs sold. When drug patents expire, generic companies use the formulas to make generic versions. In 1995, patents expired on brand-name prescription drugs with estimated sales of $10 million. Increasingly, large pharmaceutical companies produced both generic and brand-name drugs.

[58] "Mylan Is Glad It Opened This Can of Worms," *Business Week,* September 18, 1989, p. 30.

take a fresh look at regulations, and revamp the structure of the FDA. In fact, in April 1991, four FDA employees went to jail for accepting bribes from generic drugmakers.

Then presidential politics stirred the murky waters. When President Bush extended his regulatory moratorium in the spring of 1992, Madison, Shapiro, and every other generic or brand-name drugmaker had to operate without clear direction or standards. They had to develop policies that would protect them if existing regulations were enforced or new regulations were imposed.

After the 1994 congressional election, the Republican majority in Congress tried to develop legislation to streamline the FDA's approval policies. In part, they wanted to allow companies to hire outside contractors to review drug or medical devices they wanted to market. Advocates of the change argued that thousands of people would die each year because drugs and medical devices that might save their lives were tied up with expensive and overly long approval processes. Critics of the legislation said the proposals went much too far and seriously compromised consumer safety. Dr. David Kessler testified the legislation would undermine the laws enacted to protect consumers.

How much power would the 1997 Congress wield and how would its actions affect Beta?

APPENDIX
U.S. REGULATORY AGENCIES

Major Regulatory Agencies

Consumer Product Safety Commission
Environmental Protection Agency
Equal Employment Opportunity Commission
Federal Communications Commission
Federal Deposit Insurance Corporation
Federal Energy Regulatory Commission
Federal Reserve System
Federal Trade Commission
Food and Drug Administration
National Labor Relations Board
Occupational Safety and Health Administration
Securities and Exchange Commission

Other Regulatory Agencies

Architectural and Transportation Barriers Compliance Board
Commodity Futures Trading Commission
Farm Credit Administration
Federal Election Commission
Federal Housing Finance Board
Federal Maritime Commission
National Credit Union Administration
National Mediation Board
National Transportation Safety Board
Nuclear Regulatory Commission
Pension Benefit Guaranty Corporation

Postal Rate Commission
Resolution Trust Corporation
Small Business Administration
United States International Trade Commission
United States Postal Service

Departmental Agencies

Department of Agriculture.
Agricultural Marketing Service
Agricultural Stabilization and Conservation Service
Animal and Plant Health Inspection Service
Commodity Credit Corporation
Farmers Home Administration
Federal Grain Inspection Service
Food and Nutrition Service
Food Safety and Inspection Service
Foreign Agricultural Service
Forest Service
Federal Crop Insurance Corporation
Packers and Stockyards Administration
Rural Electrification Administration
Soil Conservation Service

Department of Commerce.
Board of Export Administration
Economic Development Administration

International Trade Administration
National Institute of Standards and Technology
National Oceanic and Atmospheric Administration
Patent and Trademark Office

Department of Defense.
Army Corps of Engineers

Department of Energy.
Conservation and Renewable Energy
Economic Regulatory Administration
Environment, Safety and Health
Environmental Restoration and Waste Management
Fossil Energy
International Affairs and Energy Emergencies

Department of Health and Human Services.
Family Support Administration
Health Care Financing Administration
Office for Civil Rights
Office of Human Development Services
Office of the Inspector General
Public Health Service
Regional Offices
Social Security Administration

Department of Housing and Urban Development.
Bureau of Indian Affairs
Bureau of Land Management
Bureau of Reclamation
Department of the Interior
Government National Mortgage Association
Minerals Management Service
National Park Service
Office of Community Planning and Development
Office of Fair Housing and Equal Opportunity
Office of Housing
Office of Surface Mining Reclamation and Enforcement
United States Fish and Wildlife Service
United States Geological Survey

Department of Justice.
Antitrust Division Civil Rights Division
Bureau of Prisons

Criminal Division
Drug Enforcement Administration
Immigration and Naturalization Service
Office of Justice Programs
United States Parole Division

Department of Labor.
Employment Standards Administration
Employment and Training Administration
Mine Safety and Health Administration
Office of Labor–Management Standards
Pension and Welfare Benefits Administration
Veterans' Employment and Training Service

Department of Transportation.
Federal Aviation Administration
Federal Highway Administration
Federal Railroad Administration
Maritime Administration
National Highway Safety Administration
Office of Aviation Analysis
Office of Aviation Enforcement and Proceedings
Office of Commercial Space Transportation
Office of Hearings
Office of Intergovernmental and Consumer Affairs
Office of International Aviation
Research and Special Programs Administration
Saint Lawrence Seaway Development Corporation
United States Coast Guard
Urban Mass Transportation Administration

Department of the Treasury.
Bureau of Alcohol, Tobacco and Firearms
Comptroller of the Currency
Department of Veterans Affairs
Internal Revenue Service
Office of Thrift Supervision
United States Customs Service

Regulatory Oversight and Coordination.
Administrative Conference of the United States
General Accounting Office
Office of Management and Budget
Regulatory Information Service Center

CHAPTER 10

PHILANTHROPY AND CORPORATE GIVING

This chapter focuses on philanthropy and cause-related marketing. Philanthropic giving is a major business in the United States. Individuals, foundations, and corporations all contribute to a vast panoply of causes from the extreme political right to the fringes on the left. Philanthropy helps support constituencies and organizations that are not funded by federal, state, or local governments and also those that are government funded but have inadequate resources.

In recent years, many corporations have tied their marketing programs and products to social causes. Increasingly they are using their marketing function to promote political and social agendas important to top managers or to potential customers. All countries have some form of philanthropic activity, and many also embrace cause-related marketing. This chapter examines the programs and strategies used by two of the United States' largest trading partners: Great Britain and Japan.

CASE: UNITED WAY

United Way of America is a network of more than 2,000 local chapters that collect contributions through the workplace. Employees make workplace donations and often authorize payroll deductions for local charities. About one cent of every dollar donated to local chapters goes to the United Way of America's national association in Alexandria, Virginia. The national organization helps the affiliates with activities such as advertising and training. In 1992, affiliates donated $29 million to United Way of America; however, the way some of that money was spent gave rise to a tremendous amount of negative publicity.

In February 1992, William Aramony was forced out of his job as president of United Way of America. Newspapers and other media across the United States uncovered a number of Aramony's activities that eventually led United Way's board to ask for his resignation.

Why did the media single out Aramony for criticism, and what was so noteworthy about his situation?

The *Washington Post* and *Regardie's Magazine* of Washington, D.C., reported that Aramony had been using contributions to finance an extravagant personal lifestyle. The stories focused on Aramony's salary and benefits package of $463,000, his travel habits, and entertainment paid for by the charity.

The newspapers described Aramony's lavish lifestyle. His chauffeured cars cost United Way of America more than $90,000 a year. On two occasions, he flew on the Concorde to Europe at a cost of $41,000. Whenever he traveled, he went first-class.

While president, Aramony unilaterally authorized the formation of two spin-off organizations incorporated as profit-making enterprises. One of these companies, Partnership Umbrella, Inc., bought him an apartment on New York City's Upper East Side and a Florida apartment, together valued at $1.3 million. Partnership Umbrella refused to disclose its finances despite the full disclosure policies of the standard-setting agency, the National Charities Information Bureau. The other affiliate, Sales Service/America, hired Aramony's son Robert as its top executive even though professional fund-raisers asserted that he was not qualified.[1]

The public outcry was loud and furious against what many perceived as Aramony's excesses. Economic and social concerns at that time made Aramony's actions seem especially flagrant. First, there was the public perception of appropriate conduct for the head of a nonprofit organization. According to an editor of the *Nonprofit Times,* a monthly trade publication, "The average Joe or the average Jane who makes maybe $25,000, when they see someone working for a charity, that's supposed to be mission-driven, they think these people should be doing it for the love of the mission and not to make money."[2] Clearly a disparity existed between the average donor's perception of United Way's mission and the reality of its operations.

Second, this happened at a time when the U.S. economy was in a recession. Many of the communities in which United Way campaigned were suffering job losses and the threat of more layoffs. People who were themselves barely surviving economically were exhorted to give to those less fortunate.

A third concern was that donors could not designate the specific charities to which their money would go. Various stakeholder groups had very different visions of what United Way should support and were not reluctant to make their voices heard. They wanted to target their donations to causes they liked and away from those they disliked. In Rochester, New York, for example, the local offices of Planned Parenthood had been a beneficiary of United Way for 20 years. In 1991, it announced the opening of an abortion clinic at the same time the United Way campaign got under way. Antiabortion groups promptly mounted a movement to deny donations to the local United Way.

Historically, United Way supported very few environmentally oriented philanthropies even though by 1991 those organizations were the fastest-growing category of charities soliciting workplace donations. At the same time that United Way chapters in Los Angeles, San Diego, and San Francisco were having a hard time raising funds, Earth Share of California enjoyed a 42 percent increase in gifts. Critics accused United Way of being old-fashioned, out of touch, and unresponsive to donors' concerns.[3]

By the beginning of 1993, United Way had lost its position as the blue chip of charities. For the first time since 1946, contributions were down. Local chapters cut budgets and extended campaigns. In some cities, such as San Diego and Denver, donations were behind 1991 levels by as much as 30 percent.

After William Aramony's departure, former Peace Corps director Elaine L. Chao took over as president of United Way of America. Chao instituted new policies covering financial controls, governance, travel expenses, and donors' choice. Managers accounted for their budgets to senior vice-presidents and were monitored on a monthly basis. In turn, outside auditors reviewed the senior vice-presidents' expenses.

Fifteen new seats on the board were created for officials from local chapters. Local officials were appointed to six new steering committees, including budget, ethics, and compensation committees. At the same time, the administrative staff was reduced from

---

[1] F. Barringer, "The United Way Board Discusses Leaders," *New York Times,* February 27, 1992, p. A2.

[2] F. Barringer, "Pay for Charity Leaders Raises Uneasy Question," *New York Times,* March 16, 1992, p. A12.

[3] F. Barringer, "United Way Says Slump and Scandal May Bring Sharp Drop in Donations," *New York Times,* November 20, 1992, p. A14.

275 to 186 employees. Travel expenses were severely curtailed. All business trips, including the president's, were at coach fares, and meal allowances were imposed on everyone.

For the first time, local chapters initiated programs that allowed donors to target their contributions to the charity of their choice, whether or not it was an official United Way agency. Many corporations matched their employees' donations with corporate gifts.[4]

Aramony was not the only highly paid head of a tax-exempt institution. According to the *Chronicle of Philanthropy,* 37 of the biggest 100 charitable foundations paid their chief executives more than $200,000 in salary and benefits. The median salary in 1991 was $155,000. Three foundations, the W. M. Keck Foundation, the J. Paul Getty Trust, and the Ford Foundation, paid their top executives even more than United Way paid Aramony.[5] But these foundations were not publicly supported.

In June 1995, William Aramony was sentenced to seven years in prison for fraudulently diverting $1.2 million of United Way's funds to pay for his romance with a teenager and other personal benefits. United-Way's former chief financial officer Thomas J. Merlo and Stephen J. Paulachak who also served as CFO received prison sentences and fines for running Partnership Umbrella.[6]

Writing in *Public Relations Journal,* Rayna Skolnik noted that the United Way incident brought nonprofit organizations under new scrutiny. She pointed to a general loss of public confidence in government and other organizations and institutions and noted the public wants to know far more about where the money is going and how it will be used.[7]

---

[4] T. Segal and C. Del Valle, "They Didn't Even Give at the Office," *Business Week,* January 25, 1993, pp. 68-69.

[5] "Philanthropic Pay," *The Wall Street Journal,* September 8, 1992, p. A1.

[6] K. W. Arenson, "Ex-United Way Leader Gets 7 Years for Embezzlement," *New York Times,* June 23, 1995, p. A14.

[7] R. Skolnik, "Rebuilding Trust," *Public Relations Journal,* September 1993, pp. 29–32.

Questions

1. What are appropriate benchmarks for the salary and benefits structure for top managers of charities? How can charities attract outstanding managers while responding to the concerns of donors?

2. Should the standards of compensation for employees of nonprofit institutions, such as universities and hospitals, differ from those for employees of charitable organizations such as the National Wildlife Foundation, Greenpeace, or United Way? If so, why and how? If not, why?

3. As a class project, volunteer for a fund-raising campaign. Find out what methods the charity uses to solicit funds. Are you as a fund-raiser, informed about how funds are allocated? What proportion of the funds is used for administration, and what portion goes directly to the designated recipients? What promises does the charity make with respect to how your donation is used?

Charitable Organizations

Organized charitable institutions began to proliferate at the end of the 19th century. Four ministers calling themselves the Associated Charities organized the first Community Chest in 1887.[8] Four years later, 15 similar orga-

---

[8] J. R. Seely et al., *Community Chest: A Case Study in Philanthropy* (Toronto: University of Toronto Press, 1957), p. 17.

nizations had formed. By 1919 there were 40 Community Chests, and by 1929 the number had grown to 350.[9]

Company Towns

The establishment of company towns proved to be notable exceptions to the generally limited involvement of companies in community welfare. In the 1880s, George M. Pullman, who made a fortune building railroad passenger cars, invested $8 million to build the company town of Pullman outside Chicago. The town provided housing, recreational, and church facilities for employees, all built at company expense. Heald noted that the company benefited greatly from his investment:

> Pullman's motives were practical, too. Outstanding among them was the desire to attract skilled labor beyond the immediate vicinity of Chicago's trade unions and union organizers. His philanthropy was further tempered by a determination to realize a profit in good times or bad. Pullman saw no inconsistency or impropriety in permitting the company-built church on the town square to stand vacant when no group could raise the money to rent it at a rate which would assure a 6 percent return on investment.[10]

While Pullman's primary concern was to avoid union interference, other founders of company towns were more interested in improving living conditions for employees. For instance, in 1909 Metropolitan Life Insurance Company donated money to build a hospital to serve its employees. When a disgruntled stockholder filed a suit against Metropolitan Life, the courts found in favor of the company on the grounds that "by benefiting the workers, the gift benefited the company."[11]

Mutual self-interest led the Young Men's Christian Association (YMCA) and the American railroads to work closely together between 1872 and 1903. The YMCA movement needed physical facilities, and the railroads needed a moral, healthful environment for traveling employees. The railroads contributed over half of the $1.8 million needed to build the 113 YMCA buildings constructed by 1903.[12]

Other industries also supported the YMCA, and in the years before World War I, the growth in company giving for community-related welfare and social programs was closely associated with the work of the YMCAs. Thus, the YMCA was a key institution in gaining legitimacy for corporate giving.

Two other events ensured legitimacy for corporate giving: First, the Revenue Act of 1935 allowed a deduction of up to 5 percent of pretax income

---

[9] M. T. Heald, *The Social Responsibility of Business: Company and Community, 1900–1960* (Cleveland: Press of Case Western Reserve, 1970), p. 122.

[10] Ibid.

[11] R. L. Thomas, *Policies Underlying Corporate Giving* (Englewood Cliffs,NJ: Prentice Hall, 1966), p. 53.

[12] P. Williams and F. E. Croxton, *Corporate Contributions to Organized Community Welfare Sources* (New York: National Bureau of Economic Research, 1930), p. 52.

for charitable contributions (this allowance was raised to 10 percent during the Reagan administration). The second major event was a 1953 Supreme Court decision. The case, *Smith* v. *Barlow,* involved a small New Jersey manufacturing company that had given $1,500 to Princeton University to test the legal definition of acceptable tax-deductible corporate contributions.[13] A stockholder filed suit, but the court found the contribution acceptable.

Individual Giving

Corporate giving is a 20th-century phenomenon. Earlier, individual philanthropy was considered a more appropriate means of giving than corporate donations. Most of the so-called captains of industry such as Rockefeller, Carnegie, Frick, Morgan, and Vanderbilt gave very large sums from their personal fortunes.

These donations were not always appreciated, as the following anecdote shows. In 1905, a missionary group refused a $100,000 gift from John D. Rockefeller (even though, as it turned out, the group had sought the aid). The group disparaged the tainted money, criticizing Rockefeller's business methods.

> In a subsequent incident following the 1906 San Francisco earthquake and fire, Mr. Rockefeller sent large sums of money to subordinates in San Francisco to be used as they saw fit. One of the Standard Oil managers, who specialized in clergymen, gave a number of them bank orders of $150 each but told them he wanted it distinctly understood that this was tainted money. One of the clergymen replied, "The taint wears off the moment it passes from your hands into ours." Another stated, "It's the motive that makes money tainted or not." The third one commented, "All money is tainted." The fourth said, "Tain't enough!"[14]

Andrew Carnegie had such strong negative feelings about corporate giving and such a great commitment to individual giving that he wrote *The Gospel of Wealth and Other Timely Essays* that was published in 1900. He mused about the administration of wealth and concluded that the duty of a rich person was "to set an example of modest, unpretentious living . . . to provide modestly for the legitimate wants of those dependent upon him; and . . . to consider all surplus revenues which come to him . . . to administer in the manner which, in his judgment, is best calculated to produce the most beneficial results for the community."[15]

Carnegie went on to disparage indiscriminate charity. He suggested the rich should give to institutions that would build healthy habits among the less

---

[13] Thomas, *Policies Underlying Corporate Giving,* p. 53.

[14] K. G. Patrick and R. Eells, *Education and the Business Dollar: A Study of Corporate Contributions Policy and American Education* (New York: Macmillan, 1969), p. 4.

[15] A. Carnegie, *The Gospel of Wealth and Other Timely Essays,* ed. E. C. Kirkland (Cambridge, MA: Belknap Press, 1962), p. 25.

fortunate. These institutions included universities, public libraries, hospitals, parks, meeting and concert halls, swimming pools, and churches.[16] Carnegie apparently never considered it appropriate to use corporate money for other social causes. Like many other philanthropists, he believed people should be helped only by providing facilities that would allow them to help themselves. He and other philanthropists earned great social and civic prestige.

Individual Giving in the 1990s

Individual and household giving still generate the highest percentage of total philanthropic activity in the United States. In 1990, 75 percent of U.S. households donated a total of $122.6 billion to charities. Adjusting for inflation, Americans gave more than three times as much as they did in 1955. More than 96 percent of this money stayed in the local communities.

According to Independent Sector, a Washington-based group representing the nation's nonprofit institutions, of those households that gave, each donated an average of $978 to a variety of causes, including religious institutions, the environment, health care, education, homelessness, the arts, and nuclear disarmament. Fifty-three percent of charitable gifts went to religious organizations, 10 percent to education, 9.6 percent to human services, and 8 percent to health care.[17]

By 1994, individual giving patterns had changed. The Independent Sector reported that 3.4 percent fewer Americans volunteered their time in 1993 than in 1991. Americans also gave less per household to charitable causes than in the recent past. In 1993, Americans donated $880 per household, nearly $98 less than the 1990 figure.[18]

Two years later, in 1995, American households were giving even less. *The Independent Sector* reported that only 68 percent of households made monetary gifts in 1995, the smallest percentage in nearly a decade. Seventy-five percent of the households surveyed said they were worried about having enough money in the future.[19]

Even though fewer households were giving money, total household charitable giving rose 2 percent in real terms between 1993 and 1995. Middle-class and wealthy households gave more. Almost 90 percent of those with household incomes above $100,000 made charitable contributions, averaging 3.4 percent of their incomes. Affluent givers deducted the value of these gifts from their income tax, a benefit not available to poorer households.

The Chronicle of Philanthropy reported in June 1995 that Americans gave a total of $129.9 billion to charity in 1994. Of all gifts to charity,

---

[16] Ibid., pp. 32–47.

[17] F. Baringer, "In the Worst of Times, America Keeps Giving," *New York Times,* March 15, 1992, p. E6.

[18] "Less Money and Time for Charity, Study Says," *New York Times,* October 20, 1994, p. A22.

[19] G. Koretz, "Fewer at the Charity Ball," *Business Week,* October 28, 1996, p. 36.

Exhibit 10–1 Giving in 1994

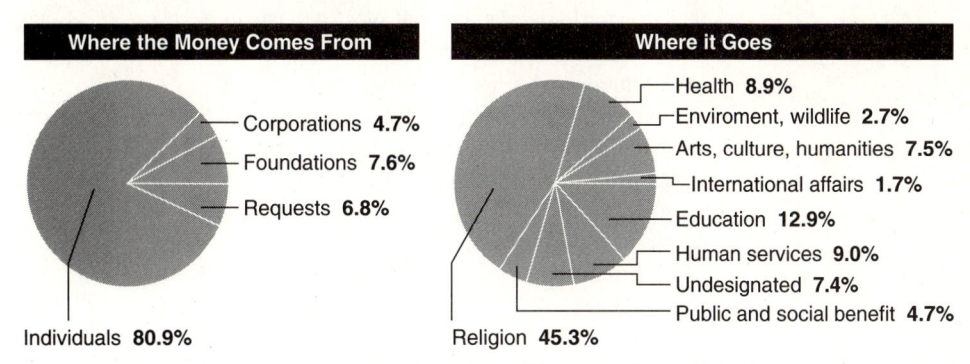

Where the Money Comes From
- Corporations 4.7%
- Foundations 7.6%
- Requests 6.8%
- Individuals 80.9%

Where it Goes
- Health 8.9%
- Enviroment, wildlife 2.7%
- Arts, culture, humanities 7.5%
- International affairs 1.7%
- Education 12.9%
- Human services 9.0%
- Undesignated 7.4%
- Public and social benefit 4.7%
- Religion 45.3%

Source: Giving USA, reprinted in *Chronicle of Philanthropy.* June 1, 1995, p. 21.

individuals gave 81 percent. However, charities faced rising costs that were barely met by increased giving of 3.89 percent over 1993 donations. Social-services groups actually experienced a drop in donations. They raised 6.1 per cent less than in 1993. Arts and cultural organizations also had a hard time. Although they received 1.2 percent more in dollars than in 1993, it was not enough to keep up with inflation.

The biggest increase in giving in 1994 was to groups that provided international relief from famine and disease. The wars in Rwanda and Bosnia appeared to have stimulated increased giving. Supporters of the environment gave 11 percent more in 1994. Fund-raisers believed that Bill Clinton's and Al Gore's strong support of the environment accounted for the rise. Colleges and private schools also did fairly well in 1994. Donations rose 8.5 percent to $16.7 billion and as soon as the stock market boom began in 1996, contributions jumped dramatically. In Exhibit 10–1, we show where charitable donations came from and where they went in 1994.

Individuals give more than money to charities and causes; they give their time, energy, and expertise. A survey by the Gallup Organization and Independent Sector, a Washington-based association of nonprofit organizations, estimated that 93 million Americans did some form of volunteer work in 1995 on their own or through their companies.[20]

Beginning in the 1970s, some small high-tech companies offered job candidates social service sabbaticals as part of a benefit package. In 1996, the

---
[20] J. Mathews, "AT&T to Pay Employees for Volunteering," *Boston Globe,* September 22, 1996, p. E3.

Conference Board, a New York-based management and economic research organization, reported that about 5 percent of Fortune 500 companies had these formal social service leaves. American Express, IBM, Time Inc., Wells Fargo, and Xerox had different terms and criteria for employees who wanted to volunteer.

Xerox began to offer extended leaves in the mid-1970s. Employees had to be employed full time and to have been with the company for at least three years. Fully paid sabbaticals lasted for as long as a year. Joseph M. Calahan, vice president of the Xerox Foundation that sponsored the company's social service sabbaticals, noted that "if companies want to attract and keep good people, they have to adapt their culture and business to attract a workforce that is changing."[21]

American Express also offers a sabbatical program to full-time employees with a minimum of 10 years' tenure. In addition, applicants must have had good performance reviews for at least three years. Richard Schack, an 18-year employee went on a six-month sabbatical during which he created a computer database for an AIDS outreach program. He said he "needed to feel that the work [he] was doing had a social impact as opposed to a shareholder impact."[22]

AT&T decided to implement a different model. In November 1996, the corporation unveiled a social service program that gave all its 127,000 employees one paid day off for volunteer work during the next year. This was the nation's largest corporate commitment to community service. A company spokesperson said he expected the program to total 1 million hours of volunteer time. On November 21, several thousand AT&T employees in 16 states and the District of Columbia assisted at child and elder care programs, repaired homes in housing projects, and served hot meals to the homeless. The executive development director of AT&T Foundation said employee surveys showed rising frustration with the lack of time for volunteerism. Company executives decided a volunteer program might ease the strain and strengthen company ties with local communities.[23]

The Political Controversy

Charities are very diverse and reflect a wide variety of interests and commitments. They include universities, health organizations, young people's groups, religious organizations, and food banks. This mix of organizations changes according to the nation's economic condition, the prevalence of particular diseases, the growth or wane of religious fervor, and international catastrophes. The list of leading charitable contributions will probably look quite different by the end of the millennium.

---

[21] M. Vickers, "Keeping Valued Employees by Letting Them Go, for a While," *New York Times,* September 22, 1996, p. F11.
[22] Ibid.
[23] Mathews, "AT&T," p. E3.

In June 1995, Speaker Newt Gingrich declared that America needed to dismantle the welfare system and turn over its functions to private charities. He called for every church and synagogue in the United States to adopt a homeless person for six months and for all Americans to contribute three hours a week to volunteer services.

His critics who administered charities observed that the nation was no longer composed of tightly knit neighborhoods and communities. Instead it rested on a vast array of organizations from neighborhood settlement houses to national organizations like the Red Cross and Salvation Army. These entities, run by professionals, provided far less in support of social services and funds than the government itself.

While many charities depend on volunteer labor and donations, they were even more dependent on government money. A comprehensive 1989 study found that federal, state, and local governments spent about $96 billion on basic social services such as welfare, housing, and aid to children. If Social Security and Medicare and other government spending for pension plans, medical care, and education were included, the government spent almost $1 trillion.[24]

A major study by the Independent Sector in 1995 showed that proposed cuts would be very severe for nonprofit voluntary organizations. If implemented by the year 2002, federal support of nonprofits would be about $197 billion, or 21 percent below 1995 levels. Proposed legislation from both the House and Senate would result in consolidation of 60 job training programs, a cut of 50 percent for the National Endowments for the Arts and Humanities, major restructuring of welfare programs, and reduction of the Community Development Block Grant program by 50 percent.[25]

As we have seen in other contexts, the Republican Congress was unable to implement most of its agenda. However, as the 1996 elections loomed, President Clinton made it clear there would be major changes in government's role, particularly in federal welfare support. In August 1996, he signed the Personal Responsibility and Work Opportunity Reconciliation Act. This legislation gave the states broad authority over welfare programs. It replaced Aid to Families with Dependent Children that had provided funds directly to 12.8 million people, including 8 million children. The new law required able-bodied adults on welfare to find jobs within two years and limited the period a person could receive welfare during a lifetime. The law slashed spending on food stamps by $24 billion and cut Supplemental Security Income (SSI) to a substantial number of legal immigrants—most of whom were elderly or disabled.

---

[24] K. W. Arenson, "Gingrich's Vision of Welfare Ignores Reality, Charities Say," *New York Times,* June 4, 1995, p. A1.

[25] "Serious Implications for Charities of FY 1996–2002 Budget Resolutions," *Responsive Philanthropy,* Spring 1995, p. 14.

EXHIBIT 10–2   Giving in 1995

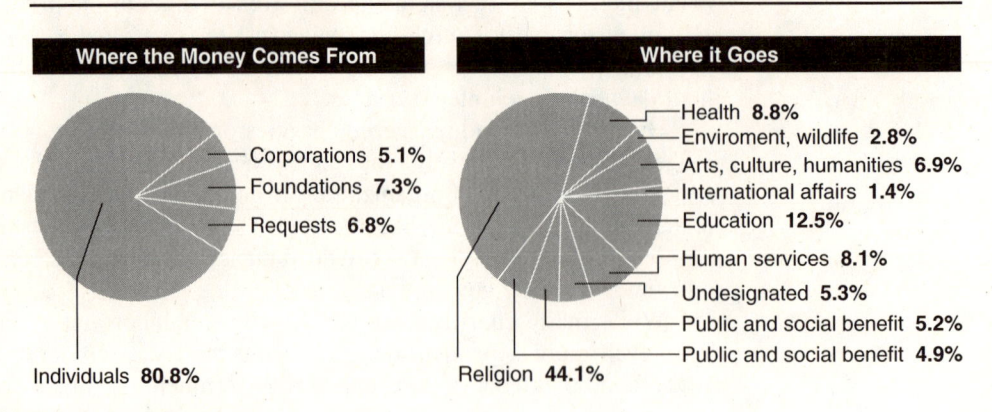

Where the Money Comes From
- Individuals 80.8%
- Corporations 5.1%
- Foundations 7.3%
- Requests 6.8%

Where it Goes
- Health 8.8%
- Enviroment, wildlife 2.8%
- Arts, culture, humanities 6.9%
- International affairs 1.4%
- Education 12.5%
- Human services 8.1%
- Undesignated 5.3%
- Public and social benefit 5.2%
- Public and social benefit 4.9%
- Religion 44.1%

Source: Giving USA, reprinted in *Chronicle of Philanthropy*. May 30, 1996, p. 29.

President Clinton said that he had reservations about the law and was particularly upset by the size of the food stamp cuts and immigrant provisions. He vowed to fix those aspects of the law before they were implemented. Some charity leaders said the welfare overhaul posed the most severe challenge they had to face since the early years of the Reagan administration. Leaders of Catholic Charities USA, the Children's Defense Fund, and Second Harvest condemned the new law. They cited a study by the Urban Institute, a Washington research group, that estimated the law would push 2.6 million people below the poverty line.[26]

Giving in 1995

The November 1996 election results maintained the tension between the Democratic executive branch and the Republican Congress. When Newt Gingrich was installed as speaker of the new 105th Congress in November 1996, he sounded a far more conciliatory note than he had in 1994. Compromise, not confrontation, seemed to be on his mind and the minds of other legislators. It seemed possible that both sides might be willing to ameliorate aspects of the welfare bill that worked against legal immigrants and children.

As a general rule, a strong economy meant more charitable giving. In 1995, charitable donations jumped 11 percent over 1994. The total of $143 billion was the biggest yearly increase since 1986. After adjusting for inflation, the real increase was 7.8 percent, the largest gain in a decade. In Exhibit 10–2, we show where charitable donations came from and where they went in 1995.

---

[26] D. Marchetti, "Reeling from Welfare Overhaul," *Chronicle of Philanthropy*, September 5, 1996, p. 38.

The American Association of Fund-Raising Council (AAFRC) reported that some charities did better than others. As in 1994, donations to *human services* fell. Donations were down to $11.7 billion or down 3 percent after adjusting for inflation. This category included disaster relief agencies such as the Red Cross.

Arts, culture, and humanities groups also fared poorly, continuing the decline of the previous year. Congress cut federal subsidies for the arts by more than one-third and continued to debate whether to continue financing the National Endowment for the Arts. Reduced government support did not result in increased nongovernmental donations. Private giving to these groups rose less than 3 percent to $10 billion, just keeping pace with inflation. It appeared that donations to the arts were in trouble because the number of people interested in arts performances declined. New research studies found that older people were more likely to attend artistic performances. Younger people preferred rock music, television, and the movies to theater, classical music performances, and museums. An aging population faced higher ticket prices and growing demands on their resources. Institutional and individual donors were asked to offset more and more of the deficits run up by most cultural organizations.[27]

A study by the National Endowment for the Arts concluded that younger Americans were unlikely to attend live performances of classical music, opera, and dramatic theater with the same intensity as the previous generation. Interest in the performing arts appeared to diminish with each generation. One sociologist said, "We're talking about a massive shift in taste and tradition: from a generation of 'war baby' cultural highbrows to future generations of cultural 'omnivores' younger Americans who think Patsy Cline, reggae, B.B. King, and hip-hop are as important as the New York Philharmonic."[28]

Public and social benefit philanthropies realized the largest gains, 17 percent or 14 percent after inflation. This category included research, public policy organizations, community development, advocacy organizations, and charities that collected goods for other charities.[29] Giving USA said the major reason for the rise was the inclusion of gifts in kind such as office equipment, computers, and software.

Donations to *environmental and wildlife-preservation* organizations rose to $4 billion, an increase of 10 percent after inflation. The rise reflected the increased lobbying and fund-raising efforts of groups supporting these causes. After the 1994 congressional attempt to eliminate or diminish protection of the environment, support for environmental and wildlife preservation organizations rebounded.

---

[27] J. Miller, "Aging Audiences Point to a Grim Arts Future," *New York Times,* February 12, 1996, p. A1.

[28] Ibid., p. C12.

[29] K. W. Arenson, "Donation to Charities Rose 11% Last Year, Report Says," *New York Times,* May 23, 1996, p. A24.

Health charities revamped their fund-raising strategies in the mid-1990s and found their donations rose by 9.2 percent to $12.6 billion. Some, like the American Lung Association, promoted planned gifts. The increase in income from bequests went up 44 percent in 1996. Until that time, the lung association relied almost exclusively on direct mail solicitations. The American Lung Association's CEO said, "What is driving our record year this year is our ability to shift from the old culture to a much more diversified approach."[30]

International groups had the worst record for 1995, a 6.6 percent decline. Some groups attributed the decline to donor fatigue while others said prospective givers were worried about the general state of the economy. Relief agencies agreed that people seemed to respond to front-page emergencies but were more focused on events at home. Save the Children and CARE found that direct mail campaigns were less effective compared to previous years.[31]

Exhibit 10–3 shows giving patterns in different categories from 1975 through 1995 in current and constant dollars.

New Models for Nonprofit Organizations: The Arts as an Example

Joanne Scheff and Philip Kotler, writing in the *Harvard Business Review,* suggest that the continuing decline in support for the arts can be ameliorated by creative action. Their model can be applied to other nonprofits as federal support and other traditional sources of funds diminish.

As noted earlier, nonprofit performing arts have fallen on hard times. Things were very different from the mid-1960s to the mid-1980s. During that period, contributions from foundations and individuals were generous and growing. New orchestras and theaters proliferated as did management staffs, performance facilities, and wages and benefits for performers. By 1987, ticket revenues for nonprofit performing arts organizations were greater than for sporting events.

Today, government spending has declined, audiences are smaller and still shrinking, and operating costs are rising. Donations from business foundations and corporations increasingly are predicated on how effective arts organizations are at becoming leaner and more responsive to donors' business objectives. Scheff and Kotler pose the question: How can arts organizations succeed in this environment and fulfill their artistic mission? One solution, they posit, is to create *strategic collaborations.* "Distinct from short-term, project-oriented sponsorships, strategic collaborations are intensive, durable commitments created for mutual gain; they require significant investment by all parties of time, energy, and emotion."[32]

---

[30] J. Murawski, "A Banner Year for Giving," *Chronicle of Philanthropy,* May 30, 1996, p. 29.

[31] Ibid., p. 30.

[32] J. Scheff and P. Kotler, "How the Arts Can Prosper through Strategic Collaborations," *Harvard Business Review,* January–February 1966, pp. 52–62.

EXHIBIT 10–3 Uses of Donations, 1978–96
(In billions)

	Religion		Education		Human Services		Month		Arts		Public and Social Benefit	
	Current Dollars	Constant Dollars	Current Dollars	Constant Dollars	Current Dollars	Constant Dollars	Current Dollars	Constant Dollars	Current Dollars	Constant Dollars	Current Dollars	Constant Dollars
1975	$12.81	$41.33	$2.83	$9.13	$2.94	$9.49	$3.61	$11.65	$1.56	$5.03	$0.79	$2.55
1976	14.18	42.62	3.28	9.86	3.02	9.08	3.92	11.78	2.27	6.82	1.03	3.10
1977	16.98	47.16	3.62	10.05	3.57	9.91	4.09	11.36	2.32	8.44	1.22	3.39
1978	18.35	47.25	4.11	10.58	3.87	9.97	4.52	11.61	2.10	6.18	1.08	2.78
1979	20.17	48.00	4.54	10.80	4.48	10.66	4.94	11.76	2.73	6.50	1.23	2.93
1980	22.23	47.82	4.96	10.67	4.91	10.56	5.34	11.49	3.15	6.78	1.46	3.14
1981	25.05	48.90	5.77	11.26	5.62	10.97	5.79	11.30	3.66	7.14	1.79	3.49
1982	28.06	50.63	6.00	10.83	6.33	11.42	6.15	11.10	4.96	8.95	1.68	3.03
1983	31.84	53.82	6.65	11.24	7.16	12.10	6.68	11.29	4.21	7.12	1.89	3.19
1984	35.55	57.18	7.29	11.73	7.88	12.68	6.84	11.00	4.50	7.24	1.94	3.12
1985	38.21	58.54	8.17	12.52	8.50	13.02	7.72	11.83	5.08	7.78	2.22	3.40
1986	41.68	60.72	9.39	13.68	9.13	13.30	8.44	12.30	5.83	8.49	2.45	3.57
1987	43.51	61.04	9.84	13.80	9.84	13.80	9.22	12.93	6.31	8.85	2.87	4.03
1988	45.15	60.25	10.23	13.65	10.49	14.00	9.58	12.78	6.79	9.06	3.21	4.28
1989	47.77	60.51	10.95	13.87	11.39	14.43	9.93	12.57	7.50	9.50	3.84	4.86
1990	49.79	59.89	12.41	14.93	11.82	14.22	9.90	11.91	7.89	9.49	4.92	5.92
1991	53.92	61.74	13.45	15.40	11.11	12.72	9.68	11.08	8.81	10.08	4.93	5.65
1992	54.91	60.24	14.29	15.67	11.57	12.69	10.24	11.23	9.32	10.23	5.05	5.54
1993	56.29	59.60	15.40	16.30	12.47	13.20	10.83	11.46	9.57	10.13	5.44	5.76
1994	60.21	61.90	16.61	17.08	11.71	12.04	11.53	11.85	9.68	9.96	6.05	6.22
1995	63.45	63.45	17.94	17.94	11.70	11.70	12.59	12.59	9.96	9.96	7.10	7.10

Source: Giving USA, represented in *Chronicle of Philanthropy*, May 30, 1996, p. 29.

Partnering with Other Arts Organizations. There are substantial crossover opportunities among audiences that attend jazz, theater, and dance performances. Arts marketers can put together special subscription packages combining art forms. Researchers have found that joint subscriptions and box office collaboration create economies of scale while acquiring new patrons that more than offset any loss to another organization.

- **Cutting Costs to Improve Quality.** Organizations also can achieve economies of scale by combining administrative functions, production expenses, marketing, dealing with boards, and raising money. Instead of having multiple directors and offices for small organizations, staff and physical administrative space can be combined.
- **Collaborating with Nonprofits Outside the Arts.** Scheff and Kotler point to the example of the Saint Louis Symphony Orchestra that developed a community partnership with neighborhood African American churches. This collaboration, called In Unison, gives free membership to the churches and their congregations if participating congregations agree to purchase 20 or more tickets at a 50 percent discount to six of the nine concerts in the package of concerts.
- **Collaborating with Businesses.** Although corporate budgets for the arts are shrinking overall, arts organizations can solicit noncash contributions in the form of management expertise, volunteers, technology such as computer software, and other products. In return, businesses demonstrate good citizenship and community goodwill. Companies also receive market exposure when arts organizations use their logos on mailings and other items. The authors point to the collaboration between EDS Corporation and the Detroit Symphony Orchestra (DSO). When the DSO toured Europe, the conductor and staff members carried portable computer notebooks bearing EDS logos.
- **Collaborating with Multiple Organizations.** Organizations that band together can carry out projects they could not support individually. For example, six Chicago-based foundations banded together to build a Music and Dance Theater for a dozen performing arts groups.
- **Sharing Contributions to Increase the Pie.** In 1992, David Packard, the chairman of Hewlett-Packard, helped organize a fund made up of 10 large arts organizations and a consortium of smaller ones. This fund earmarked 15 percent of the money for paying off deficits and 73 percent for endowments. The remaining 12 percent went to a venture fund to support new activities through one-year interest-free loans. Each organization raised more money than it would have raised alone and "the project's strategy of meeting all the financial needs of the organizations and of supporting the arts

community as a whole has created a focus on investing in the stability and future of the arts community."
- **Tie-In Promotions.** Arts groups can benefit from collaborating with local restaurants, parking garages, and museum shops.

Forging Viable Partnerships. Success depends on the following:

- **Setting Goals.** The initiating organization should decide on primary long-term objectives such as targeting new audiences, reducing overhead, and developing a capital drive. Goals should be set for each participating organization as well as the whole collaboration.
- **Building Consensus.** Organizations should develop consensus and agree on whether that means a unanimous vote or a majority vote.
- **Building Trust.** Scheff and Kotler say trust is the single most important factor for success and is the key to consensus building and effective communication.
- **Communicating.** Regular meetings and frequent communication among member organizations helps build and keep trusting relationships. Good communication with outside constituents such as the community at large also is critical.
- **Designing Leadership and Involvement Structures.** The alliance should be a partnership of equal and supportive members with clearly designed leadership roles.
- **Committing Adequate Resources.** Partnerships must commit enough money to administrative functions because collaborations require a tremendous amount of time and energy.[33]

Individual Charitable Giving

Private foundations and charities usually are funded by a single individual or family. Many of the foundations that are public today were started as private foundations by people with a net worth of less than $1 million. These foundations are nonoperating. That means they do not do their own research or provide services directly; rather, they give money to other charities of the founder's choice. About 30,000 private foundations in the United States support many different causes and activities.

Some people endow foundations for taxation purposes. Legally, a taxable estate is reduced by the endowment of the foundation. An individual who endows a foundation also receives a current income tax deduction of up to 30 percent of adjusted gross income. The law stipulates that one must disburse at least 5 percent of the foundation's total assets each year. The only tax burden on the foundation itself is a 1 to 2 percent excise tax.

---

[33] Ibid.

Anyone who wants to undertake such an endeavor should hire a good lawyer and an experienced accountant. The founder will need their help in drafting the articles and filing with the Internal Revenue Service (IRS). The IRS applies multiple tests to ensure that the foundation does not qualify as a public foundation. The lawyer and the accountant also can help establish the required trust agreements.[34]

Historically most personal foundations have chosen to support noncontroversial causes. They subsidize medical research, higher education, and secular good works of religious groups. A few (usually the largest) have made some important new contributions to the philanthropic movement. The Ford Foundation donated the seed money for the Public Broadcasting System and both the Rockefeller and Ford foundations were significant contributors to environmental causes.

The Henry M. Jackson Foundation of Seattle funded a case study of land-use conflicts in the Pacific Northwest and gave Grantmaker Forum on Community and National Service $15,000 to establish itself as a national clearinghouse and convener of regional meetings for grant makers involved in community and national service.

The Charles Stewart Mott Foundation gave $32,500 to promote ethnic reconciliation between the Muslim and Croat populations and others in Bosnia; $22,350 to carry out a six-month assessment of the Ukraine's political, economic, and foreign and security policy. This same foundation also gave $25,000 to promote public participation in trade negotiations in the Western Hemisphere, particularly as they pertained to pollution prevention; $20,000 to the Congress of National Black Churches for a national conference on black philanthropy; and $100,000 to the Center on Fathers, Families, and Public Policy to examine the legal and social services available to low-income noncustodial fathers who have never married.[35]

Sharon L. Monsky decided to establish a foundation to find a cure for her own illness, scleroderma, which primarily affects women of childbearing age. The cause is largely unknown, and the genetic link, while present, is not fully understood. At the time Monsky began the foundation, there was no cure, no treatment, and very little research under way.

Monsky formed the Scleroderma Research Foundation in the mid-1980s. By 1990, the foundation had raised $750,000 from companies such as Apple Computer, American Airlines, and Gap, Inc. From her experience, Monsky developed some helpful rules:

- Keep your goals short range and attainable.
- Create a board that includes people with business contacts.
- Enlist celebrities whenever possible.

---

[34] J. Warner, "Foundations: They're Not Just for Rockefellers," *Business Week,* April 13, 1992, p. 103.

[35] "Giving," *Chronicle of Philanthropy,* November 29, 1996, p. 21.

- Hire a good, competent office staff.
- Ask for help; don't try to do everything by yourself.

Monsky applied these rules so successfully that she was able to attract volunteers and create a lobbying strategy to increase federal research. By all reports, she achieved far more than anyone could have expected in creating awareness of the affliction and developing research for its treatment and cure.[36]

The Margus family of Boca Raton, Florida, created a charity called the A-T Children's Project. Two of Brad and Vicki Margus's four sons had ataxia-telangiectasia. Their charity raised nearly $2 million to find a cure for the rare degenerative brain disease. The Margus's strategy was to pursue the most prominent scientist in the field, focus on research, keep costs low, and get families whose children have the disease active in raising money. The A-T Children's Project organized a worldwide symposium for scientists to share the latest information and to award research grants.

Most rare-disease charities are not as successful. The National Association for Rare Disorders is a federation of 136 nonprofit groups to raise money for rare or obscure diseases. A disease is considered rare if it affects fewer than 200,000 people in the United States. The organization notes that few, if any, small rare disease groups receive money from the government, large foundations, or United Ways. Generally, the money from those sources goes to diseases that affect large numbers of people. In 1996, for example, the government spent $117 million to find a cure for lung cancer. The small charities cannot even afford the $3,000 annual fee to join the Combined Health Appeal that raises money through on-the-job drives. Most rare disease charities raise less than $500,000 a year.[37]

Some private charities and foundations are not successful and do not fulfill the expectations of the founder. Michael Jordan of the Chicago Bulls basketball team set up Heal L.A. in 1993 as a charitable foundation that would provide mentoring and antidrug programs for children. In March 1996, Jordan announced that he was closing it down. What happened? Michael Jordan's personal fortune from his Bulls contract and personal endorsements was estimated at $200 million in 1996. Because his name was associated with success and winning, there was a general expectation that the foundation would thrive.

Jordan was very involved with some of the charity's activities. He helped design its Education Club that focused on helping fifth and sixth graders to do better in school and help their communities. Teachers across the country nominated students for the program and monitored their progress for two months. The foundation selected 50 students to spend a day with Michael Jordan. The foundation also held several black-tie events and a golf tournament to raise money.

---

[36] M. Lev, "Success Comes to a Start-Up Charity," *New York Times*, November 6, 1990, p. D5.

[37] D. Marchetti, "Fighting Little-Known Diseases," *Chronicle of Philanthropy,* April 4, 1996.

The foundation had its critics. In 1995, an NBC-owned television station in Chicago accused the Jordan foundation of directing only 33 percent of revenues to charitable causes. According to the National Charities Information Bureau, a watchdog group, 60 percent is considered a minimum for reputable charities and the average is 75 percent. An examination of the charity's tax returns listed only $219,000 as program services expenses. This figure was equal to one-third of the foundation's total revenue for the year. The foundation was unwilling to disclose how the money was used. The National Charities Information Bureau asserted it was unusual for foundations to have more than one paid staff member on their boards. The Jordan foundation had two staff members on its eight-person board, one of whom was Michael's sister Roslyn.

Finally, documents showed that Jordan had given only $9,420 between 1993 and 1995. His corporate sponsors such as Quaker Oats and Gatorade-had contributed more than $1 million and the Chicago Bulls had donated more than $200,000. Despite the allegations, there was no evidence of deliberate wrongdoing. In announcing the disbanding of the charity, Jordan alluded to the high administrative costs and his disappointment in meeting his goals. John Edie of the Council on Foundations commented, "If you are a multimillion-dollar star and you want to do something to give back to the community, there are a lot of options." Edie suggested giving to local community trusts that funnel the money to local charities and provide oversight. Early in 1996, Jordan wrote a check for $2 million to the James Jordan Club (named after his murdered father) which is a local branch of the Boys and Girls Clubs of America. He said, "Every dollar we give will go directly to help others, undiluted by administrative costs that come with running a foundation."[38]

Corporate and Large Foundations

The creation of corporate and other nonprivate foundations has been one of the most dramatic developments in corporate giving. Of the estimated 1,500 corporate foundations in 1980, 1,095 were created between 1950 and 1961.[39] Some of the Fortune 500's largest industrial firms now have foundations.

There were two reasons for the rapid growth of corporate foundations. First, excess-profits taxes instituted during World War II and the Korean War led companies to seek to reduce taxes. By contributing to a corporate founda-

---

[38] P. D. Samuels, "Celebrity Foundations in Glare of the Spotlight," *New York Times*, March 31, 1996, p. F10.

[39] F. E. Andrews, "Introduction," *The Foundation Directory*, 3rd. ed. (New York: Russell Sage Foundation, 1967), p. 29.

tion, a firm could reduce its taxes even if the foundation gave little of the money away. Because too many foundations were simply accumulating dollars, the law was changed, and foundations were required to pay out annually the equivalent of 5 percent or more of their assets.[40]

Second, according to legal scholar Marion R. Fremont-Smith, the advantages of a foundation were "stability of giving despite instability in company earnings; better planning, particularly with regard to long-term commitments; and greater efficiency through centralized administration and more independent review of solicitations, including isolation of company officers from customer pressure."[41]

In 1985, as stock prices rose, the nation's 2,400 foundations gave record amounts. By 1987, foundation giving had reached an all-time high with contributions of $6.38 billion, an 8.1 percent increase over the previous year.[42] Despite this increase, however, foundations accounted for only 6.9 percent of total giving in 1988.

In 1984, Congress enacted a law of 10 years' duration that gave a generous tax deduction to foundation donors who gave stock. The law, which ran until December 1994, was not extended. Why did Congress decide to put a time limit on the tax break for stocks? The Treasury Department did not like the provision because it believed that there were abuses of private foundations and that the money did not get into the hands of charities. The Congressional Joint Tax Committee estimated that keeping the full deduction in place cost the government about $280 million in lost tax revenue over five years.[43]

In the period leading up to the December 31 deadline, wealthy people rushed to make contributions. Highly appreciated stock was one of the most common types of assets donors used to set up private foundations. Until that date, donors could deduct the current full market value of appreciated stock. The full market value was worth a great deal. For every $100,000 of appreciated stock given to a charity or foundation, most donors could avoid about $45,000 in tax payments. On January 1, 1995, they would be allowed to deduct only the amount they originally paid for publicly traded stock. Financial advisers to the wealthy urged their clients to take advantage of the full deduction before the end of the year.

A new kind of foundation emerged in the aftermath of the 1994 election. Conservative foundations stepped up their push for fundamental changes in the government. With increased visibility and public recognition, the foundations concerned themselves with how best to capitalize on their ideas about

---

[40] K. Teltsch, "Charity Donations Set a Record in '85," *New York Times,* May 7, 1986, p. C13.

[41] M. R. Fremont-Smith, *Philanthropy and the Business Corporation* (New York: Russell Sage Foundation, 1972), p. 69.

[42] K. Teltsch, "Increase in Charitable Donations in '87 Was Lowest in 12 Years," *New York Times,* May 26, 1988, p. 18.

[43] J. Murawski, "A Rush to Donate to Foundation," *Chronicle of Philanthropy,* November 1, 1994, p. 7.

welfare reform, health care, crime, and education. The executive director of the JM Foundation in New York suggested this was the time to cut the size of government. His foundation made grants of $300,000 to research centers that focused on state policy issues. He noted that "the state centers have played a tremendous role in questioning what the role of government should be and then in promoting more private-sector responses to public problems."

Newt Gingrich tapped Robert L. Woodson, Sr., to assemble a team of Washington-based nonprofits to advise Congress about cutting spending on federal poverty programs and at the same time helping more poor people become economically self-sufficient. Woodson selected 28 activists representing community efforts to build and renovate housing, nurture small businesses, work with abused children and gangs, and deal with substance abuse. Many of these activists espoused the view that foundations should identify and support similar organizations nationwide rather than impose models of organizations that relied heavily on government support.[44]

Much conservative energy was dedicated to ending federal support for the National Endowment for the Arts and National Endowment for the Humanities. At a House Appropriations subcommittee hearing, in January 1995, conservative critics attacked the federal agencies as intellectually corrupt and against mainstream American values. William J. Bennett, former secretary of education; Lynne V. Cheney, former head of the National Endowment for the Humanities; and Edwin J. Delattre, dean of the School of Education at Boston University urged Congress to withdraw all funds from the endowments. In 1995, the government allocated $167.4 million to the arts endowment and $177.5 million to the humanities.

Conservative critics testified that their funding should be left entirely to private sponsors. Ms. Cheney said the agencies subsidized many works that made political statements "rather than revealing truth or revealing beauty." William Bennett said the two agencies corrupted the arts and humanities, causing them "to deteriorate or decline from accepted standards." He said these agencies subsidized people who seemed less interested in creating art or fostering knowledge than in "ridiculing and antagonizing mainstream American values." Although he had supported the endowments in the past, Bennett said he now found the agencies too corrupt to be saved.[45]

In July 1995, the House voted to eliminate the National Endowment for the Arts for two years and to eliminate the National Endowment for the Humanities in 1998. The action then moved to the Senate for more debate.[46]

---

[44] S. G. Greene and J. Moore, "Conservative Foundations on the Move," *Chronicle of Philanthropy,* February 23, 1995, p. 1.

[45] R. Pear, "Actor Urges House Panel to Spare Money for the Arts," *New York Times,* January 25, 1995, p. A15.

[46] J. Gray, "House Accord Would Kill Arts Endowment by 1997," *New York Times,* July 14, 1995, p. A21

In August the Senate refused to go along and voted to increase the endowments for the two agencies by $11 million each. The Senate measure instituted strict provisions on how the money was to be spent and barred financing of any project considered obscene or pornographic or denigrating religion. Even with these increases, the agencies faced significant cuts from current budgets.[47]

Conservative groups and foundations continued to gain influence in Congress throughout 1995. The newer groups such as the Competitive Enterprise Institute and the New Citizen Project were much more assertive than older groups like the Heritage Foundation. The National Center for Policy Analysis promoted private alternatives to government programs. It pushed a plan to give tax credits to people who contributed to local social-service organizations. The Center for Effective Compassion tried to encourage policies that favored faith-based charities. The Capital Research Group published books and articles questioning the way philanthropy works. It decided that groups such as the American Cancer Society, the National Audubon Society, and the Council for Advancement and Support of Education were too liberal to merit corporate support. The New Citizenship Project focused on challenging President Clinton's national service plan and lobbied to eliminate AmeriCorps.[48]

The 1996 election that returned a Republican Congress and a Democratic President promised more of the same. Conservative and liberal groups vied for the donor dollar, each side promising to reflect basic American values. Those involved with the allocation of funds were unclear about which side, if either, would prevail.

How Is Your Money Spent?

As noted in the United Way case, William Aramony used donations to support his lavish lifestyle. Many charities use most of the money they receive to raise even more money. Few Americans know what proportion of their charitable donations is allocated to the cause, how much is used for administration, and how much is used to raise still more money. In fact, charities vary considerably in what they spend on each activity. Until recently, most Americans have been rather indifferent toward the way their charitable contributions have been spent. Some charities have been able to spend huge amounts on administrative costs without being held to account. Occasionally, this indifference can have catastrophic effects.

---

[47] J. Gray, "Senate Increases Arts Money, but Also Imposes Strict Limits," *New York Times,* August 10, 1995, p. B6.
[48] V. Stehle, "Conservative Centers Set Agenda on Charities," *Chronicle of Philanthropy,* September 21, 1995, p. 1.

Case: The Foundation for New Era Philanthropy

In 1982, John G. Bennett, Jr., founded a Philadelphia-based consulting firm he called the Center for New Era Philanthropy. The center provided management training and help to hundreds of nonprofit groups in the United States and Europe. In 1989, Bennett began the Foundation for New Era Philanthropies (New Era). Although called a foundation, it did not meet the accepted definition of a foundation as an endowed organization that invests its earnings to make gifts.

New Era focused on giving free technical advice to nonprofits on how to better manage their assets and qualify for more gifts. Bennett was well respected and admired in the nonprofit community. His seminars were well attended and he quickly rose through Philadelphia's philanthropic circles. He was invited to join the boards of organizations such as the Philadelphia Orchestra gifts committee and the One-to-One Partnership Foundation, a youth mentoring program.

In 1992, Bennett embarked on a new program he called the New Concepts in Philanthropy Fund. The Seminary of the East, a Baptist organization, was one of the first to get involved in this scheme. Glenn Blossom, the founder of the seminary, learned from an acquaintance that a charity called New Era had been approached by a wealthy philanthropist. This philanthropist, who remained unnamed, was willing to give money to match as much as $75,000 for worthy causes such as Blossom's seminary. The acquaintance introduced Blossom to Bennett who explained the offer. Bennett told Blossom that he would have the opportunity of finding donors willing to send New Era checks for at least $25,000 to participate in the match. New Era would keep the money for six months. After six months, the philanthropist would match the money and it would all be given to the seminary.

Within two weeks, Blossom raised $500,000 from donors attracted by the promise of matching funds. Six months later, the matching funds came through and Blossom's seminary received the entire amount promised. Blossom, delighted with the outcome, began to contact other church groups and individuals, urging them to participate. By April 1993, dollars were flowing into New Era and circulating through the seminary and Blossom's church. Blossom and the seminary's president, Russell Rosser, suggested that groups they introduced to New Era give thank offerings of 5 percent.

Several other consultants also solicited funds for New Era. Every six months, as promised, New Era doubled the participants' money. No one but Bennett knew who was matching the money. Bennett continued to seek clients in religious organizations. These nonprofits, which rarely qualified for secular foundation grants, were delighted to get involved with New Era's matching program. Robert Andriga, president of the 90-member Coalition for Christian Colleges and Universities said of the program, "It's almost a gift from heaven, in a religious sense."[49]

By mid-1993, museums, universities, and major organizations were interested. Bennett's good reputation and New Era's unique matching component attracted organizations as prestigious as the Academy of Natural Sciences in Philadelphia, the University of Pennsylvania, and the Philadelphia Public Library. Bennett told individual philanthropists they could double their contributions to worthy causes as beneficiary donors. Only Bennett knew the identities of the anonymous donors; eventually, 150 people became beneficiary donors.

Although some auditors and a few nonprofit board members urged caution, supporters pointed out that New Era had never failed to double the money. They persisted in their support even though tax records were incomplete.

Although New Era was incorporated in October 1989, it did not file any tax returns until February 1993. Moreover, New Era never received Internal Revenue Service permission to file late. Some began to ask why participants had to deposit money with New Era for six months before it doubled. They also wondered why the money was in a standard brokerage account that New Era could access instead of an escrow account.

Tony Carnes, vice president of the International Research Institute on Values Changes, a nonprofit

---

[49] S. Stecklow, "How New Era's Boss Led Rich and Gullible into a Web of Deceit," *The Wall Street Journal*, May 19, 1995, p. A1.

research group in New York state, was skeptical about New Era's dealings from the beginning. In July 1993, on behalf of his group, Carnes wrote to the office of Pennsylvania's attorney general suggesting the office examine New Era. In his letter he said, "We certainly hope that the foundation turns out to be legitimate, but we also want the public, particularly the compassionate people entrusting their money to New Era, protected."[50]

Pennsylvania officials said there was no law to prevent a pyramid or Ponzi scheme. State officials asked Bennett to meet with them and informed him that New Era had to register with the state's charity board. Shortly thereafter, Bennett informed groups they would deal directly with New Era, not with the church or seminary. According to a New Era document, participants had to be sponsored by a beneficial donor. Each group would have to undergo an extensive organization assessment to determine how much money would be offered in a match.

The groups' officials, including its person in charge of financial affairs would have to meet with Bennett at New Era offices. The fund-raising range of opportunity for matches would be between $50,000 and $500,000 in even $50,000 increments. If an organization failed to provide the full amount, it would be excluded. The document informed potential participants that the anonymous donors insisted on the six-month period, not New Era. Despite these stipulations, $100 million flowed into New Era in 1994 and Bennett asserted 1995 would bring $150 million.[51]

On May 15, 1995, New Era filed for bankruptcy. The court filing stated that New Era had estimated assets of $80 million but owed $551 million to groups and individuals. The victims included wealthy philanthropists such as John C. Whitehead, a former co-chairman of Goldman, Sachs & Co.; Laurance S. Rockefeller, and Vivian Weyerhaeuser Piasecki, a member of the paper company family and a University of Pennsylvania trustee.

In fact, it was very difficult to find out what New Era owed. Lawyers for New Era reported Bennett did not seem to understand his own financial condition. They said that New Era had received "in excess of $400 million" from donors but that claims exceeded that amount.[52]

Why did respectable charities get involved with New Era? The Nature Conservancy, a large and highly respected charity thought it had done its homework. One of the conservancy's largest donors made a $15,000 donation to its Latin American and Caribbean program through New Era. According to the Nature Conservancy's president and CEO, the donor urged Bennett to meet with conservancy officials to discuss the possibility of additional gifts from New Era. From the beginning of 1992 to October 1994, the conservancy said it received $140,000 from New Era. In mid-1994, New Era told the conservancy about matching funds through the New Concepts in Philanthropy Fund. New Era offered the conservancy the opportunity to match $3 million, up to $1 million a year in 1994 through 1996. New Era's insistence on holding the money for six months caused some consternation among the organization's officers. They visited New Era's headquarters outside of Philadelphia, checked references, obtained New Era's tax filings, and spoke to members of Prudential Securities that handled most of New Era's funds. New Era explained that it held the money for six months because the interest was used for operating expenses. Even though its concerns were addressed, the conservancy insisted its funds be placed in a segregated account rather than being commingled with most of New Era's other money. Eventually New Era agreed to segregate the money and the conservancy's executive board authorized a $1 million investment in New Era. Individual donors and family foundations agreed to pass the money to New Era. The $1 million with its matching payment was supposed to have been repaid in December 1995. Instead, the conservancy's segregated account was turned over to a bankruptcy trustee along with the other funds and it was unclear when, if ever, it would be returned. Despite the conservancy's diligence, the organization stood to lose $2 million.[53]

Why are charities susceptible to scams? Very often, managers are inexperienced in commercial dealings and are motivated by altruism. Usually, they do not have skeptical and experienced outside board members or strict audit standards. Even more

---

[50] Ibid., p. A8.

[51] Ibid.

[52] S. Stecklow, "Crumbling Pyramid," *The Wall Street Journal,* May 15, 1995, p. A1.

[53] G. B. Knecht, "How the Nature Conservancy Fell into New Era's Trap," *The Wall Street Journal,* May 31, 1995, p. B1.

important, they are constantly pressured for money. Although most states regulate charities, none has the staff to examine all the nonprofits that register with them. Experts on charities agree that donors often cannot get sufficient information to make sure their money is used as they wish.

The National Center for Nonprofit Boards asked 1,200 charity chief executives to cite the weaknesses of their governing bodies. The officers mentioned that boards rarely participated in fund-raising. The question arises, therefore, whether the institutions' professional fund-raisers were reluctant to question recommendations that came from trusted board members or donors. As the Nature Conservancy example shows, a major donor initiated the relationship.[54]

Many donors assume that state and federal regulators will help find charity wrongdoing. State regulators complain that the Internal Revenue Service (IRS) does not give them enough help in curbing abuses. The IRS says it does not have enough employees to thoroughly check out applications from groups wanting tax exemptions; neither does the IRS keep a close eye on charity tax returns. The IRS claims that if the public wants better oversight it should be willing to pay for more inspectors and audits. A federal law prevents the IRS from giving out too much information about its investigations of people or organizations. Some charity activists assert the IRS needs to do more audits and check out groups that apply for charity status. They note that Congress can grant the IRS the power to levy penalties on charities and nonprofits that break the law. At present the only way the IRS can punish a nonprofit is to take away its tax exemption—a step it rarely takes.[55]

In June 1995, Arlin M. Adams, a retired judge, was appointed bankruptcy trustee for New Era. He was given the task of sorting out the charity's financial affairs and persuading New Era creditors and grant recipients to pay back the money they received.[56]

In November 1995, John Bennett made his fiirst comments since bankruptcy. In a videotape, Bennett told contributors he took full responsibility for the collapse but did not mention any of the anonymous donors who supposedly kept the program going. In January 1996, he agreed to turn over $1.2 million in property, cash, and securities to Judge Adams. The anonymous donors never existed; Bennett used the money he received from new donors to pay existing beneficiary donors, many of whom were wealthy and influential. He then capitalized on the prestige of these individuals to attract others.

In October 1996, a federal grand jury indicted Bennett on 82 counts including charges of mail fraud, money laundering, and filing false tax returns. If convicted he could face more than 900 years in jail and a $28 million fine. Bennett's lawyers claimed he was legally insane when he ran New Era and claimed injuries suffered in a 1984 automobile accident were responsible for his behavior.[57]

The New Era scandal profoundly affected the trust wealthy donors had in charities. A poll of 292 people who gave at least $10,000 to charity in 1995 discovered that the scandals had made almost 99 percent of them "highly skeptical of claims made by fund-raisers and nonprofit executives." Nearly 70 percent said they increased their reliance on professional advisers such as lawyers and accountants to help them select the charities.

---

[54] N. R. Axelrod, "Why Charities Were Vulnerable to New Era Scheme, *Chronicle of Philanthropy,* June 15, 1995, p. 42.

[55] E. Greene and G. Williams, "Asleep on the Watch," *Chronicle of Philanthropy,* July 27, 1995, p. 1.

[56] S. Stecklow, "Retired Judge Will Sort Out New Era Mess," *The Wall Street Journal,* June 29, 1995, p. B1.

[57] "Federal Grand Jury Indicts Founder of New Era Philanthropy Fund," *Chronicle of Philanthropy,* October 17, 1996, p. 33.

[58] A. L. Cowan, "The Gadfly Who Audits Philanthropy," *New York Times,* October 7, 1990, p. F9.

NCIB

Prospective donors can find out where their money goes by contacting the National Charities Information Bureau (NCIB) in New York City. Founded in 1918, the bureau initially helped the public assess the effectiveness of World War I relief organizations. Over the years it evolved into a rating and standard-setting agency for the nonprofit sector. The bureau generates about

300 reports on 400 agencies each year. Many of the individuals, corporations, and foundations that use the bureau's research reports also contribute to its annual operating budget. A vice president for the American Cancer

---

EXHIBIT 10-4   NCIB Home Page

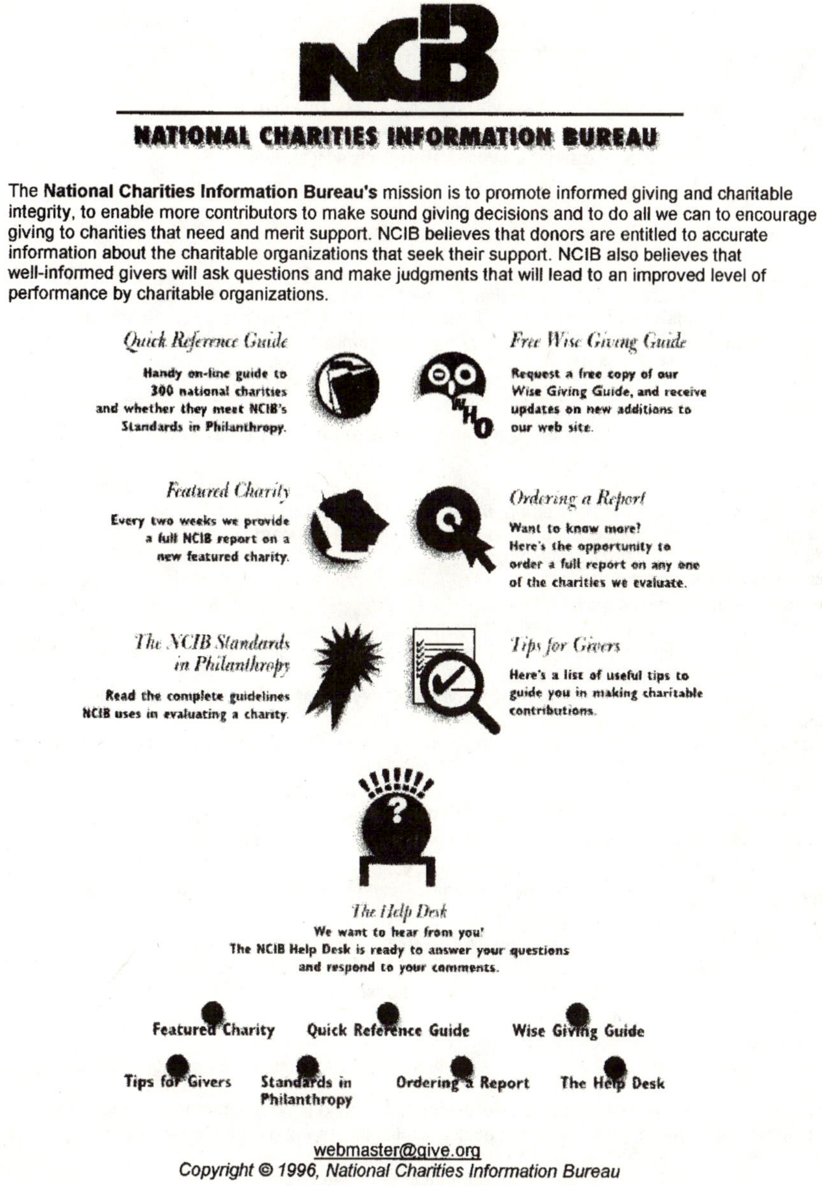

NATIONAL CHARITIES INFORMATION BUREAU

The **National Charities Information Bureau's** mission is to promote informed giving and charitable integrity, to enable more contributors to make sound giving decisions and to do all we can to encourage giving to charities that need and merit support. NCIB believes that donors are entitled to accurate information about the charitable organizations that seek their support. NCIB also believes that well-informed givers will ask questions and make judgments that will lead to an improved level of performance by charitable organizations.

Quick Reference Guide
Handy on-line guide to 300 national charities and whether they meet NCIB's Standards in Philanthropy.

Free Wise Giving Guide
Request a free copy of our Wise Giving Guide, and receive updates on new additions to our web site.

Featured Charity
Every two weeks we provide a full NCIB report on a new featured charity.

Ordering a Report
Want to know more? Here's the opportunity to order a full report on any one of the charities we evaluate.

The NCIB Standards in Philanthropy
Read the complete guidelines NCIB uses in evaluating a charity.

Tips for Givers
Here's a list of useful tips to guide you in making charitable contributions.

The Help Desk
We want to hear from you! The NCIB Help Desk is ready to answer your questions and respond to your comments.

Featured Charity   Quick Reference Guide   Wise Giving Guide
Tips for Givers   Standards in Philanthropy   Ordering a Report   The Help Desk

webmaster@give.org
Copyright © 1996, National Charities Information Bureau

Society, commenting on the work of the NCIB, observed "They're sort of a self-appointed watchdog organization that charities allow themselves to be regulated by."[58] The site gives a variety of options from which to choose

---

EXHIBIT 10–5   NCIB Home Page

NCIB Standards in Philanthropy

NCIB evaluates national charities according to the nine basic standards and informs contributors through evaluative reports (see Featured Charity for a sample) about individual agencies.

NCIB does not advise whether to give to any particular charity. Contributors are encouraged to familiarize themselves with NCIB Standards, and then decide for themselves the importance of an organization's compliance with or variation from those Standards. The information and analysis published by the NCIB is furnished to assist contributors in making informed decisions and is not intended to endorse or disparage the organization.

Governance, Policy and Program Fundamentals

1. Board Governance
The board is responsible for policy setting, fiscal guidance, and ongoing governance, and should regularly review the organization's policies, programs and operations. The board should have
a. an independent, volunteer membership;
b. a minimum of 5 voting members;
c. an individual attendance policy;
d. specific terms of office for its officers and members;
e. in-person, face-to-face meetings, at least twice a year, evenly spaced, with a majority of voting members in attendance at each meeting;
f. no fees to members for board service, but payments may be made for costs incurred as a result of board participation;
g. no more than one paid staff person member, usually the chief staff officer, who shall not chair the board or serve as treasurer;
h. policy guidelines to avoid material conflicts of interest involving board or staff;
i. no material conflicts of interest involving board or staff;
j. a policy promoting pluralism and diversity within the organization's board, staff, and constituencies.

2. Purpose:
The organization's purpose, approved by the board, should be formally and specifically stated.

3. Programs:
The organization's activities should be consistent with its statement of purpose.

4. Information:
Promotion, fundraising, and public information should describe accurately the organization's identity, purpose, programs, and financial needs.

5. Financial Support and Related Activities:
The board is accountable for all authorized activities generating financial support on the organization's behalf:
a. fund-raising practices should encourage voluntary giving and should not apply unwarranted pressure;
b. descriptive and financial information for all substantial income and for all revenue-generating activities conducted by the organization should be disclosed on request;
c. basic descriptive and financial information for income derived from authorized commercial activities, involving the organization's name, which are conducted by for-profit organizations, should be available. All public promotion of such commercial activity should either include this information or indicate that it is available from the organization.

6. Use of Funds:
The organization's use of funds should reflect consideration of current and future needs and resources in planning for program continuity. The organization should:
   a. spend at least 60% of annual expenses for program activities;
   b. insure that fund-raising expenses, in relation to fund-raising results, are reasonable over time;
   c. have net assets available for the following fiscal year not usually more than twice the current year's expenses or the next year's budget, whichever is higher;
   d. not have a persistent and/or increasing deficit in unrestricted net assets.

Reporting and Fiscal Fundamentals

7. Annual Reporting: An annual report should be available on request, and should include
   a. an explicit narrative description of the organization's major activities, presented in the same major categories and covering the same fiscal period as the audited financial statements;
   b. a list of board members;
   c. audited financial statements or, at a minimum, a comprehensive financial summary that 1) identifies all revenues in significant categories, 2) reports expenses in the same program, management/general, and fund-raising categories as in the audited financial statements, and 3) reports all ending balances. (When the annual report does not include the full audited financial statements, it should indicate that they are available on request.)

8. Accountability:
An organization should supply on request complete financial statements which
   a. are prepared in conformity with generally accepted accounting principles (GAAP), accompanied by a report of an independent certified public accountant, and reviewed by the board; and
   b. fully disclose economic resources and obligations, including transactions with related parties and affiliated organizations, significant events affecting finances, and significant categories of income and expense; and should also supply
   c. a statement of functional allocation of expenses, in addition to such statements required by generally accepted accounting principles to be included among the financial statements;
   d. combined financial statements for a national organization operating with affiliates prepared in the foregoing manner.

9. Budget:
The organization should prepare a detailed annual budget consistent with the major classifications in the audited financial statements, and approved by the board.

- Featured Charity
- Quick Reference Guide
- Wise Giving Guide
- Tips for Givers
- Ordering a Report
- The Help Desk
- HOME

webmaster@give.org
Copyright © 1996, National Charities Information Bureau

including a quick reference guide to 300 national charities. It features a new charity every two weeks and tells home page visitors which charities give most of their money directly to the causes they represent. See Exhibit 10–4. The NCIB Standards for Philanthropy also can be accessed through the home page. Exhibit 10–5 outlines the governance, policy, and program fundamentals of the organizations.

The Internet is an excellent medium for nonprofits. Exhibit 10–6 has a list of web sites for corporate and private donors and grant seekers. The Foundation Center site gives information on the fund-raising process. It tells how to write a proposal, has a glossary of philanthropic terms, and online grant application forms. The Council on Foundations has information on how to begin a foundation. The Philanthropy Journal Online provides an index of nonprofits with a list of hypertext links to the Web sites of nonprofit organizations.

Exhibit 10–6

"WHERE TO GO"

- PRILANTHROPY JOURNAL ONLINE
  http://www.philanthropy-journal.org/
- GIVE FIVES VOLUNTEERING LINKS
  http://www.Indepsec.org/give5/g5volunteer.html
- DAVID LAMB'S PROSPECT RESEARCH PAGE
  http://weber.u.washington.edu/-dlamb/research.html
- INTERNET NONPROFIT CENTER'S NONPROFIT LOCATOR
  http://www.nonprofits.org/library/gov/irs/search_irs shtml
- BETTER BUSINESS BUREAU.
  http://www.bbb.org/^1689971598/council/about/pas.html
- FOUNDATION CENTER. http://www.fdncenter.org/
- INTERNET PROSPECTOR. http://plains.uwyo.edu/~prospect/
- NATIONAL CHARITIES INFORMATION BUREAU. http://www.give.org/
- COUNCIL ON FOUNDATIONS. http://www.cof.org/
- SALVATION ARMY. http://www.salvationarmy.org/
- AMERICAN RED CROSS. http://www.redcross.org/
- FORD FOUNDATION. http://www.fordfound.org
- OPERATION SMILE, http://www.operationsmile.org/
- CITY HARVEST, http://www.riverhope.org/cityharv/
- NATIONAL BLACK UNITED FRONT. http://www.nbuf.org/
- INTERNAL REVENUE SERVICE. http://www.irs.ustress.gov/
- AMERICAN LUNG ASSOCIATIONS CHRISTMAS SEALS.
  http://christmasseals.org

Source: New York Times, December 2, 1996, p. D4.

The Strategic Marketing Approach to Corporate Giving: Doing Well by Doing Good

Cause-Related Marketing

P. Rajan Varadarajan and Anil Menon generalize the strategic marketing approach to marketing social issues.[59] *Cause-related marketing* (CRM) is a marketing program that links charitable contributions to the firm's products and/or services. The authors note that for many years companies have tried to enhance their corporate images by publicly supporting worthy causes. Firms use CRM to achieve a variety of objectives, including to

- Gain national visibility.
- Promote corporate image.

---

[59] P. R. P. Varadarajan and A. Menon, "Cause-Related Marketing: A Coalignment of Marketing Strategy and Corporate Philanthropy," *Journal of Marketing* 52, July 1988, pp. 58–74.

- Thwart negative publicity.
- Pacify consumer groups (indirect external stakeholders).
- Generate incremental sales.
- Promote repeat purchases.
- Promote multiple-unit purchases.
- Promote more varied usage.
- Increase brand awareness.
- Increase brand recognition.
- Enhance brand image.
- Broaden customer base.
- Reach new market segments.
- Increase retail activity.

CRM is a strategic management tool because top managers are involved in key decisions about the program, have a long-term commitment to it, and invest substantial resources. To be effective, CRM must evaluate performance based on objective criteria such as profitability, market share, dollar sales volume, and so on. However, Varadarajan and Menon acknowledge that many less quantifiable goals are much harder to measure. CRM, it must be remembered, is a strategy to sell more of the product, not to make philanthropic contributions.[60]

Nevertheless, CRM is a tool managers can use to incorporate philanthropy into the routine workings of the firm and do well by doing good. Beginning in the early 1980s, corporate officers began to look more closely at the strategic implications of their giving programs. Some tried to direct their giving programs into areas that would directly generate business and tie their products to the causes in which they were interested. The strategic focus was particularly important in the marketing function.

Rangan, Karin, and Sandberg examined the efforts of managers in charge of developing marketing strategies for social-change efforts. These efforts included antidrug campaigns, community development programs, or recycling initiatives. When the strategies relied on conventional consumer-goods marketing methods to promote their missions, they were not particularly effective.[61]

Social marketers encountered a variety of obstacles to achieving their goals. In many cases, *the target community opposed the changes being advocated.* The authors pointed to the results of a family-planning campaign in Bangladesh. A massive campaign to curb population growth was disappointing. Most Bangladeshis did not understand the long-term benefits to the country. They saw, instead, that there would be fewer children to support them in their old age because they expected some of their children to die in

---

[60] Ibid.

[61] V. K. Rangan, S. Karim, and S. K. Sandberg, "Do Better at Doing Good," *Harvard Business Review,* May–June 1996, pp. 42–54.

infancy from disease or later from natural catastrophes such as typhoons. In addition, Bangladeshi social custom dictated that the parents of the bride had to present the groom's parents with a cash gift. To balance the cash flow, most parents believed they should have roughly as many daughters as sons. Other Bangladeshis, primarily Muslims, objected to family planning on religious grounds. It was not surprising that the campaign failed.

In other cases, *for the target community, the adoption costs exceeded the tangible benefits.* For example, there is no question that chlorofluorocarbons (CFCs) destroy the ozone layer. If companies stopped producing CFCs, millions of lives would be saved worldwide; however, the cost would be very high for CFC-producing companies. In 1989, it was estimated that the largest dozen companies would have to bear a cost of $500 million each. Without government or other organizations to compensate producers, most companies would find the cost prohibitive. The companies that stopped producing CFCs first would bear the greatest costs since their outlay would put them at a competitive disadvantage.

The authors suggest a framework that encourages social marketers to adopt a cost-benefit analysis in advocating change. *Costs* include time, effort, and any organizational or personal psychological discomfort. *Benefits* include all nonmonetary advantages that individuals or organizations may gain if they adopt the recommended behavior. For example, with a recycling initiative, the community is the primary beneficiary, society as a whole is better off, and individuals are secondary beneficiaries of society's improvement.

It is not easy to make the distinction between primary and secondary beneficiaries because the lines between individual and societal benefits overlap. Nevertheless, the authors say, it is important to make the effort to define beneficiaries as specifically as possible so that the marketing plan will be most persuasive for the particular initiative.[62]

Earlier in the chapter, we pointed to the synergies that occur when arts organizations combine to raise money. Similar synergies are possible when nonprofits develop ties with for-profit corporations in cause-related marketing efforts. A. R. Andreasen notes, however, there are risks in these partnerships. A nonprofit may find itself linked to a company whose goals or business practices are incompatible. The nonprofit may become hostage to an overpriced, superficial campaign. Whenever nonprofits think of themselves as full partners in the cause-marketing campaign, however, they approach the alliances with a clear understanding of bottom-line issues. Nonprofit managers "will assess their organizations' strengths and weaknesses and understand exactly how their organizations can add value to for-profit partners. They will investigate many companies and identify those that stand to gain the most from an alliance. And they will take an active role in shaping a partnership and monitoring its progress at every stage."[63]

---

[62] Ibid., p. 44.
[63] A. R. Andreasen, "Profits for Nonprofits: Find a Corporate Partner," *Harvard Business Review,* November–December 1996, pp. 47–59.

Once the nonprofit has taken a hard look at its own strengths and weaknesses, it should assess its potential corporate partner ethics and the extent to which a cause-related marketing program would complement the corporation's goals and increase its profits. In general, the nonprofit should look for the following in a corporate partner:

- The company's CEO and senior executives are enthusiastic about the partnership and will champion it.
- The company will allocate sufficient funding and people to the alliance.
- The corporation indicates it is willing to maintain the initial cause-related marketing campaign for an extended period of time.
- The corporation is willing to continue the partnership beyond the initial campaign.
- The corporation appears enthusiastic about involving its employees as well as suppliers, dealers, and franchisees in the cause-related marketing program.
- The corporation appears unlikely to place undue restrictions on the nonprofit's activities or otherwise interfere with its operations.

As Andreasen points out, although nonprofit alliances can be difficult to work out, they can have great payoffs for both partners. As he says, "Cause-related marketing is about marketing, but it is also about finding new ways to improve people's lives."[64]

Murray and Montanari propose a model marketing approach to responsive management (MARM), shown in Exhibit 10–7.[65] They recommend the marketing department be accountable for social responsibility, because corporate social policies and behaviors are products offered to stakeholders. They argue that a firm's range of products could be extended to include all social goods.

Step 1 in the marketing orientation portion of the model identifies both direct and indirect stakeholders using marketing research techniques, historical data, and managers' personal judgments.

Step 2 specifies the marketing mix variables (product, place, price, and promotion) associated with each stakeholder group. In the case of product, "offerings of the firm should focus on important social morality issues that can be addressed by the firm and may include actions such as energy conservation, supporting local charities, engaging in fair hiring practices."

Step 3, determining and implementing social responsibility activities, consists of deciding on a set of activities based on "technological feasibility, management capacity, cost-effectiveness, and strategic relevance." Murray

---

[64] Ibid., p. 59.
[65] K. B. Murray and J. R. Montanari, "Strategic Management of the Socially Responsible Firm: Integrating Management and Marketing Theory," *Academy of Management Review* 11, October 1986, pp. 815–27.

EXHIBIT 10–7   Continuous Management Model of Social Responsibility Activities

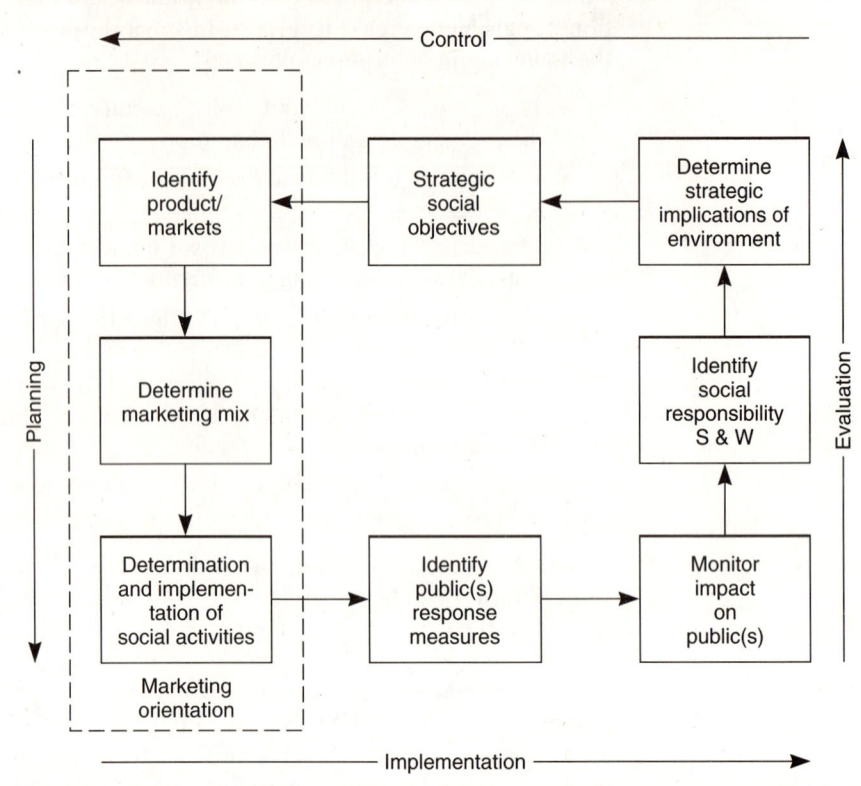

```
              ←———————————— Control ————————————
      ┌ ─ ─ ─ ─ ─ ─ ─ ─ ─ ─ ─ ─ ─ ─ ─ ─ ─ ─ ─ ┐
      │  ┌──────────┐   ┌──────────┐   ┌──────────┐  │
      │  │ Identify │   │ Strategic│   │ Determine│  │
   P  │  │ product/ │◄──│ social   │◄──│ strategic│  │  E
   l  │  │ markets  │   │objectives│   │implications│ │  v
   a  │  └────┬─────┘   └──────────┘   │of environ. │ │  a
   n  │       │                        └─────▲────┘  │  l
   n  │       ▼                              │       │  u
   i  │  ┌──────────┐                   ┌────┴─────┐ │  a
   n  │  │ Determine│                   │ Identify │ │  t
   g  │  │ marketing│                   │  social  │ │  i
      │  │   mix    │                   │responsib.│ │  o
      │  └────┬─────┘                   │  S & W   │ │  n
      │       │                         └─────▲────┘ │
      │       ▼                               │      │
      │  ┌──────────┐  ┌──────────┐    ┌──────┴───┐  │
      │  │Determin- │  │ Identify │    │ Monitor  │  │
      │  │ation and │──│public(s) │───▶│ impact   │  │
      │  │implemen- │  │ response │    │   on     │  │
      │  │tation of │  │ measures │    │public(s) │  │
      │  │social    │  └──────────┘    └──────────┘  │
      │  │activities│                                │
      │  └──────────┘                                │
      └ ─ ─ ─ ─ ─ ─ ─ ─ ─ ─ ─ ─ ─ ─ ─ ─ ─ ─ ─ ─ ─ ─┘
         Marketing orientation
              ———————————— Implementation ————————————▶
```

Source: K. B. Murray and J. R. Montanari, "Strategic Management of the Socially Responsible Firm: Integrating Management and Marketing Theory," *Academy of Management Review* 11, no. 4 (October 1986), p. 822.

and Montanari argue that the MARM model focuses on the notion that corporations and society are interdependent and have mutual goals. It efficiently allocates the company's resources and increases the firm's strategic options. The model also focuses on quantifying and measuring results, a major weakness in most companies' strategy.

An International Perspective on Charitable Giving

So far, we have been concerned with charitable giving in the United States, a country that is unique in its approach to philanthropy. No other country in the world relies so heavily on individual and corporate philanthropy to solve social problems. Each culture approaches the concept of philanthropy very differently.

Like the United States, some other countries have well-developed structures through which individuals and corporations donate money or in-kind services and goods. Most European countries, however, relegate primary responsibility for social issues to government. Countries in Asia, the Middle East, and Africa depend on an extended family structure to provide a variety of support services.

Many developing countries rely on international charities to provide basic social services. Sometimes even a consortium of such organizations is inadequate. Famines in Africa, for example, are so profound that no single government structure, charitable organization, or even international group could cope with the devastation without massive intervention.

In this section, we examine the British and Japanese approaches to philanthropy. Great Britain and Japan are two of our major trading partners. Their philanthropic activities at home and in the countries in which they invest are very different in scope and ideology. Like the United States, both countries have developed programs consistent with their own histories, government structures, and competitive needs.

The British Example

Great Britain, like many other European countries, has relied heavily on local and national government funds to support social causes. As social spending diminished in the 1980s, philanthropy was forced to take up the slack. Today philanthropy has become a big business in its own right. In the late 1980s and early 1990s, philanthropic organizations burgeoned to support health issues, care of the elderly, child advocacy, the environment, and other causes.

The Charities Aid Foundation, an oversight group, reported that in 1990 the top 10 fund-raising charities were the National Trust, the Royal National Lifeboat Institution, Oxfam, the Imperial Cancer Research Fund, the Cancer Research Campaign, the Salvation Army, the Save the Children Fund, Barnados, Help the Aged, and the Guide Dogs for the Blind Association.[66]

The mix of top charities is uniquely British. Britain's mainland is an island nation with a deep historical tradition, few natural resources, and a comprehensive government social welfare program. Reflecting these characteristics, philanthropic giving supports the natural environment and architectural preservation, the coastline and shipping, and relief of hunger worldwide.

Britain's charities, unlike those in the United States, are monitored by a national oversight body, the Charity Commission. Created by the Charities Act, the commission is charged with policing against fraud and ensuring that trustees carry out their responsibilities properly. Until the new Charities Act was passed in March 1992, the commission's powers were relatively weak.

---

[66] "No Free Lunch," *Economist,* August 29, 1992, pp. 52, 54.

The new legislation charged the government with drawing up precise rules to increase transparency, reducing the number of fraudulent fund-raisers, and monitoring corporate giving more closely.

In Great Britain, a fund-raiser is defined as anyone, including a company, that is rewarded for soliciting on behalf of a charity. Rewards can take the form of up-front payments for services, income from licensed product sales, or endorsements. Under the rules, fund-raisers must draw up legal contracts with the charities they represent. They also must reveal to prospective donors and to the public how much of the money collected will go to the charity itself.

The 1992 Charities Act also greatly strengthened trustees' responsibilities. As in the United States, typical trustees of philanthropic organizations are middle-aged, white, Anglo-Saxon Protestant men from professional backgrounds. Organizational agendas reflected the interests of these trustees, but until 1992 they provided few guidelines for their oversight function.

A report published by the National Association for Voluntary Organisations and the Charity Commission found that many of Great Britain's one million trustees had no idea what their duties were. Although trustees had major legal, financial, and managerial responsibilities under the 1992 act, only 20 percent received a formal introduction to the work of the organization and fewer than 15 percent received training directly related to their work. This absence of formal procedures was due to the rapid growth of philanthropy and the shift of social services from government to the private sector in the late 1980s and early 1990s. Britain's regulatory and legal structure failed to keep pace with this transition. Full-time professional managers who took over much of the management of charities left voluntary workers and trustees unsure of their roles and responsibilities.

The Charities Act called for radical changes in trustee recruitment and training. It charged the Charity Commission with ensuring that trustees received training in committee work, decision making, negotiating, and related skills. One trustee described it, "Start as an energetic ignoramus; make every possible mistake for five years; leave as an exhausted expert."[67]

In 1994, the National Lottery Charities Board (NLCB) completely changed the charitable environment and became the market leader. Proceeds from National Lottery were allocated to charities by the NCLB. Roughly half of every pound spent in the lottery was earmarked for charity. By the end of 1995, the National Lottery Charities Board, with an annual budget of around $400 million, was well on its way to becoming the single largest charitable donor in the United Kingdom. By 1996, there were more than 180,000 registered charities in the country and more than 15,000 individual applications for grants received by the NCLB. Preliminary data showed that the

---

[67] A. Pike, "Good Intentions Are Not Enough," *Financial Times,* September 28, 1992, p. 9.

large organizations such as the Red Cross and Oxfam had record years while small charities did not do as well.

Advocates of charitable giving noted major changes in the environment within which charities operated. By 1995, charities were forced to deal with changes in management methods, accounting principles, and investment strategies. As in the United States, British charities had come to rely on government funding as their main source of income. Throughout the 1990s, charities sought funding directly from the government rather than the private sector.

Charities also had to deal with rules established by the European Union. Under the European Union regulations, which cover the United Kingdom, lottery money counted as general government revenue. Charities could not claim cash for projects already receiving lottery money if that led to more than 50 percent of the cost of that project being paid from the government. The European Union, therefore, limited the amount charities could claim.

Within a year after lottery donations began, there was a 10 percent drop in the number of people reporting a donation to charity. The National Council for Voluntary Organisations (NCVO) calculated that in 1995, charities overall lost about $522 million. Charity fund managers seemed to agree that the lottery was, in the words of a manager, "one of the least efficient ways of raising money for good causes yet devised."[68] As a lottery operator noted, people did not buy lottery tickets to help charities; they bought tickets to become millionaires. At the same time, they reduced their individual charitable giving under the assumption that the lottery provided sufficient funds to the appropriate charities. Demos, an independent think tank, conducted an exhaustive study on charities and concluded wide-ranging changes were needed not only within charities themselves but also in public attitudes toward and involvement in voluntary work.[69]

The Japanese Example

Japanese philanthropic activities are beginning to receive a great deal of attention at home and abroad. Japanese society is facing many structural changes. As in all industrialized countries, the population is aging rapidly and values are changing. Lifetime employment, which at its peak applied to less than 40 percent of the population, is rapidly disappearing.

In 1990, people ages 65 and over made up 25 percent of the population. According to Japan's Ministry of Health and Welfare, by the year 2020 half the Japanese population will be over age 65. The percentage of national

---

[68] M. Suzman, "Some Donations May Be Lost Forever," *Financial Times,* December 11, 1995, p. 14.

[69] M. Suzman, "Call for New Legal Framework," *Financial Times,* December 11, 1995, p. 14.

income spent on supporting the elderly will be enormous. The Japanese government, while pledging to help those who need it, is urging Japanese corporations and individuals to develop and expand their philanthropic activities.

Japanese culture supports group rather than individual activity so it is not surprising that corporations are being asked to shoulder much of the philanthropic burden. The Keidanren is an overarching organization of Japanese businesses. Established under the Occupation forces in 1946, the Keidanren quickly became the consensus-building unit among large corporations. Its members meet regularly and transmit industry's views to the government. It has immense influence over public policy and the corporate community. In 1990, the Keidanren announced that corporate philanthropy was the fourth pillar of corporate strategy along with contributions to consumers, shareholders, and employees. A resolution adopted at the Keidanren's General Assembly called for establishing a new public image for private corporations joining society under the slogan, "New economic democracy."

The implementation of this call was uniquely Japanese, focusing heavily on philanthropy outside Japan. The Keidanren itself raised money for a variety of activities. In Japan, it helped establish the Foundation for Cultural Heritage, the National Assembly for Youth Development, and the Sports Fund Foundation. Abroad, it contributed to the construction of the Japanese galleries of the British Museum and the Metropolitan Museum of Art in New York. It also contributed to the Japan Festival '91 in Britain. The Keidanren's Council for Better Corporate Citizenship (CBCC) devoted its activities to overseas corporate philanthropy. The CBCC's goal was to help the efforts of Japanese companies abroad to integrate more closely with the societies in which they operate. An unstated goal was to improve the image of Japanese firms operating abroad. The CBCC held seminars on community relations and minority problems in overseas communities.[70]

Japanese corporations and managers are beginning to take this new charge more seriously. Charitable contributions by Japanese companies tripled between 1976 and 1989. According to a survey by Asahi Mutual-Life Insurance Company, Japanese companies donated $3.13 billion to charities in 1989; however, only 10 percent of Japanese companies participated. Some Japanese observers believed companies made corporate contributions because they want to avoid overseas criticism that they did not share the concerns of the communities in which they operated abroad. They noted that charity was not part of the Japanese culture and predicted it would be a temporary phenomenon.[71]

---

[70] "Keidanren Promotes Corporate Philanthropy," *Keidanren Review,* no.126 (December 1990), pp. 8–9.

[71] S. Alexander, "Japanese Firms Embark on a Program of Lavish Giving to American Charities," *The Wall Street Journal,* May 23, 1991, p. B1.

By the end of 1995, the critics' observation that Japanese were not big givers was borne out. The Secretary General of the Japan Philanthropic Association noted, "The idea of philanthropy or charity has not become part of the culture yet."[72] There is, in fact, no exact word in Japanese meaning the English equivalent of *charity*. The closest word, *jizen,* implies that the wealthy are obliged to make some gesture toward poor people but middle-class people have no obligation to those less fortunate.

Some of the most important Japanese charities have no precise equivalent in the West. For example, by November 1995, nearly 19 million Japanese had enrolled in an International Volunteer Savings program at the post office. Twenty percent of the interest on deposits of $30 million was donated to social programs in developing countries. In 1995, Japanese bought more than 500 million New Year's postcards sold for the benefit of disaster victims, medical research, and other causes. Despite these examples of charitable giving, Japanese volunteer and give at far lower levels than people in other developed countries. The chief of Japan's Salvation Army remarked that "this is not an altruistic society. Buddhism does not teach that you are your brother's keeper. It teaches that you should take care of yourself. That's what's been drilled into people over the years."[73] In addition to self-sufficiency, other factors influence public giving. Organized religions collect and give far less than in other countries. In addition, Japanese laws discourage the growth of nongovernmental social service organizations, a primary source of social service volunteers elsewhere. In sum, Japanese charitable institutions do exist, and do make contributions to those in need. The level of giving, however, is lower because the national ideology does not enthusiastically support philanthropic giving.

Summary

Over the past 100 years, Americans have changed their approach to philanthropy. In the 19th century, wealthy people gave to causes that helped individuals develop the skills they needed to help themselves. Individuals continue to give to philanthropic causes, but as society has become more complex, the number of charities and nonprofit institutions has grown.

Today individuals give even though most are not wealthy and many are only marginally more affluent than those to whom they give. People support a vast variety of causes, many of which are linked to religious and educational institutions. Increasingly, however, the environment and social welfare organizations are receiving a greater proportion of funds than they did a decade earlier. As women's wages have increased, women have given more in money and in time to causes associated with gender and family issues.

---

[72] C. A. Radin, "Japan's Take on Giving," *Boston Globe,* December 22, 1995, p. 2.
[73] Ibid.

Charitable organizations such as foundations have grown in size and scope throughout the 20th century. In the early days, some foundations supported company towns. In recent years, tax law revisions and court decisions have supported the establishment of private or public foundations through which corporate funds and individual fortunes have been funneled.

The U.S. legal and regulatory systems have not closely monitored how philanthropic donations are used. Nonprofits can legally give as little as 5 percent of donations to the causes for which the money was raised. Watchdog agencies are now tracking many of these charities and disseminating information on their allocation of funds.

Corporations continue to give even when profits fall. They are increasingly recognizing the benefits of tailoring their giving to their marketing programs and fostering public awareness of their good citizen role. Cause-related marketing has become big business.

It is not always clear what ethical considerations are attached to corporate giving or whether a company's motives or products should be considered before its money is accepted. Does the good done by the money outweigh the harm caused by the product? Each country's culture is unique and influences the structure and goals of its philanthropic programs. As countries invest across borders, they are expected to become participants in one another's social structures. The extent to which they participate in cross-border giving depends largely on how important philanthropy is to their images in the host country.

Questions and Projects

1. Choose three charitable organizations whose causes interest you. Find out what proportion of their income goes to the cause being promoted. Learn how each charity does its marketing to you and to others. Discover how each targets potential donors.

2. Volunteer your services for a fund-raiser. You might take part in a phone campaign, a school fund-raiser, or a mail solicitation. Analyze the material you are asked to convey to potential donors. Does it accurately reflect the aims of the cause? Are all parts literally and figuratively truthful? Is the potential donor misled in any way? If so, how? If there are any discrepancies, what is your ethical responsibility to call attention to them?

3. What role are corporate foundations likely to play during the late 1990s? Why do you think so?

4. Choose a product associated with a particular cause. Examine the marketing campaign to see how effectively the target audience is identified and persuaded to buy the product. Ben & Jerry's ice cream and Aveda personal care products are two companies whose products and causes are intertwined. (Don't forget to taste test Ben & Jerry's ice cream as well as examine its program!)

5. Choose a country outside the United States and examine its approach to philanthropy.

6. To what causes do you think businesses should give?

7. As head of corporate giving, you are worried about having sufficient profits at the end of the year. Make an argument to the CEO for cutting your company's contributions to a corporate minority day care program.

8. Devise a cause-related marketing program using the MARM structure.

9. Contact a Fortune 500 firm and interview a corporate giving officer. Find out what the individual does, to whom she reports, and how she is evaluated.

10. Contact a local merchant who gives to charity. Find out how he selects the charity and determines the amount to give.

Beta Case 10
Community Support and Philanthropy

Brian Madison was delighted. He had been asked to join the board of directors of the National Arts Stabilization Fund (NASF). The founding donors of the fund were the Ford Foundation, the Andrew W. Mellon Foundation, and the Rockefeller Foundation. Madison would join a distinguished group of business leaders that included Robert Allen, former president of AT&T; Jack Kemp, candidate for vice president of the United States and former secretary of Housing and Urban Development; and Juanita M. Kreps, former U.S. secretary of commerce. Madison was especially pleased that he would be working with Kenneth N. Dayton, a member of the fund's Affiliates Council.

The NASF, which began in 1983, was dedicated to the following goals:

- To strengthen the long-term financial health of selected national and regional organizations of artistic merit.
- To encourage arts organizations to adopt a balance-sheet strategy as a means of identifying financial priorities and quantifying long-term fund-raising goals.
- To assist arts organizations in developing effective management systems by providing technical assistance.
- To improve the ability of arts organizations to withstand financial stress.
- To promote a better understanding of the range of basic capital resources required to stabilize arts organizations in the United States.
- To change the public's perception of the ability of arts organizations to manage their financial affairs in a prudent and businesslike fashion.
- To demonstrate that fiscal responsibility and artistic integrity are compatible and mutually supportive.[74]

Madison was pleased with his appointment to the board for several reasons. First, he was a patron of the arts in Detroit and looked forward to supporting a cause that was personally meaningful to him. More important, Madison believed he would be able to bring to the NASF his expertise in strategic planning and fiscal accountability. He was impressed by the performances of arts organizations in the four localities in which NASF currently operated.

Boston was the first NASF stabilization project. A local consortium of business interests had joined with NASF and solicited 33 corporations for funds. Of those approached, 31 contributed. By 1987, NASF had awarded grants aggregating more than $3.5 million to five Boston arts organizations. Part of this grant money was used to liquidate the organizations' debts; the rest was used to establish restricted working capital reserves.

In Kansas City, Missouri, NASF signed an agreement with a consortium of foundations and corporations to create a $4.4 million project for the arts. Kansas City was selected because of its aggressive leadership in the local philanthropic community.

Arizona was the first statewide program and the third project. The Flinn Foundation, Arizona's largest grant-making organization, began a three-year pilot program in the arts. In January 1987, NASF earmarked $1.5 million to strengthen the financial position and managerial skills of Arizona's cultural organizations.

Seattle was the fourth locality to receive NASF help. The Seattle Arts Fund Committee set about raising $5 million to be contributed to NASF for a local stabilization project.

By 1996, however, companies were scaling back on cash donations and switching their support to marketing spnosorships funded mainly by their advertising and promotion budgets. Brian Madison was intrigued by the possibilities of developing corporate sponsorship programs for the NASF.

---

[74] National Arts Stabilization Fund, "The First Phase," (New York, 1987), p. 5.

As he contemplated the task ahead, Madison decided he would make every effort to ensure that Detroit was the next NASF city. In addition, he determined he would dedicate Beta to a contributions program that would enhance its reputation as a market-driven company with a bottom-line approach to philanthropy. At the next board meeting, scheduled in two weeks, Madison wanted to propose a program that would emphasize Beta's commitment to the community and, he hoped, enhance the company's market position as well. He wondered what that program should be.

PART III

Managing People and Social Issues

Expertise in managing people and allocating resources to support them is an important determinant of a firm's success. The three chapters in Part III deal with the many issues that directly affect employees in the internal direct segment of the stakeholder influence map. Employees, and society as a whole, expect companies to provide physical, psychological, and economic support. Stakeholders also expect companies to create an environment in which employees perceive they are treated fairly and given opportunities to grow, meet challenges, and find satisfaction.

CHAPTER 11
WORKPLACE ISSUES FOR THE LATE 1990s

CASE: JENNIFER STILLS' WORKDAY

Note: The Jennifer Stills case covers issues in Chapters 11, 12, and 13.

Jennifer Stills is the young human resources manager for Prime Office Equipment, a company that manufactures, sells, and services a wide variety of high-quality office equipment. As she unlocked her office at 6:30 one Monday morning, she mused that nothing in her educational experience had prepared her for the complexity of this job. Stills had majored in international relations in college, but she knew she had very little chance of using her academic experience in the workplace. When she graduated, she took a job with a head-hunting firm that placed administrative and secretarial personnel in a wide variety of local companies and industries. She quickly developed a strong client base, mastered interviewing techniques, and discovered she had an uncanny ability to choose the right candidate for the job. After three years, she had learned as much as she could from this job and decided to switch to corporate human resources. She had developed excellent contacts in the business community and had several offers from which to choose. Prime was Stills's first choice because she would be the company's first full-time human resources manager. Until now, the company had kept very few records, had sketchy employee policies, and did a dismal job of recruiting and dealing with the human resources function. Stills recognized the tremendous learning opportunities Prime offered. She would be able to set up systems, develop policy, and work with top management. She was also a bit uneasy, because she was inexperienced in many aspects of the job.

Stills was pleased with the company's willingness to let her set flexible hours. As a morning person, she liked to get to work early and leave by 4 P.M. She also liked being able to work at home on weekends and in the evenings, which gave her more autonomy in her personal life. Her benefits were good and her salary well above the wages of her college peer group.

Stills knew this was going to be a frantically busy day. She had spent the weekend going through the resumes of 200 applicants for customer service representative jobs. She had selected 60 applicants to interview by Monday and had to call each one to set up an interview. She had to make 15 offers by Thursday.

At 7 A.M. Reed Lawrence, her boss, poked his head into her office and told her the security officer had caught an employee trying to steal hundreds of dollars worth of computer software late Friday afternoon. Could Reed summarily fire the alleged thief? What was company policy? What did the law require? He asked Stills to get back to him within the hour.

A few minutes later her assistant Jeff arrived and he and Stills began reviewing some of the voice mail messages left over the weekend. Taken in order, the messages were

- A welder in the factory reported to her supervisor that she had just tested positive for AIDS. The welder was distraught and didn't know what to do. The supervisor asked if he could arrange a meeting with the welder and Stills to discuss the company's AIDS policy, its short-term and long-term disabilities policy, and medical benefits. The supervisor wanted this meeting held first thing Monday morning.
- A customer service representative left a message informing Stills that she was now in her ninth month of pregnancy and wanted to know when she could start her maternity leave.
- A phone representative wanted to know whether her husband, who had lost his job and had a nervous breakdown, was covered under her medical plan.
- Dorothy, the receptionist, wanted to talk immediately about Chuck, the inventory manager. He had called her honey again and told her she ought to shorten her skirts because she had such nice legs. Her message to Jennifer stressed that she had asked him repeatedly not to call her familiar names or comment on her anatomy.
- Bob Trask, Prime's president and CEO, had left a message at 10 P.M. on Friday. He wanted to talk about layoffs in the furniture department. Should Prime offer more comprehensive outplacement services? Were the company's present policies sufficient? "Before I forget," he added, "my son thinks we ought to consider subsidizing day care for employees. What's our current policy? Would you look at what the competition does, how much it would cost Prime, and send me a memo by Tuesday at 4:00 P.M.?"
- Diane Forbes, the company lawyer, with whom Stills had an excellent relationship and on whom she relied for advice, had left a message saying she had accepted a job with another firm. Forbes said she was sorry to leave Stills at this time. She knew Stills needed legal advice on Jean Tyrone's claim that Prime practiced racial discrimination. Tyrone had just filed a formal complaint with the State Commission against Discrimination.
- Leroy Aspin had left his message on Sunday. While cleaning the floor in the employee kitchen, he slipped in a pool of leftover oil and broke his left ankle. He angrily informed Stills that he was going to sue Prime for every penny it had.
- The last message came from Tim Strunk's sister. Strunk, who worked on the showroom floor, was hit from behind by a truck while riding his motorcycle home from work on Friday evening. He was killed instantly. The wake was being held that afternoon, and his sister hoped Stills would handle all the details for her and the Strunks' two young children. Would she please notify Strunk's co-workers, find out about benefits, and let the family know as soon as possible?

Stills momentarily wondered why she had ever gone into human resources. The issues she faced affected many lives and were profoundly important. She had to be an expert in just about everything. Her on-the-spot judgments had to be correct, she had to know when she needed outside advice, and she had to know how to handle the emotional needs of multiple stakeholders. She was fortunate that her personal life was in such good order and her husband Marc was so understanding and sympathetic.

Questions

1. If you were Jennifer Stills, which issues would you handle first? Make a decision on each issue with which she has to deal.
2. How should a company develop a strategy for handling workplace issues? Looking back to Chapters 2 and 3, which elements of strategy formulation and implementation can be applied?
3. What priorities should a company set regarding human resources issues? What makes some issues more important than others?

A Changing Labor Force

This chapter and the two that follow discuss the important workplace issues with which Jennifer Stills deals every day. Stills would readily agree that the problems she must solve today are very different from those she would have faced five years ago.

The composition of the U.S. labor force already differs substantially from that of past decades. As demographics change, adult white males make up a smaller percentage of the workforce. They are being replaced by a much more diverse group, including Asians, African-Americans, Hispanics, women, teenagers, and older people. These new workers are experiencing some of the same workplace issues their white male predecessors did. They also present their companies with new challenges.

The changing family structure placed new demands on management. In 1940, 9 in 10 American households were married-couple families. In 1992, slightly more than 50 percent fit that description. In 1993, single parents headed 1 in 10 households.[1] A study of women ages 18-44 who had never married revealed that 24 percent were mothers, an increase of 9 percent since 1983. Overall, 47 percent of single-mother families lived in poverty compared to 8.3 percent of families with two parents.[2]

In 1996, *Time Magazine* reported that 30 percent of men and 20 percent of women were single as they entered their thirties. Projections were that a typical population of 1,000 American women would have 2,046 children, a figure below replacement level. Population growth would depend on immigration.[3] Single women, homosexual couples, unrelated adults, and parents whose grown children have returned to the family home identify themselves as family units and are now demanding the benefits and services hitherto reserved for traditional male-headed households.

Working parents, whether single or married, are pressing for quality child and family care, better health benefits, and more flexible working conditions. Firms are exhibiting increased concern for workers by generating new corporate programs to meet employees' needs. Companies that correctly assess employee concerns, plan strategically to address them, and implement policies carefully make better use of their human resources and enhance workers' productivity. Those that react only to the most pressing demands as they occur use their human resources far less effectively.

---

[1] J. Gaines, "In Pursuit of the Unmarried Life," *Boston Globe,* June 24, 1993, p. 1.
[2] J. DeParle, Internet [from *New York Times,* July 14, 1993, pp. A1,A9].
[3] A. Hacker, "Meet the Median Family," *Time,* January 29, 1996, p. 43.

Employee Privacy

Employee privacy always has been a workplace issue. In the 19th century, managers involved themselves in every aspect of employees' lives. For example, in Lowell, Massachusetts, mill girls were required to go to church on Sunday and were chaperoned by the owners of the boarding houses in which they were required to live.

As we note in Chapter 6, George Pullman, the railroad sleeping car magnate, built a company town south of Chicago. In his town, company spies delved into every aspect of employees' lives, even reporting on domestic spats and visitors' political leanings. In the early 20th century, Ford Motor Company sent social workers to employees' homes to assess whether workers' lifestyles made them worthy of the yearly bonus. Companies continued to intrude in employees' private lives, but until computer technology became commonplace, they were constrained by the time and effort required to collect meaningful data.

In the mid-1970s, the *Harvard Business Review* interviewed Frank T. Cary, then chairman of the board and CEO of IBM. IBM had instituted a privacy code that went far beyond legal requirements in protecting employees from the collection and improper use of personal data. The company gathered only the information it needed to make initial employment decisions and conduct periodic performance evaluations. IBM did not concern itself with employees' off-the-job behavior unless it interfered with their regular job assignments. From the time managers were hired, IBM made clear the principles the company followed. All IBM employees were expected to bring code infringements to management's attention.[4]

IBM's policy was unusual in the 1970s. Most corporate upper-level managers agreed that an employee could object to a company policy on workplace privacy but maintained the company had the right to fire the employee for objecting. Although many companies now ascribe to policies like IBM's, changes in management ideology and technological advances have raised new concerns about employee privacy.

Today computers can gather so much information that virtually nothing about an individual is truly private. Computers also can store information about employees easily and inexpensively. As personnel files proliferate and companies accumulate more and more data, employees are becoming increasingly concerned about how the information is collected and used.

The Privacy Act of 1974 was the first major piece of federal legislation designed to protect employee privacy. This act aimed to "make sure that records maintained by federal agencies on individuals were accurate, complete and relevant." The legislation also created the Privacy Protection Study Commission to examine the rights of state government, local government,

---

[4] Interview conducted by D. E. Ewing, "IBM's Guidelines to Employee Privacy," *Harvard Business Review* (September–October 1976), pp. 82–90.

and corporate employees. In its 650-page report, the commission determined that corporations had far more power than government to affect employee privacy.[5]

A 1993 series in the *Boston Globe* explored the issue of privacy at home and in the workplace. Correspondents were able to obtain enormous amounts of data on individuals through a variety of sources. A Florida-based firm asserted it could track down medical records and unpublished phone numbers in minutes. The president of the company said, "There's such a vast storage of information and now with the computer, those with the right programs and ingenuity are putting it together. We can get almost anything." He observed, "The privacy factor is horrible. There is no privacy."[6]

An ongoing Louis Harris poll shows how the public's attitude toward privacy has changed. In 1970, when the poll was first taken, respondents were asked whether they were concerned about invasion of their privacy. Thirty-four percent reported they were either somewhat or very concerned. In 1977, 64 percent were concerned; in 1990, 79 percent were concerned; and in 1993, 83 percent of the 2,506 respondents reported they believed their privacy was being invaded. In this poll, the latest available, 67 percent were concerned about companies using public lists to sell their products, and 80 percent objected to individuals' ability to obtain public records on others. The two explanations respondents gave for their concern was distrust of institutions and abuses of technology.[7]

Companies collect information ranging from employees' cholesterol levels to the kinds of cars they own. Although the law and individual company policies restrict the use of this information, the potential for invasion of privacy still exists. Very few companies share with employees their reasons for intrusiveness and surveillance. As data collection techniques have become more sophisticated and uncertainty about how the data may be used grows, many employees are becoming increasingly apprehensive.

Some companies take strong measures to protect employee records and confidential data. Atmel Corp. of San Jose, California, manufactures semiconductors. In 1995, Atmel had $634 million in sales and employed 3,000 people in the United States and Europe. Employee files, in paper form, are locked in cabinets and cannot be pulled by anyone except a human resource department approved clerk. None of the folders can be taken out of the department. Medical records are kept in a separate file cabinet and cannot be seen by anyone outside of the human resources department. Atmel avoids using Social Security numbers and uses its own employee identification system—a policy adopted by only 30 percent of U.S. firms. The company is working on constructing fire walls to keep intruders out of its computerized record-keeping system.

---

[5] "New Push for Employee Privacy," *Dun's Review,* March 1979, p. 112.

[6] L. Tye, "No Private Lives," *Boston Globe,* September 6, 1993, p. 1.

[7] Ibid., p. 13.

Atmel protects its own equipment and property as diligently as it protects employee privacy. Managers tell employees exactly what information they can have on their computers and how they can use E-mail and voice mail. They also remind employees that their desks, lockers, and file cabinets are company property and can be searched. In practice, employees are not monitored unless the company has good reason to suspect wrongdoing. The company's corporate manager of human resources says, "You have to strike a balance. As an employer, it's necessary to create a secure environment and avoid liability, but it's also important to create a positive atmosphere and one in which creativity and innovation can flourish."[8]

The Government and Privacy

In 1993, the Clinton administration demonstrated concern about electronic eavesdropping on telephone calls and electronic mail. The administration developed measures to ensure privacy consistent with the government's right to eavesdrop for law enforcement and national security reasons only.

To prevent unauthorized eavesdropping, the government proposed a new system to encode voice and computer transmissions. The device, a Clipper chip, was designed by researchers at the National Security Agency in cooperation with the National Institute of Standards and Technology, a civilian agency responsible for setting computer standards for nonmilitary government applications. The design of the Clipper chip allows law enforcement and intelligence agencies and civilian services like the Internal Revenue Service to eavesdrop on electronically scrambled telephone and computer conversations. FBI officials and the National Security Agency feared that terrorists, child pornographers, and drug lords would be able to communicate in complete privacy in the absence of an eavesdropping mechanism.

Industry violently rejected the idea of the Clipper chip, fearing the government would intrude in business dealings. Corporations also pushed vigorously for the right to use and export sophisticated encryption devices to guard its corporate secrets. Most encryption programs use public-key cryptography. Senders can use a single key on their computers to garble a message. Only the recipient with the corresponding private key can decipher it.[9]

Although the Clinton administration offered compromising measures, industry rejected them. In fact, it would have been nearly impossible for the U.S. government to maintain its ban on encryption device sales abroad. By 1996, NTT, Japan's telephone giant and the Japanese subsidiary of RSA, an American encryption company, had developed and sold encryption chips in 15 countries.[10]

---

[8] S. Greengard, "Privacy: Entitlement or Illusion?" *Personnel Journal,* May 1996, p. 83.
[9] J. Carey, "Big Breakthrough or Big Brother," *Business Week,* November 18, 1996, p. 88.
[10] "Encryption: Silence of the Bugs," *Economist,* June 8, 1996, p. 65.

In October 1996, the administration capitulated and allowed firms to export even the most sophisticated cryptography. The main condition was that companies maintain access to their own encryption keys and agree to provide them to the government in response to warrants or court orders. Over the next several months, the administration issued preliminary regulations.

A computer industry group—the Business Software Alliance, including Apple Computer, IBM, Microsoft, and nine other companies—blasted the Clinton administration in December. Charging the administration had modified its October policy, the alliance said the agreement was doomed unless the changes were rescinded. The alliance insisted it was unreasonable to force manufacturers to give the government detailed information on how much money they are spending to develop software that can be descrambled, details of how they will market the software, and records of how many employees will be working on the project.

An industry executive asserted, "We don't want the government coming in and telling us how we have to tailor our programs on cryptography." The industry rejected administration assertions that law-enforcement authorities had a legitimate need to gain access to encrypted documents and that foreign agents and criminals could abuse the software. Privacy advocates also expressed their concerns, noting that they would oppose any encryption policy that would give the government the ability to snoop on private conversations and data transmissions. All sides agreed it would be some time before they could reach common ground.[11]

Polygraph Testing

Until 1989, many companies used lie detectors in preemployment screening and investigations of workplace theft. Legislators, civil liberties groups, medical personnel, and corporate organizations all had very different perspectives on whether polygraph tests worked and whether they should be used.

Many scientific and medical groups asserted that polygraph responses were often unconnected to the questions being asked and, thus, resulted in false conclusions. Increasing numbers of legislators and civil liberty groups objected to the tests for a variety of ideological and practical reasons. Polygraph operators, however, insisted their results were accurate. Even though many managers had confidence in the tests, others questioned whether the results were accurate enough to justify their use given possible adverse legal action.

In November 1987, the U.S. House of Representatives approved a bill that severely restricted the use of polygraphs to screen job applicants or test employees in private industry. In March 1988, the Senate approved a similar

---

[11] B. Ziegler, "Computer Group Blasts U.S. for Altering Pact Regulating Encryption Software," *The Wall Street Journal,* December 6, 1996, p. B2.

bill. Congress rejected the Reagan administration's assertion that polygraphs were valuable tools in combating business theft. Finally, in December 1988, Congress enacted a law making illegal approximately 80 percent of polygraph applications in the workplace. The Employee Polygraph Protection Act banned all random polygraph examinations and most uses for preemployment screening. With only a few exceptions, the law prohibited an employee from being dismissed, disciplined, or discriminated against solely for refusing to submit to a polygraph examination. The act did not regulate psychological honesty tests, medical tests for drugs, or the ability of law enforcement authorities to use polygraphs in their own investigations.

Today, an employer can ask a worker to take a polygraph test only if the worker has access to missing or damaged company property and if the employer notifies the worker in writing that there is a reasonable suspicion that she was involved in the loss or damage. The test cannot include any questions about personal beliefs or sexual behavior.[12] Current employees cannot be discharged or disciplined solely on the basis of the test results or on their refusal to take the test. If a test is administered and a person is either not hired or is fired, the employer may be required to prove there were reasons, other than the result of the lie detector test, for this action. Most employers believe that the use of polygraphs is not good policy except in extreme circumstances. Strong employee protection requirements make employers legally liable for its misuse and raise the specter of litigation and employee distrust.[13]

As soon as polygraph use was restricted, a new external indirect stakeholder emerged. Security companies marketed written tests for assessing employee honesty and began pushing their wares more aggressively. Although these tests had been around since the 1940s, when they were initially developed for the military, corporations had not used them widely. Stakeholders who objected to lie detectors used the same arguments to draft legislation to prohibit written tests.[14]

States began banning the tests in the early 1990s, charging they were overly intrusive and some discriminated disproportionately against minorities. In late 1990, the congressional Office of Technology Assessment issued a report that cast doubt on whether these so-called integrity tests worked as advertised.[15]

Security companies were not deterred, however. Wackenhut Corporation, for example, acquired marketing rights to a written honesty test called

---

[12] "Use of Polygraph in Hiring Is Curbed by U.S.," *New York Times,* December 28, 1988, p. A13.

[13] K. A. Kovach, "The Truth About Employers' Use of Lie Detectors," *Business and Society Review,* Spring 1995, pp. 65-69.

[14] C. Harlan, "Written 'Honesty' Tests Attract Interest as Polygraph Ban Begins," *The Wall Street Journal,* January 3, 1989, p. B4.

[15] G. Fuchsberg, "Integrity-Test Firms Fear Report Card by Congress," *The Wall Street Journal,* September 20, 1990, p. B1.

Phase II Profile and advertised the test in trade publications for security personnel.[16] Pinkerton Investigation Services advertised in the human resources publication, *Personnel Journal,* offering preemployment checks and introducing IntelliView, a "computerized interview system that helps add structure to the process—provides important documentation." Pinkerton also offered a hiring guide it called "an invaluable source of information about hiring practices, promoting honest behavior in the workplace and various types of employee investigations."[17]

Electronic Surveillance in the Workplace

The Fourth Amendment to the U.S. Constitution bars the government from unreasonable search and seizure of an individual's written material kept at home. Electronic surveillance in the workplace has different rules. As workplace technology has become more sophisticated, employers have developed new techniques to intrude in employees' work. A 1987 congressional report concluded organizations were monitoring nearly 7 million employees, many times without employees' knowledge. Nearly 90 percent of the 110 firms surveyed for the report collected electronic performance data on employees. Some insisted the data were used only for planning and cost control, but other firms acknowledged they were used for employee evaluations.[18]

As usage of electronic communication has increased in the workplace, so has employer surveillance. Companies are free to listen in on employees' telephone conversations, access their personal computer data, go through their E-mail messages, and videotape their activities. The computer magazine, *Macworld,* surveyed 301 companies from various industries. Investigators found supervisors in 22 percent of the companies surveyed had examined employees' computer files, E-mail, or voice mail. In companies with 1,000 or more employees, the number rose to 30 percent.[19] Supervisors insisted they were only trying to prevent theft or were simply measuring performance.

Less-skilled people involved in telephone sales or data processing are those most likely to be electronically monitored. Such jobs include airline reservations, telephone service, data processing, and insurance prospecting. Technology is so highly developed that it is possible for a firm to automatically count a computer operator's keystrokes as a measure of productivity.[20]

Some companies that do not listen in on conversations do keep track of the number of telephone calls each employee makes. Personal calls made

---

[16] Harlan, "Written 'Honesty' Tests," p. B4.

[17] "Smart Tools of the Trade," is an advertisement of Pinkerton Investigations Services. This ad was placed in *Personnel Journal* (May 1993), p. 54.

[18] R. Gelbspan, "The Boss May Be Listening," *Boston Globe,* November 30, 1987, p. 41.

[19] L. Tye and M. Van Schuyver, "Technology Tests Privacy in the Workplace," *Boston Globe,* September 6, 1993, p. 13.

[20] L. Smith, "What the Boss Knows about You," *Fortune,* August 9, 1993, p. 93.

while at work can cost a large company millions of dollars a year. Phone monitoring systems print out a record of every call, the telephone number of the recipient, and the contact time of the call.[21]

Many employees report that constant monitoring creates tremendous job stress; some think a company that monitors mistrusts its employees. Employers insist quite the contrary; they argue that monitoring is a tool to help employees do their jobs better. Employers claim monitoring even reduces worker stress if supervisors use the data to provide regular, positive feedback. Companies that monitor are within their legal rights. Under federal privacy laws, companies can listen in as long as eavesdropping is part of an established, ongoing performance evaluation program.[22]

Smart badges are one of the newest technological advances in monitoring. Olivetti patented an electronic identification card that is clipped onto an employee's clothing each morning. The badge emits infrared signals read by sensors placed around the building in which the employee works. The sensors are wired to a computer that collects and distributes information on the employee's whereabouts.

Such badge technology has tremendous potential applications in the U.S. workplace, both positive and negative. It can instantly route telephone calls to the phone closest to a badge wearer. Badges can allow access to secure laboratories. For example, the Media Laboratory at the Massachusetts Institute of Technology has electronic doors that open automatically for badge wearers. Smart-badge systems can locate doctors in hospitals immediately without paging or beeping.[23]

Although badges may facilitate efficiency and control, they also can invade employees' privacy. Managers often find these badges convenient and timesaving. Lower-level employees may resent the constant monitoring of their whereabouts and their activities.

E-Mail and Privacy. E-mail has revolutionized communication in the workplace. Many employees think their messages are private and cannot be retrieved when they are deleted from their electronic mailboxes. However, any E-mail on tape can be accessed at will by the employer.

According to a survey of corporate communicators from 93 Fortune 500 companies, 42 percent of all employee communications was through E-mail by 1996. Many employees do not know their employers have access to E-mail messages and any attachments. Increasingly, these attachments include strategic corporate plans, employee performance appraisals, and computer-aided designs.

---

[21] Ibid.

[22] "Memo to Workers: Don't Phone Home," *Business Week,* January 25, 1988, p. 89.

[23] P. Coy, "Big Brother, Pinned to Your Chest," *Business Week,* August 17, 1992, p. 38; L. Smith, "What the Boss Knows about You."

Often E-mail is backed up on magnetic tapes that employers can review at will. Deleting messages on screen does not remove them from taped files; indeed, messages may be recoverable for months or even years after they are sent or received. Recipients can forward, copy, and print messages, thus increasing the chance of violating employees' privacy.

Many employees do not understand the implications of "flaming" or sending negative comments about others through E-mail. For example, if an employee sends a message to another employee commenting negatively about someone else, the sender may be held liable for defamation or discrimination if the third person believes the information was used against him.[24]

Organizations own the computer hardware, software, and the networks employees use for their E-mail. Firms argue that they have the right to review any files because the equipment is a company asset. In addition, they say, companies pay for any personal messages sent through E-mail; while the individual E-mail message may cost very little, the cost of all employee E-mail may be substantial.

Although only 20 percent of companies monitor employees' E-mail, if employee theft and disloyalty increase, more companies may turn to monitoring. Legislation covering privacy and E-mail is still in the early stages of development. Most disputes dealing with employee E-mail privacy invoke the Fourth and Fourteenth Amendments of the U.S. Constitution. The purpose of the Fourth Amendment is to protect individuals from unreasonable searches and seizures by the federal government. The Supreme Court has ruled the Fourteenth Amendment makes the fundamental constitutional provisions of the Bill of Rights (the first ten amendments) applicable to the states. Both amendments prohibit unreasonable searches and seizures by state governments. Although public sector employees have some constitutional protection under the Fourth and Fourteenth Amendments, employees of private businesses are not covered unless a criminal investigation is taking place.[25]

In 1996, members of Congress introduced legislation in the U.S. House and Senate to set guidelines for workplace E-mail. The legislation proposed the following:

1. *Permitted Monitoring.* Employers would be permitted to monitor employees whose tenure was less than five years if all the employees in the group were monitored.
2. *Notice of Monitoring.* Employers would have to notify employees of what data are obtained, when, how, and why. Job candidates must be told in the first interview they could be monitored. Notice was not required if there was reasonable suspicion of wrongdoing.

---

[24] K. J. Lang and E. Davis, "Personal E-Mail: An Employee Benefit Causing Increasing Privacy Concerns," *Employee Benefits Journal,* June 1996, pp. 30–33.

[25] Ibid., p. 31.

3. *Prohibited Monitoring.* Employees with more than five years' tenure could not be monitored without just cause.
4. *Data from Monitoring.* Employees must be allowed to review data obtained. The employer could disclose the information to others only if the employee gave written consent. Also, there must be a legitimate need to perform work functions, such as a court order being carried out or the data being required for a law enforcement investigation. If the employee were a public official, the information could have a direct impact on public health and safety.

To date, no legislation has been passed. There is still a significant gap between employees' expectations of E-mail privacy and legal realities. Good management practices mandate that employers make policies explicit and clear in handbooks, memos, and discussions. If employers do not address E-mail privacy concerns, pressure will mount for legislators and courts to eliminate ambiguity.

Stress

Stress is a pervasive workplace issue that sometimes escalates into employee violence. A number of factors cause stress; some are inherent in today's general work environment, and others are job specific. In general, the stress level is rising in nearly all businesses and in most jobs. Employees have to make decisions so quickly that they have no time to recharge. One stress therapist noted, "Twenty-five years ago, we had more intermittent stress. We had a chance to bounce back before we encountered another crisis. Today, we have chronic, unremitting stress."[26]

Employees at every level appear to be stress victims. Managers as well as hourly workers blame stress for health and personal problems. Some observers trace the current concern about workplace stress to the wave of corporate restructuring and cost cutting that began in the early 1980s.

Between 1977 and 1988, Fortune 500 companies cut 2.8 million employees from their payrolls and encouraged many more to take early retirement or pay cuts. A manager at U.S. Steel noted, "Around here, we refer to a guy who brings his lunch on Friday as an optimist."[27]

As the economy lagged in the early 1990s, Americans worked harder to maintain their standard of living. In a 1991 Northwestern National Life Insurance survey of 600 U.S. workers, 46 percent of respondents rated their jobs as highly stressful. Thirty-four percent said their jobs were so stressful that they were thinking of quitting.[28]

---
[26] A. Miller, "Stress on the Job," *Newsweek,* April 25, 1988, p. 40.
[27] T. F. O'Boyle, "Loyalty Ebbs at Many Companies as Employees Grow Disillusioned," *The Wall Street Journal,* July 11, 1985, p. 27.
[28] A. Farnham, "Who Beats Stress Best—and How," *Fortune,* October 7, 1991, p. 71.

The Gallup Organization conducted a 1996 poll on stress in the workplace. It asked employees how often they were stressed out at work. Twenty-five percent reported they were stressed daily; an additional 12 percent said they were stressed almost every day. Stress levels were higher among professional and clerical workers than among manual workers and those engaged in business and sales.[29]

In 1988, 37 percent of employees thought their workloads were excessive. In 1995, 44 percent reported excessive workloads. In 1988, 22 percent frequently worried about being laid off; in 1995, 46 percent were worried. Seventy-three percent believed their jobs were secure if they performed well in 1988. In 1995, only 50 percent had the same expectation.[30]

Workers blamed stress for a variety of physical ailments. In states that allowed workers to sue due to job-connected stress, stress-related compensation claims skyrocketed. Three types of stress-related illnesses are categorized for workers-compensation purposes:

- A job-related physical trauma that leads to a mental disorder.
- Job-related mental stress that causes a physical problem.
- Mental illness with no related physical problem.

Some states are more generous than others in compensating workers for stress-related illness. In 1990, California had some of the nation's most liberal compensation laws. The state paid $380 million to both employed and unemployed workers claiming stress-caused insomnia, headaches, and other physical problems.[31] California has tightened its laws since then by raising the standards of compensation for stress. Before 1993, a worker had to show that 10 percent of her stress was related to work. After 1993, work had to be more than 50 percent of the cause of stress.[32]

Stress is particularly prevalent in jobs that require a great deal of customer contact or long hours in front of a computer. These jobs often are boring and require high, easily measurable output. Other high-stress jobs require instant decision making or involve life-threatening situations. Some examples of high-stress occupations are inner-city high-school teacher, data processor, police officer, air traffic controller, miner, medical intern, stockbroker, customer service/complaint representative, and secretary.[33]

The consequences of stress-related problems are often very costly for employers. According to the National Council on Compensation Insurance,

---

[29] T. D. Schellhardt, "Company Memo to Stressed-Out Employees: 'Deal with It,'" *The Wall Street Journal,* October 29, 1996, p. B1.

[30] Ibid.

[31] R. Grover, "Say, Does Workers' Comp Cover Wretched Excess?" *Business Week,* July 22, 1991, p. 23

[32] C. Kedijijian, "How to Combat Workplace Stress," *Health and Safety,* April 1995, pp. 37–38.

[33] A. Miller, "Stress on the Job," p. 43.

employees who brought legal action against companies in 1987 accounted for about 14 percent of occupational disease claims in 1988, up from only 5 percent in 1980.[34] By 1995, 70 to 90 percent of visits to primary care physicians were for stress-related problems. Stress accounted for more than half of the workdays lost each year to absenteeism; 60 to 80 percent of industrial accidents were stress-related.[35]

People interpret stress subjectively, especially at the managerial level. What may cause one manager to have a nervous breakdown is challenging and exciting for another. Most people, however, react positively to a supportive environment and to top management that seeks to reduce rather than magnify stress-producing factors. Jobs that give employees control, autonomy, and time to enjoy home and family life are less stressful than those that demand total devotion and military-style discipline.

Some companies, albeit a minority, actively try to raise stress levels because they believe stress leads to higher productivity. PepsiCo used to create a high-pressure environment designed to weed out stress-prone people early in their careers. PepsiCo moved its managers from job to job and place to place whenever it chose. It expected managers to put in a seven-day workweek to achieve measurable results quickly. Those who complied enjoyed a variety of rewards, including first-class air travel, huge bonuses, and a magnificently appointed health club. When told he was not PepsiCo material, a terminated manager asked his reviewer why he had failed. The reviewer looked him straight in the eye and said, "You're not enough of a bastard."[36]

Most human resource experts, however, recommend that managers become more flexible and help employees balance work and family. A 1993 study of Johnson & Johnson showed employee morale and productivity increased when the company offered help in resolving work and family conflicts. Fifty-eight percent of employees surveyed said stress-reducing policies such as flextime and family leave policies weighed heavily in their decision to stay at the company.[37]

The trucking industry implemented an outsource service focusing on reducing stress. Employee Advisory Resource (EAR) is a 24-hour, 365 days a year telephone service that provides counseling on issues such as emotional stress, family finance, legal questions, work problems, and substance abuse. Loram Maintenance of Way, Minnesota, builds and operates equipment used to maintain railroad tracks. The company, whose workers must be away from home for long periods, attributes a nearly 50 percent reduction in turnover to EAR.[38]

---

[34] Ibid., p. 41.
[35] C. Kedijijian, "How to Combat Workplace Stress," p. 36.
[36] B. Dumaine, "Those Highflying PepsiCo Managers," *Fortune,* April 10, 1989, p. 80.
[37] M. Galen, "Work and Family," *Business Week,* June 28, 1993, p. 82.
[38] J. D. Schutz, "New Counseling Service Offers Drivers a Friendly 'EAR'," *Traffic World,* April 1, 1996, p. 27.

Employee-assistance programs (EAPs) like EAR are very useful in reducing stress before it reaches a critical point. Companies can develop EAPs themselves or outsource them. Experts advise companies to help workers find a way out of their stressful situations through counseling, friendship, and communication. Supervisors should be trained to recognize signs of stress and refer employees to EAPs rather than trying to handle the situation themselves. Robert Gordon, a Northwestern University clinical psychologist notes, "The causes of a person's stress are as complicated as his or her own personality."[39]

Workplace Violence

Companies are finding that employees may turn to violence when they cannot relieve their stress. The Centers for Disease Control report that murder is now reaching epidemic proportions as a workplace problem. Between 1980 and 1988, homicide accounted for 12 percent of workplace injury deaths.[40] In 1994, there were 1,071 workplace homicides accounting for 16 percent of workplace injury deaths. Homicide was the second-leading cause of work-related fatalities overall and the leading cause of workplace deaths for women.[41]

Workers at most risk were cab drivers, police officers, security guards, workers in grocery stores, gas station attendants, and bartenders. The Department of Labor reported that robbery was the most common motive for murders. Family disputes accounted for 5 percent of workplace murders. About 1 in 10 murders is the result of a business dispute. About 1 million Americans were killed by workplace violence in 1995.[42] Dr. Linda Rosenstock, director of the National Institute for Occupational Safety and Health declared in 1996, "We have an epidemic of violence on the job."[43]

Companies are just beginning to deal with the connection between domestic abuse and violence on the job. Until recently, companies assumed that domestic violence was none of their business. In 60,000 incidences of on-the-job-violence, however, the victims knew their attackers intimately and in some cases, companies faced legal consequences. If a woman has a restraining order against a potential attacker, a company may be held liable if it does not protect her in the workplace. Although courts rarely direct companies to enforce restraining orders, more than a dozen companies including the

---

[39] T. D. Schellhardt, "Company Memo to Stressed-Out Employees," *The Wall Street Journal,* p. B8.

[40] "Labor Letter," *The Wall Street Journal,* June 15, 1993, p. A1.

[41] "U.S. Offers Ideas to Reduce Violence on Job," *New York Times,* March 15, 1996, p. A15.

[42] B. Meier, "When Abuse Follows Women to Work," *New York Times,* March 10, 1996, p. 11.

[43] M. Elias, "Epidemic of Violence on the Job at Record High," *USA Today,* July 9, 1996, p. 3A.

Polaroid Corporations, Liz Claiborne, Inc., and Marshall, Inc., formed the National Workplace Resource Center on Domestic Violence. This model program develops programs and policies for employees who have suffered domestic abuse. The companies give counseling and sometimes may move employees who fear for their lives to new jobs in other locations.[44]

Murder is only the most dramatic manifestation of the much larger problem of workplace violence. Companies routinely deal with on-site beatings, stabbings, rapes, suicides, and assorted psychological trauma.

Experts on workplace violence attribute the increase to downsizing in the late 1980s and recession in the early 1990s. They also point to domestic upheavals and even to workers' exposure to toxic chemical substances. An article in *Security Management* noted more than 9 million workers are routinely exposed to solvents. Solvent exposure causes a variety of side effects, including uncontrollable rages, severe mood swings, reduced inhibitions, and unfounded feelings of physical strength. The author urged security officers to be alert to this problem and document all instances of solvent exposure.[45]

In 1990, *The Wall Street Journal* reported on revenge in the office. Management consultants, managers, and psychologists reported the workplace was on the way to becoming "a breeding ground for vengeful acts."[46] One employee, who had been demoted after years with a high-tech company, was found with a loaded gun in his company's parking lot. He was waiting for the supervisor he held responsible for the demotion. In 1996, a postal worker shot and killed a supervisor who had dismissed and testified against him in an arbitration.[47]

Although present or former employees commit most office homicides and other acts of violence, workplaces are vulnerable to anyone who holds a real or imagined grudge. Experts note that pressures and deadlines have always been part of office life. However, in the past it was easier for employees to cope. Employment was more stable and families were more supportive. Today society is less supportive and life in and out of the workplace has become more unpredictable and, hence, more stressful.

Increasingly, corporations are being held responsible for creating safer workplaces. In recent years courts in more than a dozen states have ruled that employers can be held as negligent if dangerous workers are hired. At the same time, privacy laws have made it difficult for employers to use exhaustive job screening tests. GTE Data Inc. faced a dilemma with Joe Hindman; the firm fired Hindman when he brought a loaded gun to work. Hindman claimed the firing was illegal because the gun incident was the result of a chemical

---

[44] Ibid.

[45] J. J. Prince, "Fuming over Workplace Violence," *Security Management,* March 1993, p. 64.

[46] L. A. Winokur, "Sweet Revenge Is Souring the Office," *The Wall Street Journal,* September 19, 1990, p. B1.

[47] "An Ousted Postal Worker Kills His Supervisor," *New York Times,* December 20, 1996, p. A34.

imbalance in his brain that made him disabled. A federal judge in Tampa, Florida, ordered a jury trial saying, "When poor judgment is a symptom of a mental or psychological disorder, it is defined as an impairment that would qualify as a disability under the ADA [Americans with Disabilities Act]. Although a second judge dismissed the case, employment-law specialists called the initial ruling a nightmare that might protect potential killers.[48]

Guidelines for Preventing Workplace Violence

In 1996, the U.S. Occupational Safety and Health Administration (OSHA) issued *Guidelines for Preventing Workplace Violence for Health Care and Social Services Workers.* OSHA noted the guidelines were not new standards or regulations; they were designed to be advisory and informational. Although this particular document focuses on health care and social service workers, the directives are applicable to any workplace. OSHA developed four main components of this program:

- **Management Commitment and Employee Involvement**
  Management commitment includes the endorsement and visible involvement of top management. Management must show organizational concern for employees' emotional and physical safety and health. Top management must make sure that all managers, supervisors, and employees understand their obligations to prevent workplace violence. Management must create a comprehensive program of medical and psychological counseling and debriefing for employees experiencing or witnessing assaults or other violent incidents.

  Employee involvement should include understanding and complying with a program designed to promote prompt and accurate reporting of violent incidents. Employees should participate in a continuing education program that covers techniques to recognize potentially violent behaviors and how to respond to them appropriately.

- **Written Program** The program should create a clear policy of no tolerance for workplace violence, verbal and nonverbal threats, and related actions. It should ensure there are no reprisals against an employee who reports workplace violence. It should require records of incidents to assess risk and measure progress. The program should also outline a comprehensive plan that establishes linkages with law enforcement representatives and others who can help to prevent and lessen workplace violence. The written plan should assign responsibility, authority, and funding for the program to individuals or teams with appropriate training and skills.

---

[48] E. Felsenthal, "Potentially Violent Employees Present Bosses with a Catch-22," *The Wall Street Journal,* April 5, 1995, p. B1.

- **Worksite Analysis** The company should create a task force or team composed of senior management, operations, employee assistance, security, occupational safety and health, legal, and human resources staff. The team should review all injury and illness records and workers' compensation claims to identify patterns of assaults that could be prevented. All the data should be tabulated to target the frequency and severity of incidents to establish a baseline for measuring improvement. Other businesses, trade associations, and community and civic groups should be asked about their experiences with workplace violence to help identify trends of injuries and incidents. The company should give employees a questionnaire or survey to get their ideas on the potential for violent incidents and to identify or confirm the need for improved security. The review process should also include feedback and follow-up. Independent reviewers such as safety and health professionals, law enforcement, security specialists, and others may offer advice.

The team or coordinator should analyze incidents, including the characteristics of assailants and victims, an account of what happened before and during the incident, and relevant details of the situation and its outcome. The team also should obtain police reports and recommendations. Part of the analysis should be to identify jobs or locations with the greatest risk of violence as well as processes and procedures that put employees at risk of assault. The team or coordinator should note the physical risks of any building lighting problems, absence of phones, and areas with previous security problems.

- **Evaluation** An evaluation program should include establishing a uniform violence reporting system. It should analyze trends and rates in injuries or fatalities caused by violence relative to initial or baseline rates. The evaluation process should include keeping abreast of new strategies to deal with violence. Management should share workplace violence prevention program evaluation reports with all employees.[49]

Medical Issues in the Workplace

Federal law, state law, and company policies all affect individuals' services, treatment, and work environment. In this section, we address three of the most prevalent issues where managerial decision making and medical concerns overlap: substance abuse, policy toward physically challenged or

---

[49] Internet [http:www.osha.gov/oshpubs/workplace] "Guidelines for Preventing Workplace Violence for Health Care and Social Service Workers—OSHA 3248-1996."

handicapped workers, and AIDS. The law designates a number of physical conditions as handicaps and offers limited job protection, medical care, and access to special working conditions.

Substance Abuse

Substance abuse is a pervasive corporate problem. In 1988, the National Institute on Drug Abuse and other groups estimated that at least 10 percent of the workforce suffered from some form of substance abuse. American industry was losing nearly $100 billion a year to drugs and alcohol in the form of absenteeism, workforce turnover, and rehabilitation services.[50]

The Rehabilitation Act of 1973 classified substance abuse as a handicap. Under that law, an employer cannot discriminate against an employee addicted to drugs or alcohol unless other factors are involved. The act extends to any company with federal contracts that provides goods or services exceeding $2,500.

Before hiring a job candidate, an employer can condition employment on the results of a medical exam for drug or alcohol addiction if all prospective employees undergo the same exam. The employer can use the results only to verify the employee's ability to perform the job. Once a person is hired, an employer is limited in taking actions against an employee with a substance abuse problem. Unless an employer can demonstrate that an employee's current drug or alcohol abuse (1) prevents the employee from performing the duties of the job or (2) causes the employee to constitute a direct threat to property or the safety of others, the employer cannot fire or otherwise discriminate against that person.[51]

Drug use is clearly illegal and can be detected in routine screening tests. Alcohol consumption, however, is legal and socially sanctioned. Unlike drugs, alcohol is quickly metabolized and hard to detect several hours after consumption. It is difficult to define the point at which alcohol consumption becomes alcohol abuse. However, it is an equally pernicious workplace problem. The stakeholder influence map in Exhibit 11–1 shows some multiple stakeholders in the substance abuse issue.

By the mid-1990s, drug testing was widespread in larger companies. In January 1993, 84 percent of the corporate members of the American Management Association (AMA) had drug-testing programs. AMA members, mostly large corporations, account for 25 percent of all American workers.[52]

In 1994, new federal Transportation Department regulations doubled the number of workers required to be tested for drugs and alcohol. The rules,

---

[50] J. Hoerr, "Privacy," *Business Week,* March 28, 1988, p. 61.

[51] CCH editorial staff, *Drugs and Alcohol in the Workplace* (Chicago: Commerce Clearing House, 1989), p. 48.

[52] I. A. Lipman, "Fight Drugs with Workplace Tests," *New York Times,* July 18, 1993, p. F15.

EXHIBIT 11–1
Stakeholder
Influence Map:
Substance Abuse

	Direct	Indirect
External	Insurers	Federal government Local governments State government Chamber of Commerce American Medical Association Credit bureaus Civil liberties group Testing companies
Internal	Managers Employees	Unions

which took effect in January 1995, imposed drug and alcohol testing on 7.5 million workers, up from 3.5 million earlier. The tests applied to a wide range of jobs from the drivers of school buses and trucks to small businesses to airline pilots and attendants.[53]

Stakeholders, concerned about employee privacy, note drug tests are not foolproof. Although critics claim urine tests are more reliable than blood tests, employees can still switch or alter urine samples. Testing cannot distinguish between the one-time user and the hardened addict. Even when an employee is drug free, many legal substances may cause the sample to be suspect. A flu patient who took a dose of Tylenol Plus 3 with codeine could still test positive for drugs three weeks after recovery. In some cases, an employee who drank a cup of herbal tea or ate a piece of poppy seed cake for breakfast tested positive for drugs.

Even when drug tests are correctly conducted and interpreted, their cost to the company is very high. Small companies or companies that hire large numbers of young workers for low-wage, unskilled jobs such as security guards may well find that level of cost unacceptable.[54]

Corporations find they must make a series of decisions about testing. First, a company must decide whether to test applicants, employees, or both. Second, once the firm decides to test, it must decide how often to test. Procedures must ensure fair administration and proper interpretation. In

[53] A. Newman, "Drug-Testing Firms Face Pluses, Minuses in New Rules," *The Wall Street Journal,* March 15, 1994, p. B4.
[54] A. Kupfer, "Is Drug Testing Good or Bad?" *Fortune,* December 19, 1988, p. 134.

some companies, unions may object to any procedures no matter how sophisticated or accurate they are. Employees who test positive may sue the company, which can be very costly even if the company wins the suit. Third, when an employee tests positive, the firm must deal with the issue of rehabilitation.

Disabled Workers

In 1989, Congress passed the Americans with Disabilities Act (ADA), a sweeping antidiscrimination bill.[55] Prior to the passage of this act, workers with disabilities were minimally protected by three pieces of legislation: the Civil Rights Act of 1964, which bars discrimination on the basis of race, sex, or national origin; a 1973 law prohibiting the federal government, federal contractors, or entities that receive federal funds from discriminating against people with disabilities; and a 1988 housing law forbidding discrimination in the sale or rental of housing. The Equal Employment Opportunity Commission (EEOC) administers the ADA. It writes the guidelines for enforcing the act and negotiates with other federal and state agencies regarding specific coverage and implementation.

A 1985 Louis Harris & Associates poll showed 74 percent of people with disabilities shared "a common identity" and 45 percent believed they were "a minority in the same sense as are blacks and Hispanics." In 1980, a worker with a disability made only 77 percent of a nonchallenged colleague's earnings; in 1984, he made only 64 percent as much. The 1985 Harris poll found 70 percent of working-age people with disabilities were unemployed and two-thirds of that number were prevented from working because they faced discrimination in hiring or lacked transportation.[56]

Even though one-fifth of the nation's population has some form of disability, ranging from mental retardation to total physical immobility, people with disabilities had never demonstrated in the streets for civil rights as did women, Hispanics, and African-Americans. In the mid-1980s, however, more enlightened attitudes toward disabilities supported change and the development of new legislation. People with disabilities were more independent and better educated than in the past. Newly created independent-living centers became advocacy sites. The onslaught of the AIDS epidemic added thousands of involuntary recruits to the ranks of physically challenged people.

During the 1988 presidential campaign, candidate George Bush endorsed a bill extending civil rights legislation to people with disabilities. At the end

---

[55] We use the term *disabled* in this section because it is the term used by the government in legislation. Readers may find other terms such as *physically* or *mentally* challenged more acceptable.

[56] J. P. Shapiro, "Liberation Day for the Disabled," *US News & World Report,* September 18, 1989, pp. 20–23.

of that year, Senator Lowell Weicker, then senator from Connecticut and father of a Down's syndrome child, introduced the first version of the bill. Senator Ted Kennedy of Massachusetts, whose son had lost a leg to cancer and whose sister was mentally retarded, proclaimed, "This legislation will go down as one of the most important accomplishments in the history of the Congress."[57]

Under the ADA, the legal definition of a disabled person is anyone who meets one or more of the following criteria: (1) has a physical or mental impairment that substantially limits one or more major life activities, such as walking, seeing, hearing, speaking, breathing, learning and/or working; (2) has a record of an impairment such as having been hospitalized or treated for the condition in the past; and (3) is regarded by others as having an impairment. At the time the ADA was signed into law, about 43 million people having one or more of 1,000 mental or physical conditions qualified as disabled.[58]

As Exhibit 11-2 shows, the ADA set up a timetable for adaptations for people with disabilities. Beginning in July 1992, more than one-half million businesses with 25 or more employees had to comply with a new set of regulations mandating accessibility to public property, job sites, public transportation, and telephone communication.

Many companies reported their actual investments were very small compared to the benefits of compliance. For example, a blind United Parcel Service (UPS) worker became a computer programmer and trainer. He used a voice synthesizer and headset attached to his computer to convert the words on his screen to speech. UPS paid about $11,000 for special equipment, but it gained a very productive worker. A UPS spokesperson said the company looked on the ADA as an opportunity.[59]

In July 1994, 500,000 employers (with 15 to 24 employees) came under the ADA. Some employers were worried that they might encounter a situation in which an employee was unable to climb the stairs to a second-floor office and might demand the employer install an elevator. Under the law, this situation was unlikely to occur. A business did not have to make a concession to an employee if it were too costly or disruptive. Some employers still grumbled that the courts had yet to decide what constituted a financial hardship for the employer but most were prepared to make accommodations to their workers' needs.[60]

---

[57] S. F. Rasky, "How the Disabled Sold Congress on a New Bill of Rights," *New York Times,* September 17, 1989, p. E5.

[58] F. S. Hall and E. L. Hall, "The ADA: Going beyond the Law," *Academy of Management Executive* 8 (1994), no. 1, pp. 17–32.

[59] P. T. Kilborn, "Big Change Likely as Law Bans Bias toward Disabled," *New York Times,* July 1992, p. 1.

[60] J. A. Tannenbaum, "More Small Employers Must Adhere to Disabilities Act," *The Wall Street Journal,* July 25, 1994, p. B2.

EXHIBIT 11–2 Major Requirements of the Americans with Disabilities Act

ACCOMMODATIONS

Public facilities must be made accessible to the disabled.

Jan. 26, 1992: Buildings and businesses employing over 25 people must actively strive to eliminate barriers to disabled individuals.

July 26, 1992: Businesses employing 25 or fewer people, but having annual revenue over $1 million must conform.

Jan. 26, 1993: Buildings constructed for occupancy after this date must be accessible to the disabled.

EMPLOYMENT

Employers may not discriminate against qualified, disabled individuals in hiring, promoting, compensating, or training. Employers must make necessary adaptations to the workplace. Companies having fewer than 15 employees are exempt.

July 26, 1992: Companies employing over 25 people must comply.

July 26, 1994: Companies employing 15 to 24 people must comply.

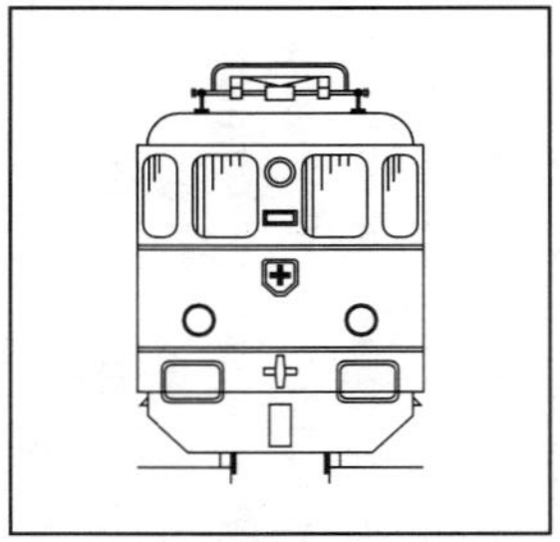

TRANSPORTATION

New buses, trains, and subway systems must be wheelchair accessible.

Jan. 26, 1992: New vehicles built for public bus and train systems must be wheelchair accessible.

July 26, 1993: Rail stations must be made wheelchair accessible.

July 26, 1995: One car per train must be wheelchair accessible.

July 26, 1996: Private transportation providers must purchase accessible vehicles. Small operators are exempt.

July 26, 1997: Small operators must comply.

TELEPHONES

Telephone companies must provide, to the extent possible, relay services allowing hearing- or voice-impaired individuals to use ordinary telephones.

July 26, 1993: Companies should have telecommunications services available 24 hours a day to hearing and voice impaired individuals.

EEOC and employment specialists advised businesses to take steps to avoid lawsuits and improve job prospects for workers with disabilities. They advised managers to take a new look at all hiring, firing, and promotion practices and follow these rules:

- *Don't ask job candidates or their references about applicants' disabilities.* The law does not allow a prospective employer to even mention physical limitations.
- *Don't ask about the following before you offer a job:* medical history; prescription drug use; prior workers' compensation or health insurance claims; work absenteeism claims; worker absenteeism due to illness; and past treatment for alcoholism, drug use, or mental illness. The law does allow companies to ask health-related questions after a candidate has accepted the offer as long as management asks the same questions of all applicants in the job category.
- *Don't require a job candidate to take a medical exam before you offer the job or require current employees to take medical exams unless the business has a specific reason for the request.* A company cannot withdraw a job offer based on a medical exam except for a job-related reason, such as the need to have an employee available every day for a specific time period.
- *Don't refuse to hire people because you are concerned that they or their dependents with disabilities will cost you more in health insurance.* Keep in mind that you can refuse to cover preexisting conditions as long as they do not completely exclude employees with disabilities or their disabled dependents from your health insurance plans.[61]

The Supreme Court ruled that self-insured employers can reduce their coverage for treatment of AIDS because they are not subject to state insurance law requirements that would bar this action. This decision was based on the Federal Employee Retirement Income Security Act (ERISA) rather than on the ADA. However, the EEOC is developing health coverage rules for AIDS under the ADA and has specifically been charged with deciding whether the ADA allows employers to discriminate in insurance coverage among AIDS and other physical illnesses such as cancer and heart disease.[62]

- *Revise all union contracts to reduce conflicts between the ADA and seniority rules.* The law is unclear about whether it is mandatory to fill a vacancy with a worker who has a disability if a more

---

[61] J. S. Lublin, "Disabilities Act Will Compel Businesses to Change Many Employment Practices," *The Wall Street Journal,* February 7, 1992, p. B1.

[62] F. Swoboda, "New U.S. Disability Law Taking Shape," *Boston Globe,* January 5, 1993, p. 43.

experienced worker is senior under union rules. The National Labor Relations Board and the Equal Employment Opportunity Commission are working out the rules on this and other union-related issues.

- *Take a tough stand with employment agencies by demanding that at the least they obey the law.* A firm can be liable for its employment agency's actions. Agencies' employment ads must comply with the ADA and offer services such as a special telephone number for hearing-impaired people.[63]

The ADA and Litigation. Between July 1992 and June 1993, 11,760 complaints of employment discrimination were brought under the act; successful plaintiffs won $11 million.[64] As the ADA evolved, claims were filed over issues the framers never intended the law to cover. Phrases used in the act were sometimes ambiguous. It is difficult to tell what constitutes "reasonable accommodation" and "undue hardship." A lawyer said, "It's like a recipe for bread when they don't tell you how much flour or yeast to use. But the penalty if you don't make a good loaf is a violation of the law."[65]

In 1996, Lynn Gansar, a former New Orleans television anchor claimed she was fired after her station learned she was receiving fertility treatments. Ms. Gansar filed a lawsuit against WDSU-Television Inc., claiming her discharge violated the ADA. Gansar said she asked the television station to allow her to skip her 5 P.M. broadcast for a few weeks while she received her hormone shots at 4 P.M. The parent Pulitzer Publishing Co. decided to fire Gansar instead. She charged they were worried that she would make more demands if she became pregnant.

Although Gansar lost her case, District Judge James Alesia allowed Charline Pacourek to proceed with her case. Pacourek had lost several days' work when she was undergoing fertility drug therapy. Judge Alesia rejected her employer's contention that infertility was not a disability that limited a major life activity. The judge found that reproduction is a major life activity, even though it isn't done as frequently as "walking, breathing, speaking, and working." The judge concluded that common sense suggested that major life activity should be defined broadly in these cases since "none of us, nor any living thing would exist without reproduction."[66]

In a unique case, a professor at a midwestern university collected his mother's Social Security checks for five years after she died. When the school

---

[63] Lublin, "Disabilities Act Will Compel Businesses to Change," p. B1.

[64] B. Wade, "Slow Going for Disabled on Private Buses," *New York Times,* August 29, 1993, p. XX3.

[65] E. Felsenthal, "The Disabilities Act Is Being Invoked in Diverse Cases," *The Wall Street Journal,* March 31, 1993, p. B1.

[66] M. A. Jacobs, "Women Seek Infertility Benefits under Disabilities Law," *The Wall Street Journal,* June 12, 1996, p. B7.

fired him, he filed a suit under the ADA claiming his criminal behavior on the job was due to the disability of clinical depression.[67]

In May 1995, the city of Bellevue, Washington, threatened to levy a $4,500 fine on Papagayo because the strip club did not have a wheelchair lift attached to the stage for performers. An exasperated representative of the company that hires the strippers condemned the government policy: "It's just asinine. If you can't dance, why should you even be on a stage?"[68]

As the EEOC continues to clarify the ADA's language and to more closely define policies, the workplace will change for mentally and physically challenged people. Advocates, many of whom have disabilities themselves, are becoming more vocal in their demands for access to quality jobs and fair remuneration. They are demanding that workplaces be equipped with better wheelchair ramps, raised-letter signs, accessible light switches, and a wide range of other modifications.

AIDS in the Workplace

AIDS is one of the most pervasive and difficult workplace issues. As we noted in Chapter 2, companies deal with economic, social, technological, and legal and political environments. Exhibit 11–3 shows the environmental impact of AIDS in all four sectors.

The increasing presence of AIDS in the workplace has crystallized a number of concerns for both employers and employees. By late 1988, more than 1.5 million people had tested positive for the HIV virus that causes AIDS. Of 2,000 companies with more than 50 employees surveyed in 1988, 10 percent had at least one worker with AIDS. Among firms with more than 10,000 employees, 59 percent had one or more workers with AIDS.[69]

All observers agree the number of AIDS cases is increasing and companies must address the cost of medical treatment. In 1992, 365 life and health insurance companies responded to a poll asking how much they had paid out in AIDS claims. The poll, conducted by the American Council of Life Insurance and the Health Insurance Association of America, reported respondents paid $1.4 billion in claims. This was a 7 percent increase over 1991 and four times as much as in 1986, the year first surveyed. Group health claims showed the largest increase, up 15 percent to $525 million. The figures do not include payments made directly to self-insured employees or claims paid by Blue Cross–Blue Shield.[70]

---

[67] E. Felsenthal, "The Disabilities Act Is Being Invoked in Diverse Cases," *The Wall Street Journal,* March 31, 1993, p. B1.

[68] J. Bovard, "The Disabilities Act's Parade of Absurdities," *The Wall Street Journal,* June 22, 1995, p. A16.

[69] B. Harrison, "AIDS Enters the Office," *Financial Times,* January 20, 1993, p. 8.

[70] "Insurers Pay $1.4b for AIDS Claims," *Boston Globe,* August 10, 1993, p. 35.

EXHIBIT 11–3 Environmental Forces Affecting Social Issues Strategy for Companies in High-AIDS Environments

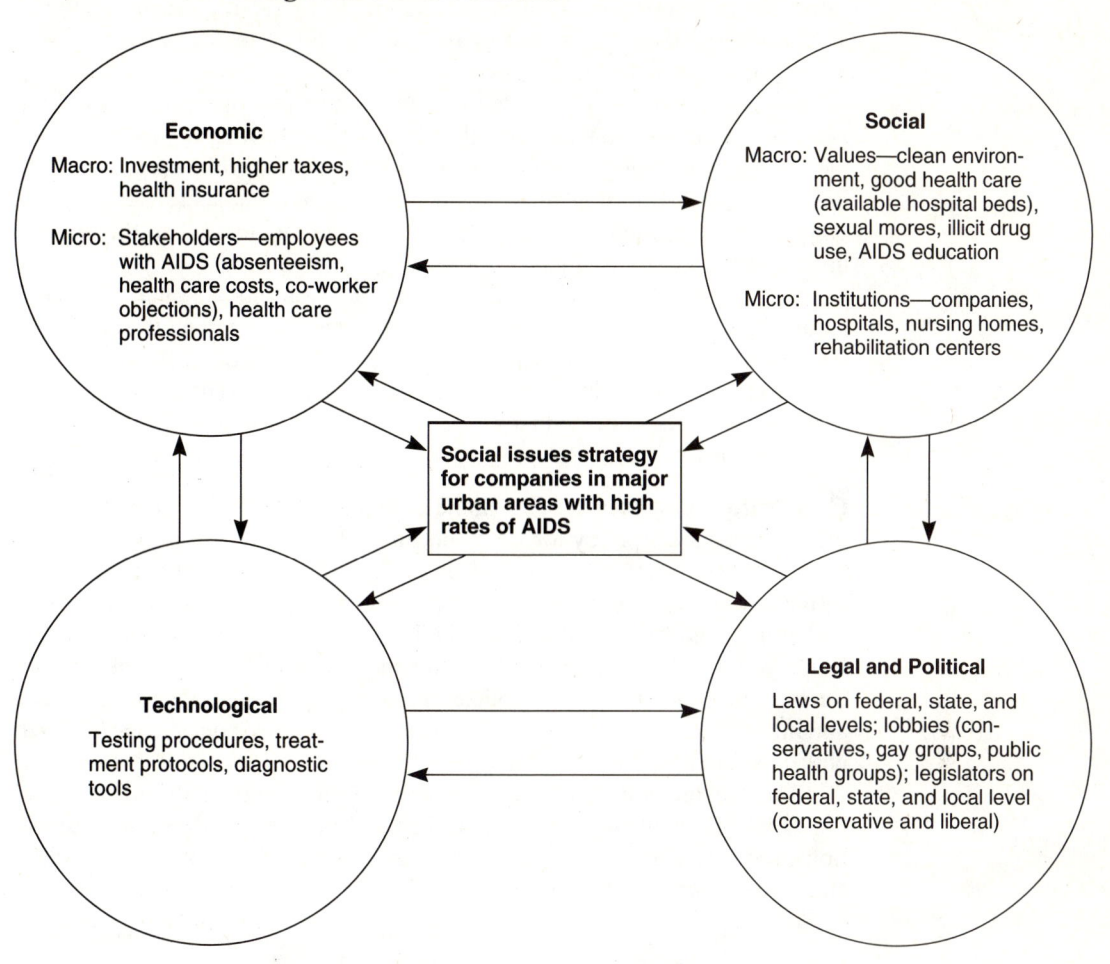

Economic

Macro: Investment, higher taxes, health insurance

Micro: Stakeholders—employees with AIDS (absenteeism, health care costs, co-worker objections), health care professionals

Social

Macro: Values—clean environment, good health care (available hospital beds), sexual mores, illicit drug use, AIDS education

Micro: Institutions—companies, hospitals, nursing homes, rehabilitation centers

Social issues strategy for companies in major urban areas with high rates of AIDS

Technological

Testing procedures, treatment protocols, diagnostic tools

Legal and Political

Laws on federal, state, and local levels; lobbies (conservatives, gay groups, public health groups); legislators on federal, state, and local level (conservative and liberal)

Title I of the Americans with Disabilities Act covers employees infected with the HIV virus. The act prohibits employers, employment agencies, labor organizations, and joint labor–management committees from discriminating against individuals with AIDS or ARC (AIDS-related complex). The act does not require that the infected person manifest symptoms of the disease. Title I applies to job application procedures, hiring, promotion, discharge, training, employee compensation, and other terms and conditions of employment.[71]

States have different fair employment laws that apply to people infected with AIDS. In many states, including Florida, Massachusetts, and Kentucky, employers cannot require an AIDS test as a condition of employment. In

---

[71] *AIDS in the Workplace* (Chicago: Commerce Clearing House, 1990), p. 5.

Minnesota, public employers are prohibited from discriminating against any employee or job applicant because of the person's sexual orientation or AIDS infection. In Rhode Island, a prospective employer can require an AIDS test as a condition of employment only if it can demonstrate a "clear and present danger of the AIDS virus to others."[72]

In practice, an employer can exclude someone from a job only if the person cannot perform the essential tasks associated with that job. For example, an AIDS-afflicted employee who normally stands while checking books out of a library cannot be disqualified if he can do the job sitting down. The employer is required to make a "reasonable accommodation" to the individual's needs and requirements.

On the other hand, an employer need not accommodate the individual if it can show accommodation would impose undue hardship on the business's operation. For example, a hospital need not keep an AIDS-afflicted nurse in an operating room setting where patients may be at risk. The hospital may be required to place the nurse in a job elsewhere in the hospital where she could not infect others accidentally.

Corporate Policy for AIDS. Some companies argue they do not need to develop a separate policy for AIDS because this illness is like any other and covered by the same policies and procedures. Many people are still uninformed about how the HIV virus is passed, how the disease affects people over time, and how it affects an individual's ability to perform his job. Employers without explicit policies are more vulnerable to charges of discrimination. Clearly written policies minimize employee uncertainty, fear, and mistrust. Even if a company does not have a written policy, an articulated philosophy can be very helpful.

The Washington, D.C.-based National Leadership Coalition on AIDS issued the following 10 principles for the workplace. More than 580 corporations, unions, religious and voluntary organizations representing 3.5 million employees have adopted them.

- Persons with HIV infection, including AIDS, have the same rights, responsibilities, and opportunities as others with serious illnesses or disabilities.
- Our employment policies comply with federal, state, and local laws.
- Our employment policies are based on the scientific fact that persons with HIV infection, including AIDS, do not cause risk to others in the workplace through ordinary workplace contact.
- Our management and employee leaders endorse a nondiscrimination policy.
- Special training and equipment will be used when necessary, such as in health care settings, to minimize risks to employees.

---

[72] Ibid., pp. 73–74.

- We will ensure that AIDS education is provided to all of our employees.
- We will endeavor to ensure that education takes place before AIDS-related incidents occur in our workplace.
- Confidentiality of persons with HIV infection and AIDS will be protected.
- We will not screen for HIV as part of preemployment or workplace physical examinations.
- We will support these policies through their clear communication to all current and prospective employees.

Family and Child Care Benefits

Family and child care are two of this decade's most pressing workplace issues. Changing demographics are responsible for this profound attitudinal change. As we note throughout this book, women, single parents, and dual-career couples dominate the workforce. They are searching for child care at the same time they are trying to cope with the problems of aging parents. The adult workforce today is a sandwich generation, caught between the needs of young and elderly dependents. In 1990, only 10 percent of more than 1 million firms with more than 10 employees offered help with child care needs.[73] Help for dependent elderly family members was even harder to find. In the late 1980s, a coalition of interest groups began to push for a federal family leave bill.

The Family Leave Bill

Although the Reagan and Bush administrations declared their commitment to family values, they opposed implementation of a national family leave bill. In 1990, when President Bush vetoed a family leave bill, Congress lacked the votes to override his veto.

In 1991, 11 of the nation's leading corporations announced they would join with more than 100 smaller businesses to collaborate on a $25.4 million project to help provide their employees with care for children and aging family members. The companies were IBM, American Express, Exxon, Eastman Kodak, Xerox, Travelers Corporation, Johnson & Johnson, Amoco, Allstate Insurance, Motorola, and AT&T. These companies financed 300 local programs in 44 cities. The programs included new child care centers, in-home care for elderly family members, vacation programs for school-age children, and vocational training for at-home mothers.

---

[73] L. T. Thomas and J. E. Thomas, "The ABCs of Child Care: Building Blocks of Competitive Advantage," *Sloan Management Review* (Winter 1990), p. 31.

In a joint statement the companies said, "The basic principle guiding our collaboration is the belief that we can accomplish more by working together than by working alone."[74] A spokesperson for IBM, which initiated the collaboration in the spring of 1991, declared, "These are family issues, not women's issues . . . . We have to attract and retain the best people we can find, more and more of whom have issues regarding their family lives."[75]

In September 1992, the House of Representatives approved a watered-down version of the 1990 family leave bill and once again sent it to the White House. This bill applied only to employers with 50 or more employees. The Women's Legal Defense Fund, a major backer, estimated that 300,000 workers had lost their jobs since 1990 because there was no federal family leave bill. Some Republicans warned the president a veto would hurt his chances of reelection. Bush retorted that he supported the family leave bill in principle but would veto it because it would impose new employee benefits on business groups. He maintained employees and employers could voluntarily work out an agreeable policy without legislation from Washington.[76]

President Bush vetoed the measure. While campaigning for a second term, he presented his own plan to grant small businesses tax breaks if they gave workers family medical leave. His opponent, Bill Clinton, strongly supported the federal bill and promised to sign it if elected.

The Senate vote overrode President Bush's veto but the House delayed the vote until the election was won. In February 1993, President Clinton won an early victory when the House approved the family leave bill. The bill had to go back to the Senate, because Senate Republicans had tacked on a measure pertaining to homosexuals serving in the military.

On February 5, 1993, 71 senators voted for and 27 opposed the family leave bill, and President Clinton signed it into law.[77] It went into effect on August 5, 1993. Exhibit 11–4 details the basic points of the Family Leave and Medical Act of 1993.

Child Care

The rapid increase in the number of women in the paid labor force and the prevalence of single mothers are among the most significant social changes of the past two decades. In August 1993, the U.S. Bureau of the Census reported that single motherhood was on the rise. In 1982, 15 percent of unwed women between the ages of 18 and 44 bore a child. In 1992, 24 percent of women in that age group became mothers.

---

[74] T. Lewin, "Top Businesses Join in Plan to Provide Dependent Care," *New York Times,* September 11, 1992, p. A26.

[75] Ibid.

[76] M. Kranish, "Family Leave Bill Is Sent to President," *Boston Globe,* September 11,

[77] A. Clymer, "Family-Leave Bill Passes the Senate and Nears Signing," *New York Times,* February 5, 1993, p. A1.

EXHIBIT 11-4 The Family Leave and Medical Act of 1993

Employees' Rights and Obligations
1. Employees are allowed to take up to 12 weeks of unpaid leave in any 12-month period for the birth or adoption of a child; to care for a child, spouse, or parent with a serious health condition—or for the worker's own health condition that makes it impossible to perform the job.
    Employees must have worked at least 25 hours a week for the company for at least one year prior to applying for the leave. They are also required to give their employers 30 days' notice for foreseeable leaves.
2. Employees must be returned to their old jobs or equivalent positions upon returning to work. An equivalent position must have the same pay, benefits, and working conditions and must involve the same or substantially similar duties and responsibilities.
3. Employees can keep their health benefits during the leave, as though they were still employed, but the employer is not required to pay workers' salaries. An employee may choose not to retain health coverage during the leave but must be reinstated on the same terms when he returns to work.
4. The employee cannot collect unemployment or other government compensation while on leave.

Employer's Rights and Obligations
1. Any employer with fewer than 50 workers is exempt.
2. An employer can deny leave to a salaried employee within the highest-paid 10 percent of its workforce if letting the employee take the leave would create "substantial and grievous injury" to the business operations.
3. An employer may require the employee to provide medical certification or opinions needed for the leave.
4. The employer may ask the employee to repay the health care premiums paid by the employer during the leave if the employee does not return to work.

Sources: A. Clymer, "Family-Leave Bill Passes the Senate and Nears Signing," *New York Times,* February 5, 1993, p. Al.; "Nutter, McLennen & Fish Client Advisory," February 9, 1993.

Substantial differences occurred across racial lines. In 1982, out-of-wedlock births as a percentage of all births among women between ages 18 and 44, were 10 percent among white women and 49 percent among African-American women. A decade later, 17 percent was white and 67 percent was African-American.

There were also differences across educational lines. More educated women had children out of wedlock. In 1992, 11 percent of unmarried mothers had some college education, and 8.3 percent had a managerial or professional occupation. In 1982, only 5 percent were professionals. Lesbians are a growing segment of this educated, more affluent group of single mothers. Although the Census Bureau's definition does not consider their households to be traditional, many are part of two-parent families.[78] The escalation of births to single women, including lesbians, slowed in 1995 and 1996.

---
[78] T. Mashberg, "More Mothers Unwed, Unwistful," *Boston Globe,* July 15, 1993, p. 1.

Child care needs continued to grow regardless of marital status. In 1994, the Labor Department reported that 60 percent of all mothers with children under the age of six were in the labor force. Ten million American preschoolers needed child care while their mothers worked in the paid labor force. Much of the care was provided by relatives. Stay-at-home fathers, older siblings, and grandparents provided 41 percent of child care arrangements. For the 59 percent of children in child care outside the family structure, the situation was grim and getting grimmer. In 1995, the media reported that American child care was in crisis. Working parents at all income levels were leaving their children in settings that jeopardized their health and safety. In 1995, economists and child-development experts at four universities conducted a study of 400 day care centers. The study entitled *Cost, Quality, and Child Outcomes in Child Care Centers* found that 73.3 percent of the centers provided mediocre care. Mediocre care was defined as meeting children's basic needs, providing some warmth and support, but offering few learning experiences. More than 12 percent of day care centers received unacceptable ratings because they did not meet children's safety needs, there was no warmth or support from adults, and learning was not encouraged. Only 14 percent of the centers fully met health and safety needs, encouraged learning, and furnished close relationships between adults and children.[79]

The investigators tried to discover why good child care was so hard to find. They concluded that cost was the single largest factor. On average it cost a center almost $5,000 per year, excluding donations, to provide services for one child. That represented 8 percent of the 1993 median U.S. family pretax income for a dual-earner family and 23 percent of household earnings with a single parent working full time. Strong competition in a local market kept prices down but depressed quality. The study noted that centers had little incentive to raise quality because they would have to spend more to lower ratios between children and adults. They also would have to hire better-educated teachers. There was a wide gap between investigators' and parents' assessment of what constituted quality child care. Parents overestimated the quality of the care children received. Ninety percent of parents rated programs as very good, while trained observers rated most of them poor to mediocre.[80]

In 1996, *Business Week* conducted its first poll on work and family strategies. Together with Boston University's Center on Work & Family, the magazine rated companies on their family-friendly strategies including child care. The survey found that large-scale corporate expenditures helped create good child care facilities and gave parents the flexibility to tend to children's needs. The companies surveyed were drawn from the *Business Week* 1000 publicly traded firms. The first questionnaire graded companies on their

---

[79] M. Galen and M. McNamee, "Honey, We're Cheating the Kids," *Business Week*, February 20, 1995, p. 38.

[80] Ibid.

self-described programs, flexible work arrangements, and organizational infrastructure. A second questionnaire was delivered to 500 randomly selected employees at each company. Some companies such as IBM, Corning, and Johnson & Johnson refused to participate even though they were known for their family-friendly policies. Other companies, questioning methodology and fairness also refused to take part. In alphabetical order, the top 10 family-friendly companies were Dupont, Eddie Bauer, Eli Lilly, First Bank Tennessee, Hewlett-Packard, Marriott International, MBNA America Bank, Merrill Lynch, Motorola, and Unum Life Insurance. First Bank Tennessee, with 8,000 employees, received the top rating overall. Employees said there was a powerful companywide commitment to family issues although the bank paid less than industry leaders. First Tennessee developed worker teams that set their own schedules and promoted flexibility. The company provided on-site child care or furnished vouchers for off-site care. Job-sharing and fitness centers were other benefits that reflected the company's view that family concerns affected business results.

Elder Care

The Family and Medical Leave Act also helped adult children cope with aging parents or dependents. Adult day care centers multiplied tenfold between the mid-1980s and 1990s. By 2030, 20 percent of the population will be over the age of 75. The number of elderly parents per adult child will nearly double and families will need to provide 80 percent of long-term care.[81] In 1989, 3 percent of medium and large enterprises offered elder care programs compared to 31 percent in 1993. Small firms were much less likely to offer elder care; in 1992, only 1 percent of companies with fewer than 100 people had programs.[82]

A 1995 study by the Family and Work Institute in New York found that working caregivers were holding full-time jobs while adding more than 15 hours a week to assist elderly relatives. Fifty-six percent said they worried at the office about their elderly dependents and 48 percent telephoned more than usual to check up on them. Thirty-seven percent arrived late at work or had to leave early and 37 percent felt their productivity was affected by the demands of elder care.

Job mobility is affected by concerns over aging parents. Search firms increasingly find that prospective employees consider elder care as a factor in whether they will relocate. Rather than hire a less desirable candidate, a few companies such as Apple Computer sometimes agree to pay for moving elderly relatives. A 1996 survey of employees at eight large companies noted that 37 percent of those who identified themselves as providing care for an

---

[81] M. O. Kirk, "Need Extra Care for an Aging Parent? Maybe the Boss Can Help," *New York Times,* August 20, 1995, p. F9.
[82] Ibid.

elderly relative said they were not interested in relocating. By comparison, 26 percent of all employees said they would not be interested in moving. Cris Collie, executive of the Employee Relocation Council said, "This [elder care] was not on our radar screen a few years ago . . . but the growth in concern is astronomical."[83]

Health Care

Health care is one of the country's most pressing social issues. The United States spends more on health care than any country in the world. In 1992, health care spending rose to 14 percent of the nation's gross national product (GNP). The Department of Commerce estimated it would continue to rise by 12 to 15 percent each year unless the system was reformed.[84] A 1994 Louis Harris & Associates poll found that Americans were much more dissatisfied with their system than the Germans or Canadians. Only 18 percent of Americans thought their health care system worked well compared to 30 percent of Germans and Canadians. Twenty-eight percent of Americans believed the health care system needed to be completely rebuilt. Half thought the nation spent too little on health care and 83 percent worried about too much bureaucracy.[85]

During his 1992 campaign, presidential candidate Bill Clinton promised to develop a new national health care plan to serve all stakeholders. After the election, he charged Hillary Rodham Clinton with developing the plan. A national debate had been raging even before the 1992 election. In April 1991, the *New York Times* published a five-part series entitled "The Price of Health." Researchers found most Americans had health insurance coverage through their jobs. Federal, state, and local governments accounted for 40 percent of all health care spending.[86]

Medicare covered all elderly people, including those who could afford other forms of insurance. The very poorest people were covered by Medicaid, but half the population with incomes below the poverty line were still too affluent to qualify. About 33 million Americans, or 13 percent of the population, had no coverage. Of this number, most were low-income workers and their families. Tens of millions more had such limited policies that a major illness could wipe out all of their financial assets.

By the end of the 1995 fiscal year, Congress and President Clinton seemed exhausted by the impasse on health care reform. The president's plan was severely rejected by big business and Congress early in 1994. The House

---

[83] J. H. Bobrzynski, "For More and More Job Seekers, an Aging Parent Is a Big Factor," *New York Times,* January 1, 1996, p. 1.

[84] "Too Sick to Wait," *Economist,* January 16, 1993, p. 30.

[85] "Grading U.S. Health Care," *Business Week,* February 5, 1996, p. 26.

[86] E. Eckholm, "Rescuing Health Care," *New York Times,* May 2, 1991, p. A1.

and the Senate debated and debated, finally offering their versions of Medicare and Medicaid overhaul bills. In Medicare, both the House and Senate plans tried to control costs by shifting beneficiaries into private plans, holding down payments to doctors and hospitals, and raising premiums. Each Medicare plan was expected to save about $270 billion over seven years. House Republicans wanted to offer a better package to health maintenance organizations and other private health care plans than Senate Republicans.

House and Senate plans tried to control Medicaid costs by ending the guarantee of aid to every poor person who qualified. They proposed continuing block grants to states to give states enormous authority to decide who would receive which benefit. Legislators expected both plans to save about $182 billion over seven years.[87]

Managed care through health maintenance organizations (HMOs) was a critical component of health care reform. In a managed care system, participants agree to use a certain group of designated physicians, specialists, and hospitals. They may go outside the system but must bear the costs themselves. An insurance company manages this network by obtaining volume discounts from the physicians and ensuring that they do not order unnecessary tests or treatments.[88]

In October 1995, House Republicans passed legislation to curb Medicare spending and encourage the elderly to turn to private managed care organizations from the traditional government plan that had been in place since 1965. President Clinton threatened to veto the measure saying that the bill "will eviscerate the health system for our older Americans."[89] A *New York Times* poll taken immediately after the vote showed the American public feared the Republican plan and did not believe it would produce a balanced budget by 2002. The survey of 1,077 adults showed the public overwhelmingly shared the Republican belief that the states would do better than the federal government in setting rules for health care.[90]

Two weeks before the December deadline for the next budget, President Clinton and Congress were still at loggerheads. Both sides vowed there could be no deal without a major compromise on Medicaid and Medicare. Although Medicare generated the most acrimonious disputes, experts considered the disagreements on Medicaid to be much greater. On Medicaid, the biggest question was whether to preserve a basic federal guarantee of health coverage for the needy or to let the states design their own programs with lump sums of federal money. Republicans and the administration had huge

---

[87] A. Clymer, "So Many Measures, So Little Time," *New York Times,* September 25, 1995, p. A12.

[88] W. E. Sheeline, "Taking on Public Enemy No. 1," *Fortune,* July 1, 1991, pp. 58–59.

[89] A. Clymer, "House Votes to Curb Costs on Medicare by $270 Billion; President Promises a Veto," *New York Times,* October 20, 1995, p. A1.

[90] A. Clymer, "Americans Reject Big Medicare Cuts, a New Poll Finds," *New York Times,* October 26, 1995, p. A1.

differences in ideology. Both sides were engaged in political posturing over the role of the federal government and the amount of discretion the states should have in determining coverage.

Finally, in April 1996, the Senate unanimously passed a significant health insurance reform bill. By a 100-0 vote, the Senate agreed to a modest measure to guarantee access to health insurance to those who suffered from preexisting medical conditions or who lost or left their jobs. The bill also prevented insurance companies from denying coverage to companies because of the health care status of an employee. It made costs for long-term care tax deductible and increased the health care tax deduction for the self-employed. Although the House and Senate versions still had some differences, most observers thought there was progress toward a compromise. Senator Kennedy (D-Mass.), a sponsor of the bill, called it a "constructive step forward."[91]

In August 1996, the House approved the Senate version of the health insurance bill by a vote of 421-2. According to House Speaker Newt Gingrich, the legislation represented, "the market-oriented free choice of citizens we think is so important in order to improve and strengthen the health system." On August 21, 1996, President Clinton signed the Health Insurance Portability and Accountability Act that made no mention of Medicare or Medicaid. Major provisions of the act

- Required group insurance plans to cover employees with preexisting medical conditions within a year of starting a job.
- Prohibited group insurance plans from dropping coverage for a sick employee, or for a business with a sick employee.
- Required insurance companies to make individual coverage available to people who leave group plans.
- Set up, on an experimental basis, some tax-deductible medical savings accounts for small businesses, the self-employed, and the uninsured.
- Expanded tax-deductibility for health insurance premiums for the self-employed to 80 percent, up from 30 percent, by 2006.[92]

Medicare and Medicaid funding was incorporated into the 1997 domestic budget appropriation bills passed on the eve of the 1996 election. A sweeping new welfare bill made almost no changes in Medicaid. Republicans said they would "bow to political reality and seek incremental reforms if President Clinton did not change his position."[93] The Medicare discussion was likely to continue indefinitely.

---

[91] C. Black, "Senate OK's Health Care Safeguard," *Boston Globe,* April 24, 1996, p. 1.

[92] S. Ugelow, "Clinton Signs Bill to Secure Health Benefits," *The Wall Street Journal,* August 22, 1996, p. A16.

[93] J. Gray, "Senate Approves a Big Budget Bill Beating Deadline," *New York Times,* October 1, 1996, p. A1.

By the beginning of 1997, health care costs were barely increasing. In the 12-month period ending September 1996, the National Bureau of Labor Statistics reported that employers paid just seven-tenths of a percent more to buy health care for their workers than a year earlier. Employers were aggressively trying to squeeze the excess out of the health system and were negotiating steep discounts with managed care insurance companies. Hospitals also made money-saving moves and consolidations. As Harvard University health economist David Cutler observed, "Doctors aren't going to become basketball players . . . if they're paid 30 percent less, they'll grumble and take it."[94]

Medium- and large-size employers provided health insurance to 82 percent of their full-time, permanent workers, less than the 92 percent in 1989. The U.S. Census Bureau said 4 to 6 million people were without health insurance for all of 1995, 7 million more than in 1989. High-school graduates were twice as likely to lack health insurance as college graduates. Who would pay the health care bill for those who were uninsured? With Medicare costs rising much more quickly than private-sector costs, Congress was likely to revisit the still unresolved Medicare issue early in its 105th session.

[94] Firms Cut Health Costs, Cover Fewer Workers, "*The Wall Street Journal,* November 11, 1996, p. A1.

Summary

Workplace issues of the 1990s have their roots in earlier decades. As the United States shifted from a manufacturing- to a service-oriented society, the composition of the workforce changed and new stakeholders emerged. Innovative technologies gave employers new tools with which to assess employee performance. Computerization of employee files and electronic devices allowed employers to compile huge masses of data about each employee without his explicit consent.

The polygraph, or lie detector, is used much less frequently today, but written tests are being used to identify potential problem employees. Electronic surveillance is used very widely, particularly to monitor employees in low-skilled jobs. Innovations like the smart badge promise new opportunities to track workers' activities. E-mail privacy issues are still unresolved.

Stress on the job is a major workplace problem. It costs companies in terms of absenteeism, lower productivity, and hostility. Unfavorable economic conditions, family problems, and productivity pressures exacerbate stress. In the most extreme cases, stress can lead to worker aggression and even homicide.

Companies face a variety of medical issues, many of them difficult to resolve. Substance abuse has grown over the past decade. Companies cannot discriminate against workers with substance abuse problems. Rehabilitation programs have proven effective in returning workers to productivity.

Individuals with disabilities have shown more activism in the 1990s. Their efforts were given impetus by the passage of the Americans with Disabilities Act in 1990 and its subsequent implementation. Generally, companies have discovered it costs comparatively little to meet national guidelines, and they have expanded their pool of productive employees. The courts are still trying to interpret the act's exact meaning, but EEOC guidelines should clarify Congress's intent.

HIV infection and AIDS will present employers with major challenges for the foreseeable future.

Companies of all sizes will have to deal with the social and financial burdens created by AIDS. The Americans with Disabilities Act is explicit regarding how employers must accommodate AIDS patients. Legal issues such as insurance coverage are still being worked out through the courts.

Family and child care are two of the most pressing workplace issues of the 1990s. Many baby boomers are caring for small children and elderly parents at the same time. Although the Family Leave and Medical Act of 1993 provides short-term help, companies are just beginning to tackle this concern. They have not come up with universally acceptable answers. It remains to be seen whether the federal government will develop its own plan or the government and corporate America will work together to provide these essential services.

The government is developing a health care policy to bring basic coverage to most Americans regardless of income or job status. This issue is tremendously complex and has engendered strong stakeholder controversy. A new model will present huge opportunities for some industries and will probably diminish opportunities for others. Overall, a profound national reorientation is under way that will take considerable time to evolve.

Projects

1. You are the CEO of a highly regarded security firm. You have taken on a new client who requires 30 additional security personnel to guard per premises. Develop a recruitment and training plan that satisfies your own standards for high-quality, well-trained personnel and still meets your customer's six-week deadline. Pay particular attention to standards of employee reliability, honesty, and expertise. Discuss how you will meet those standards without violating the new recruits' privacy.

2. As the human resources manager in a medium-size computer firm, you collect data on employee absences. You notice that during the past year, many of the firm's engineers have been reporting sick for one or two days at a time. Absenteeism is clearly up, but you don't really know why. Office gossip leads you to think the engineers are feeling stressed and anxious about changes in the firm's environment. Analyze the economic, social, legal and political, and technological environmental factors for the high-tech industry. Devise a plan to reduce stress and restore a more productive working environment.

3. In your community, find three companies that will let you interview their benefits manager. Before the interview, draw up a questionnaire that will give you information about each company's choice of health care programs. Find out what decision process the company used and whether it has changed health care plans in the past two years. If the company has changed plans, ascertain what led to that change. Based on your interview, draw some conclusions about the companies' decision rules in selecting a health care plan. If you have an opportunity, interview employees to find out what they want from their health care plan and whether they are satisfied.

Questions

1. Discuss the benefits and drawbacks of a drug-testing program for a company's truck drivers.

2. Discuss the factors that create the greatest stress in (*a*) a word processing job and (*b*) a marketing management job.

3. *a.* What would be the ideal form of child care in this country? Discuss alternatives.
   b. Discuss the appropriate role of the local, state, and federal governments in providing that ideal form of child care.

Beta Case 11
Workplace Issues for the 1990s

John West, Beta's vice president of human resources, usually looked forward to his routine of having a quiet early morning cup of coffee and a sweet roll at the kitchen table before he left for work. This morning, West was distracted by the papers he had brought home the previous night in preparation for today's meeting with Sam Powell, vice president of the Biotechnology Division. Powell had requested the meeting to report he had discovered some very serious breaches in his division's security system.

Powell's division was developing the new drugs everyone hoped would generate Beta's future profits. Secrecy was imperative in developing new products. Earlier in the week, a concerned employee had told Powell he suspected two co-workers were leaking Beta's secrets to the competition. "These turkeys are both druggies," he told Powell. "The money they get for the secrets goes right up their noses."

Powell was stunned by this graphic description of security violations. Beta did not have a random drug-testing program, and Powell had no idea what to do next. He questioned the suspects, but both denied any wrongdoing.

This is a potentially disastrous situation, thought West. We are not talking about petty theft; we are talking about the future of the company and a drug problem of unknown proportions. I've got to get my legal facts straight and then make some important policy decisions.

CHAPTER 12

EQUAL EMPLOYMENT AND AFFIRMATIVE ACTION

CASE: DIVERSITY TRAINING

Reed Lawrence, Prime Office Furniture's CEO, was concerned that the company promoted too few women and minorities. He suggested to Jennifer Stills that she organize a workshop to increase sensitivity among the company's department heads. Jennifer consulted with several diversity training companies and collected a number of their frequently used exercises. One exercise instructed supervisors to discuss stereotypes they had heard or used about women and minority group members. Although Stills had some concerns about using this exercise and bringing unpleasant stereotypes to the surface, experts assured her that usually it was very positive to acknowledge prejudice and deal with it openly.

Jennifer sent a memo to each of Prime's 10 department heads asking them to reserve a full morning the following Wednesday. Nine of the department heads were men; none was African-American, Asian, or Hispanic. Sue Fielding, head of the accounting department, was the only female in the group. She was 50 years old and had worked for Prime since her college graduation.

Stills hoped that a breakfast of juice, bagels, doughnuts, and coffee would create the right informal atmosphere. After everyone had eaten, they got down to work. She explained the exercise to the participants and stressed its purpose was to help stereotypes surface but not to attack or criticize any person or group.

"Women cry when they're criticized," one manager said.

"Blacks are lazy," said another.

"Hispanics just want to take life easy," declared a third.

Sue Fielding kept silent. She thought, "Why should I open my mouth? I've worked really hard to get where I am, and nothing I say is going to make these guys behave differently. If I say that white males are self-centered, insensitive to gender issues, or exclude people who don't look like them, they'll gang up on me. Even worse, they'll remember it for years after this session is over."

John Martin, head of the paint department, stood up. "You know," he said, "I really hate being here. I feel as if we are dumping on all the groups that aren't represented in this room. What good does it do to talk about people who aren't here to defend themselves?"

"No way!" said Tom Johnson. "Minorities get all the benefits. We are catering to them instead of giving the jobs to the people who can do them best."

Jennifer Stills realized the exercise was definitely not going the way she had anticipated. She glanced at Fielding's stony face and knew she would get no help there. She did not want to create an in-group and an out-group. Instead of bringing people together, this exercise was polarizing the participants.

391

Questions

1. What should Stills do? Should she stop the exercise where it was?
2. Should Stills try to focus the conversation differently? If so, how?
3. Should Stills ask Fielding directly for her input?
4. In retrospect, should Stills have refused to do the training herself? Should she have told Reed she felt more comfortable bringing in a professional trainer?

A Level Playing Field

Managers use the term *level playing field* to describe the business environment in which they would like their firms to compete. It means all players' chances of winning are based solely on their talents and abilities. When used to describe a firm's environment, the concept of a level playing field is fairly recent. Applicants of equal ability and qualifications have not always had the same access to employment and, in some cases, still do not. Promotions and pay are not color- or gender-blind. In the past, employers could terminate workers on a whim for reasons that had nothing to do with job performance. Since the passage of the Civil Rights Act of 1964, Congress and the courts have strengthened employees' rights.

This chapter discusses the historical background of landmark employment legislation and the issues companies and employees have faced in the past 30 years. These issues include race and gender discrimination, sexual harassment, and age discrimination.

Civil Rights Act of 1964

Background

The first major piece of legislation for equal opportunity in employment dates from World War II, when President Franklin D. Roosevelt issued Executive Order 8802. This order prohibited racial discrimination in employment by companies with federal contracts. It established the first Fair Employment Practices Committee (FEPC). The effects of the order were widespread because most manufacturing companies were operating under federal wartime contracts.[1]

When large numbers of young white men left the factories to go off to war, blacks and women were hired into jobs for which they previously were not considered. Once peace was declared, many of the blacks and women were fired so that returning white servicemen could reclaim their jobs. Although the FEPC was disbanded at the end of the war, some legislators and

---

[1] S. M. Gelber, *Black Men and Businessmen* (Port Washington, NY: Kennikat Press, 1974), p. 24.

other stakeholders continued to agitate through the late 1940s and the 1950s for a permanent federal FEPC law. States and cities did pass FEPC laws, but nothing was done on the federal level.[2]

A number of companies took steps to end discrimination in hiring during the postwar period. They were motivated by two convictions: First, they believed business, rather than government, could best solve social problems. Second, they were convinced that if they failed to address the issues voluntarily, Congress would pass restrictive and possibly oppressive legislation.

However, there were glaring disparities between the treatment of blacks and whites. In the 1950s, equal opportunity was a privilege enjoyed primarily by white males. Rosa Parks, an African-American sparked the civil rights movement that promoted equal opportunity. In December 1955, Parks, a department store employee, refused to give her seat on the bus to a white man. Although her actions were not directly related to equal opportunity, Martin Luther King, Jr., and his followers used the incident as the rationale for a bus boycott which they followed with years of demonstrations and marches. The media brought the struggle for racial equality into living rooms around the country.

The public grew increasingly aware that basic workplace rights were the prerogative of only one segment of the population: white men. This awareness led to a renewed call for federal equal rights legislation. Race was the primary focus of the civil rights struggle. Women active in the civil rights movement were told to put their gender demands aside until the primary issues of racial discrimination were settled.

Employee Qualifications

Throughout the early 1960s, most proponents of equal job opportunities emphasized the hiring of qualified employees without regard for race or ethnicity. This color-blind perspective on equal opportunity prohibited overt discrimination against racial and ethnic groups. However, some claimed it fostered a more subtle form of discrimination because it failed to right past wrongs. No special attention was paid to those people who had been considered unqualified for employment because of past discriminatory practices.[3]

By the early 1960s, it was clear that voluntary policies had failed to make a substantial dent in black unemployment. Blacks and other stakeholders called for affirmative action to make up for past inequities.

In 1961, President John F. Kennedy issued Executive Order 10925 establishing the President's Commission on Equal Employment Opportunity (PCEEO). The commission had the power to investigate complaints and enforce a ban on discrimination by federal contractors. In addition, the order required government contractors to "take affirmative action to ensure that

---

[2] P. S. Foner, *Organized Labor and the Black Worker, 1619–1973* (New York: Praeger Publishers, 1974), pp. 269–70.

[3] Gelber, *Black Men and Businessmen,* p. 165.

applicants are employed and that employees are treated during employment without regard to their race, creed, color, or national origin."[4] The PCEEO could terminate contracts of noncompliant employers, prevent them from obtaining further government contracts, and recommend that the Department of Justice bring criminal or injunctive action against them.

Title VII of the Civil Rights Act of 1964

Title VII extended many provisions of Executive Order 10925. The act covered all employers of 25 or more people, employment agencies, and labor unions with 25 or more members. It also added a prohibition against gender discrimination.[5]

Title VII, which took effect in 1965, was amended in 1972 and again in 1979. As amended, it covered nearly all employers with more than 15 employees except private clubs, religious organizations, and Native American reservations. Section 703(a) of Title VII was the most important provision. It stated, in part, "It shall be an unlawful employment practice for an employer (1) to fail or refuse to hire or discharge any individual, or otherwise to discriminate against any individual with respect to his compensation, terms, conditions, or privileges of employment, because of such individual's race, color, sex or national origin."[6] The amendments did not change the intent of the law; they merely broadened its scope and made it more inclusive.

Title VII provided that employers did not have to hire employees if it were unreasonable to do so. It declared, "Nothing contained in this title shall be interpreted to require any employer . . . to grant preferential treatment to any individual or to any group because of the race, color, religion, sex, or national origin of such individual or group on account of an imbalance which may exist with respect to the total number or percentage of persons of any race, color, religion, sex, or national origin employed by any employer."[7] The law also stated, "Notwithstanding any other provision of this title, it shall not be an unlawful employment practice for an employer to apply different standards of compensation, or different terms, conditions, or privileges of employment pursuant to a bona fide seniority or merit system . . . provided that such differences are not the result of an intention to discriminate."[8]

The 1964 Civil Rights Act emphasized equal opportunity for the individual. Employers were not required to give preferential treatment; indeed, they

---

[4] Ibid., p. 140.

[5] Bureau of National Affairs, *The Equal Employment Opportunity Act of 1972* (Washington, D.C.: U.S. Government Printing Office, 1973), p. 1.

[6] Subcommittee on Labor, Committee on Labor and Public Welfare, U.S. Senate, *Compilation of Selected Labor Laws Pertaining to Labor Relations, Part II* (Washington, D.C.: U.S. Government Printing Office, 1974), p. 591.

[7] Ibid., p. 610.

[8] Ibid., p. 612.

were expressly forbidden to do so. The act viewed discrimination as an intentional, calculated act to exclude some people from work.

Equal Employment Opportunity Commission (EEOC)

In 1965, Congress created the Equal Employment Opportunity Commission (EEOC) as an independent agency to implement antidiscrimination legislation. The EEOC was composed of five commissioners, not more than three of whom could belong to the same political party. The president appointed the commissioners and the Senate confirmed them for five-year terms. The EEOC also had a presidentially appointed general counsel who served for four years. As with other federal agencies, Congress specified the basic criteria EEOC was to use in implementing congressional directives.[9] Exhibit 12–1 lists the major responsibilities of the EEOC.

In 1990, President Bush appointed Evan Kemp, Jr., as chairman of the commission. Kemp, who was confined to a wheelchair with a polio-type disease, vowed to be the chairperson for all Americans. His appointment was concomitant with the passage of the Americans with Disabilities Act. When Kemp resigned, longtime commissioner Tony Gallegos became acting chair and served for 18 months. Very little was accomplished during the period in which the agency waited for a permanent chair.

On October 3, 1994, Gilbert Casellas assumed the chairmanship. The agency itself was experiencing major problems; more than 100,000 private sector cases were waiting to be heard. The EEOC experienced a $5 million

---

EXHIBIT 12–1 Major EEOC Responsibilities

- Prohibit employment discrimination on the basis of race, color, national origin, religion, or sex.
- Prohibit employment discrimination based on pregnancy, childbirth, or related medical condition.
- Protect men and women against pay discrimination based on sex.
- Protect workers age 40 or older from arbitrary age discrimination in hiring, discharge, pay, promotions, and other aspects of employment.
- Prohibit discrimination against individuals with disabilities within the federal government.

Also, the EEOC

- Coordinates all federal equal employment efforts.
- Oversees all affirmative action plans to eliminate discriminatory practices.
- Has jurisdiction over federal employees' complaints concerning equal employment.

Source: "Equal Employment Opportunity Commission," *Federal Regulatory Directory,* 6th ed. (Washington, D.C.: Congressional Quarterly, 1990), p. 109.

---

[9] J. R. Fox, *Managing Business–Government Relations* (Homewood, IL: Richard D. Irwin, 1982), p. 612.

shortfall in its $223 million annual budget, and had 526 fewer employees than in the previous year. In a 1995 interview, Casellas declared that while he had to do a great deal of internal housekeeping to restore public confidence and pride in the agency, "We have made enormous progress. . . . Some would say we have performed miracles."[10]

When an individual complains to the EEOC, the agency processes the complaint in three phases:

1. *Investigation.* The EEOC may examine the complaint itself or refer it to a state EEOC agency if that state has EEOC laws that meet federal standards. Usually the state or federal agency interviews the people involved and examines relevant records. Both state and federal EEOCs can compel companies to produce information they want. Once the EEOC collects the information, the agency decides whether there is probable cause to believe the employer has violated Title VII.

2. *Conciliation.* If the EEOC does not find probable cause, it ends the process and tells the complainant she can file a private suit in federal district court. If the EEOC finds probable cause, it undertakes the process of conciliation or negotiation. The complainant, the employer, and the EEOC try to work out a compromise acceptable to all parties and consistent with Title VII's requirement that the employer compensate the victim for the discrimination suffered.

3. *Litigation.* If the two sides cannot reach an agreement, the EEOC may litigate by filing suit against the employer in federal district court. Usually, however, the EEOC drops the case unless it has an excellent chance of winning. The complainant still retains the right to sue in federal district court.[11]

Affirmative Action

President Kennedy's Executive Order 10925 was the first order to use the term *affirmative action.* This order declared employers should make sure qualified minority group members were informed of job openings and had an equal chance to be hired. President Johnson's Executive Orders 11246 (issued in 1965) and 11375 (1967) required companies with federal contracts to have affirmative action programs that recruited workers on a nondiscriminatory basis. Companies with federal contracts worth over $50,000 and with

---

[10] Internet [http://www.careerspot.com/c4/kleiman/fc4kl065.htm]; [http://www.fpmi.com/eeobulletin/Casellas/html].

[11] J. Ledvinka, *Federal Regulation of Personnel and Human Resource Management* (Boston: Kent Publishing, 1982), pp. 30–31.

50 or more employees had to develop and put into effect written affirmative action programs.[12]

Department of Labor guidelines issued in February 1970 emphasized that affirmative action programs should be result oriented. Further guidelines, under Revised Order No. 4, were issued 11 months later. They stated, "An acceptable affirmative action program must include an analysis of areas within which the contractor is deficient in the utilization of minority groups and women, and further, goals and timetables to which the contractor's good faith efforts must be directed to correct the deficiencies and, thus, to increase materially the utilization of minorities and women, at all levels and in all segments of his workforce where deficiencies exist."[13]

The order said further, "Affirmative action programs must contain the following information: . . . An analysis of all major job classifications at the facility, with explanation if minorities are currently being underutilized in any one or more job classifications (job 'classification' herein meaning one or a group of jobs having similar content, wage rates, and opportunities). 'Underutilization' is defined as having fewer minorities or women in a particular job classification than would reasonably be expected by their availability."[14]

Although these guidelines applied only to federal contractors, the EEOC and the courts interpreted the Civil Rights Act as having similar provisions so that most large employers were affected. What began as equal opportunity came to mean statistical parity.[15]

The benchmark for minority employment became the proportion of the minority group in question living in the area or of the overall workforce in the Standard Metropolitan Statistical Area (SMSA) surrounding a business. The emphasis of affirmative action shifted from discrimination against individuals to discrimination against an entire class of people. For example, if the area in which a plant is located had 20 percent African-American residents or workers, a company should aim for a workforce that was 20 percent African-American at all levels, not only the lowest ones. Evidence of discrimination was either a conspicuous underrepresentation of women or minority group members among a company's employees or concentration of these groups at the lower levels of employment.

The law did not require companies to hire unqualified workers. It did require them to go beyond the Civil Rights Act of 1964 and undertake an active search for qualified minorities, women, and people with disabilities to

---

[12] U.S. Equal Employment Opportunity Commission, *Affirmative Action and Equal Employment: A Guidebook for Employers,* vol. 1 (Washington, D.C.: U.S. Government Printing Office, 1974), p. 13.

[13] Ibid., vol. 2, p. D-28.

[14] Ibid.

[15] N. Glazer, *Affirmative Discrimination: Ethnic Inequality and Public Policy* (New York: Basic Books, 1975), pp. 33-49.

Exhibit 12–2 Steps in an Affirmative Action Plan

An employer must:
- Conduct a utilization analysis that shows (1) the percentage of the employer's workforce that belongs to the group in question and (2) the percentage of the available labor supply in that group.
- Determine which employment policies are contributing to the underutilization of the target group.
- Establish goals, timetables, and plans for action increasing the utilization of the target group in deficient areas.
- Apply good-faith efforts to meet the goals. The term *good faith* is nonspecific and usually means the company must make a real effort to remedy underutilization.
- Take steps to meet goals in the next planning cycle if they are not met in the current one.
- Report progress to the OFCCP.

Source: N. Glazer, *Affirmative Discrimination: Ethnic Inequality and Public Policy* (New York: Basic Books, 1975), pp. 33–49.

fill positions. Employers also were expected to upgrade the skills and utilization of these same groups. Affirmative action required the employer to make as wide a search as possible for qualified applicants and to upgrade present target group employees. The Office of Federal Contract Compliance Programs (OFCCP) monitored the effort. Exhibit 12–2 shows the steps in an affirmative action program.

Landmark Supreme Court Decisions

Despite the profusion of legislation, guidelines, and court decisions, ambiguities and other problems with the implementation of affirmative action programs persist. To some white males, the preferential treatment being given to women and minority group members amounts to reverse discrimination. Affirmative action guidelines usually dictate that if a white man, a woman, and a minority group member are equally qualified for a job, an individual in one of the latter two groups should be hired because these groups are likely to be underrepresented in the firm.

After the passage of the Civil Rights Act of 1964, a number of lawsuits were filed claiming companies were discriminating in favor of women and minorities and this reverse discrimination violated the act. However, in April 1975, the New York State Supreme Court declared remedial legislation to be legal.

The severe recession of the early 1970s hindered company efforts to hire women and minority group members. Because seniority was the basis for layoffs and firings—at least in unionized companies—the recently hired women and minority group members were the first to lose their jobs.

During this period, the proportion of recently hired women and minorities declined sharply. Some of these fired employees filed suits, claiming the seniority system discriminated against them because it enabled white male workers to keep their jobs while members of other groups were fired.

Minority group employees contended their low seniority stemmed from prior discrimination. Companies considered several remedial alternatives, including laying off women and minority workers in the same proportion as the company's overall layoff and paying minority workers' salaries until those employees could be called back to work.[16]

However, layoffs by percentage violated seniority rules that were an important part of most union contracts. Because management implemented workforce reductions to save money, remedial payments to laid-off workers could defeat the reduction's purpose. Lower court decisions were mixed until 1984, when the Supreme Court upheld seniority as a legal basis for layoffs.

There are several landmark cases on reverse discrimination. The four most important are (1) *Allan Bakke* v *Regents of the University of California,* (2) *U.S. Steelworkers, etc.* v *Weber;* (3) *Memphis Fire Department* v *Shotts;* and (4) *City of Richmond* v *J. A. Croson.*

Allan Bakke v *The Regents of the University of California*

Allan Bakke, who contended he was refused admission to medical school because of reverse discrimination, brought his case before the California Supreme Court. The school to which he had applied, the University of California at Davis, had a special admissions program for minorities. Of the 100 openings for entering classes in 1973 and 1974, 84 were filled by the usual admissions process. Nonwhite applicants received preference for the remaining 16 places.

The university admitted the 16 minority applicants who had college grades and standardized examination scores well below those of the white applicants. Bakke asserted this program violated the U.S. Constitution's Fourteenth Amendment rights of equal protection to everyone regardless of color. The California Supreme Court, in a six-to-one decision, banned minority quotas in the graduate schools of California's state system.[17]

The University of California appealed the decision to the U.S. Supreme Court. The Court split five to four on the decision, supporting the California court's order admitting Bakke to the medical school. The Supreme Court held the admissions program of the University of California at Davis violated Title VI of the Civil Rights Act of 1964, which forbade racial discrimination in programs or activities receiving federal financial assistance.

The Court also ruled, however, that a university could take race into account in admissions in the same way it considered geography, athletic ability, or other special talents. As a result of the inconclusive Bakke decision,

---

[16] *Business Week*, March 9, 1976, p. 166.
[17] *Allan Bakke* v *The Regents of the University of California* 553 P, 2d 1152 (1976).

the EEOC issued new guidelines. It would not support charges that companies were violating the civil rights of white men in cases where reasonable affirmative action programs favored women or minorities.

The Bakke case had a postscript. The 1980 medical school class at the University of California at Davis had no African-Americans; in 1981, only two enrolled. Although the school made numerous offers, African-Americans rejected them. Apparently the Supreme Court's decision to admit Bakke was the single most important factor in the candidates' decision.[18]

United Steelworkers, etc. v *Weber*

In 1974, Brian Weber, a white man, was a lab analyst at a Kaiser Aluminum and Chemical plant in Gramercy, Louisiana. Kaiser and the United Steelworkers agreed to establish a program to train workers for high-paying, skilled craft jobs. At least 50 percent of the trainees were to be minority group members. Kaiser had not been ordered to establish such a program, but both the company and the union wanted to improve minority participation to head off government interference. The federal government had already observed that at Kaiser Aluminum, "prior to 1974, there were fewer than 2 percent blacks among craft workers . . . compared with a 39 percent black labor force in the area."[19]

When Brian Weber applied to the new training program, he was turned down in favor of minority group members with less seniority. Weber sued on grounds that the 1964 Civil Rights Act clearly prohibited discrimination against anyone on the basis of race. The Fifth Circuit Court of Appeals agreed with Weber, but the case was appealed to the Supreme Court.[20]

By a five-to-two majority, the Court ruled that employers could voluntarily give preferences to minorities and women in hiring and promoting for traditionally segregated job categories. In a concurring opinion, Justice William Brennan noted the Kaiser plan did not require the discharge of any white workers and did not pose an absolute barrier to their promotion. He described the plan as a "temporary measure" designed "simply to eliminate a manifest racial imbalance."[21]

Memphis Fire Department v *Stotts*

In 1980, the city of Memphis agreed to integrate its fire department by filling half of its vacancies with African-Americans. In 1981, the city suffered a

---

[18] W. King, "School Still Feels Bakke Effect," *New York Times,* December 6, 1981, p. A2.

[19] *The Wall Street Journal,* June 28, 1979, p. 30.

[20] For a review of lower court decisions in this case, see B. Lindemann Schlei and P. Grossman, *Employment Discrimination Law, 1979 Supplement* (Washington, D.C.: Bureau of National Affairs, 1979), pp. 194–96. The Supreme Court decision may be found in the *Supreme Court Reporter* 99, no. 18 (July 15, 1979), pp. 272–31.

[21] *The Wall Street Journal,* June 28, 1979, p. 30.

major budget crisis and had to lay off some city employees under the last hired, first fired rule that was part of its seniority plan. About 40 firefighters lost their jobs. The local district court ordered the city to modify its seniority plan to protect the African-American firefighters hired under the 1980 affirmative action plan. Because 15 of the 40 were African-American, the plan would have reversed the movement toward an increased percentage of African-Americans on the force.

In 1984, the Supreme Court had to decide whether the lower court had exceeded its authority by requiring the city to protect the African-American firefighters. The Reagan administration lobbied furiously against the affirmative action protection and for the seniority plan. The Supreme Court sided with Reagan administration policy. Six Supreme Court justices ruled the district court had exceeded its powers and the existing seniority plan, with its last hired, first fired provision, should stay intact.[22] Justice White wrote for the majority, "Title VII protects bonafide seniority systems and it is inappropriate to deny an innocent employee the benefits of his seniority in order to provide a remedy in a pattern or practice suit such as this."[23]

City of Richmond v *J. A. Croson*

In 1983, the Richmond City Council, five of whose nine members were African-American, passed a plan designed to increase the participation of minority firms in public works projects. The council heard testimony that although half of the city's residents were African-American, only 0.67 percent of its prime construction contracts had been awarded to minority businesses. The plan (called a set-aside) required that prime contractors subcontract at least 30 percent of the dollar value of each contract to one or more minority business enterprises. Minority was defined as at least 51 percent owned and controlled by African-American, Hispanic, Asian, Native American, Eskimo, or Aleut citizens.

In 1983, J. A. Croson Company, a white-owned mechanical plumbing and heating contractor, challenged the plan. Croson had lost a bid to supply toilets for the city jail because he could not certify he would use a minority-owned subcontractor. The city denied Croson's request for a waiver of the 30 percent set-aside.

The U.S. Court of Appeals for the Fourth Circuit, in Richmond, ruled the Richmond ordinance violated white contractors' constitutional rights to equal protection of the law. In January 1989, the Supreme Court ruled six to three to uphold the lower court ruling. In effect, the Supreme Court said laws favoring African-Americans over whites had to be judged by the same constitutional test that applied to laws favoring whites over African-Americans.

---

[22] "A Ruling That Could Roll Back Affirmative Action," *Business Week,* July 2, 1984, p. 31; L. Greenhouse, "Bias Remedy vs. Seniority," *New York Times,* June 14, 1984, p. A12.

[23] Supreme Court Decides Seniority, Not Race, Should Govern Layoffs," New York Times, pp. 1, B2.

Justice O'Connor, who wrote the majority opinion, noted that no racial discrimination, even that undertaken for a laudable purpose, is benign. She added, "Racial classifications are suspect, and that means that simple legislative assurances of good intention cannot suffice."[24]

Equal Opportunity and Affirmative Action in the 1980s

Decisions in the Memphis and Richmond cases were consistent with the Reagan and Bush administrations' philosophies. As soon as the Reagan administration took office, it abruptly reversed equal employment opportunity (EEO) and affirmative action enforcement. Raymond Donovan, Reagan's labor secretary, said he and the president believed in affirmative action but "not the push-pull, slap-punch, police approach."[25]

In 1982, William Bradford Reynolds, head of the Justice Department's Civil Rights Division, announced he hoped to get the Supreme Court to reverse its decision in the Weber case.[26] He expanded on his statement, spelling out the administration's philosophy: "By elevating the rights of groups over the rights of individuals, racial and sex preferences are at war with the American ideal of equal opportunity for each person to achieve whatever his or her industry and talents warrant. This kind of 'affirmative action' needlessly creates a caste system in which an individual must be unfairly disadvantaged for each person who is preferred."[27]

In 1986, Attorney General Edwin Meese III declared, "The idea that you can use discrimination in the form of racially preferential quotas, goals and set-asides to remedy the lingering social effects of past discrimination is nothing short of a legal, moral and constitutional tragedy."[28] Despite the administration's unequivocal opposition, the Supreme Court still supported some affirmative action programs.

Corporate restructuring in the mid-1980s eliminated large numbers of management-level jobs. Particularly hard hit were staff support positions heavily populated by African-Americans and women. Public affairs, community relations, and human resource jobs were the first to go. In 1987, the Black Executives Agency (BEA), an association of African-American directors of social service agencies in New York, tried to organize a meeting with

---

[24] L. Greenhouse, "Court Bars a Plan Set Up to Provide Jobs to Minorities," *New York Times,* January 24, 1989, pp. A1, 16, 19; E. Bronner, "A Plan to Help Minority Firms Is Struck Down," *Boston Globe,* January 24, 1989, pp. 1, 7.

[25] "The New Bias on Hiring Rules," *Business Week,* May 25, 1981, p. 123.

[26] B. R. Bergmann, "An Affirmative Look at Hiring Quotas," *New York Times,* January 10, 1982, p. A1.

[27] L. Denniston, "Changes in Affirmative Action Policy," *Boston Globe,* January 5, 1982, p. 9.

[28] S. Taylor, Jr., "Breaking New Ground on Affirmative Action," *New York Times,* May 21, 1986, p. A28.

African-American executives of major corporations. They dropped their plans for the meeting because so many African-American managers had lost their jobs. John N. Odom, director of the BEA, observed, "The ranks of blacks in corporations have been so decimated there just wouldn't be enough people to come."[29]

The Supreme Court's 1989 ruling on the Richmond set-aside program cast doubt on set-aside programs in 190 cities and 36 states. In March 1989, for example, the Supreme Court used the precedent of the Richmond decision to reject two additional affirmative action plans, one in Michigan and the other in Florida. Many observers concluded that this and subsequent decisions sounded the death knell of affirmative action. Gelvin L. Stevenson, chairman of CommonWealth Capital Group, Inc., observed the "ruling will be a major setback for minority firms and for minority employment . . . Affirmative action cracked open a door, and now it's shutting . . . Affirmative action has finally allowed qualified blacks . . . to start doing business. It did not level the playing field, it let them onto the playing field."[30]

The Civil Rights Act of 1991

In October 1990, the Democratic Congress, dismayed and angered by Reagan Supreme Court appointments and decisions, submitted a new civil rights bill to the White House. That legislation would have made it easier for victims of job discrimination to sue and collect damages. President Bush promptly vetoed the bill, asserting it encouraged unacceptable hiring and promotion quotas.

In May 1991, Democratic leaders outlined a compromise worked out by members of the House Judiciary Committee. They changed the legislative language of the bill to conform to language negotiated by the Business Roundtable and the Leadership Conference on Civil Rights. The new language allowed employers to defend employment practices as necessary if they bore a substantial and manifest relationship to the jobs at issue. The bill prohibited the use of discriminatory employment testing and the adjustment of test scores on the basis of race, color, sex, national origin, or religion.

Eleanor Holmes Norton, who headed the EEOC under President Carter, wrote a thoughtful editorial on the issue of quotas in *The Wall Street Journal*. She pointed out that quotas were explicitly barred in the language of the bill and damage awards were rare and small. Yet the Bush administration persisted in raising quotas as a scare tactic. Norton wrote, "[The quota scare] poisons the racial atmosphere already polluted by racial incidents and by

---

[29] C. H. Deutsch, "The Ax Falls on Equal Opportunity," *New York Times,* January 4, 1987, p. F1.

[30] *The Wall Street Journal,* February 9, 1988, p. 1.

EXHIBIT 12–3 Civil Rights Act of 1991

Disparate impact: Disparate impact deals with suits involving hiring or promotion practices. Tests that seem fair on the surface but have a disparate impact may result in a company hiring, for example, proportionately more whites than African-Americans or more men than women. These tests and other practices sometimes result in "unintentional discrimination" cases.

In a 1989 case, *Wards Cove Packing* v *Antonio,* the Supreme Court held that once complainants had shown a disparate impact had resulted from an employment practice, they still had to prove there was no business necessity for the practice.

Under the new act, once disparate impact was proven, the burden of proof shifted from the complainant to the employer. The concept of disparate impact was written into law for the first time. It said employers must show employment practices were "job related for the position in question and consistent with business necessity." The act eliminated the standard set by *Wards Cove* and ordered the courts to interpret the law as it existed before that decision.

Discrimination and harassment: In the 1989 case *Patterson* v *McLean Credit Union,* the Supreme Court held that the right to sue for damages for racial job discrimination under an 1866 law did not apply to on-the-job harassment or other forms of discrimination after someone was hired. Under the new act, the *Patterson* decision was rejected and the 1866 reconstruction law was clearly defined as applying only to hiring, firing, promotions, and all other terms of employment.

Victims of intentional discrimination or harassment based on sex, religion, national origin, or disability were protected under the 1964 Civil Rights Act. The 1964 law was amended to allow complainants to sue for back pay, compensatory damages, and punitive damages.

Reopening old discrimination cases: In the 1989 case *Martin* v *Wilkes,* the Supreme Court ruled that since some white firefighters in Birmingham had not been parties to two earlier suits challenging discrimination in the city's fire department, they had a right to go into court later to attack hiring and promotion practices. People could not sue to reopen employment cases if they had actual notice of the decree at the time it was entered and a reasonable opportunity to object if their cases were adequately represented in the original case.

Source: T. Noah and A. R. Karr, "What New Civil Rights Law Will Mean," *The Wall Street Journal,* November 4, 1991, p. B1; "The Compromise on Civil Rights," *The New York Times,* October 26, 1991, p. 7.

---

the mutual suspicion between blacks and whites that is the legacy of retrenchment, resistance, and resentment on racial issues that began in the 1980s."[31]

President Bush promptly denounced the bill. He charged the Democratic leadership with proposing a quota system that would allow employers to establish personnel systems based on numbers rather than merit. The White House promptly moved to ease even further federal regulations intended to prevent discrimination in employment tests. Civil rights leaders, lobbyists, and Democratic members of Congress were furious. The Leadership Conference on Civil Rights, an umbrella lobbying organization, called President

---

[31] E. H. Norton, "Quota Scare Must Not Destroy Civil Rights Bill," *The Wall Street Journal,* May 16, 1991, p. A17.

Bush's remarks "almost Orwellian" in the way they turned the truth about quotas upside down.[32]

On June 6, 1991, the Civil Rights Act passed the House of Representatives with a vote of 273 to 158, exactly the same number of votes the earlier bill had received. The White House capitulated almost immediately and declared the quota issue dead. President Bush now supported a measure he had adamantly opposed. He dropped his assertion that the measure would lead employers to hire racial minorities on the basis of strict percentages to avoid lawsuits charging indirect discrimination.

The proposed new law extended for the first time punitive damages to victims of employment discrimination based on sex or disability as well as on race. It also countered seven Supreme Court decisions, most of them from 1989, that made it more difficult for job bias plaintiffs to win lawsuits. With no objections from the administration, Congress passed the act and it was signed into law.

Legal experts quickly pointed out that the most important aspect of the new law was not racial discrimination but sexual discrimination. They declared that as a practical matter, people claiming racial discrimination were already able to sue under a separate law. The 1991 bill's biggest impact was the increased likelihood that women complaining of sexual discrimination would come forward with claims.[33]

Changing Views of Affirmative Action, the Mid-1990s and Beyond

The 1994 Republican Contract with America declared war on affirmative action and racial-preference policies. During the early and mid-1990s, the Supreme Court also became more conservative in its approach. Justices Rehnquist, Scalia, Thomas, Kennedy, and O'Connor appeared willing to roll back federal affirmative action. Although the court seemed unlikely to dramatically reverse affirmative action policies, legal analysts predicted justices would be likely to require programs to be more narrowly tailored to remedy past discrimination.

The debate about the role of race and gender in America grew more and more divisive after 1994. A slow-growing economy, stagnant middle-class incomes, and corporate downsizing all contributed to the anxiety over who would get hired and fired. One side argued that all Americans deserve equal opportunities. Connie Rice of the NAACP Legal Defense and Education

---

[32] A. Clymer, "Bush Denounces Civil Rights Bill Advocated by House Democrats," *New York Times,* May 31, 1991, p. A1; S. A. Holmes, "White House Changes in Job Discrimination Rules," *New York Times,* May 31, 1991, p. B6.

[33] S. Faison, Jr., "Rash of Sex-Bias Suits Seen After Rights Act," *New York Times,* November 30, 1993, p. 1.

Fund asserted, "We tried color-blind 30 years ago, and that system is naturally and artificially rigged for white males . . . . If we abandon affirmative action, we return to the old-boy network."[34] The other side countered with the argument that hard work and merit should prevail over race, gender, religion, or birthright. Many contended that women and racial minorities were no longer disadvantaged simply because of race and gender. William Bennett, former education secretary, declared that toxic race relations aggravated by affirmative action lead to a damaging resegregation in which society is even more color-conscious.[35]

Public opinion seemed to support the growing anti-affirmative-action sentiment. A 1995 *Fortune* magazine poll of CEOs at the nation's largest industrial and service companies found only 52 percent of the 200 respondents described the results of affirmative action programs as good or very good, down 68 percent from a similar poll taken in 1989.[36]

The California Plan

The debate over affirmative action was greatly exacerbated by a California legislative initiative. Early in 1995, two San Francisco-based academics decided to initiate action to eliminate affirmative action programs in California. Professors Glynn Custred and Thomas Wood declared that affirmative action programs were never meant to be permanent and that they had accomplished their purpose. They proposed the following referendum:

"Neither the State of California nor any of its political subdivisions or agents shall use race, sex, color, ethnicity or national origin as a criterion for either discriminating against, or granting preferential treatment to, any individual or group in the operation of the State's system of public employment, public education or public contracting."[37]

Even critics agreed that the bill, known as the California Civil Rights Initiative, would pass overwhelmingly if presented to voters. They asserted that if California passed the bill it would encourage other states and Congress to apply the rollback to the private sector. As it stood, its passage would mean that millions of dollars in annual contract set-asides for minorities and women-owned businesses would disappear. The state government could not consider race, sex, or ethnicity in hiring or promotion. The University of California would not give admission preference to blacks or Hispanics.[38] A

---

[34] "Affirmative Action on the Edge," *US News & World Report,* February 13, 1996, p. 35.

[35] Ibid.

[36] J. P. Pinkerton, "Why Affirmative Action Won't Die," *Fortune,* November 13, 1995, pp. 191–92.

[37] B. D. Ayres, Jr., "Conservatives Forge New Strategy to Challenge Affirmative Action," *New York Times,* February 16, 1995, p. A1.

[38] B. McGrory, "Californians Lead Affirmative Action Challenge," *Boston Globe,* February 12, 1995, p. 1.

March 1995 poll of California voters showed that two out of every three voters favored a ban on affirmative action.[39]

In June 1995, California Governor Pete Wilson, a Republican contender for the presidential nomination, took the dramatic step of unilaterally scrapping affirmative action programs. His executive order eliminated about 150 advisory panels designed to help blacks and women win state contracts and employment; repealed executive orders issued by the three preceding California governors that promoted affirmative action programs; and asked public universities to consider only merit in awarding jobs and contracts.[40] The order was framed into Proposition 209 that called for an end to racial and gender preferences in state hiring, contracts, and education.

In mid-July 1995, the University of California regents voted to support Wilson's order over the objections of the university's top administrators. A California study predicted that black enrollment at Berkeley, the flagship campus, would fall from 6.4 percent to 1.4 percent; Hispanic enrollment would fall from 15.3 percent to 5.6 percent; Asian enrollment would rise from 42 percent to well over half the class; and white enrollment would gain slightly from 30 percent to about 34 percent.[41]

Three days after the Board of Regents voted, the White House announced that the university had made a terrible mistake and that the Justice Department would begin a review of the $2.5 billion flowing annually into the nine campuses of the University of California system. Officials at the university suggested there might be loopholes in the regents' decision that would allow them to substitute socioeconomic factors for race or sex, thereby mitigating the effect of the order.[42]

Immediately after President Clinton's defense of affirmative action, the regents began to debate whether to stop admitting students, hiring professors, and awarding contracts on the basis of race and sex. In January 1996, university officials declared they would delay the new policy by a year to apply to freshmen entering in 1998 rather than 1997. New guidelines for hiring without preference took effect in January 1996.

Proponents of Proposition 209 went on a campaign to export its goals and ideology to other states and institutions. By early March, the University of Texas' bitter affirmative action situation was resolved by a Federal Appeals court that ruled race-based admissions practices were unconstitutional. The University of Texas had been sued by four white applicants who had been rejected by the school's law school. Their scores had been higher than some

---

[39] B. D. Ayres, Jr., "California Acting on Affirmative Action," *New York Times,* March 26, 1995, p. 24.

[40] A. Pertman, "Wilson Order Ends Affirmative Action in California," *Boston Globe,* June 2, 1995.

[41] A. Dembner, "Academic Leaders Uphold Affirmative Action," *Boston Globe,* July 22, 1995, p. 1.

[42] B. D. Ayres, Jr., "Obstacles Arise to Switch by California on Diversity," *New York Times,* July 24, 1995, p. A1.

African-American and Hispanic students who had been admitted. The Fifth Circuit Court of Appeals declared that the University of Texas could not use different admission standards for minority students than it used for white applicants. Immediately, the entire 15-school system of the University of Texas temporarily suspended admissions.[43]

At the same time, a seven-year investigation by the Office of Civil Rights of the U.S. Department of Education concluded that the aggressive affirmative action program at Berkeley was legal and did not discriminate against white students. The Department of Education reported that the school's affirmative action program "employed no quotas or set-asides and all students, regardless of race or national origin, competed with all other students."[44]

With affirmative action scuttled at the University of California and University of Texas, other states began to reexamine their positions on affirmative action in state universities and offices. Some states like Pennsylvania and Arizona tried to enact legislation to outlaw affirmative action. In South Carolina, campaigns were launched to amend the state constitution or gather ballots for a November vote. In Colorado, the governing board of the university curtailed some, but not all, affirmative action programs.[45]

California's Proposition 209 passed handily on November 5, 1996, but was quickly bogged down in court challenges. Legal specialists expected court challenges to last for years before the measure reached the Supreme Court.

At the end of November 1996, U.S. District Judge Thelton E. Henderson in San Francisco blocked enforcement of Proposition 209, declaring there was a strong probability that opponents would show the measure was unconstitutional. He issued a temporary restraining order that barred Governor Wilson and Attorney General Dan Lungren from enforcing the proposition. Governor Wilson was furious, calling Judge Henderson's ruling "an affront to common sense" and to California voters.[46]

Judge Henderson extended his order on December 7, ordering the California University system to retain preferences until December 16 when the court was scheduled to hear arguments for a preliminary injunction against the enforcement of the initiative.[47] Despite the California ruling, Florida Representative Charles Canady announced he would reintroduce a bill

---

[43] S. C. Gwynne, "Undoing Diversity," *Time,* April 1, 1996, p. 54.

[44] P. Applebome, "Two Decisions Reflect Bitter Conflict Surrounding University Affirmative Action Policies," *New York Times,* March 22, 1996, p. A12.

[45] W. H. Honan, "Organized Efforts to End Affirmative Action Grow Nationally," *New York Times,* March 31, 1996, p. 30.

[46] M. Dolan, "Judge Blocks California Ban on Affirmative Action Efforts," *Boston Globe,* November 28, 1996, p. 1.

[47] "Ban Extended on Affirmative Action Measure," *New York Times,* December 7, 1996, p. 10.

designed to end racial preferences in federal law. His Equal Opportunity Act of 1996:

- Barred the use of racial and gender preferences in federal contracting and subcontracting, in federal employment, and in other federally funded activities.
- Barred the federal government from requiring or encouraging federal contractors or subcontractors to grant racial or gender preferences.
- Defined preference as an advantage of any kind, including quotas, set asides, goals, timetables and other numerical objectives.
- Protected the federal government's ability to engage in nonpreferential outreach, recruiting, and marketing efforts.[48]

With the election of Clinton and the certainty of four more years of a Democratic president, many GOP members expressed reluctance to get behind Canady's bill. The prospect of pressing this issue became particularly unappealing after the White House announced the administration would join a challenge to Proposition 209's constitutionality.

On December 28, 1996, a Justice Department official declared, "The argument is not that affirmative action is constitutionally required . . . It is not that affirmative action can never be repealed or that it is always appropriate as a matter of policy." Instead, the Justice Department said it would make the more limited argument that in approving the ballot measure, the voters illegally denied minorities and women the ability to seek redress from state and local institutions for past discrimination.[49]

As the Clinton administration began its second term, the affirmative action measure begun in California was still unresolved. It was likely that other states would take up the same issues and pass resolutions that would wind up slogging their way through the judicial system. No one expects to see a resolution in the foreseeable future.

Race Discrimination: The Case of Texaco

In 1994, six Texaco company employees brought a suit on behalf of 1,500 other minority employees asserting that Texaco systematically discriminated against minority employees in promotions and fostered a racially hostile environment. Early in 1996, the EEOC issued a finding that Texaco did not promote black employees because of their race. At that time Texaco disputed the finding saying the government did not take into account the full scope of the company's promotion policies.

---

[48] G. F. Seib, "GOP Congress Debates an Attack on Affirmative Action," *The Wall Street Journal,* December 10, 1996, p. A24.

[49] S. A. Holmes, "Clinton Decides to Join a Fight on Preferences," *New York Times,* December 18, 1996, p. 1.

Court papers filed in White Plains, New York, disclosed that Richard A. Lundwall, the coordinator of personnel services, secretly recorded August 1994 conversations about the pending suit. Lundwall, who was responsible for keeping minutes of the conversation apparently wanted to ensure their accuracy. After Lundwall was dismissed by Texaco in August 1996, he contacted the plaintiff's lawyers and gave them the tapes.

On November 4, 1996, the *New York Times* reported the existence of the tapes and published excerpts included in court records. According to the tapes, Robert Ulrich, Texaco's treasurer, referred to a key document saying, "All it could do is get us in trouble. That's the way I feel. I would not keep anything." Lundwall agreed, "Let me shred this thing and any other restricted version like it." Ulrich later urged caution about withholding some documents noting, "I don't want to be caught in a cover-up. I don't want my own Watergate here." Why were these executives discussing destruction of evidence in a federal suit? The tapes referred to diversity and characterized minorities in extremely offensive and derogatory terms.[50]

Federal prosecutors had already issued subpoenas seeking evidence including the audiotapes. When the *New York Times* piece was published, they immediately opened a criminal investigation to determine whether the senior company executives actually had destroyed the documents.

Texaco officials were in an extremely awkward position; although they had not heard the tape recordings yet, they were forced to respond to published reports. Peter I. Bijur, the company chairman, was described as absolutely livid about the words quoted on the tapes. He told employees he had directed a review of all Texaco's programs for diversity and equal opportunity. He also told the company's human resources department to adopt programs for attracting and keeping minority employees.[51]

The company faced an additional problem as the value of its stock fell 3 percent the day after the revelation about the tapes. Large institutional investors expressed concern about how the company would be perceived and what steps top management would take to handle the issue. H. Carl McCall, the New York State Comptroller and trustee of the common retirement fund, wrote to CEO Bijur saying, "I'm looking for reassurance for me and other stockholders that what appears to have happened here was not prevalent in the company."[52] Bijur replied immediately declaring the company denounced the "alleged behavior in very strong terms."[53]

---

[50] K. Eichenwald, "Texaco Executives, on Tape, Discussed Impeding Bias Suit," *New York Times,* November 4, 1996, p. A1.

[51] K. Eichenwald, "U.S. Inquiring into Texaco's Actions in Suit," *New York Times,* November 5, 1996, p. D1.

[52] K. Eichenwald, "Civil Rights Groups Ask U.S. to Join Texaco Bias Suit," *New York Times,* November 6, 1996, p. D2.

[53] P. Fritsch, "Fund Trustee Rebukes Texaco for Racist Remarks," *The Wall Street Journal,* November 6, 1996, p. A4.

The next day Bijur announced the suspension of J. David Keough, who had been at the meeting where the shredding of evidence had been discussed, and Peter Meade, assistant general manager of the fuel and marine marketing department. The company also ended benefits to Richard A. Lundwall and retired treasurer Robert Ulrich.[54]

Bijur said Texaco was adopting a program to express its regret for what happened and to improve the company's employee diversity effort. Those familiar with Texaco's policies pointed to the difference between published policies and actual workplace practices. They noted the company said all the right things. For example, a booklet called "Texaco's Visions and Values" states, "The company believes that a work environment that reflects a diverse workforce, values diversity, and is free from all forms of discrimination, intimidation, and harassment is essential for a productive and efficient workforce. Accordingly, conduct directed toward any employee that is unwelcome, hostile, offensive, degrading, or abusive is unacceptable and will not be tolerated."[55]

Reality and rhetoric at Texaco were very different. Of the 873 executives at Texaco who made more than $106,000 annually, only 6 or 0.7 percent were black. A Labor Department audit in 1996 found that minority employees waited longer for promotions and were less likely than whites to receive evaluations that helped their careers. Minority-group accountants, for example, took 6.1 years to achieve their positions; whites were named to those same jobs after 4.6 years. Following the audit, the agency ordered Texaco to compensate minority employees for lost wages and to revise the appraisal system.

Leonard J. Bierman, former acting director of the federal agency that monitored affirmative action programs of federal contractors like Texaco, wrote, "Deficiencies in the affirmative-action programs suggest that Texaco is not committed to insuring comprehensive . . . compliance with the company's affirmative-action responsibilities." Texaco executives admitted under oath that the corporate office did not exercise any oversight of affirmative-action programs. In a 1995 sealed deposition, Vice President for Human Resources John D. Ambler testified, "There is nobody that is responsible for every business unit."[56]

Within a week after the original revelation, Texaco entered formal talks to bring a quick end to the 1994 race-discrimination suit. Lawyers for the employees sought $71 million in back pay for about 1,400 black Texaco employees. The $71 million figure was based on Texaco payroll records from

---

[54] K. Eichenwald, "Texaco Punishes Executives for Racial Comments and Plans to Destroy Papers," *New York Times,* November 7, 1996, p. D2.

[55] K. Eichenwald, "The Two Faces of Texaco," and "What Texaco Says and What it Does," *New York Times,* November 10, 1996, p. A1.

[56] Ibid., p. F10.

1990 to 1994. If the case went to trial, a jury could potentially award each plaintiff as much as $300,000, raising Texaco's liability to $500 million.[57]

By mid-November 1996, civil rights leaders such as Jesse Jackson and Emanuel Cleaver, second national president for the National Conference of Black Mayors, were calling for a boycott of Texaco. Responding to the boycott initiative, Texaco shares fell $2 on the New York Stock Exchange. However, other civil rights advocates such as Dennis Walcott, president of the New York Urban League and Kweisi Mfume, president and chief executive of the NAACP, advised waiting for Texaco's plan of action.[58]

On November 16, Texaco agreed to the nation's largest settlement in a racial discrimination case. The company agreed to pay $140 million to resolve the federal lawsuit. Of the cash portion, $115 million was earmarked for a pool to benefit the company's minority employees. The company agreed to grant pay increases of about 10 percent to those employees. The settlement would be monitored by a federal court for five years. Texaco CEO Peter Bijur said, "Texaco is committed to developing and instituting specific, effective policies that will ensure that discrimination is wiped out wherever it may be, and that will expand the positive economic impact we can have on the minority community."

The company also agreed to make changes in the way it did business, including a plan to turn over authority for reorganizing its personnel operations to a new task force. The task force was given the authority to evaluate employment policies and practices and to develop new procedures on hiring and promoting minority workers. It was composed of three Texaco appointees, three people appointed by the plaintiffs' attorneys, and a chairperson who had to be approved by both sides. Its first efforts were the creation of a diversity and sensitivity training program as well as the development of a mentoring program.[59]

Peter Bijur appointed Willie M. Stanfield, a black Texaco employee, as an assistant to the chairman. Bijur also ordered managers to plan to do more business with African-American-owned banks, advertising firms, vendors, and contractors. The decisive steps taken by Bijur encouraged investors. Stock closed up $2.75 per share after Bijur's announcements.[60]

Richard A. Lundwall was the first person to face criminal charges related to the Texaco case. On November 19, he was arraigned for obstruction of justice in federal district court in White Plains, New York. Lundwall was

---

[57] A. Sullivan and P. Fritsch, "Texaco Is Trying to Reach a Settlement in 1994 Racial-Discrimination Lawsuit," *The Wall Street Journal,* November 11, 1996, p. A3.

[58] K. Eichenwald, "Rights Groups Urge Boycott of Texaco," *New York Times,* November 13, 1996, p. D1.

[59] K. Eichenwald, "Texaco to Make Record Payout in Bias Lawsuit," *New York Times,* November 16, 1996, p. A1.

[60] "Texaco to Pay $176.1 Million in Bias Suit," *The Wall Street Journal,* November 18, 1996, p. A1.

quickly released on $50,000 bond without entering a plea. Legal experts did not expect Lundwall to be tried. They agreed that prosecutors would seek his cooperation with a grand jury into allegations that Texaco officials withheld or destroyed documents.[61]

On December 18, 1996, civil rights leaders announced they would drop their boycott. Joseph E. Lowery, president of the Southern Christian Leadership Conference, called Texaco's response, "A new era, a new message to America, corporate or otherwise." Peter Bijur said the company had committed itself to additional initiatives. It would increase its minority employees to 29 percent from 23 percent by 2000. Black employment would go up to 13 percent from 9 percent and the number of women would go from 32 percentto 35 percent. Texaco would try to nurture employees by financing a nationwide internship and scholarship program to develop minority students for managerial careers in engineering, physical science, and other areas important to the petroleum business. All employees would undergo diversity training and would have access to an ombudsman to whom they could report concerns.[62]

The Equal Employment Opportunity Commission (EEOC), which was not included in the settlement talks filed a motion to intervene, an action that temporarily stalled Texaco's implementation of the plan. After several weeks of discussion, the EEOC agreed to stop its intervention in the settlement but announced it would take an active oversight role. The agreement between the EEOC and Texaco made it clear that the EEOC did not rule out further legal action if Texaco failed to carry out any of its promises. In a draft agreement between Texaco and the EEOC, the agency proposed a five-year oversight, the same period during which the court-mandated task force would function. The EEOC said that if the task force and Texaco disagreed and had to seek court intervention, the agency also would participate in the legal proceedings.[63]

In January 1997, Texaco agreed to allow the EEOC to monitor its employment practices. Under the agreement, Texaco makes yearly reports to the EEOC on its hiring and promotion of racial minorities and gives details about each applicant for the position. The EEOC can examine Texaco's records and interview employees and applicants.[64]

The Texaco case focused stakeholder attention on corporate diversity programs across the nation. Some major civil rights organizations planned more confrontation, boycotts, and litigation. Wade Henderson, executive

---

[61] A. Sullivan and P. Fritsch, "Ex-Official of Texaco Is Charged," *The Wall Street Journal,* November 20, 1996, p. A3.

[62] K. Eichenwald, "Texaco Plans Sweeping Program for Minority Opportunities," *New York Times,* December 19, 1996, p. D1.

[63] A. Sullivan, "EEOC Plans Oversight of Texaco after Race-Bias Case Is Settled," *The Wall Street Journal,* December 31, 1996, p. 12.

[64] A. Reifenberg, "Texaco Agrees to Report to EEOC on Promotion of Racial Minorities," *The Wall Street Journal,* January 6, 1997, p. B5.

director of the Leadership Conference on Civil Rights observed, "The Texaco incident does have the potential to catalyze the civil rights movement into a more aggressive campaign."[65]

Corporate directors who usually paid very little attention to diversity issues, began to scrutinize management's diversity efforts in the immediate aftermath of the Texaco settlement. B. Kenneth West, an outside director of Motorola declared that the Texaco uproar represented "a wake-up call for thinking boards." Directors of companies such as Chase Manhattan, Columbia Gas System, Warner-Lambert, and Westinghouse Electric took new notice of their companies' diversity policies. However, *The Wall Street Journal* observed that there was a very good reason diversity issues were not high on board agendas; the boards themselves were not very diverse. Women and minorities accounted for less than 12 percent of all directors of the nation's 878 biggest public companies in 1996. In a climate of waning support for affirmative action, some recruiters noted the search for women and minority board candidates was slowing down.[66]

Sexual Harassment

In recent years, women have fared better than minorities in the courts in terms of access to jobs and promotions. But they face a special problem—sexual harassment in the workplace. In 1980, the EEOC wrote its guidelines defining sexual harassment as

> [unwelcome] sexual advances, requests for sexual favors, and other verbal or physical conduct of a sexual nature . . . when (1) submission to such conduct is made either explicitly or implicitly a term or condition of an individual's employment, (2) submission to or rejection of such conduct by an individual is used as the basis for employment decisions affecting such individual, or (3) such conduct has the purpose or effect of unreasonably interfering with an individual's work performance or creating an intimidating, hostile, or offensive working environment.[67]

This definition prohibited two specific types of sexual harassment: (1) situations in which sexual harassment created a hostile work environment and (2) cases in which a supervisor demanded sexual favors in exchange for job benefits.[68]

Men and women generally agree on the actions that constitute sexual harassment, but they have very different views of its impact. In a 1988 study

---

[65] K. H. Hammonds, "Texaco Was Just the Beginning," *Business Week,* December 16, 1996, p. 34.

[66] J. S. Lublin, "Texaco Case Causes a Stir in Boardrooms," *The Wall Street Journal,* November 22, 1996, p. B1.

[67] 29 C.F.R. 1604, 11(a) (1987).

[68] *Shrout* v *Black Clawson,* 689 F. Supp. 774, 780 (1988).

EXHIBIT 12–4 AT&T's Antiharassment Policy

It is company policy that all employees have a right to work in an environment free of discrimination, which encompasses freedom from sexual harassment. A.T.&T. prohibits sexual harassment of its employees in any form.

Such conduct may result in disciplinary action up to and including dismissal. Specifically, no supervisor shall threaten or insinuate either explicitly or implicitly that any employee's submission to or rejection of sexual advances will in any way influence any personnel decision regarding that employee's employment, evaluation, wages, advancement, assigned duties, shifts or any other condition of employment or career development.

Other sexually harassing conduct in the workplace, whether physical or verbal, committed by supervisors or non-supervisory personnel is also prohibited. This includes repeated offensive sexual flirtation, advances, propositions, continual or repeated abuse of a sexual nature, graphic verbal commentary about an individual's body, sexually degrading words to describe an individual and the display in the workplace of sexually suggestive objects or pictures.

Employees who have complaints of sexual harassment should in appropriate circumstances report such conduct to their supervisors. If this is not appropriate, they should seek the assistance of their equal opportunity complaint investigator. Where investigations confirm the allegations, appropriate corrective action will be taken.

of business school graduate students, 46 percent of the men surveyed thought women would be flattered by actions that constitute sexual harassment; only 5 percent of the women agreed.[69]

Some companies have taken steps to ensure that their workplaces remain free of discrimination and specifically, sexual harassment. As Exhibit 12–4 shows, AT&T has a corporate policy that clearly defines sexual harassment and sets up a process to deal with sexual harassment charges. The exercise of defining the problem and drawing up a policy helps sensitize and protect all employees, men as well as women.

Two major sexual harassment cases in the mid-1990s took place in subsidiaries of non-U.S. companies. Both cases, one at Mitsubishi Motor Manufacturing of America and the other at Astra USA, point to the difference in perceptions of the actions that constitute sexual harassment and to the importance of companies complying with U.S. law.

Mitsubishi Motor Manufacturing of America, Inc. (MMMA)

In April 1996, the Equal Employment Opportunity Commission (EEOC) sued Mitsubishi Motor Manufacturing of America, a unit of Mitsubishi

---
[69] A. Bennett, "Managing," *The Wall Street Journal,* August 5, 1988, p. 18.

Motors of Japan. Mitsubishi was one of Japan's giant trading companies with global sales of about $38.2 billion annually. Worldwide, it was involved in nearly every industry from banking to shipbuilding. The U.S.-based automaker was a very tiny part of the company with only one assembly plant in this country. At the time of the suit, 70 Japanese—including the chief executive and president—were working in the plant. Only one member of the U.S. company's board was American.[70]

The EEOC said hundreds of women employees had suffered physical and mental abuse since 1990. In 1994, two dozen women had sued the company through a private attorney alleging similar incidents. That suit was still going through the courts when the new suit was filed. The EEOC began a 15-month investigation immediately. The commission concluded the allegations had merit and futilely tried to settle with Mitsubishi. When MMMA refused to settle, the EEOC concluded it had no alternative but to sue the company. The EEOC announced that as many as 700 women may have been affected by the conduct and that each woman could be awarded statutory damages of $300,000.

The 1996 class-action suit filed in Peoria, Illinois, listed a variety of complaints by women who worked in the automobile assembly plant in Normal, Illinois. The women charged that men grabbed their genitals and breasts, called them bitches and whores, and subjected them to drawings of female body parts on car fenders.

Most of the alleged harassment took place in the plant's production and maintenance areas and involved line workers, their immediate supervisors, and lower-level management. The director of the EEOC's regional office, John Rowe, said the EEOC was concerned about the incidents but was even more concerned with MMMA's knowledge of the behavior and the fact that it took no action to remedy the situation.

Gary Shultz, the company's vice president and general counsel said the U.S. government was politically motivated in bringing the suit. Shultz also stressed the company's procedures called for swift punishment of anyone violating sexual discrimination or harassment procedures.[71]

MMMA refused to admit any wrongdoing and began a grassroots attack on the EEOC. The company offered to shut down the production line for a day, pay full wages, charter a bus, and supply lunch to permit workers to attend a rally outside the Chicago EEOC office. The company had a sign-up sheet for workers who planned to attend the rally and could identify those who chose not to go. Shultz declared he wanted to see a backlash and wave of outrage by Mitsubishi's loyal workers. Eventually 3,000 took advantage of the day off.

---

[70] R. Sharpe, "A Mitsubishi U.S. Unit Is Taking a Hard Line in Harassment Battle," *The Wall Street Journal,* April 22, 1996, p. A1.

[71] R. Sharpe, "EEOC Sues Mitsubishi Unit for Harassment," *The Wall Street Journal,* April 10, 1996, p. B1.

Mitsubishi Motors in Japan, which could have vetoed the strategy, supported Shultz's hard line. The parent company's stand was unusual. Most Japanese companies tried very hard to be sensitive to anything that might attract unwanted attention. In this case, Japanese government officials joined company officials in asserting the EEOC was simply trying to justify its existence. A company attorney charged the plaintiffs with promiscuous sexual behavior.

In May 1996, 10 congresswomen met with Larry Greene, executive vice president of procurement and government affairs for MMMA. They had sent a letter to CEO Takahisa Komoto complaining about the tactics MMMA used against the women who claimed sexual harassment. Greene told Representative Patricia Schroeder (D-Colorado) that the company would seek outside help to improve its practices. He also gave the representatives a letter from Komoto vowing to pursue a mutually satisfactory resolution of the EEOC lawsuit.[72]

Business Week investigators called MMMA's actions "just the most recent example showing that companies haven't yet learned how to do that" [handle sexual harassment]. They pointed to several factors that predisposed Japanese companies to be insensitive in dealing with many issues in their subsidiaries. One factor was the us versus them mentality that persists in Japan. Most Japanese companies are torn between micromanaging their overseas subsidiaries and abrogating all decisions to the subsidiary managers. The authors note that Japanese multinationals do not attract top local talent because the career path is limited to Japanese.

Japanese companies at home paid very little attention to sexual harassment issues. Many leading manufacturing companies had no internal rules outlawing such conduct and were loath to provide help for female workers who were harassed. According to a 1995 poll of working women taken by the Japanese prime minister's office, 41.3 percent of respondents reported they had been sexually harassed. In most cases, women who complained were fired. Women who brought sexual harassment suits in Japan could be charged under criminal law with slander or public indecency.[73]

When the EEOC filed its suit against the MMMA, corporate counsel Gary Shultz received free rein to handle the situation. Prior to joining MMMA, his only professional experience was running a two-person law firm in Bloomington, Illinois. Shultz reported to Tsuneo Ohinouye, a 40-year veteran engineer of Mitsubishi Motor Company who had limited experience in U.S. human resource issues. Shultz exacerbated the tension within the company by telling employees their jobs would be in jeopardy if they did not present a united front against the suit.[74]

---

[72] R. Sharpe, "Mitsubishi Official Answers Complaint of Congresswomen," *The Wall Street Journal,* May 1, 1996, p. B5.

[73] "Japan Slow to Tackle Sex Harassment," *Financial Times,* May 13, 1996, p. 6.

[74] E. H. Updike and W. J. Holstein, "Mitsubishi and the 'Cement Ceiling,'" *Business Week,* May 13, 1996, p. 62.

In May 1996, the Reverend Jesse Jackson said that his National Rainbow Coalition and Operation Push would join with the National Organization for Women to start picketing Mitsubishi dealerships. Leaders from the groups met with lawyers at the EEOC in Chicago to show support for the agency's suit. MMMA said it regretted the groups' actions and hoped they would "take the time to learn all the facts and understand our efforts to build a model workplace."[75]

Within days, the company hired former Labor Secretary Lynn Martin to conduct a comprehensive review of its workplace policies. Martin, who was a consultant at the Deloitte & Touche accounting firm, said she would not investigate individual complaints of sexual harassment nor would she try to explain MMMA's actions. She asserted that she had complete independence. The company continued to say that it wanted to solve the problem but attorneys for the EEOC reported no indication of any interest in a settlement.[76]

By June, pressure was mounting on the company to settle the allegations. Although the boycott had only limited effect, Mitsubishi dealers were worried. A major dealer in Chicago figured it would be better to close his doors in support of the boycott than suffer the longer-term fallout from bad publicity. The controversy threatened to spill over onto the other 40 companies in the Mitsubishi group. The consumer-electronics company and other units pushed Mitsubishi Motor Manufacturing of America to cooperate with the EEOC and settle the suit.[77]

In June 1996, the company asked a federal court to dismiss the government's lawsuit claiming it took reasonable and prompt steps to deal with the harassment claims. John Row of the EEOC said the argument was frivolous. This case was expected to drag on for some time to come. Because this case was likely to become the largest sexual harassment case in U.S. history, there were very high stakes on both sides.[78]

Astra USA, Inc., and Sexual Harassment

When Astra AB, a Swedish pharmaceutical firm with a Massachusetts subsidiary, encountered charges of sexual harassment, it adopted quite a different strategy from Mitsubishi's. On April 28, 1996, the Astra USA board voted to suspend Lars Bildman, president and chief executive officer, of the Massachusetts firm. A spokesperson for the board said that members were alerted to the charges by an investigative reporter for *Business Week* who had interviewed employees. After the reporter met with executives, the parent company sent its senior executives to talk to employees and conduct an

---

[75] "Mitsubishi Picketing Concerning Lawsuits Is Readied by Groups," *The Wall Street Journal,* May 8, 1996, p. B3.

[76] R. Sharpe, "Mitsubishi Chooses Ex-Labor Secretary to Review Policies," *The Wall Street Journal,* May 15, 1996, p. B8.

[77] P. Elstron and S.V. Brull, "Mitsubishi's Morass," *Business Week,* June 3, 1996, p. 35.

[78] Internet [http://www.civiljustice.com/mitsudis.htm].

investigation of its own. As a result of the investigation, Bildman was replaced by Jan Larrson, executive vice president of the Swedish parent.[79]

A few days later, Bildman's lawyer defended him saying that the number of sexual harassment claims filed while he was president was extraordinarily low. This comment came hours after Kimberly Cote, a 31-year-old Cambridge woman, tried to reopen a 1994 settled sexual harassment claim against Bildman and Astra, its Swedish parent company. She claimed that the company fraudulently bought her silence by telling her that no other actions were pending.

Cote joined Astra as a trainee in the fall of 1992 and left a year later. In her original suit she charged a supervisor propositioned her and retaliated by giving her negative evaluations when she turned him down. At the time she settled, Cote said she did not know that other women had grievances. Had she known, she asserted, she would never have settled the original complaint.[80] She charged the company falsely claimed she was alone in making allegations of sexual harassment. In her suit, Cote reported that at one large meeting, an Astra vice president who reported directly to Bildman told trainees that "there are 24 hours in a day, and Astra requires you to divide them into three equal segments: eight for work, eight for socializing and drinking, and eight for yourself."[81]

The *Business Week* article, which appeared on May 13, 1996, said its reporters interviewed more than 70 former and current employees and discovered a "disturbing pattern of complaints" during much of Bildman's 15-year tenure at Astra USA. It noted that Bildman and other senior managers at Astra did not respond to *Business Week's* requests for interviews and as the article went to press, Bildman categorically denied the allegations in a written statement.

Apparently socializing was very much a part of the Astra training environment. Upper management hosted three or four open-bar nights a week for recruits. Women reported that George Roadman, a vice president running sales and marketing for the company's hospital division, called female recruits in their rooms and invited them down to the bar. It was widely acknowledged that managers made assignments based on the social skills recruits showed at the bar. Managers including Bildman and Roadman invited women to nights on the town. Women told *Business Week* investigators that they were inexperienced and really didn't know what was appropriate or inappropriate in a business training setting.

According to the investigators, the harassment continued after training was over. At national sales meetings, Bildman and top executives hosted

---

[79] D. Lewis, "Astra Chief Suspended after Harassment Charge," *Boston Globe,* April 30, 1996, p. 39.

[80] D. Lewis and K. Blanton, "Astra Executive Defended," *Boston Globe,* May 2, 1996, p. 55.

[81] L. Johannes, "Astra Unit Faces Sexual-Harassment Suit," *The Wall Street Journal,* p. B1.

after-hours parties. One party in 1991 got so out of control the police were called. Hotel officials reported that "their behavior was unbelievably unprofessional."

Vice presidents from the parent company allegedly exhibited the same behavior on business trips from Sweden. Women reported they were groped, squeezed, and kissed despite their protestations. Some lower-level managers began to exhibit the same behavior as their bosses; other male managers were appalled. One male rep said he was so angry he eventually quit the company. He told the investigator, "I felt powerless and embarrassed as a man." A group of male managers approached their boss and told him they were worried about the impact the harassment was having on morale and their own reputations. Reportedly they were told that no one criticized Bildman.[82]

Despite the fact that Astra had a written sexual harassment policy, complaints went on for years and usually were settled quietly. As the investigation widened, George Roadman and Ed Aarons, a high-ranking sales director, were relieved of their responsibilities and replaced by new managers.

In mid-May the federal EEOC began to investigate the allegations. Four EEOC complaints were already pending: Two were sexual harassment claims filed in 1995. A total of 16 legal or internal complaints were brought by employees during Bildman's presidency.[83] In a May 13 letter the EEOC asked Astra for extensive information including copies of the company's sexual harassment policy, lists of sales representatives, and information about settlement agreements the company signed with employees who complained of sexual harassment.[84]

On May 14, Jan Larsson, the interim CEO of Astra USA appointed a new head of human resources to report directly to him. He also set up a hotline at the company's headquarters in Marlborough, Massachusetts, to receive calls from employees who could speak anonymously to investigators.[85]

Internal Astra investigators began to look into whether Bildman had improperly ordered one of the company's contractors to perform $330,000 in renovations at his home and whether he used company funds to maintain a fleet of cars. A 37-page federal lawsuit filed by four men and two women employed in the Westborough company, alluded to bookkeeping irregularities. One manager reported that a member of Bildman's top staff told him that three sets of books were kept: "One for the Swedes, one for ourselves, and one for the auditors."[86]

At the end of June 1996, Astra USA announced it had fired Lars Bildman without compensation for having engaged in "inappropriate behavior" at

---

[82] M. Maremont, "Abuse of Power," *Business Week,* May 13, 1996, pp. 86–98.
[83] K. Blanton, "U.S. Launches Astra Harassment Probe," *Boston Globe,* May 11, 1996, p. 1.
[84] "Astra USA Inc. Says EEOC Requests Data in Harassment Probe," *The Wall Street Journal,* p. B8.
[85] K. Blanton, "New Astra CEO Makes Changes," *Boston Globe,* May 14, 1996, p. 39.
[86] D. E. Lewis, "Astra Allegedly Forced Workers to Keep Silent," *Boston Globe,* May 31, 1996, p. 1.

company parties and for using $2 million in company funds for personal vacations and renovations to his home. The company also disclosed that Bildman's financial misconduct was being investigated by the U.S. Justice Department. George Roadman was finally fired for "inappropriate behavior." Two other executives, Edward Aarons, director of institutional business, and Anders Lonner who headed the company's Swedish marketing operations, resigned as a result of the probe.[87]

In mid-September, Astra AB announced that an executive from its Canadian subsidiary, Ivan R. Rowley, would become the new head of Astra USA. By the end of December 1996, Rowley was busy making major changes in the Astra USA corporate culture.

He developed training seminars in sexual harassment and expanded the human resource office under a new woman vice president. Lynn Tetrault announced that by June 1997, the department would have as many as 15 employees. An employment lawyer was hired to investigate complaints of harassment. A work-family task force was in the process of developing programs to help Astra's nearly 1,500 employees balance work and personal lives. Workplace specialists observed that this was a good start.

The president of the American Institute for Managing Diversity cautioned that Astra had looked at the branches of the problem without addressing the basic root assumptions associated with it. He suggested the company conduct a cultural audit to examine current practices. Ann Vincola, national director of work-life consulting at Coopers & Lybrand suggested developing a "road map for a diversity strategy for the next two to three years . . . putting women in roles of responsibility so they can move up the ladder should be part of that plan."[88]

The cases of Mitsubishi and Astra illustrate how two companies reacted when faced with sexual harassment problems. Both companies are likely to be tied up in litigation for years but their public images and working environments are likely to be quite different. Public perception of their strategy in dealing with sexual harassment charges may have a considerable effect on their profitability and on their attractiveness as prospective workplaces. How substantial their financial penalties will be remains to be seen.

Age Discrimination

The EEOC also administers the Age Discrimination in Employment Act (ADEA). The act protects workers between ages 40 and 70 from arbitrary age discrimination in employment. When Congress passed the ADEA in 1967, the law covered people up to age 65; in 1978, the age limit was raised to 70.

---

[87] L. Johannes, "Astra USA Fires Bildman from Top Post," *The Wall Street Journal,* June 27, 1996, p. A3.

[88] D. E. Lewis, "Going a New 'Way,'" *Boston Globe,* December 4, 1996, p. C1.

The ADEA encompasses issues of hiring, firing, pay, promotion, and fringe benefits. It does not cover cases in which age is a bonafide occupational qualification.

In 1990, the Older Workers Benefit Protection Act (OWBPA) was signed into law. This act prohibited discrimination based on age in connection with all employee benefit programs. It reestablished the requirement that benefits for older workers be the same as for younger workers, except to the extent the employer can show a greater cost is attached to providing for older workers.[89]

Under the OWBPA, companies can ask outgoing workers to sign a promise, or waiver, not to sue for age discrimination. To be legal, a waiver must meet the following requirements:

- The company must give workers some kind of compensation in addition to the benefits and severance pay they would ordinarily get.
- The waiver must be in plain English, not legal jargon.
- The waiver cannot cover issues arising after the date of the waiver.
- The company must suggest the employee talk to a lawyer.
- The company must give the employee at least 21 days to sign the waiver and 45 days if the employee is leaving because of mass layoffs or buyout incentives. Employees have seven days after signing to change their minds.
- Employers must give employees a list of job titles and ages of everyone potentially affected by the cutback, including people who were not fired.
- Employers must specifically refer to the Age Discrimination in Employment Act in their discussions with employees.[90]

In the spring of 1993, the U.S. Supreme Court ruled that employers are not necessarily barred from firing older workers to avoid paying them pensions. Such firings would violate the age bias law only if age rather than years of service were the actual reason for the firing. Writing for the majority, Justice Sandra Day O'Connor observed, "It is the very essence of age discrimination for an older employee to be fired because the employer believes that productivity and competence decline with old age. When the employer's decision is wholly motivated by factors other than age, the problem of inaccurate and stigmatizing stereotypes disappears."[91]

In April 1996, the Supreme Court ruled that older workers who lost their jobs to someone younger had a claim of illegal age discrimination even when the replacement workers were also older than 40. This ruling strengthened the federal law against age discrimination at a time when thousands of

---

[89] *Labor Law Legislative Update* (Boston: Nutter, McClennan & Fish, 1991), p. 1.

[90] J. Woo, "Ex-Workers Hit Back with Age-Bias Suits," *The Wall Street Journal,* December 8, 1992, p. B1.

[91] L. Asseo, "Court Limits Age-Discrimination Law," *Boston Globe,* April 21, 1993, p. 47.

workers were losing their jobs to downsizing. The original suit was brought in North Carolina by a 56-year-old salesman whose boss told him he was "too damn old for this kind of work." The supervisor said it was time to get some young blood into the company. Two days later, the firm reorganized the sales force and fired the plaintiff, James O'Connor. Two lower courts dismissed the suit because O'Connor's replacement was over 40 years old.

The Supreme Court rejected the view that replacing O'Connor did not amount to illegal age discrimination because both he and his replacement were covered by the Age Discrimination in Employment Act of 1967. Speaking for the court, Justice Antonin Scalia said, "So long as the employee lost out because of his age," he suffered age discrimination. The fact that he was replaced by another person over 40 was "utterly irrelevant."[92]

Age discrimination suits proliferated in the mid-1990s as restructurings and downsizing continued. At Westinghouse Electric Corporation about 12,000 mostly older workers lost their jobs. In mid-1996, a class-action suit was filed by the EEOC on behalf of 250 workers aged 40 or older who were dismissed by a former Westinghouse defense unit. Westinghouse did not have a corporatewide policy for layoffs and left severance up to individual business managers. John Bergen, senior vice president for corporate relations at the company noted the basic policy was that it didn't discriminate but in a "performance culture, you want to let people know there is a reward for high performance. Some people move to the top, some don't."

John Ryder, a 30-year Westinghouse employee, won a $241,909 judgment in an age-discrimination suit against Westinghouse. Ryder, an assistant controller was talking with his boss's secretary when he was unexpectedly called into his boss's office and told his career would be over in five months. He was replaced by a woman in her 30s who assumed his duties under a different title.

Ryder knew other veteran employees who had been dismissed but they had been given consultant contracts or severance bonuses after signing documents waiving their right to file suit against Westinghouse. Ryder was not offered a consultancy or severance bonus and was not asked to sign a waiver. Ryder retained a lawyer and filed in U.S. District Court in Pittsburgh in November 1993. Ryder's attorney, who was handling a separate age-discrimination suit against Westinghouse, was given a copy of a company memo written in September 1994. The memo discussed the need to hire "younger individuals" and get the "blockers" out of the way. In the Ryder case, Westinghouse argued that the memo could not be used as evidence because it was written after Ryder's dismissal. However, the judge allowed it to be admitted on the ground that it indicated the company's state of mind at the time Ryder was fired.[93]

---

[92] D. G. Savage, "High Court Ruling Boosts Age Bias Law, "*Boston Globe,* April 2, 1996, p. 1; L. Greenhouse, "Justices Say Age Bias Can Occur Even When One Over-40 Worker Replaces Another," *New York Times,* April 2, 1996, p. A14.

[93] P. Thomas, "Restructurings Generate Rash of Age-Bias Suits," *The Wall Street Journal,* August 29, 1996, p. B1.

In November 1996, a $13 million settlement ended one of the nation's largest age-discrimination suits. This suit affected 2,000 former employees of Martin Marietta Corporation (now part of Lockheed Martin). The settlement also called for rehiring 450 former employees who were victims of age discrimination and for the company to hold retraining courses and to provide outplacement services for employees laid off between January 1990 and December 1994.[94] The EEOC lawsuit, which was originally filed in May 1994, claimed Martin targeted employees age 40 and older for major layoffs during a five-year period beginning in 1990.

As large companies like AT&T and Eastman Kodak trim their workforces and remove entire levels of older workers, experts observe that age-discrimination suits are likely to outnumber sex-discrimination suits in the near future. They note that middle managers who earned high salaries are particularly prone to sue because they have a great deal to gain by going after lost wages.

A lawyer who specializes in age discrimination suits warns companies that if it can be inferred that age is the basis for layoff decisions, a flashing light goes off at EEOC agencies for potential age discrimination suits.[95] Age discrimination suits can be very costly to companies; most settlements run from $50,000 to $400,000 per employee.

Managing an Aging Workforce

In an *Academy of Management Executive* article, Robert J. Paul and James B. Townsend point out that by the year 2000, nearly half of all Americans will be older than 45 and more than 36 million will be over 65 years of age. They say American business tends to undervalue the importance and experience of older workers. Forty million Americans age 60 and older have more than 1 billion years of cumulative work experience that should not be wasted. They suggest managers follow these guidelines for employing older workers:

- *Talk with your legal department.* You should discuss the ADEA and its amendments, the Senior Community Service Employment Program of 1973, the Employee Retirement Income Security Act (ERISA), the Job Training Partnership Act of 1982, the Social Security Act and its amendments, and the Tax Reform and Budget Conciliation Acts of 1986.
- *Review your strategic plan.* The HRM manager should forecast personnel needs to determine whether the company has adequate policies on recruitment, orientation, retention, and retirement.

---

[94] "Firm to Pay $13m to Settle Age Bias Suit," *Boston Globe,* November 22, 1996, p. D2.

[95] K. G. Salwain, "EEOC Gets Settlement from McDonnell in Crackdown on Age-Biased Layoffs," *The Wall Street Journal,* March 2, 1993, p. A4.

- *Reconsider your human resource policies.* Older workers should be accommodated by using flexible benefits and work schedules, part-time work, and incentives for continued employment. The company also should consider arrangements with older workers such as consulting, seasonal work, reduced hours with reduced pay, job sharing, compressed workweeks, expanded or reduced shifts, voluntary demotions, and job rotation.
- *Think about job redesign.* The company should consider individual job preferences of older workers. Older workers are proficient at teaching, counseling, research, long-range planning, security, arbitration, and other tasks. Jobs that require accuracy, judgment, and reason are more appropriate than those that require speed, innovation, and creativity.
- *Provide for career-long training.* Training for older workers should take place in a nonthreatening environment that builds confidence for learning new skills. Verbal assurances, adequate learning time, and privacy are important.
- *Examine your benefit plans.* Make sure older workers have a choice of insurance plans, pension credits, extended leaves, and vacation days to meet their needs.
- *Reconsider incentives.* Older workers may have different incentives than younger workers. Stress recognition of accomplishments, financial rewards, and peer recognition instead of promotions and more responsibility.
- *Ensure that performance appraisal programs are current.* These data form the basis for many personnel decisions.[96]

Making the Most of Diversity

In their *Harvard Business Review* article, "Making Differences Matter: A New Paradigm for Managing Diversity," David A. Thomas and Robin J. Ely insist that diversity programs fail or do not fulfill their promise unless a company recognizes preconditions:

1. The leadership must understand that a diverse workforce will embody different perspectives and approaches to work and must value a variety of opinions and insights.
2. Corporate leadership must recognize both the learning opportunities and the challenges that the expression of different perspectives presents for an organization.

---

[96] R. J. Paul and J. B. Townsend, "Managing the Older Worker—Don't Just Rinse Away the Gray," *Academy of Management Executive* 7, no. 3 (1993), pp. 67–74.

3. The organizational culture must create a expectation of high standards of performance from everyone.
4. The organizational culture must stimulate personal development.
5. The organizational culture must encourage openness.
6. The culture must make workers feel valued.
7. The organization must have a well-articulated and widely understood mission.

Thomas and Ely say leadership's vision of the purpose of a diversified workforce is critical to the successful implementation of a company's program. A high-level commitment to creating an environment of organizational trust is essential if the company is to resolve tensions quickly and effectively.[97]

---

[97] D. A. Thomas and R. J. Ely, "Making Differences Matter: A New Paradigm for Managing Diversity," *Harvard Business Review,* September–October, 1996, p. 79–90.

Summary

The passage of the Civil Rights Act of 1964 fundamentally changed companies' criteria for hiring, firing, and rewarding employees. The act established the Equal Employment Opportunity Commission (EEOC) to write and administer rules and regulations. The EEOC's job is to investigate employees' discrimination charges and litigate on their behalf if the charges were sufficiently grave.

Affirmative action, a policy embodied in a series of executive orders, goes beyond equal treatment. It is directed primarily at minorities and women and requires companies to redress past discrimination. The Office of Federal Contract Compliance Programs monitors corporations' affirmative action efforts and suggests models for formulating and implementing programs.

Since the mid-1970s, the Supreme Court has ruled on several precedent-setting affirmative action cases. Over the past 15 years, the ideological composition of the court has changed, and so has the direction of its decisions. The Supreme Court of the early 1990s was far more conservative and less likely to support affirmative action cases than the pre-Reagan era Court. Some recent decisions have upheld affirmative action for women, but minority programs have fared poorly.

The Republicans' 1994 Contract with America helped precipitate a more conservative discussion of affirmative action. California was the first state to challenge affirmative action in a referendum. Public opinion polls showed growing support for the dismantling of affirmative action policies on the state and national level.

Although more women have entered the workforce and are moving upward through the management hierarchy, they are still encountering difficulties, including sexual harassment. The law prohibits sexual harassment, but it is very difficult to prove and the EEOC is reluctant to take cases to court. Some companies have instituted procedures and policies aimed at diminishing sexual harassment. As with all other issues of social responsibility, top management's commitment is critical. Programs that foster fair and equitable treatment benefit all employees.

The passage of the Age Discrimination in Employment Act protects workers between ages 40 and 70 from discrimination in hiring, firing, pay, and promotion. In recent years, more and more employees have been filing grievances under this act. Faced with expensive pensions and health costs, companies are trying to find ways to minimize their burden. But firms face an indefinite future of court-mandated payments and damages if they are found guilty of violating age discrimination regulations.

Questions

1. Even if top management is committed to an affirmative action program, middle managers and supervisors often resist implementation. Suppose you are the head of personnel for a large manufacturing company. Send the CEO a memo suggesting how to secure middle-management support.
2. Discuss the problems women face in the workplace, and determine what issues, if any, are unique to women. How do women's issues differ from those of minorities and elderly workers? How do they differ, if at all, from the issues men face?
3. How should a company assess its social performance in the area of affirmative action?
4. Since the passage of the Civil Rights Act, how has government policy affected the law's implementation? Discuss the role of the Supreme Court in determining civil rights issues.
5. What are the elements of a good and effective diversity program?

Projects

1. Contact the EEOC in your state to find out what it does to monitor the status of minorities in the workplace.
2. Find out from your state or the federal EEOC how it decides which cases to litigate and which cases to drop.
3. Conduct a diversity awareness workshop in class. As a semester-long project, pick a diversity issue with which you are not familiar. Some examples might be problems of gay and lesbian employees, people with disabilities, elderly people, women, African-Americans, Hispanics, or other minorities. Interview members of their lobbying or support groups and write a comprehensive paper. The paper should include the problems described by the chosen group, relevant legislation, and a personal statement about what you have learned. Examine your own stereotypes and assess whether they have changed as a result of the project. You may do this project individually or in small groups.

BETA CASE 12
EQUAL EMPLOYMENT AND AFFIRMATIVE ACTION

Joan McCarthy, vice president of public affairs at Beta, decided she had put off the woman issue long enough. Shortly after she joined Beta, McCarthy and her task force found women were substantially underrepresented in the ranks of top management, craftspeople, and service workers. In fact, she remembered the only category in which women were fully represented was office, clerical, and staff. In 1983, only 3.66 percent of Beta's managers and professionals were women; in 1995, that number had grown to only 4.12 percent.

McCarthy reflected that not one woman had made it through the managerial ranks to the vice president level in more than a decade. Even she had been hired from outside the company to fill the public affairs position. Of all the vice presidential slots in companies, public affairs was the one most likely to be held by a woman or minority group member.

The glass ceiling against which Beta's women managers banged their heads as they tried to rise was clearly intact. Certainly women had been at Beta long enough to have made it higher up the ladder. McCarthy decided to do a little research before she discussed the matter with John West, vice president of human resources. She wondered why upward mobility at Beta was so low. Was it because the women were undervalued? Was it because they did not do their jobs as well as the men? Were they stalled because of factors that had little or nothing to do with Beta?

McCarthy studied data on women in a variety of managerial and professional jobs. A 1996 study by Catalyst, a nonprofit women's research group, showed that women held about 2 percent of the power positions in the nation's 500 largest U.S. companies. Catalyst defined power by title, by paycheck, and by responsibility for the bottom line.[98]

McCarthy's research on the status of women in the nation's large pharmaceutical firms found Beta was consistent with the norm in number of women in top positions. Over the next several weeks, McCarthy discussed the women issue with several of the top male managers at Beta. Generally they prefaced their responses with "Of course, we don't mean you, Joan, but." Some observed women were not interested in sports or other topics men liked to talk about informally. Many were afraid women would get emotional if they had a professional disagreement. A few mentioned their wives would object if they had to travel with a woman.

Overwhelmingly, the men agreed they did not want to hire or promote women because if the women had children, they would want special privileges. All the training and time invested in them would be lost if the women did not come back to work or had extended maternity leaves.

Women who returned to work after childbirth frequently found their performance evaluations were far lower than before. Staff cuts and management overhauls gave companies the opportunity to save money by firing employees whose personal circumstances might require special attention. Some companies had family-friendly policies but women who took advantage of them were frequently sidetracked. Robin Ely, a scholar specializing in gender and race relations, commented in the Catalyst study that although some companies had family-friendly policies, they were not very good at implementing them.

As McCarthy pulled into her driveway after an exhausting day, she reflected on her conversations with male colleagues and on her other findings. The month she had spent on this issue had been intensely unsettling. She was very concerned about women's access to top management jobs and dismayed at her male colleagues' attitude toward women with families.

After working 14-hour days for the last 10 years, McCarthy and her husband were contemplating starting a family. Although she had every intention of continuing to work after her child was born, she wondered whether she would find herself relegated to another job. She also wondered whether her colleagues' treatment of her would change when her pregnancy became obvious.

---

[98] J. H. Dobrzynski, "Somber News for Women on Corporate Ladder," *New York Times,* November 6, 1996, p. D1.

CHAPTER 13
Unions, Occupational Safety, and Health

Case: Jennifer Stills and Workplace Safety

Jennifer Stills hated mornings like this. Betsy Stanford, an employee in the customer service department, was still causing a problem. Six months ago, Stanford fell in the parking lot and claimed her back was broken. Physicians' diagnoses were inconclusive. One corroborated the claim, while two others said she had simply suffered a very bad sprain. All agreed she had recovered sufficiently to return to work. However, Stanford refused, insisting she was in terrible pain and could not sit for the long periods her job required.

When the accident occurred, Stills notified the state workers' compensation board and Prime's insurance company. Stanford was still receiving 66 percent of her pay from the insurance company. Because she refused to return to work, Prime filed for arbitration with the state board of industrial accidents. Josh Charles at the board told Stills the arbitration could drag on for as long as two years, during which time Prime's insurance company would have to continue to pay. Stanford said she was willing to settle for $15,000 and leave the company.

Stills was very annoyed that over the past six months her time had been taken up by someone who just wanted to make money at Prime's expense. She was sure Stanford never intended to come back to her job. Stills was thoroughly disgusted with a system that rewarded a malingering employee at the expense of the company.

Questions

1. What responsibility should a company have toward a worker who appears to be taking advantage of an inefficient legal system?
2. Should Jennifer Stills recommend fighting the issue to its conclusion regardless of how long it takes?
3. If Prime gave Betsy Stanford the $15,000, what message would it send to other employees?

The Changing Work Environment

Before 1970, American workers relied on a combination of labor union intervention, voluntary corporate responsibility, state law, and luck to make the work environment even moderately safe. Across industries, union organizers pressed business organizations to raise wages, improve benefits, and implement workplace safety standards. Unions were workers' only consistent major advocates for workplace safety.

After Congress passed the Occupational Safety and Health Act in 1970, federal and state governments assumed major responsibility for rule setting and enforcement of workplace safety. The federal Occupational Safety and Health Administration (OSHA) and state OSHAs have gone through periods of minimal activity as well as times when standards were enforced. Much of their effectiveness depends on budget allocations and political commitment to their role in safety enforcement.

Labor Unions

U.S. workers were slower than Europeans to organize labor unions. The United States never developed a politically active working class. The tightly knit, highly structured European guild system was incompatible with an America of boundless land, abundant natural resources, and an unshakable belief in individualism.

In colonial America, workers had little need to form labor unions to preserve or improve working conditions. In the few formal associations of employees, workers were limited to a single craft such as shoemaking or carpentry because

- The market for the employer's product was local and usually not competitive.
- Workers had close contact with their employers and often shared the same living quarters. Therefore, they tended to resolve their differences amicably.
- Skilled labor was in short supply. A formal apprentice system stipulated that workers could not be fired without good reason.
- Land was cheap and dissatisfied workers could always move west to become farmers or practice their crafts in new surroundings.
- The ratio of labor to resources was low, enabling many people to afford luxuries.

The Development of Nationwide Unions

Workers began to unionize in the early 19th century, when the influx of unskilled immigrant labor forced them to compete for wages. Since then, unions' membership and vitality fluctuated with the nation's economic peaks and depressions. When the economy prospered, so did the unions. Recessions and depressions, which created intense job competition, sapped unions' strength and solidarity.

In 1827, workingmen's associations of several crafts joined together under one umbrella organization to push for political and industrial goals. Their first objective was to shorten the workday from 12 to 10 hours. Some participants in the union movement diluted economic and workplace safety concerns with social goals, such as free education, woman suffrage, and abolition of imprisonment for debt. These early efforts at organization were short-lived because workers could not agree whether economic or social goals were more important.

The depression of 1837 virtually wiped out union activity and an influx of Irish immigrants during the 1840s fostered increased wage competition. With the return of economic prosperity in 1850, however, the unions regained strength, concentrating on issues of higher wages and a shorter workday. Labor leaders began to press for standardized wages and developed common bargaining demands.

The Civil War (1861–1865) brought a new spurt of union activity. By the end of the war, 2 percent of the northern population was unionized, up from less than 1 percent four years earlier. Workers became more interested in joining unions because (1) more immigrant competitors were working for low wages; (2) changing technology was replacing workers with machines; and (3) prices were rising faster than wages, lowering workers' standard of living.

William Sylvis of the Iron Moulder's Union formed the National Labor Union in 1866. He made the first attempt to unite all unions into a single federation of American labor. A collection of farmers' groups, woman suffragists, and blacks promoted the eight-hour day, female suffrage, and free libraries. Because many of the goals were social and the participants had very little in common ideologically, the union quickly folded.

In 1873 business collapsed into a five-year-long depression and once again unions disbanded. Employers, sensing a chance to smother unionism entirely, engaged in lockouts, hired spies to identify union organizers, and employed strikebreakers.

A secret organization called the Noble and Holy Order of the Knights of Labor emerged from the embers of the union movement. Organized in 1869, the Knights of Labor was a huge general union of skilled and unskilled workers. When good economic times returned in the 1880s, its charismatic leader, Terence Powderly, embarked on an organizing campaign. By 1886, the Knights of Labor had 700,000 members. However, this union, like its predecessors, fell apart. Skilled and unskilled workers had very few common interests in the various political, economic, and social issues of the time. By 1900, the union had virtually disappeared.

Unlike earlier unions, the American Federation of Labor (AFL), founded in 1886 and led by Samuel Gompers, was a well-organized federation of craft unions that concentrated on economic goals rather than political or social issues. Membership in trade unions grew rapidly in the early 1900s, reaching 5 million in 1920.[1]

During World War I, economic growth and labor shortages facilitated union growth. As unions grew stronger, business owners applied countervailing pressure through trade associations. Fearing that organized labor would usurp their prerogatives to determine wages and workplace conditions, business leaders actively campaigned against the unions. The National Association of Manufacturers (NAM), founded in 1895, became the most notable antiunion trade association. Management used blacklists, yellow-dog contracts (agreements by employees that if hired they would not join a union), strikebreakers, and accusations of communist infiltration to fight the burgeoning unions.

Some employers took a more subtle approach to undermining unions and began to offer worker benefits such as profit-sharing plans, pension plans, unemployment benefits, guaranteed wages, and employee stock ownership. They made it quite clear to workers that they were granting privileges, not conceding rights to the labor unions.

The stock market crash of 1929, followed by the Depression of the 1930s, ended public support for antiunion activity. As the epidemic of unemployment spread across the country, public opinion turned in favor of organized labor in a remarkable and fundamental change of attitude. The Depression was so profound that people looked to labor unions as their only hope.

Franklin D. Roosevelt's election and the establishment of the New Deal signaled a new attitude toward organized labor. The Norris–LaGuardia Act, passed in 1932, ended the use of injunctions and made yellow-dog contracts unenforceable. Prior to this act, when a company was struck or workers formed picket lines, government could get a court order called an injunction to force strikers to return to work.

Employers still were not obliged to recognize unions as bargaining agents for employees. Unions lobbied Congress to pass a law requiring employers to deal with them. In 1935, the National Labor Relations Act (better known as the Wagner Act) set up the National Labor Relations Board (NLRB) to hear union appeals and peacefully resolve disputes between labor and management.

In 1935, John L. Lewis, unhappy about the craft orientation of the AFL, combined his United Mine Workers of America with several other unions to form the Congress of Industrial Organizations (CIO). The CIO promoted the idea of industrywide unions instead of the AFL federation. After a massive membership drive and successful strikes against the automobile and steel industries, most large businesses began to recognize industrial as well as craft unions. Over the next 15 years, the AFL and CIO spent huge sums of money competing for new members. Finally, in 1955, they decided to call a truce and

---

[1] S. Cohen, *Labor in the United States,* 4th ed. (Columbus: Charles E. Merrill, 1973), p. 51

merged into one labor movement, the AFL–CIO. George Meany was elected president and represented the interests of more than 16 million workers.

Not all post-World War II legislation was prolabor. In the chill of the Cold War, employers again charged that communists were involved in union leadership and that American productivity was jeopardized by unions' monopolistic control. In 1947, they persuaded Congress to pass the Taft–Hartley Act over President Harry Truman's veto. The act broadened employers' range of options in dealing with unions and further defined and limited the rights of employees. It also gave the president the right to declare a national emergency if, in his judgment, a strike created major health or safety problems. A court order could force strikers to go back to work for a cooling-off period of 80 days while both sides tried to resolve their differences. This provision was used 35 times between 1947 and the early 1980s.

During the 1970s, the percentage of unionized members in the total workforce declined from 29.3 percent in 1968 to 24.9 percent in 1979. The growth of nonunion operations in construction, trucking, and mining accounted for some of the decline. Other reasons for membership decline included growth in high-technology, science-based, and service industries. Workers in these industries did not have a tradition of union activity as did in steel and automobile workers. In addition, employers in the new industries strongly resisted union efforts to organize.[2]

Union Activity in the 1980s

Union membership dropped sharply between 1980 and 1985. As noted earlier, deregulation and recession in the early 1980s, coupled with a shift from manufacturing to service industries, were major factors in the decline. The Bureau of Labor Statistics reported 23 percent of wage and salary earners belonged to unions in 1980. Four years later, only 18.8 percent of that population held union membership.[3]

Realizing its power was rapidly eroding, the AFL–CIO executive council met to develop a new strategy. The council acknowledged new issues had emerged that required innovative approaches. Unions began to stress concerns for pay equity, day care, advancement for women, office automation, job security, and health and safety in the workplace. A prominent labor leader commented that labor would have to confront corporations "not as streetfighters but as professional opponents."[4]

In the 1980s, unions and management leaders began working together over workplace issues and compensation. Some corporate boards, like their counterparts in Europe, appointed worker-directors. Former United Auto

---

[2] E. M. Kassalow, "The Future of American Unionism: A Comparative Perspective," *Annals of the American Academy of Political and Social Science* 473, May 1984, pp. 52–63.

[3] W. Serrin, "U.S. Cities Continued Drop in Union Membership," *New York Times*, February 8, 1985, p. B5.

[4] L. M. Apcar and C. Trost, "Realizing Their Power Has Eroded, Unions Try Hard to Change," *The Wall Street Journal*, February 21, 1985, p. 1.

Workers (UAW) President Douglas A. Fraser became the first union director of a major corporation when he joined the Chrysler Corporation board in 1980. The trend toward union participation on boards began to change the historically adversarial relationship between labor and management. A more cooperative relationship between labor and management emerged for the first time in American labor relations.

In 1988, unions faced major problems in negotiating for increased pay as wages took a backseat to job security. The Conference Board (a business research organization) anticipated union pay hikes would average 2.5 percent, half the rate of inflation. In a period of weak unions, fierce foreign competition, and widespread restructuring, unions had very little clout. Lower pay in a secure job was clearly preferable to no job at all. Unions still expressed concern about workers' health and safety, but they more frequently left enforcement to government regulators and inspectors.

Many union leaders believed President Ronald Reagan set the tone for the decade when he broke the Professional Air Traffic Controllers' strike and its union in 1981. Management prevailed over organized labor in other industries as well. Steel union membership declined by half during the 1980s. Greyhound Bus Lines strikers lost their battle when the company went into bankruptcy. At Continental Airlines, Frank Lorenzo broke the pilots' union and tried to repeat the process at Eastern Airlines.[5] Douglas Fraser observed, "Unions will have to offer innovative and different services. We can expand the employee assistance programs . . . and social services. They have to be available near where people work to do much good."[6]

By 1990, unions no longer dominated major industries like automobiles, steel, and rubber. Audrey Freeman, a labor economist at the Conference Board, said 39 percent of all people represented by unions were in the public sector, and it [the union movement] will probably be over by the end of the decade [in the year 2000].[7]

The recession of the early 1990s did little further damage to the union movement. Most unions already had dealt with the restructuring of the 1980s and with sharp cuts in jobs and pay. Productivity had even risen in many industries. At USX (formerly the U.S. Steel Corporation), management had made massive cuts in employee compensation already and slashed its unionized workforce by more than one-half. Although the United Steelworkers union was not happy with the company's 1991 offer of an 8 percent pay raise over four years, at least unionized workers' wages were likely to match inflation.[8]

---

[5] J. Holusa, "Unions Are Expanding Their Role to Survive in the 90s," *New York Times,* August 19, 1990, p. F12.

[6] Ibid.

[7] Ibid.

[8] A. Bernstein, "Been Down So Long," *Business Week,* January 4, 1991, p. 31.

Labor in the 1990s

Labor leaders were very disappointed with labor's losses in the early 1990s and were very apprehensive about their future under the 1994 Republican Congress. Thirty-three union presidents and leaders gathered at the AFL–CIO's executive council meeting in February 1995. They expected to hear from Clinton administration officials but their top agenda item was to discuss whether to replace Lane Kirkland as president of the AFL–CIO. Kirkland, who succeeded George Meany in 1979, had demonstrated little inclination to work with management to improve productivity or enhance union clout by forming coalitions with church, environmental, or community groups.

In May 1995, Gerald McEntee, president of AFSCME (the public employees' union), and John J. Sweeney, president of the service employees' union, led a move to replace Kirkland. Organized labor was involved in an internecine quarrel that threatened to break out into open rebellion against established leadership.[9]

In July, the leadership issue that threatened to drag on and on was dramatically resolved. George Becker of the United Steelworkers of America; Samuel P. Yokich, president the United Automobile Workers (UAW); and George G. Kourpias, president of the nearly half million members of the International Association of Machinists and Aerospace Workers, joined the two powerful service union presidents in calling for Lane Kirkland's resignation. Shortly after Kirkland agreed to resign, the steel workers, automobile workers, and machinists declared they would merge over a five-year period.

The merger would create a 2 million-member megaunion with a strike support fund of more than $1 billion. Sweeney, who was in line to succeed Kirkland; AFL–CIO Secretary-Treasurer Thomas R. Donahue, who would complete Kirkland's term; and Kirkland himself all supported the merger.[10]

By fall 1995, organized labor began to win some small battles thanks to a shift in strategy. For the first time in decades, unions poured resources into organizing campaigns for low-wage workers whom they previously ignored. For the first time, they courted chicken pluckers, street sweepers, and toilet scrubbers. Many of these jobs paid less than $15,000 a year for full-time work.

AFL–CIO leadership pledged to send out organizers and spend as much as $20 million on organizing. Lane Kirkland had spent virtually nothing on attracting new members. Instead the union had focused on national politics and foreign affairs as policy issues. Labor historians noted the new strategy and drew parallels between the 1990s and the 1930s. In the depth of the Depression, low-wage workers also had been written off. However, they rose

---

[9] L. Kaufman, "Union Solidarity Forever? Sorry, Not This Year," *Newsweek,* May 22, 1995, p. 62.

[10] P. T. Kilborn, "Three Big Unions Are Set to Merge, Creating a Giant," *New York Times,* July 28, 1995, p. A1.

up in the face of intense employer opposition and by the end of World War II had organized nearly every major manufacturing sector.[11]

In October, 78 AFL-CIO labor unions represented by more than 1,000 voting delegates, gathered in New York City to choose Lane Kirkland's successor. For the first time the election was contested. Thomas R. Donahue, Kirkland's deputy, and John J. Sweeney vied for the job of president of the AFL-CIO. Both candidates promised big increases in spending, staff, and training to overthrow Republican incumbents in the 1996 congressional election. Donahue said he would assign 50 specially trained workers to congressional districts three months before the election.[12] Sweeney vowed to create a separate AFL-CIO organizing department, expand the AFL-CIO Executive Council from 33 to 45 vice presidents, and bar people over 70 years of age from running for top offices.[13]

On October 16 the rank and file chose John Sweeney over Thomas Donahue. Sweeney received 7.3 million votes to Donahue's 5.7 million. The new Executive Council included more women and minorities, increasing the proportion from 17 percent to 27 percent. Sweeney immediately declared he would transform the AFL-CIO into a confrontational voice for American workers. In his acceptance speech, Sweeney declared, "The most important thing we can do . . . is to organize every working woman and man who needs a better deal and a new voice."[14]

With the election over, labor turned toward organizing. The Supreme Court gave organized labor a big boost when it ruled unanimously that union organizers who took or sought jobs with nonunionized employers with the goal of persuading co-workers to join the unions were protected by federal labor laws. The decision upheld a policy of the National Labor Relations Board (NLRB) stipulating that employers who tried to root out those union workers could be charged with unfair labor practices.[15]

In January 1996, Sweeney named Richard Bensinger, former chief of the AFL-CIO's training institute for organizers, as the union's new organizing chief. Bensinger was promised a budget of $20 million in addition to power and influence. He announced he would adopt some of the tactics of the 1960s civil rights movement in organizing today's workers. He also said he would advocate civil disobedience actions in situations where employers fired workers trying to organize their shops. Unless new members joined the unions,

---

[11] G. P. Zachery, "Some Unions Step Up Organizing Campaigns and Get New Members," *The Wall Street Journal,* September 1, 1995, p. A1.

[12] P. T. Kilborn, "Delegates of Labor Gather Battered but Now Buoyant," *New York Times,* October 22, 1995, p. A1.

[13] R. L. Rose and G. P. Zachery, "Labor Chief's Top Job: Resuscitation," *The Wall Street Journal,* October 23, 1995, p. B1.

[14] S. Greenhouse, "A Big Job for Labor," *New York Times,* October 27, 1995, p. A28.

[15] L. Greenhouse, "High Court Protects Union Organizers from Dismissals," *New York Times,* November 29, 1995, p. B11.

Bensinger said, he saw no end to the long-term deterioration of wages earned by many workers.[16]

In a new program to change the AFL-CIO's stodgy image, the union hired 1,000 college students and other young people during the summer to work in cities, help unionization drives at nursing homes and apparel factories, and to work for prolabor political candidates. The Union Summer program was modeled after the Freedom Summer programs of the 1960s when young people went South to work in the civil rights movement.[17]

As the nation prepared for a summer of political campaigning, Sweeney sent out an additional 1,000 organizers to mobilize women and minorities. Sweeney and organized labor could not count on unified Democratic support. In this election year, many Democrats were conservative on social issues such as crime, gun control, abortion, and affirmative action. A February 1996 report for the AFL-CIO found that "union members are profoundly cynical about—and disengaged from—contemporary politics." The report also remarked that "many workers see both the Democratic and Republican [parties] as failed institutions."[18]

Republican campaign committees and business lobbies filed a complaint with the Federal Election Commission protesting the unions' campaign fund raising. The U.S. Chamber of Commerce and about 40 of Washington's business lobbies undertook a coordinated fund-raising drive to keep Congress in probusiness hands.[19] They said it was illegal for the AFL-CIO to make a 15 cent per capita monthly assessment on each of its 78 unions. This money was added to more than $40 million in voluntary contributions from union members to political action committees.

Despite the 1996 Republican victory in the Congress, Sweeney said his central goal had always been to reawaken the sleeping labor giant. Republican detractors were quick to retort. Representative Dick Armey of Texas, the House majority leader, said union members should be furious that so much money was spent for so little result. He asserted that the unions spent more than $100 million on the campaign. Union leaders called the figure ludicrous and put their campaign costs at $35 million.

The Republicans began immediately to prepare legislation to inhibit labor's campaign spending. They wanted a law passed to require unions to get written permission from members before using their dues for political purposes. Union leaders characterized the Republic rhetoric as hypocritical. If

---

[16] G. P. Zachery, "Chief AFL-CIO Organizer to Try Civil-Rights Tactics," *The Wall Street Journal,* February 8, 1996, p. B1.

[17] S. Greenhouse, "Labor Uses an Old Idea to Recruit the Young," *New York Times,* February 25, 1996, p. 23.

[18] B. B. Auster and W. Cohen, "Rallying the Rank and File," *U.S. News & World Report,* April 1, 1996, p. 26.

[19] P. T. Kilborn, "Republicans Are Up in Arms at Labor's Political Rebirth," *New York Times,* April 3, 1996, p. A1.

union spending was such a failure, they asked, why were the Republicans trying to implement legislation to prevent it in the future?[20]

As President Clinton started his second term, organized labor was well positioned to pursue ambitious goals. Sweeney's agenda included using the AFL-CIO to soften the new welfare reform bill, particularly that portion denying benefits to immigrants. He was also committed to providing health insurance to children and developing a more family-oriented policy. Sweeney struck a conciliatory note as he promised to work with moderate Republicans to "make them aware of the issues that workers are confronted with."[21]

Organized labor in the United States appeared to be on the upswing in the mid-1990s. A contract was concluded in the acrimonious tire controversy and the automakers completed their negotiations with the United Auto Workers. The United Farm Workers (UFW) shifted 40 percent of its resources into organizing and recruited thousands of new members. The United Food & Commercial workers recruited more than 70,000 new members in 1996 and won 13 elections in a row to organize workplaces. Other unions, observing these successes, also shifted resources into recruiting new members. Garment workers won new members in the South by upping organization efforts 50 percent. Oil and chemical workers set up a separate organizing unit, boosting spending from 1 to 11 percent of the budget. Service employees, the fastest growing national union, expected to triple its growth by pushing local unions to spend at least 20 percent of their budgets on recruitment.[22] For the time being, at least, labor and business were talking productively and had a common goal of industrial harmony.

For nearly two years, rubber workers around the United States had boycotted, picketed, and excoriated Bridgestone/Firestone because it forced workers to accept 12-hour shifts. When workers struck in July 1994, the giant tire company hired permanent replacements. Finally in November 1996, the United Steelworkers of America, which represented the rubber workers, announced it had reach an agreement with the company. The company promised to reinstate strikers who had been displaced and to give their first across-the-board raise since 1982. The union agreed to end its picketing and radio ads urging consumers to boycott Firestone products.[23]

The United Auto Workers and the Big Three automobile manufacturers completed their negotiations in December 1996. For the first time in years, the Big Three started a three-year contract in good financial shape. Each automaker promised to maintain 95 percent of the 1996 UAW hourly posi-

---

[20] S. Greenhouse, "Despite Setbacks, Labor Chief Is Upbeat over Election Role, "*New York Times,* November 15, 1996, p. A20.

[21] S. Greenhouse, "Organized Labor Outlines Ambitious Goals for the Next Congress," *New York Times,* December 17, 1996, p. A17.

[22] A. Bernstein, "Sweeney's Blitz," *Business Week,* February 17, 1997, pp. 56–62.

[23] S. Greenhouse, "Accord Is Reached in Dispute at Bridgestone," *New York Times,* November 7, 1996, p. A16.

tions. There were exceptions for jobs lost because of productivity gains, market-share declines, and the sale of uncompetitive plants. Each worker received a lump sum of $2,000 the first year of the contract. In the second and third years of the contract each worker was to receive a 3 percent wage increase. Under the terms of the contract, health maintenance organizations (HMOs) would provide health care for UAW members. In year three, workers could switch to traditional indemnity coverage. Limits were removed on how much retired UAW members could earn while receiving full pension benefits. Monthly pensions over the life of the contract increased by $265 to $2,295.

When talks had opened six months earlier, all parties had been pessimistic about reaching a smooth settlement, especially at General Motors where productivity was well behind Ford and Chrysler. GM's relations with the UAW had become touchy during a local strike over outsourcing in March 1996. The strike briefly shut down the entire North American operations. GM, which had taken a hard line on farming out its parts-making work to nonunion shops, finally capitulated after Ford and Chrysler reached agreements. Frank Joyce, the UAW's top spokesman, said, "This is a visionary contract in the way it combines and addresses the interlocking needs of the present, past, and future workers with the Big Three. It's a win–win for both of us."[24]

European Labor Issues

The relative harmony that prevailed in U.S. labor relations was absent as European unions clashed with governments over a variety of issues. European labor unions faced a difficult economic climate in 1995. Workers blamed a borderless European Union for soaring unemployment. Governments tried to cut social benefits to bring budgets in line with the Maastrict Agreement leading to a single currency. State-owned companies that had been sheltered from competition were being privatized and slimmed down. Strikes were rampant across Europe as labor union members demonstrated in the streets.

French Labor. During late autumn 1995, France suffered a series of crippling strikes. Prime Minister Alain Juppé promised tough reforms and deregulatory policies to enable France to meet the 1999 deadline for a European monetary union. He claimed France's $65.5 billion debt would destabilize the nation's financial markets. Unions demanded that the government continue to protect its state-run monopolies.

The French government proposed to reorganize the state-owned national railroad network along those lines dictated by the European Union. The government also planned to review special pension provisions for railroad workers that allowed some to retire at the age of 50. The railroad workers'

---

[24] R. Blumenstein and N. M. Christian, "UAW Contract Appears to Provide Win–Win Situation," *The Wall Street Journal,* December 9, 1996, p. B6

union demanded the government retract the reorganization plans before they would end the strike.

Universities were also hotbeds of union activity. The French government announced universities would receive $400 million in credits in 1995 and $74 million in extra funding. The government also proposed hiring 2,000 more teachers and 2,000 extra administrative personnel. Student organizations found this proposal inadequate and demanded increased spending of $10 billion over the next five years.

The government proposed raising premiums for unemployed people and pensioners by 2.4 percent over the next two years. Public-service sector workers, like those in the private sector, would have to work 40 years, instead of 37.5 years to collect pensions. The government also proposed raising income tax rates in 1996 by 0.5 percent. All but one French labor union rejected the proposals and demanded withdrawal of the entire plan as a condition of ending the strikes.[25] When the government refused to budge, strikers shut down the railways, post office, and electric and gas utilities. Transit worker strikes created huge traffic jams in Paris.[26]

The strikes spread through the first week of December immobilizing the trains, subways, and buses. Strikers blocked planes from landing at Orly airport, forcing Air France to cancel flights. Government ministers promised to talk to the unions but vowed they would not retreat on reforms or promise increased spending for universities. Tourists who usually flocked to France for the Christmas season, stayed home or went elsewhere.[27]

As the strikes intensified, a government spokesman told reporters officials would enter talks with the strikers but the government would not change its mind about overhauling the Social Security system to bring down the debt.[28] Finally Juppé agreed to talk with the railroad strikers but the discussion only hardened their position. On December 13, hundreds of thousands of French demonstrators took to the street demanding Juppé completely abandon his austerity plan and resign. Nearly 41 percent of France's teachers joined the strike, sanitation workers refused to pick up garbage, and newspapers were not published.[29]

The government agreed to drop cutting back pension benefits for public employees and gave up on its plan to trim the rail system. Finally, on December 16, railway workers agreed to end their walkout. Juppé conceded that

---

[25] N. C. Nash, "Leader Calls Cutbacks Vital for French Role in Europe," *New York Times,* December 8, 1995, p. A1.

[26] T. Kamm and D. Lavin, "French Stand Tough against Strikers to Prove Readiness for Monetary Union," *The Wall Street Journal,* November 30, 1995, p. A16.

[27] Y. M. Ibrahim, "Strike Protesting Government Cuts Growing in France," *New York Times,* December 2, 1995, p. 1.

[28] Y. M. Ibrahim, "As Strike Intensifies, French Government Stands Firm," *New York Times,* December 5, 1995, p. A6.

[29] Y. M. Ibrahim, "Strikes in France Surge as Demands by Unions Stiffen," *New York Times,* December 13, 1995, p. A1.

railroad workers' pension rules would allow retirement at the age of 50 and 37.5 years of service. Workers continued to be angry but believed they had won on the most important issues.[30]

Commentators wondered whether the French strikes were likely to spread elsewhere in Europe. Conflicts in principle and tradition were behind the strikes. Governments across Europe were cutting spending, privatizing state-owned companies, and deregulating to meet the goal of monetary union and global competition. Many Europeans saw these policies as an attack on their way of life that had always included high-quality, inexpensive services such as transportation and mail service. Henri Vacquin, a French sociologist remarked, "The government has put its finger on the most sensitive part of France's fears. The power of the free market has run smack into the notion of public service."[31]

After a relatively quiet spring and summer, labor unrest rose in France in the autumn of 1996. Union leaders called for strikes but Prime Minister Juppé and President Jacques Chirac reminded citizens of the government deficit and the need to keep it to the European Union-imposed level of 3 percent of the Gross National Product. Despite threats of massive action, French unions were unable to galvanize workers into large-scale demonstrations and strike activity petered out.[32]

German Labor. In 1993, German workers staged wildcat strikes and blockaded the autobahns to protest corporate restructuring. IG Metall, Germany's largest union with 3.3 million workers, announced it would fight companies' cancellation of national union wage and vacation contracts. The companies had canceled the national contracts for the first time. IG Metall, which covered automobile and machine tools workers, had lost 116,000 jobs between May and July 1993. Observers noted that as many as 60 percent of German industrial jobs were threatened by Eastern European, Asian, and U.S. competition. Labor costs in Germany were running 25 percent higher than in the United States and 33 percent higher than in Japan.[33] As one official commented, "There's such discontent in Europe, it takes very little to set it off."[34]

By 1995, Germany's collective bargaining system was unraveling. Membership in IG Metall had fallen off and participants on both sides criticized the bargaining system's one industry, one wage scale, and one set of

---

[30] C. R. Whitney, "Crowds Dwindle as France's Three-Week Strike Loses Steam," *New York Times,* December 17, 1995, p. 16.

[31] T. Kamm and D. Lavin, "The Strikes in France May Pose a Challenge for European Union," *The Wall Street Journal,* December 22, 1995, p. A1.

[32] C. R. Whitney, "In France, Leaders Brace for the Worst from Unions," *New York Times,* September 29, 1996, p. 44.

[33] G. E. Schares, "Time to Leave the Cocoon?" *Business Week,* October 18, 1993, p. 46.

[34] S. Troy, J. Rossant, and P. B. Oster, "Strike Fever Hits Europe," *Business Week,* November 8, 1993, p. 51.

negotiations approach. Although employers seemed loath to abandon the system altogether, many were making side deals with workers. Robert Bosch GmbH, a diversified industrial company, got its workers to agree to more flexible hours after it said it would build a plant in Scotland. Daimler-Benz negotiated with officials in France, Germany, Britain, and the Czech Republic. It decided to make its cars in Germany only after workers accepted wage increases well below the nationally negotiated level.[35]

In September 1995, Germany's biggest employers' federation, Gesamtmetall canceled its agreements with IG Metall on pay and holidays. Employers told workers that labor costs were too high and the usual raises in pay were out of the question. Union officials called employers' actions a declaration of war. This level of acrimony between the two sides was new and heretofore uncharacteristic in Germany.

However, the industrial climate in Germany was changing. There were enormous differences in productivity and unemployment between the former East Germany and the rest of the country. In addition, new high-technology and service sector industries were not as eager to organize as more traditional industries. German workers, the highest paid in Europe, also had the shortest working hours. Overall unemployment was 9.2 percent and absenteeism was double that in the United States.[36]

In the beginning of 1996, Chancellor Helmut Kohl and his advisors sat down with union and employer representatives to discuss the best way to revive business activity. Union membership had fallen 20 percent since 1992. The German gross domestic product (GDP) grew less than 2 percent in 1995 and unemployment was increasing. Unions were continuing to threaten strikes if wages were not increased; employers believed they had given enough and were unwilling to compromise.[37] The government proposed a number of reforms including the following:

- A cutback in unemployment benefits.
- A reduction of sick pay from 100 percent to 80 percent of basic wages.
- A limitation of state-subsidized cures at health resorts to three weeks every four years instead of four weeks every four years.
- A gradual rise in the retirement age for women from 60 to 63 years and for men from 63 to 65 years.

Despite their previously militant stance, unions compromised with the Kohl cabinet in February. Precipitated by an appreciating German mark, an

---

[35] "Put Germany Back to Work," *Economist,* October 23, 1995, p. 18.

[36] G. Steinmetz, "German Firms Sour on System That Keeps Peace with Workers," *The Wall Street Journal,* October 17, 1995, p. A1.

[37] K. L. Miller, "Are the Easy Times Gone for Good?" *Business Week,* January 29, 1996, p. 48.

economic crisis slowed production, caused industry layoffs, and fostered a new climate of compromise. Unions agreed to raise the early-retirement age to 63 from 60 in exchange for government's promise that a new full-time job would be created for every two older workers who moved into a new half-time work status. Business leaders agreed that they would do their best to create new jobs but could not make any promises.[38]

In April 1996, the head of the employers' organization announced talks had collapsed. German unions vowed to begin a public campaign against government welfare and employment reforms. Dieter Schulte, head of the German trade union federation, accused the Kohl government of buckling under to big business and turning its back on the welfare state.[39]

A reporter for *The Economist* wondered whether the German social market system was broken. Germany's policy of co-determination or *Mitbestimmung* put workers on boards and gave unions a say in the way companies were run. It was part of a network of arrangements that had traditionally fostered close ties between workers and managers. In 1996, some of the biggest companies were in the process of expanding their production abroad and even middle-sized companies were shifting production to central and eastern Europe. Foreign firms, reluctant to pay high German wages, invested elsewhere. Four million Germans were unemployed, the highest number since the 1930s. *The Economist* questioned whether the changes would produce a newer version of the old model or whether the entire union–management–government structure would collapse.[40]

In October 1996, major German corporations cut sick pay by 20 percent as soon as the law went into effect even though workers' contracts did not expire until 1997. Sick pay, the most generous in Europe, had direct costs of $46 billion in 1995, up from $36 billion in 1990. A spokesman for Siemens figured the immediate cut would save the company about $249 million a year. Workers were enraged and union representatives insisted the law required employers to continue under the old rules until new contracts were negotiated. Not so, said executives, passage of the law automatically allowed changes in the union contract.[41]

More than 100,000 engineering workers all over Germany went out on strike over the sick pay issue. Despite this show of militancy and even though they were able to stall implementation of the sick leave changes, German trade unions were forced to become more flexible. In their four-day congress meeting in mid-November 1996, trade unions voted the biggest overhaul of

---

[38] M. Marshall, "Germany's Depleted Unions Show Clout," *The Wall Street Journal,* February 15, 1996, p. A10.

[39] P. Norman and W. Munchau, "Setback on German Work Unity," *Financial Times,* April 25, 1996, p. 1.

[40] "Is the Model Broken?" *The Economist,* May 4, 1996, pp. 18–19.

[41] E. L. Andrews, "New Hard Line by Big Companies Threatens German Work Benefits," *New York Times* October 1, 1996, p. A1.

their manifesto since World War II. The delegates capitulated to a new economic reality and approved the concept of *regulated choice,* under which unions accepted the principle of flexibility in union contracts.[42]

By February 1997, 4.66 million workers were unemployed and the unemployment rate had climbed to 12.2 percent overall; the former East Germany had a nearly 20 percent unemployment rate. The rising unemployment rate raised new doubts about the German economy's ability to generate new growth. Chancellor Kohl had an additional problem. To qualify for the European monetary union, Germany had to keep its budget deficit to less than 3 percent of the GDP in 1997, down from the 3.9 percent in 1996. Politicians and business executives attacked Kohl's coalition, calling it feeble-hearted.[43]

Labor movements in Europe struggled to maintain their power in difficult circumstances. Union memberships declined, governments developed policies to keep their budget deficits down, and the social fabric threatened to unravel. The security of social welfare was undermined as governments worked toward forming a monetary union.

Labor unions in the United States had already dealt with restructuring, mergers, and downsizing. They had adjusted their expectations to the reality of the marketplace in ways that their European counterparts had not. They had a sympathetic president in the White House and a solid economy. Perhaps even more important, they had leadership that understood the competitive environment that would prevail into the next millennium.

Occupational Safety and Health

Development of Worker Health and Safety Concerns

Throughout most of the 19th century, employers rarely concerned themselves about occupational safety and health. During the early days of the Industrial Revolution, accidents were common in many occupations. Machines had few, if any, protective devices. Local newspapers in mill cities such as Lowell, Massachusetts, reported horrendous accidents on a nearly daily basis. It was quite common for mill workers to be seriously injured when their hair or clothing got caught in machinery. With depressing regularity, Lowell workers fell into the water-driven turbine pits and were swept to their deaths in the Merrimack River.

Miners and construction workers were maimed or died by the thousands in the 19th century. Railway brakers had to clamber to the tops of trains to use the hand brakes; rarely did a braker retire with all 10 fingers. Open vats

---

[42] W. Muchau, "German Unions Dump Left-Wing Dogmas," *Financial Times,* November 16–17, 1996, p. 2.

[43] E. L. Andrews, "German Unemployment Soars, Worsening Choices for Kohl," *New York Times,* February 7, 1997, p. D3.

of chemicals were left on factory floors, where employees inhaled the fumes or even fell into the vats. In the days before antibiotics and tetanus shots, a cut finger could be a death warrant. In 1925, the *Monthly Labor Review* reported that one-third to one-half of all electric line workers were killed on the job.[44]

Although accidents were more dramatic than complaints from long-term exposure to chemicals, the effects were no less frequent nor incapacitating. Workers suffered debilitating ailments such as "brass chills," "painter's colic" (from lead poisoning), and "grinder's consumption" (lung diseases acquired from inhaling dust).[45] Hatmakers were poisoned by the mercury they used to cure beaver pelts. Even fictional characters like the Mad Hatter in Lewis Carroll's *Alice in Wonderland* exhibited symptoms of real-life hatters' occupational ailment.

Before 1900, companies and unions did very little to make the workplace safer. There were several reasons for their apathy. Calvinist ethics promoted a general sense of fatalism and the expectation that life would be full of tribulation and adversity. Although skilled workers were in chronically short supply in the United States from the colonial era on, large numbers of unskilled immigrant workers were available to take the places of incapacitated employees. Training requirements were minimal and experience was unnecessary. Companies made the economic decision to replace workers rather than install safety mechanisms to protect them.

Employees and employers ascribed to three doctrines that U.S. courts generally accepted. These doctrines made it difficult for workers to recover damages when they sued their employers. Legal fees were so high that even in the rare cases in which workers won, they actually kept little, if any, of the awards. The doctrines were as follows:

- *Assumption-of-risk doctrine.* Employers held that when workers took jobs, they were aware of and accepted the risks involved.
- *Fellow-servant doctrine.* The employer was not responsible for an employee's injury if the injury was caused by a co-worker's negligence. For example, if a worker did not sufficiently tighten a steam valve and a co-worker was scalded, the employer could not be held responsible.
- *Contributory negligence doctrine.* Whenever an accident occurred, the employee was at least partially responsible. The courts generally assumed injured workers had demonstrated some degree of negligence.

The concept of workers' compensation was established in Germany in the 1880s, but it was not until 30 years later that Congress passed the first United States' workers' compensation law. Early laws required employers to

---

[44] *Monthly Labor Review,* May 1925, p. 172.
[45] W. B. Caitlin, *The Labor Problem in the United States and Great Britain* (New York: Harper & Row, 1935), p. 193.

carry insurance to pay for injuries. If they did not have insurance, they would have to pay damages out of their own pockets. Although employers were obliged to assume responsibility for job-related injuries, they could handle safety issues as they saw best.[46]

Some states passed laws against unsafe working conditions, often after a tragedy such as the Triangle Shirtwaist Company fire in New York City on March 25, 1911. One hundred fifty employees, mostly young women, were killed either directly in the fire or when they jumped from the top floors of the building to the sidewalk below. Bodies were found heaped against emergency doors that were bolted "to safeguard employers from the loss of goods by the departure of workers through fire exits instead of doors."[47]

In the aftermath of the fire, the New York state legislature set up a factory-investigating commission whose findings led New York and other states to enact comprehensive safety legislation. In the absence of federal legislation, safety regulations remained the province of the states. But in many states, laws did not allow inspectors to enter workplaces against the wishes of management. Inspectors were few and poorly trained, and employees were denied access to inspection reports.

Occupational health was more difficult to define and legislate than were accidents. Although it was common knowledge that miners and textile workers suffered respiratory problems, the connection was hard to prove in court. Employers tended to blame alcoholism for symptoms that are now known to have been brought on by industrial diseases.[48]

It was difficult to establish that illness was work-related because the effects of exposure to toxic substances often do not appear until years later. Even after symptoms appeared, it was easy to blame other, nonwork-related causes for the illness. For example, in 1978, 20 workers at an Occidental Chemical Company plant in Lathrop, California, were sterilized by exposure to the pesticide dibromochloropropane. Although researchers knew the chemical caused sterility in animals, 16 years passed before Dow Chemical Company and Shell Oil, which made the chemical, acknowledged it caused sterility in people.[49]

In the 1950s and 1960s, many American corporations created the position of safety director and stressed educating employees in safe workplace habits. During this period, manufacturing processes introduced new chemical compounds, and the number of illnesses and accidents began to rise. After

---

[46] R. A. Buchholz, *Business Environment and Public Policy: Implications for Management and Strategy Formulation* (Englewood Cliffs, NJ: Prentice Hall, 1986), pp. 342–43.

[47] M. B. Schnapper, *American Labor: A Pictorial Social History* (Washington, DC: Public Affairs Press, 1972), p. 358.

[48] A. Hamilton, *Exploring the Dangerous Trades* (New York: Harper & Row, 1948), pp. 5–6.

[49] V. Cahan, "The Overhaul That Could Give OSHA Life under Reagan," *Business Week,* January 19, 1981, p. 88.

Ralph Nader and others pointed out serious flaws in industrial safety practices, public concern mounted about the hazardous substances to which workers were exposed.

The Occupational Safety and Health Act

In 1964, Congress held public hearings that criticized the weak enforcement of workplace safety and health. In 1968, President Lyndon Johnson asked Congress to enact comprehensive federal safety and health legislation. Business strongly opposed the measures, charging the federal government was infringing on states' rights.

Johnson's successor, President Richard Nixon, introduced the Occupational Safety and Health Act that Congress passed in 1970. The act gave states the option to administer standards set by the federal government. In 1971, the federal government created the Occupational Safety and Health Administration (OSHA) to administer federal government standards; see Exhibit 13–1. Twenty-three states immediately created their own OSHA

EXHIBIT 13–1   Occupational Safety and Health Administration

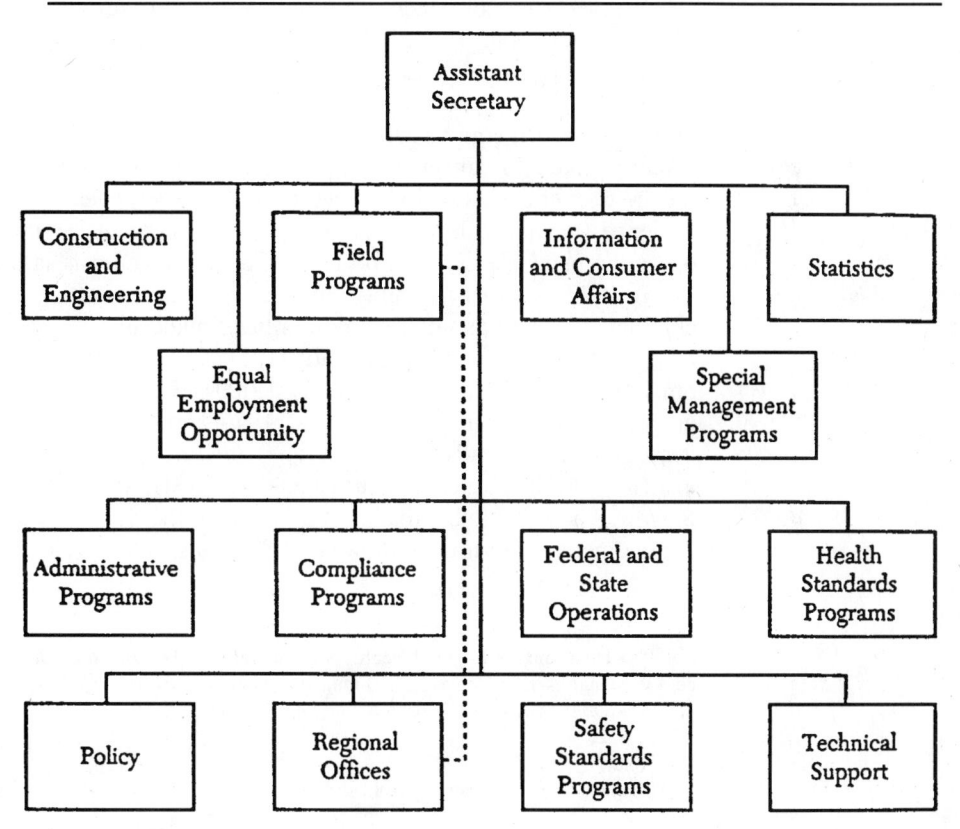

```
                          ┌─────────────┐
                          │  Assistant  │
                          │  Secretary  │
                          └──────┬──────┘
        ┌────────────┬───────────┼────────────┬────────────┐
   ┌────┴────┐  ┌────┴────┐ ┌────┴────┐ ┌─────┴─────┐ ┌────┴────┐
   │Construction│ │ Field  │ │Information│ │           │ │Statistics│
   │   and    │  │Programs│ │and Consumer│ │           │ │         │
   │Engineering│ │        │ │  Affairs  │ │           │ │         │
   └─────────┘  └────────┘ └───────────┘ └───────────┘ └─────────┘
                    ┌──────────┐         ┌───────────┐
                    │  Equal   │         │  Special  │
                    │Employment│         │Management │
                    │Opportunity│        │ Programs  │
                    └──────────┘         └───────────┘
   ┌─────────┐  ┌──────────┐  ┌──────────┐  ┌──────────┐
   │Administrative│ │Compliance│ │Federal and│ │  Health  │
   │  Programs  │ │ Programs │ │   State   │ │Standards │
   │            │ │          │ │Operations │ │ Programs │
   └────────────┘ └──────────┘ └──────────┘  └──────────┘
   ┌─────────┐  ┌──────────┐  ┌──────────┐  ┌──────────┐
   │  Policy │  │ Regional │  │  Safety  │  │Technical │
   │         │  │  Offices │  │Standards │  │ Support  │
   │         │  │          │  │ Programs │  │          │
   └─────────┘  └──────────┘  └──────────┘  └──────────┘
```

programs that were "at least as effective" as the federal health and safety regulations.[50] Specifically, OSHA had responsibility to

- Encourage employers and employees to reduce workplace hazards and implement new or improve existing safety and health programs.
- Provide for research in occupational safety and health and develop innovative ways to deal with occupational safety and health problems.
- Maintain a reporting and record-keeping system to monitor job-related injuries and illnesses.
- Develop mandatory job safety and health standards and enforce them effectively.
- Provide for the development, analysis, evaluation, and approval of state occupational safety and health programs.[51]

OSHA began to develop health and safety standards from existing federal regulations and from standards established by groups such as the American National Standards Institute and the National Fire Protection Association. In its first month of operation, OSHA adopted more than 4,000 health and safety rules, some of which were outdated and irrelevant. Businesses complained bitterly that the penalties for violation were unfair and the cost of compliance was unnecessarily burdensome. Paperwork and documentation requirements were enormous and time-consuming.[52]

Between 1974 and 1976, OSHA set stringent health standards for substances linked to cancer and lung disease. OSHA required employers to reduce worker exposure to the lowest possible levels even when there was no evidence that those levels were necessary to prevent significant risk. The operating principle was that no level of a carcinogen was safe.[53]

In 1977 the Carter administration adopted a cost-cutting strategy. Carter eliminated standards advisory committees made up of research, business, labor, and government representatives. These committees defined and recommended health standards. Nearly 1,000 safety standards were revoked during the first month of fiscal year 1977 and the number of inspections decreased dramatically.

In 1978, the Supreme Court ruled on an OSHA-related case, *Marshall* v *Barlow*. The court found that an employer had the right, based on the Fourth Amendment, to refuse to allow an OSHA inspector to enter the premises

---

[50] "Occupational Safety and Health Administration," *Federal Regulatory Directory,* 6th ed. (Washington, DC: Congressional Quarterly, 1990), p. 380.

[51] *All about OSHA*, rev. (Washington, DC: U.S. Department of Labor, OSHA 2056, 1982), p. 2.

[52] Ibid.

[53] Cahan, "The Overhaul," p. 88.

unless the inspector had a search warrant. In practice, very few businesses demanded warrants, and inspections went on without them.[54]

Fines for OSHA violations were very low. The Interagency Task Force on Workplace Safety and Health reported in 1978 that "an inspection system alone cannot rely on indirect costs, embarrassment, or inconvenience to convince recalcitrant employers to invest in safety and health." The report suggested that fines for violators should run into the thousands of dollars.[55] Yet in 1981, the average fine for a serious violation was still only $800.

Presidential candidate Ronald Reagan promised to abolish OSHA, but settled for appointing Thorne G. Auchter as a commissioner. Auchter, like Reagan, was dedicated to reducing government involvement in workplace health and safety.

The Reagan and Bush Years

In April 1981 the White House issued new policies. OSHA would have to measure potential worker health risks against the costs to business of meeting required health standards. In effect, OSHA was required to conduct a cost-benefit analysis of workplace safety measures. OSHA also was directed to give businesses more options for meeting standards. In pragmatic terms, businesses could issue earplugs to workers in a noisy environment instead of having to reduce noise levels.[56]

In 1982, penalties assessed by OSHA fell by 65 percent. OSHA Chairman Auchter ordered federal investigators not to investigate workplaces in states that had their own OSHA programs. He declared, "This Administration is committed to using federal intervention as the last, not the first, resort in solving problems."[57] Business executives were delighted, noting they could now focus on the big picture instead of nitpicking.

Workplace fatalities continued to rise throughout the mid-1980s. In 1984, workplace deaths rose to 3,740 from 3,100 a year earlier. Occupational injuries and illnesses climbed to 5.4 million from 4.85 million. Between 1980 and 1985, workplace inspections declined by 40 percent in U.S. factories and between 1980 and 1986, OSHA issued only three new standards covering toxic materials.[58]

Union officials placed the blame squarely on the administration. Eric Frumin, health director of the Amalgamated Clothing and Textile Workers

---

[54] Ibid.
[55] Ibid., p. 89.
[56] S. E. Teeley, "Reagan Plan Would Slash OSHA Role," *Boston Globe,* April 12, 1981, p. 12.
[57] "As Regulation Relaxes, Critics Flex Their Muscles," *Business Week,* April 12, 1982, p. 44B.
[58] T. Lewin, "Archives of Business," *New York Times,* March 23, 1986, p. F8.

Union, observed, "OSHA under Reagan is a disaster. They have virtually abandoned the responsibility Congress gave them to set standards and then vigorously enforce them."[59]

As the Reagan administration drew to a close in 1988, none of the stakeholders in the workplace safety issue was satisfied. Companies charged the agency with petty rule making. Labor unions and employee lobbying groups accused OSHA of internal disarray and lax enforcement. They noted the agency had only 1,000 inspectors to cover nearly 5 million employers. Margaret Seminario, the AFL-CIO's health and safety director, charged that "when you get behind the headlines and banners, you see thousands of workers being killed every year from occupational injuries and scores of thousands suffering from occupational disease, and OSHA doesn't have a coherent plan on how to deal with those problems." The President's Council of Economic Advisers expressed the administration's philosophy: "Government . . . has no clear advantage over workers, labor unions and employers in using this information to determine appropriate levels of workplace safety or the best way to reduce hazards."[60]

In 1989, the National Safety Council reported on a disturbing trend. Along with rising productivity, the workplace was becoming more dangerous. Permanent work-related disabilities jumped 16 percent between 1986 and 1987, from 60,000 to nearly 70,000. In manufacturing industries, injuries and illnesses climbed nearly 12 percent. Safety experts suspected the increase was much greater, citing industry's propensity to underreport industrial accidents.[61]

In 1989, the Bush administration appointed Gerard Scannell as OSHA commissioner. Scannell, the former safety chief at Johnson & Johnson, proposed new rules and guidelines. Scannell's efforts successfully reduced workplace fatalities. He also increased the maximum penalty for willful violation from $10,000 to $70,000. Even so, critics continued to point to OSHA's poor inspection record. In July 1991, there were only 1,290 U.S. OSHA inspectors for 6 million work sites.[62]

Hoping to harness OSHA's newfound energy, Senator Howard Metzenbaum (D-Ohio) introduced a bill to revamp OSHA. He sought criminal penalties of up to five years in prison for employers who willfully caused bodily harm to employees. OSHA's existing rules allowed criminal prosecution only where negligence led to death. The Bush administration vigorously opposed the bill and prevented it from coming to a vote.[63]

---

[59] P. Perl, "Corporate Experience Can Be Hazardous to Your Health," *Washington Post National Weekly Edition,* September 8, 1986, p. 33.

[60] K. B. Noble, "The Long Tug-of-War over What Is Hazardous," *New York Times,* January 10, 1988, p. E5.

[61] C. Ansberry, "Workplace Injuries Proliferate as Concerns Push People to Produce," *The Wall Street Journal,* June 16, 1989, p. A1.

[62] D. Lewis, "Is It Time to Revamp OSHA?" *Boston Globe,* July 5, 1991, p. 1.

[63] Ibid.

Standard-setting efforts were very expensive and met strong corporate resistance. Presidents Reagan and Bush gave the White House's Office of Management and Budget (OMB) unprecedented authority to delay or kill proposed OSHA standards. The White House also sent lawyers to the Supreme Court to support industry challenges to the economic feasibility of OSHA standards on lead and cotton dust levels.

Although Scannell improved standard setting, he did very little to speed up enforcement. In 1992, only about 11 percent of employees benefited from regular safety inspections, and state agencies were chronically underfunded and understaffed.

Almost all investigations focused on the most dangerous industries, including construction, oil and gas extraction, maritime industries, and some dangerous manufacturing operations. Even with this narrow focus, OSHA inspectors saw fewer than 1 in 10 high-hazard job sites in a given year.

In a 1992 *Technology Review* article, Charles Noble suggested the following reforms:

- OSHA should accelerate standard-setting processes.
- OSHA should develop timetables for rule making and set priorities for that process.
- Where feasible, OSHA should adopt generic regulations, that is, across-the-board rules covering related problems. Generic standards could be applied to chemical substances with similar properties or to toxic chemical monitoring and worker education programs.
- The National Institutes for Occupational Safety and Health (NIOSH) should have its responsibilities, status, and funding strengthened. Congress created NIOSH to play a lead role in researching workplace hazards and developing exposure criteria for OSHA, but often its recommendations were ignored.
- Congress should ensure that the OMB could not use political influence to manipulate cost-benefit tests or assumptions about potential dangers.
- Congress should strengthen the Occupational Health and Safety Act's criminal penalties and give government the authority to seek felony charges against employers who willfully exposed workers to bodily injury.[64]

OSHA and the Clinton Administration

In April 1993, President Clinton appointed Joseph Dear, then director of Washington State's Labor and Industries Department, to head OSHA. Dear, who had run Washington's OSHA agency since 1987, inherited a federal

---

[64] Ibid.

agency badly in need of reform.[65] The agency's compliance staff of 1,120, was 25 percent below the number of inspectors when Reagan took office. OSHA's computer system was antiquated and unable to target the work sites with the greatest safety risks.

Dear's greatest challenge was political; how would he manage a sweeping overhaul of safety laws proposed by liberal Democrats? The Democrats, under Senator Edward Kennedy's leadership, proposed that employers with 11 or more workers be required to form joint labor–management safety and health committees with elected representatives. Supporters said the proposal would promote the kind of cooperation between labor and management that the administration wanted. Big business opposed this measure, calling it a sham for union organizing.[66]

The Clinton–Gore government streamlining plan, released in September 1993, drew fire from those on both sides of the workplace safety issue. Vice President Al Gore's task force on workplace safety proposed the Labor Department "let employers self-certify health and safety standards." Margaret Seminario, AFL-CIO safety and health director, was no happier with Clinton's proposal than she had been with the Reagan policies years earlier. She said, "This idea was tried under the Reagan administration. It failed because companies lied on their safety reports. Finally the policy was abandoned. It shouldn't be tried again."[67]

Edward Kennedy (D-Mass.), chairperson of the Senate's Labor and Human Resources Committee, was stunned by the self-certification proposal. As author of the proposed labor–management safety councils, he opposed the notion that companies police themselves. Vice President Gore's task force suggested giving employers two options for "certified self-inspection." OSHA would set reporting standards and conduct random audits and inspections to ensure compliance. The first option would be to let companies hire outside parties to conduct safety inspections. Alternatively, companies could train and certify employees to conduct inspections.[68]

In 1996 OSHA's Priority Planning Process Overview paper concluded OSHA and its 25 state partners had "substantial success" in fulfilling their mission.[69] OSHA's regulatory strategy and priorities were to develop rules and create ways of intervening to make industry safer. The five-point regulatory strategy was designed to:

---

[65] "Joseph Dear Selected by President Clinton to Be Head of OSHA," *The Wall Street Journal,* April 2, 1993, p. A4.

[66] D. Frost, "Stepping into the Middle of OSHA's Muddle," *Business Week,* August 2, 1993, p. 53.

[67] M. Vaillancourt, "OSHA Reform Plan Draws Fire," *Boston Globe,* September 9, 1993, p. 43.

[68] Ibid.

[69] Internet [http://www.osha.gov/].

1. Identify clear and sensible priorities.
2. Focus on key building block rules.
3. Eliminate or fix confusing and out-of-date standards.
4. Emphasize plain language.
5. Rely on cooperative partnerships.

Repetitive Stress: A Workplace Safety Issue

A spate of repetitive-stress injury (RSIs) claims began to flood the courts in the early 1980s. More and more workers filed damage claims. RSIs plagued a number of industries in which people repeated the same small motions. In the meatpacking industry, for example, 800 out of 10,000 full-time employees reported RSIs. The *Newspaper Guild* found 4.5 percent of its membership, more than 1,500 people, claimed they suffered repetitive-stress injuries. About 63 percent of operators polled by Communications Workers of America experienced wrist and hand pain. Twenty percent had been diagnosed with tendinitis or carpal tunnel syndrome (a hand and wrist nerve disorder).[70]

Most lawsuits were filed by reporters, data processors, and telephone operators against *manufacturers* such as AT&T and Unisys because under workers' compensation laws, workers were barred from suing their own companies. Aetna Life & Casualty estimated workers' compensation claims and other expenses from these injuries cost employers $20 billion a year.[71]

By early 1995, it was clear OSHA's rule-making activities had stalled. The federal OSHA and its California counterpart were scheduled to issue standards to prevent arm, wrist, shoulder, and back injuries in November 1994. The written standard would have required employers to take preventive action and would help OSHA fine companies with high injury rates. Opposition came from two major stakeholder groups: businesses and Republican leaders in Congress. Businesses objected to provisions that would require them to pay for additional medical care or implement ergonomics programs (the science of adjusting workplace conditions to it employees' physical needs). Republican members of OSHA's oversight committee suggested states would do a better job of enforcement than the federal government. Joseph Dear remarked, "This is a climate which is difficult at best for regulatory proposals . . . we're approaching this with extreme care."[72]

In March 1995, the Clinton administration circulated a draft of proposed regulations covering repetitive-stress syndrome. Administration officials

---

[70] B. Goldoftas, "Hands That Hurt," *Technology Review,* January, 1991, pp. 43–50.

[71] M. Gales, "Repetitive Stress: The Pain Has Just Begun," *Business Week,* July 13, 1992, pp. 42–44.

[72] E. Felsenthal, "Delays Thwart Two Efforts to Enact Rules on Repetitive-Stress Injuries," *The Wall Street Journal,* February 14, 1995, p. B7.

were very careful not to antagonize OSHA's relationship with the newly installed Republican Congress. Chairman Dear laid out a timeline that meant the final regulatory proposal would not be ready until 1996. This modest draft would affect 2.6 million workplaces, fewer than half the 6.1 million sites originally intended. The businesses targeted by the proposal only involved workplaces in which the worker made the same motion every few seconds for at least two hours at a time and in which the worker lifted heavy objects repeatedly during a work shift. Employers with 10 or more workers would have a year to fix problem jobs.[73]

Opponents of OSHA's standards argued that ergonomics was costly and time-consuming for business and was based on questionable science. Republican House Majority Whip Tom DeLay declared, "The way to get bureaucrats' attention is to cut their budget. I've been fighting OSHA's silliness for years."[74] Supporters pointed to the experience of L. L. Bean, Inc., in Freeport, Maine. L. L. Bean gave ergonomic training to many of its 4,000 workers and designed workstations to make them easier on hands and backs. Over a four-year period, the company reduced by 50 percent its number of lost-time claims from musculoskeletal disorders. Noting that Bean's policy was voluntary, OSHA's opponents recommended all implementation be left to businesses. OSHA replied that voluntarism was an insufficient response to the rising number of cases of repetitive-stress injury. Union representatives pointed out that most companies made changes only after OSHA cited them and levied fines.[75]

Much to the surprise and anger of many congressional Republicans, the House narrowly rejected business leaders' efforts to prevent the Labor Department from developing new worker-safety rules to guard against repetitive-stress injuries. In the middle of the 1996 campaign, 35 Republicans joined the Democrats in approving the measure.[76]

On November 14, 1996, California's Occupational Safety and Health Standards Board adopted a draft ergonomics regulation that was far less stringent than the measure it had adopted in 1994. Nevertheless the new draft measure brought California into compliance with a court-ordered deadline resulting from a lawsuit filed by the California Labor Federation. Although this measure was the first ergonomics standard in the United States, it was far less comprehensive than organized labor had hoped. This new standard was applied only when two workers performing identical tasks at the same work site were diagnosed with similar injuries within a 12-month period.[77]

---

[73] A. Q. Nomani, "White House Circulates Draft of Rules by OSHA on Repetitive-Stress Injuries," *The Wall Street Journal,* March 21, 1995, p. B4.

[74] S. Lohr, "Waving Goodbye to Ergonomics," *New York Times,* April 10, 1995, p. F1.

[75] Ibid.

[76] D. Rogers, "House Rebuffs Effort to Prevent OSHA from Developing Repetitive-Stress Rules," *The Wall Street Journal,* July 12, 1996, p. A4.

[77] Internet [http://www.afia.org:80/FL_ARTS/FL_Cal.html] "California Adopts Landmark Ergonomics Standard."

Doug Adams, safety coordinator of the San Diego School district, complained that, "At a time when schools are struggling to buy new textbooks . . . spending even one dollar on an experimental ergonomics regulation is an injudicious use of funds." Tom Rankin, of the California AFL-CIO thought the measure didn't go far enough. He said, "It is an unenforceable standard. Any employer can say, 'Sorry, the work wasn't identical'."[78]

After the 1996 election, Clinton renewed his administration's efforts to develop new rules to prevent repetitive-stress injuries at work. By the end of 1996, OSHA estimated that payments would total $20 billion a year to compensate workers for repetitive motion injuries. Related costs like absenteeism could bring the 1997 total to $100 billion. Secretary of Labor Robert Reich announced that the government would continue to enforce the statute requiring employers to maintain workplaces free of recognized hazards until new regulations could be written.[79]

In a spirit of conciliation toward Republicans and business interests, in January 1997 OSHA and the National Institute for Occupational Safety and Health sponsored a two-day conference that brought together business groups, workers, and medical experts. The purpose of the conference was to discuss programs for preventing repetitive-stress motion injuries.[80]

In anticipation of new federal regulations, North Carolina tackled the problem of repetitive-stress injuries. Instead of forcing companies to take measures, North Carolina officials implemented a Department of Labor initiative called the Cooperative Assessment Program. This program gave volunteer companies three years to improve ergonomics while protecting them from fines. Pepsi-Cola Bottling Company and National Gypsum decided to participate in the new program.[81]

Pepsi already had started an ergonomics programs five years earlier. The company offered aerobics classes, safety and training courses, education, and medical plans. The aerobics classes cost very little, but the company spent about $30,000 to substitute shrink-wrapping machines for manual labor. Bob Landers, Pepsi's safety director acknowledged that, "you can drop $1,500 in a heartbeat . . . but you can make dramatic improvements at very little cost." Landers apparently meant that it was all too easy to spend large amounts of money to address workplace problems but sometimes small expenditures also could achieve substantial results.

National Gypsum redesigned its entire customer service center. This 53-workstation department cost $78,000, included ergonomically designed

---

[78] Internet [M. Fordahl, "California Board Adopts Nation's First 'Ergonomics Standard,'" *Breaking News,* November 15, 1996].

[79] Internet[http://www.freep.com] C. Burrell, "Government Promises Action on Repetitive-Motion Injuries," *Detroit Free Press,* December 17, 1996.

[80] S. Lohr, "Administration Renews Efforts on Prevention of Repetitive-Motion Injuries," *New York Times,* December 11, 1996, p. A24.

[81] Internet [J. Overstreet, "Companies Get Handle on Injuries," *Business Journal of Charlotte,* January 20, 1997].

chairs and computer keyboard wrist pads. The additional cost above a conventional renovation was very small. Director of Safety and Health Wes Harkens pointed to additional ergonomic measures in the manufacturing plants. He noted the company reduced heavy lifting where possible. The company also reduced the weight of bags used to transport raw material and invested in machinery to move the bags.[82]

Although some companies voluntarily adopted ergonomically sound practices, most waited for the federal government to issue guidelines and make site visits.

Management Strategy for Workplace Safety Issues

Managers rarely learn in school how to implement health and safety programs, and many have no experience in assessing the costs and benefits of workplace safety. As with any social issue plan, introducing occupational safety and health measures is likely to meet organizational resistance. Health and safety are emotional issues because accidents and illness bring intense personal suffering and financial loss to victims and their families. They also add to worker compensation costs, disrupt productivity, increase downtime, and add to hiring and training costs. Further, unfavorable press can follow accidents and seriously impair a firm's image in a community or throughout the country.[83]

The U.S. government, the Minerva Education Institute, and U.S. corporations jointly sponsor a variety of educational activities to encourage business schools to educate prospective managers about occupational health and safety. The institute makes specific recommendations about how companies can use their control systems to monitor progress and assess costs of worker safety programs. It recommends that corporate managers ask themselves the following series of questions as they plan, organize, and control for workplace safety.

Planning. How do other companies develop a corporate philosophy regarding safety and health matters? How do these philosophies incorporate public affairs, media interaction, regulations, and litigation?

How do managers in high-hazard industries comply with occupational and environmental safety and health standards? What actions do they take to ensure they have relatively few adjustments to make when these standards and other requirements become effective?

How do managers in high-hazard industries set occupational health and safety goals, and to what extent is the staff involved in the goals' exercise? How does the company measure goals?

---

[82] Ibid.
[83] *Research in Occupational Safety and Health for Business Schools: A Resource Guide* (Cincinnati: Minerva Education Institute, 1988), pp. 1–20.

What constitutes a reasonable budget within an organization for activities of a specified size, mission, hazard category, and geographic spread of operations?

Organizing. Within the organization, where is the most effective place to locate the safety and health function? Should it be located under operations, personnel, employee relations, or some other department?

To what extent do joint labor–management safety and health committees within an industry influence management decisions about occupational safety and health matters? Can such committees be structured for greater effectiveness? If so, how?

Controlling. Managers should examine the effects of variations in economic conditions on issues relevant to workers' health and safety. For example, why and how does a recession affect the injury and illness experiences of workers within specific industries? How can such effects be minimized?

Managers should examine the costs of compliance with provisions of the Occupational Safety and Health Act in (1) a low-risk industry, (2) a moderate-risk industry, and (3) a high-risk industry. They should also assess the impact of the Americans with Disabilities Act.

Managers should investigate both budgetary and nonbudgetary methods of control as they relate to the safety and health function within an organization. They should ask: What are the strengths and limitations of each method? Should both methods be used? If so, in what balance?

Managers should try to calculate dollar losses due to safety and health incidents. They should assess the benefit mechanisms of setting up special accounts for this purpose and ask how the accounts would be handled in internal financial and managerial accounting reports. Top managers must devise their plan to effectively communicate the benefits to middle managers and employees and assess costs to the company.

Summary

The unionization movement in the United States was disorganized and weak until the 1930s. In a country of high social and physical mobility and abundant land, workers had very little incentive to organize. The early unions emphasized social goals rather than economic aims. This approach divided rather than united America's diverse ethnic, social, and religious groups. Finally, in the 1930s, New Deal legislation provided protection for the AFL and CIO and fostered the aims of organized labor. As the U.S. economy concentrated on service and high-technology industries, labor unions lost much of their clout and effectiveness. From 1996 on, the labor union movement gained in strength. Under new leadership, unions organized the old, the young, and even those on welfare. Job security and other issues became more important than a rise in the weekly paycheck.

Workplace safety and health has never been a corporate priority in the United States. Although some companies have voluntarily incorporated occupational safety and health programs, most companies have responded to legislation and the regulations of the Occupational Safety and Health Administration (OSHA). OSHA activities have been both praised and criticized.

Stakeholders hotly debate the agency's effectiveness in reducing accidents and illness in the workplace. Most observers agree reporting procedures and recordkeeping have improved workers' compensation, but much more progress is needed.

Questions

1. Why did the union movement have less impact in the United States than in Europe?
2. How do U.S. unions compare in structure and goals with Japanese unions? (To answer this question, you should research the unique relationship between Japanese unions and companies.)
3. How are European unions likely to fare as the European Union works toward monetary integration? What are the major structural and ideological differences between U.S. unions and their European counterparts?
3. What predictions can you make about how unions will do in the remainder of the 1990s? What information led you to these conclusions?

Projects

1. In the 1990s, OSHA, the meatpacking industry, and its unions disagreed vehemently about safety and working conditions in plants. Research this issue and write a three-page paper about it. Make recommendations to management in a one-page executive memo.
2. OSHA has been a highly controversial agency. Interview the safety director of a local company to determine advances in the measurement of occupational health and worker safety and the extent to which OSHA has contributed to them.

Beta Case 13
Unions and Workplace Safety

Donald Drees, Beta's president and COO, could not believe that clerical and office workers were threatening to unionize. The Service Employees Union of America was passing out literature describing the hazards of video display terminals (VDTs). Beta had succeeded in keeping labor union activity to a minimum by providing competitive wages, safe working conditions, and generous benefits.

Daphne Malone, Drees's assistant, came back from lunch with a manila envelope full of union material. "May I see that propaganda?" Drees asked. Malone silently handed him the packet. Drees began to read:

Danger from Your VDT
Did you know that nearly 40 million workers, 15 million of whom are women, receive and process information on video display terminals? VDTs cause miscarriages. The Northern California Kaiser-Permanente Medical Care program found twice as many miscarriages among those women who remembered spending long hours in front of screens while pregnant than among those who did not. Many occupational health and technology experts warn that babies of women who work in front of VDTs may be harmed by very-low-frequency, pulsed, nonionizing electromagnetic radiation.

Even if you are not planning to have a baby, do you know that you risk severe hand and wrist damage from the repetitive motions you must use in your work?

Dress read a little farther, then threw the paper on his desk. "Daphne," he snapped, "get me Bob Mobley!" Drees fidgeted with a paper clip until Mobley, the corporate counsel, answered. "Hello, Bob, we've got trouble," Drees began. "The union's trying to organize the women who work on the VDTs. The union is saying pregnant women are going to have miscarriages unless they wear lead aprons or are transferred to some other noncomputer work. They're also predicting all sorts of vision and hand problems for VDT workers. Do we know whether the union is telling the truth? Are we liable if an employee has a miscarriage and sues? What do you think the chances are that the union will be successful? We've got to tell Brian about this issue so we can plan our strategy."

PART IV Consumer Welfare

Part IV covers consumer information and product safety. Chapter 14 discusses the evolution of the consumer movement, issues of information dissemination, and product promotion. Chapter 15 explores product safety, total quality management, and the role of the Consumer Product Safety Commission (CPSC).

To survive, businesses must build trusting relationships with consumers. Customer retention is a major concern in our highly competitive business environment. Customer retention begins before the sale is made by providing appropriate information about the firm's products or services.

Consumers need good information to make sound buying decisions. The better the quality of information, the better able the consumer is to choose among buying options and the more likely the consumer is to be happy with the final choice.

Consumer welfare is both a societal obligation and a necessity for business success. If a product is unsafe or its advertising misleading, all the stakeholders involved with that product suffer. We define consumer welfare as providing products and services of appropriate quality to prospective buyers in an honest and comprehensive manner to ensure to a reasonable degree their safety, well-being, and satisfaction. Consumer welfare and the welfare of the firm are inextricably linked.

CHAPTER 14
CONSUMERS AND INFORMATION

CASE: WHAT YOU DON'T KNOW ABOUT DRUGS...

In August 1996, *U.S. News & World Report* published an article entitled, "Danger at the Drugstore." The article noted that the public regards pharmacists as highly admired professionals. Pharmacists fill about 2 billion prescriptions a year and are widely regarded as the individuals who are most likely to catch physicians' errors in prescribing. Pharmacists point out that they have a six-year training period and are much more knowledgeable than physicians about drug properties and interactions.

A poll by *U.S. News & World Report* in conjunction with Georgetown University School of Medicine, however, found many of the nation's pharmacists failed to protect consumers against dangerous interactions of prescription drugs. Investigators tested 245 pharmacists in Philadelphia, Houston, Columbus, San Francisco, Denver, Indianapolis, and suburban New York. More than half of all pharmacists did not warn consumers that if they took two drugs together they risked illness or even death although each drug was safe when taken alone. In one case, the interaction between two drugs was so dangerous that the pharmacists should not have filled the prescription. Yet, one-third of the pharmacists filled the prescriptions for both drugs without any comment to the patient.

Pharmacists in independent drugstores accounted for nearly two-thirds of the pharmacies that failed to warn consumers even though half the stores represented in the sample were independent. Pharmacists in low- and lower-middle-income areas warned customers much less frequently about even the most potentially deadly interactions than those in more affluent neighborhoods.

The pharmacists who were surveyed agreed that their failure to catch the dangerous drug interactions was indefensible. Although they conceded the mistakes should have been caught, they insisted insurers should be held partially responsible. Rising costs and increased competition in the retail pharmacy industry pressured employers to build higher volume to compensate for lower prices. Pharmacists noted they often work 12 hours a day with few—if any—breaks; they also are expected to oversee poorly trained assistants and technicians.

In some cases, pharmacists are legally liable for failure to warn. In 1990, a federal law was passed requiring pharmacists to offer counseling to all Medicaid (elderly) patients. Since then, more than 40 states have passed laws to extend the counseling requirement to all patients. In 1996, a Michigan State Court of Appeals ruled that pharmacists assumed a legal duty to advise consumers when they implemented and advertised a computer system that checked for adverse drug interaction before filling a prescription.

Pharmacists insisted doctors should be responsible for identifying drug interactions. In fact, when one doctor prescribed two interacting drugs, pharmacists said they were much less likely to question that doctor's judgment than if two doctors were involved. Between 3 and 10 percent of doctors prescribe conflicting drugs. Drug manufacturers, the federal Food and Drug Administration, and pharmacists say this points to serious gaps in physician training in pharmacology. Pharmacists place some of the blame on drug companies that look for the positive impact without examining potential side effects from drug interaction.

A 1996 law required pharmacists to distribute uniform and easy-to-understand information with every new prescription or refill by the year 2006. Dr. John Gans, executive vice president of the American Pharmaceutical Association, noted the profession found itself significantly challenged and said, "You [the consumer] have to manage your own care."[1]

Consumers who want to find information on their own should look on the Internet [http://www.pharminfo.com]. This page has links to drug information, publications, meeting highlights, discussion groups, disease centers, and additional pharmacy links. Healthtouch at [http://www.healthtouch.com] gives consumers and health professionals information about prescription or over-the-counter medications. Its health resource directory has links to a variety of health associations and organizations, many of which give information on drug use and contraindicated combinations of drugs. The Institute for Safe Medication Practices is a nonprofit organization committed to preventing errors in medication. Its Internet address is [http://www.geohealthweb.com/ISMP/]. Consumers can use home page links to national and international reports on medication errors and get answers to questions about their own medications through the organization's E-mail address at *ismpinfo@ismp.org*.

---

[1] The above came from S. Headden, "Danger at the Drugstore," *U.S. News & World Report,* August 26, 1996, pp. 45–53.

Questions and Exercises

1. Should legislators be responsible for passing laws to make sure pharmacists are legally liable for any reactions to contraindicated drugs prescribed by physicians?
2. Should legislators pass laws to make physicians responsible for knowing whether patients use contraindicated drugs?
3. How would you find additional information on drug interaction using the Internet?
4. Interview pharmacists at your neighborhood drugstore chain. Ask them what special training, if any, they have had in tracking customers' prescriptions for drug interaction. What is their store policy?

Consumerism

The term *consumerism* was not widely used until the 1960s, although consumer organizations flourished from the 19th century onward. We cover the early period of the consumer movement in Chapter 8's discussion of the development of American regulatory legislation.

The role of marketing and government regulation to cover its practice increased after the turn of the century. The 1920s ushered in the era of modern marketing. Consumers were inundated with billboard, magazine, and newspaper advertising. Radio, the new medium, also promoted new and exciting products. Automobiles, refrigerators, vacuum cleaners, and phonographs sold briskly, but consumers had to purchase them with very little real information. Whatever information was available came from manufacturers and retailers, both marketer-dominated sources.

Concerned about the objectivity of these sources, some consumers began organizing groups to press for scientific product testing and uniform product standards. In 1927, Stuart Chase and F. J. Schlink wrote *Your Money's Worth* in which they strongly criticized companies' high-pressure sales tactics and suggested that consumers sponsor organizations to conduct scientific product testing. In 1929, Consumers' Research, Inc., began scientific testing of new products in its laboratory. Around this time, a few major department stores and trade associations also formed testing laboratories.

The Great Depression heightened consumer awareness of price and value. People became more determined to get the best and safest buys for their money. The New Deal under Franklin D. Roosevelt responded to consumer pressure. Legislators reinforced the Pure Food and Drug Act and extended the powers of the Food and Drug Administration to ensure that the food and drug industries met consumer demands.

By the late 1930s, the business community had become very wary of the growing power of consumer groups. The Advertising Research Foundation, a trade association, commissioned George Gallup to conduct a survey assessing the impact of the consumer movement. In 1940, Gallup reported the movement had generated substantial support, particularly among more educated and upper-income consumers. Gallup concluded the consumer movement would be likely to grow because of its strength among influential groups.[2]

During the 1940s, the consumer movement was dormant as people focused on the war effort. It flourished again in the 1950s and blossomed fully in the 1960s. President John F. Kennedy's Consumer Message to Congress in March 1962 outlined needed reforms in existing programs and suggested new initiatives in product safety, particularly in food and drugs. His Consumer Bill of Rights had four major components:

- *The right to safety.* The consumer has the right to be protected from dangerous products and from the thoughtless actions of other consumers.
- *The right to be informed.* The consumer has the right to easily available, accurate information to use in making buying decisions.
- *The right to choose.* The consumer has the right to select among products from competing firms.

---

[2] R. O. Herrman, "The Consumer Movement in Historical Perspective," in D. A. Aaker and G. S. Day, eds. *Consumerism: Search for the Consumer Interest,* 2nd ed. (New York: Free Press, 1974), pp. 10–18.

- *The right to be heard.* The consumer has the right of access to some person or some group that will respond to legitimate complaints about abuses in the marketplace and about products that do not meet expectations.

In the late spring and summer of 1965, the government held hearings on tire and auto safety. Manufacturers argued that drivers, not they, were responsible for auto safety. A few months later, Ralph Nader came out with *Unsafe at Any Speed* in which he presented evidence that faulty engineering, construction, and design were to blame for many auto accidents. General Motors (GM) tried to undermine Nader's credibility, even hiring private detectives to stage a seduction scene to bring Nader's integrity into question. When GM's tactics became public, the backlash was so great that Congress had enough consumer support to pass safety legislation easily.

Between the 1960s and 1980s, numerous incidents heightened public awareness about product safety. As television became a fixture in nearly every home, people heard about product problems on TV news programs as soon as they occurred. While there was enormous publicity about unsafe or harmful products, the agencies set up to protect consumers paid relatively little attention to the quality of information marketers provided to consumers.

The Reagan administration was a low point for consumerism. Business organizations such as the Business Roundtable and the U.S. Chamber of Commerce aggressively pursued the business agenda. Consumer groups seemed to have run out of steam.

As the Bush administration took office in January 1989, consumerism was infused with new life. Suddenly Ralph Nader and consumer groups were back in the headlines with new initiatives and new programs. Exhibit 14–1 shows the broad range of public-interest and consumer groups under Nader's umbrella organization. The U.S. Public Interest Research Group (PIRG) is perhaps one of the most interesting. It is the national organization for state PIRGs organized on college campuses. The state PIRGs are lobbying groups that provide a training ground for young people interested in environmental and consumer rights issues. In some states, they have had a considerable impact on legislation and obtained the respect of local politicians. In Massachusetts, for example, Masspirg had an ambitious 1997 legislative program. Among its goals was passage of the following bills:

- *Citizens' Right to Know Bill* that would require clear warning labels on consumer products containing significant amounts of chemicals linked to infertility, birth defects, cancer, and other serious health threats.
- *Bottle Bill* that would place a five-cent deposit on juice and iced tea containers and other no-deposit beverage containers.

EXHIBIT 14–1 Consumer Groups

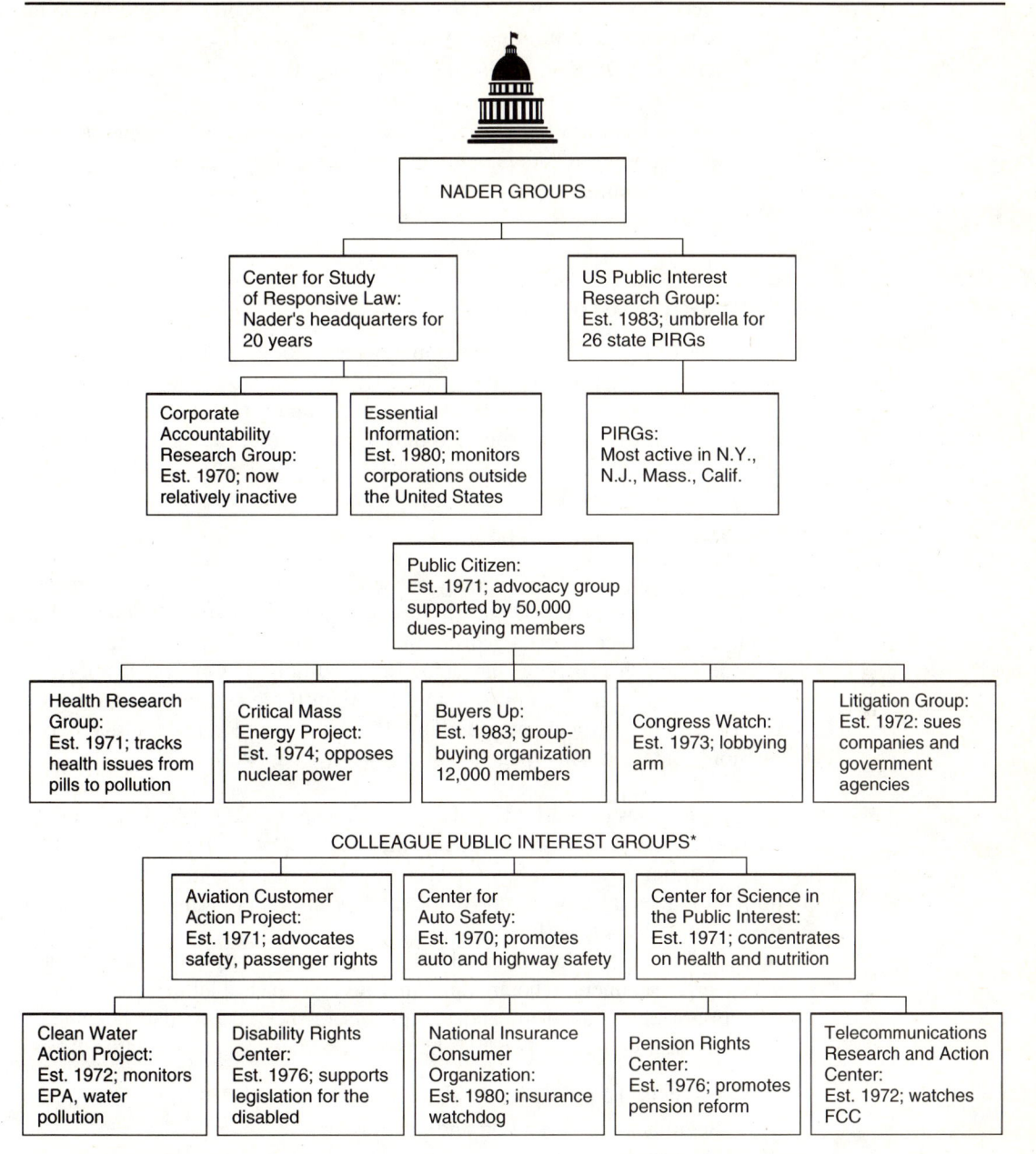

NADER GROUPS

Center for Study of Responsive Law: Nader's headquarters for 20 years

- **Corporate Accountability Research Group:** Est. 1970; now relatively inactive
- **Essential Information:** Est. 1980; monitors corporations outside the United States

US Public Interest Research Group: Est. 1983; umbrella for 26 state PIRGs

- **PIRGs:** Most active in N.Y., N.J., Mass., Calif.

Public Citizen: Est. 1971; advocacy group supported by 50,000 dues-paying members

- **Health Research Group:** Est. 1971; tracks health issues from pills to pollution
- **Critical Mass Energy Project:** Est. 1974; opposes nuclear power
- **Buyers Up:** Est. 1983; group-buying organization 12,000 members
- **Congress Watch:** Est. 1973; lobbying arm
- **Litigation Group:** Est. 1972: sues companies and government agencies

COLLEAGUE PUBLIC INTEREST GROUPS*

- **Aviation Customer Action Project:** Est. 1971; advocates safety, passenger rights
- **Center for Auto Safety:** Est. 1970; promotes auto and highway safety
- **Center for Science in the Public Interest:** Est. 1971; concentrates on health and nutrition
- **Clean Water Action Project:** Est. 1972; monitors EPA, water pollution
- **Disability Rights Center:** Est. 1976; supports legislation for the disabled
- **National Insurance Consumer Organization:** Est. 1980; insurance watchdog
- **Pension Rights Center:** Est. 1976; promotes pension reform
- **Telecommunications Research and Action Center:** Est. 1972; watches FCC

Source: *Fortune,* May 22, 1989, p. 112.

- *Clean Energy Bill* that would require coal and oil power plants to meet existing clean air standards and require utilities to sell a minimum amount of energy from clean, renewable resources.
- *ATM Fee Disclosure Bill* that would require on-screen disclosure of the fee the consumer will be charged for using an ATM.
- *Environmental Crimes Bill* that would strengthen environmental law enforcement by allowing courts to seize assets used or profits gained in the commission of an environmental crime.[3]

Regulation and Consumer Protection

In this section, we discuss the two major regulatory agencies that deal with consumer information and safety: the Federal Trade Commission (FTC) and the Food and Drug Administration (FDA). Chapter 15 covers the responsibilities of the Consumer Product Safety Commission, the independent consumer watchdog agency established in 1972.

The Federal Trade Commission

The FTC is an independent agency headed by five commissioners nominated by the president of the United States and confirmed by the Senate. The commissioners serve seven-year terms and the president chooses the FTC's chairperson. The current chairman, Robert Pitofsky, took office in April 1995. To avoid partisan politics, no more than three commissioners can be from the same political party. Exhibit 14–2 shows the Federal Trade Commission's Internet home page at [http://www.ftc.gov:80/]

Responsibilities of the FTC. The FTC is responsible for issues relating to competition, consumer information, and consumer protection not covered by the Consumer Product Safety Commission. It deals especially with advertising that makes false or deceptive claims to consumers. Exhibit 14–3 shows the organization of the FTC.

The FTC warns consumers about phony jewelry, pyramid schemes, inaccurate price scanners, scholarship scams, and green card lottery scams. Consumers are encouraged to send complaints to the FTC E-mail hot line at *consumerline@ftc.gov*. The FTC has the following consumer-related duties:

- Protects the public from false and deceptive advertising.
- Regulates the packaging and labeling of consumer products to prevent deception.

---

[3] *Masspirg Bulletin*, Winter 1997, p. 2.

Chapter 14   Consumers and Information   **469**

EXHIBIT 14–2   Federal Trade Commission Web Page

Federal Trade Commission
6th Street and Pennsylvania Avenue, N.W
Washington, D.C. 20580

Welcome to the Home Page for the Federal Trade Commission World Wide Web Server.

■ What's New?

- **Regulatory Reform:** Franchise Rulemaking [NEW]
- Fortuna-Alliance Update [NEW]
- "Fighting Consumer Fraud: The Challenge and the Campaign"
- **Consumer Alert!** Beloved...Bejeweled...Be Careful: What to Know Before You Buy Jewelry
- Spread the Word about Telemarketing Fraud
- Scholarship Scams
- **Procurement Announcement:** Trash and Debris Removal Services

■ News Releases

- German and Brazilian Piston Manufacturers Agree To Pay Largest Every Penalty for Failure to File for U.S. Antitrust Review
- FTC Seeks Public Comment on Proposed Notices of New Rights and Duties under the Fair Credit Reporting Act

■ FTC Weekly Calendar

■ Commission Actions
■ Speeches
■ Conferences, Hearings, Workshops
■ Staff Reports

■ Antitrust/Competition Issues

■ FTC ConsumerLine: *Facts for Consumers*
■ FTC BusinessLine: *Facts for Businesses*

■ Consumer Protection Rules and Guides
■ Links to Other Sites

■ The Federal Trade Commission

■ Regional Offices

Please send consumer complaints or comments to: consumerline@ftc.gov
Please refer technical problems or comments to: webmaster@ftc.gov
Rev. Thursday, February 27, 1997 01:44 EST
geh/jps

EXHIBIT 14–3 Organization of the FTC, January 1993

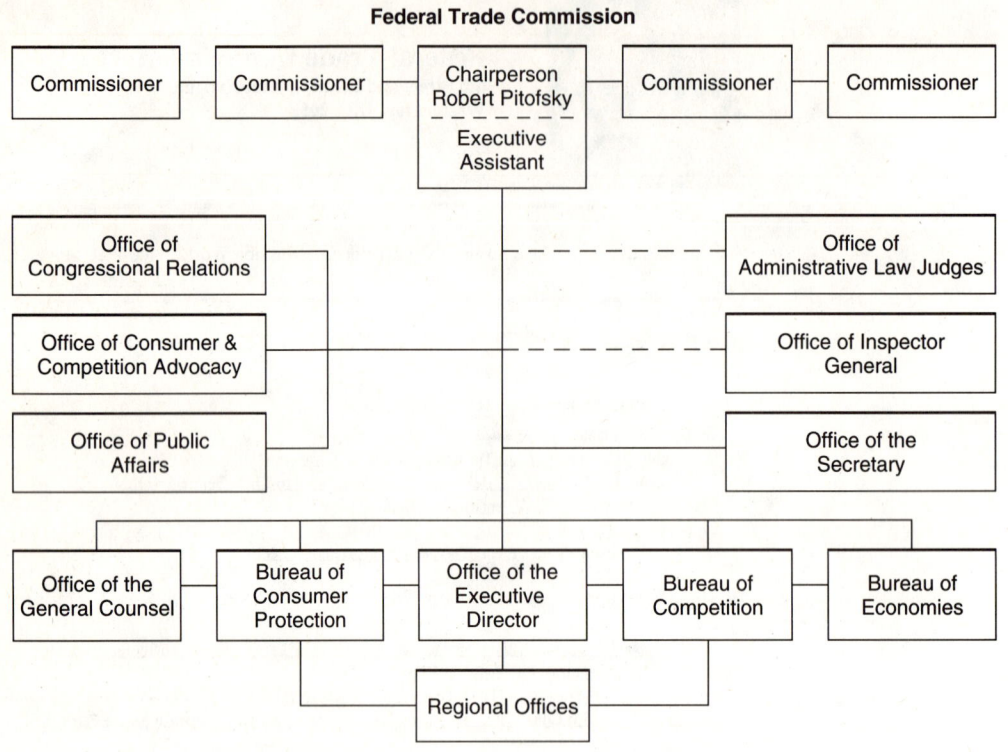

Federal Trade Commission

- Commissioner
- Commissioner
- Chairperson Robert Pitofsky / Executive Assistant
- Commissioner
- Commissioner

- Office of Congressional Relations
- Office of Consumer & Competition Advocacy
- Office of Public Affairs
- Office of Administrative Law Judges
- Office of Inspector General
- Office of the Secretary

- Office of the General Counsel
- Bureau of Consumer Protection
- Office of the Executive Director
- Bureau of Competition
- Bureau of Economies

- Regional Offices

Source: *FTC Directory,* January 1993 (updated)

- Informs consumers and industry about major FTC decisions, programs, statutes, and rules defining the legality of certain business practices.
- Prohibits credit discrimination on the basis of sex, race, marital status, national origin, age, or receipt of public assistance.
- Requires sellers to give consumers notice of their three-day cancellation rights for sales made away from the seller's place of business, such as door-to-door sales.
- Requires nondepository creditors, including retailers and finance companies, to give borrowers accurate and complete information about the true cost of credit.
- Prohibits sending unordered merchandise to consumers and then charging for it.
- Requires that consumers ordering merchandise through the mail be informed if shipment cannot be made by the promised date (or

within 30 days). Customers must then be given the opportunity to agree to a new shipping date or to cancel the order and receive a full refund.

As noted earlier, the pre-World War II antimonopoly activities of the FTC are covered in Chapter 8. In this chapter, we focus on the agency's consumer-related functions.

The FTC was inactive during the World War II years, but in the late 1940s it began to investigate consumer complaints of deceptive advertising. The courts supported the FTC's activities in this area, and deceptive advertising quickly became one of the agency's main targets.

The FTC's responsibilities grew after Congress passed the Wool Products Labeling Act, the Fur Products Labeling Act, the Textile Fiber Products Identification Act, and the Flammable Fabrics Act in the 1940s. In the 1970s, responsibility for the Flammable Fabrics Act was shifted to the Consumer Product Safety Commission.

In the 1950s and 1960s, the FTC's major task was to warn the public about the hazards of smoking. In 1964, the FTC tried to enforce a rule that would have required cigarette packages and advertising to carry a health hazard warning. Successful lobbying by the tobacco industry resulted in weakened legislation called the Federal Cigarette Labeling and Advertising Act (1965). However, industry pressure did not prevail for long. In 1969, the Public Health Cigarette Smoking Act prohibited cigarette advertising on radio and television and mandated stronger health warnings on cigarette packages. Successive laws continued to strengthen and expand antitobacco legislation. In 1986, the Smokeless Tobacco Act added chewing tobacco and snuff to the list of products banned from television and radio advertising. Antitobacco lobbying groups continue to succeed in fostering regulation and restriction of tobacco use.

FTC Leadership. Richard Nixon's administration rejuvenated the FTC's activities with the 1969 appointment of Caspar Weinberger as chairperson. Under Weinberger and his successor, Miles Kirkpatrick, the FTC hired activist lawyers, updated rules, and placed greater emphasis on consumer affairs. During this period, the FTC's activities antagonized many of the industries it scrutinized. Some businesspeople charged the FTC was pandering to consumers at their expense.

President Jimmy Carter's appointee, consumer advocate Michael Pertschuck, continued to press for consumer protection. An angry House of Representatives tried to stall industrywide rule making in 1977. The House attached a requirement to the FTC's authorization bill directing the FTC to submit proposed trade regulation rules to Congress for approval before they took effect.

The Senate and President Carter objected, calling a legislative veto unconstitutional because it encroached on the executive branch's authority. A stalemate among the executive branch, the Senate, and the House held up funding for the FTC. Finally, in 1980, a compromise agreement authorized FTC funds, but also allowed a two-house veto of the commission's rules. The 1980 bill also restricted FTC rule making authority over commercial advertising to cover deceptive (but not unfair) practices. The bill forbade the FTC to go forward with studies of the insurance industry and children's advertising.

The House and Senate skirmishes were not over. They continued until 1989, when the Senate passed a bill to reauthorize the FTC. This bill also imposed curbs requiring the FTC to notify Congress before it gave testimony or made comments before any other federal or state body.

Throughout the 1980s, the FTC's budget was whittled down and personnel cut from 1,800 under Pertschuk to fewer than 900 under his successors James Miller III and Daniel Oliver.

President Bush appointed Janet Steiger, who at the time seemed inclined to make the commission more active, particularly in the area of merger and antitrust. Steiger vowed to look hard at the advertising and marketing of tobacco products, the alcohol industry, and food advertising and labeling. Her successor, Robert Pitofsky, the FTC's 54th chairperson, was a professor and antitrust scholar at the Georgetown University Law Center when President Clinton nominated him. Since he took office in 1995, he has been increasingly concerned about economic rather than political goals of FTC legislation.

The Concept of Materiality in FTC Rulings on Advertising. The issue of *materiality is* key to FTC involvement in a claim. The FTC is empowered to rule on advertisements only if they are both deceptive and material. If a company's claim is not important to the buyer (that is, material), the FTC has no power to take action regardless of how far the ad stretches the truth.

Section 5(*b*) of the Federal Trade Commission Act of 1914 incorporates the concept of materiality into the FTC's standard of deceptive advertising. Under the U.S. system, regulatory agency rulings are tested and refined by the judicial system. Some rulings eventually make their way to the Supreme Court that decides their constitutionality.

In FTC rulings tested in the 1930s, the courts ruled that purchasers were entitled to receive what they intended to buy. The FTC's materiality test rested solely on whether the deceptive claim was likely to induce purchase. The FTC was charged with protecting the public interest by stopping unfair trade practices before the public was injured. In 1938, Congress amended the FTC Act to include a definition of false advertisement that made a direct reference to materiality:

> [The term *false advertisement* means] an advertisement, other than labeling, which is misleading in a material respect; and in determining whether any advertisement is misleading, there shall be taken into account (among other things) not only representations made or suggested by word, design, device, sound, or any combination thereof, but also the extent to which the advertise-

ment fails to reveal facts material in light of such representations or material with respect to consequences which may result from the use of the commodity to which the advertisement relates.[4]

This clause clarified any potential conflicts between the duties of the FTC and those of the Food, Drug, and Cosmetic Act, now the FDA. It focuses the FTC on what advertisers say about the product or service rather than on the attributes of the product or service itself. It also recognizes that omitting facts, like making false statements, is deceptive.

In 1964, the FTC expanded the range of conditions under which omissions of information were considered material and that justified the FTC's action ordering a company to make an affirmative disclosure:

- Where the seller has created in consumers' minds a false impression of the quality or merits of a product.
- Where undisclosed facts are made material by virtue of affirmative claims by the seller.
- Where the seller has made no affirmative claims about country of origin, but consumers believe and prefer that the product be from a country other than its actual origin.
- Where the seller has made no affirmative claim about safety, but the product is hazardous and the hazards are not disclosed.

The Supreme Court heard a number of cases testing these conditions. Through its decisions, the court granted greater regulatory latitude to the FTC in determining materiality, allowing the commission to presume materiality under any reasonable circumstances.

The judicial finding concerning an Anacin ad illustrates this precedent. The ad falsely implied (but did not explicitly state) that Anacin contained a secret ingredient other than aspirin. In 1981, an administrative law judge decided that a significant difference in price between Anacin and plain aspirin constituted materiality. If consumers were willing to pay more, the judge reasoned, they must have believed there was a difference in the product's effect, and this difference was important enough to induce them to pay the higher price.

By the early 1980s, the FTC's power to infer materiality was so broad that most advertisers could not effectively defend an argument claiming immateriality. When James Miller III became the FTC chairperson, he asked Congress to amend the FTC Act to more closely define deceptive acts or practices. In his testimony, Miller said, "I believe that we should allocate our resources only to cases in which consumers have been hurt." In effect, if that standard prevailed, it would return FTC powers to their 1938 parameters. Miller won a new definition of deception and a modified definition of materiality. The new definition of materiality states, "A 'material' misrepresentation or practice is one which is likely to affect a consumer's choice or conduct

---

[4] Wheeler-Lea Act, 1938, Pub. L. No. 447, 52, Stat.111.

regarding a product [and] material information may affect conduct other than the decision to purchase a product."

The Case of Telemarketing Fraud. In 1996 the FTC formed alliances with the Federal Bureau of Investigation (FBI), the U.S. Postal Service, the National Associations of Attorneys General (NAAG), the North American Securities Administrators Association (NASAA), and state and local authorities. Together, they battled the old problem of consumer fraud with a new high-tech twist. Con artists were telemarketing through the Internet, direct mail, and television; they also used desktop publishing and other sophisticated techniques to sell their wares.

Congress laid the legislative groundwork for the collaborative approach when it enacted the Telemarketing Consumer Fraud and Abuse Prevention Act of 1994. This legislation directed the FTC to issue a ruling covering telemarketing sales and authorized states to enforce the rule in federal court. The FTC issued the Telemarketing Sales Rule, effective December 1995, that allowed enforcers to bring suit against fraud operators in federal district court and to obtain nationwide injunctions.

During 1996, the FTC, the U.S. Postal Service, and 25 states and the District of Columbia worked together to deal with telemarketing abuses.[5] Nearly 100 federal district court cases were brought by the FTC between October 1995 and December 1996. The fraudulent sales in these actions cost consumers more than $250 million a year and more than $700 million over the life of the schemes.

The Telemarketing Complaint System, a consumer complaint database operated by the FTC and National Association of Attorneys General showed that 89 percent of all 1996 complainants reported they were victimized by out-of-state enterprises. California and Florida were the two states generating the most telemarketing complaints. Quebec, Canada, was the third largest geographic area.

Senior citizens are particularly vulnerable to telemarketing schemes. In 1996, an American Association of Retired Persons (AARP) survey of people 50 years or older showed that 57 percent were likely to receive calls from telemarketers at least once a week. College-educated older people were more likely to receive the calls than their less-educated counterparts or those with lower incomes. More than half the respondents reported they could not distinguish a legitimate telemarketer from a fraudulent one.

Older Americans fell victim to prize promotion scams in disproportionate numbers. In 1996 the National Fraud Information Center (NFIC), a project of the National Consumers' League, reported prize promotion complaints represented more than 40 percent of all complaints logged into the system. The fraudulent prize promoters disguised themselves as legitimate businesses but never delivered worthwhile goods. These companies solicited

---

[5] Internet [http://www.ftc.gov:80/reports/Fraud/preface.htm] "Letter from the Chairman."

charitable contributions in return for a prize. The FTC found that 85 percent of a randomly selected group of victims were 65 or older.

According to the FTC, the solicitor told the prospective victim something like the following:

> Now, naturally, Jean, with no monetary requirement on that guarantee in mind, we are going to ask two things from you. They're both very simple. First, we'd like to get permission to use your name after you receive your award so we can show the rest of our customers who got what in this big promotion. Secondly, we want you to take or renew your choice of five top national magazines from us at a savings of up to 50 percent off the newsstand prices. . . . But more importantly, Jean, than anything else, you are absolutely guaranteed and must receive one of those five fabulous awards and nothing else.[6]

In 1996, U.S. attorneys and more than a dozen attorneys general prosecuted a multifaceted effort led by the Department of Justice against telemarketing scams that specifically targeted older Americans; nearly 80 percent of the victims were elderly. AARP members posed as consumers to record fraudulent sales pitches for evidence. In December 1995, nearly 400 telemarketers were arrested and by the end of 1996, 800 individuals were charged with federal crimes for telemarketing. More than 160 of these people were convicted and sentenced to an average of 30 months in prison.[7]

The Food and Drug Administration

The Food and Drug Administration (FDA) is an agency in the Department of Health and Human Services (HHS). The FDA home page on the Internet is [http://www.fda.gov:80]. The Secretary of HHS appoints the FDA commissioner, who does not have to be confirmed by the Senate. Seven associate commissioners are responsible for legislation and public information; planning and evaluation; management and operations; and regulatory, health, and consumer affairs.

Responsibilities of the FDA. As we discussed in Chapter 8, the Food and Drug Act of 1906 was the first piece of legislation to protect the public from potential health hazards created by adulterated and mislabeled foods and drugs. The Department of Agriculture's Bureau of Chemistry administered the act from 1907 until 1927, when the department's newly created Food, Drug, and Insecticide Department took over this responsibility. In 1931, the new agency's name was changed to the Food and Drug Administration.

---

[6] Internet [http://www.ftc.gov:80/reports/Fraud/fraudcon/htm] "Telemarketing Fraud Against Older Consumers."
[7] Ibid., p. 4.

EXHIBIT 14-4 Organization of the Food and Drug Administration

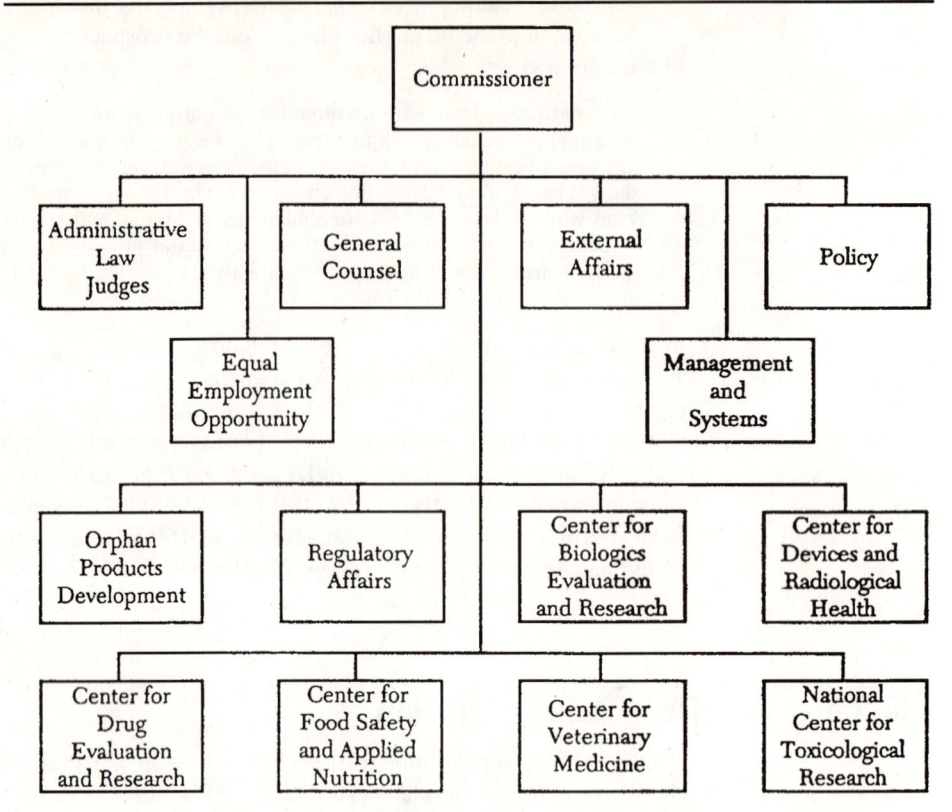

```
                              Commissioner
        ┌──────────────┬──────────┴──────────┬──────────────┐
  Administrative     General              External         Policy
   Law Judges        Counsel               Affairs
                         │                     │
                       Equal              Management
                     Employment              and
                     Opportunity           Systems
        ┌──────────────┬─────────────────────┬──────────────┐
     Orphan         Regulatory          Center for       Center for
    Products          Affairs            Biologics       Devices and
   Development                          Evaluation      Radiological
                                        and Research       Health
        ┌──────────────┬─────────────────────┬──────────────┐
   Center for      Center for            Center for       National
     Drug          Food Safety           Veterinary      Center for
   Evaluation      and Applied            Medicine      Toxicological
   and Research     Nutrition                             Research
```

Source: "Food and Drug Administration," *Federal Regulatory Directory,* 6th ed. (Washington, DC: Congressional Directory, 1990), p. 312.

Exhibit 14-4 shows the FDA's organization chart. The FDA

- Regulates the composition, quality, safety, and labeling of food, food additives, colors, and cosmetics, and conducts some research in those areas.
- Monitors and enforces regulations through inspection of food and cosmetic producers' facilities; also oversees advertising and media reports by investigating consumer complaints.
- Regulates the composition, quality, safety, effectiveness, and labeling of all drugs for human use and establishes scientific standards to carry out this task.
- Requires premarket testing of new drugs and evaluates new-drug applications and requests to approve drugs for experimental use.
- Develops standards for the safety and effectiveness of over-the-counter (OTC) drugs.

- Develops guidelines for proper drug-manufacturing practices and makes periodic inspections of drug-manufacturing facilities in the United States and abroad.
- Monitors the quality of marketed drugs.
- Recalls or seizes products that violate federal laws and pose human health hazards.
- Conducts research and establishes standards for the manufacturing and use of biological products; inspects and licenses biological products.
- Regulates the safety, effectiveness, labeling, and pretesting of medical devices.
- Conducts research on the effects of radiation exposure and determines standards for radiation-emitting products.[8]

In 1938, the passage of the Food, Drug, and Cosmetic Act greatly increased the FDA's powers. A year earlier, 100 people had died from taking a miracle drug called *elixir of sulfanilamide*. There was nothing wrong with the sulfanilamide itself, but its manufacturer, S. E. Massengill Company, had dissolved the drug in ethylene glycol, which is poisonous. To prevent a similar tragedy, the new act required that a manufacturer prove the safety of a new drug and its ingredients before the FDA would allow the drug to be placed on the market.

In 1940, the FDA moved from the Department of Agriculture into the Federal Security Agency, a new agency formed to protect the public health. This agency was incorporated into the Department of Health, Education, and Welfare (HEW) in 1953. In 1979, HEW was split into a new Department of Education and Department of Health and Human Services (HHS).

When the Bush administration took office, the FDA was widely regarded as one of the most professionally run regulatory agencies in the federal government. President Bush reappointed Reagan's commissioner, Frank Young, in 1989. Within a year, a payoff scandal in the FDA's Generic Drugs Division drove Young out of office. The Generic Drugs Division was downgraded and folded into the agency's Center for Drug Evaluation.

In February 1991, HHS Secretary Louis W. Sullivan appointed Dr. David Kessler FDA commissioner. Most observers agreed this was a crucial period for the FDA. The effects of the scandal still lingered. The agency's staff was smaller than it was a decade earlier although demands on it had grown. By 1991, the FDA had responsibility for the safety and effectiveness of a vast range of products, the value of which totaled one-quarter of the

---

[8] "Food and Drug Administration," *Federal Regulatory Directory,* 6th ed. (Washington, DC: Congressional Directory, 1990), pp. 290–303.

Exhibit 14–5 FDA Issues, 1996–1997

January 1996:	The FDA approves olestra, a fat substitute for use in snack foods.
April 1996:	The FDA announces a move to streamline and reduce approval costs for medical devices.
August 1996:	The FDA sends the White House new antismoking regulations for final review.
October 1996:	The FDA reports that its process for approving new drugs and medical devices has been significantly speeded up.
February 1997:	The FDA proposes new improved labels for over-the-counter drugs.
February 1997:	The FDA's ban on tobacco sales to youngsters under age 18 takes effect.

nation's GNP. However, the FDA budget was only $690 million a year, about the same as that of Albert Einstein Hospital in New York City.

Kessler immediately announced that over the next two years, he would create a team of 100 criminal investigators to pursue cases of fraud. He also announced that his top priorities were to strengthen enforcement and eliminate the multilayered approval process for new drugs and medical devices.[9]

Within a few months, Kessler began a sweeping review of 400 food and drug safety measures that had been proposed but never acted on between 1960 and 1990. He also embarked on a reorganization plan to divide the FDA into five management centers. In addition, he created a new policy center to ensure that proposed regulations were written and issued promptly.

Some consumer groups and federal officials questioned whether the FDA had adequate powers to protect the public from dangerous drugs and medical devices. They pointed out that the FDA did not do any of its own testing but relied entirely on the results submitted by manufacturers. The FDA was also the only federal agency without subpoena power. Without that power, the FDA could not force drug companies to turn over documents when its suspicions were aroused.

Over the past several years, the FDA has become much more active and assertive in a variety of issues. Exhibit 14–5 lists some of the issues the FDA took up in 1996 and 1997. In November 1996, David Kessler resigned as FDA commissioner and in February 1997 was appointed dean of the Yale University School of Medicine. Deputy Commissioner for Operations, Michael A. Friedman was chosen acting commissioner.

Consumers' Sources of Information

Despite myriad regulations covering nearly every product and process, most consumers assume they must take some responsibility for protecting themselves by learning about products they buy. What do consumers need to know, and how do they go about acquiring and using the necessary information?

---

[9] P. J. Hilts, "New Chief Vows New Vitality at F.D.A.," *New York Times,* February 27, 1991, p. A12.

Consumers use a variety of sources of information. They also vary considerably in the amount of detail they want to know about the products they buy.

There is compelling evidence that many consumers are in a hurry to buy and are unwilling to use a great deal of energy to seek the perfect purchase. Often they "satisfice," that is, gather just enough information to make themselves believe they have made an acceptable decision. In some circumstances, the information needed to make a perfect purchase is simply not available.

A variety of resources are available to consumers willing to make the effort to become better informed. Very often, however, people rely on their accumulated experience, general knowledge, and informal recommendations as their major sources of product information.

Although marketer-dominated sources of information are usually the most prevalent, consumers do not always see those sources as the most reliable, trustworthy, or objective. A number of objective or unbiased publications specialize in providing detailed and comparative information about products. Some consumers rely on information from private testing laboratories, such as Consumers' Union and Consumers' Research.

Other popular information sources include the consumer magazine, *Changing Times,* and certain newspaper columns. A growing number of books aim to help consumers buy insurance, food, automobile repairs, prescription drugs, and many other products and services. The U.S. Government Printing Office publishes specialized reports from federal consumer agencies and also furnishes comparative test data on consumer products bought with public funds.

Consumers Index is a guide to product evaluations and information sources. Published each quarter by Pierian Press in Ann Arbor, Michigan, it aims at individual consumers and the education/library community. The publishers emphasize articles that reflect the financial or physical health and well-being of consumers, libraries, and educational institutions. *Consumers Index* divides its subjects into 17 main groupings. It provides general information about the products and addresses a variety of relevant information categories designed to help consumers make better decisions.

Better Business Bureaus (BBBs) are also good sources of information, especially about local businesses. In 1911, John I. Romer, publisher of *Printer's Ink,* suggested that local advertising clubs form vigilance committees. These committees worked to eliminate abuses in advertising codes and to create and set advertising standards.

In 1912 George Coleman, a Boston advertising executive, formed the National Vigilance Committee to extend the effort to regional and national advertising. This group became an independent corporation in 1926 and changed its name to the National Better Business Bureau. An overarching Council of Better Business Bureaus was formed in 1970, when the National Better Business Bureau and the Association of Better Business Bureaus International merged.

Exhibit 14-6 Better Business Bureau Home Page

The Better Business Bureau®
Helping Consumers and Business to Maintain an Ethical Marketplace

U.S. & CANADA

BBB Services Online
- Alerts & News
- Business Report Databases
- Charity Reports & Standards
- Dispute Resolution
  - Online Complaint Forms
- Resource Library
- Locate a BBB

Sitemap/Search

Click on the logo for information about our new program--- coming soon!

BBBOnLine

About the BBB
- Programs & Services
- Advertising Review Programs
- Membership Rosters & Information
- Frequently Asked Questions
- How to Reach Us

"Our mission is to promote and foster the highest ethical relationship between businesses and the public..."

The Better Business Bureau provides instant access to business and consumer alerts as well as helpful resources. Plus, you can file a complaint online and more. This web site is provided by the Council of Better Business Bureaus, Inc., and the BBB system of over 150 Bureaus located throughout the United States and Canada.

BBB Services Online:
Alerts and News: The latest consumer warnings and other news from the BBB
Business Report Databases: How to obtain a BBB report on a business
Charity Reports and Standards: How to obtain a BBB report on a charity
Dispute Resolution: How BBBs help resolve marketplace disputes Here's where to find online complaint forms
Resource Library: BBB consumer buying guides and business publications
Locate a BBB: Find the BBB serving your community

About the BBB
Programs and Services: How BBBs work for businesses and consumers.
Advertising Review Programs: BBB programs to promote ethical advertising and selling practices
Membership Rosters & Information: How and why to join the BBB, membership standards, and how to obtain member rosters
Frequently Asked Questions: Frequently Asked Questions About the BBB
How to Contact the CBBB
The BBBOnLine Program: Information about the BBB system's new program to build consumer confidence in the online marketplace

Click on the torch (upper left) from any page to return to this home page

In the coming months, this site will be growing and changing. Please check back often to see what's new. Add a 'bookmark' now to make it easy to return.

Council of Better Business Bureaus
4200 Wilson Blvd., Suite 800
Arlington, VA 22203-1804
Phone: (703) 276-0100
Fax: (703) 525-8277

The name Better Business Bureau is a registered service mark of the Council of Better Business Bureaus, Inc. Only those non-profit organizations that meet CBBB standards and are approved for membership in the CBBB are authorized to use the name 'Better Business Bureau'.

Copyright © 1996, 1997 Council of Better Business Bureaus, Inc. All rights reserved.

Comments to webmaster: jpond@cbbb.bbb.org
This address for webmaster/site related mail only: **business reports are not avaliable through this address**

EXHIBIT 14–7 Better Business Bureau Alerts

The Better Business Bureau® U.S. & CANADA

Locate a BBB | Alerts & News | Resource Library | Business & Charity Reports
Resolving Disputes | Member Info | About the BBB | Advertising Review Programs

SEARCH SITEMAP FEEDBACK

BBB Alerts

The Better Business Bureau places a high priority on disseminating accurate, valuable information that helps consumers and businesses make informed decisions in today's marketplace. This Alerts and News area includes the most time-sensitive and newsworthy types of information, while the Resource Library contains publications of more general and ongoing value to both consumers and businesses.

Alerts
Alerts are urgent warnings to notify consumers and businesses about recently discovered, fraudulent business scams or are brief advisories to help the public know how to deal with specific buying decision situations.

January 1997

Scam hitting hotel guests (1/30/97)
Beware of Door-To-Door Contractors Soliciting Repair Work (1/30/97)
Business Opportunity Scams on the Internet (1/21/97)
Businesses Hit by Telemarketing Con Artists (1/17/97)
National Consumer Alert: Stimulator Pain Killing Device (1/9/97)
Dallas BBB Warns Consumers Nationwide About Phone Slamming (1/7/97)
New Year's Resolution: Avoid These Scams (1/7/97)
Don't Let Disaster Strike Twice: Beware of Cons After Natural Disasters (1/6/97)

Businesses, Beware of "900" Phone Scams (1/6/97)

December 1996

CPA Firms Targeted with Deceptive Internet Services Invoice
Internet Computer Sales Company Forced out of Business Following Postal Investigation
Beware of Bogus Fliers Announcing Baby Formula Settlements
Fraudulent Customs Telemarketers Targeting Seniors
"Environmental Protection Enforcement Agency" Restaurant Scam
The Federal Trade Commission Issues Alert on Pyramid Schemes
Holiday Shopping Tips for the 1996 Season

November 1996

Magazine Distribution Company Using Dubious Telemarketing Techniques
CD-ROM Directory Listing Scam

BBBs are private, nonprofit, self-regulatory agencies. From its Virginia headquarters, the council disseminates information about charitable solicitations and performs consumer education and public information functions. Exhibit 14–6 shows the home page of the Better Business Bureaus at [http://www.bbb.org]. The BBB issues alerts to consumers and businesses to better inform their decision making. See Exhibit 14–7 for the alerts issued between November 1996 and January 1997.

What Is Good Information?

Consumers have become more sophisticated over time. Raymond Bauer pointed out over 30 years ago, "As the persuaders become more sophisticated, so do the people to be persuaded. One way of reading the history of the development of techniques of persuasion is that the persuaders have been in a race to keep abreast of the developing resistance of the people to be persuaded."[10] Bauer's words have been prophetic.

Business generates a huge volume of material to influence consumers to buy particular products and services. Consumer advocates assert that full disclosure of every aspect of the product is necessary for the consumer to make a wise choice.

The term *full disclosure* means different things to different people. To most it means disclosure of the hazardous characteristics of a product, such as its poisonous or inflammable nature. A second meaning is the disclosure of terms-of-sale information, component ingredients, and net contents. The statement of a product's performance characteristics is a third kind of disclosure. Full disclosure also may require a statement about the ratings of product-testing agencies and whether the products subscribe to industry codes or practices. There is no widespread consensus on the definition of full disclosure because costs as well as benefits are associated with additional disclosures. Perhaps the materiality concept is the best guideline for what a marketer should disclose.

Advertising

Advertising Goals

Advertising is "any form of nonpersonal presentation of ideas, goods, and services by an identified sponsor."[11] The goal of advertising is to make potential customers *aware* of the product's existence and then to *inform* those customers of product characteristics leading to a favorable *purchase* decision. The firm's goal is to have consumers insist on purchasing its brand.

---

[10] R. A. Bauer, "The Limits of Persuasion," *Harvard Business Review* 36, September–October 1958, p. 105.

[11] P. Bagozzi, *Principles of Marketing Management* (Chicago: Science Research Associates, 1986), p. 372.

Advertising is big business. In the United States, thousands of advertising agencies do billions of dollars worth of business each year. In 1940, advertising expenditures in all media in the United States were $2 billion. In 1978, they totaled around $43 billion and in 1986 they reached $55 billion. The advertising industry estimates the average American family is exposed to more than 1,500 ads per day on television, in newspapers and magazines, and on radio. With the growing popularity of Internet use, companies are targeting people even more closely. For example, a person who logs into a home page on car purchases is bombarded with car-related products and services.

Do all these ads directly result in sales? The answer is, obviously not. Sometimes sales are not the primary object of advertising. A company may simply be trying to increase awareness of its brands in a particular market or to build a positive company image and then rely on personal selling to close the deal. Whether or not the company uses ads to generate sales, only a small percentage of those ads' content has any meaningful effect on consumers' buying decisions.

A 1968 study by Raymond A. Bauer and Stephen A. Greyser concluded that the average American adult was aware of 76 advertisements a day in the major media.[12] Of that total, 84 percent of the ads were not notable enough for people to categorize their reactions or the strength of their feelings. It is unlikely that people's ability to assimilate information has changed in the 25 years since that study was conducted; rather, their willingness to assimilate information from advertising has likely decreased as sources proliferate.

Nevertheless, advertising is ubiquitous and uses the most advanced audiovisual and psychological techniques to reach consumers. Thirty-five years ago, historian David M. Potter argued, "Advertising now compares with such longstanding institutions as the school and the church in magnitude of its social influence. It dominates the media, it has vast power in the shaping of popular standards and is really one of the very limited group of institutions which exercises social control."[13] The power and sophistication of advertising companies and the media have grown enormously since Potter made his observation. Yet it is clear that people do not believe every advertisement they read or hear. In fact, some advertisements do a company much more harm than good.

Deceptive Advertising

Advertising claims and techniques of personal selling can be deceptive. No universally accepted definition of deceptive advertising exists. A working definition states that *deceptive advertising* occurs when the advertisement in some people's minds differs from the reality of the situation and adversely affects those consumers' buying behavior. Although some advertisements

---

[12] R. A. Bauer and S. A. Greyser, *Advertising in America: The Consumer View* (Boston: Harvard University Press, 1968), pp. 385–86.

[13] D. M. Potter, *People of Plenty* (Chicago: University of Chicago Press, 1954), p. 167.

Exhibit 14–8 Generic Standards for Advertisers

- Who is your audience? The nature of the audience will be a factor in determining whether an advertisement is deceptive. Advertisements directed at vulnerable groups such as children receive closer scrutiny than others. However, in reviewing misleading advertising, the FTC does not always adopt law schools' traditional "reasonable person" standard. Rather, they can be concerned with the public, "that vast multitude which includes the ignorant, the unthinking and the credulous, who, in making purchases, do not stop to analyze, but are governed by appearances and general impressions." In summary, the appearances and general impressions you convey to the lowest common denominator—the audience segment that is more likely to be influenced by an impression gleaned from a first glance and not tempered by mature reflection or judgment—may be controlling.

- The FTC will view an advertisement in its entirety; total net impression governs. A headline will outweigh any subsequent disclaimers or clarifying material.

- Literal truth will not save your advertisement if it is misleading when read in the context of the entire advertisement. Here you must avoid deception by half-truth or the failure to disclose material facts. The advertisement usually does not have to state all the facts, but must contain a reasonably complete statement.

- An advertisement may be found false and deceptive if either of two possible meanings is false.

- Expressions of subjective opinion (puffery) are not actionable unless they convey the impression of factual representations or relate to material terms. Opinion of the superiority or the merits of a product seems to be generally acceptable until the phrase becomes a fact. "We believe (an opinion) that our razor blades will never cut your face (fact)." The claim of fact may cross the line from puffery to deception. Likewise, exaggerating the qualities of a product is usually permissible, but assigning qualities that do not exist reaches too far. Stating that you're the "number one" seller requires substantiation with supporting evidence and documentation.

- If you are employing a mock-up that is not an accurate representation of a consumer experience, it must not pertain to the product you are specifically selling.

- All research quoted must be significant and must have been professionally obtained through state-of-the-art research techniques.

- You have a *continuing* obligation to make sure all your material claims are substantiated, including test results, price claims, and endorsements.

Throughout its history, the FTC has tried to follow the ideal that its regulation would serve two objectives—to provide useful and truthful data and to maintain effective competition. One way to accomplish this is to enforce minimal standards of marketplace compliance such as the examples above. Another way is to affirmatively encourage broader consumer information.

Source: R. J. Posch, Jr., *The Complete Guide to Marketing and the Law* (Englewood Cliffs, NJ: Prentice-Hall, 1988), pp. 391–92.

contain explicit falsehoods, more frequently advertisements are not explicitly false. Even then, however, consumers may misinterpret the message or perceive that it is deceptive.[14] Exhibit 14–8 outlines some generally accepted principles that help clarify what constitutes a deceptive practice.

Deceptive sales practices have come under increasingly heavy criticism. Such practices as bait-and-switch, lowballing (advertising a price lower than the price that will actually be charged for the product), fear selling, chain referral selling, and free gimmicks are increasingly being brought under control by strengthened state laws and city ordinances. Most of these practices are not subject to federal control, because the perpetrators do not engage in interstate commerce. Even when they do, they generally affect too few consumers to meet the public-interest requirements for federal action.

Counterfeit Products. Some producers use misinformation and engage in outright fraud by selling counterfeit products under famous brand names such as Gucci, Cartier, and Apple Computer. The company that developed a trademark or other intellectual property and the consumer who has purchased an inferior product bear the cost. Most often the culprits are developing-country producers hoping to cash in on American, European, or Japanese design and technology. Some of these products are sold only in the counterfeiters' home countries; other faux products enter world trade. Counterfeiting and foreign violation of intellectual property rights remain a very serious problem for companies in the industrialized countries.[15]

U.S. government and industry studies found American companies lost $200 billion in worldwide sales in 1996 because of Chinese, Taiwanese, South Korean, Vietnamese, and Russian counterfeiting. In mid-1996, the Clinton administration reported evidence that a large number of previously undiscovered Chinese factories were producing their own versions of American software, videos, and music. For more than a year, the Clinton administration threatened to impose trade sanctions on goods from China if the government did not crack down on the practice. This latest revelation led the American government to announce retaliatory action against more than $2 billion in Chinese imports to the United States. The administration noted it had repeatedly warned that it would remove China's Most-Favored-Nation status that gave the Chinese preferential tariffs unless they took action to stop the violations.

Chinese officials immediately threatened to issue counter-sanctions against American goods. A top-level Chinese official warned that the more pressure the United States applied, "the less opportunities the United States will have in the Chinese markets."[16]

---

[14] D. A. Aaker, "Deceptive Advertising," in D. A. Aaker and G. S. Days, eds. *Consumerism: Search for Consumer Interest,* 2nd ed. (New York: Free Press, 1974), p. 137.

[15] D. Stipp, "Farewell, My Logo," *Fortune,* May 27, 1996, p. 128.

[16] D. E. Sanger, "U.S. Says It Finds Pirating by China Is on the Increase," *New York Times,* May 8, 1996, p. A1.

U.S. and Chinese negotiators entered intense, public, and often acrimonious discussions over what this country called broad violations of an agreement previously reached on the piracy issue. In May 1996, the United States announced it would release a trade sanction hit list. Chinese textiles, electronics, and toys worth more than $3 billion would be slapped with punitive tariffs if the widespread piracy of compact disks, videos, and software continued. By focusing on China's huge textile, toy, and electronics industries, the administration hoped to convince China it meant business and to enhance American credibility with other Asian nations.

John Yochelson, head of a Washington agency that worked on developing U.S. strategy, declared, "In any trade conflict, you have to show you mean business by hitting your trading partner where it hurts." The process of imposing sanctions took on some attributes of a formalized dance with each partner knowing the step that would come next. This process had worked a year earlier when the United States announced a 100 percent tariff on more than $1 billion of Chinese cellular telephones and sporting equipment. Sanctions were averted at the last minute when the Chinese government raided retail stores and factories where pirated goods were being made.

Under the U.S. process, retaliatory action begins when the United States publishes an initial list of sanctions. This action is followed by a 30-day period during which U.S. importers and retailers can argue that the proposed sanctions will harm their businesses or consumers. The list is cut by one-third of its dollar value and, if all negotiations fail, sanctions are imposed. The process is intentionally drawn out to allow the other side time to enforce its intellectual property laws.[17]

Chinese and U.S. negotiators remained intransigent until it was clear to the Chinese government that sanctions would, indeed, go into effect. At the last minute, the Chinese government agreed to crack down on the factories and the United States lifted its threat of sanctions. Both sides acknowledged how difficult it was to control the production and flow of pirated goods.

Compact Disk (CD) plants in the southern province of Guangdong were backed by the Chinese Army and the Public Security Bureau. CDs that cost pirates 36 cents to make were sold in Hong Kong for $4.30 each. A used CD press that could produce 2 million disks a year cost about $400,000. New presses that cost $1.5 million could make nearly 7 million disks a year. Experts in Hong Kong said there were more than 100 presses in China and that two or three European-made presses were smuggled into Guangdong each month. They estimated Chinese production of pirated CDs totaled 200 million in 1996.[18]

---

[17] H. Cooper and K. Chen, "China's Textiles to Top U.S. Hit List of Sanctions Aimed at Curbing Piracy," *The Wall Street Journal,* May 14, 1996, p. 22.

[18] J. Barnathan, "A Pirate under Every Rock," *Business Week,* June 17, 1996, pp. 50–51.

By mid-May 1996, the immediate crisis was over. Secretary of State Warren Christopher told reporters the administration strongly supported the continuation of Most-Favored-Nation status for China. He acknowledged that the Chinese government had not lived up to the 1995 agreement and stressed that "intellectual property is one of our principal products to sell abroad, and we simply cannot abide a situation where there is wholesale piracy of American ideas. . . . Nevertheless," he emphasized, "we have resolved some problems and quieted some tensions."[19]

The Chinese situation points out the problem companies and consumers have in determining the attributes of a product. As more and more manufacturing becomes globalized, industrialized countries are applying pressure on developing countries to protect intellectual property. However, even when all the labeling laws are followed and no intent to defraud exists, it may be difficult for consumers to judge a product by its advertising or labeling.

Food Labels. The Food and Drug Administration, the Department of Agriculture, and the Federal Trade Commission all monitor and regulate food advertising. Even with oversight by three federal agencies, consumers sometimes received conflicting information or information they could not understand. Some labels were so full of confusing detail that the average consumer was unable to exercise the right to know guaranteed in the Consumer Bill of Rights.

Although information has been readily available on an item's label, often it was neither relevant nor accurate. Many food producers used the word *lite* or *light* to describe their product. The average consumer did not know whether the product was light in color, light in calories, or light in texture. Light beer could be a 12-ounce can of Michelob Light, which had 134 calories, or Miller Lite, which had 95. Schaefer regular beer had 139 calories, just 5 calories more than Michelob Light.[20]

The Bush administration announced the first major changes in food labels in many years. Health and Human Services Secretary Louis W. Sullivan said, "The grocery store has become the Tower of Babel, and consumers need to be linguists, scientists, and mind readers to understand the many labels they see."[21]

The administration's food label bill called for mandatory nutrition labeling on nearly every food product. After a year of public discussion, companies would be required to provide information about amounts of saturated fat,

---

[19] Internet [http://www.usia.gov:80/abtusia/posts/HK1/wwheb09.html] "Transcript: Christopher Interview on PBS Lehrer Newshour."

[20] C. Schaeffer, "Food Labels: The Hype behind the Type," *Changing Times,* July 1989, p. 38.

[21] P. J. Hilts, "U.S. Plans to Make Sweeping Changes in Labels on Food," *New York Times,* March 8, 1990, p. A1.

fiber, and cholesterol and the percentage of calories coming from fat. Booklets at stores would give consumers the same information about fresh fruits and other produce. The plan also would give formal definitions for *low-fat* and *high-fiber,* thereby taking the responsibility for those designations away from manufacturers or processors.

In May 1990, the food label bill passed the House Energy and Commerce Committee and the Senate Labor and Human Resources Committee and went to the floor of the House and the Senate. Finally, in October, the Senate passed the bill that had been approved by the House three months earlier. It remained for the president to sign the bill and the FDA to write the detailed regulations for more than 14,000 food products. Scheduled to go into effect in May 1994, the bill had a relabeling cost of about $40 million.

In April 1991, the Department of Agriculture announced it would coordinate its efforts with the FDA by requiring meat and poultry processors to list nutritional data. The proposal covered processed meat and poultry products from chicken soup to lunch meat. Labels would contain calories, total fat, saturated fat, cholesterol, protein, sodium content, and serving size. Supermarkets and retail stores would be requested to supply similar information for fresh meats and poultry.[22]

The involvement of the Department of Health and Human Services, the Department of Agriculture, the FDA, and Congress pointed out the complexity of interactions among various jurisdictions. Congress was not asked to pass labeling legislation on fresh meats and poultry that went into processed foods. Therefore, a sausage pizza could be under the jurisdiction of the Department of Agriculture that regulated pork, while a cheese pizza might come under the FDA that covered dairy products. The Federal Trade Commission that regulated advertising might allow food companies to use terms in television commercials that the FDA and the Department of Agriculture would not permit on labels.

In June 1991, the FDA targeted labeling practices of the juice industry. It decided to require companies to list percentages of each juice in blends as well as the total percentage of juice in juice cocktails and punches. The proposal covered about 3,000 products including fruit sparklers, sparkling cider, carbonated fruit drinks, soft drinks, and carbonated waters.

Consumer groups were delighted with the FDA proposal. Bruce A. Silverglade of the consumer advocacy group the Center for Science and the Public Interest noted that juice processors would have to make major labeling changes. Under the old rules, juice blend drinks could be identified as tropical guava or passion fruit drinks even though most of their liquid was plain apple juice.

Manufacturers were given one month to comment on the rules and required to have new labels by November 1991. A New Jersey manufacturer

---

[22] B. Ingersoll, "USDA Proposes Nutritional-Data Rules for Labels on Processed Meat, Poultry," *The Wall Street Journal,* April 2, 1991, p. B5.

noted her company would have to change 2,500 labels to comply with the new rules. She doubted the nation's printing presses could handle her company's requirement and those of all the other juice manufacturers in time to make the deadline.[23]

For the most part, consumers were pleased they would have access to so much new information. About half of all consumers said they depended on labels to decide which foods to buy. A casual stroll through the supermarket, however, showed how easily consumers could be deceived. Budget Gourmet Light and Healthy Salisbury Steak was labeled *low fat,* but derived 45 percent of its total calories from fat. Diet Coke and Diet Pepsi each contained more than the one calorie per can listed on the label. Post Fruity Pebbles contained no fruit at all, and Mrs. Smith's Natural Juice Apple Pie contained artificial preservatives.

Nearly half of all consumers reported they were highly skeptical about the information they read on grocery packages. Medical experts said they were right to be concerned and pointed to the inherent dangers in mislabeled food. For someone with heart disease, high blood pressure, or diabetes, inaccurately labeled quantities of salt or sugar in a product could have fatal consequences. A spokesperson for the American Dietetic Association noted-some Stouffer diet products contained almost half the total amount of salt allowed daily on a salt-restricted diet. Stouffer labeled the salt content in grams rather than milligrams (one thousandth of a gram).[24]

Although a dispute between Bush administration officials briefly delayed label implementation, in December 1992 the administration gave the plan the green light. Dr. David Kessler, kept on by the Clinton administration, continued the FDA's aggressive consumer education plan. It seems clear that the food labeling law that went into effect in May 1994 greatly enhanced consumers' ability to choose products based on their actual contents and attributes.

The Food and Drug Administration now clearly defines terms such as *light,* which can mean two things:

> First, that a nutritionally altered product contains one-third fewer calories or half the fat of the reference food. If the food derives 50 percent of its calories from fat, the reduction must be 50 percent of the fat. Second, that the sodium [salt] content of a low-calorie, low-fat food has been reduced by 50 percent. In addition, 'light in sodium,' may be used on food in which the sodium content has been reduced by at least 50 percent. The term 'light' can still be used to describe properties such as texture and color, as long as the label explains the intent—for example, 'light brown sugar' and 'light and fluffy'.[25]

---

[23] T. Golden, "Juice Label Asked by F.D.A," *New York Times,* July 2, 1991, p. D1.
[24] C. Gorman, "The Fight over Food Labels," *Time,* July 15, 1991, pp. 50, 52–59.
[25] Internet [http://vm.cfsan.fda.gov/~dms/qa-lab8j.html.] Excerpted from *FDA Booklet, May 1995: The New Food Label.*

Green Products. Earth Day 1990 marked the beginning of a flood of environmentally sound products. Since then, many companies have asserted their products or services are environmentally sound or environmentally friendly. Often however, it is very difficult for consumers to make reasoned judgments about whether such claims are valid.

In 1990, for example, John Hancock Life Insurance Company boasted that its $53 million Freedom Environmental Fund was a good way to "participate in the coming environmental mobilization." A consumer advocate group in California sent letters to the SEC charging the Hancock fund deliberately misled the public because Waste Management Inc., a company with multiple Environmental Protection Agency violations, was one of the fund's biggest investments. The fund manager insisted there were no perfectly environmentally pristine companies and Waste Management ran the cleanest landfills in the business.

Environmental fund managers rode the tide of public interest in the wake of the *Exxon Valdez* debacle. The Merrill Lynch Environmental Technology Trust opened two portfolios of pollution cleanup stocks. Within a few days after the first one opened, the trust reached its $50 million goal.

Organizations as well as individuals questioned their portfolio managers about companies' environmental records. The director of the Prudential-Bache Capital Funding Group's social research service reported the environment was the single most important social issue among institutional investors.

Assessing a company's green credentials becomes very complicated when that company both pollutes and cleans up the pollution. DuPont Company, for example, makes chlorofluorocarbons (CFCs) that contribute to global warming. On the other hand, DuPont promised to phase out CFCs by the year 2000 and developed new substitute technologies. How does a consumer decide whether to buy DuPont stock or invest in a fund that holds this stock?

Some investors use an independent screening service to ensure that their investments are environmentally clean. The screening service researches and eliminates funds that own any of the 150 major toxic waste dumps identified by the World Wildlife Foundation or that own the stock of firms identified as environmental culprits.

Many experienced investors were skeptical about the green craze. Some warned consumers not to be taken in but instead to contribute some of their traditional investment profits to organizations that clean up their local areas. Most experts agree environmental investing requires consumers to make trade-offs between profitable investments and environmental commitment.[26]

Economists who have studied the effects of product manufacturing have concluded that common sense doesn't really help people assess what helps or hurts the environment. In some cases, recycling actually used more energy

---

[26] E. C. Gottschalk, "Investments Promoted as Ecologically Clean Pop Up Like Weeds," *The Wall Street Journal,* April 10, 1990, p. A1.

and created more pollution than the alternatives. The use of plastics versus paper illustrates that point. Ecologists and environmental action groups warned consumers that plastics were "environmental enemy No. 1." They urged consumers to ask for paper cups at fast-food restaurants and to choose cardboard containers over plastics in the supermarket.

Lester Lave, director of the Green Design Initiative at Carnegie Mellon University, traced the effects of paper manufacturing through the entire economy. This analysis captured everything from the fuel burned in chain saws that cut down the trees, to pollution generated by factories making tires for the trucks that delivered papers to the supermarket. Lave and his associates concluded that a plastic cup took half as much energy to make and resulted in 35 percent fewer pounds of toxic chemicals released into the environment. They noted that a plastic cup weighed one-sixth as much as a paper cup and used much less plastic than a paper cup used paper.[27]

The Federal Trade Commission is still working on guidelines for the use of environmental marketing claims. It issued its Guides for the Use of Environmental Marketing Claims in July 1992. The guides included a provision for public comment and review in 1995. By the end of 1996, the commission had concluded its general review of the guides and was looking for added information on how to define *recyclability* more precisely. The FTC noted that the guides benefited consumers by "stemming the tide of spurious environmental claims; bolstering consumer confidence; increasing the flow of specific and accurate environmental information to consumers, enabling them to make informed purchasing decisions; and encouraging manufacturers to improve the environmental characteristics of their products and packaging."[28]

In the early 1990s, the green craze spread to other countries. Governments established panels to judge the truthfulness of companies' claims. In Great Britain, the Independent Television Association, a trade group representing Britain's independent television companies, devised guidelines for green television commercials. The Advertising Standards Authority, the trade group for press advertisements, advised companies not to make absolute claims. This group suggested advertisers call a product environmentally *friendlier* rather than simply environmentally friendly. It also suggested advertisers tell the consumer what attributes make the product green. For example, an ad should state that a product has no CFCs or is biodegradable rather than simply environmentally sound.[29]

In 1995, the European Union (EU) agreed on environmental standards for a wide range of products. Critics pointed out that the EU's ecolabel did not necessarily give consumers more or better information. They noted that

---

[27] S. Budiansky, "Being Green Isn't Always What It Seems," *U.S. News & World Report,* August 26, 1996, p. 42.

[28] Internet [http://www.ftc.gov:80/WWW/os/9610/16cfr260.htm] "Guides for the Use of Environmental Marketing Claims," *Federal Trade Commission 16CFR Part 260.*

[29] "Friendly to Whom," *Economist,* April 7, 1990, p. 83.

products at the top end of the market conformed to the label's requirement but there was no way to show their superiority. A producer of washing machines said, "The ecolabel is not a mark of supreme excellence—instead it is a great leveller." The United Kingdom's Consumers' Association was concerned that consumers were being confused rather than enlightened by the label. A spokesman remarked, "The Ecolabel system does not suppress labels that manufacturers and shops give their own products and that is confusing to buyers who find it difficult to distinguish between official and unofficial marks."[30]

McDonald's. When eco-stakeholders pressured companies to adopt environmentally sound practices, McDonald's, which generated mountains of trash, became a prime target. Polystyrene hamburger boxes became the symbol of a throwaway society. Environmentalists agreed it took hundreds of years for those boxes to rot. Earlier McDonald's had tested a pilot program to collect and recycle the polystyrene boxes. The program failed because most customers carried the boxes out of the restaurant and discarded them elsewhere. Customers eating in the restaurants were confused when confronted with multiple bins for trash. Even when the hamburger boxes were cleaned and recycled, they had very limited use.

Young people, McDonald's largest consumer group, became its severest critics. During 1989 and 1990, schoolchildren demonstrated outside the restaurants and wrote thousands of letters to corporate headquarters. McDonald's management had to respond and enlisted the environmentalists' help. In August 1990, the company signed an agreement with the Environmental Defense Fund (EDF), an environmental research and lobbying group. The EDF and McDonald's agreed to work together to reduce the company's trash output. Initially McDonald's wanted to continue trying to recycle the hamburger boxes, but the EDF suggested the company concentrate on reducing the amount of packaging material. McDonald's took EDF's advice and announced it would replace the polystyrene box with a quilted wrap made from a layer of tissue between a layer of polyethylene and a sheet of paper. Although the wrap could not be recycled, it was only 10 percent as bulky as the box and used far fewer natural resources. Initially the EDF wanted McDonald's to use washable plates instead of disposable containers. McDonald's managers resisted, pointing out that outlets served two to three times as many people per square foot as a conventional restaurant did. They also argued that dishwashers use water, detergents, and energy.

The alliance between McDonald's and the EDF has flourished. McDonald's adopted a policy of "reduce, reuse, and recycle." Some experiments to reduce waste worked, while others did not. Consumers found that when the company narrowed its straws to save paper, their milk shakes were too thick

---

[30] J. Harding, "Sticking Point for Fresh Green Products," *Financial Times,* March 29, 1995, p. 10.

to suck through the new straw. However, when McDonald's reduced the size of its napkins, consumers did not use more napkins.

Recycling efforts continue with McDonald's experiments in composting. Almost half the waste from a typical restaurant consists of food scraps and paper that eventually can be used for fertilizer. In time, McDonald's should be able to dispose of nearly 80 percent of its trash without adding to landfills. By redesigning its packaging, McDonald's reduced material use by more than 3,000 tons in 1994 and used more than 200,000 tons of recycled packaging. It also reached its target of $1 billion of recycled purchases five years ahead of schedule.[31]

The Future of the Green-Product Movement. Manufacturers say it is too soon to tell whether the current consumer apathy toward green products is temporary or more lasting. The Roper Organization found green products have not gained mass acceptance. Some people do not like the appearance, texture, or performance of recycled products and paper in particular. Although disposable diapers are a major contributor to landfills, most parents are unwilling to switch to cloth diapers.

Price seems to be the biggest obstacle to the widespread use of green products that usually are more expensive. Consumers report they would buy environmentally sound products if they were the same price as or cheaper than conventional products, but they are reluctant to pay a premium for them.

Some companies have found innovative ways to address both environmental concerns and price issues. Procter & Gamble, for example, reduced the amount of plastic it used and at the same time saved consumers money. P&G's refillable laundry detergent and fabric softener bottles have gained market share because they are cheaper for the manufacturer, retailer, and consumer and incidentally are environmentally sound. Virtually all detergent manufacturers now offer more concentrated products that save packaging material.

Consumers are bombarded by information, some of which is unreliable and much of which is confusing. Government agencies such as the Food and Drug Administration and Federal Trade Commission have tried to make this information more understandable to the layperson and more accurate. Over time they have achieved considerable success. This discussion of what constitutes an ecologically sound product, however, is far from over.

Summary

For a century, consumers have been concerned about access to product information and the quality of that information. As the number of available products has increased, potential sources of information also have proliferated. Organized consumers' groups help publicize information about unsafe or harmful products.

---

[31] McDonald's Annual Report, 1995, p. 13.

After World War II, consumer movements grew in both size and influence. The Federal Trade Commission and the Food and Drug Administration are the two key government agencies dealing with consumer protection. In some instances their duties appear to overlap, but together they dictate industry rules and regulations for consumer protection. They oversee advertising, labeling, and content requirements, allowing consumers to make more confident choices based on more accurate information.

Consumers use a variety of sources to get the information they want and need. Often they do not have complete information about their product choices and have to question what constitutes reliable information or complete disclosure about a product.

Advertisers try to attract new customers and keep old ones. Nearly all consumers are bombarded with far more product information than they can use or are willing to absorb. Many consumers are sophisticated enough to reject messages in advertisements that are obviously misleading.

Food labeling is one of the FDA's major responsibilities. Although food product labels in the United States are more comprehensive than those in most other countries, they still provide too little information for consumers to make really informed choices. The standards that took effect in 1994 improved labels and eliminated much of the confusion over contents and dietary requirements.

Consumers' desire for environmentally sound products has created new offerings of goods and services in the United States and abroad. Nevertheless, consumers are ambivalent about green products; price seems to be the major impediment to mass acceptance of these products. However, manufacturers and advertisers are finding innovative ways to make standard products greener at little or no extra cost.

Questions

1. Define consumer welfare. What are the various issues involved in consumer welfare?
2. What are the major sources consumers might use to obtain product information? What are the costs associated with using each source?
3. What are the Federal Trade Commission's responsibilities with respect to advertising?
4. What are the Food and Drug Administration's responsibilities to consumers?
5. Evaluate the Federal Trade Commission's concept of materiality. What are the pros and cons of a position that all information is material?

Projects

1. Buy several magazines available at the supermarket checkout counter. Carefully read the advertising copy for over-the-counter drug ads. List the ads and any copy you consider deceptive or potentially deceptive. Use these ads as a basis for class discussion.
2. Find out whether your state has passed legislation against deceptive advertising. Contact your state office for consumer affairs to find out what the state government has done to protect consumers. Ask how your state and the federal government work together on this issue.
3. Find out the procedure by which one registers a complaint with the Federal Trade Commission or the Food and Drug Administration.

BETA CASE 14
CONSUMERS AND INFORMATION

February 26, 1997, was an important day for Beta. The Food and Drug Administration (FDA) announced that if all went as the agency planned, the labels on all nonprescription drugs would be simplified by mid-1999. Dr. David Kessler, the outgoing commissioner of the FDA, noted that 125,000 over-the-counter drugs would come under the new regulations. These drugs accounted for about $18 billion in sales with the number going up as the FDA shifted more drugs from prescription to nonprescription status.

The new label format included:

- Uniform, standardized headings, subheadings, and a standardized order of information.
- Simplified language for certain words or phrases, for example: *throw away* instead of *discard; lung* instead of *pulmonary;* and *hole in* instead of *perforation.*
- Bulleted, easier-to-read format, including a readable type size and type style.

CEO Brian Madison and Chief Operating Officer Donald Drees were pleased that their own hard work had paid off. For the past several years, they had been part of an industry committee that worked with the FDA to develop the new rules. They agreed with Secretary of Health and Human Services Donna Shalala's comment that the propensity of Americans to treat themselves was troublesome. They had seen the *American Pharmaceutical Association's Handbook of Nonprescription Drugs* and its estimate that four times as many health problems were handled by consumers treating themselves with over-the-counter-drugs than by consumers seeing a doctor. In their meetings with the FDA and other pharmaceutical company representatives, they often discussed the problems people created when diagnosing and medicating themselves without fully understanding the medications' side effects and interactions. Elderly people used about 30 percent of all the over-the-counter drugs; by the year 2000, this group was expected to account for as much as half of the sales.

Although generally pleased by the new regulations, Drees and Madison were very concerned about the added cost Beta would have to incur to comply with the new regulations. The FDA estimated the cost for the industry at $14 million. The Nonprescription Drug Manufacturers Association put the cost at about $100 million although it acknowledged the cost could be less if drug makers coordinated scheduled changes with the new regulations. While Beta's executives had worked collegially and diligently with the FDA, there was no doubt that giving consumers information that was easier to use would place a substantial burden on the company. Drees and Madison wondered what trade-offs they had made in the name of good corporate citizenship.

C H A P T E R

15   PRODUCT USE ISSUES

Chapter 14 discussed what companies should do to ensure that consumers have the right information about the quality and other attributes of products they buy. This chapter discusses issues of product quality. It covers the major trends in quality management and examines the role of the Malcolm Baldrige Award, ISO 9000, and ISO 14000 in fostering quality among U.S. companies.

Chapter 15 also describes the components of product quality, the evolution of product safety, company liability, and the changing legal environment for managers and consumers injured by defective products. As we shall see, companies are liable when their products do not perform as expected. Quality management is essential as a competitive weapon as well as a critical skill for avoiding product liability lawsuits.

CASE: GENERAL MOTORS AND ITS PICKUP TRUCKS

Between 1973 and 1987, General Motors Corporation (G.M.) made its GMC and Chevrolet pickups with side-mounted dual gas tanks placed outside the frame rails. In 1988, G.M. altered the trucks' design and put a single tank inside the frame.

In November 1992, the media began to draw attention to the fact that when the trucks with dual gas tanks were hit from the side, they were more likely than other pickups to burst into flames. By the time the problem was widely known, G.M. was involved in more than 100 lawsuits and had made payments of over $1 million. Families of the more than 300 people who were killed claimed it was because of the safety defect. At the end of 1992, however, 4.7 million of those trucks were still on the road.

G.M. documents suggest that prior to 1983, the company tried to better protect the fuel tanks. Federal rules mandated that fuel tank systems must be able to withstand a collision from the side with another vehicle moving at 20 miles per hour. According to G.M.'s director of engineering analysis, after the company installed a plastic shield around the tank, the truck passed a 50-mile-an-hour crash test.

G.M.'s critics demanded a recall, claiming the plastic shield was only a Band-Aid fix. They asserted the test results did not take into account the buildup of corrosion and rust around the fuel tank that made the trucks much more likely to catch fire as they aged.[1] General Motors told the media it would resist any decision to recall the trucks. Company spokespersons said a recall would be illegal and would represent ad hoc regulation.

On November 17, 1992, the television program "Dateline NBC" showed crash tests in which a 1977 Chevrolet CK pickup ignited when hit from the side by a car going 30 miles per hour. A 1980 G.M. truck, subjected to the same test, did not catch on fire.

On December 9, the National Highway Traffic Safety Administration (NHTSA) sent a letter to G.M. asking whether the company had conducted its tests on cars that differed from those sold to the public. The NHTSA also asked G.M. to supply missing and incorrect data concerning failed tests. These moves meant the agency believed there was a reasonable possibility that G.M. would issue a recall.

G.M. called the tests rigged and unfair. NBC later admitted the network had used sparking devices to ignite the gas tank but maintained the results would have been the same had the devices not been used. In January, NBC told G.M. the vehicles used in the demonstration had been destroyed and thus could not be examined.[2]

Early in February 1993, G.M. suffered another public relations disaster. A Georgia state jury found the automaker responsible for the death of teenager Shannon Moseley. Moseley was burned to death when his 1985 GMC Sierra pickup was hit in the side and burst into flames. A former G.M. safety engineer, the chief witness against the company in the Moseley case, told the jury the company had intentionally hidden knowledge of the safety defect. Regardless of whether or not NBC had staged the crash test, public opinion against G.M. was mounting. The jury awarded Shannon's parents, Thomas and Elaine Moseley, $105 million in damages.[3]

Within a few days of the verdict, G.M. adopted a tough, stonewalling strategy to deal with the Moseley case and the NBC segment. Regarding the jury verdict, G.M. accused "plaintiff attorneys and others of creating a poisoned public and litigation climate in which an objective engineering evaluation and fair assessment are very hard." Commenting on the NBC program, Harry J. Pierce, G.M.'s executive vice president and general counsel, asserted that the company was cooperating with the NHTSA and that the crash test was a blatant deception.[4]

NBC capitulated and made an on-the-air apology to General Motors on February 9. Nevertheless, G.M. announced it was suspending advertising on all NBC news programs, although it did agree to drop a suit it had filed a few days earlier.

G.M. executives were delighted with NBC's apology, stating they and the company had been vindicated. G.M. continued to resist any pressure to recall the 4.7 million older trucks. Although it maintained the pickup trucks were safe, the company issued a recall for a different problem in March. Nearly 2 million full-size pickup trucks and large sports-utility vehicles made between 1988 and 1993 were called in to replace defective hoses that could spark and cause a fire under the body. G.M. admitted it had received reports of 400 incidents, including some minor fires that started when transmission fluid ignited near the catalytic converter.

G.M., safety critics, and the federal government faced an impasse. On April 7, 1993, safety advocates called a news conference in Washington. They suggested a practical and relatively inexpensive solution to the safety problems in the trucks. Clarence Ditlow, director of the Center for Auto Safety, noted that G.M. could solve the problem without bankrupting itself. For little more than $200 million, G.M. could install a protective cage around the side-mounted gas tanks. Ditlow released an internal G.M. document that described the side-mounted tanks as potential leakers. The same document, released to G.M. salespeople in the late 1980s, touted the new inside frame design, claiming it reduced the chance of fuel spillage. G.M. called the document a fluke.[5]

On April 9, 1993, NHTSA formally asked G.M. to recall the 4.7 million pickup trucks and correct the fuel tank design. This recall request was the fourth

---

[1] B. Meier, "Data Show G.M. Knew for Years of Risk in Pickup Trucks' Design," *New York Times,* November 17, 1992, p. A1.

[2] M. Maynard, "G.M. Suit Attacks NBC Report," *USA Today,* February 9, 1993, p. A1.

[3] P. Applebome, "G.M. Is Held Liable over Fuel Tanks in Pickup Trucks," *New York Times,* February 5, 1993, p. A1.

[4] D. P. Levin, "In Suit, G.M. Accuses NBC of Rigging Crash Tests," *New York Times,* February 9, 1993, p. B6.

[5] D. Lavin and B. Ingersoll, "G.M. Is Offered Plan to Resolve Truck Dispute," *The Wall Street Journal,* April 7, 1993, p. B1.

largest in the agency's history and was the first formal step toward a mandatory recall. William A. Boehly, NHTSA's top enforcement officer, said placement of the side-mounted tanks created a risk of a crash fire 2.4 times greater than the risk in a comparable full-size Ford or Dodge pickup. NHTSA gave G.M. until the end of April to explain why the trucks should not be recalled. In response, G.M. issued a statement claiming the trucks met "all applicable safety standards and General Motors does not agree with any suggestion that they should be recalled because of their side-mounted tanks."[6]

On April 30, G.M. rejected the recall request. G.M. officials said that if they honored NHTSA's request, all of the company's past and future products could be exposed to government action. GM's position drew support from those who had charged the government with inconsistent and lax policies. After all, they noted, NHTSA acknowledged that the trucks were safe overall and that GM's internal testing was even more stringent than the government's.

G.M. and its supporters charged that government policy changed unfairly after President Clinton entered the White House. G.M.'s critics responded that under Presidents Reagan and Bush, safety inspectors had worried more about the expectations of political employees who ran the agency than about product safety. The new secretary of transportation, Federico Peña, vowed to make public safety his top priority and to use recalls to implement his policy. With neither side willing to budge, NHTSA and G.M. seemed to be hunkering down for a protracted fight.

The issue was economic as well as moral and ethical. NHTSA estimated that if all 4.7 million trucks remained on the road until the year 2003, 50 to 60 more people would die in them. If a recall actually cost the estimated $1 billion, G.M. might spend $16 to $20 million to save one life. Today, government agencies value a life at $3 to $7 million, depending on the victim's age, gender, and profession.[7]

The case dragged on without resolution until April 1995 when a Philadelphia federal appeals court threw out the settlement of a huge class-action lawsuit brought by the owners of 5.7 million G.M. pickup trucks with side-mounted gas tanks. Owners would have received $1,000 coupons good for the purchase of new G.M. pickups. The class-action suit charged that the owners suffered economic loss because the public perceived the trucks to be unsafe and, therefore, worth less on a trade-in or sale. The court ruled the coupons were merely "a sophisticated marketing program" and returned the case to a lower court.[8]

In September 1995, the Moseley case and four other injury or death suits were settled. As noted earlier, the Moseleys had won a $105 million judgment against G.M. in 1993. The case was overturned on appeal and a retrial scheduled for late in 1995. The Moseleys and other plaintiffs were influenced by a Department of Transportation action. In December 1994, the Department of Transportation decided to settle with G.M. rather than press its demand that the remaining 6 million trucks with side-mounted gas tanks be recalled. G.M. admitted guilt in unrelated safety cases and paid $51 million in fines. The Moseleys followed the Department of Transportation precedent saying, "The government didn't want to spend the next 10 years in court fighting General Motors and neither did we. We're tired, too."[9] Only cases of economic loss remained in the court system.

In October 1995, the Supreme Court decided not to hear General Motor's request to revisit the issue of the $1,000 coupons. The justices said they would not review a ruling by the Philadelphia federal appeals court covering millions of G.M. customers who said the trucks were diminished in value because of the safety flaws. General Motors said it was disappointed in the Supreme Court action but it seemed likely that the company would not press the matter further in the lower courts.[10]

In July 1996, G.M. agreed to the coupon scheme in which the company would issue more than 5 million $1,000 coupons toward the purchase of a new G.M. car or light truck, except Saturns and electric vehicles. Truck owners who did not want a new G.M. vehicle could sell the transferable certificates. G.M. also agreed to contribute $4.1 million to fund research into

---

[6] F. Swoboda and W. Brown, "G.M. Refuses Request to Recall Pickups," *Boston Globe,* April 10, 1993, p. 1.

[7] A. E. Serwer, "G.M. Gets Tough with Its Critics," *Fortune,* May 31, 1993, pp. 90–97.

[8] N. M. Christian, "G.M. Truck Pact Is Overturned by U.S. Court," *The Wall Street Journal,* April 18, 1995, p. A3.

[9] R. Smothers, "G.M. Settles 4 Lawsuits over Safety of Pickup Trucks," *New York Times,* p. A16.

[10] P. M. Barrett, "G.M. Fails to Persuade Supreme Court to Consider Reinstating Truck Accord," *The Wall Street Journal,* October 3, 1995, p. A3.

fuel-system safety in vehicles built between 1991 and 1996.[11]

In December 1996, a Louisiana judge approved a settlement that required G.M. to pay about $28 million in fees and expenses to plaintiffs' attorneys and former objectors [those who objected to the 1995 settlement] in addition to providing the 5 million $1,000 coupons. Company attorneys said they might appeal the $28 million assessment. This legal battle promises to continue as new lawsuits involving the side-mounted trucks are filed.[12]

---

[11] G. Stern, "G.M. Weighs Appeal of Fees Set by Judge in Truck Pact," *The Wall Street Journal,* December 27, 1996, p. A3.

[12] Ibid.

Questions

1. Did G.M. adopt a wise strategy in dealing with the safety problem?
2. If you were G.M.'s chief counsel, what legal issues would you need to take into account?
3. How should a company handle situations in which public opinion is clearly against them?
4. Was there a single most ethical position open for G.M. to take?
5. How well does the U.S. legal system work in cases such as this?

Product Quality

When producers and consumers talk about *product quality,* they often have very different concepts of the term's meaning. How do managers know when they have made a product of acceptable quality? How can they set product quality goals for their companies and determine when those goals have been met?

Industry discussions about product quality have become tremendously significant in the 1990s. During the 1970s and 1980s, American consumers lost confidence in the ability of the nation's manufacturers to make high-quality products. Japan's success, which came at the expense of U.S. producers, drove home the importance of quality production. Manufacturers and service companies looked back to the postwar period, when product quality advocates were ignored by American manufacturers but eagerly listened to by Japanese companies.

History of Quality Control

W. Edwards Deming. In 1950, W. Edwards Deming became a leader of the Japanese quality-control initiative. Deming exhorted managers on both sides of the Pacific to concentrate on continuous improvement of products and services, to innovate, and to commit resources to ongoing quality improvement. Quality, he stressed, had to be built into all goods and services.

Deming's key to quality management was statistical process control (SPC). Deming acknowledged that some variation from product to product was inevitable, but managers could use statistical probability to distinguish an acceptable variation from a problem situation.[13]

Joseph M. Juran. More than 30 years ago, Joseph M. Juran wrote the *Quality Control Handbook*. He, too, had a significant impact on Japanese quality control. Juran said that *quality* was another term for "fitness for use." This means that people who use a product or service should be able to count on it to perform up to their expectations. If a person ships a package from New York to California, it should arrive within the time period specified by the shipper and in the same condition in which it was sent. Juran identified five major dimensions of fitness for use: quality of design, quality of conformance, availability, safety, and condition after it reached customers' hands. Juran developed an analytical method to identify areas needing improvement. He advocated a cost-of-quality (COQ) accounting system that defined avoidable and unavoidable costs. Avoidable costs resulted from product defects and manufacturing process failures. In other words, with proper quality control, the manufacturer could avoid having to refinish a piece of furniture or a car body. Unavoidable costs were those associated with sampling, sorting, and inspection procedures. Juran assumed that as the number of defects continued to decrease, failure costs approached zero.[14]

Armand Feigenbaum. In the mid-1950s, Armand Feigenbaum introduced the idea of total quality control (TQC). This approach called for the establishment of interfunctional teams from functional business areas such as finance, marketing, engineering, and manufacturing. In Feigenbaum's view, every functional area and activity of the firm should be focused on producing the best-quality product at the best price to the consumer.[15]

David A. Garvin. In the 1960s and 1970s, U.S. companies adopted various quality control procedures but failed to keep pace with foreign competitors in Germany and Japan. In 1987, David A. Garvin noted the United States was falling behind and suggested that companies ask themselves tough questions about how much quality is enough and what quality looks like from the customer's perspective. He proposed eight critical dimensions of quality that could serve as a framework for strategic analysis. Garvin suggested that

---

[13] A. March, "A Note on Quality: The Views of Deming, Juran, and Crosby," Harvard Business School #9–687–011, pp. 1–4.

[14] D. A. Garvin, "Competing on the Eight Dimensions of Quality," *Harvard Business Review*, November–December 1987, pp. 101–9.

[15] R. B. Chase and N. J. Aquilano, *Production and Operations Management: A Life Cycle Approach* (Homewood, IL: Richard D. Irwin, 1989), p. 166.

companies use this framework to explore opportunities to distinguish their products from those of other companies.[16] The following discussion elaborates on this framework.

Eight Dimensions of Quality

Performance. Performance refers to a product's primary operating characteristics. In a bank, for example, it includes how quickly a service representative handles a customer's needs and how efficiently problems are resolved. Consumers judge the performance of a microwave oven by how evenly and quickly it cooks food. To a typical consumer who buys a self-defrosting refrigerator, the fact that the refrigerator keeps food cold and does not build up a wall of ice in the freezer is not sufficient evidence of product quality. Other operating characteristics are whether the compressor is quiet, the motor is energy saving, the refrigerator is easy to clean, and shelves are sturdy and easy to adjust.

Consumers do not always agree on what constitutes high quality in refrigerators, because their needs differ. Some people are more concerned about an appliance that operates quietly than about energy-saving features. Generally good performance includes objective technical attributes of the product as well as subjective personal judgment. Safety is a critical attribute of performance that Garvin does not explicitly include in his formulation. However, if making a refrigerator more energy efficient also makes it more likely to catch fire, the energy-saving quality is negated. As is pointed out later in this chapter, a company ignores the product's or process's safety aspect at its peril.

Features. Features are a product or service's bells and whistles. Sometimes it is difficult to draw the line between a product's primary performance and its secondary features. For example, some consumers have no need for a browning element in a microwave oven because they use the oven only to warm up conventionally cooked food or leftovers. A home computer that has enough power for only word processing may be sufficient for one consumer, but another may need much more power to run graphics software or complex spreadsheets. A customer may use the teller at the bank to process transactions but not use the advice of the bank's service representative on buying certificates of deposit or investing in mutual funds.

To many consumers, the more features built into the product or service, the more favorable their perception. To others, the greater the number of features, the greater the likelihood that something will go wrong. Let us return to our earlier example of the refrigerator and add ice and chilled-water dispensers on the outside door; an ice maker inside the freezer; separate

---

[16] D. Garvin, "Competing on the Eight Dimensions of Quality," pp. 104–8.

butter, egg, meat, and vegetable bins; and an electronic voice that tells the owner when the door has been left ajar. Some consumers would consider the quality of this refrigerator better than that of its basic, no-frills counterpart; others would not. Individual preference thus plays a major role in assessing quality in performance and features.

Reliability. Reliability is the probability that the product will function properly for a reasonable period of time. Even within the same brand, some individual items are more reliable than others. One refrigerator will not need a major repair over its lifetime, while another, of the same brand, will be a constant source of trouble. Items that need very frequent repairs are called lemons. The more features that are built in and the greater the number of interrelated parts that depend on one another to function, the more likely a product is to malfunction.

Unreliable products can result from a variety of factors. The product may be badly designed, materials may be shoddy, workmanship may be poor, or some unexpected variable may crop up in its use. To most consumers, the longer the product is out of service and the more expensive it is to fix, the more important the issue of reliability becomes. If the copier in a busy office breaks down, a restaurant's ovens malfunction, or an airplane's engine stalls in flight, reliability becomes the product's most important attribute. On the other hand, if a light bulb burns out or an electric toothbrush stops working, the consumer's concern about reliability is much less pressing.

Conformance. Conformance is the degree to which the product's design and operation meet established standards. All products have established specifications that constitute a central point. Consumers will tolerate a certain amount of deviation from that point as long as it stays within an acceptable range. Sometimes, consumers tolerate a fairly wide deviance. For example, one can of minestrone soup may have 15 chunks of onion and seven pieces of potato, while another has 12 chunks of onion and nine of potato, yet both are still acceptable to most consumers. At other times, conformance is more important. A person with heart trouble can tolerate only a very small margin of deviation in medication. Also, consumers in different countries have different expectations of conformance. Although Japanese consumers expect every seam of a garment to be stitched perfectly; American consumers are less exacting.

Durability. Durability is the amount of use a consumer gets from a product before it reaches the point at which replacement is preferable to repair. Many consumers make the decision to purchase a particular item or brand on the basis of its estimated life. Retailers and consumer magazines frequently provide information about products' expected longevity. A product's life can be affected significantly by the frequency and intensity of operation and the attention given to its maintenance. A car whose oil is rarely changed breaks down and wears out more quickly than one maintained according to the manufacturer's recommendations. Likewise, a humidifier is less likely to clog up with dust when its filters are changed regularly.

Increasingly consumers are throwing away products they used to repair. Calculators, portable radios, hair dryers, videocassette recorders, and even television sets can cost more to repair than their initial purchase price. In addition, the inconvenience of doing without a product while it is in the repair shop for a long period may be sufficient reason for the consumer to choose to discard it. Even for products that are thrown away, the initial purchase price may have been low enough that the consumer believes the product was of sufficient quality given its features.

In other instances, a consumer or a company discards a product because it has become obsolete. An obvious example is major airlines' substitution of jet planes for propeller-driven aircraft; here, obsolescence was selective. Airlines still use propeller-driven planes for short trips and wherever runways are too short to accommodate jets. Note that faster travel did not make conventional jets obsolete when the supersonic Concorde was introduced. Although the Concorde cut trans-Atlantic flying time in half, other considerations were more important. The Concorde's tendency to make sonic booms, its cramped quarters, and its expensive operation diminished its attractiveness for mass transportation.

Automobile manufacturers used to be extremely successful in persuading consumers that their current cars were obsolete. Some consumers traded in their cars every two years to get the newest style. In 1972, Ralph Nader wrote, "The stylists' . . . function has been designated by automobile company top management as the prerequisite for maintaining the annual high volume of automobile sales—no small assignment in an industry that has a volume of at least $20 billion every year." The stylists are responsible for most of the annual model changes that promise consumers new automobiles. It is not surprising, therefore, to find this newness is almost entirely stylistic in content and that engineering innovation is restricted to a decidedly secondary role in product development.[17]

When styling was the paramount purchase determinant, durability mattered little. Consumers traded in their cars before the autos needed major repairs. As automobiles became more expensive, consumers changed their car-buying habits, however. Many consumers recalculated the elements of product quality. Serviceability, reliability, and performance became more important than style. As this change occurred, Japanese cars became more attractive to a sizable segment of consumers.

Even in the ever-changing fashion industry, consumers are paying more attention to durability in their clothes. In 1987, designers and manufacturers tried to revive flagging sales by switching their new lines from the long skirts

---

[17] R. Nader, *Unsafe at Any Speed: The Designed-In Dangers of the Automobile* (New York: Grossman Publishers, 1972), p. 211.

of the earlier 1980s to miniskirts. In 1993, they switched back to long skirts. To the fashion industry's dismay, women did not replace their wardrobes. They simply added the new long fashions to their existing wardrobes. Some even took their long skirts out of closets where they had been stored for five years or longer. Others wore both short and long skirts interchangeably, no longer looking to designers as arbiters of fashion.

Serviceability. Serviceability is the speed, courtesy, competence, and ease of repair. How much time will it take to fix a broken product? Consumers often find the repair process frustrating and sometimes infuriating. Many consumers feel like the physician who called his plumber on a Saturday to report that the only toilet in the house was stopped up. The plumber advised the physician to drop two aspirins down the toilet and call her on Monday. When repair people are courteous, quick, and efficient, consumers attribute higher quality to the company's product.

Aesthetics. Aesthetics refers to how the product looks, feels, tastes, and smells. Chocolate candy manufacturers always refer to mouth feel in judging quality. High-quality leather goods always have a distinctively appealing scent. Because people have individual aesthetic preferences, companies have to develop their own niches.

Perceived Quality. Consumers often get their information about quality from advertising copy, acquaintances, television, and other indirect sources. Many make buying decisions with imperfect information and sketchy data. Often a product's reputation is based on perceived quality that may in fact belong to an older model or an established company image rather than the intrinsic quality of that product.

Total Quality Management

In the 1960s and 1970s, U.S. industry focused on the cost of making a particular product or service rather than on its quality. Companies believed they had to choose between quality and cost reduction or cost maintenance; when costs went down, profit would increase. Firms made very little effort to involve employees or customers in production decisions. The assumption was that management knew best.

Japanese companies had a different mind-set when they approached cost, quality, and employee involvement issues. Japanese consumers demanded higher-quality products than American consumers. Japanese manufacturers had to ask themselves how they could provide high quality and still keep costs low. Many times, they found that with clever engineering, higher quality could lead to lower costs. Japanese firms looked to their customers' needs to drive quality improvements and were far more customer directed than their U.S. counterparts.

As Japanese productivity continued to improve in the 1970s and 1980s, U.S. performance declined. The three major reasons for Japanese companies' excellent performance were

1. They achieved a major competitive advantage by reducing the time needed to complete processes.
2. They adopted a habit of continuous improvement.
3. They focused first and above all on the customer.

Finally, in the early 1980s, U.S. companies realized that if they were to keep their global market share, they would have to develop new leadership skills. They would have to take a multifaceted approach to the technical, physical, and behavioral aspects of their businesses. By the mid-1980s, *total quality management (TQM)* was touted as the new, best approach to remedy U.S. industries' problems. Typically the major elements of TQM were as follows:

- *Technical expertise,* including just-in-time manufacturing. Companies experimented with reducing lead times, work-in-process inventories, and finished-goods inventories. They demanded that suppliers deliver defect-free parts as they were needed and that suppliers assume the task of inspection before delivery. Predictability and conformance were the watchwords.
- *Organizational development* techniques fostered better team management and greater team interdependence. Management focused on building the interpersonal relationships that would lead to more effective strategic decision making.
- *Strategic approaches* to markets and customers that defined and clarified the important organizational imperatives.
- *Concern for the customer* is the element that makes the organization look outward rather than inward. Companies recognized the negative results from offering poor-quality products. They shared customer feedback with employees so that all organization members could be involved in product improvement.

In short, TQM is a form of organizational change. Organizational change drives the process of quality improvement. Often a change agent triggers the process. The change agent may be a person (usually the CEO), competition, customer demand, a new start-up venture, or a restart. Competitors and demanding customers influence CEOs to change their perceptions and actions.[18]

---

[18] D. M. Lascelles and B. G. Dale, "Quality Improvement: The Motivation and Means of Starting the Process," in *Quality Management Handbook,* ed. M. Hand and B. Plowman (London: Butterworth-Heinemann Ltd., 1992), pp. 22–23.

The Malcolm Baldrige National Quality Award

In 1987, President Reagan's secretary of commerce, Malcolm Baldrige, died in a rodeo accident. An award was established in his memory to encourage American businesses and other organizations "to practice effective quality control in the provision of their goods and services."

Award criteria have two result-oriented goals: to project key requirements for delivering ever-improving value to customers and, at the same time, to maximize the overall productivity and effectiveness of the delivering organization. To achieve these goals, the organization must have in place a set of values that addresses and integrates the overall customer and company performance requirements.

The National Institute of Standards and Technology (NIST), a branch of the Department of Commerce, manages the Baldrige Award. Any for-profit company in the United States or its territories is eligible to apply. Governments—federal, state, or local—are not eligible, nor are not-for-profit companies, trade associations, and professional societies. Each year, two awards for each of these categories may be given: manufacturing, service, and small business (fewer than 500 full-time employees). However, there is no obligation to give all six awards unless companies meet the criteria.

Each fall, NIST chooses a board of examiners from a pool of applicants. The board tries to provide a balance among a number of constituencies such as universities, trade associations, government agencies, health care organizations, and industry. The board of examiners assesses companies' performances in the areas of leadership, information and analysis, strategic quality planning, human resource development and management, management of process quality, quality and operations results, and customer focus and satisfaction.

In the first stage of the award process, the company must pass a review. In the second stage, at least four members of the board of examiners and a senior examiner review each applicant. A panel of judges decides which firms go on to the third stage, the site visit review. In this stage, five board members and a senior examiner visit the site over three or four days to verify information and clarify issues. In the final stage, the panel of judges recommends award recipients to NIST. Then NIST presents the judges' recommendations to the secretary of commerce, who presents the award.[19]

1996 Winners of the Malcolm Baldrige Award. In October 1996, President Clinton and Commerce Secretary Mickey Kantor announced the winners of the Baldrige Award. They were ADAC Laboratories (manufacturing category); Dana Commercial Credit Corporation (service category); Custom

---

[19] Bureau of Business Practice, *Profiles of Malcolm Baldrige Award Winners* (Boston: Allyn and Bacon, 1992), pp. 61–64.

Research Inc. (small business category) and Trident Precision Manufacturing Inc. (small business category). Secretary Kantor extolled the activities of these companies, saying "They represent a new breed of American business, grounded in traditional business values—including putting customers first, trusting employees, building quality into products and services, and being responsible corporate citizens—but with a focus on the future and a passion for continuous improvement. They are models for how people and organizations will operate and work, now and well into the next century."[20]

In its Internet winner profile, Dana Commercial Credit Corporation (DCC) describes its business and details the achievements that led to the award. DCC provides leasing and financing services to a broad range of business customers in chosen market niches. Among other activities, it leverages leases for power generation facilities and real estate properties; customizes programs assisting vendor-manufacturers in selling products such as in-store photo processing labs; and customizes private-label leasing programs that aid computer manufacturers, distributors, and dealers in selling systems.

DCC points to its quality and business performance achievements. Over time it met or exceeded key customer requirements in completing and closing transactions on time. Customers rated DCC services between a 4 and 5 on a 5-point scale. Each DCC employee received 48 hours of education in accounting, law, interpersonal communication, quality, and marketing. DCC promoted all its senior managers and 95 percent of middle managers from within. With more than 2,000 competitors, DCC ranked number 11 with 0.6 percent of the market.[21]

Custom Research Inc. (CRI), an award winner in the small-business category, is a full-service national marketing firm with business-to-business, consumer, and medical market clients. CRI, a privately owned corporation, ranked 36th in size in a $4 billion industry and had 105 employees in three locations in the United States. Since 1988, feedback from clients showed steady improvement and by 1996, 70 percent of clients said the company exceeded expectations. Managing work through technology-driven processes is key to CRI's success. The company uses a nine-step process of delivering customized proposals and projects to clients. Cycle time for data tabulation dropped from two weeks to one day because of integrated software systems. CRI delivered 99 percent of its final reports and 96 percent of its data tables to clients on time. Ninety-four percent of CRI's employees agreed that "All things considered, this is a good place to work." The national norm of employee satisfaction was 76 percent for business service companies.[22]

ADAC Laboratories was the winner in the manufacturing category. This firm designs, manufactures, markets, and supports products for health care

---

[20] Internet [http://www.quality.nist.gov/docs/winners/96win/nist.htm] "Malcolm Baldrige National Quality Award 1996 Winner," p. 1.
[21] Ibid.
[22] Ibid.

customers in nuclear medicine, radiation therapy planning, and health care information systems. ADAC's achievements include a strong customer focus. All executives are expected to spend 25 percent of their time with customers in personal interactions. ADAC measures service quality by its service cycle time, the total time for getting a system back into operation. Since 1990, the average cycle time has declined from 56 to 17 hours. Revenue per employee rose from about $200,000 in 1990 to almost $330,000 in 1995. Overall, ADAC achieved a 65 percent greater efficiency than its nearest competitor. ADAC's employee training and education program is standardized and strongly focused on process. Twice weekly quality meetings are open to all employees, customers, and suppliers.

Trident Precision Manufacturing Inc. was a second winner in the small business category. It is a privately held contract manufacturer of precision sheet metal components, electromechanical assemblies, and custom products. The company develops tooling and processes to manufacture components and assemblies designed by its customers in various industries. Its quality and business performance achievements include a positive trend in on-time delivery from 87 percent in 1990 to 99.4 percent in 1995. Trident's custom products had zero defects between 1993 and 1995. Since 1992, departmental work teams had 100 percent participation. Sales per employee rose from $67,000 in 1988 to $116,000 per employee in 1995. General Dynamics Corp. awarded Trident its Supplier Excellence Award, reflecting strong customer satisfaction. Trident works with potential customers to ensure that no material required for their projects poses safety or health risks.

These four winners all demonstrated continuous improvement in many areas; they met the three national purposes of the Baldrige award:

1. To help elevate quality standards and expectations.
2. To facilitate communication and sharing among and within organizations of all types based on common understanding of key quality requirements.
3. To serve as a working tool for planning, training, assessment, and other uses.[23]

ISO 9000

In 1986, the International Organization for Standardization (ISO) developed five universal quality standards called ISO 9000. The purpose of ISO 9000 is to set common specifications for a wide range of products and services and to accredit those products and services that meet the standards. Countries participating in ISO 9000 include all of the European Community (since 1989), the European Free Trade Association (EFTA), Japan, and the United

---

[23] Bureau of Business Practice, p. 16.

States. ISO is headquartered in Geneva, Switzerland, and is nongovernmental. Although not a part of the United Nations, ISO does have technical liaisons with some UN agencies. As an independent body, ISO has issued more than 40,000 certificates in 95 member countries. Member countries voluntarily participate in nearly 1,000 technical committees and subcommittees that develop and revise international standards covering service industries as well as manufacturing.

Many companies now require their suppliers to become registered with ISO 9000 or 9001. ISO 9001 applies to industries involved in the design and development, manufacturing, installation, and servicing of products or services. A company that complies with ISO 9000 or 9001 promises a solid Quality Assurance System.[24]

Companies begin the accreditation process by consulting a 100-page ISO 9000 guidebook. This book directs companies to document how workers perform every function affecting quality. Then companies institute mechanisms to ensure that workers follow through on stated routines. They develop internal teams to check that procedures are followed in each of 20 functions, including design, process control, service, purchasing, inspection and testing, and training.

When a company decides it has these processes in place and operating, the International Standards Organization sends independent auditors to inspect the company; if it passes, ISO awards the company a certificate of compliance. The auditors are certified by agencies in their own countries; for example, the Registrar Accrediting Board licenses U.S. auditors. The accreditation process can take as long as 18 months to complete and can cost a company more than $200,000.

ISO 9000's underlying concept is that companies can standardize certain generic management practices consistently to produce products at a given level of quality. While ISO 9000 does not mandate that a company raise its quality, it forces the firm to follow a uniform standard in its production.

U.S. companies with European subsidiaries are well aware of the benefits of certification. For example, the 3M subsidiary in France has been responding to its customers' requirement for ISO 9000-registered products since 1989. Additional companies conforming to these standards include Volkswagen, DuPont, Eastman Kodak, Renault, Corning, Exxon Chemicals, Sandoz, and many others. Government ministries and departments also have made ISO 9000 a requirement for their large contract suppliers. The U.S. Department of Defense and the Food and Drug Administration, for example, mandate that their suppliers be registrants.

Pall Corporation of New York recognized the importance of ISO 9000 several years ago. Hyman Katz, corporate vice president of quality assurance and regulatory affairs at Pall Corporation, noted that his company began its

---

[24] Internet [http://www.exit109.com:80/~leebee/] "Welcome to ISO Easy!" p. 1.

efforts to comply with ISO 9000 in its U.K. manufacturing plants in 1987. The company, which makes filters and other fluid clarification devices that remove contaminants, has manufacturing facilities worldwide. If its operations did not comply with ISO 9000, prospective purchasers would not be assured of a fixed standard of quality and might look to Pall's competitors for that assurance.[25]

ISO 9000 requirements contribute to a TQM process, and the process requires documentation and product assessment, two important aspects of TQM. But total quality management goes beyond ISO 9000 by dealing with issues such as leadership, strategic planning, and employee empowerment.

Sybase, Inc:. A Company That Ate the Elephant One Bite at a Time

Located in Emeryville, California, Sybase is the seventh largest software engineering firm in the world. In 1997, it was the only independent company to become ISO 9000 certified in more than 80 percent of its engineering in the United States. Malcolm L. Mcfarlane, vice president of corporate quality at Sybase, Inc., chronicled the company's effective implementation of ISO 9001/TickIT.

The TickIT program was created by the government of the United Kingdom to provide a method for registering the software development systems based on the ISO 9000-3. The ISO 9000-3 standard is entitled "Quality management and quality assurance standards—Part 3: Guidelines for the application of ISO 9001 to the development, supply, and maintenance of software." The TickIT program turns guidelines for the development, supply, and maintenance of software into a compliance standard.

Mcfarlane notes that any mention of ISO boosts attendance at quality seminars; even so, most attendees are predisposed to think of certification as a hopeless thicket of rules and a commitment to large expenditures of money. In his experience, there are major benefits to a software group willing to make an honest investment in ISO 9001TickIT. Mcfarlane says that audits identify weak areas and time schedules are developed to fix problems. "Things get better—all over. No magic, just a company in alignment with its customers and a shared direction for improvement."

Mcfarlane said any champion of ISO 9000 in a software company has to be able to laugh at himself if he wants to champion an ISO 9000 program. As he noted, the comic strip "Dilbert" likened the ISO 9000 directions in the "big honkin' binder" to a "dead raccoon." Mcfarlane believes people lose credibility if they get angry at programmer humor that deprecates the value of ISO 9000. He notes that the ISO golden rule is "if the process doesn't make long-term business sense, stop and rethink your interpretation of the standard and reconsider

---

[25] Bureau of Business Practice, pp. 7–11.

your alternatives." Mcfarlane also mentioned the importance of picking a registrar who will provide flexible but firm added value to the company.

In pursuing ISO 9000 goals, companies often make the following common mistakes. One is setting schedules that are too long. Sybase set a tight schedule; the manufacturing group that was the first unit in the process was certified within six months of starting the process.

A second mistake companies make is to delegate responsibility too low in the organization. Mcfarlane recommends assigning a senior manager at least half time to each major group to be certified. That manager must be accountable for the group's success. Sybase got temporary help from a consultant who translated ISO language and attitudes. More important, however, was that the executives were strongly involved. Sybase established an eight-member steering committee composed of three members of the executive staff, local experts, and management. Project leaders presented their progress and got frequent feedback.

A third mistake that large companies make is trying to train and certify the company all at one time. "Eating the elephant one bite at a time" is the philosophy that works. Mcfarlane notes that early groups provide documentation that can be used by trailing organizations thereby shortening implementation schedules even further. At Sybase, groups that were lagging behind were tightly tracked. If they reported the same scores over time, the steering committee invited them to discuss their issues. In some cases, they were given additional resources.

A fourth mistake is assigning writing procedures to someone already committed to other projects. The best strategy is to dedicate a technical writing resource to the team. Budgets also have to be allocated for ISO-associated activities such as reviews, training, and internal auditing. At Sybase, the first draft of its *Quality Policy Manual* was written in two weeks. Twenty meetings were held, one for each section of the standard, and resources were dedicated to completing the documentation on a tight schedule. A technical writer was assigned to the project to complete the documentation, perform the review process, and implement the documentation delivery system.

A fifth error Mcfarlane noted was that some companies are not doing enough training. Sybase emphasized the importance of determining and making highly visible metrics, such as defects, cycle times, and productivity. Employees got the feeling that ISO really brought improvements rather than empty documentation.

Mcfarlane concluded the process of becoming ISO 9001/TickIT certified was worth the cost and provided a "vehicle for introducing permanent change, measuring its effects, and making it stick." It provided a common language and direction for process and measurement and a long-term positive contribution to the bottom line.[26]

---

[26] Internet[http://www.exit109.com/~leebee/case01.htm] "Eating the Elephant One Bite at a Time."

ISO 14000

The International Organization for Standardization (ISO) had such great success with ISO 9000 that it began to assess the need for international environmental management standards in the following areas: controlled and uncontrolled emissions into the atmosphere, discharges into water, land contamination, and waste disposal. Although many countries already had national and regional standards, ISO formed the Strategic Advisory Group on the Environment in 1991. The group was charged with considering whether an international standard could:

- Promote a common approach to environmental management similar to quality management.
- Enhance organizations' ability to attain and measure improvements in environmental performance.
- Facilitate trade and remove trade barriers.[27]

In 1992 ISO's Technical Board formed a new committee, TC207, to develop standards for environmental management, environmental auditing, environmental performance evaluation, environmental labeling, life-cycle assessment, and environmental aspects in product standards. See Exhibit 15–1 for the proposed standards.

The standards apply to all types and sizes of organizations but do not have absolute environmental performance requirements. Organizations with similar activities but very different environmental management systems and performance still can comply with ISO 14001. Environmental Management Systems (EMS) (ISO14001) require the company to create an environmental policy that is fully supported by senior management. It must outline the policies of the company to the staff and the public and must stress a commitment to continuous improvement in compliance with environmental legislation.

The environmental policy must be written and publicized in nontechnical language to be widely understood. It should provide both an overview of the company's activities on the site and a clear picture of the company's operations. The company must make public the environmental objectives that have the greatest environmental impact. The program constitutes the plan to achieve specific goals or targets on the route to a specific goal and describes the realistic and achievable objectives. The EMS establishes procedures, work instructions, and controls to ensure that the policy is being implemented and that targets are achievable. Periodic audits ensure that the EMS is effective and is meeting specified goals. The audits also provide information on practices that are different from current procedures or offer an opportunity for improvement. A management review process ensures that the EMS suits the company's objectives and is operating effectively.[28]

---

[27] Internet [. . . g.eng.clemson.edu/pub/tqmbbs/iso9000/iso14000.txt] M. Harmon, "First There Was ISO 9000, Now There's ISO 14000," *Quality Digest,* 1994, pp. 1–8.

[28] Internet [http://www.quality.co.uk/quality/iso14000.htm#history], "Introduction."

EXHIBIT 15–1   ISO 1000 Proposed Standards

Standard	Title/Description
14000	Guide to Environmental Management Principles, Systems, and Supporting Techniques
14001	Environmental Management Systems—Specification with Guidance for Use
14010	Guidelines for Environmental Auditing—General Principles of Environmental Auditing
14011	Guidelines for Environmental Auditing—Audit Procedures—Part 1: Auditing of Environmental Management Systems
14012	Guidelines for Environmental Auditing—Qualification Criteria for Environmental Auditors
14013/15	Guidelines for Environmental Auditing—Audit Programs, Reviews, and Assessments
14020/23	Environmental Labeling
	Environmental Labeling—Practitioner Programs—Guiding
14024	Principles, Practices, and Certification Procedures of Multiple Criteria Programs
14031/32	Guidelines on Environmental Performance Evaluation
14040/43	Life Cycle Assessment General Principles and Practices
14050	Glossary
14060	Guide for the Inclusion of Environmental Aspects in Product Standards

Source: Internet [http://www.quality.co.uk/quality/iso14000.htm#history] "ISO 14000 Introduction," p. 4.

Many corporate observers think that ISO 14000 will become the new standard for managing environmental responsibilities. U.S. companies, which were slower than Europeans to adopt ISO 9000 standards, are more enthusiastic about starting early on ISO 14000. Joe Cascio is IBM's program director of environmental health as well as the safety standardization and chair of the U.S. technical advisory group to TC207. Cascio believes, "Major corporations are going to make this [ISO14000] a requirement of their suppliers." Ross Stevens, DuPont's manager of corporate issues agrees, noting his company created a new policy for safety, health, and the environment using early-stage ISO 14000 standards as a guide. Stevens encourages any company to start looking at the standards because customers will demand it. Joel Charm, AlliedSignal's director of corporate occupational health and safety said his company was adding ISO 14000 to its internal audit program "to see where each plant stands." Charm said ISO 14000 "will be a requirement for doing business in Europe" and predicted it will also become a requirement for ISO 9002 certification within a few years. Charm noted that preparing for ISO 9000 certification costs companies about $500,000. In his view, companies already registered by ISO 9000 should have to pay only about $50,000 for ISO 14000 because systems and documentation are already in place.[29]

---

[29] R. Begley, "Environmental ISO Standard Adds to Management Tasks," *Chemical Week*, April 5, 1995, pp. 45–47.

Regulation of Product Safety

Consumers have become increasingly concerned about the safety of the products they buy and use. As we discussed in the previous chapter, the concept that a product should be safe under reasonable use is fairly new, but generally accepted. Manufacturers cannot ignore safety-in-use considerations in their quest to offer products that satisfy other quality dimensions.

In 1972 Congress passed the Consumer Product Safety Act that created the Consumer Product Safety Commission (CPSC). As an independent regulatory body, CPSC is charged with protecting the public against unreasonable risk of injury by unsafe products. The CPSC also supervises regional offices and testing laboratories around the country. Based in Washington, D.C., the commission has five members appointed by the president. Ann Brown has headed the CPSC since 1994. Her recent initiatives emphasize public education, better use of CPSC resources, and redefining the agency's direction. Exhibit 15-2 shows the Consumer Product Safety Commission's organization chart. CPSC's duties are to

- Develop and enforce uniform safety standards for consumer products, including design, construction, content, performance, and labeling.
- Initiate and monitor recalls of products deemed to be hazardous.
- Help industry develop uniform safety standards.
- Help consumers evaluate comparative safety standards of consumer products.
- Promote and conduct research and investigation into the causes and prevention of injury, illness, and death caused by consumer products.
- Help minimize the conflicts among local, state, and federal product safety laws.

In the first six years after CPSC's creation, the commission issued more than 1,200 recalls affecting over 7 million specific products.[30] Recalled products included toys, electrical appliances, and clothing. The commission banned such products as flammable contact adhesives, products containing asbestos, flammable clothing, and unstable refuse bins. Most of these actions resulted from negotiations between the CPSC and the companies producing the products. Of the 600 actions taken by the commission, fewer than 10 required court action.[31]

In 1981, the first year of the Reagan administration, Congress passed Consumer Product Safety Amendments that gave industries the right to develop their own safety standards. The Reagan administration's real goal was to abolish the CPSC, but it settled for slashing the commission's budget and appointing inexperienced commissioners.

---

[30] *New York Times*, February 9, 1979, sec.3, p. 1.
[31] W. Guzzardi, Jr., "The Mindless Pursuit of Safety," *Fortune*, April 9, 1979, p. 60.

EXHIBIT 15-2 Organization Chart for the Consumer Product Safety Commission

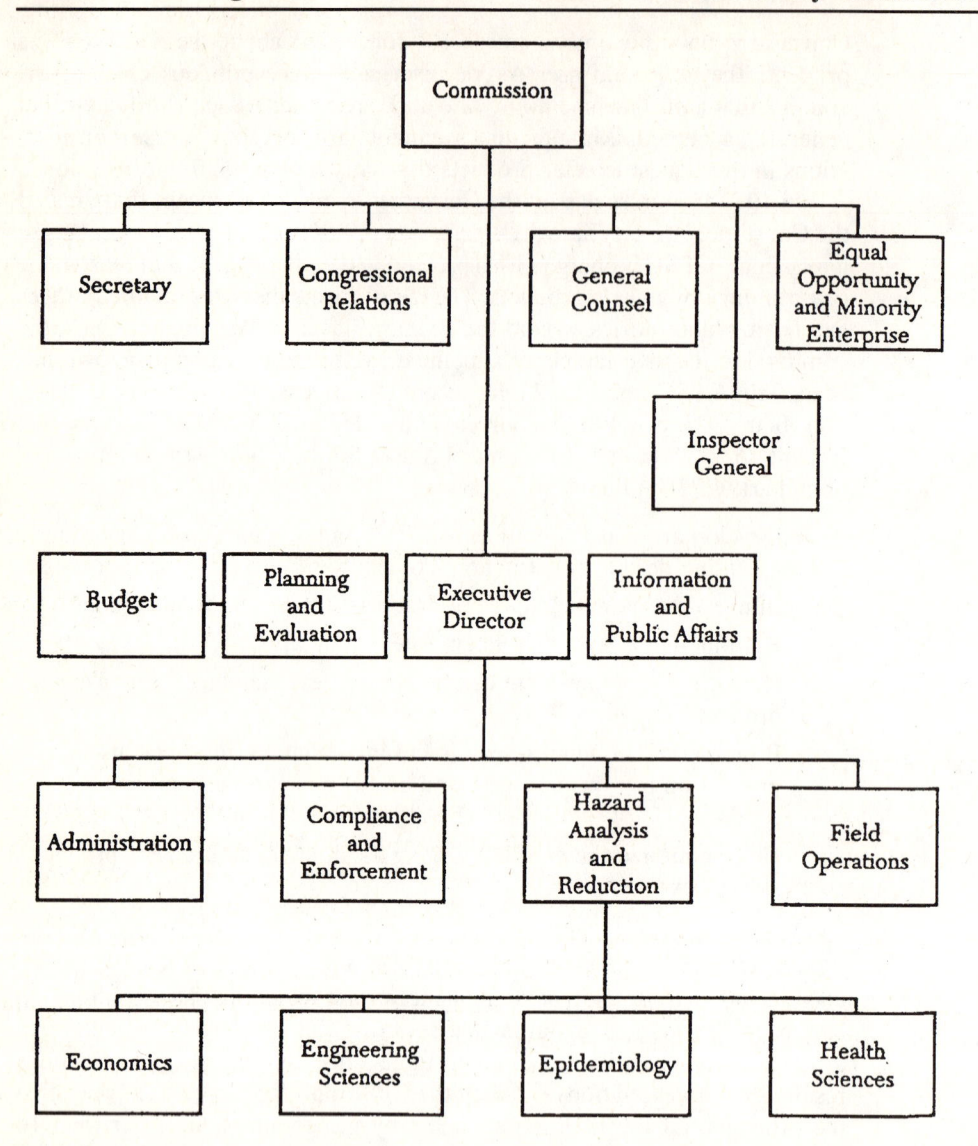

```
                              ┌──────────────┐
                              │  Commission  │
                              └──────┬───────┘
         ┌────────────┬──────────────┼──────────────┬────────────────┐
   ┌─────┴─────┐ ┌────┴──────┐ ┌─────┴─────┐ ┌──────┴──────┐ ┌───────┴────────┐
   │ Secretary │ │Congress-  │ │           │ │  General    │ │Equal Opportunity│
   │           │ │ional      │ │           │ │  Counsel    │ │and Minority     │
   │           │ │Relations  │ │           │ │             │ │Enterprise       │
   └───────────┘ └───────────┘ │           │ └──────┬──────┘ └─────────────────┘
                               │           │        │
                               │           │  ┌─────┴──────┐
                               │           │  │ Inspector  │
                               │           │  │ General    │
                               │           │  └────────────┘
   ┌─────────┐ ┌───────────┐ ┌─┴─────────┐ ┌─────────────┐
   │ Budget  │ │Planning   │ │ Executive │ │Information  │
   │         │ │and        │ │ Director  │ │and Public   │
   │         │ │Evaluation │ │           │ │Affairs      │
   └─────────┘ └───────────┘ └─────┬─────┘ └─────────────┘
         ┌──────────────┬──────────┼──────────────┬──────────────┐
   ┌─────┴──────┐ ┌─────┴──────┐ ┌─┴─────────┐ ┌──┴─────────┐
   │Administra- │ │Compliance  │ │  Hazard   │ │   Field    │
   │tion        │ │and         │ │ Analysis  │ │ Operations │
   │            │ │Enforcement │ │ and       │ │            │
   │            │ │            │ │ Reduction │ │            │
   └────────────┘ └────────────┘ └─────┬─────┘ └────────────┘
         ┌──────────────┬──────────────┼──────────────┐
   ┌─────┴─────┐ ┌──────┴─────┐ ┌──────┴─────┐ ┌──────┴─────┐
   │ Economics │ │Engineering │ │Epidemiology│ │  Health    │
   │           │ │Sciences    │ │            │ │  Sciences  │
   └───────────┘ └────────────┘ └────────────┘ └────────────┘
```

Source: *Federal Regulatory Directory*, 7th ed. (Washington DC: Congressional Quarterly, 1994) p. 59.

Between 1981 and 1989, the CPSC's budget fell from $42.1 million to $34.5 million. In mid-1989, its budget was approximately the same as it had been 15 years earlier.[32] Its staff shrank from 978 members in 1981 to 519 in 1989.[33] When George Bush took office in 1989, the commission had only two members, one of whom was the acting chairperson, Anne Graham. Graham observed that the reliance on voluntary standards became "a signal for everything to go in slow motion."[34]

Over the past several years, consumer groups have criticized the Consumer Product Safety Commission for the length of time it takes to complete investigations. The commission's rules require that it give manufacturers a chance to review and dispute data; CPSC cannot release preliminary data to the public.

To enhance its responsiveness, the CPSC established a toll-free hotline to

1. Report unsafe products or a product-related injury.
2. Find out whether a product has been recalled.
3. Learn how to return a recall product or arrange for its repair.
4. Get information on how to use a consumer product safely.
5. Receive information about ordering CPSC publications.

Consumers can E-mail the CPSC at info@cpsc.gov or access the commission's web page at http://www.cpsc.gov.

The Legal Environment

Prior to 1916, U.S. product liability law was based on the concept of *privity*. Privity meant that if a negligent manufacturer made an unsafe product, the consumer's only legal recourse was to sue the firm. If the consumer bought the product from an intermediary such as a wholesaler or retailer, the manufacturer was immune from liability for negligence.[35] While the privity concept might have been appropriate when a consumer bought a product directly from the craftsperson who made it, it did not serve the public interest in a time of mass production and mass distribution.

The courts ended privity with the case of *MacPherson* v *Buick Motor Company*. In that case the defendant, Buick Motor Company, sold a car to a

---

[32] J. Bodnar, "Whatever Happened to the Consumer Movement?" *Changing Times*, August 1989, p. 50.

[33] M. D. Hinds, "Troubles of a Safety Agency: A Battle to Keep Functioning," *New York Times*, March 18, 1989, p. 52.

[34] Ibid.

[35] R. J. Posch, Jr., *The Complete Guide to Marketing and the Law* (Englewood Cliffs, NJ: Prentice Hall, 1988), p. 3.

retailer who in turn sold it to Mr. MacPherson. As MacPherson was driving the car, one of its wooden wheels crumbled. Buick had bought the wheels from a manufacturer that had not inspected them prior to the sale. The charge was negligence rather than fraud because there was no intent to deceive. Even though it sold the car to a retailer, the court found that Buick was guilty because it was responsible for the finished product and should have tested the component parts.[36] Once privity was no longer applicable, the issue of product safety was thrown open to judicial interpretation.

Theories of Product Liability

Negligence

Negligence is the failure to exercise reasonable care in manufacturing or selling a product, resulting in injury to a person or property. The concept of reasonable care extends to all parts of the production and distribution process, including the salesperson who presents the product to the consumer. For example, if a salesperson overpromotes a product, thereby causing the consumer to overlook warning labels, the salesperson can be found guilty of negligence.

When products are sold to vulnerable consumers such as children or the elderly, companies have to be particularly careful. A company can be guilty of negligence if it fails to warn the user about potential hazards. A company may make a toy that may be perfectly safe for a five-year-old child, but not for her two-year-old sibling. Unless the toy carries a warning about dangers to toddlers, the manufacturer or retailer may be guilty of negligence.

Warnings may not be enough if the product is still dangerous in normal use. The Consumer Affairs Committee of the Americans for Democratic Action published a report in 1988 criticizing the CPSC for pitiful ineptitude in overseeing toy standards. The report asserted that with ordinary use, toys caused 131,000 injuries in 1987. The ubiquitous baby walker alone caused nearly 21,000 injuries.[37]

In 1992, the Institute for Injury Reduction, a nonprofit group founded by trial attorneys, said the CPSC tested fewer than 1 percent of all toys for sale. Its report claimed that in 1991, 67 children were killed by toys and 163,000 were injured. The institute's president urged the Clinton administration to reverse Reagan and Bush cutbacks and give the CPSC more money and staff to expand its testing and recall programs.[38]

---

[36] Ibid., p. 5.

[37] T. Ahern, "Consumer Group Warns Shoppers of Hazardous Toys," *Boston Globe,* November 22, 1988, p. 3.

[38] R. Green, "1 in 6 Toys Tested by U.S. Is Unsafe for Children, Group Says," *Boston Globe,* November 19, 1992, p. 6.

In mid-1992, the Consumer Product Safety Commission decided not to ban balloons, marbles, small balls, crayons, and other toys that failed to carry labels warning that toddlers could choke on the objects. According to statistics, less than one death results from the sale of 1.5 billion marbles each year, and an average of six deaths occur from yearly sales of 1.2 billion balloons.

The CPSC decided the effectiveness of warning labels could not be demonstrated for these products. It also noted that studies of labeling indicate it has no effect on the use of common products that have obvious hazards. The CPSC staff concluded multiple warning labels would be necessary for any product that contains both marbles and balloons or balloons and small balls.[39]

Toy labeling has gotten more and more explicit as manufacturers try to protect themselves against lawsuits. In 1997, a Batman costume had the following label: "PARENT: Please Exercise Caution—FOR PLAY ONLY: Mask and chest plate are not protective: cape does not enable user to fly." The Snow Works Super Boggan, a simple four-foot plastic sled had a large warning label glued near the top. It advised users to wear a protective helmet at all times, to allow no more than three riders at a time, and not to ride "while lying on the stomach or back or while standing." The warning label exhorted the sledder to avoid trees, stumps, rocks, branches, or man-made obstacles, and not to use the sled near streets, roadways, or driveways because "it does not have brakes." In addition, the user should not use "any motorized or nonmotorized vehicle" to pull the sled.[40]

To avoid accusations of negligence, manufacturers are labeling every product possible with the most obvious warnings. In 1997, about 90 percent of product liability cases filed included an allegation that a manufacturer had failed to warn the consumer of significant and foreseeable dangers.[41] There is considerable debate over whether consumers read all these warnings. Roger L. McCarthy, a human-factors engineer who studied the relationship between people and products collected more than 3,500 articles about the effectiveness of warning labels. So far, McCarthy has not found one reliable study that documented a reduction in accidents because of a warning on a product.

A Washington lawyer who defends companies against product liability claims said that juries have become much more sympathetic to injured plaintiffs over the past two decades. A company's best defense is a good warning that accomplishes three things: gets the consumer's attention, describes the danger in vivid terms, and gives specific information on how to avoid the injury.

The 1995 Child Safety Protection Act required retailers and manufacturers to report any hazards to the CPSC as soon as they were aware of it—even

---

[39] C. Lochhead, "Child Safety Bill Is Hard to Swallow," *The Wall Street Journal,* July 7, 1992, p. A14.

[40] J. M. Broder, "Warning: A Batman Cape Won't Help You Fly," *New York Times,* March 5, 1997, p. A1.

[41] Ibid.

if no one had been injured—or face a maximum $125 million penalty. Anxious to avoid bad publicity or law suits, companies quickly acted on their own. Toy makers, consumer groups, and government agencies agreed that the greatest danger to children was parents or other child minders who inadequately supervised the age-appropriateness of toys or ignored warning labels.[42]

Design Defect

Manufacturers are legally bound to design products with reasonable care. Even if a product is carefully made, it may be defective because it is unreasonably dangerous to use. Manufacturers are responsible for anticipating the way a product will be used and designing it so it can be put to use safely. Manufacturers are not expected to use designs that are impractical or prohibitively expensive; therefore, a balance exists between the likelihood that injury will occur and the cost of taking precautions to ensure that it does not.

The Case of Automobile Air Bags. Federal and auto industry officials first suspected that air bags could injure or kill children and small adults almost 30 years ago. However, the government did not disclose the information because it wanted to win public acceptance of air bags, thinking the benefits would outweigh the negative consequences. Industry sources were no more forthcoming than the government. A 1969 research paper by General Motors noted that "a small child close to an instrument panel from which an air cushion is deployed may . . . be severely injured or even killed."

In 1991 the National Highway Traffic Safety Administration (NHTSA), an agency under the Transportation Department, warned parents that children in infant safety seats should not be placed in the front seat where an air bag could deploy. NHTSA officials met with auto executives to assess several years of road-testing cars with air bags. At the meeting, NHTSA said it was aware of a few cases in which the deployment of an air bag was believed to cause the death of an occupant at crash speeds slower than 10 miles an hour. A NHTSA memo of the meeting showed that federal and industry officials agreed that "the potential for bad press in these few cases could cause a lot of harm to the public's positive perception and receptiveness to air bags." Finally in 1996, NHTSA publicly stated that air bags could cause injuries and death.[43] The air-bag standard required bags powerful enough to protect an unbelted dummy the size of an average man in a 30-mile-per-hour head-on crash. On impact, the bag opened with a burst of speed up to 200 miles per hour.

In November 1996, NHTSA decided to allow drivers to have air bags disconnected and to permit manufacturers to make air bags that inflate more

---

[42] A. Brooks, "Warnings on Toys Are Often Ignored, Causing Injuries," *New York Times,* March 13, 1997, p. C2.

[43] W. Brown and C. Skrzycki, "Air-Bag Risk Seen since '69," *Boston Globe,* p. C1.

slowly. The decision to allow manufacturers to make a slower-inflating air bag represented a safety trade-off. Unbelted adults had less protection in high-speed crashes but slowly inflating bags were less harmful to children and small adults in lower-speed accidents. NHTSA also announced plans to require automakers and their suppliers to make smart air bags and install them in cars and trucks sold in 1998. The new air bags would automatically tailor their deployment to individual crash circumstances and the size of the occupant. These smart bags would have ultrasound sensors to transmit sound waves to determine the size and position of the occupant. The sensors could even tell whether a child was facing forward or backward. Another sensor in the front of the car could tell seat belts to tighten before an impact. A dual-stage air bag could inflate in several stages depending on how severe the crash was and whether the occupant's belt was fastened.[44] Discussions about air bags and children's car seats were linked because the standard air bag could injure or kill a child in its car seat even when that seat was secured to the front seat of the vehicle.

Early in 1997, federal regulators decided to change the way children were strapped into cars. The National Highway Traffic Safety Administration reported that 80 percent of child seats were secured in cars incorrectly. The agency estimated 600 children under five years of age died each year in crashes because they weren't properly restrained. Most child seats were strapped in by belts designed to fit loosely around an adult until there was a crash. Child seats were not held tight enough and allowed the child and the seat to move in a crash.

NTSHA proposed rules backing a General Motors design that changed the way safety seats were attached to the cars. The new design required carmakers to install fixtures so that the seats would no longer depend on seat belts. Instead, new child seats have two straps that buckled to latches mounted between the seat cushion and seat back. A tether strap attached to the top of the child seat would hook onto a spot near the rear window to reduce the child's head movement in a crash. G.M. estimated its proposal would increase the cost of a $55 seat to $100 but would add little or nothing to the purchase price of a car.[45]

In March 1997, regulators came under pressure from automobile and insurance companies objecting to the Clinton administration's proposal to let auto mechanics and dealers disconnect air bags. NHTSA found itself caught in a policy debate between liability and personal choice. Ford, Chrysler, General Motors, and Allstate, fearing they would be held responsible for injuries if air bags were disconnected, pressured the agency not to implement the new rule. In a letter to Transportation Secretary Ronald Slater, executives

---

[44] R. Meredith, "U.S. Agency Plans to Reduce Danger Posed by Air Bags," *New York Times,* November 23, 1996, p. 1.

[45] A. Q. Nomani, "Regulators Plan Safety Rules for Child Seat," *The Wall Street Journal,* February 13, 1997, p. B1.

of 26 companies representing auto, insurance, and air bag interests argued that air bags were designed to work with seat belts; as a result, consumers would not be properly protected by their seat belts if they disconnected their air bags. Automakers said the best way to handle the situation was to instruct parents to buckle their own seat belts and secure the children in the rear of the car.[46]

On March 14, NHTSA told car manufacturers they were now permitted to make bags that opened with less force. Automakers were pleased with the new rule that allowed them to reduce air bags' force by up to 35 percent. They said the change would be made on all cars by the end of the 1988 model year. Dr. Ricardo Martinez, the agency administrator said the change would "preserve the benefits of air bags while minimizing the risk to children and smaller adults."

Consumers Union and other safety advocates said NHTSA had taken the wrong approach. They pointed out that many air-bag deaths came from crashes at low speeds, sometimes less than 10 miles per hour. The new rule set no minimum speed below which the bag would not deploy. They suggested the government require manufacturers to install air bags that would not open in low-speed collisions.[47]

The discussion of air bags and child safety was far from over. All sides agreed that children should be placed in the rear of a car in a seat firmly secured to the automobile frame and that all adults should wear safety belts at all times in a moving vehicle. However, the various factions could not agree on the degree of responsibility the individual consumer should assume. Should manufacturers be required to supply sufficient restraint in cases where consumers refused to take responsibility for their own and their children's safety?

Warranty

A *warranty* indicates the seller's willingness to stand behind its product. A seller that issues a written warranty assumes responsibility for a specific time for the quality and suitability of the goods sold. A written warranty must be given at the time of sale and must be a part of the sale; the consumer must not have to pay any additional fees for the warranty.

Sellers are not required to offer warranties regardless of the price or type of product. Once the seller issues a written warranty on a product that costs more than $10, however, that warranty must be designated as a full or a limited warranty. A *full warranty* promises the consumer that a defective product will be replaced or fixed in a reasonable period of time. A *limited*

---

[46] A. Q. Nomani and G. Stern, "Clinton's Air-Bag Proposal Faces Delay by Regulators after Industry Pressure," *The Wall Street Journal,* March 11, 1997, p. A5.

[47] M. L. Wald, "New Government Rule Seeks to Stem Danger from Air Bags," *New York Times,* March 15, 1997, p. 11.

warranty promises less than the stipulations of a full warranty. For example, a seller may decide to issue a limited warranty that covers parts but not service.

Strict Liability

Under strict liability standards, the company is held to more exacting standards than it is under negligence or design defect standards. The quality of the product is the key issue.[48] A manufacturer of a defective product may be held responsible for an injury caused by a product "regardless of privity, foreseeability, or due care."[49] The injured party must show only that the manufacturer or seller was connected with a defective product, the product was dangerous when it was sold, and it caused injury. Under strict liability, everyone in the distribution chain is responsible for the safety of the product.

The United States has the most litigious legal climate in the world. Courts have been willing to compensate injured parties with huge settlements. Although Vice President Dan Quayle railed against the legal profession and large monetary awards in the Bush administration, he was unsuccessful in effecting change. The 1994 Republican Congress tried to pass legislation to cap punitive damages. The Senate and House each produced versions of bills that curbed product liability lawsuits. President Clinton vowed to veto any measure that limited damage awards in lawsuits over faulty products. The discussion over a product liability law that would be acceptable to the administration and Congress continued into Clinton's second term with no resolution in sight.

---

[48] F. W. Morgan, "Marketing and Product Liability: A Review and Update," in *Contemporary Moral Controversies in Business,* ed. A. P. Iannone (New York: Oxford University Press, 1989), pp. 353–64.

[49] Posch, *The Complete Guide,* p. 14.

CASE: CELLULAR PHONES AND ELECTROMAGNETIC FIELDS: ARE THESE PHONES SAFE?

Cellular phones were sold commercially for the first time in 1984. By November 1992, more than 10 million people subscribed to the service. In January 1993, David Reynard of St. Petersburg, Florida, appeared on CNN's "Larry King Live" show. Reynard announced he was suing a phone maker, NEC America, and a GTE subsidiary, GTE Mobilnet. He asserted his wife had developed brain cancer and died because she used a cellular phone.

A few days later, Reginald Lewis, chairperson of TLC Beatrice Company, died of brain cancer and Michael Walsh, a top executive at Tenneco, Inc., was diagnosed with the disease. People also remembered Lee Atwater's death from brain cancer; as George Bush's campaign manager, Atwater had used a cellular phone incessantly.

Cellular phone transmitters operate at very high frequencies at one-half to three watts of power. Unlike car phones and low-powered cordless home phones, cellular phones place the radio transmitter beside the user's head. Scientists know radio waves enter the brain as they seek out the nearest transmitter site, but they do not know whether those waves are harmful.

Most research has centered on the effects of low-frequency electromagnetic radiation from power lines and video display terminals rather than from cellular phones. Scientists do agree that cellular phones create only a negligible risk due to heat or thermal damage to tissues. There are no hard data on the effects of radio waves from cellular phones, however.

Within hours after Reynard's charges were made public, cellular phone manufacturers vehemently denied the product posed health risks. Edward F. Staiano, president of the cellular phone division of Motorola, said independent studies showed "no existence of health risks from the use of cellular phones." His judgment was echoed by the president of a communications market research firm, who called the charges a tempest in a teapot.[50]

Scientists pointed out that consumers are exposed to the dangers of electricity in many other ways and recommended means to avoid exposure. M. Granger Morgan, head of the Department of Engineering and Public Policy at Carnegie Mellon University, offered some tips for avoiding electric and magnetic fields (EMFs):

- Don't use electric blankets, electric mattress pads, or waterbed heaters. Older designs of these products create strong magnetic fields. If you are determined to warm your bed, preheat it, then unplug the devices. Remember that newer devices have low-field electricity.
- Don't sleep next to bedside clocks or fans. They also produce strong magnetic fields.
- Switch to wind-up clocks, or place motorized clocks across the room.
- Ask your local utility company to measure electric fields around your bedroom, and place your bed in the area of the lowest field.
- If you use a computer, put at least 24 inches between you and it. Get strong reading glasses if you need them to see the screen.
- Don't stand near your dishwasher, refrigerator, clothes dryer, or oven.
- Don't use a hair dryer.

Morgan acknowledged at the bottom of his list, "once you have done whatever seems reasonable to you, then it is probably wise to forget about it."[51]

Shifting the public's attention to the dangers of other products did not stop the cellular phone controversy. Cellular phone companies hastened to assure consumers that health risks were minimal. However, the companies acknowledged they were caught in a dilemma. They had no way of knowing whether the health risk was real or imagined. They had to decide quickly whether to address negative news stories or ignore the issue. In fact, there was very little information, either positive or negative, to report. Could the

---

[50] "Motorola Denies Cellular Phone Risk," *New York Times,* January 26, 1993, p. D7.

[51] "Some Tips to Reduce Exposure to Electricity," *USA Today,* February 4, 1993, p. 13A.

firms be held legally responsible if sued for selling an unsafe product? Had they protected themselves against problems that might surface years later?

In mid-1994, the National Cancer Institute (NCI) announced it would conduct a comprehensive study of the environmental and genetic causes of brain cancer. Researchers planned to address the question of whether hand-held cellular phones contributed to the disease. They planned to collect information on handheld, car, or transportable cellular phone use; duration of use; and frequency of use. They planned to make a distinction between cordless phones commonly used in homes and cellular phones operating at a higher frequency and power. A final report was expected sometime in 1997.[52]

Cellular phone use has spread remarkably in recent years but there is currently very little discussion of its potential danger. Apparently, the cellular phone scare did not have staying power because people find it difficult to believe danger exists if they cannot see, feel, hear, or smell it or if the consequences are deferred.

At the end of 1996, the public concern over the hazards of electromagnetic fields seemed to be resolved. A three-year study by a 16-member panel of the National Research Council concluded that evidence "does not show exposure to these fields presents a human-health hazard." The panel noted an enormous paradox however. Children living near high-current power lines in Denver got leukemia at 1.5 times the expected rate. The study found that the higher a house's rating, the greater the chance a child would get leukemia. However, when the researchers measured EMFs, they found that fields were no higher in homes with leukemia cases than in homes without. The studies were forced to use a stand-in for EMF exposure. It was nearly impossible to continuously monitor actual EMFs inside thousands of homes and to reconstruct the past exposure of a child who contracted leukemia. The stand-in was a wire-code rating that reflected a home's distance from a power line and the size of wires close by. Some panel members suggested other risks might account for the findings on childhood leukemia. High ratings were characteristic of older homes, homes in dense developments, and homes in high-traffic areas. They urged further study taking these factors into account. As the NRC noted, it found an absence of proof, not proof of absence of risk.[53]

To avoid all sources of electromagnetic exposure, a person must stop using or alter the use of the conveniences that make life pleasant and easy, with no assurance that the effort is worthwhile.

---

[52] Internet [http://graylab.ac.uk/ NCI_To_Study_Brain_Tumors_and_Their_Causes.html]

[53] D. Glick and M. Hager, "The Force Is with You," *Newsweek*, November 11, 1996, p. 67.

Questions

1. Should cellular phone companies lease or sell their products if they cannot guarantee their use will not harm consumers?
2. Is a warning label on the headset sufficient to absolve the companies from responsibility?
3. Based on the information in the case, would you stop using a cellular phone if you had one? If not, what data would convince you to stop?

Summary

The term *product quality* has many meanings; however, some basic elements and criteria define product quality. Until the 1990s, the issue of product quality was taken more seriously in Japan and Europe than in the United States. The dimensions of quality are performance, features, reliability, conformance, durability, serviceability, aesthetics, and perceived quality.

Total quality management (TQM) became a national obsession in the late 1980s as American companies lost market share. The major elements of TQM are technical expertise, organizational development, strategic approaches, and concern for the external customer. Many companies have applied for the Malcolm Baldrige Award for Quality. The award process is difficult and time-consuming, but it provides important organizational feedback.

Companies are using ISO 9000 and ISO 14000 standards as benchmarks for quality worldwide. ISO 9000 is the standard the European Community uses across countries to ensure standardization of quality, and ISO 14000 ensures environmental quality. U.S. companies and government agencies are adopting the standards to enhance their competitiveness abroad.

Product quality and TQM are liability and safety concerns as well as competitive issues. A good quality-management program considers how and by whom the product will be used and whether such use will be safe. Such a program will not sacrifice safety for other elements of performance. Unsafe products, as well as poor-quality products, negatively affect a firm's profits.

The Consumer Product Safety Act created the Consumer Product Safety Commission (CPSC) to enforce uniform safety standards, monitor product recalls, help develop safety standards, evaluate safety standards, promote safety research, and minimize legal conflicts. Over the years, its activities have responded to political pressures and funding concerns.

Privity was the original legal basis for product liability law. When privity was eliminated as a legal concept, product liability law developed on a state-by-state basis. The theories of product liability include negligence, design defects, warranty, and strict liability.

Liability laws are in a state of transition. Although the Reagan, Bush, and Clinton administrations tried repeatedly to pass a uniform federal law, stakeholders successfully thwarted those efforts. There is still no resolution although all sides vow they want to reduce the huge sums awarded by courts.

Questions

1. What are the basic elements of product quality?
2. What is the significance of the Malcolm Baldrige Award? What benefits accrue to the winners?
3. How are ISO 9000 standards important to U.S. competitiveness?
4. How are ISO 14000 standards important to U.S. competitiveness?
5. What are the duties of the Consumer Product Safety Commission as delegated by Congress? How effective has the commission been?
6. What is the legal concept of privity?
7. What are the theories of product liability?
8. Are manufacturers of marbles or balloons exercising reasonable care when they make those products? Should a toy store be charged with negligence if it sells a marble or balloon to a parent whose child puts it in his mouth and chokes? What constitutes reasonable care in making and selling these products?

Projects

1. Suppose you are a toy manufacturer. Write an executive memo to your staff defining what product safety should mean in your industry.
2. Talk to a lawyer in your city or town who deals in product safety issues. Ask her what legal trends seem to be emerging.
3. Call your state legislator's office and find out your state's laws regarding product safety.

BETA CASE 15
PRODUCT USE ISSUES

Robert Mobley, general counsel for Beta, was having a terrible day. Not only was the March downpour flooding his new basement family room, but problems were mounting at the office. In January, Mobley was notified that one of Beta's products, E-Targa, a form of vitamin E, may have been responsible for the deaths of four premature babies in a Boise, Idaho, hospital. Beta, which had distributed the solution to hospitals the previous July, at first attributed the deaths to routine nursery problems. In August and September, when other hospitals began to report deaths, Beta took the solution off the market. Now, Mobley discovered, parents of the infants had filed a class-action suit against Beta.

Vitamin E is an important nutrient for premature babies, but it is not very effective when taken orally. Babies' immature stomachs cannot handle oral doses, and their limited muscle area makes intramuscular injections impractical. E-Targa, however, was in a solution that could be injected directly into the veins.

Beta had not sought Food and Drug Administration (FDA) approval for E-Targa because, in Mobley's opinion, the drug was not new. Although the means of dispensing it to infants was an innovation, the substance was simply a variation of others that had been on the market for years.

When Beta found out about the deaths in January, Mobley recommended the company not inform the FDA. According to the law, any company that markets a product needing federal approval must report severe reactions within 15 working days of its discovery. Since Beta had not asked for or received approval for the drug, the reporting requirement was not clear.

Doctors at the Boise hospital did not raise a red flag by reporting the deaths to the FDA. They did call the regional FDA office to find out whether E-Targa had been approved, but they did not mention any problems. They also notified a prominent pediatrician whose close ties to the FDA, they thought, would lead him to inform the agency.

The Food and Drug Administration had been told repeatedly that the solution was being marketed without approval, but it took no action until it learned about the mounting death toll. FDA officials explained that vitamin E had been used safely for decades and that its intravenous form was similar to that of other vitamin E products. Moreover, the entire class of vitamins was under review, and it would be premature to act on an individual vitamin.

Now, Mobley mused, he, Beta's board of directors, and Brian Madison would have to decide how best to handle the impending lawsuits.

PART V

THE ENVIRONMENT

The two chapters in Part Five cover the critical topics of the domestic and international environments. Governments, corporations, special interest groups, and individuals are concerned about the problems of our shrinking ozone layer, toxic waste disposal, and the disappearing rain forests even as they create and perpetuate those problems. Stakeholders have tremendous potential to either ameliorate or exacerbate environmental problems.

Managing the environment is a global problem that becomes increasingly difficult as economic development progresses. Without a doubt, economic development has improved the standard of living of people around the world. As Exhibit V shows, however, economic development has come at a high cost to the environment. Even though the World Bank published this exhibit's information in 1992, the world still faces significant environmental problems that adversely affect health and productivity.

Despite the lack of a global system of regulation to deal with environmental issues, countries are forging multilateral agreements as they seek to create international guidelines for environmental remediation. Although experts disagree about the effectiveness of Earth Summit meetings and treaties, there is no doubt that concern is widespread and growing.

EXHIBIT 16–V **Principal Health and Productivity Consequences of Environmental Mismanagement**

Environmental Problem	Effect on Health	Effect on Productivity
Water pollution and water scarcity	More than 2 million deaths and billions of illnesses a year attributable to pollution; poor household hygiene and added health risks caused by water scarcity.	Declining fisheries; rural household time and municipal costs of providing safe water; aquifer depletion leading to irreversible compaction; constraint on economic activity because of water shortages.
Air pollution	Many acute and chronic health impacts: excessive urban particulate matter levels are responsible for 300,000–700,000 premature deaths annually and for half of childhood chronic coughing; 400 million–700 million people, mainly women and children in poor rural areas, affected by smoky indoor air.	Restrictions on vehicle and industrial activity during critical espisodes; effect of acid rain on forests and water bodies.
Solid and hazardous wastes	Diseases spread by rotting garbage and blocked drains; risks from hazardous wastes typically local but often acute.	Pollution of groundwater resources.
Soil degradation	Reduced nutrition for poor farmers on depleted soils; greater susceptibility to drought.	Field productivity losses in range of 0.5–1.5 percent of gross national product (GNP) common on tropical soils; offsite siltation of reservoirs, river-transport channels, and other hydrologic investments.
Deforestation	Localized flooding, leading to death and disease.	Loss of sustainable logging potential and of erosion prevention, watershed stability, and carbon sequestration provided by forests.
Loss of biodiversity	Potential loss of new drugs.	Reduction of ecosystem adaptability and loss of genetic resources.
Atmospheric changes	Possible shifts in vector-borne diseases; risks from climatic natural disasters: diseases attributable to ozone depletion (perhaps 300,000 additional cases of skin cancer a year worldwide; 1.7 million cases of cataracts).	Sea-rise damage to coastal investments; regional changes in agricultural productivity; disruption of marine food chain.

Source: *World Development Report: Development and the Environment* (New York: Oxford University Press, 1992), p. 4.

CHAPTER 16 ENVIRONMENTAL ISSUES

CASE: BUYING AND SELLING THE RIGHT TO POLLUTE

In the summer of 1991, the Chicago Board of Trade voted to create a private market for buying and selling rights to emit sulfur dioxide. The Clean Air Act of 1990 required the Environmental Protection Agency (EPA) to allot pollution allowances to individual plants. A unique feature of this act was the provision that a plant exceeding clean air requirements could sell pollution rights, while a plant that did not meet those requirements could buy those rights rather than having to invest in additional pollution control equipment. To see how the trading system works, see Exhibit 16–1.

The act left to power station operators the task of deciding how to meet clean air requirements. The clean air allowance program has two phases:

- *Phase I* took effect in 1995 and required the 110 most heavily polluting power plants in 21 states to reduce their total sulfur dioxide emissions to about 60 percent of their aggregate 1980 levels of 8.9 million tons a year.
- *Phase II* takes effect in the year 2000 and affects about 800 additional, less heavily polluting, plants. Phase II cuts annual sulfur dioxide emissions to less than half of their 1980 level.[1]

---

[1] B. Durr, "Creating a Future for Pollution," *Financial Times*, July 24, 1991, p. 8.0

The Chicago Board of Trade devised a plan that would permit it to begin trading cash forward contracts in 1993. These contracts were promises to deliver allowances after the EPA issued them in 1995. The Chicago Board of Trade also asked the Commodity Futures Trading Commission for permission to establish an ongoing futures market that would allow anyone to gamble on emissions rights in 25-ton allotments up to three years in advance.

In theory, a utility might buy 100 contracts due in 1999. The utility would then have the right to emit an extra 2,500 tons of sulfur dioxide that year. A potential seller might be the owner of an old coal plant due to be closed in

Exhibit 16–1 The Pollution Rights Trading System

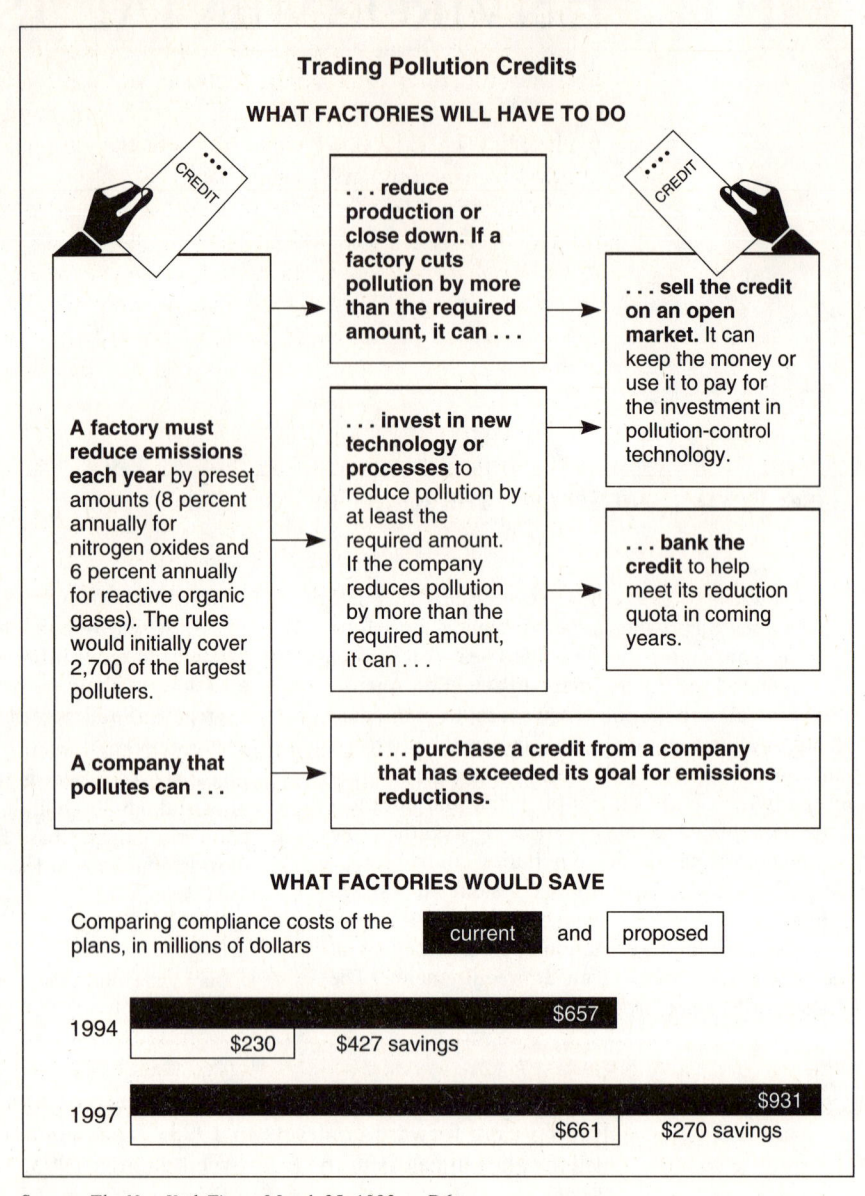

Trading Pollution Credits

WHAT FACTORIES WILL HAVE TO DO

A factory must reduce emissions each year by preset amounts (8 percent annually for nitrogen oxides and 6 percent annually for reactive organic gases). The rules would initially cover 2,700 of the largest polluters.

A company that pollutes can . . .

. . . reduce production or close down. If a factory cuts pollution by more than the required amount, it can . . .

. . . invest in new technology or processes to reduce pollution by at least the required amount. If the company reduces pollution by more than the required amount, it can . . .

. . . purchase a credit from a company that has exceeded its goal for emissions reductions.

. . . sell the credit on an open market. It can keep the money or use it to pay for the investment in pollution-control technology.

. . . bank the credit to help meet its reduction quota in coming years.

WHAT FACTORIES WOULD SAVE

Comparing compliance costs of the plans, in millions of dollars — current and proposed

1994: $657 / $230 $427 savings

1997: $931 / $661 $270 savings

Source: *The New York Times,* March 25, 1992, p. D6.

1999. Another participant in the market might be the mutual funds manager of a brokerage house; she may expect the price of allowances to fall and be prepared to gamble the assets of the fund.

Experts estimated that contracts initially would trade at about $400 per ton, although their value might fluctuate with the changing demand for electricity or with new developments in scrubber technology. The price per ton would not exceed $2,000 because that was the amount of the fine for each ton emitted over a company's legal limit.[2]

In March 1992, the state of California decided to adopt a market approach to pollution. The South Coast Air Quality Management District began to work out the details. Exhibit 16-1 shows what factories would have to do and what they would save by adopting the plan. The underlying principle was to reduce total emissions in the most cost-effective way.[3] The district also planned to allow trading in emissions of hydrocarbons, nitrogen oxide, and sulfur oxide by 1994.

Wisconsin Power and Light Company entered into a deal to sell pollution rights to the Tennessee Valley Authority (TVA) and Duquesne Light Company in Pittsburgh. In May 1992, the TVA bought from Wisconsin Power and Light the right to emit 10,000 tons of sulfur dioxide. Wisconsin Power and Light, which had shifted to a lower-sulfur fuel, agreed to reduce its emissions 10,000 tons below the requirements of the 1990 Clean Air Act. The TVA got additional time to install scrubbers or replace the sulfur dioxide with cleaner fuel. Duquesne Light Company bought the right to emit up to 25,000 tons of sulfur dioxide.

The state of Massachusetts also hopped on the emissions trading bandwagon by setting up a stock market-like system to buy and sell emission rights. The Massachusetts plan was similar to the Chicago Board of Trade model but did not include a formal auction; instead, trading would be left to private brokers. The Massachusetts system allowed trade in all kinds of pollution in addition to sulfur dioxide.[4]

The first Chicago Board of Trade auction took place on March 29, 1993. By this time, the EPA had distributed 5.7 million permits among the 110 worst polluters. Each permit allowed a discharge of 1 ton of sulfur dioxide per year to be used between 1995 and 2000. The auction was based on sealed bids from power companies, coal producers, environmentalists, and smokestack industries. When the auction was over, traders discovered that successful bids ranged between $122 and $439 per ton of sulfur dioxide. Experts agreed the prices were substantially lower than the cost of developing technology for reducing emissions under the 1990 Clean Air Act.

---

[2] P. Passell, "A New Commodity to Be Traded: Government Permits for Pollution," *New York Times,* July 17, 1991, p. A1.

[3] R. W. Stevenson, "Trying a Market Approach to Smog," *New York Times,* March 25, 1992, p. D1.

[4] S. Allen, "State Touts Give-and-Take on Clean Air," *Boston Globe,* January 8, 1993, p. 1.

There have been unexpected consequences of the trading mechanism. In New York, a utility cleaned up more than required and made the excess emission credits available to utilities in the Midwest. New York State tried to intervene because Midwestern emissions were blown right back into New York.[5]

How well has the market worked? When Congress was debating emissions limits, utilities predicted that a 1-ton allowance would sell for $1,000 or more; some even said $1,500. The Environmental Protection Agency said $500 to $600 was more realistic. In 1995, the price of a 1-ton allowance was less than $140. In 1992, when the first trades were made, the price was $250 and prices have dropped steadily since. A columnist for *E/The Environmental Magazine* concluded the market for the right to pollute had hit rock bottom. He noted that the 1996 auction drew as many buyers from high-school ecology clubs, and environmental groups as serious utilities.[6]

Environmental groups, led by Greenpeace, adopted the strategy of buying pollution rights then retiring them. For instance, businesses in Los Angeles must acquire smog credits for the right to release pollution into the air. The credits are traded on an open market, but the total number decreases each year. This system raises the prices and gives business incentives to conduct cleaner operations. A California Group called SmogBusters buys credits from the Los Angeles smog market and retires them with the Air Quality Management District so they can never be used again. SmogBusters announced in 1996 that it planned to buy more credits from the market, removing nitrogen oxide and sulfur oxides from the air.[7]

An official of the federal General Accounting Office admitted that the trading system needed "fine-tuning and more effective regulations to ensure that emissions really are reduced." He observed, "Right now, there's no guarantee about where the allowances are going. A pattern of trading could develop in which one region of the country suffers over another."[8]

---

[5] M. L. Wald, "Acid-Rain Pollution Credits Are Not Enticing," *New York Times,* June 5, 1995, p. A11.
[6] Internet [http://www.emagazine.com/2curr3.html], J. Bradley, "Buying High, Selling Low," *E/The Environmental Magazine,* July–August 1996.
[7] Internet[http://www.voyagepub.com/publish/stories/0996air0.htm]
[8] Internet[emagazine]

Questions

1. If the pollution rights trading concept is broadly applied, what result will the market produce?
2. What are the implications of this plan for labor? Will companies sell their pollution rights, close plants, and move to Mexico or other developing countries where pollution is less controlled?
3. Could this pollution permit model apply to automobile emissions? What elements would such a plan entail?
4. What potential does this model have for global or regional agreements, such as NAFTA?

History of Air and Water Pollution

Pollution and cities developed together. In the first century B.C., the Romans built one of the first sewer systems to protect Rome's municipal water supply. In the 13th century, London had such a severe smoke control problem that city officials passed a law forbidding the burning of coal when Parliament was in session. By the 18th century, most large European cities were still drawing drinking water from rivers. Sewers did little to remove the effluvia from city streets.[9]

As the Industrial Revolution gathered steam in the 1830s, industrial pollution began in England and Scotland. Factory jobs brought many people into cities ill-prepared to house them. These jobs also brought sickness and pestilence. To employers, workers' health problems were important only because they interfered with worker productivity. In the early 19th century, town leaders passed strict environmental controls. Gradually, as controls became more expensive to implement, industrialists pressured officials to allow increasing amounts of solid waste particles to be released into the air and water.

In the United States, pollution and industrialization also went hand in hand. Factories and cities dumped untreated sewage directly into lakes and rivers. Regular epidemics of typhoid, yellow fever, and dysentery ravaged 19th-century American cities. As industrialization progressed through the 20th century, smoke and chemical by-products poured out of pipes and chimneys, automobile exhausts filled city streets with haze, and hazardous waste dumps proliferated.

In the mid-1960s, environmentalists and other concerned stakeholders, realizing environmental pollution could irrevocably damage the nation's natural resources and the health of its people, began to pressure Congress for remedial legislation. The environmental movement and subsequent regulation came out of the same ideology that led to the establishment of regulatory bodies, such as OSHA, EEOC, CPSC, and others discussed in earlier chapters.

At first, environmental regulatory groups were scattered among government agencies and executive departments. They did not work closely with one another, nor did they coordinate activities. Finally, in 1969 and 1970, Congress reorganized environmental affairs oversight into two bodies, the Council on Environmental Quality (CEQ) and the Environmental Protection Agency (EPA).

---

[9] F. Braudel, *Capitalism and Material Life, 1400–1800* (New York: Harper & Row, 1973), pp.159–62.

Regulatory Agencies

Council on Environmental Quality (CEQ)

In 1969 Congress established the three-member Council on Environmental Quality (CEQ). As part of the executive office, the council's task was to recommend to the president new policies for improving environmental quality. CEQ also administered the environmental impact process when federal agencies prepared their statements. The council's role was limited to the executive branch, and the council was not involved with industry or with other stakeholders.

Environmental Protection Agency (EPA)

Prior to 1970, separate programs for control of air pollution, water pollution, pesticides, radiation, and waste management were scattered among independent agencies and executive departments. President Nixon sent to Congress a reorganization plan that combined all programs into a new, single agency, the Environmental Protection Agency (EPA). The EPA is now an independent agency in the executive branch; its organization and reporting relationships are depicted in Exhibit 16–2.

The EPA's mission is to control and lessen pollution in the areas of (1) air, (2) water, (3) solid waste, (4) pesticides, (5) radiation, and (6) toxic substances. Congress charged the EPA with integrating efforts in research, monitoring, standard setting, and enforcement. In short, the EPA was "designed to serve as the public's advocate for a livable environment."[10]

The EPA encourages voluntary compliance by government agencies, private industry, and communities. It also urges state and local governments to meet local standards. The EPA is authorized to intervene if state and local agencies fail to develop or implement effective plans to reduce pollution. The EPA's Office of Enforcement and Compliance Monitoring oversees enforcement activities. It gathers and prepares evidence and conducts enforcement proceedings for water quality, air pollution, radiation, pesticides, solid waste, toxic substances, hazardous waste, and noise pollution.[11]

The EPA starts enforcement proceedings by notifying an alleged polluter of a violation. If the violation is not corrected, the EPA begins informal negotiations with the polluter. If the situation cannot be resolved, the hearings become public. Finally, the EPA can initiate civil proceedings in a U.S. district court to force compliance. It can file criminal charges if a polluter engages in certain activities, including willfully discharging waste into waterways, dumping toxic waste, and deliberately falsifying environmental reports.

---

[10] U.S. Government Manual (revised June 1988), p. 527.

[11] "Environmental Protection Agency," *Federal Regulatory Directory,* 6th ed. (Washington, DC: Congressional Quarterly, 1990), pp. 71–105.

EXHIBIT 16–2 Environmental Protection Agency

U.S. Environmental Protection Agency

- Administrative Law Judges
- Cooperative Environmental Management
- Civil Rights
- Executive Support Office
- Small and Disadvantaged Business Utilization
- Executive Secretariat
- Science Advisory Board
- Pollution Prevention Policy
- Environmental Appeals Board

ADMINISTRATOR / DEPUTY ADMINISTRATOR

- Associate Administrator for Regional Operations and State/Local Relations
- Associate Administrator for Communications, Education and Public Affairs
- Associate Administrator for Congressional and Legislative Affairs

- Assistant Administrator for Administration and Resources Management
- Assistant Administrator for Enforcement
- General Counsel
- Assistant Administrator for Policy, Planning and Evaluation

- Assistant Administrator for International Activities
- Inspector General
- Assistant Administrator for Research and Development

- Assistant Administrator for Air and Radiation
- Assistant Administrator for Prevention, Pesticides and Toxic Substances
- Assistant Administrator for Water
- Assistant Administrator for Solid Waste and Emergency Response

- Region I Boston
- Region II New York
- Region III Philadelphia
- Region IV Atlanta
- Region V Chicago
- Region VI Dallas
- Region VII Kansas City
- Region VIII Denver
- Region IX San Francisco
- Region X Seattle

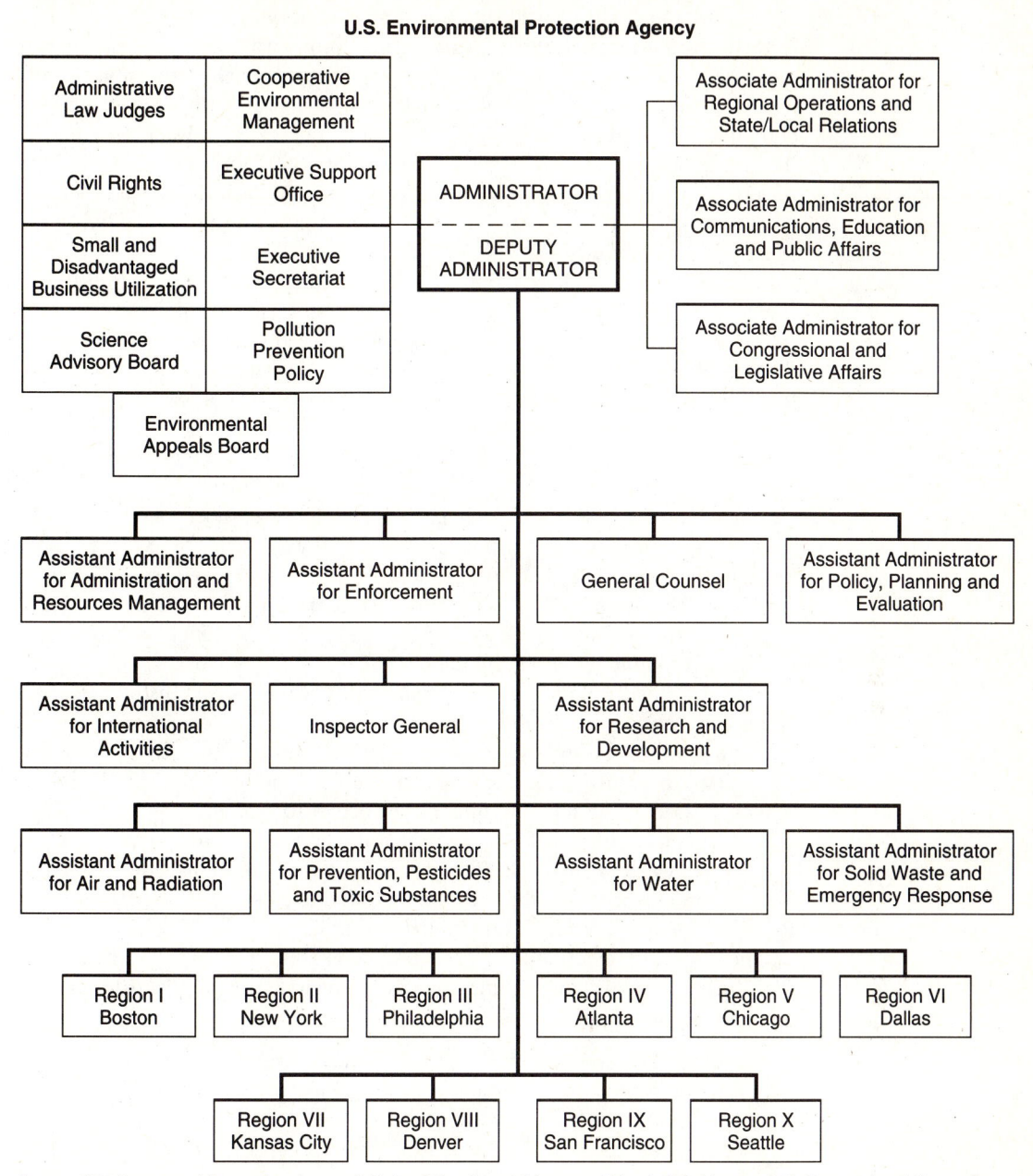

Source: "Environmental Protection Agency," *Federal Regulatory Directory,* 7th ed. (Washington, DC: Congressional Quarterly, 1994); p. 91.

EPA History. During the 1970s, the EPA actively designed and implemented environmental policy but in the early 1980s, the agency became highly politicized and fractious. EPA administrator Anne McGill Burford was very critical of environmental laws. Claiming she simply was applying cost-cutting measures to reduce the agency's budget, Burford slashed the number of enforcement cases slated to be heard by the courts. She insisted voluntary compliance with regulations was preferable to coercion. In December 1982, the House of Representatives cited Burford for contempt for refusing to turn over documents on Superfund management. Although the action was subsequently dropped, the EPA suffered tremendous political damage. Finally, in March 1983, Burford resigned.

William Ruckelshaus, who was the first administrator of the EPA in 1970, replaced Burford. He led the agency into a quieter, scandal-free period, although the Reagan administration largely ignored many of his recommendations. Ruckelshaus was very frustrated by his inability to get the administration to address certain issues such as acid rain. How to allocate the cost of cutting sulfur dioxide emissions was at the heart of the problem. The Reagan administration took the side of the coal and utility industries, maintaining there was insufficient data about acid rain to warrant intervention.

In November 1984, Ruckleshaus resigned and was succeeded by Lee M. Thomas who stepped up the agency's activities. During 1987, the EPA brought the largest number of legal actions in its history, referring 372 civil cases and 59 criminal cases to the Justice Department.[12] Nevertheless, environmentalists continued to charge that the EPA favored business, while industrialists complained incessantly about unreasonable controls.

George Bush, who stressed environmental affairs during his presidential campaign, chose William Reilly to head the agency. The former president of the Conservation Foundation and the World Wildlife Fund, Reilly was the first person from the conservation community appointed to the EPA in its 19-year history. The new administration began to formulate policy to deal with the main problems of the environment: clean air, clean water, and toxic and nuclear waste. During the four years of the Bush administration, Reilly's views often clashed with those of industry and even more heavily with Vice President Quayle's Council on Competitiveness.

Following his election in 1992, Bill Clinton appointed Carol M. Browner, Florida's secretary of environmental regulation, to lead the EPA. Administrator Browner issued her priorities:

- To quicken the pace of EPA decision making across a wide range of issues from water pollution to pesticide use.

---

[12] P. Shabecoff, "EPA Set in Pollution Cases," *New York Times,* December 9, 1988, p. A24.

- To improve management of the Superfund used to clean up toxic waste and end monetary waste. (We discuss this fund later in the chapter.)
- To restore credibility to the EPA and its programs.[13]

Within a few weeks of taking office, Browner concluded the EPA had a total lack of management. She found agency contracts suffered from cost overruns and highly paid professionals caring for lab animals. Millions of dollars had been misallocated and improperly spent in laboratories across the United States.

Experts on the environment shared Browner's view. They noted that environmental laws developed since 1980 had created a tangle of regulations that cost industry more than $100 million per year and cost the government $40 billion annually. Many of the laws were not backed by sound research or cost-benefit analysis.

Industry leaders, government officials, and environmentalists all argued for a new environmental policy that was more reflective of real risk than of the public's perception of risk. All observers agreed the toxic waste program and the Superfund were the most wasteful programs of all.

Administrator Browner discussed the agency's priorities and accomplishments in *The U.S. EPA's 25th Anniversary Report, 1970–1995*. She stressed the EPA's commitment to reinventing the way it provided environmental protection and explored new directions to implement programs "fairer, faster, and more cost-efficiently." Reinvention meant focusing on results and providing flexibility and incentives to encourage innovative solutions. Browner stressed the need to form co-regulatory partnerships with states and Native American tribes. She also wanted to find ways to make it easier to implement integrated approaches for managing environmental quality at facility, industry, and community levels.[14]

Clean Air

The first major federal legislation for controlling air pollution was enacted in 1955. It left most of the responsibility for clean air to individual states. States were required to file State Implementation Plans (SIPs) to show how they would meet acceptable concentrations of particular pollutants. In 1970, Congress passed the Clean Air Act. The act mandated federal regulation and enforcement of federal air quality standards and emission thresholds

---

[13] K. Schneider, "New Type of Watchdog for the EPA," *New York Times,* December 17, 1992, p. B20.

[14] Internet[http://www.epa.gov/25year/intro.html]

through the EPA. States were still required to develop their own SIPs and work with the EPA to achieve them.

Congress passed a subsequent Clean Air Act in 1977, but implementation stalled. Interagency conflict, which had lessened after Burford's departure, reemerged. Industry dragged its heels and state plans were routinely delayed. An EPA official observed, "We were beset with interagency politics, and we just stopped requiring states to provide attainment demonstration. Since we have not pressured the states, the states have not pressured industry."[15]

In the 1980s, the EPA devised two mechanisms to foster industry compliance. First, some plants were allowed to pretend they operated under a bubble. They could measure the total quantity of pollution gathered under the bubble rather than the quantity emitted by each smokestack. They could then use their own discretion in working toward reducing total pollution. The second mechanism allowed companies to buy and sell pollution credits. If a company shut down a smokestack that emitted particulate matter, it could sell that amount of pollution credit to another company that could use the credit instead of reducing its own pollution.

In 1987, Congress began to push for more and stricter clean air laws. States cracked down on the dirtiest polluters, the steel and utility companies. This flurry of activity was due in part to the development of new technology that could pinpoint polluters more precisely and clean up emissions more efficiently. Although the 1977 act badly needed revising, Congress was unable to muster enough support to do so.

In 1989, after more than a decade of legislative stalemate, the Bush administration declared, "we will make the 1990s the era for clean air," and proposed a greatly revised Clean Air Act. The proposal addressed three critical clean air issues:

- *Acid rain.* The plan suggested a 10-million-ton (nearly 50 percent) reduction in emissions of sulfur dioxide from coal-burning electric power plants by the year 2000. It also proposed a 2-million-ton-per-year (1 percent) reduction in nitrogen oxides. When midwestern smokestacks emit sulfur and nitrogen oxides, the emissions travel long distances and change chemically. Eventually particles fall on Canadian and Northeast lakes and forests as acid rain, snow, or smog. Under the proposed law, companies would be free to decide how to meet EPA goals. They could use scrubbers that chemically remove sulfur residue from smokestacks; they could burn coal with lower sulfur content; they could encourage consumers to conserve electricity; or they could adopt new technologies.

- *Selling the right to pollute.* As we discussed earlier in the chapter, polluters who exceeded the reduction requirements could sell or

---

[15] C. H. Deutsch, "The Pollution Hounds Get Ready to Pounce," *New York Times,* September 6, 1987, p. F6.

transfer their pollution rights to other companies within the same state. The pollution rights would be bought and sold like securities, with brokers managing the parties.

- *Ozone reduction.* Ozone in the stratosphere protects the earth from harmful ultraviolet radiation. On earth, ozone is a main component of smog and causes serious respiratory problems. Sunshine acts on nitrogen oxides and volatile organic compounds to produce what an environmental physician called "pound for pound . . . by far the most toxic of the usual outdoor pollutants."[16] Motor vehicle exhausts, bakeries, dry cleaners, petroleum refineries, and paint shops all contribute to ozone pollution. New measures would place stricter controls on motor vehicle tailpipe emissions and encourage the use of clean-burning motor fuels like methanol. The 20 cities with the worst ozone problems would have to reduce pollution by 3 percent per year.

As soon as the Bush proposal became public, stakeholders such as members of Congress, environmentalists, and state officials pointed out its shortcomings. Most contended it did not go far enough in limiting automobile emissions. Some criticized possible loopholes in smog reduction. The congressional Office of Technology Assessment reported the EPA was overly optimistic and unrealistic about how rapidly cities could reduce urban ozone pollution.[17] On the other hand, some industry spokespeople, especially automobile manufacturers, asserted the measures were too burdensome. As Congress began its debate on the new bill, the only issue on which all stakeholders agreed was that strict and prompt measures to restore clean air were critical.

The Clean Air Act of 1990

On November 16, 1990, George Bush signed the first new clean air act in 13 years. The proposed acid rain provision went into effect along with the permits to pollute. The early estimate of the initial price to pollute of between $1,000 and $2,000 per ton was grossly inflated, as noted in the case at the beginning of the chapter.

The ozone depletion provision mandated the complete phaseout of chemicals that deplete the ozone layer by the year 2000. Motor vehicles had to conform to new standards. The Clean Air Act lowered the limit on smog producing hydrocarbon emissions by 40 percent and nitrogen oxide emissions by 60 percent. A new program phased in alternative-fuel cars for fleets. The act mandated onboard canisters to trap vapors during refueling and doubled extended warranties on emissions control equipment to 100,000 miles. The act also required factories to install technology to reduce the release of nearly

---

[16] E. Faltmayer, "Air: How Clean Is Clean Enough," *Fortune,* July 17, 1989, p. 59.
[17] "Bush's Clean-Air Plan Is Seen Falling Short," *Boston Globe,* July 18, 1989, p. 58.

200 toxic chemicals by the year 2000. Finally, chemical safety boards would be formed to investigate chemical release accidents.[18]

Late in 1996, the EPA recommended tighter national standards for emissions of the chemicals that form smog and soot; see these in Exhibit 16–3. Under the proposal, hundreds of communities that complied with the Clean Air Act could fall out of compliance. The EPA estimated that more than 100 million people would be affected by the new rules and the steps needed to meet the goals would cost between $6.6 and $8.5 billion a year for at least a decade. The agency estimated the benefits would be between $51 and $112 billion a year, mostly in the form of reduced medical costs and lower absenteeism from work and school and because tens of thousands of premature deaths linked to particulate air pollution would be averted.[19] Browner asserted that "this is one of the most important decisions I will make to protect public health in this country." The new standards, which changed the premise upon which clean air standards were based, had to be reviewed by both houses of Congress and the courts before they could be implemented.

Within days after the new guidelines were issued, John H. Chafee (R-Rhode Island) questioned whether the health benefits of the stricter standards were great enough to justify the cost. In a draft letter to Carol Browner, Senator Chafee called for setting aside the Clean Air Act's presumption that quality air standards were to be based on public health considerations, not costs. He noted that a 1995 law gave Congress the right to review all new major federal rules and to block those that were too big a burden on business.[20]

The discussion over the proposed legislation was not scheduled to reach closure before fall of 1997 and political jockeying would go on even longer. Regardless of the outcome of this particular program, there was no doubt that the nation's air was cleaner than it had been 25 years earlier. In December 1996, the EPA announced that U.S. air overall was about 30 percent cleaner than it had been in 1971. There were dramatic declines in sulfur dioxide emissions that contributed to acid rain. Increased use of cleaner-burning reformulated gasoline contributed to a sizable drop in the number of toxic air pollutants. The concentration of carbon monoxide, mainly from automobile exhausts, fell 10 percent between 1994 and 1995, its biggest year-to-year drop.[21]

---

[18] M. Kranish, "Bush Signs Historic Clean Air Act," *Boston Globe,* November 16, 1990, p. 3.

[19] J. H. Cushman, "Administration Issues Its Proposal for Tightening of Air Standards," *New York Times,* November 28, 1996, p. A1.

[20] J. H. Cushman, "Surprise Senate Challenge to Pollution Plan," *New York Times,* December 7, 1996, p. 8.

[21] Nation's Air 30 Percent Cleaner than 25 Years Ago, EPA Reports," *Boston Globe,* December 18, 1996, p. A29.

EXHIBIT 16-3 Sorting It Out
Understanding the Ozone and Particulate Pollution Standards

	Existing Standards	Proposed Standards	Health Effects	Where It Comes From
OZONE A highly irritating, colorless gas that is the main component of smog. It is formed by reactions between nitrogen oxides and hydrocarbons in the atmosphere. Near the ground, ozone is a serious pollutant, not to be confused with the stratospheric ozone layer that protects the earth from ultraviolet radation.	Ozone should not be allowed to exceed 120 parts per billion in the air for one hour.	Would limit this kind of pollution to 80 parts per billion over an eight-hour period.	Ozone and fine particles can both damage lung tissues and aggravate existing respiratory diseases, such as asthma and bronchitis. Children, outdoor workers, and the frail elderly could be especially at risk from breathing polluted air.	Hydrocarbons like the volatile organic compounds that evaporate from petroleum products and nitrogen oxides that come from burning fossil fuels can form into both ozone and particulate matter. There are many other sources of particulate matter, and both types of pollution come generally from combustion of fuels by power plants, factories, and automobiles.
PARTICULATE MATTER These complex mixtures of particles and vapors can be emitted directly into the air or are formed in the atmosphere when chemicals like hydrocarbons, sulfur oxides and nitrogen oxides combine.	Limited to 10 microns in diameter or less (a human hair is about 70 microns thick), to no more than 150 micrograms per cubic meter of air measured daily and an annual average of no more than 50 micrograms per cubic meter.	Would limit smaller particles, of 2.5 microns or less, to concentrations of 50 micrograms per cubic meter daily and 15 micrograms per cubic meter annually.		

Source: "Sorting It Out," *New York Times*, November 28, 1996, p. B20.

The Clean Car

In 1991, California passed a clean air act that was far more stringent than the federal act passed a year earlier. By 2003, all new cars sold in California can produce no more than one-fifth of the pollution emitted by 1991 automobiles.

California quickly became the laboratory in which carmakers experimented in making the automobile of the future. None of the major manufacturers was willing to give up a market of 1.7 million car and truck sales per year. The manufacturers realized the California law represented the wave of the future and its standards were likely to be adopted in much of the United States and eventually overseas. Any company that achieved a technological breakthrough in reducing pollution would have a competitive advantage.

By the end of 1994, some state law makers and governors were in open revolt about the EPA requirement that emissions testing be done only at central testing sites. The agency believed the central site was more effective in measuring tailpipe emissions than neighborhood gas stations where cars in many states were tested. Administrator Browner capitulated to the states' objections to the new requirement fearing the issue would spark a debate in Congress about amending the Clean Air Act. The EPA agreed that states would be given several options. A state could require that only older, presumably dirtier-running cars go to the central site. Under one option, some cars that failed at a central facility and were repaired at the neighborhood service station, could be retested at the same station.[22]

Automakers tried electric power, methanol power, natural gas, and other systems using fuel cells. To use any of these new power sources, nearly all the parts that powered the car, from fuel injection systems to hoses, had to be redesigned. The major carmakers settled on these alternatives as the most promising.

Electric Cars. Electric cars, which run on batteries, produce no emissions at all; in fact, some prototypes have no exhaust pipes. Electrically powered cars require different motors, drivetrains, and battery systems than conventional automobiles. In 1991, the average operating cost of an electric car was estimated at 25 to 36 cents per mile. The cars had a driving range of 50 to 120 miles before they had to be recharged for six hours. Fiat's Electra was the only electric car on the market made by a major manufacturer. Retailing for $22,000, the Electra had a top speed of 45 miles per hour and ran out of power after 100 miles.

Batteries were the major environmental problem posed by electric cars. Existing electric car batteries were filled with toxic lead acid, cost about $1,500 each, and had a lifetime use of 2,000 miles. Early in 1992, ABB Asea

---

[22] M. L. Wald, "EPA to Allow Flexibility in Auto Emission Testing," *New York Times*, December 10, 1994, p. 8.

Brown Boveri, a Swiss–Swedish company, and Britain's Chloride Silent Power, Ltd., began pilot production of a more ecologically sound, lightweight, sodium-sulfur battery. Test results were promising and it appeared a commercial product could be ready by 1994.

In April 1993, the Big Three automakers announced they were discussing collaborating to build an electric car. All three companies already had expensive prototypes with limited driving range and high price tags compared to conventionally powered autos. The last time these companies had worked together was in the early 1960s, when the first pollution control rules were proposed. At that time, the Justice Department raised antitrust questions that led the companies to drop their joint effort. In 1984, the rules were changed, and today manufacturers are exempt from antitrust complaints as long as they notify the Justice Department and the Federal Trade Commission of their activities in advance. As managers of the carmakers pointed out, there was no possibility of antitrust violation because there was no market to monopolize.

By the end of 1995, the Big Three automakers were battling behind the scenes for domination of the emerging market for so-called zero-emissions vehicles. They still presented a united front in the fight against state laws that required them to sell electric cars beginning in 1998. The American Automobile Manufacturers, the trade organization, argued that batteries were too weak to appeal to consumers because cars ran only about 100 miles before needing to be recharged. The association also claimed the electric car would cost $20,000 more than a comparable gas-powered car.

Privately, the Big Three told California regulators they could begin selling the cars in 1996. Company representatives told the California Air Resources Board they could mass produce up to 5,000 electric cars in late 1996 and 1997, and another 14,000 in 1998. Automobile company officials saw no contradiction between their campaign against sales quotas and their readiness to sell electric cars. They argued that they wanted to develop a business in electric cars but not be governed by state rules.[23]

Governor Pete Wilson, looking at a run for the presidency, began to back away from the California requirement that by 1998, 2 percent of all cars sold in the state be electrically powered. Wilson urged the California Air Resources Board to prepare a rule to suspend the requirement and to gradually increase production of zero-emissions vehicles to 10 percent by 2003. The new proposal also called for automakers to stop spending millions of dollars trying to defeat the zero-emissions vehicle requirements. In 2003, all car companies that sold more than 3,000 vehicles a year statewide would have to comply with the regulation. Automakers immediately applauded the move but critics in California and elsewhere were outspoken in their opposition. The executive director of the California Public Interest Research Group

---

[23] S. Allen, "Automakers Race to Rule Market in Electric Cars," *Boston Globe*, December 5, 1995, p. 1.

accused Governor Wilson of "selling out the environment, high-tech business, and consumers to support his generous patrons in the oil business."

The federal Clean Air Act gave states the choice of either following its rules on automobile emissions or adopting California's which were the strictest in the nation. Massachusetts and New York officials who had promised to follow California's lead in moving to electric-powered cars, expressed their disappointment in the Wilson plan. Governor William Weld of Massachusetts was quoted as saying, "We think the California Air Resources staff made the wrong decision, but that decision does not bind Massachusetts." Governor George Pataki, whose mandate on electric cars was tied to California's actions, expressed his support for the previous policy but experts noted it could mean that New York law would change automatically, requiring a return to the previous 2 percent level.[24]

In January 1996, General Motors unveiled its electric Saturn EV1 passenger car. The EV1 was equipped with standard features such as dual air bags, antilock brakes, CD player, and cruise control. G.M. said the car would be priced in the mid-$30,000 range and would be marketed primarily to male professionals interested in the new technology and anxious to adopt the latest electronic hardware. G.M. Chairman John Smith called it a car for "people who never want to go to a gas station again." He said that when auto industry historians looked back they would see this car as the first in a new generation of vehicles. G.M. planned to offer the car to customers in warm climates. The energy needed to heat the passenger compartment made the car impractical elsewhere.

General Motors also planned to market an electric truck in the 1997 calendar year. The truck would be marketed first to government agency and utility company fleet buyers. It would look like all other Chevrolet S-Series pickup trucks but would be powered by a battery pack located under the vehicle.[25]

In mid-February 1996, G.M. announced that initially EV1s would be leased, not sold. The car's program manager said, "There are so many things in this car that when it comes to the finance side, we wanted to keep things simple. We wanted the driver to feel as little risk as possible." Saturn planned to treat EV1 drivers as members of an exclusive club. Lease fees were planned to run between $450 and $600 a month. A separate company, Edison EV, would lease the home chargers.[26]

On March 29, 1996, the California Air Quality Board voted to substantially water down its requirement for electric vehicles over the next several

---

[24] L. M. Fisher, "California Is Backing Off Mandate for Electric Car," *New York Times*, December 26, 1995, p. A14.

[25] B. Skillman, "G.M. Announces Plans for Electric Cars," *The Weekly Tab*, January 30, 1996, p. 1, Transportation Section.

[26] R. Blumenstein, "G.M. to Lease, Rather than Sell, Electric Cars," *The Wall Street Journal*, February 15, 1996, p. B6.

years. The new rules eliminated the earlier requirement that 2 percent of California's vehicles sold in 1998 and beyond be zero-emission. The Air Resources Board directed its staff to sign a memorandum of agreement between California and seven auto manufacturers to establish a technology partnership. The partnership would put nearly 3,750 zero-emission vehicles on California roads by 2003. The agreement also committed automakers to marketing cars nationally by 2001 that met tougher emission standards than currently required for new California cars. The vote did not affect the requirement that 10 percent of all new cars and light trucks sold in California be electric beginning in 2003.[27]

As the EV1 and other electric cars were test driven and came on the market, they received mixed reviews. The EV1's performance was enthusiastically received. One driver noted the EV1 gave a swift, silent, and vibration-free driving sensation. He reported the car was almost as different from an internal combustion car as a computer was from a typewriter. He also noted there was no maintenance schedule. There was no oil to change, and no air filters, spark plugs, or fan belts to replace. There was no timing belt, no muffler, no fuel injection, no clutch or transmission, and no fuel line to freeze in the winter. An average driver who drove 36,000 miles could expect to spend about $80 on wiper blades and windshield washer fluid.[28]

A columnist for *U.S. News & World Report* called the EV1's performance in traffic stunning. Like other reviewers, he noted that the car's driving range was limited by its battery power. G.M. said the 2,970-pound car should go 70 miles in the city and 90 on the highway before needing to be recharged. When the air conditioner was used, the car went just about 40 miles before it needed recharging. The reviewer noted that when he had driven Ford's experimental Ecostar electric vehicle under similar conditions it went more than 80 miles around town but was powered by a very expensive experimental battery that could not yet be produced commercially. The four-passenger Honda EV due to come on the market in 1997 could go 125 miles without a recharge but reportedly had glacial acceleration.

In this reviewer's view, electric cars were not a sure thing. Although EVs were likely to get a great deal of news coverage, "it's unlikely that a car with the throaty throb of a V-8 engine will soon seem as quaint as a locomotive that goes 'choo-choo-choo.'"[29] A writer for *Financial Times* noted that the public's adoption of electric vehicles would be slow until there were a sufficient number of recharging stations along the road.

---

[27] F. Rose, "California Eases Environmental Rules for Introduction of Zero-Emission Autos," *The Wall Street Journal,* April 1, 1996, p. B8; M. L. Wald, "Electric Cars in California Are Set Back," *New York Times,* March 30, 1996, p. 6.

[28] M. L. Wald, "What's the Buzz? G.M.'s Electric Car Is Headed to Showrooms," *New York Times,* March 10, 1996, p. F10.

[29] W. J. Cook, "Look, Mom, No Gas," *U. S. News & World Report,* September 30, 1996, p. 52.

Diane Wittenberg, electric vehicles president at Edison utilities, accused carmakers of forgetting their debt to the utilities that helped them get their vehicles on the road. She noted that as competitive pressure built among carmakers, they began to withhold information from the utilities that had helped them commercialize the cars. She pointed out that initially utilities helped foster consumer acceptance of electric vehicles. As the vehicles were commercialized, however, new players from the automobile companies did not recognize or value the relationship with power suppliers. Wittenberg reminded the auto industry, "We have a couple of years to go before we can afford the luxury of not pulling together."

Howard Levin, an executive of San Diego Gas & Electric, pointed out that "carmakers had to maintain very close relationships with utilities so that they could be involved before, during, and after the vehicle's purchase. Owners needed to have their home chargers rewired and remetered before connecting the cars. As the use of electric cars increased, a network of public fueling stops needed to be created, although new battery technology was likely to extend the range of the vehicles."[30]

Clean Water

The Rivers and Harbors Act of 1899 was the earliest act prohibiting pollution of navigable waters or adjoining banks without a permit. Throughout the first half of the 20th century, Congress passed other antipollution water acts, but none was as far reaching or comprehensive as the federal Water Pollution Control Act of 1972. This act, administered by the EPA, set national standards for reducing water pollution. The EPA defined pollutants as solid waste, incinerator residue, sewage, garbage, sewage sludge, munitions, chemical wastes, radioactive materials, and a variety of other substances.

Clean Water Act of 1972

The states and the EPA had to work together to draw up comprehensive plans for river basin and regional water-quality planning.[31] The act, which came to be known as the Clean Water Act of 1972, called for national action to create "fishable, drinkable, swimmable" waters. It required industries and cities to clean up their sewage and led to the establishment of a national, multibillion-dollar water treatment program.

---

[30] C. Parkes, "A Hesitant Debut for the Electric Car," *Financial Times,* January 6, 1997, p. 4.

[31] *Toward Cleaner Water* (Washington, DC: Environmental Protection Agency, 1974), p. 5.

In 1977, Congress passed amendments to the 1972 legislation that tightened rules dealing with the discharge of toxic chemicals into water supplies. Environmentalists thought the amendments were too lax, while industry representatives contended that costs for compliance were prohibitive.[32]

When the bill came up for renewal in 1982, the Reagan administration proposed what it called minor revisions. Environmentalists immediately pointed out that the Reagan proposal threw out the rule mandating national standards for treatment of industrial wastes discharged into municipal water systems. It also extended the time limit for cleanups for four years and doubled the time limit for industry pollution permits.[33]

Contention among the EPA, the Reagan administration, Congress, and other stakeholders continued throughout the 1980s. When President Reagan vetoed a $20 billion 1987 bill aimed at cleaning up the nation's water, Congress promptly overrode his veto. The bill enjoyed enormous popularity with politicians because it provided $18 billion in aid to state and local governments for construction of sewage treatment plants through 1994.[34]

At the end of the Reagan years, the United States Geological Survey reported that although most of the nation's underground water was of good quality, contamination was on the rise. Industrial waste, garbage dumps, septic tanks, underground storage of gasoline, and agricultural pesticides all contributed to increasing contamination.

Coastlines near major cities came under major assault from contamination. In New York City, for example, household waste mixed with rainwater was eventually conveyed through 6,200 miles of pipeline to treatment plants. During storms when the capacity of the treatment plants was overwhelmed, millions of gallons of raw sewage flowed into the city's harbors and along nearby shorelines. The city estimated that if more than three-quarters of an inch of rain fell, the system discharged 500 million gallons of mixed, untreated sewage. New York City was no different than Boston or any other old cities with antiquated sewage treatment systems.

Pollution affects waterways and the fishing industry in every part of the United States. Experts say some of the most valuable food fish are threatened with commercial extinction. Commercial fishers would catch so few fish that the effort would not be worth the cost. Between 1986 and 1991, the finfish and shellfish catch off the lower 48 states declined by 500 million pounds.

Nearly half of the U.S. population lives within 50 miles of a coastline. Due to population pressure, the coastal wetlands in which fish breed are

---

[32] P. Shabecoff, "New Rules for Clean Water: Attacks on 2 Fronts," *New York Times,* June 29, 1992, p. A20.

[33] "15 Changes Asked in U.S. Water Act," *New York Times,* May 28, 1982, p. A12.

[34] B. Weintraub, "Clean Water Bill Passed by House after Reagan Veto," *New York Times,* February 4, 1987, p. A1.

disappearing. Bays and estuaries are polluted with sewage, runoff from fertilizers and pesticides, and factory wastewater. More than one-third of the nation's shellfish beds are closed at any time because of pollution.

In March 1995, a bipartisan group in the House of Representatives began to consider major changes to the Clean Water Act of 1972. The House Committee, led by the Republican supporters of the Contract with America, tried to reshape the part of the law that dealt with preserving the wetlands from development. They narrowly defined what kinds of lands qualified for wetlands protection. The new proposal did not aggressively try to control polluted runoff. Instead, it left states to manage the effort through voluntary measures and repealed the Coastal Zone Management Act, the only law that allowed some states to enforce controls on polluted runoff.[35] Bud Shuster (R-Pennsylvania) said, "If the election was about anything, it was about our reforming government control, top-down government regulations and clean water is one of the areas crying out for reform."

The Clinton administration and Democratic leaders strongly opposed the measure. The president vowed to veto the House bill, and Administrator Carol M. Browner said the bill "undermined 20 years of success in our clean water programs."[36]

On May 16, 1995, the House approved far-reaching changes to the Clean Water Act. It was the first vote in the 104th Congress to rewrite whole sections of a major conservation law. The bill, which relaxed pollution controls in dozens of programs, was a surrogate for the much broader and highly ideological debate over the role of the federal government. The bill's antiregulatory sponsor, Bud Shuster, called EPA officials "environmental Gestapo." Representative Richard J. Durbin (D-Illinois) responded, "The references to Gestapos and heavy-handed tactics by the federal agencies fuels the gross national paranoia, which we see so much of in this country."[37]

The bill went on to the Senate with the threat of a Clinton veto. President Clinton characterized the bill as a Dirty Water Act, saying the water quality would go straight down the drain if the legislation became law. In 1996, the 104th Congress ended its session without amending the Clean Water Act.

As the 105th Congress began its term, two major studies assessed the state of water resources. In the first study, two private organizations, the Environmental Working Group and the U.S. Public Interest Research Group analyzed the EPA's annual inventory of industry's self-reporting toxic discharges. Since the passage of the Clean Water Act, about 60 percent of the nation's rivers, lakes, and coastline had been made fishable and swimmable.

---

[35] John H. Cushman, Jr., "House Group Set to Revamp Law Cleaning Water in U.S.," *New York Times,* March 23, 1995, p. A22.

[36] J. H. Cushman, Jr., "Rewritten Clean Water Act Gains in House," *New York Times,* May 12, 1997, p. A2.

[37] J. H. Cushman, Jr., "House Votes Major Changes in Clean Water Act from 70s," *New York Times,* May 17, 1995, p. A1.

However, from 1990 to 1994, about 1.5 billion pounds of chemicals were released into the nation's streams, lakes, and along coastlines. The effluence contained arsenic and other heavy metals that could cause cancer and diseases of the nerves and reproductive system. The legal dumping was only a fraction of overall dumping from sewage plants, utilities, mines, and municipal incinerators.[38]

A National Oceanic and Atmospheric Administration (NOAA) study monitored the discharge into waterways or use of 14 chemicals and compounds that had been outlawed or restricted. The NOAA study found that pollution levels had fallen at more than 100 sites along the U.S. coastline since 1986. Scientists monitored oysters and mussels at 154 sites from coast to coast. They found 217 decreases in chemicals and 41 increases. The greatest number of decreases were for chlordane, PCB, DDT, and cadmium. The greatest increases were for mercury, lead, zinc, and arsenic. The administration concluded that despite the decline in pollution, the situation was still serious and results should be "interpreted as indicating that ongoing human activity is increasing the chemical contamination."[39]

Safe Water Drinking Act

The 1976 guidelines established by the Safe Water Drinking Act required the EPA to establish levels at which 83 specific pollutants posed absolutely no risk to human health and to set safe levels for another 25 pollutants every three years. The law additionally required utilities to reduce pollutant levels in tap water to as close to the no-risk levels as possible, using the best technology they could find.

In April 1993, a General Accounting Office (GAO) report found state programs to ensure the safety of drinking water were in shambles. Forty-five states had failed to comply with EPA directives to evaluate all components of their public water systems. Blame for this situation was placed squarely on the EPA, which for many years had failed to request enough money from Congress to allow the states to meet the requirements.[40]

Environmental officials agreed the situation was as dismal as the GAO study depicted. Nationally, states failed to check half of the large water systems and 20 percent of the smaller ones to ensure they were not contaminated by pesticides or sewage runoff. States did not check their systems as often as the EPA required, a situation that was graphically brought to public attention when, in 1993, the city of Milwaukee's water supply became

---

[38] M. Satchell, "Pollution Count," *U.S. News & World Report,* September 30, 1996, p. 20.

[39] W. J. Broad, "Survey of 100 Coastal Sites Shows Pollution Is Declining," *New York Times,* January 21, 1997, p. C4.

[40] M. Wines, "Senate Acts to Loosen Rules on Purity of Tap Water," *New York Times,* May 20, 1994, p. A12.

contaminated by the protozoan cryptosporidium. Four hundred thousand people became ill and some with other medical conditions died.[41]

In May 1994, the Senate voted to amend the Safe Drinking Water Act. It decided that purity standards it had voted to support in 1986 were too tight. The Senate concluded that many of the nation's 200,000 water systems could not afford the technology and many systems served too few customers to warrant massive intervention. Many of the no-risk deadlines had not been met. Despite the Milwaukee episode, the problem of cryptosporidium in water supplies had not been remedied or even addressed. Cancer-causing contaminants still posed a major threat to water supplies.

The new bill included a $6.6 billion revolving loan fund—$600 million to be used in 1994—to help utilities buy the necessary equipment to meet federal purity standards. The EPA said the total cost was about $8.5 billion; utilities said it was much greater.

The bill also allowed small water systems to get waivers to allow them to filter pollutants with less than state-of-the-art technology. Instead of the no-risk requirement on cancer-causing pollutants, the bill said that if a utility could save money on water treatment without significantly *raising* the cancer risk, it could seek a waiver to do so.

Environmentalists were very upset about the Senate's actions. They called it a victory for the pesticide lobby and financially strapped water companies. Drinking-water experts noted it was difficult to say which side was right because data on the health effects of drinking water were poor.

The extension of the Safe Drinking Water Act finally received unanimous House approval in June 1996. The bill gave the EPA more flexibility in deciding which contaminants to regulate most closely and increased federal financial aid to states and local water agencies to help them comply. A major change in the 1986 law ended the requirement that the EPA expand the list of regulated contaminants by 25 additional substances every three years. How to balance costs and benefits of regulations was one of the most divisive questions under discussion. This bill called for cost-benefit analysis but did not bind the EPA's regulatory decisions on the basis of that analysis.

The Senate already had passed similar legislation just before the 1994 election. As the 1996 election approached, Republicans in Congress tried to present a more moderate environmental image. Carol Browner supported the bills saying, "This legislation reflects the kind of bipartisan commitment to public health and environmental protection that the president has called for."[42] On August 6 President Clinton signed the bill into law.

---

[41] M. D. Hinds, "Survey Finds Flaws in States' Water Inspection," *New York Times,* April 15, 1993, p. A14.

[42] J. H. Cushman, Jr., "Environment Bill's Approval Now Likely after Panel's Vote," *New York Times,* June 7, 1996, p. A27; T. Noah, "Major House Subcommittee Approves Revision of Safe Water Drinking Act," *The Wall Street Journal,* June 7, 1996, p. B7.

Hazardous Waste

In 1980, the EPA estimated that at least 57 million metric tons of the nation's total waste could be classified as hazardous. Hazardous waste emissions that contaminate air and water come under EPA jurisdiction. In a 1973 report to Congress, the EPA recommended passage of a federal law to regulate disposal of this waste on land. This law was the Resource Conservation and Recovery Act (RCRA). Subtitle C of RCRA imposed strict controls over the management of hazardous waste over its entire life cycle from cradle to grave. Some estimated the costs of complying with RCRA would exceed the combined costs of the Clean Air and Clean Water Acts. The RCRA program included:

- Identification of hazardous waste.
- Standards for generators and transporters of hazardous waste.
- Performance, design, and operating requirements for facilities that treat, store, or dispose of hazardous waste.
- A system that issues permits to such facilities.
- Guidelines describing conditions under which state governments can carry out their own hazardous-waste management programs.[43]

In 1980, Congress created a Superfund of $1.6 billion to clean up oil and chemical spills and abandoned toxic waste dumps such as Love Canal. The money for the fund came from taxes on petroleum and chemical companies, from fees on polluting substances, and from the U.S. Treasury. Over the years, the Superfund has had problems maintaining and increasing its funding levels. Oil and petroleum manufacturers wanted to shift the burden to manufacturers as a whole. Public support for the Superfund prevailed, however, and by 1989 the EPA had $8.5 billion in the cleanup program.

The Superfund, like other environmental programs, was caught in the post-1994 election wranglings. The Superfund law had been amended in 1986 and extended in 1991. In 1994, five committees of the Democratic Congress reached consensus on a revision with support of the chemical industry, environmentalists, and insurers. Put aside in the flurry of business at the close of the 103rd Congress, the bill never came to the floor. When the 104th Congress took office, it had more pressing items on its agenda.

The Clinton administration, acknowledging some of the Superfund's programmatic weaknesses, proposed changes in 1995. The administration identified four problems with the 1980 bill:

1. It did not provide a clear standard for remediated sites to meet and did not specify what level of risk was acceptable after the site was cleaned up.

---

[43] *Everybody's Problem: Hazardous Waste* (Washington, DC: Environmental Protection Agency, 1980), p. 10.

2. The law did not require that the site's probable future be considered in setting the standards or choosing the remedies. In most cases, regulators required that the site be cleaned up enough for any use from industry to schools.
3. The law imposed most of the burden of liability on current owners. An owner could be held liable even if it had not contributed at all to the contamination.
4. The people most involved in the decision-making process were not consulted. This was particularly true for low-income people and minorities who lived near the sites.

The Clinton administration's proposals required the EPA to:

- Issue national goals for the protection of human health and the environment to be applied at all sites covered by the law.
- Develop generic cleanup standards for the specific hazardous substances, pollutants, and contaminants most commonly found at these sites.
- Define cost-effective, generic remedies for the different types of sites, and establish procedures for selecting a remedy at a particular site.
- Issue a standard protocol for risk assessment using realistic assumptions.
- Allow the people affected to more fully participate in the selection of remedies.[44]

The administration told tens of thousands of minor polluters they would not be required to help pay for cleaning up sites and exempted thousands of less serious polluted sites from the program. Many formerly polluted sites were returned to industrial use because of cleanups done in the two previous administrations.

The federal government's authority to collect the tax that financed the trust fund from oil and chemical companies lapsed on December 31, 1995. After three years of effort, Congress had failed to reach agreement on how to restructure the program and how to split the cleanup costs between private companies and the federal government.

In January 1996, workers were sent home from hundreds of Superfund sites because the Environmental Protection Agency ran out of money to pay contractors and agency supervisors. But the crisis went far beyond the budgetary impasse that had cut off funding. Congressional committees struggled, without success, to write a bill that determined how the program would

---

[44] T. P. Grumbly, "Lessons from Superfund," *Environment* 37, no. 2 (March 1995), pp. 33–34.

be financed in the future and how liability would be apportioned among polluters. Congress also had to decide how clean a site needed to be for the job to be considered completed.[45]

In March 1996, Senate Republicans presented their version of the Superfund bill. Like the House bill, the Senate measure would drastically scale back the degree to which chemical companies, insurers, and other businesses would be required to pay for hazardous waste site cleanup. Like the House proposal, the Senate version eliminated most industry liability prior to 1987. No new taxes were included to pay the government's added cleanup costs environmentalists estimated at $1 billion.[46] The congressional impasse seemed likely to continue as the 105th Congress tried to find common ground with the stakeholders and their political agendas.

Waste Reduction

Recycling: A Strategy for Reducing Waste

Recycling is a partial solution to ameliorating the waste disposal problem. Public opinion and political pressure are working against the opening of more landfills and the operation of more incinerators. Therefore, converting the waste into a reusable commodity offers some promise of reducing the absolute amount of waste. In 1988, about 18 percent of municipal waste was recycled; however, 80 percent of solid waste in municipal garbage could be recycled. As a solution to waste disposal, recycling has both supporters and detractors.

In 1991, George C. Lodge and Jeffrey F. Rayport concluded that government and industry would have to work together if recycling were to succeed.[47] They noted business, government, environmentalists, and ordinary citizens were all trying to do the right thing. However, these stakeholders' combined efforts were disappointing because there was no coordination in matching the supply of waste for recycling and the demand for recycled output.

Different stakeholders had different agendas and sometimes worked at cross-purposes. Lodge and Rayport observed that many packaged-products manufacturers would have liked to switch to recycled plastics but worried that the supply might not be of sufficient volume or quality. Recyclers, on the

---

[45] J. H. Cushman, Jr., "Federal Program to Clean Toxic Waste Sites Is in Turmoil," *New York Times,* January 15, 1996, p. A1.
[46] T. Noah, "Superfund Plan Is Revised by GOP for Senate Action," *The Wall Street Journal,* March 25, 1996, p. A10.
[47] G. C. Lodge and J. F. Rayport, "Knee-Deep and Rising: America's Recycling Crisis," *Harvard Business Review,* September–October 1991, p. 133.

other hand, would have had to make expensive capital investments to process plastic, with no clear assurance of demand stability.[48]

Lodge and Rayport recommended the EPA set up a foundation operated on a regional and national level to design and manage a recycling infrastructure. The foundation would have the following tasks:

- Setting standards and establishing definitions for environmentally acceptable products and packaging, including recycling, recycled content, and reuse.
- Developing and promoting a national philosophy and perspective on recycling, including recognizing the need for cradle-to-grave product responsibility and championing fairness in the burdens and benefits of recycling.
- Creating and administering green product certification through an ecolabeling system.
- Establishing a standard coding system for materials to facilitate recycling.
- Recommending packaging and product design to promote the manufacture of easily recycled products from consumer goods to automobiles.
- Identifying and outlawing packages that were environmentally unacceptable.
- Instituting a national container-deposit law to promote recycling in both rural and urban areas and to raise funds for the further development of the national infrastructure.
- Funding research projects in waste reduction.
- Implementing incentives and penalties to stimulate recycling, such as deposit fees, tax credits, and fees on virgin materials.
- Creating markets for recycled materials by developing procurement incentives for businesses and government agencies.
- Designing education programs to make children more aware of the benefits of recycling and proper waste management.[49]

In 1994, *Consumer Reports* published a guide to the best ways to recycle what can be recycled and to dispose of the rest safely and efficiently. The magazine asked whether recycling was worth the effort. It concluded that recycling helped to keep garbage out of landfills and incinerators but it had its limitations. Recycling could not solve the problems of disposal of toxic metals and hazardous waste. On the other hand, making new products out of recycled materials almost always produced much less air and water pollution

---

[48] Ibid.
[49] Ibid., p. 139.

and used much less energy than making the products out of virgin raw material.

Cities and towns often found recycling programs were costly and difficult to implement. Most communities with curbside pickup used separate trucks and containers for recyclables and garbage. They had to buy trucks and sorting equipment and hire people to run them, thereby increasing labor and equipment costs. Garbage trucks squashed or compacted what they collected but recycling trucks didn't because compacting made it difficult to sort the material later. Therefore, recycling trucks filled up before they reached maximum weight load.

Most municipalities collected recyclable containers in one bin or bag and papers in another. Eventually, they all went to a materials recovery facility (MRF) where they were sorted by hand, or by machine if possible. Then materials were sent on to the factories that reused them. When the costs of building and running the MRFs were combined with collection and sorting, often they were higher than the value of the recycled material.[50]

The Wall Street Journal looked at curbside recycling and tried to assess costs and benefits. It observed that one-third of U.S. households sorted their garbage for collection by curbside recycling. Although recycling made people feel good, the cost was high. The *Journal* debunked some of the mythology about recycling.

- *Myth:* Without curbside pickup, consumers wouldn't recycle.
  Reality: Recycling efforts such as paper drives, buybacks, and drop-off centers, preceded the recycling movement and were much less costly. Paper drop-off programs in the early 1980s were widespread in California resulting in 45 to 50 percent of newspapers being collected in paper drives that didn't require curbside collection.
- *Myth:* The United States is running out of dump sites.
  Reality: In 1995, the U.S. Conference of Mayors said cities had on average 16.5 years of capacity remaining and the major waste companies had a total of more than two billion tons of space available.
- *Myth:* Consumer trash is overwhelming us.
  Reality: Consumer trash gets a great deal of attention but is only a tiny part of the waste problem. Commercial trash totals 22.9 million tons a year; consumer drop-offs, buyback, and paper drives total 8.3 million tons, and curbside collections account for 5.1 million tons.[51]

One major problem still confounding recycling advocates is the paucity of backward channels of distribution for most waste. Backward channels are

---

[50] "A Guilt-Free Guide to Garbage," *Consumer Reports,* February 1994, pp. 92–97.

[51] J. Bailey, "Curbside Recycling Comforts the Soul, but Benefits Are Scant," *The Wall Street Journal,* January 9, 1995, p. A1.

simply reverse distribution systems in which materials flow from the user's discard pile to a reprocessor and back to a manufacturer. Backward channels work well for aluminum cans and automobile batteries. Virtually all new automobile batteries are made with recycled lead. Wherever such backward channels are well-established, there are likely meaningful economic motivations to recycle.

Alternative Fuels: Another Strategy for Reducing Waste

Generating energy is a major source of pollution. Another alternative to reducing waste and by-products of fossil fuel is for companies to adopt new, nonpolluting or less polluting fuels.

Wind Power. In the early 1980s, wind power seemed to promise a way to generate electricity without using fossil fuels and without leaving any waste by-products. In 1991, Iowa-Illinois Gas & Electric Company and Windpower Inc. teamed up to develop wind farms. They proposed a joint venture to put wind turbines on agricultural land in Iowa. Using clusters of giant propellers, the turbines powered generators that produced electricity. This technology was a great improvement over older machines. The president of Windpower's parent company, Kenetech, Inc., predicted that the 1990s would be a transition decade for wind power and that wind power would contribute as much as 10 percent of the nation's electricity by the year 2010.[52]

Within a year, new technology made wind power even more attractive as an alternative power source. A comparison of wind-powered and oil-fired plants showed that the cost of wind turbine production from capital investment to operation and maintenance was about 5 cents per kilowatt-hour, about half the average retail price for power nationwide. A kilowatt-hour is enough electricity to light ten 100-watt bulbs for one hour. In contrast, at an oil-fired plant, the same amount of electricity costs 5 cents in fuel alone.

In 1995, wind still cost five cents a kilowatt hour to produce. Capital investment, operation, and maintenance expenses were all additional costs. For fossil fuel plants already in operation, the generation costs were lower. For new operations in areas where the wind was sufficient, however, wind turbines potentially were a cheaper alternative.

In March 1997, Houston-based Enron Corporation announced the world's largest wind power project. Enron's wind power subsidiary agreed to build 150 propellered wind turbines to supply the MidAmerican Energy Company, Iowa's largest electric utility. The turbines will stand on masts 15 stories tall and have about the same wing span as a Boeing 747. The project will cost about $100 million and go into operation at the end of 1998. The

---

[52] D. Stipp, "Wind Farms May Energize the Midwest," *The Wall Street Journal,* September 6, 1991, p. B1.

new project will produce power for 4 to 4.5 cents a kilowatt-hour. At this rate, wind power will be more efficient than nuclear, coal, and oil-fired plants but not as efficient as the newest natural gas plants.[53]

The negative aspect of wind farms is that they change the landscape visually and kill birds that wander into the propellers. A 1995 U.S. Fish and Wildlife study concluded that the wind farm in Altamont Pass in California killed more than 500 raptors in two years including 78 golden eagles.[54] In addition, because winds vary in intensity, backup is required, and technology for backup systems requires further development.

Hydroelectric Power. The technology of hydroelectric power dates back to the mid-19th century. Today less than 20 percent of the electricity generated worldwide comes from hydroelectric plants. In areas with appropriate water sources, such plants are economically competitive with fossil fuel plants. However, rivers must be dammed for hydroelectric generation, and some stakeholders charge that the resulting ecosystem damage is an unacceptably high price for this kind of power.

Solar Power. Since the oil shortages of the 1970s, solar power has become a more popular alternative for heating homes and small businesses. However, very few utilities outside of California have integrated solar energy into their grids. At this writing, solar energy for commercial use is still considerably more expensive to generate than electricity from traditional fossil fuels like coal and oil. If new solar technologies continue to advance, projected costs for solar-powered, grid-connected systems could be cut in half by the end of the century. Within 20 years, solar thermal systems could occupy a significant niche in a portfolio of electricity-generating utilities.[55]

Even though solar energy may not replace fossil fuel in the United States, American companies are making money exporting solar panels. Since the oil shocks of the 1970s, the federal government has awarded research grants totaling $1.4 billion to companies developing solar power. Solar panels made in the United States are in use all over Southeast Asia and Latin America. In some areas, huge solar plants are being designed by American companies to provide supplemental power for thousands of homes. By 1996, U.S. companies had 30 percent of the worldwide market, making the United States the world's biggest center of solar manufacturing. Companies export 70 percent of their products, up from 50 percent in 1993.

---

[53] A. R. Myerson, "Enron Wins Pact to Supply Power from Wind Turbines," *New York Times,* March 20, 1997, p. D2.

[54] J. Bailey, "Carter-Era Law Keeps Price of Electricity Up in Spite of a Surplus," *New York Times,* May 17, 1995, p. A1.

[55] D. C. White, C. J. Andrews, and N. W. Stauffer, "The New Team: Electricity Sources without Carbon Dioxide," *Technology Review,* January 1992, pp. 43–50.

Residential installation costs in the United States were cut in half between 1986 and 1996, when the typical residential installation cost between $10,000 and $20,000. Energy consultants say that when the cost gets down to $6,000, the initial outlay and financing expenses will become competitive with traditional fuels.[56]

Thermal Energy. Thermal energy can be tapped from several natural sources. Hot-water reservoirs lie about a mile underground in an area along the Pacific Rim called the Ring of Fire. This area and the Mediterranean area are volcanically active and can be exploited for small-scale energy sources. In fact, steam from geysers already supplies much of San Francisco's electricity.

Hot dry rock mining is another geothermal option. According to scientists, a gigantic furnace lies under the earth holding 30 times as much energy as all the gas, oil, and coal deposits combined. A project is under way at Los Alamos National Laboratories in New Mexico to develop an electricity-generating plant. Wells are driven from the surface into the rocks, whose temperature reaches 400 degrees Fahrenheit. Under high pressure, cold water is forced through cracks in the hot rocks and then pumped back to the surface. When the plant is operating commercially, the hot water will heat butane, which will drive turbines. In the West, the costs should be competitive with those for conventional electric plants.

Recycling and use of alternative fuels will help decrease the amount of carbon dioxide and other pollutants released into the air and lower the volume of hazardous waste requiring cleaning. Despite all these efforts, we will continue to generate waste, use large quantities of fossil fuel, and have to deal with the by-products of an industrial economy. Hazardous waste disposal is, and will continue to be, a major industry in the United States and all industrialized countries.

A Systems Approach to Waste Minimization

Every product goes through a life cycle from its creation to the end of its useful life. The steps in this cycle involve the participation of separate organizations that have little incentive, other than economic, to coordinate their efforts to minimize waste.

The problem of pollution control and decreasing access to dumping sites has engendered interest in finding ways to minimize the amount of effluence and waste we create. The Society of Environmental Toxicology and Chemistry (SETAC), founded in 1979, is a professional organization that brings together environmental scientists, engineers, academics, government

---

[56] J. E. Halpert, "U.S. Industry Harnesses the Sun and Exports It," *New York Times*, June 5, 1996, p. D1.

officials, industry representatives, and public-interest groups to discuss issues of environmental management and develop solutions to environmental problems. SETAC members try to develop holistic procedures for studying environmental consequences associated with the cradle-to-grave life cycle of products or processes. As Exhibit 16–4 shows, SETAC has developed a life-cycle assessment approach as a tool to help identify, assess, and solve the environmental concerns associated with products, processes, and activities. At the 1990 SETAC annual meeting, participants developed the above framework. The major stages were (1) raw materials acquisition; (2) manufacturing, processing, and formulation; (3) distribution and transportation; (4) use/reuse/maintenance; (5) recycling; and (6) waste management. Each stage received inputs of materials and energy and produced outputs of materials or energy that move to the next phase and release waste into the environment. Energy sources might include natural gas, petroleum, coal, hydroelectric power, solar energy, wind, and wood. Waste was defined as material having no beneficial use.

Companies and governments can still use this assessment model to establish baselines of information about a system's overall resource requirements, energy use, and emissions. They also can identify points within the life cycle as a whole, or within a given process, at which they can achieve the greatest reduction in resource requirements and emissions. Finally, they can compare the system inputs and outputs associated with alternative processes.[57] Since this model was developed, SETAC's Life Cycle Assessment Advisory Group continued to develop cases dealing with life-cycle assessment in North America and Europe, to refine definitions of terms, allocate costs within the life cycle more accurately, and seek business involvement in its activities.[58]

Waste Management

Congress passed the Resource Conservation and Recovery Act (RCRA) in 1976. RCRA substantially revamped federal regulation of solid waste disposal and created the first comprehensive federal regulatory program for the systematic control of hazardous waste. RCRA originally amended the Solid Waste Disposal Act (1965). It was reauthorized in 1984 with the Hazardous and Solid Waste Amendments and was amended in 1988 to include the management of infectious waste.

RCRA regulates solid waste including both the garbage households and offices generate and more hazardous chemical waste produced by industries.

---

[57] *Workshop Report of the Society of Environmental Toxicology and Chemistry: A Technical Framework for Life-Cycle Assessment* (Washington, DC: SETAC Foundation, 1991), pp. 1–27.

[58] Internet[http://www.setac.org/mar1ca.html] "SETAC Foundation Life-Cycle Assessment Newsletter."

EXHIBIT 16–4 A Technical Framework for Life-Cycle Assessment

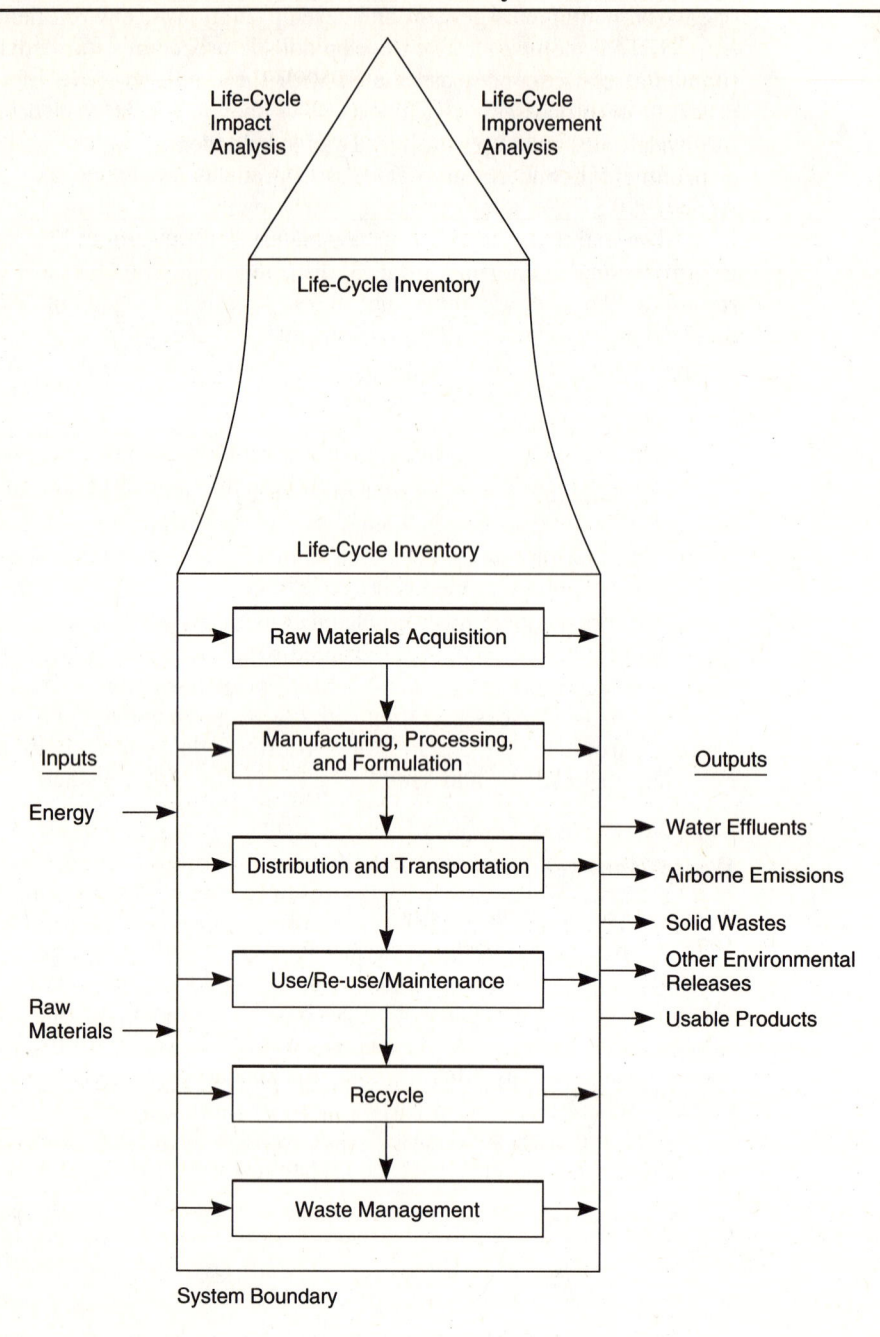

```
                    /\
                   /  \
          Life-Cycle   Life-Cycle
           Impact      Improvement
           Analysis    Analysis
                 /      \
                /_____\
               |          |
               | Life-Cycle|
               | Inventory |
                \          /
                 \        /
                  _____/
               |              |
               | Life-Cycle   |
               | Inventory    |
               |  ┌────────────────────┐   |
         ────▶│ Raw Materials Acquisition │────▶
               |  └────────────────────┘   |
               |            ↓              |
               |  ┌────────────────────┐   |
 Inputs  ────▶│ Manufacturing, Processing,│────▶  Outputs
               |   and Formulation        │
               |  └────────────────────┘   |
 Energy ────▶  |            ↓              |  ────▶ Water Effluents
               |  ┌────────────────────┐   |  ────▶ Airborne Emissions
         ────▶│ Distribution and Transportation │────▶
               |  └────────────────────┘   |  ────▶ Solid Wastes
               |            ↓              |  ────▶ Other Environmental Releases
               |  ┌────────────────────┐   |  ────▶ Usable Products
         ────▶│ Use/Re-use/Maintenance  │────▶
 Raw           |  └────────────────────┘   |
 Materials ──▶ |            ↓              |
               |  ┌────────────────────┐   |
         ────▶│       Recycle             │────▶
               |  └────────────────────┘   |
               |            ↓              |
               |  ┌────────────────────┐   |
         ────▶│   Waste Management      │────▶
               |  └────────────────────┘   |
               └──────────────────────────┘
                     System Boundary
```

Source: *Workshop Report of the Society of Environmental Toxicology and Chemistry: A Technical Framework for Life-Cycle Assessment* (Washington, DC: SETAC Foundation, 1991), title page.

RCRA also regulates medical waste and underground storage tanks that contain hazardous substances.

The Environmental Protection Agency enforces RCRA and issues the regulations that cover creation, transportation, treatment, storage, and disposal of hazardous waste. The EPA sets the management standards for hazardous waste generators and treatment, storage, and disposal facilities and must issue a permit before hazardous waste can be treated, stored, or disposed.

RCRA encourages public participation in all phases of its programs. It requires that:

- Citizens have access to information obtained by a state or EPA during an inspection of a hazardous waste facility.
- Citizens are allowed to participate in the permitting process from the beginning.
- Citizens may bring suits against anyone whose hazardous waste management activities may constitute an "imminent hazard, risk, or substantial endangerment in the past or present."
- Citizens may bring suits against anyone who may be violating a RCRA permit, standard, or requirement.
- EPA or the state must notify local officials and post signs at sites that pose imminent and substantial threats to human health and the environment.[59]

The EPA controls the selection of technology for cleanup treatment and can hold a company liable for years after if a job said to be complete later is found to be inadequate. Waste cleanup and removal has been slow and expensive, but new technologies—partly supported by the Superfund—are beginning to make the task easier. Development of these processes created a new, multibillion-dollar waste disposal consulting and engineering industry.

Between 1986 and 1988, 16 waste management firms went public. Chemical Waste Management's profits grew from $25 million in 1985 to $115 million in 1988.[60] By 1992, the rosy financial picture changed. The economic recession reduced the volume of waste that needed to be collected, treated, and discarded. Companies lost their enthusiasm for cleanup projects. According to the industry newsletter *Environmental Business Journal,* revenue growth slowed to 10 percent in 1990 and 2 percent in 1991. Industry experts recommended that waste management companies explore recycling as a new endeavor.

The big waste management companies grew bigger during the early and mid-1990s. Waste Management Technologies (WMX) became North

---

[59] Internet [http://www.em.doe.gov/fs/fs2a.html] "Resource Conservation and Recovery Act."

[60] "The Big Haul in Toxic Waste," *Newsweek,* October 3, 1988, pp. 37, 39.

America's leading waste management and recycling company. It operated in 380 of the nation's top 500 markets. It provided recycling, collection, processing, and transfer and disposal services to more than 750,000 commercial customers and about 12 million households. Between 1971 when it was founded, and 1997, WMX grew from a local Oak Brook, Illinois, solid waste company to an international giant serving North and South America, Europe, the South Pacific, and Asia. It had five operating groups: Waste Management, Inc. (WMI); Chemical Waste Management (CWM); Rust International, Inc.; Wheelabrator Technologies, Inc. (WTI); and Waste Management, International plc.[61] In 1996, WMX acquired USA Waste Services, the nation's third largest waste hauler and Sanifill, a landfill operator.

Allied Waste Industries (AWT), a small Tennessee waste management company, bought Canada's Laidlaw for $15 billion becoming the fourth largest waste group in the United States. In 1996, AWT carried out the following projects: it was an ISO 14001 registrar for Lockheed Martin's Ocean Radar & Sensor Systems; controlled waste management for the Port of Aqaba in Jordan; evaluated technical proposals for Indonesia's national environmental data management system; was a expert witness on a Kentucky PCB contamination case; evaluated a site for a Tennessee factory owner; was selected as one of five U.S. companies for a pilot program to certify U.S. registrars for ISO 14000; completed engineering of metals sludge detoxification plans; and prepared a business plan for hazardous waste treatment in Hungary.[62]

Despite this consolidation and growth, stockholders pressured the waste management industry to restructure and consolidate. In February 1997, WMX announced it would cut 3,000 jobs and $300 million in costs by 1999 and would sell $1 billion worth of assets.

Browning-Ferris, the nation's second largest waste management group had a net loss of $101 million on revenues of $5.8 billion in the year ending September 1996. Like WMX, Browning-Ferris decided to retrench internationally. It sold non-core businesses and its Italian operations, and closed unprofitable recycling centers.

The unrestrained growth of the biggest waste companies during the 1990s was partly to blame for these problems. The companies spent more than $20 billion to acquire companies and new waste dumps. This strategy produced overcapacity and put pressure on profits. As mentioned earlier, although recycling looked profitable in the early 1990s, it became much less profitable as the cost of collection and processing rose sharply in 1996 and 1997. Waste companies that avoided recycling and concentrated on the solid waste business have done well and continue to prosper.[63]

---

[61] Internet [http://www.naco.org/members/corp/wmx.htm] "NACo-Waste Management, Inc."

[62] Internet [http://www.mindspring.com/~awms/projects.html] "Representative Experience."

[63] Waste Management: In the Dumps," *Economist,* February 8, 1997, p. 68.

Radioactive Waste in the United States

Many stakeholders do not realize radioactive contamination comes from a number of sources other than nuclear power plants. Weapons facilities, hospitals, and laboratories all generate huge volumes of contaminated material. The three levels of radioactive waste are low, intermediate, and high. Each has different potencies and poses varying levels of danger to the public.

Low-Level Waste. Workers in hospitals, nuclear plants, and other industries generate a considerable proportion of radioactive waste. Such waste contaminates clothing, tools, and cooling and cleaning water. Although its radioactivity is short-lived, its volume is enormous. In 1980, Congress passed legislation aimed at making states responsible for disposal of low-level radioactive waste generated in state.

In 1985, Congress amended the law to require that states unable to dispose of the waste would have to take possession of the waste and be held liable for any damages resulting from their failure to do so. This law was to go into effect in 1996.

State governors had a major role in crafting the 1985 law and gave it their unanimous support. They and members of Congress agreed it was unfair for Washington, Nevada, and South Carolina (which had existing dump sites) to serve as the dumping grounds for the entire nation's low-level radioactive waste.

As New York State proceeded to choose potential dump sites, the Not-In-My-Backyard (NIMBY) syndrome hit residents in the targeted areas. In 1990, New York State sued the federal government, alleging that Congress had trampled on state sovereignty by putting itself in charge of issues that should have been reserved for state legislative and executive bodies.

The Supreme Court heard the case in 1992 and was sympathetic to New York's argument. Justices Sandra Day O'Connor and Anthony M. Kennedy suggested that Congress could no more require the states to assume the burden of nuclear waste than it could make states legally liable for all crimes committed with handguns within their borders.

In June 1992, the Supreme Court ruled in a six-to-two decision that it was unconstitutional for Congress to hold states responsible for the waste. Justice Sandra Day O'Connor, who wrote the decision, based it on the 10th Amendment, which provides that powers not expressly given to the federal government are "reserved to the states" or to "the people."[64]

By 1993, only South Carolina and Washington State accepted low-level radioactive waste. In May, New York officials announced that due to local opposition, they were putting their search for a local dump site on hold. South Carolina, which had been accepting 84 tractor-trailers full of New York waste

---

[64] L. Greenhouse, "High Court Eases States' Obligation over Toxic Waste," *New York Times,* June 20, 1992, p. 1.

per year for eight years, finally lost patience. South Carolina officials announced they might cancel their contract with New York, leaving 200 hospitals, nuclear power plants, research laboratories, and companies with no place to dump their by-products. As in many other states, the NIMBY syndrome left New York without a storage plan for the future and producers of waste with an uncertain future. A medical researcher at the University of Rochester noted uncertainty over disposal of radioactive isotopes might jeopardize his $6 million AIDS grant.[65]

In autumn 1996, the Department of Energy completed an 84,000-page report on a nuclear dump site in southeastern New Mexico. A network of vaults carved out of salt were designed to become the world's first underground low-level nuclear waste dump. The first truckloads were scheduled to arrive at the end of 1997 and continue through 2003. For 100 years after that people would be kept away by signs and fences identifying the site. The Energy Department concluded the waste would be safe for 10,000 years.[66]

Intermediate-Level Waste. Intermediate-level waste includes reactor components, resins, heavily contaminated equipment, and waste by-products. Low- and intermediate-level radioactive waste usually is buried in pits or sealed in concrete.

High-Level Waste. Spent fuel from reactors presents the gravest problems in storage. Uranium-238 that comes from nuclear fuel and waste has a half-life of 4.5 billion years.

The accidents at Three Mile Island and Chernobyl focused the world's attention on nuclear contamination and how it could and should be handled. For most Americans, the immediate concern was whether U.S. facilities were really safe. Despite loud and repeated assurances from the nuclear energy industry, people were reluctant to build more nuclear plants. A less dramatic but more realistic concern was how nuclear plants would deal with their waste once they were too old to be operated safely.

As we discussed at the beginning of Chapter 3, the 15 plants closed by 1993 operated for an average of 12.7 years, although they had been licensed for 40 years. The questions were how to dismantle old utilities and what the cost would be. The Nuclear Regulatory Commission (NRC) requires utilities with nuclear plants to put aside as much as $135 million per plant to pay for dismantling costs. A Stanford University study concluded that by the beginning of 1993, utilities should have set aside a total of $33 billion. The NRC estimated only $4 billion actually had been collected.[67]

---

[65] S. Lyall, "Failing to Build a Dump, New York Faces Shutout," *New York Times,* May 21, 1993, p. A1.

[66] J. Brooke, "Underground Haven or a Nuclear Hazard," *New York Times,* February 6, 1997, p. A14.

[67] R. Johnson and A. de Rouffignac, "Nuclear Utilities Face Immense Expenses in Dismantling Plants," *New York Times,* January 25, 1993, p. A1.

Fort St. Vrain in Colorado was the first fully operational nuclear power plant to be taken apart in pieces. Built in the 1970s, the plant had suffered a variety of small problems that caused frequent shutdowns. After cracks developed in the reactor's steam tubes, the plant's owner, Public Service of Colorado, decided it should be decommissioned and dismantled.

This facility, which had cost $224 million to build, was small compared to many others around the nation. Yet the cost of taking it apart was estimated at $333 million, and the technology needed was not always obvious. Engineers sometimes had to create models to figure out how to take the plant apart. The utility's customers will pay for the dismantling until the year 2005.

How to dispose of nuclear spent fuel has been an issue since the end of World War II. In the early days of the nuclear age, there was little concern about safe disposal. In 1983, the Nuclear Regulatory Commission, conducting a routine check of old records, unexpectedly found a 6.5-acre radioactive dump site in Wayne, New Jersey. Between 1948 and 1960, the Atomic Energy Commission—the predecessor of the Nuclear Regulatory Commission—had conducted atomic bomb research on the property. Radioactive sludge left behind grew into open mounds that were exposed to rain and runoff.

The research facility left nearly 2,000 tons of waste on the ground or buried in pits. Radiation eventually leached into a local stream adjacent to residential housing.[68] Finally, in 1982, Congress set guidelines for burying radioactive waste. By that time, more than 8,000 tons of highly radioactive spent fuel was piled up at power plants. Most of the waste was still held in the shallow pools initially designed to store it for only several months.

The military, which created 80 percent of high-level waste, stored its residue in huge steel tanks in Washington State, South Carolina, and Idaho. A new military waste site, to be developed at a cost of $700 million, was under the New Mexico desert near Carlsbad. The first ventilator shafts were sunk and excavation of storage rooms began in 1983.

Environmentalists protested any attempt to ship radioactive waste over land to the disposal facility. Politicians, responding to public antipathy to nuclear waste, exhibited the NIMBY syndrome. Governor Cecil Andrus of Idaho was so determined to keep it out of his state that in 1987 he ordered a boxcar of radioactive waste to be stopped at the Idaho border and sent back to the Rocky Flats nuclear weapons plant in Colorado.

In 1988, the Department of Energy announced there were cracks in the 300-foot-long rooms of the New Mexico storage facility. Disposal of plutonium-contaminated clothing, equipment, solvents, and other waste stalled. Worried about environmental safety, Congress refused to transfer ownership of the land from the Department of the Interior to the Department of Energy.[69]

---

[68] R. Hanley, "Atom Waste Found in Town in Jersey," *New York Times,* June 8, 1983, pp. A1, B4.

[69] K. Schneider, "Safety Questions Still Delay Nuclear Waste Plant," *New York Times,* June 13, 1989, p. A23.

By 1993, the Department of Energy had fallen 12 years behind its deadline for opening a facility in Nevada. Utilities around the country were desperate to find storage sites for high-level waste. The Boston Edison-owned Pilgrim plant applied to the Nuclear Regulatory Commission to increase its storage capacity by two-thirds, allowing it to operate until its license expired in the year 2010. Pilgrim and the now closed Yankee Rowe plant in western Massachusetts together stored more than 400 tons of high-level nuclear waste by mid-1993. On-site storage raised concerns that if cooling water were suddenly lost, the resulting fire could melt the metal casings that enclosed the uranium fuel pellets.[70]

By 1997, the problem of a dumping site for high-level radioactive waste was still under discussion. The Energy Department said it could not keep its promise to dispose of the waste by January 31, 1998, the date agreed on by the DOE and nuclear utility companies. Deputy Energy Secretary Thomas P. Grumbly told the Senate Energy Committee the Yucca Mountain site in Nevada would not be ready until at least 2010. The utilities were faced with building expensive containers to hold their waste. They and their regulators sued in court and lobbied Congress to hold the government to its contract. It was clear that no settlement would be imminent.[71]

---

[70] S. Allen, "Pilgrim Asks to Increase Radioactive-Waste Storage," *Boston Globe,* April 8, 1993, p. 35.

[71] M. L. Wald, "U.S. Says It Cannot Meet Goal for Nuclear-Waste Disposal," *New York Times,* February 6, 1997, p. A14.

Summary

Environmental issues present stakeholders with profound challenges and dangers. Businesses, governments, environmental groups, and individuals all have a tremendous stake in promoting clean air, water, and earth.

Since the beginning of the Industrial Revolution in the early 19th century, industrial and urban waste have seriously damaged the environment. The United States has taken measures to deal with some of the worst cases of air, water, and hazardous waste pollution. The Environmental Protection Agency(EPA), established by Congress, oversees programs for control of air pollution, water pollution, pesticides, radiation, and waste management. During the 1980s, the performance of the EPA fell far short of environmentalists' expectations, but the 1990s promised to be a decade of environmental activism.

The Clean Air Act of 1970 placed clean air legislation under EPA supervision. Federal air quality standards were drawn up with state participation. The initial act and subsequent amendments were helpful in reducing air pollution. President Bush submitted his administration's proposed revision in 1989, and the Clinton administration pushed forward in enforcing the Clean Air Act of 1990. Although the new act does not satisfy all stakeholders, it addresses some critical U.S. problems such as acid rain and ozone reduction.

Clean water legislation also came under EPA authority. Progress was slow during the Reagan years, but there were some notable successes in cleaning up harbors, rivers, and lakes. Drinking water in many communities is showing signs of antiquated and inadequate filtration. Abandoned toxic waste sites, pesticides, and industrial waste contamination threaten underground water supplies.

The EPA tracks and manages hazardous waste under the Resource Conservation and Recovery Act. Congress established a Superfund designed to clean up the worst of the nation's toxic waste dumps. The EPA is still finding toxic sites abandoned years ago, and communities are trying to evaluate resulting health problems.

Waste management is now a multimillion-dollar business. Communities are insisting that companies dump their by-products in someone else's backyard. New technologies, partly funded by government, are devising ways to safely dispose of chemicals and other potentially dangerous industrial by-products.

Radioactive waste is the most hazardous waste and the most difficult to manage. It comes from a variety of sources, including hospitals, laboratories, weapons plants, and commercial nuclear reactors. The United States has not yet developed a safe means of disposing of the tremendous volume of nuclear material it has generated. In recent years, nuclear weapons plants have been cited for decades of unsafe operation and disposal of waste products. Authorities will struggle with this problem for the foreseeable future.

Questions

1. What are the duties of the Environmental Protection Agency?
2. What are some mechanisms companies can use to reduce their pollution?
3. What are the major clean air issues for the 1990s?
4. What are the major clean water issues for the 1990s?
5. What is NIMBY? What hazardous waste issues do local communities face?
6. What are the most important sources of alternative power? How realistic is this technology commercially?

Projects

1. Contact your state environmental agency. Find out how the state and federal governments work together to reduce environmental hazards.
2. Go to your city, town, or local government offices and find out about recycling policies in your community.
3. Contact an environmental lobbying group in your community. Attend meetings to find how it develops its agenda, solicits funding, and carries out its mission.
4. Choose a product of interest to you. Trace its life cycle according to Exhibit 16–4. Identify all sources of environmental contamination and recommend ways to eliminate problems.

Beta Case 16
Environmental Issues

Ken Braddock, Beta's vice president for ethical products, poked his head into Bill Parker's office. "Want any lunch?" he asked. "I'd like to run something by you." The two men walked to the executive dining room and found a corner table. After ordering a light lunch of cold turkey and pasta salad, Braddock leaned back in his chair. "Bill, I am really upset. As you know, we have a fairly large volume of toxic waste in our radiopharmaceutical division. We've been using Waste Disposal Associates to handle the material, and until recently we have been pretty satisfied with their prices and performance."

"Then what's your problem?" asked Parker.

"My problem is that Waste Disposal Associates has just been cited by the Michigan attorney general's office for violating state and federal laws covering disposal of chemical waste. According to my buddy in the State House, the newspapers are going to have this plastered across page one tomorrow morning."

"Okay, Ken, let's take this from the top," soothed Parker. "Tell me everything that is going on."

Braddock promptly launched into a recitation of the facts as he knew them. He had been called late the previous evening by a former college classmate who was an aide to the attorney general. She told him the following story.

Two employees of Waste Disposal Associates quit their jobs six months ago, then filed lawsuits against their former employer. They charged they had repeatedly reported dumping violations to their superiors. The superiors told them to either forget about it or cover it up. One employee had made a deposition in which he alleged that Waste Disposal had failed to file manifests (shipping documents) with the state of Michigan. If the manifests were not filed as the law required, the state could not track the waste. Apparently Waste Disposal drivers were dumping large amounts of toxic substances in landfills or burying them in unauthorized drums. The manager of one of Waste Disposal's own dumps had written to a company official a year ago, telling her the company's disposal practices were inviting disaster. So far, Waste Disposal's top managers have denied any wrongdoing, claiming they have not withheld manifests or authorized any illegal dumping.

"I know these people at Waste Disposal," sighed Braddock. "They are one of the most aggressive companies in the waste disposal business. They have disposal contracts from New York to Saudi Arabia. On the other hand, the lawsuits are coming in like bees to honey. Bill, I have no idea if waste is being dumped illegally. Even if it is, I don't know whether it is our waste. After all, we may not be responsible. We gave them the contract in good faith."

"Hey, Ken," Parker interrupted, "if the press finds out our waste is involved, we're going to get really bad publicity regardless of who's responsible."

"Well, what should I do?" moaned Braddock.

CHAPTER 17
THE INTERNATIONAL ENVIRONMENT

Maintaining the environment is a global problem that is exacerbated as economic development progresses. Economic growth has undoubtedly improved the standard of living across much of the globe, but at a great cost to the environment.

Clean air, clean water, and toxic waste management are not purely domestic issues; they concern every nation at every stage of development. Rivers, oceans, and wind currents carry one country's environmental problems across national boundaries. Many countries have environmental policies and regulations that govern their own institutions, but each nation's economic, legal, and social systems produce a different approach. In every country, tension exists between the cost of environmental protection and remediation and the public's economic well-being.

This chapter discusses sustainable development as an underlying concept in the discussion of the international environment. *Sustainable development* seeks to balance economic development and protection of the environment. Economic development is not a purely domestic issue; it also is linked to international trade policy. The world's most powerful trade body, the World Trade Organization (WTO), promotes an antiprotectionist agenda to foster development while still protecting the environment.

Environmental issues in the European Union, Eastern Europe, Russia, and China are linked to sustainable development and provide illustrations of private and governmental environmental decision making. The World Bank's concern about the environment and its relationship to international trade policy provides additional insight into this problem. The chapter also examines events before and after the Rio Earth Summit and their implications for multilateral environmental treaties.

Case: The Aral Sea

Before the late 1960s, the Aral Sea was the fourth largest lake in the world. By 1997, the lake covered less than half its original area and contained a quarter of its original volume. The lake used to have a fish catch of 25,000 tons a year. Now there is almost no commercial fishing at all.

The Aral Sea is a closed water system located in Central Asia between Turkmenistan, Kazakhstan, and Uzbekistan. Water flows into the sea from the glaciers high up in the mountains of the Hindu Kush and Pamir Mountains each more than 1,500 miles from the sea. Since the Pliocene Epoch more than 2 million years ago, the Aral depression has flooded and dried up as glaciers froze and melted. However, this newest dry period has nothing to do with weather conditions; it is entirely man-made.

Under Joseph Stalin, the Soviet Union developed a cotton-producing plan that diverted the Amu Tarya and Syr Darya tributaries into a number of man-made lakes, canals, and irrigation channels. The Amu darya River was cut off from the Aral Sea between 1974 and 1986 and the Syr Darya River between 1982 and 1986. Since 1986, a small flow from both rivers has resumed but is completely inadequate to replenish the sea.

The dissolution of the Soviet Union has not ameliorated the ecological disaster caused by the cotton industry. Today, Uzbekistan, Turkmenistan, Kazakhstan, and nearby Tajikistan compete for control of the scarce water supply to maintain the high yield of cotton they call white gold. Irrigated agriculture accounts for one-third of the jobs in these countries and provides an exportable crop for their cash-starved economies. In Uzbekistan, cotton accounts for nearly 80 percent of foreign earnings.

In the past decade, the summers have gotten hotter and the winters colder. Strong winds blow over hundreds of miles of Central Asia, carrying 150 million tons of salty dust filled with hazardous fertilizers and industrial toxic waste. The salts are poisonous to people, animal life, and crops. People living around the lake have abnormal levels of anemia, cancer, and respiratory diseases.

International organizations have tried to help clean up the region. In 1994, at a conference of donor states in Paris, participants agreed to invest $31 million to the Aral Sea salvation program. By 1996, $13 million had been invested and $5 million was given to Kazakhstan, Uzbekistan, and Turkmenistan for an assistance program known as Pure Water and Health.[1]

In February 1997, the World Bank pledged $380 million to help clean up the area. The leaders of five Central Asian republics held a summit to announce they would donate part of their budgets to an interregional fund to save the sea. Experts say that unless cotton cultivation is reduced sharply, all the aid in the world will not have an impact. Environmentalists agree that the lake will disappear entirely by 2010 if nothing is done to stop the environmental degradation.[2]

---

[1] Internet [http://www.Kazakhstan:Aral Sea Foundation Faces Funding Shortage . . . rferl.org/nca/news/1996/11/N.RI.961121174413.html] M. Sharipzhan, "Kazakhstan: Aral Sea Foundation Faces Funding Shortage," *Radio Free Europe*, 1996.

[2] D. Filipov, "A Sea Dies, Mile by Mile," *Boston Globe*, March 23, 1997, p. 1.

Questions

1. To what extent, if any, should the U.S. commit money and other resources toward cleaning up environmental problems such as the Aral Sea?

2. Does the United States already have policies that guide legislative initiatives to clean up environmental problems abroad?

3. What role should the World Bank and other multinational organizations play in environmental cleanup?

Sustainable Development

In 1987, a United Nations Commission chaired by Norway's Prime Minister Gro Harlem Brundtland sponsored a conference to discuss the concept of sustainable development. Since the Brundtland conference, the concept of sustainable development has become increasingly important to the discussion of the impact of economic development on the environment.

The National Research Council's definition of sustainability says that "world conservation strategy should include management of the use of a resource so it can meet human demands of the present generation without decreasing opportunities for future generations."[3] The issue of the future is crucial to the concept of sustainability.

It is very difficult to predict all the consequences of even the best intentioned actions. For example, assume a factory is built using a technology that removes a certain percentage, but not all, of the factory's effluence. It is hard to know with certainty what the long-term trade-offs are between putting people to work so they can support their families and the eventual degradation of air quality.

The notion of sustainable development demands that regulators, policymakers, private enterprise, and other stakeholders measure economic progress as precisely as possible. Current statistics on education, infant mortality, and nutrition are all important in determining a country's gross domestic product (GDP) or gross national product (GNP), both important indicators of progress. These statistics are inadequate for assessing the costs of today's economic development to future generations. When we make economic choices in the late-1990s, we pass on to future generations a wide range of physical, human, and natural capital that will determine their welfare and their legacy to future generations.

In making choices, we face unclear trade-offs between environmental protection and economic development. This chapter discusses the difficult issues involved in understanding these long-run trade-offs. The goal is to help us understand more fully what the consequences of domestic and foreign policies and multilateral treaties mean to future generations.

In 1993, T. Nagpal and C. Foltz, editors of *Choosing Our Future: Visions of a Sustainable World* developed the 2050 Project to explore common elements and differences in people's views of a sustainable future. They contacted 88 people in 47 countries and finally received 52 essays from 34 countries in five languages. Nagpal and Foltz deliberately overrepresented developing countries because they considered the views of people from industrialized countries to be well-known. The authors then conducted 19 interviews with people from 14 countries. Respondents intimated that Western

---

[3] National Research Council, Committee on Global Change, *Research Strategies for the U.S. Global Change Research Program* (Washington, DC: National Academy Press, 1990).

supporters of sustainable development didn't really understand the concept. Westerners, they charged, equated sustainability with development. By using a vocabulary connected with economic growth and efficiency, Westerners ignored the urgency of preserving human life and ecosystem health. Respondents all voiced deep concern about the fragmentation of their communities and their growing cultural detachment from the environment. A common thread in many contributors' responses was the belief that communities had to provide much better educational and employment opportunities for their children. Many asserted that wisdom came not only from books but also from traditional knowledge and customs. Some suggested the development of graduate programs in tribal languages, combining the skills of traditional healers with the expertise of modern medicine, and the establishment of regional universities that stressed integrated plans for development.[4] The authors noted that many respondents tended to romanticize and idealize the past, looking back fondly on communal decision-making, communal goals, and consensus.

Stuart L. Hart, in a thoughtful 1997 article in *Harvard Business Review,* observed that corporations faced a major challenge in helping develop a sustainable global economy. He pointed out that if all the companies in the industrialized world were to achieve zero emissions by the year 2000, the earth would still be stressed beyond its "carrying capacity." As Hart saw it, the roots of the problem were explosive population growth and rapid economic development in developing countries. These social and political issues were not within the control of any corporation. Nevertheless, corporations were the only organizations with the resources, technology, global connections, and the motivation to achieve sustainability.

Hart identified three economies: market economy, survival economy, and nature's economy. He noted that affluent societies in a *market economy* accounted for more than 75 percent of the world's energy and resource consumption and created most of the industrial, toxic, and consumer waste. Despite their heavy use of energy and materials, industrialized countries had relatively low levels of pollution because of strict environmental laws, the greening of industry, and the relocation of the most polluting industries to developing countries.

Countries in the second economy, a *survival economy* (the traditional, village-based way of life), comprised 3 billion people; Africa, India, and China will account for 90 percent of population growth over the next 40 years. The ecosystems in these countries have become degraded and continued to decline as drinkable water and fuel became less and less accessible.

---

[4] Tanvi Nagpal, "Voices from the Developing World," *Environment,* October 1995, pp. 10–15.

Millions of people migrated into overcrowded cities as their villages were devastated by erosion, floods, and drought.

The third economy, *nature's economy,* consisted of the natural systems and resources that supported the market and survival economies. Resources such as oil, metals, and other minerals were finite.

Hart thinks that depletion of renewable resources such as soil, forests, and water is the greatest threat to sustainable development. He notes that humankind uses more than 40 percent of the earth's primary productivity. As we approach the year 2000, he sees the three economies as worlds in collision, creating major social and environmental challenges. He concludes that "like it or not, the responsibility for ensuring a sustainable world falls largely on the shoulders of the world's enterprises, the economic engines of the future."[5]

Trade Policy and the Environment

In the winter of 1992, shortly before the Earth Summit meetings in Rio de Janeiro, the secretariat of the General Agreement on Tariffs and Trade (GATT) issued a report on trade and the environment.[6] The report specifically addressed the link between agriculture and trade. Its major point was that European Union (EU) and U.S. agricultural policies seriously hurt the environment. U.S. programs that aimed for higher yields per acre encouraged increased use of chemical fertilizers and pesticides. European Union countries established high tariff barriers blocking American products grown with these chemicals. GATT was concerned that protectionist groups would lobby environmentalists and persuade them to support tariff and nontariff barriers that restricted international trade.

The report specifically criticized the U.S. decision to ban Mexican yellow fin tuna because Mexico's fishing methods also killed dolphins. It warned governments not to take unilateral actions to export domestic environmental policies. GATT's position reflected its concern that the United States and other nations might use trade sanctions to force their concepts of sound environmental practices on other countries. The report claimed "such environmental imperialism would be a fast track to chaos and conflict."[7]

---

[5] S. L. Hart, "Beyond Greening: Strategies for a Sustainable World," *Harvard Business Review,* January–February 1997, pp. 68–76.

[6] GATT is an international institution whose mission is to foster trade, resolve trade disputes, and lower trade barriers such as tariffs. There are more than 125 members including all the major industrialized nations and many developing countries.

[7] D. Dodwell, "GATT Issues Warning against Environmental Imperialism," *Financial Times,* February 12, 1992, p. 3.

GATT asserted countries should set their own policies because each nation is different. No country should appoint itself the world's guardian of environmental imperatives. Talks on environmental issues should be multilateral and foster intergovernmental cooperation.

In general, GATT took the position that free trade did not contribute substantially to environmental degradation. Expanded trade was likely to lead to greater wealth and diffusion of technology, giving nations the resources with which to protect and upgrade environmental practices.[8] The World Bank agreed with this perspective, noting that "liberalized trade fosters greater efficiency and higher productivity and may actually reduce pollution by encouraging the growth of less polluting industries and the adoption and diffusion of cleaner technologies."[9]

In December 1993, negotiators concluded GATT's Uruguay Round and established a new international body, the World Trade Organization (WTO).[10] In its October–November 1996 newsletter, *WTO Focus,* the World Trade Organization discussed the 70-page report of the WTO Committee on Trade and Environment (CTE). The CTE recommended to attendees of the First Ministerial Conference in Singapore, that it continue as a regular WTO body reporting to the General Council and "work in the WTO . . . to build a constructive policy relationship between trade, environment, and sustainable development."

When the CTE detailed its work at its latest meeting in Marrakesh, it made 10 major conclusions and recommendations:

1. A commitment not to undertake trade action to offset any real or perceived competitive disadvantage resulting from other countries' environmental policies.
2. Recognition of the right of governments to establish their national environmental standards, noting that it would [be] inappropriate for them to relax existing national environmental standards or their enforcement in order to promote their trade.
3. Endorsement of multilateral solutions based on international cooperation and consensus as the best and most effective way for governments to tackle environmental problems of a transboundary or global nature.
4. Confirmation of the need to preserve the valuable scope that already exists under WTO provisions for the use of trade-related measures needed for environmental purposes, including those taken pursuant to multilateral environmental agreements (MEAs).

---

[8] Ibid.

[9] *World Development Report, 1992: Development and the Environment* (Washington, DC: The World Bank, 1992), p. 67.

[10] The WTO home page can be found at [http://www.wto.org].

5. Encouragement of greater cooperation between the WTO and relevant MEA institutions, and recognition of the positive role in granting observer status for the relevant MEAs in WTO bodies in creating clearer appreciation of the mutually supportive environmental policies.
6. Recognition that eco-labeling schemes and programs can be effective instruments of environmental policy to encourage the development of an environmentally conscious public, and a call for transparency in their preparation, adoption and application and allowing participation of interested parties from other countries.
7. Recommendation on the creation of a database, accessible to all members, of all WTO notifications of trade-related environmental measures.
8. Emphasis on the importance of market access opportunities in assisting developing countries to obtain the resources to implement national development and environmental policies.
9. Encouragement to members to provide technical assistance and transfer of technology to help strengthen the technical capacity of developing countries in monitoring and controlling imports of domestically prohibited goods.
10. Recognition of the need to respond to public interest in WTO activities in the area of trade and environment, and a recommendation to continue interaction of the WTO Secretariat with non-governmental organizations and the derestriction of all CTE documents.[11]

Reaction to the report was mixed. Singapore, on behalf of the ASEAN nations, described the report as balanced and said it represented substantial progress in clarifying trade–environment issues. The European Union(EU) was disappointed the report had fallen short of its early high ambitions. On the other hand, the EU acknowledged, the report showed the CTE was open to further exploration of the connection between trade and the environment. The United States was generally pleased and said the report made valuable contributions. It particularly applauded the agreement on greater openness. Japan, too, was generally laudatory but said the WTO had to work harder to avoid "the rule of the jungle" in the trade–environment field.[12]

While the GATT, the WTO, and World Bank positions reflect the most prevalent view of the link between the environment and trade, some argue that polluting industries will try to locate where environmental laws are more

---

[11] *WTO Focus* 13, October–November 1996, pp. 4–5.
[12] Ibid.

lax and even suggest developing countries will compete for foreign investment in dirty industries by lowering their environmental standards.

There is scant evidence for this view. Chile, for example, has few controls on industrial emissions and is open to foreign trade and investment. Its cheap and efficient labor force, rather than its lack of environmental regulations, draws multinational investment.

Increasingly management of the international environment is being seen as a multilateral problem that must be addressed quickly, effectively, and multilaterally. Individual nations no longer have the luxury of putting off environmental concerns for another day or another year.

The Environment and the European Union

Green Politics

Between 1972 and the mid-1980s, the European Community adopted several action plans that generated a spate of environmental directives. In 1987, the European Community placed the issue of the environment near the top of its agenda and member nations made an explicit commitment to move to "a high level of [environmental] protection."[13]

Nevertheless, it was difficult to achieve agreement among countries that varied so widely in their own political structures, national interests, levels of industrial development, and economic well-being. Unlike the United States, most European governments were made up of coalitions of many large and small special-interest parties.

Green parties representing environmental interests are now major players in European governments. The first national Green Party was organized in Germany in the late 1970s. It was an alliance of left-wing, ecology-oriented groups whose members had little in common other than their commitment to the environment. Despite a great deal of internal dissension, the German Green Party held its first Congress in January 1980.

On March 22, 1983, 27 Greens walked through Bonn carrying a huge rubber globe and the branch of a tree dying from Black Forest pollution. Calling themselves *die Grunen,* they entered the West German national assembly building and took seats as the first new party to be elected in more than 30 years. They insisted on being seated between the conservative Christian Democrats and the left-liberal Social Democrats. They considered

---

[13] R. Vernon, "The Triad as Policy Makers" (Center for Science and International Affairs, John F. Kennedy School of Government, Harvard University, December 1992), pp. 24–25.

themselves the political voice of citizens' movements such as ecology (anti-toxic waste, radiation, air pollution, and pro-eco development), antinuclear energy, peace (antimissile movement, demilitarization), and feminism.

Within a short time, Green parties organized in all European Community (EC) countries to agitate for an environmentally sound EC policy. Eurocrats agreed a common environmental policy was critical to a united Europe. However, they disagreed about who should pay for the policy and how to implement and enforce it.

In October 1992, EC environment ministers met to discuss their commission's green strategy for the 1990s. The ministers were concerned about how they would handle the issue of subsidiarity as applied to the environment. The Maastricht Treaty vaguely and generally defines subsidiarity as the concept that political authority should be exercised at the level most appropriate to the function in question and that government should supplement, not replace, action by individuals and families.[14]

If subsidiarity were applied to environmental policy, each country would implement its own environmental rules. Even though countries share waterways and are greatly affected by one another's airborne pollution, national rules and regulations would prevail over common EC directives. From the Greens' perspective, it was essential that all 12 nations ratify the Maastricht Treaty to ensure a common environmental policy.

By the end of December 1992, 8 of the 12 countries had ratified the treaty. Denmark voted against the Maastricht Treaty in June 1992, based partly on the fear that the EU would dilute Denmark's own high environmental standards. In May 1993, Denmark reversed its earlier vote and approved a modified treaty that included a common environmental policy.

Britain postponed its vote on the Maastricht Treaty. British Greens wanted measures considerably stronger than those proposed by the commission. They promoted a program that greened EU policies from transport to energy and pushed for the formation of a green police force to enforce common standards.

By mid-1995, the newly established European Environment Agency was recruiting staff and had offices in Copenhagen. Domingo Jimenez-Beltran, the Spanish executive director of the agency, had hired one-third of the expected workforce of 60. Jimenez declared, "The main role of the agency is to provide efficient information to the policy makers and to the public . . . to improve both decision making and public participation in the process." The agency was expected to deal with global issues such as the ozone hole and global warming. It also would address European regional issues such as acid

---

[14] The Maastricht Treaty was passed by European Community leaders in December 1991. Voters in the then 12 countries approved the treaty, changed the name of the EC to the European Union, and committed their countries to new common economic, social, political, and monetary policies.

rain, pollution of the seas, forest degradation, nature conservation, protection of the ground water, and urban pollution.[15]

The agency is unique among institutions created by the EU because its membership is not limited to EU members. Norway and Iceland were early members and Switzerland applied. Poland, Hungary, the Czech Republic, Slovakia, and Slovenia were expected to join along with the Baltic republics of Latvia, Lithuania, and Estonia.

Environmental Policy Implementation

Although all 15 current EU member countries have their own cultures, political systems, and national agendas, the EU commission and council pushed them toward a more uniform approach to the environment. Some governments voluntarily spent large amounts of money to clean up water and air, even during recessionary times and were dismayed by their neighbors who ignored the rules. They asked whether they should continue to bear the cost if other members refused.

The poorer countries charged the commission was too ambitious and imposed excessively costly rules. For example, the commission's drinking water directives came under heavy fire. The directives mandated that every trace of lead, pesticides, nitrates, and bacteria be removed, even though health risks from tiny residual amounts of these substances were unproven. The rules also dictated that the water look clear even when its safety was not affected by cloudiness.

By 1995, the EU commission had issued 200 directives on environmental management. Wealthy industrialized countries like Germany, Denmark, and The Netherlands had much stricter environmental standards and spent much more than did poorer countries such as Portugal, Greece, Spain, and, in some instances, Italy. The poorer countries believed they could not finance tougher environmental measures and assumed the richer EU countries would help them with the costs. EU environmental experts agreed a successful common environmental policy would have to address costs. The northern European countries would have to decide whether they would help the southern countries and, if so, which directives were the most important.

Corporate Involvement. Corporations inside the EU were important stakeholders in developing and implementing environmental policy. In the early 1990s, more and more companies began revealing information about their green performances. Many companies developed publications to inform stakeholders such as shareholders, employees, and local communities where they operated. Corporations in Europe did not have to comply with rules as

---

[15] H. Barnes, "Continental Mandate: The European Environment Agency," *Financial Times,* June 21, 1995, p. IV.

strict as those in the United States. However, industry realized the quality of its voluntary compliance would help shape future EU laws.

Corporate Europe took another giant step forward in March 1993. After three years of discussion, the EU commission established a voluntary eco-management system for corporations. When the commission first drafted its proposals in 1990, it recommended mandatory eco-audits for all industrial companies larger than a specified size. That scheme was rejected but negotiations proceeded.

The new, voluntary Eco-Management and Audit Scheme (EMAS) included the establishment of corporate environmental management systems. Participating companies were required to

- Establish environmental policies, goals, and management systems.
- Systematically self-assess their environmental policies through site audits at time intervals no longer than three years.
- Provide information to the public about the results of the audits.
- Have independent verification by external auditors, who would be licensed by each nation.

All audits had to contain figures on each site's pollution emissions, waste output, consumption of raw materials, energy and water, and noise levels. They had to present overall company policy, goals, eco-management policies of the site, and the name of the accredited external auditor. In return for adopting this process, companies could use a green logo to indicate their involvement as long as they did not use it on their products or promotional materials. While some critics worried that this voluntary system would be made mandatory, most companies saw the system as a positive and low-risk means of establishing green credentials, boosting their corporate image, and establishing systems the EU would eventually impose anyway.[16]

As with ISO 9000, the Environmental Management System itself required a planned comprehensive periodic audit to ensure that its operation was effective in meeting specified goals. Most companies produced an annual report and accounts describing the activities of the organization over the previous year and discussing its future plans. EMAS expected a similar system for the company's environmental performance. An externally accredited EMAS verifier reviewed and validated the company's policy statement, its program, its management system, and audit cycles. If they were all satisfactory, the verifier provided a registration number and confirmed the company's environmental statements.[17]

The EU is making rapid progress toward a comprehensive and uniform environmental policy. It still faces problems of who should bear the cost,

---

[16] A. Jack, "The Green Time Bomb," *Financial Times,* March 31, 1993, p. 14.

[17] Internet [http://www.quality.co.uk/emas.htm#Description] "The European Eco Management & Audit Scheme EMAS," 1996.

what body should implement its policies, and what responsibility it has to its newly independent neighbors in Eastern Europe.

The Environment and Eastern Europe

In 1989, the world looked in wonder at the demolition of the Berlin Wall. The Soviet Union disintegrated soon afterward, leaving the rest of its former political and economic bloc countries to establish independent governments. For the first time since the end of World War II, horrified observers saw the environmental cost of Soviet industrial policies.

Eastern Europe was a cesspool. Pollution in East Germany was so pervasive that all life was extinct in one-third of the country's waterways. Farmland was so heavily contaminated by pesticides that even hardy earthworms failed to survive. Mountain peaks were barren because acid rain had damaged 90 percent of all the trees in the country. The then West German newsmagazine *Der Spiegel* called East Germany a cauldron of poison.[18] East Germany's environmental problems were duplicated all over Eastern Europe.

In 1994, five years after the collapse of communism, the region was still decaying. Chemical works, smelters, coal mines, and power plants sent waste into the air and water in levels far higher than international standards. Toxic dumps still poisoned groundwater and raw sewage spilled into waterways.

Regional leaders struggled with the balance between economic recovery and the environment. Antipollution devices, fines, and taxes vied with jobs and employment in public policy decision making. Leaders asked whether continued pollution would bring more health problems and cleanup costs in the future. The head of Bulgaria's environment group spoke for many Eastern Europeans when he said that "the modern notion that development and environmental protection should go together has not reached here."[19]

Eastern European attitudes toward energy use were very hard to change. Under the Communists, energy was very cheap and was seen as an entitlement. People abrogated responsibility for energy to their governments, many of which were part the problem. For example, Bulgaria's minister of energy wanted to make more electricity so the utilities could make more money. He also wanted to keep the coal mines open because the mine unions were very important politically. Rejecting outright a plan from the European Bank for Reconstruction and Development to cut sulfurous brown coal fumes, he demanded money for a new power plant and even additional transmission lines.

---

[18] "East Germany: Cauldron of Poison," *World Press Review,* March 1990, p. 66.

[19] M. Simons, "East Europe Sniffs Freedom's Air, and Gasps," *New York Times,* November 3, 1994, p. A1.

Conservationists, environmentalists, and Green Party members in Eastern Europe admitted that the burgeoning market economy was wiping out any movement to reduce pollution. They noted that not only did new packaging, foam, plastic, and cans litter the landscape but also recycling programs that existed under communism had collapsed. Millions of privately owned cars fueled by leaded gasoline wiped out any reduction in pollution achieved by idle factories. Hartwig Berger, spokesman for the Green Party in Germany, declared, "There was a chance for fundamental change in the East, a chance for a new beginning . . . but so far it has been squandered."[20]

The Example of Poland

In 1983, the Polish government designated 27 geographic areas as areas of economic hazard. These danger zones covered 11.3 percent of the country's land and water mass and were home to 12.9 million people. Government officials said even the best areas of the country had suffered serious environmental damage and the worst were ecological disasters.

By 1989, pollution-related losses to forests, crops, buildings, and human health had cost Poland up to 20 percent of its national income.[21] None of Poland's waterways had drinkable water; 65 percent were loaded with salt, mercury, cyanide, and human feces. Even industries were afraid to use the water. The Vistula River was an open sewer, and 53 percent of the lakes were too polluted for industrial use.

A World Bank study found coal mines threw their untreated corrosive waste into rivers and canals. These chemicals ate right through the pipes that carried them. Coal-powered factories and utilities had no scrubbers, and very few had filters. The winds carried their airborne pollutants for miles in every direction.

Car exhausts further added to air pollution. Poland had no emissions-control regulations, and car engines burned an oil-gasoline blend that emitted up to eight times more hydrocarbons and 50 percent more carbon dioxide than plain gasoline.

Fifty percent of Poland's forests were badly damaged, and another 17 percent were ravaged by sulfur dioxide and other chemical pollutants. Eighty-three percent of Poland's farmland was highly acidic. Forty-one animal species became extinct in the 1980s, and 66 percent of the remaining species were jeopardized.

Life expectancy for men who survived infancy was lower than it had been in the late 1960s. In upper Silesia, where industry was concentrated, cancer rates were 30 percent higher than normal, respiratory disease was up

---

[20] Ibid., p. A14.
[21] L. Tye, "Poland Is Left Choking on Its Wastes," *Boston Globe,* December 18, 1989, p. 1.

47 percent, and every fourth pregnancy suffered medical complications. The infant mortality rate was 20 per 1,000 compared to 6 per 1,000 in Sweden.[22]

By 1991, the market economy had reduced the pollution level in Poland. Between the beginning of 1990 and mid-1991, the government eliminated industrial subsidies and centrally controlled energy prices. The price of gasoline was cut free to rise to world market levels. Electricity charges doubled and the price of coal rose more than 250 percent.

As the cost of energy rose, old factories became increasingly inefficient and many quickly went out of business. With the cost of energy rising, factory and utility company managers tried to find ways to burn coal more efficiently. Instead of releasing the 4.2 million tons of sulfur gas each year, they tried to recover it and sell it for profit. In Poland, market incentives cleaned up the environment more quickly than government regulation.[23]

By 1996, Poland had taken the lead in Eastern European environmental cleanup. The government estimated it would need $10 billion over the next four years for additional environmental cleanup. Poland passed strict environmental laws and created an inspection agency that levied some of the highest fines in the world. The proceeds from the fines went into cleanup funds including the National Fund for Environmental Protection & Water Management. PATKO, a unit of the fund, was a Polish–American consulting firm based in Warsaw. It matched Polish companies that needed cleanups with American companies that had the necessary technology. PATKO also located financing from Polish sources, the U.S. Export–Import Bank, the European Bank for Reconstruction and Development, and private banks. TRC Cos., an environmental consulting and engineering company based in Windsor, Connecticut, owned 48 percent of PATKO. TRC's partners were the Bank of Environmental Protection and ECO-Effect, an environmental consultant.[24]

A 1996 report by the Organization for Economic Cooperation and Development (OECD) reviewed Poland's progress.[25] The report concluded that despite substantial progress and Western involvement, Poland still had major pollution problems. Air quality was much better than it had been in 1989 but sulfur dioxide and particulate levels remained very high compared to those of Poland's OECD neighbors. The energy sector was the major source of air pollution; plants were fueled with coal and lignite that produced very high pollution levels.

Poland was a significant contributor to global warming with the sixth highest level of CO_2 emissions in Europe. However, the nation's environmental policy contained provisions to combat global warming and its leaders

---

[22] Ibid.
[23] P. Fuhrman, "Breathing the Polish Air," *Forbes,* June 24, 1991, p. 40.
[24] K. L. Miller, "Cleaning Up after Communism," *Business Week,* September 23, 1996, p. 142N.
[25] The OECD is a multilateral organization of industrialized and semi-industrialized countries that help develop social and economic policies.

ratified the United Nation's Framework Convention on Climate Change. Poland's Ministry of Environmental Protection committed itself to stabilizing CO_2 emissions at 1988 levels by the year 2000.

Poland's available water per capita was one of the lowest in Europe and its consumption per unit of gross domestic product (GDP) two to three times as high as the OECD countries. In 1996, only 37 percent of the population was hooked up to sewage treatment plants. As a result, much of Poland's available water still was seriously polluted.

Poland was one of Europe's largest sources of industrial waste both in absolute terms and as a function of GDP. In 1996, only 9.3 percent of industrial waste was treated; almost all of it went untreated into landfills. Only 26 percent of hazardous waste was treated and the rest was simply discharged into the environment.

The 27 zones of economic hazard established in 1983 were still subject to government oversight and covered 10 percent of the country. Poland's goal for nature conservation was to develop an integrated network of protected areas and to increase those areas to cover 30 percent of the country.[26] Although Poland had formidable environmental problems, it was making progress with the help of an organized international effort.

The Example of the Former Soviet Union

When people discuss the former Soviet Union and the environment, they nearly always do so in the context of the 1986 Chernobyl accident. Zhores A. Medvedev, author of *Nuclear Disaster in the Urals,* reported that prior to the Chernobyl explosion, there was virtually no discussion of the environment within the Soviet Union. The government withheld news of catastrophic accidents from the press and the populace. Few people challenged the view that central planning served the interests of environmental protection better than capitalism. The Soviet nuclear industry had no competition and no responsibility to external stakeholders. It also had no incentive to use modern, safer, but more expensive technology.

Like the Chernobyl plant, most of the other nuclear plants still in operation after the Soviet breakup were unsafe. In 1991 alone, more than 270 malfunctions occurred at nuclear plants. Russia resisted pressure to shut down even the most dangerous reactors because it had no other power source.[27]

Western experts worried about Russia's reliance on unsafe and outdated technology. In November 1992, Russian and Western technical experts got together at a meeting sponsored by the United Nations International Atomic Energy Agency. Senior Russian officials told a watchdog group of Western

---

[26] Internet [http://www.rri.org/envatlas/europe/poland/pl-conc.html#Air] "Poland: Areas of Concern," 1996.

[27] "Preventing Chernobyl II," *Business Week,* June 8, 1992, pp. 44–51.

experts that they would continue using Chernobyl-type plants indefinitely. The officials asserted that although the plants had problems, they had been made safer.

Western scientists remained skeptical, calling the plants' internal workings plumbers' nightmares. Unlike Western nuclear plants, none of Russia's plants was surrounded by a container to limit contamination due to an explosion. The chairperson of Russia's Research and Development Institute of Power Engineering, Dr. Eugene Adamov, expressed his country's tension between economic needs and safety concerns. He defended Russia's policy, saying, "Reagan and Bush set out to destroy the 'Evil Empire,' and they succeeded. Now it seems you want to destroy our economy as well. . . . What we need from you is medicine for the illness, not just [for] the symptoms."[28]

Three months after the February 1993 conference, two fires and an oil leak at Chernobyl heightened fears that safety measures were lax at this and other nuclear plants. But Chernobyl provided power to Kiev, Russia, and several Eastern European countries, including Poland, the Czech Republic, Hungary, and Romania. Even if Chernobyl were completely shut down, nobody knew how to dismantle it.[29]

In April 1996, 10 years after the Chernobyl disaster, one-fourth of the adjoining country of Belarus was still uninhabitable. The government established a fenced-in danger zone and forced people who lived inside the zone to move to housing projects in Gomel, a city 70 miles north of Chernobyl. There was no question that the accident was responsible for a rise in the cases of thyroid cancer but scientists were unable to find statistical data to prove that people who had lived within the zone had more physical illnesses than people who were not exposed to radiation.[30]

After much negotiation and jockeying, the Ukrainian government promised to close the two remaining reactors at Chernobyl by the year 2000. The condition for the closure was that the Group of Seven leading industrial countries deliver $3.1 billion in aid.

Western experts continued to stress the dangers posed by some of the former Soviet Union's reactors. The European Commission's technical assistance to the Commonwealth of Independent States group (Tacis) implemented a pilot project to give western Europe early warning of any accidental releases of radiation. The system had radiation monitors situated around nuclear stations connected by radio link to local response centers that would collect and process the data. All data would be sent automatically to response

---

[28] M. W. Browne, "Russians Planning to Continue Using Faulty Reactors," *New York Times,* November 8, 1992, p. 1.

[29] L. Hayes, "Fires at Chernobyl Heighten Safety Concerns," *The Wall Street Journal,* February 4, 1993, p. A14.

[30] M. Specter, "10 Years Later, through Fear, Chernobyl Still Kills in Belarus," *New York Times,* March 31, 1996, p. 1.

centers in Kiev and Minsk by dedicated phone lines. Summary data also would be sent to Europe by E-mail on a routine basis.[31] Despite the warning system, scientists continued to worry about accidents at other plants in Belarus and Ukraine.

In the post-Chernobyl years, the Soviet public began to confront the truth about environmental degradation. Water usage was a major problem. In the 1950s, under the Soviet regime, hydroelectric dams created reservoirs that covered a total area greater than the Netherlands. As industry and agriculture used more and more water from the 1960s on, the water table fell. Salinization and dust storms destroyed topsoil and ruined vast tracts of cultivated land. We have discussed the environmental disaster around the Aral Sea in the case at the beginning of the chapter.

Deforestation was rampant as forests disappeared at the same rate as those in Brazil. In Siberia, inefficient harvesting and erosion destroyed more than 5 million acres of trees each year.

In the provinces of Uzbekistan and Moldavia, chemical poisoning left so many children mentally retarded that the school curriculum had to be simplified. Respiratory diseases afflicted nearly all children and elderly people in the affected areas. As these and other provinces assessed the state of their own environments in the early 1990s, they began to realize the Soviet legacy was nothing short of a national tragedy.

Sumgait, a city of 300,000 people is about an hour from Azerbaijan's capital of Baku. The city was set up before World War II due to its proximity to the Caspian Sea oil fields. Statistics compiled from local hospital records between 1970 and 1990 showed an eightfold increase in the rate of children born with birth defects. The percentage of children born prematurely nearly doubled and premature babies' mortality rate more than tripled.

After the collapse of the Soviet Union, Sumgait's factories lost their captive customers and went out of business. The buildings were empty, toxic waste was thrown into the streets, sheep and goats wandered through heaps of junk. Azerbaijan, like other former Soviet provinces, hoped to attract foreign investment and United Nation money to clean up the mess.[32]

Russia's environmental future is unclear. The country is beset with political problems, a dearth of foreign currency, and food shortages. The degree to which the government seems interested in environmental cleanup is in direct proportion to outside offers of money and technological assistance. Russian peasants have a long history of endurance in times of adversity. It seems likely the present regime will count on this attribute as it deals with its economic woes.

---

[31] D. Greek, "Gamma Curtain Drawn," *Financial Times,* April 24, 1996, p. 10.

[32] P. Graff, "Plan to Save One of World's Dirtiest Towns," *Financial Times,* July 9, 1996, p. 3.

The Environment and Asia

As Asian economies gathered steam in the early 1980s, pollution reached worrisome proportions. In some small countries, like Singapore, governments regulated industrial pollution and motor vehicle exhausts. Most others exercised little or no control over toxic emissions from factories and traffic, agricultural degradation, and filthy energy sources.

A 1994 study of eight developing nations showed that the coastlines of Asia would be seriously threatened if nothing were done to stop the flow of greenhouse gases. The Climate Institute, a highly respected Washington-based advocacy group calculated that by the year 2070 much of metropolitan Manila, Philippines, could be under water. More than 3 million people would have to be relocated from Indonesia's capital city, Jakarta, and rice production in Vietnam's Mekong and Red river deltas would be seriously imperiled. The institute's director for global environmental programs predicted that "in the future, the Asian-Pacific regions with 75 percent of the world's population, will be the world's largest source of greenhouse emissions."[33]

More people are hurt by environmental damage in Asia than anywhere else in the world, simply because Asian countries have such large populations. Indonesia's population alone is more than half that in the entire EU. Asia's pollution affects nearly half the people in the entire world. To make matters potentially worse, Asia's population and cities are growing twice as fast as Europe's and North America's.

Taiwan, the Philippines, Thailand, Indonesia, Hong Kong, India, Bangladesh, and, most of all, China are ticking environmental time bombs. But what incentives do these countries have to defuse the bombs? One persuasive argument for change is to look at what will happen if these countries do not change. For everyone who breathes poisoned air, health costs grow. For every acre of land lost to erosion, people cannot eat. For each release of industrial waste into rivers, fishers lose their livelihood. Realistically, Asian environmental practices will change only when active green stakeholder movements force their governments to impose regulations on themselves.

China: A Nation in Transition

China is a vast industrializing country of more than 1.25 billion people. In the past, China's contribution to worldwide environmental degradation has been small compared to those of industrialized nations. But at its current rate of development, China has the potential to become one of the world's biggest polluters. The tension between economic development and environmental preservation is ongoing and unresolved. For the most part, questions about sustainable development have not been asked, much less answered.

---

[33] E. Lachica, "Asia Faces Increasing Pressure to Act as Global Warming Threatens Its Coasts," *The Wall Street Journal,* August 22, 1994, p. A5A.

In 1982, China's Ministry of Construction became the Ministry of Construction and Environmental Protection as the country implemented new laws on environmental and marine protection. Between 1982 and 1984, the government doubled the number of environmental monitoring stations to 650 and quadrupled the number of environmental protection workers to nearly 27,000. Most of the antipollution effort was concentrated in cities with scenic tourist sites and was financed by fines levied against offending industries.

These measures were not as impressive as they might sound. Because China was— and in many ways still is—a centrally planned economy, fines were simply allocated as costs of production and did not constitute a meaningful bottom-line penalty. Factory managers had no incentive to make environmental concerns a major issue.

In 1984, the government created the National Environmental Protection Agency. Most of its employees were minimally educated and trained. The main office in Beijing had 100 workers who analyzed pollution data but did little else. Although its 20,000 field workers had the power to shut down factories, impose heavy fines, and deny permission for construction of certain industries, they rarely did so.

In fact, national policy worked against environmental protection. Rural development was the key element of the government's economic drive. More than 15 million small local factories were built between 1978 and 1988. They raised income levels in the countryside and absorbed surplus rural labor. By 1988, these factories accounted for more than one-quarter of China's industrial output. However, they also contributed to pollution. China's National Environmental Protection Agency estimated that 40 percent of these small and midsize factories had pollution problems.

In fact, China's overall industrial development repeated the worst mistakes of England's industrial revolution. High-sulfur coal constituted more than 70 percent of all fuel consumed in China. In the late 1980s, a visitor to Hohhot, the capital of Inner Mongolia, saw and smelled the haze of greasy coal smoke hovering over this city of several million people. In the evening, cooking stoves burned charcoal, whose fumes contributed to the smog.

Water quality was no better than air quality. Tap water was not, and still is not, drinkable in most Chinese cities and towns. Work units, factories, and villages provide huge steel containers of boiled and filtered drinking water. By 1989, 29,000 miles of waterways were so heavily polluted that they no longer sustained marine life. Industrial and domestic sewage ruined nearly one-third of China's coastal fishing.

Pesticides such as DDT, long banned in the United States, were regularly used in China until the end of the 1980s. Untreated human waste was spread on the fields as fertilizer. Effluence filtered into rivers, lakes, and canals.

About 5 billion tons of topsoil washed away each year, and 1.1 million acres of farmland were covered by the concrete of encroaching cities. Original forests disappeared so quickly experts predicted at that rate, not one acre of natural forest would survive to the year 2000. Because of erosion and deforestation, deserts expanded at a rate of more than 600 square miles per year and by the year 2000 will cover twice as much area as in 1949.[34]

In 1989, a small cadre of Chinese environmentalists sounded a warning about China's virtually unrestrained economic degradation. The president of the Chinese Academy of Scientists warned there could be "a deadly threat to the Chinese population if immediate action is not taken to halt pollution."[35] In 1989, only 10 percent of Chinese families owned a refrigerator loaded with chlorofluorocarbons. What would be the effect on the ozone layer if, as the government promised, every family in China owned a refrigerator by the year 2000? Although China passed stricter environmental legislation in 1989 and 1990, enforcement remains very lax. Pollution problems are still growing. In 1991, acid rain caused nearly $3 billion in damage to crops, forests, and buildings across China. Factories were expected to pump increasing amounts of carbon dioxide into the air. The 1991 level of 15.5 million tons will rise to 1.4 billion tons by the year 2000 if air pollution is not controlled. It remains to be seen how China will balance its economic development with environmental controls. How long will it take and what price will be paid before China addresses sustainable development as a political, social, and economic concern?

China and the Three Gorges Project

The Three Gorges project was designed to build the world's largest dam on China's Yangtze River. From its inception, the Chinese government promulgated it as "a dream for generations to come." China embarked on a campaign to persuade the world that the dam was the fruition of Dr. Sun Yat-sen's dream in the 1920s. Government publications reminded readers that meticulous feasibility studies concluded that the benefits of the project far outweighed the drawbacks. On April 3, 1992, the National People's Congress approved the construction of this project. The main benefits were to come in flood control, power generation, and navigation.

The government noted that people along the middle and lower reaches of the Yangtze suffered terrible losses from flooding. The great flood of 1931 covered 150,000 acres of land and killed 145,000 people. The new dam, 575 feet high and more than 1 mile across, would create a 410-mile-long reservoir with a flood control capacity of a 100-year frequency flood.

The Three Gorges Hydropower Station would generate one-ninth of the China's total power. The Yangtze's navigation capacity would be increased from 10 to 50 million tons a year and would lower transportation costs by about 36 percent.

The government acknowledged there would be problems. About 1 million people would have to be relocated but "the relocatees find higher-paying

---

[34] C. Nickerson, "China Copies Worst Polluters," *Boston Globe,* September 20, 1989, p. 1.

[35] S. Wu Dunn, "Chinese Suffer from Rising Pollution as By-Product of the Industrial Boom," *New York Times,* February 28, 1993, p. 20.

jobs in the newly set up businesses, which are usually located within the same country [county] or city. Therefore, they feel quite at home and enjoy a better living in their new homes."[36]

The government was equally reassuring about the project's environmental impact. Although the project would affect the habitat of the Chinese river dolphin and sturgeon, the government planned to perfect artificial breeding grounds. The use of hydroelectric power would reduce soft coal use, thereby cleaning the air of carbon dioxide and sulfur dioxide.

On December 1994, the government announced the formal beginning of the project. By the end of 1995, the Chinese government and outside financing bodies had invested about $1.55 billion. More than 100 cubic meters of earth and stone had been excavated. The project's first major goal was blocking the Yangtze River in November 1997.[37]

By the time of the blocking 29,300 local residents were to be resettled. The reservoir was to affect 21 cities and counties in Hubei and Sichuan provinces. It was to completely or partially submerge two prefectural cities, 11 county seats, 114 towns, and 1,599 factories. By January 1997, 64 factories had been rebuilt and 256 additional ones were under construction.[38]

The Chinese government provided substantial funding for the Three Gorges Project but it was, by no means, the only funding institution. U.S. funding came from private banks, companies, and the Export–Import Bank, a federal agency specializing in foreign lending to support exports. In 1992, Congress revised the Ex-Im Bank's charter to include a requirement that the bank establish environmental review procedures consistent with the bank's objectives. The bank's board was authorized to grant or withhold financing support after assessing the beneficial and adverse environmental effects of the proposed transactions. In 1995, the Ex-Im Bank's environmental procedures and guidelines went into effect..

By June 1996, the Ex-Im Bank was deeply involved in an aggressive outreach effort to support U.S. exporters doing business in China. As the bank's largest customer in Asia, China had supported $3.8 billion in U.S. exports to China since 1992. It had allocated more than $10 billion in potential financing for transactions in power (conventional coal-fired, hydro, nuclear, and wind energy), aircraft, airports, telecommunications, and more.

Before the Ex-Im Bank issued letters of interest indicating the bank's willingness to provide financing to the Three Gorges Project for purchases of U.S.-made equipment, the bank reviewed financial, technical, and environmental issues raised by the project. The bank also consulted with other U.S. government agencies including the National Security Council. The bank had

---

[36] Internet [http://www.china-embassy.org/Cgi-Bin/Press.pl?105] "The Three Gorges Project: A Brief Introduction."

[37] Ibid.

[38] Internet [http://www.china-embassy.org/Cgi-Bin/Press.pl?255] "Three Gorges Resettlement Program Enters Key Stage."

a series of open meetings with exporters, nongovernment organizations, and Chinese officials and met with many members of Congress and congressional staff.[39]

Environmentalists in the United States and other countries condemned the Three Gorges Project. *Planet ENN,* an Internet environmental publication, pointed out potential problems. There was no doubt that one of the world's most scenic areas would be devastated by the dam. The Three Gorges were carved out by the river and erosion about 70 million years ago. Their spectacular beauty and cultural artifacts would be lost forever.

By October 1996, almost nothing had been done to save the cultural antiquities along the river, and Chinese art scholars were distraught. Generations of Chinese had built their temples on the rock formations towering above the Yangtze River. Shibaozhai, which means "stone rock fortress," was a threatened 18th-century 12-story pagoda. A local villager said, "Without Shibaozhai, there are only mountains and poverty here."[40] Preservationists proposed surrounding the site with an oval shaped wall to create an island in the lake and make the red pagoda a scenic focal point.

The project's chief engineer was not concerned about the loss of historical artifacts, however. He asserted that the Chinese people were not interested in cultural preservation. "To tell you the truth," he said, "the common people of China have such a low education level that they will not be able to enjoy these cultural relics, and only some of these experts will go to these museums."

In addition to the artistic loss, other environmental consequences were potentially devastating. Many experts expected silt (suspended solids) to build up in the tail of the dam, the area where the back surge of the river deposited its silt. Siltation would interfere with navigation as would the lock system. Other hydroelectric dams in China that used locks to lower and raise the water so boats could move around the dam already had experienced substantial mechanism difficulties.

The Federation of Chinese Students and Scholars in Canada provided the following story on their web site. A former director of the Chinese Academy of Science visited another project with locks similar to those planned for Three Gorges. "He asked an official of the Gezhouba project how long it would take to pass the dam. The answer was '45 minutes.' Then he asked the same question to the captain when he boarded the ship. To his surprise, the answer he got this time was 'usually 4 or 5 hours.' What made the difference? Well, the ship carrying the 'big shot' . . . would surely get lifted when they got there. But normally the ship lift will wait until 'small potatoes' fill up the chamber, and that usually takes several hours. Naturally the next question is

---

[39] Internet [http://www.exim.gov/3gorges.html.] "Frequently Asked Questions about the Three Gorges Dam Project," June 1996.

[40] P. E. Tyler, "Dam's Inexorable Future Spells Doom for Yangtze Valley's Rich Past," *New York Times,* October 6, 1996, p. 12.

how long will it 'usually' take to pass [Three Gorges Project], a much higher dam claimed to provide much greater navigation benefit?" The webmaster did not bother to respond to a question with such an obvious answer.[41]

Flood control also was questionable. Although most agreed that flooding in the middle reaches of the river would be alleviated, the area above the dam would suffer as the waters backed up. As the flow was reduced, pollution would be concentrated and saltwater would back up in the Shanghai estuary, contaminating the city's drinking water supply.[42]

Although environmentalists raised scores of objections to the Three Gorges Project, it was clear the Chinese government would go ahead as scheduled. Nearly all observers expected historical artifacts to be lost, people to be displaced, aquatic species to disappear, and accidents to happen. It was equally clear the Chinese government would bring the project to fruition and deal with problems if they arose later.

Development versus the Environment

The World Bank's study, *World Development Report, 1992,* addressed four major themes through which it explored the relationship between the environment and economic development.[43] The *Report* noted that sound economic policies can deliver environmental benefits and that government and the private sector must work together to achieve those benefits.

Since the private sector did not provide strong incentives to halt environmental degradation, the governmental role was critical. For example, when a government eliminated subsidies for fossil fuels and water, gave poor farmers property rights, and made heavily polluting, state-owned companies compete, both economic efficiency and the environment benefited.

Four Themes

Water and Sanitation. The World Bank estimates the volume of water for household use will need to rise sixfold in the next 40 years to meet demand. As people in developing countries continue to move from the countryside to cities, urban populations will triple. Currently, as much as 90 percent of the water in the least-developed countries goes to irrigation, compared to 39 percent in high-income countries. Governments around the world will

---

[41] Internet [http://theory.caltech.edu/people/ckchow/hkf/TGP1-06%3aNavigation] December 4, 1995.

[42] Internet [http://www.enn.com/feature/fe052796/feature1.htm] "China's 'Golden Waterway'," May 27, 1996.

[43] Much of the following discussion is taken from the World Bank's *World Development Report, 1992: Development and the Environment* cited in note 9.

have to reallocate water, an undertaking rife with profound political, economic, and social implications.

Most urban residents of developing countries want water piped into their homes, and many are willing to pay for it. Their governments, however, assume the people cannot bear the full cost. Therefore, governments have used their limited public resources to subsidize poorly constructed and unreliable systems. Residents who are poorly served must buy water from private vendors, paying up to 10 times what they would pay for efficiently piped water.

The World Bank recommends a variety of programs to service those unable to pay and provide a variety of options to those willing and able to pay. Two alternatives, privatization and franchising water supplies, have been successfully adopted in Africa and Latin America.

A 1995 World Bank report on water resources and management in the 21st century noted that more than 1 billion people worldwide did not have access to safe water supplies and 1.7 billion did not have access to adequate sanitation facilities. The 21st century will bring formidable challenges in water management. Rapid population growth leads to increased demands for water in agriculture and expanding urban centers. Water quality is likely to fall and pollution will create new health hazards. There may be increased international conflict over water resources as energy needs rise.[44]

The World Bank is deeply involved in water resource management. The bank assists borrowers in developing a comprehensive framework for designing water resource investments, policies, and institutions. It also tries to make sure that its individual lending programs are linked to the borrower country's priorities for reform and investment and to the bank's support program. Whenever a country makes inadequate progress or seriously misuses the resource, the bank limits its lending to operations that provide potable water for poor households or conserve water and protect its quality without drawing on the country's water resources.[45]

Water in Sub-Saharan Africa. The World Bank reviewed water issues in Africa in October 1996. It noted that about two-thirds of Sub-Saharan Africa's rural population and one-quarter of the urban population were without safe drinking water. By the year 2000, approximately 300 million Africans were likely to live in a water-scarce environment.

Sub-Saharan Africa's population was expected to exceed 1 billion people by 2025. Population growth and economic development were likely to lead to excess demand on water in most countries; the percentage of the

---

[44] Internet [http://www.worldbank.org/html/gef/text/gefceo/spewater.htm] M. T. El-Ashry, "Water Resources and Management in the 21st Century," December 13, 1995.

[45] Internet [http://www,worldbank.org/html/opmanual/ops/407Tx.html] "Water Resources Management: A World Bank Policy Paper," 1993.

population without access to clean water would increase. Urban areas, whose population has poor sanitation practices, discharge untreated wastewater causing widespread water contamination. The diarrhea death rate of 17 per thousand is the highest in the world.

The bank concluded that Africa needed integrated water resource management to reach its social, economic, and environmental goals. Countries would need to cooperate regionally and share water rationally. They would have to have a vision that encompassed economic growth, food security, and environmental stability. Political stability would be necessary for this vision to become reality. Maintaining its support of free-market forces, the World Bank exhorted the countries to develop market-like solutions and choose policies that favored economic incentives to use and price water more efficiently.

Between 1961 and 1995, cumulative bank lending to 30 countries totaled nearly $4.6 billion. During this period, lending had shifted from supporting physical infrastructure investments to operations focusing on the rehabilitation of existing facilities. Efforts focused on (a) improving urban water supplies, (b) monitoring groundwater resources, and (c) improving cost recovery. The bank assured borrowers in the region it would continue its financial and advisory support. The report's author noted, "Water gives life to Africa's people and is essential to the region's social, economic, and environmental security."[46]

Emissions from Energy and Industry. Household energy use creates indoor and outdoor pollution. In Africa and South Asia, people burn wood and plant fibers inside their homes, creating indoor pollution. In China, India, and Eastern Europe, people burn polluting soft coal. As people turn away from these polluting fuels, they will likely switch to cleaner coal, oil, gas, or electricity for cooking and heating. Making cleaner fuels available at affordable prices will accelerate the pace of such a switch.

Electric power generation accounts for 30 percent of all fossil fuel consumption worldwide. A shift to clean coal or natural gas can reduce emissions of carbon monoxide and particulates by 99.9 percent. In 1992, the World Bank recommended that all new power plants using coal be equipped with particulate matter trapping devices to clean emissions. Once installed, these traps must be well maintained.

Conversion to renewable energy sources such as solar energy and wind power also shows some promise. Each year, the earth receives about 10 times as much energy from the sun as is stored in all fossil fuel. The unit costs of solar energy have fallen by 95 percent since the early 1970s. Wind power technology is improving, and unit costs can be greatly reduced.

---

[46] Internet [http://www.worldbank.org/aftdr/findings/english/find74.htm] N. P. Sharma, "African Water Resources: Challenges and Opportunities for Sustainable Development," Technical Paper No. 331.

Vehicles account for 50 percent of oil consumption in most developing countries. They produce as much as 95 percent of lead and carbon monoxide emissions. Vehicle maintenance standards in developing countries are generally low. Without major intervention, developing-country vehicle emissions could quadruple by the year 2030. Malaysia, Singapore, and Mexico are among the countries converting to lead-free fuel. They are using a combination of market incentives such as fuel and vehicle taxes. They also are passing regulations that mandate emission standards and require manufacturers to install catalytic converters.

Industrial pollution is fairly easy to regulate if a country's plants are big enough and few in number. Ample technology is available to deal with emissions from such industries as cement, metallurgy, chemicals, paper, and pulp. In much of the developing world, however, there are thousands of small plants whose by-products are impossible to track. Smaller industries, particularly leather tanning and gold mining, are especially dangerous because they release toxic chemicals into water supplies.

Rural Environmental Challenges and Forestation. Rural people and policy makers face two major environmental challenges. The first is to prevent degradation resulting not only from growing demands for food, fuel, and fiber but also from poor management due to poverty, ignorance, and corruption. The second is to preserve forests, wetlands, coastal areas, and grasslands.

In the future, most increased food production will come from higher yields on existing farmland. But more intensive cultivation will cause environmental problems such as overfertilization and overuse of pesticides that run off into the water supply.

The World Bank recommends governments adopt policies that will strengthen local research and develop credit systems to enable farmers to make long-term investments. It also suggests governments impose taxes on pesticides to reduce their use and undertake research to develop fewer toxic substances. Farmer education, training programs, and follow-up assessments are critical.

Communal resource management is common in many developing countries. Sometimes management breaks down, resulting in overgrazed ranges, depleted woodlands, and overfished lakes and rivers. Sound communal practices can be encouraged by fostering effective leadership and legal protection. The World Bank warns, however, that nationalization of communal lands is almost never a good idea.

Whether or not nationalization makes sense, government-owned and managed land is the norm in many developing countries. Governments have sponsored settlement programs on these lands with mixed results. Countries in West Africa and the Amazon Basin have successfully allocated land to settlers, loggers, and extractive industries while continuing to protect the rights of indigenous people. However, these situations are the exception.

The impact of logging on government-owned tropical forests has been particularly destructive. In 1990, a joint report of the World Resources Institute and the United Nations found 40 to 50 million acres of tropical forest were cleared each year for agriculture and other development. The rate of loss was nearly 50 percent higher than that reported in 1980 by the United Nations Food and Agriculture Organization.

Spokespeople for the World Resources Institute suggested their estimates were probably quite conservative. In nine major tropical countries, total annual loss of forest acreage was about four times higher than estimates from 1981 to 1985. Brazil suffered the greatest loss, between 12.5 and 22.5 million acres a year. Myanmar (Burma) lost more than 500 times the 1980 estimate.[47]

The World Bank noted tropical forests were almost always owned by governments. Only governments had the authority to establish tropical forestry zones that constrained agricultural degradation and fostered managerial practices that protected biodiversity and the ecosystem. The bank recommended that governments provide economic incentives to discourage farmers, loggers, and squatters from using the land.

Proper logging procedures and policies, combined with more prudent use of cut timber, were essential. Tropical forests had to be protected to conserve soil, prevent erosion, and establish flood control. The Tropical Timber Organization found that fewer than 1 percent of tropical forests are under sustainable management. Sophisticated assessment and selection by species and size of trees and other vegetation were necessary to preserve delicate ecosystems.

In August 1996, the Consultative Group on International Agricultural Research, a United Nation-supported group, reported that poor farmers in the developing world could destroy half the remaining forest cover, with logging threatening the rest. About 38 million acres of tropical forests, or 72 acres a minute, were being destroyed by slash-and-burn farmers.

Experts agreed that solutions were hard to find in a world where poverty and population growth forced people deeper into forests to develop farm land. A World Bank official said the loss of tropical forests to farming could be stopped only by government policies combined with new agricultural practices. He suggested that government teach farmers how to cultivate more intensively and choose crops with multiple uses.

Lester R. Brown, president of Worldwatch Institute, a world resource monitoring group, argued there was little alternative to more efficient use of farmland. He noted that many countries were outrunning their resources. Population growth in large developing countries was overtaking their capacity to produce. At the same time, grain prices continued their three-decade rise.[48]

---

[47] P. Shabecoff, "Loss of Tropical Forests Is Found Much Worse Than Was Thought," *New York Times,* June 8, 1990, p. A1.

[48] B. Crossette, "Report Blames Poor Farmers for Depleting World Forests," *New York Times,* August 4, 1996, p. 9.

International Environmental Challenges. International agreements are most effective when they are based on reciprocity and address national interests. The major problem is that they are very difficult to enforce. Until recently there was no supranational body with the power to punish offenders; enforcement rested on the goodwill or moral suasion of each participant.

International Agreements on the Environment: Before Rio and Beyond

Since the early 1970s, the world population has jumped 66 percent and world economic output has doubled. During the same period, the pressures of population and industrial development have accelerated the destruction of the earth's soil, seas, forests, and wetlands at increased rates each year. In the 1980s, it finally became clear that nations had to take common action to tackle these problems.

The early international agreements focused on reducing chemicals that diminished the ozone layer and contributed to the buildup of greenhouse gases. The greenhouse effect occurs when carbon dioxide and other gases, such as methane, nitrous oxide, and chlorofluorocarbons (CFCs), trap the sun's heat in the atmosphere. The atmosphere heats up like the interior of a greenhouse. Scientists disagree about the consequences of the greenhouse effect. As we discussed earlier, some say ice caps will melt, sea levels will rise, and cities will be flooded. Rain patterns will change, turning fertile farmland into dust bowls.

In 1995, the International Panel on Climate Change (IPCC) issued a 500-page report on global warming. This respected UN-sponsored panel was made up of more than 1,500 leading climate experts from more than 60 countries. The report warned that unless the world took immediate and drastic steps to reduce the emission of heat-trapping gases, the greenhouse effect could drive global temperature up by as much as six degrees Fahrenheit by the year 2100. A rise of this magnitude would be comparable to the warming that ended the last Ice Age. Huge areas of land would be flooded by rising seas; droughts, floods, and storms would become more severe.

Why should this report be more credible than earlier ones? Climatologists test their theories by doing simulations on supercomputers. As the computer models get more sophisticated, the data analysis becomes more reliable. Until this report, the computer models had been overlooking the impact of aerosols. Aerosols are little droplets of chemicals like sulfur dioxide that are produced along with carbon dioxide when fossil fuels are burned in cars and power plants. When the scientists factored in aerosols, they found their predictions were much more accurate.

The ICCP report discussed:

- *Sea levels.* Sea levels could rise as much as 3 feet as glaciers melted and the water expanded as it warmed. Low-lying coastal areas and

river deltas could flood. Beaches would disappear along the U.S. Atlantic coast, parts of China, and the islands of the Maldives, the Seychelles, and the Cook and Marshall Islands. More than 100 million people would be displaced.
- *Warm Winters.* Although warm winters might be welcome, extremely hot summers could be lethal to the urban poor lacking air conditioning.
- *Rainfall.* Rainfall increases were likely to be spotty. Areas prone to flooding would flood more often. Drought-prone areas and deserts might become even dryer. Hurricanes would increase in number and strength. Ecosystems could be devastated and one-third of the world's forests might suffer extreme climate changes.
- *Disease.* Rises in temperature would increase the range of insect-borne diseases such as malaria, dengue fever, and yellow fever.

Some scientists scoffed at all the doomsday predictions, admonishing their colleagues and the public not to be alarmed. They argued that we needed to gather more evidence before we make any predictions or worry unnecessarily. However, they conceded that greenhouse gases were potentially very dangerous.

The great majority of scientists are seriously concerned about the consequences of global warming. Since the early 1980s, they have urged governments to take measures to reduce emissions of gases that produce the greenhouse effect. The unresolved issue is how rigorous these measures should be.

An equally serious consequence of gas buildup is the thinning and eventual destruction of the ozone layer that protects the earth from the sun's radiation. The major culprits in ozone destruction are CFCs used in aerosol cans, refrigerators, and other cooling devices such as air conditioners. Without the protection of the ozone layer in the atmosphere, the rate of skin cancer will rise and crop growth will suffer.

In 1985, the United States, Canada, the European Community, and 15 other countries signed the Vienna Convention on the Protection of the Ozone Layer and, in 1987, the Montreal Protocol. These agreements focused on eliminating CFCs and halogen gases by the year 2000.

In March 1989, 124 nations held a conference in London to discuss the greenhouse effect. Top environmental officials of the European Community called for total elimination of CFCs by the end of the century. President Bush pledged the United States would comply and would phase out their use. Hungary, Trinidad and Tobago, Zambia, the Philippines, and Malaysia promised a 50 percent reduction by the year 2000.

Three months later, the U.S. Environmental Protection Program sponsored a follow-up conference in Helsinki, Finland. Developing-country attendees based their participation on economic restructuring. The poor nations urged the industrialized countries to help them find alternatives to fossil fuel. In the keynote address, President Moi of Kenya said all nations had an obligation to protect the atmosphere, but poor nations needed financial and technological help. The Western industrialized countries and Japan stopped short of establishing a special international fund but ordered a report on the possibility of an ozone conference in London in 1990.

In June 1990, representatives of 100 countries met in London to discuss ozone depletion. Ninety-three nations agreed that by the year 2000, they would halt the production of chemicals that destroy the ozone layer. This agreement went well beyond the 1987 treaty calling for a 50 percent reduction by 1998. Developing countries were given a 10-year grace period in which to comply. The agreement created a new international body with a 14-member executive committee to administer a fund to help poorer countries make the transition to new technologies.[49]

Although the United States participated in the ozone conferences and agreed to phase out CFCs, it was less agreeable when it came to reducing carbon dioxide, the leading greenhouse gas. At the Second World Climate Conference in Geneva in October 1990, the United States, the world's largest polluter, was the only major industrialized nation to oppose specific limits on carbon dioxide emissions. An atmospheric scientist for the Environmental Defense Fund called the United States an outlaw nation.[50]

The Bush administration, reluctant to commit the United States to a policy that it believed might interfere with economic growth, invited other nations to a 1992 Earth Summit. Held under the auspices of the United Nations, one major goal of the summit was to deal with global warming. President Bush proposed that over the next 16 months, countries work on a treaty.

The Earth Summit, Rio de Janeiro

The international environmental agenda took on unprecedented dimensions. Finally, nations and their leaders recognized the seriousness of overpopulation, pollution, and the decline of natural resources. The United Nations initiative specifically addressed the conflict between economic growth and the preservation of natural resources. Heads of state and negotiators from 170 countries agreed to meet in Rio de Janeiro in June 1992 for an Earth Summit. No one thought this summit would result in easy answers. It was only the first step toward a fundamental restructuring of the industrial and social priorities

---

[49] M. W. Browne, "93 Nations Agree to Ban Chemicals That Harm Ozone," *New York Times,* June 30, 1990, p. A1.

[50] D. Dumanoski, "U.S. Is Alone at Climate Talks in Resisting Curbs on Gases," *Boston Globe,* October 29, 1990, p. 1.

of developed and industrializing countries. Agenda items were to be worked out in advance, and two treaties were to be negotiated and prepared for signing.

If meaningful progress was to be made, industrialized countries would have to reduce their dependence on natural resources and decrease pollution. Developing countries would have to cut population growth, change farming techniques, and adopt methods of development that would conserve resources and diminish harmful by-products. The summit's goal was to achieve sustainable development.[51]

The United Nations Conference on Environment and Development (UNCED) put together an 800-page agenda that the secretary of the Rio summit called "the most comprehensive international program ever proposed on environmental protection." The agenda encompassed more than 100 initiatives to be taken before the year 2000 to cut energy use, protect ocean resources, promote sustainable agricultural practices, and control toxic waste. With considerable difficulty and contention, the participants agreed to support a declaration making the eradication of poverty a global goal. They also agreed that the biggest polluters should clean up their own messes and that poorer countries should be helped to improve their standards of living in an environmentally sound way.

Summit organizers agreed active U.S. participation was critical. Throughout the preliminary negotiations, the Bush administration repeatedly threatened to boycott the summit if participants insisted on precise goals and methods for pollution reduction. A month before the meeting, it was still unclear whether President Bush would attend. He assured business leaders that he would not make a bad deal and would sign no agreements that did not protect the U.S. economy.[52] Two binding treaties were to be presented to the assembled nations: the Treaty on Global Warming and the Treaty on Biodiversity.

Treaty on Global Warming. After 10 days of talks prior to the summit, diplomats agreed on the text of a treaty to curb global warming. The Bush administration succeeded in removing limits on carbon dioxide and other greenhouse gas emissions. Environmentalists were sharply critical of U.S. negotiators who said they would not sign any accord requiring the United States to adhere to targets and timetables.

In mid-May, President Bush announced he would attend the Earth Summit and sign the global warming treaty aimed at reducing the gases that caused global warming. Vice presidential candidate Al Gore called the administration's policy one of "photo opportunities and symbols instead of real

---

[51] "Growth versus Environment," *Business Week,* May 11, 1992, p. 68.
[52] M. Wines, "Bush Likely to Go to Ecology Talks," *New York Times,* May 7, 1992, p. A1.

commitments."[53] The president's environmental advisers countered this charge, claiming the treaty set in motion a global process for stabilizing the concentration of gases at 1990 levels. Eventually 143 nations, including the United States, signed the draft treaty.

Treaty on Biodiversity. Another group of negotiators worked on an equally important treaty on biodiversity and hoped to have a draft approved before the June meeting. U.S. officials maintained the draft was unacceptable because it would force the federal government to take responsibility for wildlife preservation away from individual states. The United States also opposed the provision that made nations responsible for the environmental effects of the actions of their private companies in other countries. Administration negotiators insisted that biotechnology be considered apart from biodiversity and objected to the premise that all genetically altered organisms were inherently unsafe. They did agree in principle that developing countries should be compensated for genetic materials such as plants with cancer-treating properties.

Despite U.S. and Japanese objections, 98 nations adopted the biodiversity treaty on preserving plant, animal, and microbial species. The biodiversity treaty required developed countries to help finance and provide expertise to industrializing countries, where most of the protected species are found. Scientists warned that half the world's plant and animal species could be extinct by the year 2050 if action were not taken soon.[54]

The Meeting. As the Rio summit got under way, several issues had been settled:

- Negotiators had agreed in principle that polluters should bear the cost of pollution, poverty should be eradicated, and family planning should be promoted.
- They recognized that industrialized countries, which had created many of the problems, bore responsibility for remediation.
- They agreed, in general, to give priority to the needs of developing countries.
- They developed a $600 billion agenda to save the planet but did not specify from where the money would come.
- They agreed to try to reduce carbon dioxide and other greenhouse gas emissions to 1990 levels, but did not make such reductions mandatory.

---

[53] K. Schneider, "Bush Plans to Join Other Leaders at Earth Summit in Brazil in June," *New York Times,* May 13, 1992, p. A8.

[54] J. Perlez, "Environmentalists Accuse U.S. of Trying to Weaken Global Treaty," *New York Times,* May 19, 1992, p. C4.

- The United States committed $75 million to helping developing countries pay for the environmental agenda.[55]

The Rio summit was the largest meeting of national leaders in history. More than 35,000 participants took part in the conference, and 153 nations signed the treaties on global warming and biodiversity. In contrast, only 15 nations had signed the 1985 Vienna convention on limiting ozone-depleting chemicals.

Delegates approved three nonbinding documents: a statement to guide forestry practices, a declaration of principles on environmental policy, and Agenda 21, the massive blueprint for environmental action. The United States was the only nation that publicly refused to sign the biodiversity treaty.[56]

The Aftermath of Rio. The Rio summit left financing, timetables, and compliance mechanisms to future negotiations. The U.S. presidential election changed administrations and the government's attitude toward environmental policy. In April 1993, President Clinton announced the United States would follow a timetable to reduce the threat of global warming. Specifically, he promised to sign five executive orders directing the federal government to:

- Instruct federal agencies to change purchasing policies to use fewer substances harmful to the ozone layer.
- Commit the government to buy more American-made vehicles that use fuels such as natural gas, ethanol, methanol, and electric power.
- Require agencies to buy and use more recycled products.
- Require agencies to buy energy-efficient computers.
- Require federal offices that use toxic chemicals to publicly report their waste and releases.

President Clinton's announcement came only one day before scientists announced the ozone layer had dropped to record low levels over North America, Europe, and parts of Asia.

In 1995, 120 nations met in Berlin for the first time since Rio to talk about reducing emissions of heat-trapping industrial waste gases like carbon dioxide. The parties to the treaty agreed to begin a two-year negotiation on actual reductions in emissions after 2000. For poorer countries the stakes were very high; they needed fossil fuel to develop their economies and raise their standards of living. These countries resisted specific emission reduction targets and timetables. The planned talks on reducing greenhouse gases after 2000 were to apply only to industrialized countries and the former Soviet bloc. Developing countries softened their position by allowing rich countries

---

[55] "Summit to Save the Earth," *Time,* June 1, 1992, p. A1.
[56] P. Lewis, "Storm in Rio: Morning After," *New York Times,* June 15, 1992, p. A1.

to get credit toward meeting their reduction targets by providing technology or money to help poor countries reduce theirs. There was still considerable uncertainty among delegates about the impact of greenhouse gases. Although scientists agreed that the earth was warming, they disagreed about whether the warming was attributable to greenhouse gases.

In addition to government policy on ozone depletion, President Clinton announced he would sign the biodiversity treaty. On June 4, 1993, the president signed the Treaty on Biodiversity that created the Convention on Biological Diversity (CBD). In 1996, the CBD was still stalled in Congress. Unless it was ratified, the United States remained outside the treaty.

In March 1997 at the Rio 5 conference, Gustave Speth, head of the UN Development Program charged that the world's main industrialized countries had failed utterly to honor the commitments made in Rio. He spoke to 500 delegates from nongovernmental organizations, industry, and UN agencies who had gathered to find ways of implementing the goals set out in 1992. Speth said that big industrialized countries had made a commitment at Rio to double spending on development assistance but had actually decreased spending 20 to 25 percent in the past five years. He called for the creation of a permanent world organization to develop regional and global environmental agreements, conduct research, and promote cooperation.[57]

Internet Sources. The number of international agreements continues to proliferate since the 1972 United Nations Conference on the Human Environment. For example, the International Union for the Conservation of Nature's Environmental Law Information System (IUCN ELIS) contains information on more than 400 conservation-related treaties. Libraries cannot possibly keep up with the flood of documents that flow from secretariats. The World Wide Web offers students, faculty, and practitioners access to these documents from their own homes or offices. Exhibits 17–1, 17–2, and 17–3 and are examples of web sites from which the search can begin.

---

[57] G. Dyer, "Earth Summit Promises 'Not Kept'," *Financial Times,* March 19, 1997, p. 7.

EXHIBIT 17–1 United Nations Environment Programme

United Nations Environment Programme
Geneva Executive Center
Switzerland

Geneva is a leading center for international treaties and programmes dealing with the environment and sustainable development. Many of these activities are sponsored by the United Nations Environment Programme (UNEP). This Web site is maintained by UNEP's Information Unit for Conventions (IUC) to make information from Geneva-based sources more easily available; it also includes links to other relevant sites.

- Basel Convention on Transboundary Movements of Hazardous Wastes
- Chemicals issues (including PIC and POPs)
- Convention Calendar (view / download)
- Convention on Biological Diversity
- Convention on Climate Change
- Convention to Combat Desertification
- Convention on International Trade in Endangered Species (CITES)
- Convention on Migratory Species (The Bonn Convention)
- Financial Services Sector and the Environment
- Global Resource Information Database (GRID), Geneva and Arendal
- Intergovernmental Panel on Climate Change (IPCC)
- Ozone Secretariat (Montreal Protocol and Vienna Convention)
- Trade and the Environment
- UNEP's Regional Office for Europe
- United Nations System-Wide Earthwatch

Click here for other Web sites on environment and sustainable development.

For further enquiries, please send an e-mail to: Webmaster@unep.ch

EXHIBIT 17-2   The Ozone Secretariat WWW Home Page

The Ozone Secretariat WWW Home Page

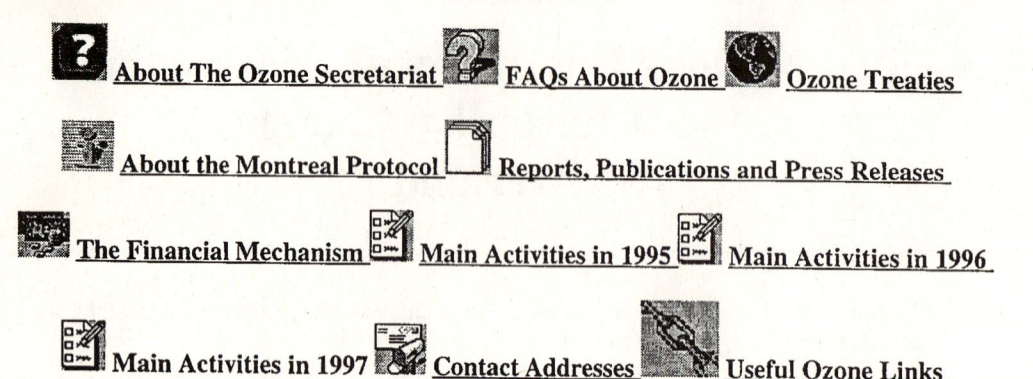

- About The Ozone Secretariat
- FAQs About Ozone
- Ozone Treaties
- About the Montreal Protocol
- Reports, Publications and Press Releases
- The Financial Mechanism
- Main Activities in 1995
- Main Activities in 1996
- Main Activities in 1997
- Contact Addresses
- Useful Ozone Links

Also take a look at what's new from the Ozone Secretariat

Ozone Secretariat Contacts....

Mr. K.M. Sarma
The Secretariat for the Vienna Convention and the Montreal Protocol
Executive Secretary
P.O. Box 30552, Nairobi, Kenya
Tel: (254-2)62-1234/62-3851
Fax: (254-2)52-1930

E-mail:
Executive Secretary: Madhava.Sarma@unep.org
Scientist: Nelson.Sabogal@unep.org
Lawyer: Gilly.Bankobeza@unep.org
Administrative Officer: Paul.Silfvenius@unep.org
Information Technology: Mohammed.Ayoub@unep.org

Last updated: 24 June 1996
Maintained by: Ozoneinfo@unep.org
URL: http://www.unep.org/unep/secretar/ozone/home.htm

EXHIBIT 17–3 International Institute for Sustainable Development–About IISD

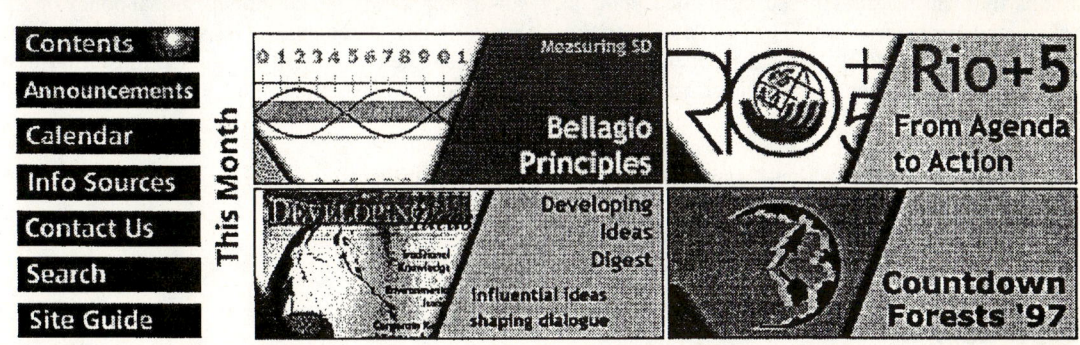

IISDnet
International Institute for Sustainable Development – About IISD

Contents
Announcements
Calendar
Info Sources
Contact Us
Search
Site Guide

This Month

Measuring SD
Bellagio Principles

Rio+5
From Agenda to Action

Developing Ideas Digest
Influential ideas shaping dialogue

Countdown Forests '97

Linkages — Our multimedia resource for environment & development policy makers

IISDnet in Feature Images
This Month
Bellagio Principles ~ Rio +5 ~ Developing Ideas Digest ~ Countdown Forests 97
** This Month **

Contents ~ Calendar ~ Information Sources ~ Search ~ Navigational Guide ~ Feedback ~ Contact Us
About IISD ~ Linkages

© International Institute for Sustainable Development

Summary

The concept of sustainable development permeates the discussion of economic development and environmental protection. Each country or region faces trade-offs and compromises in government policy in promoting environmental protection and remediation. In general, protectionism and trade barriers tend to harm sustainable development measures.

Each region faces environmental problems and develops its own measures based on unique political, social, and ideological bases. The newest industrializing nations face some of the toughest decisions about the environment. They must balance their need to raise their national economic levels against growing international pressures to ameliorate environmental problems. This chapter discusses Eastern Europe, Russia, China, and Asia in this context.

The World Bank is one of the most active and influential international bodies in suggesting policy approaches for developing countries. Its 1992 report provided developing countries with major thematic proposals for sustainable development.

In recent years, nations have begun to grapple with the possibilities for international consensus on environmental issues. The Earth Summit in Rio was a major step forward in developing global policy on the environment. It remains to be seen how its treaties will be implemented, but it signaled the seriousness with which world leaders are approaching environmental issues.

Questions

1. What is sustainable development? Choose a country in West Africa. Research that country's economic situation and suggest policies for sustainable development. Take into account the social structure, government, geography, and climatic conditions.
2. South American countries are at different stages of economic development, degree of foreign investment, and natural resource potential. Compare Brazil's environmental situation to Chile's. What are the particular problems of each country?
3. What environmental concerns would you have if you were contemplating setting up a bottling plant in Russia?
4. What should U.S. policy on participation in international environmental treaties be? Give reasons why the United States should stay out of these treaties and reasons why it should or should not participate.

BETA CASE 17
International Environment

Brian Madison was struggling with a difficult investment decision. "I guess I need to bounce this idea off someone with specific experience," he mumbled to himself. Beta was committed to developing a worldwide presence in generic drugs, many of which it produced and marketed outside the United States. The company had plants in Europe, Latin America, and Asia. Now Madison was seriously contemplating manufacturing in a plant in the Moscow suburbs. The drugs made there would be sold in Eastern European markets and in the Commonwealth of Independent States (CIS).

The whole issue began when the general manager of one of Russia's largest drug-manufacturing companies visited Detroit. Since the breakup of the Soviet Union, many managers of formerly state-owned companies were authorized to develop joint venture agreements with American and European partners. The joint ventures would be privately owned, profit-earning enterprises subject to minimal government supervision.

But Madison had read a great deal about operations in Russia. He knew that the regulatory structure in the CIS was quite advanced and developed on paper, but fell apart when it came to implementation. A large percentage of prescription drugs were mixed and ground by pharmacists rather than in production plants, so that maintaining quality control was difficult. Other investors in Russia had told him it required complex navigation through the regulatory system just to get a pharmaceutical product to market.

Madison also worried about the personal safety of his managers who might go to supervise. Organized crime, bribery, and extortion seemed to be endemic.

Madison was especially worried about one specific aspect of the regulatory system: environmental controls. Since drug manufacturing required the use of chemicals and potentially toxic compounds, would the Russian regulatory structure and process dictate the procedures for disposing of waste? If Beta entered the joint venture in a plant that had been operating for some time, would it be responsible for environmental problems created by the previous tenant?

Madison buzzed his secretary, Tom Hansen, and asked him to call Robert Mobley, the corporate attorney. "Hey, Bob, we really need to get some data on this proposal," Madison said. "Would you get your people to find out as much as you can on Russian regulation of pharmaceuticals? Also, find out what the rules are about waste disposal and other environmental issues. I have the finance department working on the financial risk, and I've contacted a firm to assess political risk. Do we know anyone who specializes in environmental risk in that part of the world?"

Mobley sighed. He knew little, if anything, about Russian environmental protection. "I guess I'm going to have to learn more than I ever thought about the international environment," he mused. "I wonder where I should start looking."

CHAPTER 18 BETA'S MANAGEMENT CHALLENGE

The last few years of the twentieth century are likely to be uncertain, exciting, anxiety producing, and for a select few top managers, incredibly lucrative. Although many experts were convinced that the downsizing and layoffs of the early and mid-1990s were over, others disagreed. Employee anxiety about job loss continued. In the last quarter of 1996, mass layoffs of 50 or more people in a single work site rose four percent over the same quarter in 1995. The number of workers involved rose two percent. This trend continued in early 1997. Job cuts in February were 20 percent higher than in February 1996.

University of Wisconsin poll takers asked a random national sample of workers the same question at three month intervals: "What do you think is the percent chance that you will lose your job in the next 12 months?" In the period ending January 1997, the average response was 17.5 percent, up from 16 percent in the survey a year earlier. Companies like Apple Computer, H. J. Heinz, and AT&T expected to continue to cut jobs.

In some companies, technology made employees obsolete. At AT&T, for example, new voice recognition technology replaced people. Between 1990 and the beginning of 1997, the company fired more than 55 percent of its operators.[1] What would Beta do about downsizing in the next year? If the company had to layoff workers, what strategy should the company adopt?

Corporate mergers and acquisitions continued through the 1990s. The number of mergers more than doubled between 1992 and 1997. In most cases, the U.S. government approved the mergers although it sometimes required the companies to make divestitures or other changes. In 1997, the Federal Trade Commission and the Justice Department released new guidelines weighing cost savings and other efficiencies in evaluating mergers. FTC

---

[1] A. Bernstein, "Who Says Job Anxiety Is Easing?" *Business Week,* April 7, 1997, p. 38.

Chairman Robert Pitofsky said, "There may be some deals that will go through, which otherwise would not have . . . the greatest impact is a transaction where the potential anticompetitive problems are modest and efficiencies that would be created are great." Merger guidelines would:

- Let companies argue to the government that cost savings and related benefits might offset potential anticompetitive effects of a merger. For example, would a merger that raises anticompetitive concerns nevertheless lead to lower prices, better services, or better products? Merging companies could argue, for example, that if they combined two factories, each of which had been operating at less than full capacity, the combination would make more efficient use of fixed assets and lead to lower prices.
- Define which cost savings and other benefits are directly attributable to the merger itself. Would they still get these efficiencies without merging?
- Clarify what companies must do to show that cost savings will result. This would be a road map for making their case before the government.
- Bring U.S. antitrust guidelines more into line with those of other countries. What regulatory climate would Beta encounter? There was no doubt that mergers and acquisitions had been rampant a few years earlier. Would there be a new threat this coming year?

Although mergers and consolidations brought layoffs and bankruptcies, the salaries and benefits for top executives continued to rise. In the middle 1990s, compensation packages for top executives changed from large increases in salaries to big packages of stock options. Options gave executives the right, at some time in the future, to purchase a certain number of shares at a price set when the options were issued. If the stock prices rose, the options became more and more valuable.

Unlike other forms of pay, options did not appear on income statements, although beginning in 1997, companies had to footnote them in their annual reports. There were less obvious costs to shareholders in these compensation plans. Many companies bought back shares then sold them to executives when they cashed in their options. If the stock was bought at top dollar, executives could pocket the difference between the option price and market price; executives got large cash outlays and a higher percentage of outstanding stock. By putting more potential shares into circulation, every shareholder realized a smaller portion of company earnings.[2]

---

[2] J. Reingold, "Executive Pay," *Business Week,* April 21, 1997, pp. 58–66; J. H. Dobrzynski, "New Road to Riches Is Paved with Options," *New York Times,* March 30, 1997, p. F1.

If stock prices fell sharply, most experts expected executives to demand higher cash salaries or lower-priced options. As long as the stock market continued to rise, executives received a windfall. Stockmarket advances through 1996 and in the beginning of 1997 resulted in a 20 percent increase in compensation. During this same time, the average worker received a 3.3 percent increase in wages.

In April 1997, the economic climate soured. The Dow Jones Industrial average was down 10 percent from its all-time high earlier in the year. During the week of April 7 alone, the market lost 134 points. Some traders attributed the bearish market to concerns about inflation and interest rates and advised investors to ride out the correction. Others saw opportunity in the market decline. Noting that the economy was generally quite strong, they suggested this was the time for investors to pick up stocks at bargain prices. In fact, no one could predict the market or anticipate its rise or fall with any degree of accuracy.[3]

Brian Madison wondered what the board would do about his compensation for the coming year. He was worried about his options package in an overvalued stock market but also was concerned about the ethics of commanding a huge raise when the average worker's wage went up less than 5 percent.

The political climate was impossible to predict. The results of regulatory and legal changes that accompanied the switch to a Republican Congress in 1994, were far less dramatic than anyone predicted. The 1996 election gave President Clinton four more years in office and assured a Republican House of Representatives at least until 1998. Although President Clinton appointed new people to government agencies and the courts and announced which policies he wanted Congress to pass, Republicans continued to hammer away at campaign spending, ethics, and budget cutting. Despite heated rhetoric on both sides, Congress was off to a slow start.

The 105th Congress that opened in January 1997 lagged far behind the "First Hundred Days" of the 104th in proposing and implementing legislation. During the first three months of the session, Senators authorized the minting of coins to honor singer Frank Sinatra and approved a resolution praising the University of Florida football team. The House of Representatives supported a judge's public display of the Ten Commandments and voted to honor former Secretary of State Warren Christopher.

Between January and April, the House was in session 27 days, less than half the 53 days in the same period of 1995. House votes in the first quarter totaled 60, down from 271 in the 1995 period. What happened to the fervor of the 104 Congress? Most observers agreed that Republican goals were much more uncertain than in 1994. Speaker Newt Gingrich's ethics problems, the

---

[3] Internet [http://cnnfn.com/markets/9704/14/marketopen/] "Dow Opens Weak," April 14, 1997.

defeat of proposed constitutional amendments for a balanced budget and term limits, and intra-party disputes over campaign financing confused and demoralized lawmakers.[4]

Were the ethical dilemmas that plagued Congress and the President going to have any effect on the way Beta did business at home and abroad? Would Beta's operations in developing countries be scrutinized to see if the company had used host government connections in inappropriate ways? Perhaps there was nothing to worry about since Congress couldn't seem to get started even at home.

Unanticipated national and international events create unstable and often unpredictable economic, political, and social environments for corporations. Proliferating technological advances add to the uncertainties but also present myriad opportunities. Beta Pharmaceuticals, like other large companies, faced numerous decisions; some had to be made immediately, others could be deferred. Beta encountered opportunities and problems and experienced accomplishments and failures. As Beta assessed its performance at its annual June board of directors meeting, it might be any large American company struggling to respond to the pressures it encountered each day.

Beta had some good years in the mid-1990s. Sales and profits were up. Research and development efforts were on schedule and stock prices rose. Although some glitches occurred, Brian Madison realized there was no getting around the fact that the recent past had been tranquil compared to the uncertainties Beta would face in the next several years.

The world's pharmaceutical companies saw the potential for good profits and growth in 1997 and 1998. Markets in Latin America and southeast Asia were fast growing. Drug companies put huge efforts into trying to persuade governments that drugs could be cost effective. The three major reasons the future seemed bright were:

- Companies argued successfully that a patient's stay in a hospital for a day or two costs thousands of dollars, therefore a drug that allowed patients to be discharged quickly deserved a high price;
- Companies convinced the U.S. government that mergers and acquisitions and subsequent job losses were a result of the pressure on profits produced by price control measures;
- New product launches took place faster than old patents expired. This reversed the trend between 1993 and 1996 in which sales of some pharmaceutical companies' best-selling drugs fell by as much as 90 percent as old patents expired and generic drug manufacturers quickly offered rivals;

---

[4] J. Calmes, "Congressional Record: Little to Show for First 3 Months," *The Wall Street Journal,* March 31, 1997, p. A16.

There were some troubling trends as well:

- The Clinton administration failed to get health care reform; therefore, pricing and regulatory environments were uncertain.
- Dr. David Kessler resigned as head of the FDA and, although there was an acting head, his permanent successor's strategy was unknown.
- U.S. health maintenance organizations (HMOs) that managed health care costs for insurers and employees were still growing quickly. HMOs demanded cost cutting measures that could lead to additional mergers and acquisitions.[5]

Waiting for the last participants to straggle into the board meeting, Brian Madison wondered whether the company could have done a better job of social issues management. He recalled how enthusiastic he and Joan McCarthy had been about implementing the social issues agenda. The public affairs department had taken its charge seriously. It had compiled several position papers and made recommendations to management on a variety of subjects. The department now had a sophisticated, complex computer program for stakeholder analysis and issue tracking. Madison and McCarthy met regularly to discuss each stakeholder priority and to try to anticipate new issues before they became problems.

But, Madison thought, no matter how well you plan, unexpected crises occur. Just look at the new problem Sam Powell's biotech division was facing with those radical animal rights people. The division was getting some fascinating and potentially lucrative results despite ups and downs in the early and mid-1990s.

The FDA had refused to approve the division's major new drug, a bioengineered version of a protein the body uses to fight infection. The FDA faulted the division on its data collection, asserting the data did not show a clear reduction in deaths among the patients who took the drug. Sam Powell, while disappointed with the FDA's decision, was determined to continue data collection and gain the agency's approval.

Powell and his staff were really excited about their new initiatives in animal bioengineering. The U.S. Patent and Trademark Office, which had imposed a five-year moratorium on approvals of animal-testing patents, resumed issuing the patents. Beta's scientists were particularly interested in producing genetically engineered mice that developed AIDS. The mice would help them and other scientists better understand the effects of anti-AIDS drugs on humans.

Powell and his people were stunned by the wave of stakeholder intervention they encountered. As soon as animal rights advocates got wind of Beta's plans, they began picketing company headquarters. They held signs accusing

---

[5] D. Green, "Tonic for Drug Companies," *Financial Times,* January 7, 1997, p. IV.

Beta of inflicting pain and suffering on laboratory animals and chanted slogans about Beta being a "killing factory." Employees were accosted, plied with literature, and accused of developing an army of small animals genetically programmed to suffer. A few activists tried to get into headquarters, and one actually punched a guard before the police intervened. Now picketers were kept away from the building's entrance, but they continued to hand out leaflets, chant, and verbally abuse employees.

Although Brian Madison was thoroughly annoyed with the activists' tactics, he acknowledged that ethical issues were involved here. In his own view, people with AIDS took precedence over mice with AIDS. He could not imagine how Beta or any other pharmaceutical company could operate without performing tests on animals. Beta's policy dictating humane treatment of animals was one of the most stringent in the industry. But, Madison privately admitted, if he were not involved in the industry, he might have a different outlook. In any case, Beta would have to deal with this whole area of animal testing very soon.

Finally, everyone was seated around the large walnut table. Madison welcomed them and moved quickly through the agenda. He had deliberately saved many of the social issues for last. He knew some problems defied quick and easy solutions. Mergers and acquisitions were, thankfully, deferrable.

His own salary situation was more immediate but would not be addressed at this meeting. The executive committee of the board of directors was due to get together the next week to discuss top management compensation. Some members of the committee were adamantly opposed to what they perceived as outrageous excess in corporate salaries. They were adamant that options and stock dilution would not be part of the compensation package. Others on the committee said it was realistic to pay a CEO top dollar to keep him or her in a very competitive environment and as long as they were legal, all forms of compensation should be considered. Everyone agreed Madison and other top managers deserved raises. The two major questions were (1) how much and (2) in what form.

Other issues involved ethical judgments that were sure to be controversial. Beta had appointed two new outside directors. One, a senior pastor with one of Detroit's largest African-American churches, was a bright, articulate man who brought a valuable perspective to meetings despite his tendency to preach rather than discuss. The other was an executive from a company that supplied some of Beta's chemical products. His expertise and breadth of knowledge had been highly beneficial to the company.

Beta had resolved the issue of document retention for historical and legal purposes. After talking to other drug company executives, Madison had concluded there would be more danger to the company if it destroyed documents than if they were kept. History aside, if Beta were involved in future litigation, dumping documents might appear to constitute a cover-up.

Madison looked down the table at Joan McCarthy and asked her to bring members up to date on issues her department had handled.

McCarthy turned to her notes. "Gentlemen," she began, "the first issue is our advertising policy." Hearing the word *gentlemen,* Madison looked around. He suddenly realized McCarthy was one of only three women in the room; the other two were secretaries. Hiring women was certainly one area in which the company had not progressed, he thought. McCarthy reviewed Beta's advertising policy and enumerated the new guidelines the company had adopted.

McCarthy went on to discuss Beta's relationship with political action committees (PACs), noting the issue had been assigned to a policy-making committee. Discussion had been contentious and difficult. Nevertheless, the committee had reached a tenuous consensus, and a subcommittee was now drafting a document that would go to top management.

After covering a few other topics, McCarthy broached an ongoing concern: "Our next item is our policy toward women." She handed out copies of recent court decisions on affirmative action, noting that courts in California and Texas were beginning to build a body of law that abandoned affirmative action. John West, vice president for human resources, interrupted, "Joan, I think that falls under my jurisdiction. As a matter of policy, we are making every effort to add qualified women in all positions. If President Clinton can appoint a woman as Secretary of State and another as Attorney General, we ought to be able to find more qualified women for top management positions."

"I agree," Madison chimed in. "Last year, we committed ourselves to bringing women into these jobs. Obviously we have not made a sufficient recruiting effort, and maybe we have fostered a climate in which women don't have sufficient upward mobility. This issue isn't going to be put aside for another year. John, you and Joan will convene a task force by next month. We are going to systematically examine our policies and implementation record in hiring, promotion, and support for women. And while we are at it, we also are going to look at how well we have done with minorities. Demographics are changing, and our workforce has to reflect these trends. By this time next year, we are going to have a plan in place that everyone in this company understands. We are going to attract the most qualified and best-trained people in the industry. It seems highly unlikely to me that all those candidates are white males."

"Wait a minute here," said the CEO of a paper goods company. He had been on the board for five years and nearly always took a contrarian position regardless of the issue. Often, his objections helped to focus discussion and bring out important opposing viewpoints. "Affirmative action has no place in the decisions of this company. We have had affirmative action laws on the books for 30 years. Surely that is enough time for anyone qualified to enter this company and succeed. We should not be giving preference to any group. Merit should be the only criterion for hiring and promotion."

For the next 20 minutes, there was heated discussion about affirmative action and whether it had a place in Beta's hiring and promotion decisions.

Finally, the subject was sent to a subcommittee for further discussion and resolution.

Over the next two hours, the board and top managers discussed a variety of matters from the likelihood of being acquired by another company, to protection of patents, to tax breaks in developing countries.

Brian Madison could not shake off his uneasiness about this portion of the meeting. When it came to social issues, the company tended to either avoid decision making or react to situations only when they reached crisis proportions.

Despite Madison's personal commitment to planning, formulating, and implementing social issues strategy, Beta had accomplished much less than he had hoped. What could he, his top managers, and the board of directors do to ensure that issues were addressed in a rational, organized way? How could Beta more effectively anticipate issues before they became crises? How could the company convey to middle managers its commitment to the process? Even more important, what policies and management mechanisms could Beta develop to ensure that middle managers were committed to social issues policies and rewarded for their implementation?

INDEX

Aaker, D.A., 465n, 485n
Aarons, Ed, 420, 421
Abandonment of strategic initiatives, 108
ABB Asea Brown Boveri, 544–545
Abbott Laboratories, 104
Academy of Management Journal, 98
Access, political power and, 241–242
Accidents, in workplace, 444–445
Acid rain, 540
Ackerman, Robert W., 114
Acquisitions, international, 11
Activist groups, 89, 99
ADAC Laboratories, Baldrige award winner, 507–509
Adamov, Eugene, 586
Adams, Arlin M., 332
Adams, Doug, 455
Adams, Henry, 25, 25n, 26n
Adams, John, 25
Adams, John Quincy, 25
Adaptability to change, 58
Administrative agencies, 254–256
Adolescents, 8–9
Advertising
  deceptive *see* Deceptive advertising
  false advertising, 472
  FTC regulation of, 472
  goals of, 482–483
  standards for advertisers, 484
  telemarketing fraud, 474
Advertising Research Foundation, 465
Aesthetics, and quality, 505
Aetna Life and Casualty Company, 11–12
Affirmative action, 396–398
  California plan, 406–409
  changing views of, 405
  in 1980s, 402–403
  Texaco case, 409–414
AFL-CIO, 433, 435–438, 450
Africa, water issues in, 594–595
AFSCME, 435
Age discrimination, 421–424. *see also* Equal employment
Age Discrimination in Employment Act (ADEA), 421–424

Age segmentation, 8–9
Aggregate household income, growth in, 6–7
Aging workforce, 424–425
Agriculture, legislative initiatives, effect of, 14
A.H. Robins, Dalcon Shield IUD and, 122
Ahern, T., 518n
AIDS, 371, 376–379
Air pollution, 539–541; *see also* Clean Air Act (1970); Clean Air Act (1977); Clean Air Act of 1990
  clean car, 544–548
  environmental mismanagement and, 530
  history of, 535
Airline industry
  deregulation, 286, 291, 303–305
  unions and, 434
Alesia, James, 375
Alexander, S., 344n
Alexrod, N.R., 332n
Alger, Horatio, 198
Allan Bakke v. The Regents of the University of California, 399–400
Allen, Frederick L., 198n, 211n, 213, 213n, 215n
Allen, Jay, 162
Allen, Robert A., compensation of, 12
Allen, Robert E., 63, 64
Allen, S., 84n, 545n, 568n
Allied Waste Industries (AWT), 564
Allison, L., 298n
Alternative fuels, 558–560
Amalgamated Clothing and Textile Workers Union, 449–450
Ambler, John D., 411
Amelio, Gilbert F., 67
America Online, 93
American Airlines, 304–305
American Association of Fund-Raising Council (AAFRC), 319
American Association of Retired Persons (AARP), 475
American Chambers of Commerce, 246
American Cyanamid, 104
American Federation of Labor (AFL), 431–433
American Home Products, 104

American Management Association, 369
American National Standards Institute, 448
American Pharmaceutical Association, 464
American Safety Razor Company of Maine, 38
Americans for Democratic Action, 518
Americans with Disabilities Act, 371–376
Anatomy of major crisis, 132
  crisis stage, 133
  postcrisis stage, 133–134
  precrisis stage, 132–133
  prodromal stage, 132–133
Anders, G., 276n
Anderson, Beverly, 261
Anderson, Fred D., 67
Anderson, Warren, 149
Andreasen, A.R., 338, 339
Andrew, C.J., 559n
Andrews, E.L., 275n, 280n, 281n, 443n, 444n
Andrews, F.E., 326n
Andrews, R., 56
Andriga, Robert, 330
Andrus, Cecil, 567
Ansberry, C., 450n
Ansoff, H. 22, 58, 59n, 86
Antitrust laws; *see also*
  Clayton Act of 1914,
  Federal Trade Commission Act of 1914;
  Sherman Antitrust Act of 1890
  Justice Department and antitrust legislation, case, 273–276
Apcar, L.M., 433n
Apple Computer 65–67
  counterfeit products, 485
Applebome, P., 408n, 498n
Appleton, Nathan, 204, 207
Aquilano, N.J., 501n
Aral Sea, case, 572
Aramony, W. 309–311, 329
Arenson, K.W., 311n, 317n, 319n
Armey, Dick, 437
Articles of Confederation, 233
Arts 319–323
Asahi Shimbun, 33
Asbestos claims, 127–128
Asia 8, 588
Aspin, Leroy, 352
Asseo, L., 422n

Assessment, model for crisis management, 131–132
Association of Southeast Asian Nations (ASEAN), 298
Assumption-of-risk doctrine, 445
Astra USA, Inc., 418–421
A-T Children's Project, 325
Atmel Corporation, 355–356
Atmospheric changes, environmental mismanagement and, 530
AT&T, 11, 63–64
  deregulation and, 291–292
  employees of, 96–97
  internet services, 93
AT&T Global Information Solutions, downsizing, 3
Auchter, Thorne G., 449
Augustine, N.R., 131, 131n, 133n, 134, 134n, 149n
Auster, B.B., 437n
Automobile air bags, 520–522
Automobile industry
  clean car, 545–548
  consumerism and, 466
  unions and, 434, 438–439
Aveda Ecological Products, 117
Ayres, B.D., Jr., 406n, 407n

Bacon, K.H., 294n
Badaracco, J. L., Jr., 167, 168n, 169, 169n, 170, 174
Bagozzi, P., 482n
Bailey, J., 557n, 559n
Bailey, S., 49n
Bailyn, B., 196n
Baker, D., 33n
Bakke, Alan, 399
Balance of payments, 41
Baldrige, Malcolm, 273, 507
Ball, George L., 134, 135, 136
Bank of England, Barings PLC case and, 156–158
Bank of Tokyo, merger of, 11
Banking Act of 1933 (Glass Steagall Act), 272, 302–303
Banking industry 212, 292–295, 301–303
Bankruptcy, Manville Corporation, 127–128
Baring, Francis, 156
Baring, John, 156
Baringer, F., 314n

619

Index

Barings PLC case, 156–158
Barnathan, J., 486n
Barnes, H., 580n
Barnett, Rosalind, 10
Barrett, A., 302n
Barrett, P.M., 499n
Barringer, F., 310n
Barshefsky, Charlene, 95
Baruch, Bernard, 214
Bateman, T.S., 112, 112n
Bates, S., 300n
Bauer, R. A., 115, 115n, 482, 483
Baxter, R., 298n
Baxter, William F., 276
Baxter Healthcare Corporation, 124
Baysinger, Barry D., 246, 246n
Beech-Nut baby food contamination crisis, 133
Begley, R., 514n
Bell Atlantic, 94–95
Bell Telephone Company, 203
Bellace, J.R., 234
Ben & Jerry's, 117
Benes, Larry, 70
Benes, Stacie, 70
Bennett, A., 415n
Bennett, J. G., Jr., 330–332
Bennett, William J., 328
Bensinger, Richard, 436, 437
Bentsen, Lloyd, 295
Berge, Dieudonnee Ten, 145n
Bergen, John, 423
Bergmann, B.R., 402n
Berke, R.L., 248n, 249n, 292n
Berle, Adolph A., 20, 20n
Bernard, Chester I., 56, 56n
Bernstein, A., 434n, 438n, 611n
Bernstein, J., 147n, 149n, 150n
Beta Pharmaceuticals, Inc., 77–81
Better Business Bureaus (BBBs), 479–482
Biddle, F.M., 38n
Bierman, Leonard J., 411
Big business, origins of, 195
before American Revolution, 195–196
communication, innovations in, 202–203
conditions supporting, 196
government role, 199
immigration, 200
natural resources, 197
population growth, 200
social environment, 198
stages of capitalism, 205–223
technology developments, 203–204
transportation revolution, 201–202
urbanism, 200–201
Bijur, Peter I., 410, 411, 412
Bildman, Lars, 418, 419, 420

Bilimoria, D., 98n
Bingaman, Anne K., 275, 276
Biodiversity
environmental mismanagement and, 530
international treaty, 602
Birth rate, unmarried teenagers, 9
Black, C., 386n
Black, R.L., 234
Blalock, D., 165n
Blanton, K., 419n, 420n
Bliley, Thomas J., Jr., 231
Blitz, J., 158n
Blossom, Glenn, 330
Blough, Roger, 219
Blumenstein, R., 439n, 546n
Board of directors, 97–99
Bobrzynski, J.H., 384n
Bodnar, J., 517n
The Body Shop, 68–71, 117
Boehly, William A., 499
Bok, Sissela, 166, 166n
Boorstin, D.J., 201n, 202n
Bork, R.H., 266n
Boroughs, D.L., 6n
Boulton, W. R., 58, 59n
Bovard, J., 376n
Bowman, Charles, 85
Boyer, B., 290n
Bradley, J., 534n
Bradsher, K., 301n, 302n, 303n
Brady, Nicholas F., 293, 294
Braudel, F., 535n
Breast implant case, 122–125
Bribery, 187
Bridgestone/Firestone, 438
Brief, Arthur, 165
Bristol-Meyers Squibb, 104, 123, 160
British Airways, 304–305
British Petroleum, 11
Brittan, Sir Leon, 96
Broad, W.B., 85n
Broad, W.J., 85n, 551n
Broder, J.M., 519n
Brooke, J., 566n
Brooks, A., 520n
Brown, Ann, 515
Brown, Lester R., 597
Brown, W., 499n, 520n
Brown & Williamson Tobacco Corp., 52–53
Browne, M.W., 586n, 600n
Browner, Carol M., 538, 539, 542, 544, 550, 552
Brull, S.V., 418n
Bryan, Richard, 85
Bryant, A., 304n
Bryner, Gary, 288, 288n
Buchholz, R.A., 23, 23n, 244n, 446n
Budiansky, S., 491n
Burford, Anne McGill, 538
Burke, James, 175
Burke, James E., 61

Burke, Jim, 151
Burns, G., 156n
Burrell, C., 455n
Burroughs Wellcome, 104
Burrows, P., 66n
Burton, T.M., 125n
Bush, George, 160, 222, 281, 371, 379, 380, 395, 403, 404, 405, 451, 538, 601
Bush administration
cable industry and, 280
clean air and, 540
consumerism in, 466
Justice Department and antitrust legislation, case, 274
national capitalism and, 220–222
Business and society, 23
Business associations, 245–246
Business decisions, ethics and, 170–173
Business ethics see Ethics
Business Roundtable, 246
Business schools, ethics and, 169–170
Business strategy, 6, 21–24
Butterfield, B.D., 12n
Buyers
bargaining power of, 94
stakeholders, 86
Byrne, J.A., 12n, 62n

Cable Communications Policy Act, 279
Cable industry
Cable Communications Policy Act, 279
regulation and, case, 279–281
Cahan, V., 446n, 448n, 449n
Caitlin, W.B., 445n
Calahan, Joseph M., 316
California Civil Rights Initiative, 406
Calmes, J., 614n
Calvani, T., 274n, 275n
Campbell, Andrew, 59
Campbell, K., 157n
Campbell, William I., 51
Campeau Company, 220–221
Canady, Charles, 408
Canterbery, E.R., 219n
Capital investment, 41
Capitalism, 15–16, corporation in evolution of, 19
nature of, 15–19 private property, 16–18
Capitalism, stages of, 205
finance, 210–215
industrial, 207–210
mercantile 206
national 216–223
petty, 206
prebusiness, 205–206

Capitalistic system, defined, 15
Captains of industry, 207
Carey, J., 296n, 356n
Carlton, J., 66n
Carman, Harry J., 196, 196n
Carmichael, Barbara, 122
Carnegie, Andrew, 199, 207, 208, 211, 212n, 313n, 313–314, 314n
Carnegie Mellon University, 491
Carnes, Tony, 330–331
Carroll, Archie B., 121, 121n
Carroll, Lewis, 445
Carter, Jimmy, 220, 285, 286, 288, 290, 403, 448, 471
Carter administration
deregulation, 285–287
health and safety standards, 448–449
Cartier, counterfeit products, 485
Cary, Frank T., 354
Cascio, Joe, 514
Casellas, Gilbert, 395, 396
Castano, Diane, 54
Castano class-action suit (tobacco), 54
Cause-related marketing, 336–340
Caux Round Table Principles for Business (CRT), 189–191
Cavanagh, Gerald F., 57, 58n
Cellular phones, case, 524–525
Censorship, 300–301
Census Bureau, aggregate household income, growth in, 6–7
Center for International Private Enterprise (CIPE), 245–246
Center for Science and the Public Interest, 488
Center for Workforce Preparation and Quality Education, 246
Chafee, John H., 542
Chandler, A. D., Jr., 197n, 202, 206, 211n, 266n
Chao, Elaine L., 310
Charitable organizations, 311–312
company towns and, 312–313
Charles, Josh, 429
Charles Stewart Mott Foundation, 324
Chase, R.B., 501n
Chase, Stuart, 465
Chase Manhattan Bank, 11
Chemical Bank, 11
Chemical Waste Management (CWM), 564

Chen, K., 486n
Cheney, Lynne V., 328
Chernobyl, 106
  high-level radioactive waste and, 566
Chicago Board of Trade, buying and selling right to pollute, case, 531–534
Child care, 353. 433 see also Family and child care benefits
Children's advertising, FTC regulation of, 472
Children's Defense Fund, 9
China
  counterfeit products from, 485–487
  environmental issues, 588–593
Chirac, Jacques, 441
Chloride Silent Power, Ltd., 545
Choosing Our Future: (Nagpal & Foltz), 573
Christian, N.M., 439n, 499n
Christopher, Warren, 487, 613
Chrysler Corporation, 3, 434
Chua-Eoan, H.G., 157n
Ciba-Geigy Ltd., 11, 104
Cities, economic polarization of, 7
City of Richmond v. J.A. Croson, 401–402
Civil Aeronautics Authority (CAA), 272
Civil Aeronautics Board (CAB), 286
Civil Rights Act of 1964; *see also* Equal Employment Opportunity Commission (EEOC)
  affirmative action, 396–398
  background, 392–393
  employee qualifications, 393–394
  Title VII, 394–395
Civil Rights Act of 1991, 403–405
Clancy, J. Barron, 136
Clark, D., 275n
Clarke, Kenneth, 158
Class action suits
  drug companies, 103–105
  Mitsubishi, 415–418
Clayton Act of 1914, 267
Clean Air Act (1970), 539–540
Clean Air Act (1977), 540
Clean Air Act of 1990, 540–543
Clean car, 544–548
Clean Water Act of 1972, 548–551
Cleaver, Emanuel, 412
Cleland, D.I., 47n

Cline, Patsy, 319
Clinton, Bill, 13, 15, 93, 160, 166, 167, 172, 222, 231, 232, 242, 247, 251, 275, 295, 296, 300, 305, 315, 317, 380, 384, 438, 451, 455, 499, 507, 523, 552, 603, 604
Clinton, Hillary Rodham, 384
Clinton administration
  encryption issues, 356–357
  Justice Department and antitrust legislation, case, 274–276
  national capitalism and, 222–223
  regulation in, 295–305
Clipper chip, 356–357
Clymer, A., 14n, 248n, 249n, 250n, 380n, 381n, 385n, 405n
Coastlines, water pollution and, 549–550
Coca-Cola, compensation of CEO, 12
Cochise, Silas, 84
Cochran, Philip L., 30, 30n
Cochran, T. C., 196, 197n, 199, 201, 210, 218, 218n
Cohen, L.P., 104n
Cohen, S., 432n
Cohen, W., 95n, 437n
Coleman, George, 479
Collective bargaining, 441–442
Collie, Cris, 384
Collins, James C., 61, 61n
Committee action on bill, 252
Common law, 233–234
Communications Decency Act, 300
Communications industry deregulation, 287
  economic growth and, 202–203
Company towns, 312–313
Compensation
  of CEOs, 12
  of nonexecutive employees, 12
  unions and, 433
Competition
  dynamic change and, 18–19
  ethics and, 168
  global, intensity of, 11
The Competitive Advantage of Nations (Porter), 18
Competitive Strategy (Porter), 59
Competitors, stakeholders, 86, 89
Compton, Ronald, 12
CompuServe, 93
Concern for customer, element of TQM, 506
Conformance, dimension of quality, 503

Congress of Industrial Organizations (CIO), 432–433
Conservative foundations, 327–329
Consolidations, international, 11
Constantine, Mark, 68
Construction workers, accidents to, 444
Consumer Product Safety Act, 515
Consumer Product Safety Commission (CPSC), 515–517, 518–519
Consumer protection
  Consumer Product Safety Act, 515
  Consumer Product Safety Commission (CPSC), 515–517
  Federal Trade Commission (FTC) *see* Federal Trade Commission (FTC)
  Food and Drug Administration (FDA) *see* Food and Drug Administration (FDA)
  pharmacists and, 463–464
  product liability law, 517–518
  product quality issues *see* Product quality
  sources of information, 478–482
Consumer Reports, recycling and, 556
Consumerism, 464–468
  business community and, 465
  consumer groups, 467
  pharmacological information, 464
  product liability law case, 230–232
  Pure Food and Drug Act, 465
  in Reagan administration, 222
  sources of information, 478–482
Consumerists, stakeholders, 86
Consumers Index, 479
Consumers' Research, Inc., product testing, 465
Continental Airlines, 434
Contract with America, 13
Contracts, ethics and, 181–182
Contributory negligence doctrine, 445
Control, ethics and, 157
Cook, T.I., 16n
Cool. W.J., 547n
Coolidge, Calvin, 214

Cooper, H., 486n
Cooperative Assessment Program, 455
Corley, R.N., 234
Corporate codes of conduct, ethics and, 168–169
Corporate directors, unions and, 434
Corporate foundations, 326–329
Corporate governance, 70–71
Corporate objectives, 64–65
Corporate political program, 242–243
Corporate political stakeholders, 237–238
  employees, 239–240
  government, 240
  industry associations, 239
  institutional investors, 240
  intellectual community, 240
  news and broadcast media, 239
  public-interest groups, 240
  shareholders, 240
Corporate restructuring, 10–13, 402–403
Corporate Strategy (Ansoff), 86
Corporations, 19–21
  administrative agencies and, 255–256
  criminal liability and, 235–237
  drug testing and, 370–371
  environmental policy implementation, 580–582
  legal processes and, 235–237
  political action committees (PACs), 247
  political power of, 240–242
  political programs of, 242–243
  proper role in society, 4
Corson, John J., 115, 115n
Cost benefit analysis, 296, occupational safety and health, 449
Cost efficiency, competition and, 18–19
Cost-of-quality (COQ) accounting system, 501
Cote, Kimberly, 419
Council of Better Business Bureaus, 479
Council on Environmental Quality (CEQ), 535, 536
Counterfeit products, 485–487
  food labels and, 487–489
Coutts & Company, 156
Cowan, A.L., 332n
Coy, P., 360n

Craig, Larry E., 250
Creative destruction, 18
Criminal liability, corporations and, 235–237
Crisis, defined, 121
Crisis audit, 148
Crisis classification, 126–128
Crisis management, 5
 anatomy of major crisis, 132–134
 crisis classification, 126–128
 Dow Corning breast implant case, 122–125
 effective, 146–149
 environmental crises, 128–129
 Exxon Valdez, 140–146
 media and, 149–152
 model for, 129–131
 Prudential Securities, Inc., 126–127, 134–140
 routine crises, 146
 team approach, 146–149
Crisis stage
 Exxon Valdez, 142–143
 major crisis anatomy, 133
 Prudential Securities, Inc., 138
Crisis team, 147–148
Crispell, D., 9n
Crocker, Charles, 207
Crossette, B., 597n
Croxton, F.E., 312n
Cultural conflicts, 47
Culture groups, charity to, 319
Current issues, 5
 age segmentation, 8–9
 corporate restructuring, 10–13
 gender issues, 10
 immigration, 7–8
 politics, 13–15
 United States economy, 6–7
Cushman, J.H., 14n, 223n, 296n, 542n, 550n, 552n, 555n
Cushman, R.E., 263n
Custom Research, Inc., 507–508
Customers, stakeholders, 89
Cutler, David, 387

Daiwa Bank Case, 33–35
Dale, B.G., 506n
Dalzell, Stewart R., 301
D'Amato, Alphonse, 151
Dana Commercial Credit Corporation, 507, 508
Darr, James J., 137
Dartmouth College v. Woodward, 20
Data collection, employee privacy and, 355
David, F.R., 179n
Davis, E., 361n

Davis, Henry, 264n
Day, G.S., 465n
Dayton Press, downsizing, 3
De Rouffignac, A., 566n
Dear, J., 451–454
Deceptive advertising, 483–485
 counterfeit products, 485–487
 food labels, 487–489
 green products *see* Green products
Deforestation, 596–598
 environmental mismanagement and, 530
Del Valle, C., 311n
Delattre, Edwin J., 328
Dellinger, Chaig, 174
Delta Airlines, compensation of CEO, 12
Dembner, A., 407n
Deming, W. Edwards, 500–501
Dempsy, P.S., 303n
Denfee, T.W., 234
Denmark, green politics, 579–580
Denniston, L., 402n
Denton, N., 157n
DeParle, J., 353n
Department of Agriculture, 488
Department of Education, 289
Department of Energy, supervision of nuclear plants, 84, 397, 455
Depression, unions and, 431
Deregulation. *see also* Regulation
 Airline Deregulation Act of 1978, 286
Derivative contracts, 156
Design defect, 520
 automobile air bags, 520–522
Desmond, E.W., 42n, 43n
Detection, model for crisis management, 129–130
Deutsch, C.H., 403, 540n
Dever, Michael K., 242
Diamon, G., 300n
Disabled workers, 371–376
 AIDS and, 371, 376–379
Discrimination *see* Equal employment
Ditlow, Clarence, 498
Diversity, 425–426
Diversity training, case, 391
Dobrzynski, J.H., 612n
Dobson, John, 164, 165n
Dodwell, D., 575n, 576n
Dolan, M., 408n
Dole, Robert (Bob), 15, 47, 167, 222, 223, 235, 251, 296
Domestic violence, workplace violence and, 365–366

Donahue, Thomas R., 435, 436
Donaldson, Thomas, 188
Donnelley Mirrors, whistleblowing, 183
Donovan, Raymond, 402
Dow Chemical Company, 446
Dow Corning, breast implant case, 122–125
Downsizing
 AT&T Global Information Solutions, 3
 blue-collar jobs, 12
 Chrysler, 3
 Dayton Press, 3
 General Motors, 3
 as socially responsible behavior, 11–12
 white-collar jobs, 12
 Wright-Patterson Air Force Base, 3
Drake, B.H., 181n
Drake, E., 181n
Drexel Burnham Lambert, Inc., 134, 147–148, 160
Drucker, Peter F., 21, 27, 31, 109,
Drug companies, 103–105
Drug testing, 108
Dumaine, B., 364n
Dumanoski, D., 600n
Dunn, C. P., 11n, 161
Dunn, S. Wu, 590n
DuPont, Henry, 209
DuPont Company, 490
Durability, and quality, 503–505
Durbin, Richard J., 550
Durkin, Martin, 219
Durr, B., 531n
Dwyer, P., 156n
Dyer, G., 604n

Earning potential, education and, 10
Earth summit, 600–604
Eastern Airlines, 434
Eastern Europe, environment, 582–587
Eaton, L., 11n
Eckholm, E., 384n
Eco-Management and Audit Scheme (EMAS), 581
Economic crime, 185–186
Economic environment, 41–43, 78
Economic polarization of cities, 7
The Economist, 280
Edie, John, 326
Education, 10, 167–170
The Education of Henry Adams (Adams), 25
Eells, R., 313n
Effective crisis management, 146–149

E.I. DuPont de Nemours, political power and, 241
Eichenwald, K., 127n, 134n, 136n, 137n, 138n, 139n, 410n, 411n, 412n, 413n
Eichner, A., 209, 210n
Eisenhower, Dwight D., 218, 219
Elder care, 383–384
Elderly
 telemarketing schemes and, 474–475
Electric cars, 544–548
Electric power generation, 595
Electronic surveillance, 359–362
Eli Lilly, 104
Elias, M., 365n, 366n
Ellison, Lawrence J., 12
Ells, Richard, 20, 20n
Elstron, P., 418n
Ely, Robin J., 425, 426, 426n
E-mail, privacy issues, 360–362
Emerson, Ralph Waldo, 16,
Employee assistance programs (EAPs), 365
Employee contracts, 181–182
Employee qualifications, 393–394
Employees; *see also* Civil Rights Act of 1964; Civil Rights Act of 1991; Workplace issues
 corporate political stakeholders and, 239–240
 equal employment *see* Equal employment
 ethics and, 161–162, 181–184
 internal direct force on company, 96–97
 nonexecutive, compensation of, 12
 stakeholders, 86
 total quality management (TQM) and, 505–506
 uncertainty and insecurity of, 4
 value systems of, 45
 whistle-blowing, 182–184
Encryption, 356–357
Enders, J., 85n
Enron Corporation, 558–559
Ensign, John R., 85
Entertainment industry, technological change and, 48
Entine, J., 68n, 70, 70n
Environment
 development and, 593–598
 European Union and, 578–582
 legislative initiatives of, 14
 trade policy and, 575–578
Environmental crises, 128–129

Index

Environmental forces on firm, 23
  performance evaluation, 24
  strategy formulation, 24
  strategy implementation, 24
Environmental issues; *see also* Air pollution; Radioactive waste; Water reduction; Water pollution
  buying and selling right to pollute, case, 531–534, 540–541
  deregulation, 285
  ethics and, 159
  hazardous waste, 553–555
  international environment *see* International environment
  in Reagan administration, 221
  recycling, 555–558
  regulatory agencies, 536–539
Environmental Management Systems, 513
Environmental mismanagement, 530
Environmental organizations, donations to, 319
Environmental policy implementation, 580–582
Environmental Protection Agency (EPA), 535–539
  deregulation in, 290
  secondhand smoke report, 50–51
Environmental scanning and analysis, 71–73
Environmentalists, 86
Epstein, E. 240, 241, 242n
Equal employment
  age discrimination, 395–396, 399–405, 421–426
  aging workforce, management of, 424–425
  diversity and, 425–426
  diversity training, case, 391
  equal opportunity in 1980s, 402–403
  level playing field, 392
  Older Workers Benefit Protection Act (OWBPA), 422
  sexual harassment, 414–421
  Supreme Court decisions, 398–399
Equal Employment Opportunity Commission (EEOC), 395–396
  Mitsubishi, 415–418
Ernst & Young, 157
Estes, Ralph, 238
Ethical codes, in mission statements, 62n

Ethics, 155, 170–173
  background, 159–163
  Barings PLC case, 156–158
  education of managers, 167–170
  employee issues, 181–184
  Ethics in Government Act, 166
  False Claims Act, 183–184
  Foreign Corrupt Practices Act, 185
  in future, 5
  ideological arguments, 163–166
  international, 184–189
  multinational corporations, 188–189
  in Reagan administration, 221
  responsibility for, 166–167
  whistle-blowing, 182–184
Ethics codes, 173, 176–181
Ethics credos, 173, 175–176
Ethics in Government Act, 166
Ethics programs, 174–175
Ethics training, 174–175
European Community, ISO 9000 and, 509
European Free Trade Association (EFTA)
  ISO 9000 and, 509
  ISO 9001 and, 510–511
European labor issues, 439
  French labor, 439–441
  German labor, 441–444
European Union
  environment and, 578–582
  GATT and, 575
Ewing, D.E., 354n
Expansion, 41
External direct forces, 92
  bargaining power, 94–95
  government agencies, 95–96
  new entrants, 92–93
  potential entrants, 92–93
  rivalry among existing companies, 93
  substitute products, 93–94
External indirect forces, 99–101
External stakeholders, 86–90
Exxon Valdez, 105, 122
  environmental crisis, 129
  green products and, 490
  internally generated crisis at, 140–146

Factory workers, accidents to, 444–445
Fahey, L., 47n
Fair Deal, 218–219
Fair Employment Practices Committee (FEPC), 392–393

Faison, A., Jr., 405n
Faison, S., 299n
False advertising, 472–473
False Claims Act, 183–184
Faltmayer, E., 541n
Families, 9
Family and child care benefits, 379
  child care, 380–383
  elder care, 383–384
Family and Medical Leave Act of 1993, 381, 383
Family Leave Bill, 379–380
Family structure, labor force and, 353
Farnham, A., 362n
Farnsworth, C.H., 289n
Farrell, J.A., 222n
Feder, B.J., 53n
Federal Bureau of Investigation (FBI), 474
Federal Communications Commission (FCC), 279–281, 287
Federal contractors, affirmative action and, 397
Federal Home Loan Bank Board (FHLBB), 271
Federal Trade Commission Act of 1914, 267–268
  materiality, 472
Federal Trade Commission (FTC), 267–268, 468–469
  deregulation in, 290
  food labels and, 487
  leadership, 471–472
  materiality, concept of, 472–474
  organization of, 470
  responsibilities of, 468–471
  telemarketing fraud, 474–475
Federated Department Stores, 220–221
Feigenbaum, Armand, 501
Fellow-servant doctrine, 445
Felsenthal, E., 367n, 376n, 453n
Fenn, Dan H., Jr., 115, 115n
Ferris, Charles, 287
Fielding, Sue, 391
Filipov, D., 572n
Finance capitalism, 210–215
Financial governance, business ethics and, 159–160
Fine, S., 216, 220n
Fink, S., 132n, 133n, 143n
Fisher, L.M., 546n
Fleming, John E., 71, 71n
Flint, A., 55n
Foltz, C., 573
Foner, P.S., 393n
Food, Drug, and Cosmetic Act, materiality and, 473

Food and Drug Administration (FDA), 465, 475–478
  breast implant case and, 122–125
  tobacco industry and, 51
Food labels, 487–489
Forbes, Diane, 352
Ford, Gerald, 220
Ford, Henry, 217
Ford Foundation, executive salaries, 311
Ford Motor Company, business ethics and, 159
Fordahl, M., 455n
Fordice, Kirk, 53
Foreign Corrupt Practices Act, 159, 185, 241
Forest Laboratories, Inc., 104
Fortune
  162, 182
Fortune 500 firms, ethics credos at, 176
Foundation for New Era Philanthropy, case, 330–336
Foust, D., 156n, 302n
Fox, D.R., 200n
Fox, J.R., 256n, 395n
Framework for strategy formulation, 59–76
  corporate objectives, 64–65
  environmental scanning and analysis, 71–73
  internal assessment, 65–67
  mission statement, 59–64
  organizational weaknesses, 67–68
  social issues visibility, 67–68
  strategic choice, 73–76
  vulnerability, 67–68
Francese, P., 7n, 9n
Fraser, Douglas A., 434
Fraud, 160
Frederick, W. C., 28
Free enterprise*see* capitalism
Free enterprise environment, global, 4
Free market system, government regulation and, 19
Freedman, A.M., 51n, 52n, 53n
Freedom Environmental Fund, 490
Freeman, Audrey, 434
Freeman, R. E. 27, 27n, 28, 29, 90, 91, 103, 105
Fremont-Smith, M. R., 327,
French labor issues, 439–441
Freudenheim, M., 104n
Frey, William, 7
Friedman, Michael A., 478
Friedman, Milton, 17, 18, 26–27, 163, 164, 166
Fritsch, P., 410n, 412n, 413n

Fritsch, P., 410n, 412n, 413n
Fritschler, A.L., 247n
Frost, D., 452n
Frum, D., 231n
Frumin, Eric, 449
Fuchsberg, G., 358n
Fuhrman, P., 584n
Full disclosure, 482
Full warranty, 522

G D Searle & Co., 104
Gaines, J., 353n
Gaines, S., 175n
Galambos, Louis, 263, 263n, 268n
Galen, M., 364n, 382n
Gales, M., 453n
Gallegos, Tony, 395
Gallup, George, 465
Gans, John, 464
Gansar, Lynn, 375
Gapper, J., 158n
Garvin, D., 501–502
Gary, Elbert H., 214
Gates, Bill, 241–242, 275
GATT, 575–578
Gelber, S.M., 392n, 393n, 394n
Gelbspan, R., 359n
Gender issues, 10
Gender roles, 10
General Accounting Office (GAO), Safe Water Drinking Act and, 551
General Agreement on Tariffs and Trade (GATT), 575–578
General Electric, 221
General Motors Corporation
  automobile air bags and, 520–522
  business ethics and, 159
  clean car and, 546
  consumerism and, 466
  downsizing, 3
  pickup trucks, case, 497–500
Georges, C., 14n
German labor issues, 441–444
Germany, green politics, 578
Geronimo, Joseph, 84
Geyelin, M., 231n
Giallourakis, M., 179n
Gibney, F., Jr., 158n
Gifford, Kathie Lee, 162
Gilbert, C., 196n, 201n, 204n
Gilbert, D. R., Jr., 103, 105
Gilbreth, Frank B., 214
Gillette, King Camp, 37–38
Gillette Corporation, 37–39
Gingrich, Newt, 13, 232, 235, 249, 303, 317, 318, 328
Giordano, Frank, 136
Giuliani, Rudolph, 151

Glaser, Carroll, 139
Glasgall, W., 156n
Glaxo, 104
Glazer, N., 397n, 398n
Glick, D., 525n
Global business environment, 4
Global markets, 11
Global warming, international treaty, 601–602
God Wants You to Be Rich, 25
Goizueta, Roberto C., compensation of, 12
Goldberg, C., 8n
Golden, T., 489n
Goldman, Alan H., 30, 30n
Goldman, E.F., 218n
Goldoftas, B., 453n
Gompers, Samuel, 431
Gore, Al, 315, 452
Gorman, C., 93n, 489n
Gormly, Sister Doris, 99
Gorsuch, Anne, 290
Gospel of Wealth and Other Timely Essays (Carnegie), 313
Gottschalk, F.C., 490n
Gould, Jay, 207
Government
  corporate political stakeholders and, 240
  economic growth and, 199–200
  ethics in, 166–167
  intervention in business matters, 17–18
  privacy and, 356–357
Government agencies
  external direct force on company, 95–96
  external indirect force on company, 99
  stakeholders, 86, 89
Government regulation
  free market system and, 19
  national capitalism and, 217–218
Graff, P., 587n
Graham, Anne, 517
Gras, N.S.B., 205, 206n, 212, 216,
Gray, Daniel H., 116, 116n
Gray, J., 328n, 329n, 386n
Great Britain, charitable giving in, 341–343
Great Society, 220
  regulation in, 282
Greek, D., 587n
Green, D., 615n
Green, R., 518n
Green Design Initiative, 491
Green politics, 578–580
Green products, 490–492
Greene, E., 332n
Greene, S.G., 328n
Greengard, S., 356n

Greenhouse, L., 401n, 402n, 423n, 565n
Greenhouse, S., 102n, 436n, 437n, 438n
Greyhound Bus Lines, 434
Greyser, Stephen A., 483, 483n
Grossman, P., 400n
Grover, R., 363n
Grumbly, T. P., 554n, 568
GTE Data Inc., 366–367
Gucci, counterfeits, 485
Guzzardi, W., Jr., 515n
Gwynne, S.C., 408n

Hacker, A., 353n
Hager, M., 525n
Hall, ⊒.L., 372n
Hall, F.S., 372n
Hall, W., 50n
The Hallcrest Report, 185
Halpert, J.E., 560n
Hamilton, A., 446n
Hamilton, Alexander, 25
Hammonds, K.H., 414n
Hampton, C., 275n
Handbook for British Managers (Croos and Witlau), 86
Hanley, R., 96n, 567n
Hanson, Kirk O., 70, 71
Harding, J., 492n
Harkens, Wes, 456
Harlan, C., 358n, 359n
Harlem, Gro, 573
Harriman, Edward H., 207, 212
Harris, Richard, 282, 282n, 285n
Harrison, B., 376n
Harrison, Jeffrey S., 88, 88n, 90
Harrison, Kenneth, 83
Hart, Stuart L., 574, 575, 575n
Harvard Business Review, 170, 574
Hawes, Anthony, 157
Hawkins, K., 290n
Hayes, L., 586n
Hays, L., 34n
Hazardous wastes, 553–555; 561–563; *see also* Radioactive waste
  environmental mismanagement and, 530
  Superfund, 553–555
Hazelton, Richard A., 124
Hazelwood, Joseph, 142, 144
Headden, S., 464n
Heal L.A., 325–326
Heald, M.T., 312, 312n
Health and safety standards, 447–449, 451

Health care, 13, 384–387
Health charities, 320
Health maintenance organizations (HMOs), unions and, 439
Healthtouch, 464
Heath, Christopher, 156
Henderson, Thelton E., 408
Henderson, Wade, 413
Henry M. Jackson Foundation, 324
Hepburn Act of 1906, 265
Herrman, R.O., 465n
Hershey, R.D., Jr., 248n
Hetter, K., 95n
Hilder, D.B., 183n
Hill, James J., 212
Hillenbrand, B., 158n
Hilts, P.J., 122n, 123n, 478n, 487n
Hinds, M.D., 517n, 552n
Hispanic population
Hitchcock, Cornish, 285
Hoerr, J., 369n
Hofer, C.W., 22n, 59n
Hoffman, Michael, 175
Hoffman-LaRoche, Inc., 104
Hofstadter, R., 200n, 213n
Hofstede, Geert, 44, 44n
Holbrook, Stewart H., 199, 207
Holcomb, J.M., 235, 236n
Holdendolph, E., 286n
Holding companies, finance capitalism and, 214
Holland, H. Russell, 144
Hollings. Ernest F., 281
Holmes, S.A., 409n
Holstein, W.J., 417n
Holusa, J., 434n
Holusha, J., 132n, 143n
Honan, W.H., 408n
Hooker Chemical Company, 159
Hoover, Herbert, 214, 270
Hopkins, Mark, 207
Horizontal combinations, 210
Hospitals, radioactive waste in, 565
House Energy and Commerce Committee, 488
Howe, R., 162n
Hrebiniak, L.G., 59n
Hughes, Everett C., 30, 30n
Hughes, J.R., 199
Human resources, 351–352
Humanities groups, charity to, 319
Huntington, Collis, 207
Hwang, S.L., 53n
Hyde, Henry J., 231

Iannone, I.A., 163n, 164n
IBM, 183, 354
Ibrahim, Y.M., 440n

Ideology
  Clinton administration, 222
  ethics and, 163–165
Ifill, G., 222n
Iguchi, Toshida, 33
Immigration, 7–8, 200
Immigration and Naturalization Service
Income
  contribution by women, 10
  stagnating, 5
Income distribution, 41
Income tax, 200
Independent drugstores, 463
Individual giving, 313–314
  individual foundations, 323–326
  in 1990s, 314–316
  in 1995, 318–320
  political controversy, 316–318
Individualism, capitalism and, 15–16
Industrial capitalism, 207–210
Industrial development, downside of, 4
Industrial pollution, 596
Industrial Revolution, 444
Industry associations, corporate political stakeholders and, 239
INFACT, 105
Inflation, 41
Ingersoll, B., 123n, 488n, 498n
Institute for Injury Reduction, 518
Institute for Safe Medication Practices, 464
Institutional investors, 240, and environment, 45–47
Insurance, product liability and, 230
Insurance industry, FTC regulation of, 472
Intellectual community, 240
Intent, corporate, 236
Interagency Task Force on Workplace Safety and Health, 449
Internal assessment, 65–67
Internal monitoring systems, 126–128
Internal stakeholders, 86
Internally generated crises, 126–127
International Association of Machinists and Aerospace Workers, 435
International business combinations, 11
International charity, 320, 340–341
  British example, 341–343
  Japanese example, 343–345

International environment, 571
  Aral Sea, case, 572
  Asia, 588
  China, 588–593
  deforestation, 596–598
  development versus environment, 593
  Eastern Europe, 582–587
  energy, pollution from, 595–596
  environment and European Union, 578–582
  environmental policy implementation, 580–582
  international agreements, 598–607
  rural environment challenges, 596–598
  Sub-Saharan Africa, 594–595
  sustainable development, 573–575
  trade policy and environment, 575–578
  water and sanitation, 593–595
International environmental agreements, 598–600
  biodiversity, 602
  earth summit, 600–604
  global warming, 601–602
  internet sources, 604–607
International ethics, 184–189
International Institute for Sustainable Development, 607
International Organization for Standardization (ISO)
  ISO 1000, 514
  ISO 9000, 509–511
  ISO 9001, 510–511
  ISO 14000, 513–514
International Panel on Climate Change (IPCC), 598–599
Internationale Nederlanden Groep (ING), 157–158
Internet, 93–99
  Better Business Bureaus (BBBs), 480–481
  Communications Decency Act, 300
  Federal Trade Commission (FTC), of, 469
  International Institute for Sustainable Development, 607
  Ozone Secretariat, 606
  regulation of, 297–301
  source of information for managers, 73
  United Nations Environment Programme, 605

Interstate Commerce Act of 1887, 262–265
Interstate Commerce Commission (ICC), 264, 286–287, 296–297
Invention, 37–38
Iron Moulder's Union, 431
Isaacs, C.N., 116, 116n
ISO 9000, 509–512

J. Paul Getty Trust, 311
Jack, A., 581n
Jackson, B., 241n
Jackson, Jesse, 412, 418
Jackson, T., 11n
Jacobs, M.A., 375n
Japan
  charitable giving in, 343–345
  economic growth of, 41–43
  social environment, 43
  total quality management (TQM) and, 505–506
Japan as Number One (Vogel), 42
Jaynes, M., 182
Jefferson, Thomas, 25
Jehl, D., 232n
Jervis, John B., 201
Jimenez-Beltran, D. 579
Job competition, 7
Job contraction, 5
Job creation, compared with layoffs, 12–13
Job insecurity, 13
Johannes, L., 419n, 421n
John Hancock Life Insurance Company, Freedom Environmental Fund, 490
Johnson, G., 84n
Johnson & Johnson, 61, 104, 128, 131, 175–176
  mission statement, 61
  Tylenol poisonings, 128
Johnson, Lyndon B., 220, 282
Johnson, Robert Wood, 175, 176
Johnson, Tom, 391
Johnston, R., 566n
Jordan, Michael, 325–326
Joseph, Fred, 147
Josephson, M., 211n
Joyce, John, 38
Joyce, W.L., 59n
J.P. Stevens, 221
Judge, P.C., 174n
Juppe, Alain, 439, 440
Juran, Joseph M., 501
Justice Department
  antitrust legislation and, case, 273–276
  cable industry and, 279
  tobacco industry and, 53

Kahn, Alfred E., 262n, 286, 290
Kamm, T., 440n, 441n
Kantor, Mickey, 185, 507, 508
Karim, S., 337, 337n, 338n
Karr, A.R., 404
Kasich, John C., 85
Kassalow, E.M., 433n
Katsh, S. M., 26, 238, 239n, 240n
Katz, Hyman, 510
Kaufman, L., 435n
Kedjijian, C., 363n, 364n
Keesal, Samuel A., 135
Keim, G. D., 242, 243, 246, 247
Keller, J., 11n
Keller, M., 271n
Kelso, James, 136
Kemp, Evan, Jr., 395
Kempner, M. W., 150, 151n, 152
Kennedy, Anthony M., 565
Kennedy, Edward (Ted), 372, 452
Kennedy, John F., 102, 219, 393
Keough, J. David, 176n 411
Kernaghan, Charles, 162
Kerwin, C.M., 272n
Kessler, D., 51, 52, 122, 123, 477, 478, 489
Khalfani, L., 174n
Kilborn, P.T., 372n, 435n, 436n, 437n
King, B.B., 319
King, Martin Luther, Jr., 393
King, W., 400n
King, W.R., 47n
Kirk, M.O., 383n
Kirkland, Edward C., 202n, 264, 264n, 313n
Kirkland, Lane, 435, 436
Kirkpatrick, Miles, 471
Kleinfield, N.R., 12n, 13n
Kluckhohn, C., 44n
Knecht, G.B., 331n
Knight, Woody, 136
Knights of Labor, 431
Knoll Pharmaceutical, 104
Kocoras, Charles P., 104
Koenig, L.W., 218n
Kohl, Helmut, 442, 444
Kolata, G., 125n
Koretz, G., 314n
Kotler, P., 320, 323, 324
Kourpias, George G., 435
Kovach, K.A., 358n
Kranish, M., 380n, 542n
Kristol, Irving, 28, 282
Krooss, H. E., 196n, 197, 200n, 201n, 204n
Kuntz, P., 250n
Kupfer, A., 370n
Kurtzman, J.A., 59n
Kuttner, Robert, 303, 303n

Index

Labaton, S., 231n, 294n
Labich, K., 162, 163n
Labor Department, compensation statistics, 13
Labor force, changes in, 353
Lachica, E., 588n
Lake Research, 6
Land, Edwin, 57
Landers, Bob, 455
Lang, K.J., 361n
Larrson, Jan, 419, 420
Lascelles, D.M., 506n
Lave, Lester, 491
Lavin, D., 440n, 441n, 498n
Law enforcement, legislative initiatives, effect of, 14
Lawrence, Reed, 351, 391
Leach, James A., 303
Leadership, 55–58
Leadership Education for Asian Pacifics, 8
Leavitt, Arthur, Jr., 134
Ledvinka, J., 396n
Lee, E.D., 221n
Leen, Mitchell, 151n
Leeson, Lisa, 157
Leeson, Nick, 156–158
Legal immigration, 8
Legal processes, 229
  administrative agencies, 254–256
  corporations and, 235–237
  informal societal rules, 234–235
  legal classifications, 234
  product liability law case, 230–232
  United States Constitution, 233–234
Legal/political environment, in social issues strategy, 47
Legislation
  action in second house, 254
  committee action, 252
  conference, 254
  final stages, 254
  floor action, 252–254
  introduction of bill, 252
  legislative process, 252
  passage of, 251
  political action committees (PACs), 247–250
  polygraph testing, 357–358
  prelegislative phase, 251
Lemonick, M.D., 301n
Lerner, Max, 17, 17n
Letwin, W., 198n
Lev, M., 325n
Level playing field, 392
Levin, D.P., 498n
Levin, Howard, 548
Lewin, T., 10n, 380n, 449n
Lewis, D., 419n, 450n, 451n
Lewis, D.E., 420n, 421n
Lewis, John L., 432
Lewis, N.A., 232n

Lewis, P., 96n, 603n
Lewis, P.H., 93n, 300n, 301n
Lewis, Reginald, 524
Liedka, Jeanne, 27, 28, 28n
Life cycle of products, 560, 562
Lifetime employment, 42
Liggett Group, 54
Limited warranty, 522–523
The Limits of Corporate Power (Millstein and Katsh), 26
Lincoln Electric, 183
Line-item veto, 14
Linowes, D.F., 115n
Lipin, S., 10n, 11n
Lipman, I.A., 369n
Litigation. 375–376, 396; *see also* Class action suits
Littlejohn, Robert, 146, 146n
Litzinger, W.D., 163n
Lloyd, H., 199
Lobbies, external indirect force on company, 99
Lobbying, political action committees (PACs), 246–247
Local communities
  external indirect force on company, 99-101
  recycling and, 557
  stakeholders, 89
Locke, John, 16, 17
Lockhead, C., 519n
Lockheed Corporation, political power and, 241
Lockheed Martin Corporation, 131, 177–178
Lodge, G. C., 555, 556n
Logging industry, 160
Lohr, S., 276n, 454n, 455n
Lonner, Anders, 421
Lorange, P., 59n
Lorenzo, Frank, 434
Los Alamos National Laboratory, 85
Loucks, V. R., Jr., 165,
Love Canal, 159
Lowell, F. C., 204, 207
Lowell, Massachusetts, mill accidents in, 444
Lowery, Joseph E., 413
Lowi, Theodore, 282
Lublin, J.S., 98n, 99n, 374n, 375n, 414n
Lucas, Robert E., Jr., 103
Lundwall, R. A., 410–413
Lungren, Dan, 408
Lyall, S., 566n
Lying (Bok), 166

Machinery, economic growth and, 204
MacPherson v. Buick Motor Company, 517–518
Macrocultures, ethics and, 155

Madison, B., 119, 613–618
Makridakis, S. G., 56, 106, 108n
Malcolm Baldrige National Quality Award, 507–509
Management, 611–618
  ethical duty of, 164
Managers
  administrative agencies and, 255–256
  education in ethics, 167–170
  effectiveness of, 5
  moral stewardship of, 167
  regulation and, 259–260
  skills of political manager, 243–244
Managing techniques, for stakeholders, 88–90
Manville Corporation, 127–128
March, A., 501n
Marchetti, D., 318n, 325n
Maremont, M., 420n
Margus, Brad, 325
Margus, Vicki, 325
Marion Merrill Dow, Inc., 104
Mark, J., 157n, 158n
Marketing, consumerism and, 464–468
Marks, J., 46n
Marshall, M., 443n
Marshall v. Barlow, 448–449
Martin, John, 391
Martin, Lynn, 418
Martinez, Ricardo, 522n
Mashberg, T., 381n
Mass merchandising, 48–49
Masspirg, 466–468
Materiality, 472–474
Mathers, J., 124n
Mathews, J., 315n, 316n
Mayer, C., 290n
Maynard, M., 498n
McCall, H. Carl, 410
McCarthy, J., 615–617
McCarthy, Roger L., 519
McCoy, C., 144n, 145n
McCraw, T.K., 271n
McDermott, D., 157n, 299n
McDonald's, 492–493
McDonough, William J., 33
McEntee, Gerald, 435
Mcfarlane, Malcolm, 511, 512
McGhan Medical Corporation, 122
McGrath, N., 186n
McGrory, B., 406n
MCI Communications, 11, 292
McMorris, F.A., 301n
McNamee, 382n
Meade, Peter, 411
Means, Gardiner, C., 20
Meany, George, 433, 435
Measurement, social assessment system, 113–114

Media
  corporate political stakeholders and, 239
  crises and, 149–152
Medicaid, 463
Medical companies, ethics and, 160
Medical issues in workplace, 368–371
Medicare, 384–387
Medvedev, Zhores A., 585
Meese, Edwin, III, 402
Meier, B., 124n, 365n, 498n
Memphis Fire Department v. Shotts, 400–401
Men, view of gender roles, 10
Menon, Anil, 337n
Mercantile capitalism, 206
Merck, 104
Meredith, R., 521n
Mergers
  airline industry, 304–305
  international, 11
  in late 1990's, 10–11
Merlo, Thomas J., 311
Metzenbaum, Howard, 450
Meyers, G. C., 132, 133n, 143
Mfume, Kweisi, 412
Miceli, M.P., 182, 184, 184n
Michigan Chemical Company, 182–183
Microcultures, 155
Middle class, 6–7
Mieher, S., 103n
Migration, caused by immigration, 7
Mikva, Abner J., 232
Miles, G.L., 185n, 186n
Miles, Robert H., 73, 75n
Milkis, Sidney, 282, 282n, 285n
Miller, A., 362n, 363n, 364n
Miller, Arjay, 172
Miller, J., 319n
Miller, James, III, 472, 473
Miller, James C., 288
Miller, K.L., 442n, 584n
Miller, Robert, 85
Miller, W., 197n, 198, 199n, 201, 210
Mills, J., 134n, 135n
Millstein, I., 26, 238, 239n, 240n
Miners, accidents to, 444
Mintzberg, Henry, 164
Mission statement, 59–64
Mitchell, A., 166n, 167n
Mitchell, T., R., 167
Mitroff, I., 121n
Mitsubishi Bank, 11
Mitsubishi Motor Manufacturing of America, Inc., 415–418
Mobil Corporation, 11
Model for crisis management, 129
  assessment, 131–132
  avoiding crisis, 131

crisis, 130
detection, 129–130
repair, 130–131
The Modern Corporation (Berle and Means), 20
Monopoly
Clayton Act of 1914, 267
Federal Trade Commission Act of 1914, 267–268
Sherman Antitrust Act of 1890, 265–267
Monsky, Sharon L., 324–325
Montanari, J.R., 339–340
Moody, Paul, 204
Moore, J., 328n
Moore, Michael, 53
Moore, Wilbert E., 30, 30n
Moral decision making, 170–173
Moral standards, 161
Moral stewardship of managers, 167
More Business Down Under, 246
Morgan, F.W., 523n
Morgan, J. Pierpont, 207, 208, 211, 212, 213
Morgan, M. Granger, 524
Morison, E.E., 201n
Moritz, T.E., 179n
Morton Thiakol, 133
Mosely, Elaine, 498
Mosely, Shannon, 498
Mosely, Thomas, 498
Moses, J.M., 128n
Motor Carrier Act of 1935, 272
Motorola, 524–525
Multilateral environmental agreements (MEAs), 576–577
Multinational corporations, ethics, 188–189
Multiple workplaces, 5
Munchau, W., 443n, 444n
Munn v. Illinois, 17
Murawski, J., 320n, 327n
Murray, H.A., 44n
Murry, K.B., 339–340
Myers, Kenneth D., 238
Myerson, A.R., 559n

Nader, Ralph, 159, 231, 292, 447, 466, 504, 504n
Nagpal, Tanvi, 573, 574n
Naik, G., 11n
Narayanan, V.K., 47n
Nash, Laura L., 170, 170n, 171, 171n, 173n
Nash, N.C., 440n
National Association of Corporate Directors, 98
National Association of Manufacturers (NAM), 245
National Association of Rare Disorders, 325

National Associations of Attorneys General (NAAG), 474
National Better Business Bureau, 479
National capitalism, 216
Bush administration, 220–222
Clinton administration, 222–223
Fair Deal, 218–219
Great Society, 220
National Industrial Recovery Act (NIRA), 217
New Deal, 217–218
New Frontier, 219
1970s, 220
progressive movement, 216–217
Reagan administration, 220–222
National Cash Register Company (NCR), 3
National Chamber Foundation, 246
National Consumers' League, 474
National debt, 5
National Endowment for the Arts, 328–329
National Endowment for the Humanities, 328–329
National Fire Protection Association, 448
National Foundation of Women Business Owners, 10
National Fraud Information Center (NFIC), 474
National Gypsum, 455–456
National Highway Traffic Safety Administration (NHTSA)
automobile air bags and, 520–522
deregulation in, 289
General Motors pickup trucks, case, 498–500
National Industrial Recovery Act (NIRA), 217
National Institute for Occupation Safety and Health, 455
National Institute of Standards and Technology (NIST), 507
National Institute on Drug Abuse, 369
National Labor Relations Act (Wagner Act), 432
National Labor Relations Board (NLRB), 432, 436
National Labor Union, 431
National Oceanic and Atmospheric Administration (NOAA), 551

National Research Council, 573
National Safety Council, 450
National Vigilance Committee, 479
National Workplace Resource Center on Domestic Violence, 366
Natural resources, economic growth and, 197–198
Near, J.P., 182, 184, 184n
Needham, Douglas, 283, 284n
Negligence, 517–518, 518–520
Nepotism, ethics and, 155
Nevins, Allen, 208, 208n
New Deal
consumerism and, 465
unions and, 432
New entrants to industry, 92–93
New products, technology and, 47
Newman, A., 370n
Newman, W.H., 59n
Newman, William H., 86, 86n, 90n
Nickelodeon/Yankelovich Youth Monitor survey, 9
Nickerson, C., 590n
Nikkei market, 156–157
Nixon, Richard, 220, 296, 447, 536
Noah, T., 404, 552n, 555n
Noble, Charles, 451
Noble, K.B., 450n
Noble and Holy Order of the Knights of Labor, 431
Nomani, A.Q., 304n, 454n, 521n, 522n
Nonprivate foundations, 326–329
Nonprofit organizations, 61, 320–323
Norman, P., 443n
Norris-LaGuardia Act, 432
North American Securities Administrators Association (NASAA), 474
Northern States Power Company, 84
Northwest Airlines, 50
Norton, E. H., 403, 404n
Not-In-My-Backyard (NIMBY) syndrome, 565, 567
Noval, V,, 51n
Nuclear Disaster in the Urals (Medvedev), 585
Nuclear energy, 106–108
Nuclear plants
radioactive waste in, 565
in Soviet Union, 585–587
Nuclear Regulatory Commission, 566–567
Nuclear waste, stakeholders and, 83–85

Nutrition labeling, 487–489
NYNEX, 94–95, 281

Oba, Mkunii, S., 42n
O'Boyle, T.F., 362n
Obsolescence, 503–505
Occidental Chemical Company, 446
Occupational safety and health
cost benefit analysis and, 449
history of, 444–447
management strategy for workplace safety, 456–457
repetitive stress, 453–456
work-related illness, 446
Occupational Safety and Health Act, 430, 447–449
Clinton administration and, 451–453
Reagan and Bush years, 449–451
repetitive stress and, 453–456
Occupational Safety and Health Administration (OSHA), 430, 447–456
O'Connor, James, 423
O'Connor, Sandra Day, 402, 422, 565
Odom, John N., 403
Odwalla, Inc., 57
Odyssey Partners, 221
Office of Technology Assessment, Clean Air Act and, 541
Oil industry, mercantile capitalism and, 209
Older Workers Benefit Protection Act (OWBPA), 422
Oliver, Daniel, 472
One parent families, 9
Oracle Corporation, 12
O'Reilly, B., 163n
Organization for Economic Cooperation and Development (OECD), 7, 584–585
Organizational change, total quality management (TQM) and, 505–506
Organizational culture, strategic management and, 55–59
Organizational development, element of TQM, 506
Organizational problems, internally generated crises and, 126–128
Organizational weaknesses, 67–68
Osaka Securities Exchange, 156–157

Ostapski, S.A., 116, 116n
Oster, P.B., 441n
Ota, Takeshi, 33
Overstreet, J., 455n, 456n
Owens, Simon, 119
Ownership interests, in corporations, 21
Ozone reduction/depletion, 541–542
Ozone Secretariet, home page, 606

Pacific Associates, 207
Pacific Telesis, merger of, 10–11
Packard, David, 322
Pacourek, Charline, 375
Palamountain, Jr., J.C., 48n
Pall Corporation, 510–511
Pare, T.P., 137n
Parks, C., 548n
Parks, Rosa, 393
Partnering techniques, for stakeholders, 88–90
Partnerships, 20
Pascale, Richard T., 45, 45n
Pataki, George, 151, 546
PATKO, 584
Patrick, K.G., 313n
Paul, Robert J., 424, 425n
Paulachak, Stephen J., 311
Pear, R., 328n
Pearce, II, John A., 61, 61n
Pena, Federico, 499
Peng, Li, 299
Pepsi-Cola Bottling Company, 364, 455
Perceived quality, 505
Performance, dimension of quality, 502
Performance evaluation, 24
Perl, P., 450n
Perlez, J., 602n
Perot, Ross, 251
Pertman, A., 407n
Pertschuck, M., 282, 284n, 471
Petit, Thomas A., 44, 44n
Petty capitalism, 206
Pfeffer, J., 237, 238n
Pfizer, 104
Pham, A., 39n
Pharmaceutical companies, ethics and, 160
Pharmaceuticals, 463–464
Pharmacia & Upjohn, Inc., 104
Pharmacists, 463–464
Philanthropy, 309
 charitable organizations, 311–313
 conservative foundations, 327–329
 corporate foundations, 326–329

Foundation for New Era Philanthropy, case, 330–336
 individual foundations, 323–326
 individual giving, 313–323
 international perspective, 340–345
 nonprivate foundations, 326–329
 strategic marketing approach, 336–340
 United Way case, 309–311
 use of money, 329
Philip Morris Co., 50–52
Piasecki, V. W., 331
Piderit, S.K., 98n
Pierce, Harry J., 498
Pike, A., 342
Pinkerton, J.P., 406n
Pitney Bowes, 183
Pitofsky, R., 468, 612
Planning for social issues, 56–57
Pointer, Sam C., Jr., 124
Poland, environmental issues, 583–585
Polaroid Corporation, 57, 183
Political action committees (PACs)
 administrative agencies and, 255–256
 external indirect force on company, 99
 lobbying and legislation regarding, 247–250
 stakeholder groups, political and legal, 246–247
Political framework of business, 237
Political processes, 229
 administrative agencies, 254–256
 corporate political power, 240–242
 corporate political program, 242–243
 corporate political stakeholders, 237–240
 passage of legislation, 251–254
 political manager, skills of, 243–244
 product liability law case, 230–232
 stakeholder groups, 245–250
Politics
 current issues, 13–15
 and international ethics, 186–187
 presidential campaign of 1996, 15
Pollack, A., 43n

Pollack, E.J., 99n
Pollution. see also Air pollution; Water pollution
 buying and selling right to pollute, case, 531–534, 535 540–541
Polygraph testing, 357–358
Pooling, 209–210
Population growth 8–9, 200–201
Population Reference Bureau, 9
Porras, Jerry I., 61, 61n
Porter, G., 264n
Porter, M. E., 18, 19n, 59, 65, 90, 92, 94, 105
Posch, R.J., Jr., 484, 517n, 518n, 523n
Post, J.E., 72n
Postcrisis stage
 Exxon Valdez, 143–146
 major crisis anatomy, 133–134
 Prudential Securities, Inc., 138–139
Potential entrants to industry, 92–93
Potter, D.M., 483n
Powderly, Terence, 431
Powell, Sam, 615
Prairie Island coalitition Against Nuclear Storage, 84
Pratt, Joseph, 263, 263n, 268n
Prebusiness capitalism, 205–206
Precrisis stage
 Exxon Valdez, 142
 major crisis anatomy, 132–133
 Prudential Securities, Inc., 134–138
Prelegislative phase of statute, 251
President's Commission on Equal Employment Opportunity (PCEEO), 393
Preston, L.E., 71n, 72n
Pricing, ethics and, 160
Prime Office Furniture, 391
Privacy
 business ethics and, 159
 electronic surveillance, 359–362
 employee privacy, 354–356
 government and, 356–357
 polygraph testing, 357–358
Privacy Act of 1974, 354–355
Private enterprisesee capitalism
Private foundations, 323–326
Private property, capitalism and, 16–18
Privatization, 4, 11

Proactivity, 75–76
Process innovations, technology and, 48
Prodigy, 93
Prodromal stage
 Exxon Valdez, 142
 major crisis anatomy, 132–133
 Prudential Securities, Inc., 134–138
Product innovations, technology and, 48
Product liability law, 517–523
 case, 230–232
 design defect, 520–522
 negligence, 518–520
 strict liability, 523
 warranty, 522–523
Product quality, 500
 cellular phones and electromagnetic fields, case, 524–525
 eight dimensions of quality, 502–505
 General Motors pickup trucks, case, 497–500
 history of quality control, 500–502
 product liability law and, 517–518
 quality, defined, 501
 regulation of product safety, 515–517
 TQM see Total quality management (TQM)
Product recalls, General Motors pickup trucks, case, 497–500
Product safety, consumer awareness of, 466
Productivity, total quality management (TQM) and, 505–506
Profit
 ethics and, 163
 as measure of success, 18
Progressive movement, 216–217
Property, private, 16–18
Proposition 209, 407
Prosperity, unions and, 431
Prudential Securities, Inc., 126–127, 130–140, 160
Public employees' union, 435
Public philanthropies, 319
Public relations
 crises and, 149–152
 Exxon Valdez, 143
 General Motors pickup trucks, case, 497–500
Public Relations Journal, 311
Public-interest groups, 240
Pujo committee, 213
Pullman, George M., 312, 354

Index

Punitive damages, product liability, 232
Pure Food and Drug Act of 1906, 268–270, 465

Quality control *see* Product quality
Quality Control Handbook (Juran), 501
Quayle, Dan, 523

Race discrimination. *see also* Equal employment
  Texaco case, 409–414
Radin, C.A., 345n
Radio
  consumerism and, 465
  deregulation, 287
Radioactive waste, 565
  high-level, 566–568
  intermediate-level, 566
  low-level, 565–566
  Nuclear Regulatory Commission and, 566–567
Railroads
  economic growth and, 197, 202
  finance capitalism and, 210–211, 212–213
  French labor issues, 439–440
  Interstate Commerce Act of 1887, 262–265
  regulation of, 262–265
Railway workers, accidents to, 444
Rains, Theodore, 135
Rand organization, 9
Rangan, V.K., 337, 337n, 338n
Rankin, Tom, 455
Rasky, S.F., 372n
Raven, Janis, 69
Rawl, Lawrence G., 142, 143, 144, 149–150, 150n
Raymond, Lee, 143
Rayport, J. F., 555, 555n, 556n
RCRA, 553, 561–563
Reactivity, 75–76
Reagan, Ronald, 166, 287, 288, 289, 296, 434, 449, 451, 549
Reagan administration
  affirmative action in, 402–403
  banking industry regulation in, 292–295
  Consumer Product Safety Commission (CPSC), 515–517
  consumerism in, 466
  deregulation in, 287–292

equal opportunity in, 402–403
Justice Department and antitrust legislation, case, 273–276
national capitalism and, 220–222
Rebello, K., 66n
Recalls, General Motors pickup trucks, case, 497–500
Recession, 41
  in Japan, 42
  unions and, 431, 434
Recycling, 555–558
Reed, Lawrence A., 122
Reed, O.L., 234
Regan, M.B., 249n
Regardie's Magazine, United Way case, 310
Regulation, 259–260
  Airline Deregulation Act of 1978, 286
  airline industry, 286, 291, 303–305
  Banking Act of 1933 (Glass Steagall Act), 272, 302–303
  banking industry, 292–295, 301–303
  business, summary, 270
  Cable Communications Policy Act, 279
  cable industry, case, 279–281
  Carter administration, 285–287
  Civil Aeronautics Authority (CAA), 272
  Civil Aeronautics Board (CAB), 286
  Clayton Act of 1914, 267
  Clinton administration, 295–305
  Communications Decency Act, 300
  communications industry, 287
  consumer protection *see* Consumer protection
  consumer regulation, 268
  in daily lives, case, 261
  defined, 259
  deregulation, 284–285
  economic agencies, 272
  Federal Home Loan Bank Board (FHLBB), 271
  Federal Trade Commission Act of 1914, 267–268
  flexibility in, 296
  functional agencies, 271–272
  Hepburn Act of 1906, 265
  history of, 262, 270–271, 282–284
  Internet, 297–301

Interstate Commerce Act of 1887, 262–265
Interstate Commerce Commission (ICC), 286–287
Justice Department and antitrust legislation, case, 273–276
Motor Carrier Act of 1935, 272
National Labor Relations Board (NLRB), 271
  in 1960s, 282–284
political and legal framework, 237
Pure Food and Drug Act of 1906, 268–270
Reagan administration, 287–292
Securities and Exchange Act of 1934, 272
Securities and Exchange Commission (SEC), 272
Sherley Amendment, 270
Sherman Antitrust Act of 1890, 265–267
social agencies, 272
telephone industry, 291–292
trucking industry, 286–287
Wheeler-Lea Amendment, 267–268
Regulatory Analysis Review Group (RARG), 285
Rehabilitation Act of 1973, 369
Reich, Robert, 455
Reifenberg, A., 413n
Reilly, A., 273n
Reilly, William, 538
Reingold, J., 612n
Relationship investing, 102
Reliability, 503
Religion, link to wealth, 24–25
Religious groups, stakeholders, 86
Religious organizations, external indirect force on company, 99
Repair, model for crisis management, 130–131
Repetitive stress, 453–456
Resource Conservation and Recovery Act (RCRA), 553, 561–563
The Responsible Company, 115
Return on investment, stakeholder effect on, 105
Reynard, David, 524
Reynolds, William Bradford, 402
R.H. Macy and Company, 221

Rhone-Poulenc Rorer, Inc., 104
Rice, Connie, 405
Richards, B., 291n
Rigdon, J.E., 124n
Rimmer, S., 3n
Rio de Janeiro, earth summit in, 600–604
Rivalry among existing companies, 93
R.J. Reynolds Industries, Inc., 50
Roadman, G., 419, 420, 421
Robber barons, 207
Roberts, S., 10n
Robertson, Pat, 248
Robin, D., 179n
Robinson, E.A., 160n
Rochester, A., 214n
Rockefeller, John D., 199, 207, 208, 211, 313
Roddick, Anita, 68–71, 117
Rodgers, T.J., 99
Rogers, D., 454n
Romer, John I., 479
Roosevelt, Franklin D., 20, 217, 218, 260, 392, 432, 465
Roosevelt, Theodore, 213, 216, 217, 269, 270
Rose, F., 547n
Rose, M., 71n
Rose, R.L., 436n
Rosenstock, Linda, 365
Rosenthal, S.B., 23, 23n
Rosoff, A.J., 234
Ross, B.H., 247n
Ross, Ralph, 44, 44n
Rossant, J., 441n
Rosser, Russell, 330
Rothenberg, R., 50n
Routine crises, 146
Row, John, 418
Rowley, Ivan R., 421
Rubber industry, unions and, 434
Rubin, Richard E., 302
Ruckelshaus, William, 538
Ruggiero, Renato, 96
Rural environment, 596–598
Russia, counterfeit products from, 485
Rust International, Inc., 564
Ryder, John, 423

Safe Water Drinking Act, 551–552
Safety director, 446
Safire, William, 86, 86n
Sager, I., 66n, 174n, 175n
Salancik, G. R., 237, 238n
Salmon, Walter J., 97, 97n
Salwain, K.G., 424n
Same gender families, 9
Samuels, P.D., 326n
Sandberg, J., 301n

629

Sandberg, S.K., 337, 337n, 338n
Sandefur, Thomas E., 52
Sandoz Ltd., merger of, 11
Sandoz Pharmaceuticals, 104
Sanger, D.E., 297n, 485n
Santoli, M., 137n
Saporito, B., 304n
Sarma, K.M., 606
Satchell, M., 551n
Savage, D.G., 423n
Sawyer, John E., 198, 198n
SBC Communication, 11
Scalia, Antonin, 423
Scannell, Gerard, 450, 451
Schack, Richard, 316
Schaeffer, C., 487n
Schares, G.E., 441n
Schechter, Loren, 134, 136
Scheff, J., 320, 323
Schellhardt, T.D., 363n, 365n
Schendel, D.E., 22n, 59n
Schering-Plough, 104
Schlei, B. Lindemann, 400n
Schlender, B.R., 42n
Schlesinger, A., Jr., 217n
Schlesinger, A.M., 200n
Schlink, F.J., 465
Schmitt, R.B., 232n
Schnapper, M.B., 446n
Schneider, K., 145n, 539n, 567n, 602n
Schramm, W., 203
Schroeder, M., 135n
Schulte, Dieter, 443
Schultze, Charles L., 285
Schumpeter, Joseph, 303
Schumpeter, Joseph A., 18, 18n
Schutz, J.D., 364n
Schwab, Charles, 211, 212
Schwartz, B., 233n
Schwartz, T., 287n
Schwartz, V.E., 231n
Scleroderma Research Foundation, 324–325
Scope of business responsibility
 global 30–31
 legal and economic, 31–32
Scott, M., 57n
Scott, Thomas, 207
Scott, William G., 167, 167n
Securities, Barings PLC case and, 156–158
Securities and Exchange Act of 1934, 272
Securities and Exchange Commission (SEC), 272
Seely, J.R., 311n
Seelye, K.Q., 223n, 249n
Segal, T., 311n
Seib, G.F., 6n, 409n
Seidenberg, Ivan, 95
Selection of alternatives
 control over, 106–108
 drug testing, 108
 nuclear energy, 106–108

Seminario, Margaret, 452
Senate Labor and Human Resources Committee, food labeling and, 488
A Sense of Mission: (Campbell and Nash), 59
Serrin, W., 433n
Serviceability, 505
Serwer, A.E., 499n
Sethi, S.P., 235, 235n, 236n
Sexual harassment, 414–415
 Astra USA, Inc., 418–421
 Mitsubishi Motor 415–418
Shabecoff, P., 144n, 538n, 549n, 597n
Shad, John S.R., 169n, 169–170
Shaefer, T.E., 163n
Shanghai Razor Blade Factory, 38
Shao, M., 53n
Shapiro, J.P., 371n
Shareholders
 corporate political stakeholders and, 240
 internal indirect force on company, 102–103
Sharma, N.P., 595n
Sharpe, A., 25n
Sharpe, R., 416n, 417n, 418n
Sheeline, W.E., 385n
Shell Oil, 446
Shellenberger, S., 10n
Sherley Amendment, 270
Sherman, Stratford P., 150, 151n
Sherman Antitrust Act of 1890, 265–267
Sherwin, D. S., 163, 164
Shipping, economic growth and, 201
Shirouzu, N., 33n
Shleifer, Andrae, 187
Shrivastava, P., 121n, 129n
Shulman, S., 83n
Shultz, Gary, 416
Shuster, Bud, 550
Sick pay, 443–444
Siconolfi, M., 136n
Silverglade, Bruce A., 488
Simison, R.L., 292n
Simmons, Hardwick, 136
Simon, Herbert A., 203, 204n
Simons, M., 582n, 583n
Simpson, Alan K., 250
Sinatra, Frank, 613
Sinclair, Upton, 269, 269n
Singapore, 61
Singapore Monetary Exchange, 156–157
Singer, I.M., 199
Sioux tribe, 84
Skilled labor, 201
Skillman, B., 546n
Skolnik, R., 311n
Skrzycki, C., 520n
Slater, Samuel, 204

Smith, Adam, 15, 15n, 19, 303
Smith, Charles T., 183
Smith, G., 12n
Smith, G.D., 195n
Smith, Guy, IV, 50
Smith, John, 546
Smith, L., 359n, 360n
Smith, Ray, 95
SmithKline Beecham, 104
Smothers, R., 499n
Social audit, 115–117
Social benefit philanthropies, 319
Social environment, 43–47
 Beta Pharmaceuticals, Inc., 78–79
 economic growth and, 198–199
Social issues, 4, 243–244
Social issues strategy
 environment of, 39–49
 tobacco industry, 49–55
Social issues visibility, 67–71
Social responsibility, downsizing, 11–12
Social responsibility debate, 24–30
 business responsibility, 30–32
Social responsiveness, 109–114
 social audit, 115–117
Social responsiveness management, 22–24
Societal expectations of teenagers, 8–9
Societal role of corporations, 4
Societal rules, legal processes and, 234–235
Society, relationship to business, 23
Society for Business Ethics, 29
Society of Environmental Toxicology and Chemistry (SETAC), 560–561
Soil degradation, environmental mismanagement and, 530
Solar energy, 595
Solar power, 559–560
Sole proprietorships, 20
Solid Waste Disposal Act, 561
Solid wastes, environmental mismanagement and, 530
Solomon, C., 144n
South Korea, counterfeit products from, 485
Soviet Union
 Aral Sea, case, 572
 environmental issues, 585–587
Specter, M., 586n
Speth, Gustave, 604
Spindle, W., 274n

Spiro, L.H., 135n
Springen, Karen, 188, 188n
Sprint, 11
St. John, Caron H., 88, 88n, 90
Staiano, Edward F., 524
Stakeholder groups, political and legal, 245
 business associations, 245–246
 lobbying and legislation, 247–250
 political action committees (PACs), 246–247
 relative power of, 4–5
Stakeholder influence map, 86–90
Stakeholders, 3, 86
 affirmative action and, 393
 analysis and management, 90–92
 classification of, 86–90
 corporate political, 237–240
 of corporation, 20–21
 drug testing and, 370
 environmental crises and, 128
 ethics and, 159, 160
 external, 86–90
 influence map for nineteenth century, 263
 internal, 86
 internally generated crises and, 126
 managing techniques for, 88–90
 mission statements and, 63
 nuclear waste and, 83–85
 partnering techniques for, 88–90
 power of, 103–108
 pressure by, 75
 product liability law case, 230–232
 recycling, 555–556
 regulation and, 283–284
 resources of, 105
 selection of alternatives, control over, 106–108
Stalin, Joseph, 572
Stamper, Chris, 67
Standard of living, 6
Standard Oil Company, 199
Stanfield, Willie M., 412
Stanford, Betsy, 429
Stanford, Leland, 207
Staples, Inc., 49
State Implementation Plans (SIPs), 539
State organizations, mission statements of, 61
States, corporation charters by, 19
Statistical process control, 501
Statute of repose, 230
Stauffer, N.W., 559n
Steadman, L.E., 195n

Stecklow, S., 330n, 331n, 332n
Steel industry, 204, 211–212, 219
Steel unions, 434
Steffans. L., 212n
Stehle, V., 329n
Steiger, Janet, 472
Steiner, G. A., 57, 115
Steinmetz, G., 136n, 442n
Steltenpohl, Greg, 57
Stern, G., 500n
Stevens, Ross, 514
Stevenson, Gelvin L., 403
Stevenson, R., 7n
Stevenson, R.W., 276n
Stills, J., 351–352, 353, 391, 429
Stipp, D., 485n, 558n
Stock market speculation, finance capitalism and, 215
Stockmeyer, Steven F., 249
Storaska, J. Frederic, 135
Strategic approaches, element of TQM, 506
Strategic choice, 73–76
Strategic collaborations, 320
Strategic management, organizational culture and, 55–59
Strategic marketing, social issues, 336–340
Strategic planning, issues management and, 121
Strategy formulation, 24
 Beta Pharmaceuticals, Inc., 77–81
 environment of, 39–55
 framework for, 59–76
 Gillette Corporation, 37–39
 strategic management and organizational culture, 55–59
Strategy implementation and evaluation, 24
 external direct forces, 92–96
 external indirect forces, 99–101
 internal direct forces, 96–99
 internal indirect forces, 101–103
 power of stakeholders, 103–108
 selection of alternatives and, 106–108
 social responsiveness, 108–117
 stakeholder analysis, 86–87, 90–92
 stakeholder influence map, 86–90
 stakeholders and nuclear waste, case, 83–85

Strategy in Action (Yavitz and Newman), 86
Strauchs, John, 185, 185n
Street, M.D., 182
Stress, 362–368
Strickland, A.J., III, 64n
Strict liability, 523
Strikes
 French, 440–441
 German, 441
Strunk, Tim, 352
Sub-Saharan Africa, water issues in, 594–595
Substance abuse, 369–371
Substitute products, 93–94
Success, profit as measure of, 18
Sullivan, A., 144n, 412n, 413n
Sullivan, Louis W., 477
Sun Microsystems, Inc., 66
Sundquist, J.L., 218n
Superfund, 553–555
Suppliers
 bargaining power of, 94–95
 stakeholders, 86, 89
Supreme Court, unions and, 436
Survival economy, 574
Sustainable development, 573–575
Suzman, M., 117n, 343n
Sweeney, J., J., 102, 435–438
Swoboda, F., 374n, 499n
Sybase, Inc., ISO 9000 and, 511–512
Sylvis, William, 431
Syre, S., 49n
Syrett, Harold C., 196, 196n

Taft-Hartley Act, 433
Tait, N., 51n, 157n
Taiwan, counterfeit products from, 485
Tannenbaum, J.A., 372n
Tanouye, E., 104n, 105n
Tashiro, H., 42n
Taxation, private foundations and, 323–326
Taylor, Frederick W., 214
Taylor, S., Jr., 402n
Team approach to effective crisis management, 146–149
Technical expertise, element of TQM, 506
Technological change, 18
Technological environment, in social issues strategy, 47–49
Technology, 5, 203–204
Teeley, S.E., 449n
Teenagers, 8–9
Telemarketing Complaint System, 474
Telemarketing Consumer Fraud and Abuse Prevention Act of 1994, 474

Telemarketing fraud, 474–475
Telephone companies of, 11
Telephone industry, deregulation, 291–292
Television industry, deregulation, 287
Teltch, K., 327n
Terrance Group, 6
Tetrault, Lynn, 421
Texaco case, 409–414
Textile industry, economic growth and, 204
The Theory of Economic Develpment (Schumpeter), 18
Thermal energy, 560
Thomas, Barbara S., 288, 288n
Thomas, David A., 425, 426, 426n
Thomas, J.E., 379n
Thomas, J.M., 290n
Thomas, Lee M., 538
Thomas, L.T., 379n
Thomas, P., 423n
Thomas, R.L., 312n
Thompson, A.A., 64n
Thompson, E., 42n
Thomson, J. Edgar, 202
Thornburgh, Richard, 273, 274
Three Gorges Project, 590–593
Three Mile Island, 106, 566
TickIT, 511–512
Time/CNN, poll on economic future, 6
Title VII, Civil Rights Act of 1964, 394–395
Tobacco industry
 adaptability to change, 59
 environments impacted, 49–55
Toffler, B. Ley, 163, 174
Tolchin, M., 242n, 280n, 283, 288
Tolchin, S. J., 283, 288
Toner, R., 250n
Total quality control (TQC), 501
Total quality management (TQM), 505–506
 ISO 1000, 514
 ISO 9000, 509–511
 ISO 14000, 513–514
 Malcolm Baldrige Award, 507–509
Townsend, James B., 424, 425n
Toys R Us, 94
Trade associations, external indirect force on company, 99
Trade organizations, source of information for managers, 73
Trade policy, environment and, 575–578

Transfer of ownership, in corporations, 21
Transparency International, 185
Transportation, 199, 201–202
Transportation Department, 369–370
Trask, Bob, 352
Triangle Shirtwaist Company fire, 446
Trident Precision, 508, 509
Trost, C., 433n
Troy, S., 441n
Trucking industry, 286–287, 364
Truell, P., 33n
Truman, Harry S, 218, 219, 433
Trusts, Sherman Antitrust Act of 1890, 265–267
Tsuda, Masahiro, 34
Tucker, M.T., 236n
TWA flight 800 crash, crisis management, 151
Tye, L., 355n, 359n, 583n, 584n
Tylenol poisonings, Johnson & Johnson, 128–129
Tyler, E.B., 44n
Tyler, P.E., 592n

Uchitelle, L., 13n
Udwadia, F., 121n, 129n
Ugelow, S., 386n
Ulrich, Robert, 410, 411
Underemployment, 5
Unemployment, 41
 German labor issues, 444
Unfair trade practices, 267–268
Union Carbide, 124
 crisis management, 149
 environmental crisis at, 129, 131
Unions, 430–433
 colonial America, 430
 communists and, 433
 decline in membership, 433
 European, 430, 439–444
 growth during WWI, 432
 internal indirect force on company, 101–102
 nationwide, development of, 430–433
 in 1980s, 433–434
 in 1990s, 435–439
 political action committees (PACs), 247
 stakeholders, 86, 89
 strategy of, 435–436
 Supreme Court and, 436
United Automobile Workers (UAW), 435, 438–439
United Farm Workers (UFW), 438

Index

United Food and Commercial Workers, 438
United Mine Workers of America, 432
United Nations Environment Programme, home page, 605
United States Chamber of Commerce, 245–246
United States Constitution, 233–234
United States economy, current issues, 6–7
United Steelworkers, etc. v. Weber, 400
United Steelworkers of America, 434, 435
United Way case, 309–311
Universities, French labor issues, 440
Unsafe at Any Speed (Nader), 159
Unskilled labor, 201
Updike, E.H., 417n
Urbanism, economic growth and, 200–201
U.S. Government Printing Office, consumer information, 479
U.S. Healthcare, Inc., merger of, 11
U.S. Postal Service, telemarketing fraud and, 474
U.S. Public Interest Research Group (PIRG), 466–468
USAir, 305
Useem, M., 243n, 244
USX Corporation, unions and, 434

Vacquin, Henri, 441
Vail, Theodore N., 203
Vaillancourt, M., 452n
Values, 55–58
  economic growth and, 198
  reciprocal transfer of, 45
ValuJet crash, environmental crisis, 129
Van Schuyver, M., 359n
Vancil, R.F., 59n
Vanderbilt, Cornelius, 208
Varadarajan, P. R.P., 336, 337n
Velasquez, Manuel, 181, 182n
Vennari, Francesco, 85
Verity, William, 273, 274
Vernon, R., 578n
Vernon, Raymond, 201, 201n
Vernon-Wortzel, H., 37n, 204n
Vickers, M., 316n
Videocassette recorders, social issues regarding, 48

Vietnam, counterfeit products from, 485
Vincola, Ann, 421
Violence in workplace, 365–368
Vishny, Robert, 187
Vogel, D., 26, 185, 200
Vogel, Ezra, 42
Votaw, Dov, 21, 21n
Vulnerability, 67–71

Wackenhut Corporation, 358–359
Wade, B., 375n
Waite, Chief Justice, 17
Walcott, Dennis, 412
Wald, M.L., 84n, 107n, 522n, 534n, 544n, 547n, 568n
Walker, Robert S., 85, 296
Wall Street Journal, 22–25, 99, 174
Wall Street Journal/NBC News, poll on economic future, 6
Wallace, C.P., 70n
Wallace, Mike, 151
Wal-Mart, ethics and, 161
Walton, C. C., 20, 26
Warner, J., 324n
Warner-Lambert, 104
Warranties, 522–523
Warsh, D., 183n
Washington Post, United Way case, 310
Waste management, 561–564
Waste Management, Inc., 564
Waste Management Technologies (WMX), 563–564
Waste reduction
  alternative fuels, 558–560
  recycling, 555–558
  systems approach to, 560–561
Water pollution
  Aral Sea, case, 572
  clean water, 548–552
  environmental mismanagement and, 530
  history of, 535
Water scarcity, environmental mismanagement and, 530
Wealth, link to religion, 24–25
Wealth distribution, 6–7
The Wealth of Nations (Smith), 15
Wealthy, C-7
Weaver, Gary R., 177, 177n
Webb, A. P., 167, 168n, 169, 170, 174

Weber, Brian, 400
Weicker, Lowell, 372
Weidenbaum, Murray L., 283n, 284, 284n, 296
Weinberger, Caspar, 471
Weintraub, B., 549n
Welch, Jack, 242
Welch, John F., 273
Weld, William, 546
Welfare, 14, 317
Wells, K., 129n, 143n
Wernham, R., 112n
Wessel, D., 6n
West, B. kenneth, 414
West Point-Pepperell, Inc., 221
Western Union, 202–203
Westin, A.F., 182
Weston, Thomas, 196
Weyerhaeuser, 160
Wheel of Competitive Strategy, 65
Wheelabrator Technologies, Inc. (WTI), 564
Wheeler-Lea Amendment, 267–268
Whirlpool, 221
Whistle-blowing, 182–184
Whistleblowing, False Claims Act, 183–184
White, D.C., 559n
White-collar jobs, downsizing and, 12
Whitehead, John C., 331
Whitelaw, K., 95n
Whitney, C.R., 441n
Wicks, Andrew, 29, 29n
Wigand, Jeffrey S., 52, 53
Wilde, Oscar, 134
Wildlife-preservation organizations, 319
Wilkins, M., 199
Williams, F., 96n
Williams, G., 332n
Williams, P., 312n
Williamson, Stephen, 57
Wilson, Graham K., 26, 26n
Wilson, P., 407, 408, 545
Wilson, Woodrow, 213, 217
Wind power, 558–559
Wines, M., 248n, 551n, 601n
Winokur, L.A., 366n
Wittenberg, Diane, 548
W.M. Keck Foundation, 311
Women
  education of, 10
  in Reagan administration, 221
  unions and, 433
Women in workforce
  child care and, 380–383
  contribution of, 10
Woo, J., 422n

Wood, Donna J., 29, 29n, 30, 30n
Woodruff's Palace Car Company, 199
Woodson, Robert L., Sr., 328
Work environment, 430
Workday length, unions and, 431
Workers' compensation, 445–446
Working parents, 353
Workplace accidents, 444–445
Workplace fatalities, 449–450
Workplace issues
  changing labor force, 353
  disabled workers, 371–379
  employee privacy, 354–362
  family and child care benefits, 379–384
  health care, 384–387
  Jennifer Stills case, 351–352
  medical issues, 368–371
  stress, 362–368
  unions and, 433
Workplace safety
  case, 429
  management strategy for, 447–457
Workplace violence, 365–368
World Trade Organization (WTO), 95–96, 571, 576–578
Wright-Patterson Air Force Base, downsizing, 3

Yamaji, Hiroki, 33
Yang, C., 274n, 375n
Yankelovich, Daniel, 13, 162
Yavitz, B., 59n, 86, 90n
Yeo, George, 299
YMCA, 312
Yochelson, John, 486
Yomuri Shimbun, 43
Young, Frank, 477
Your Money's Worth (Chase & Schlink), 465

Zachery, G.P., 436n, 437n
Zadek, S., 115n, 116, 117
Zein, Alfred M., 39
Zeithaml, C. P., 112, 242, 243, 246,
Zellner, W., 12n
Zeneca, 104
Ziegler, B., 357n
Zilg, G.C., 209n
Zinn, L., 9n
Zollers. F.E., 230n